OUT
OF
CHAOS

Other books by Louis J. Halle

Transcaribbean

Birds against Men

River of Ruins

Spring in Washington

On Facing the World

Civilization and Foreign Policy

Choice for Survival

Dream and Reality

Men and Nations

Sedge

The Society of Man

The Cold War as History

*The Storm Petrel and the Owl
of Athena*

The Ideological Imagination

*The Sea and the Ice: A Naturalist
in Antarctica*

Louis J. Halle

OUT OF CHAOS

1977

Houghton Mifflin Company
Boston

The author gratefully acknowledges the permission granted for the quotation or reproduction of copyrighted material, as follows: G. Bell & Sons, Ltd (London), from *Gothic Architecture in England & France* by George Herbert West (1911), drawings of The Complete French Cathedral, from Viollet-le-Duc, on page 470, and The Crypt, Canterbury, under Conrad's Choir, on page 474; Cambridge University Press (London), from *On Growth and Form* by D'Arcy Thompson; Curtis Brown Ltd (London), on behalf of the Estate of Roy Campbell, from "The Serf," in *Adamastor I* by Roy Campbell; Eulenburg Scores Ltd. (New York), for permission to reproduce part of J. S. Bach's Brandenburg Concerto No. 5 from Edition Eulenburg No. 282; Faber & Faber (London), from *Collected Shorter Poems 1927–1957* by W. H. Auden, and from *Collected Poems, 1909–1962* by T. S. Eliot; Harcourt Brace Jovanovich, Inc. (New York) for permission to quote from "Sweeney among the Nightingales" and "The Waste Land" in *Collected Poems, 1909–1962* by T. S. Eliot, copyright 1936 by Harcourt Brace Jovanovich, Inc., copyright © 1963, 1964 by T. S. Eliot; Harper & Row (New York), for permission to quote from *Physics & Philosophy* and *Physics & Beyond* by Werner Heisenberg, and from *The Odyssey of Homer: A Modern Translation* by Richmond Lattimore, copyright © 1965, 1967 by Richmond Lattimore; Edwin F. Kalmus, from "Kol Nidrei" by Max Bruch; William Morrow & Co., from *The Heritage of the Cathedral* by Sartell Prentice, copyright © 1936 by Sartell Prentice, the drawing of a groin vault on page 474, the drawing that shows the thrust and counter-thrust of a Gothic vault on page 476, and the drawing of the cross-section of a Gothic Church (Westminster Abbey) on page 477; C. F. Peters Corporation (New York), from "Brandenburg Concerto No. 5" (Edition Eulenburg No. 282. Reprinted by permission of C. F. Peters Corporation, sole agents for the United States.), and "Inventionen und Sinfonien" (Peters NR. 4201, copyright © 1933 by C. F. Peters. Reprinted by permission of C. F. Peters Corporation.) by J. S. Bach; Random House, Inc. (New York), from *Collected Shorter Poems 1927–1957* by W. H. Auden; *Scientific American* (New York), for permission to reproduce on page 291 a simplified version of the diagram representing evolution that accompanies "The Oldest Fossils" by Elso S. Barghoorn, copyright © 1971, in its issue of May 1971; The University of Chicago Press (Chicago), from *The Iliad of Homer* translated by Richmond Lattimore, copyright © 1951 by the University of Chicago. The diagram on page 22 was drawn by Alain Coquoz.

Library of Congress Cataloging in Publication Data

Halle, Louis Joseph, date
  Out of chaos.

  Includes bibliographical references and index.
  1. Cosmology. 2. Life. 3. Mind and body.
  4. Civilization — History.   5. Man. I. Title.
  BD511.H25   110   76-52468
  ISBN 0-395-25357-8

Printed in the United States of America

V 10 9 8 7 6 5 4 3 2 1

Preface

THIS BOOK is based on the premise that the realm of being is meaningful to the extent that we are able to view it comprehensively. Our understanding, in its degree, depends on the breadth of our knowledge; for everything, as we shall see, tends to shed light on everything else. But the knowledge we have today, although far exceeding that of our predecessors, does not serve this purpose of illumination insofar as it remains unassembled, partitioned among the minds of the specialists who respectively represent the fields into which it is divided.

From the beginning of my conscious life I have done my best to command at least a distant view of all basic knowledge. Such an undertaking is regarded with suspicion by those among the specialists who believe that the only proper view is the one that scans reality close up, moving from one detail to another. But there is more than one valid perspective. For anyone who wants to view the geography of the earth as a single whole, the general shape of South America is what counts, not the little irregularities of its coastline. In any case, the close-up and the distant views are complementary rather than contradictory. Let us have both.

In one of its aspects, this book is an exercise in perspective. As such, it will have much to say of the very small and the very large, of analysis and synthesis.

*

Despite my lifelong effort to command all basic knowledge, it is clear that I could not have written this book without the help of specialists. This applies particularly to the basic physics that is the subject of Part One. For over forty years I had suffered from my inability to grasp certain key concepts in the theory of gravitation and in quantum theory. Such physicists as I found myself in touch with either could not answer my questions or took the position that the answers were matters that only the initiated might know, as the knowledge of certain mysteries is confined to a priesthood. Then, just as I was embarking on the present work in spite of the apparently insurmountable obstacle that this presented, I was saved by what seemed like an act of providence.

Having twice read through that exemplary textbook, *Basic Physics* by Kenneth W. Ford (Waltham, Mass., 1968), I had the temerity to submit my questions to him in a letter. I speak with feeling when I report that he was the first who did not, in response to these questions, adopt the attitude I have reported above. He took the necessary pains to enlighten me, and so a correspondence began that has continued over the years. From the start, Professor Ford showed an active and helpful interest in the whole project, answering my questions, reviewing my successive chapters in draft, correcting my errors, and supporting me by constant encouragement. Without his help I could not have written Part One, and without writing Part One I could not have written this book at all.

The problem posed by basic physics was that of grasping concepts that are opposed to our common sense and hardly susceptible of expression in our common language. The problem posed by the molecular biology, genetics, and evolution set forth in Part Two was that of the complexity represented by masses of intricate detail. In preparation for writing it, I devoted ten months to the intensive study of innumerable books and scientific papers. When I did set about the composition, at the end of those ten months, I could not be confident that I would find a biologist who would do for me what Professor Ford had done. I therefore deliberately adopted the procedure of making no statement that was not obviously so without noting, for my own later information, the authority on which I had made it. Even so, it would have been impossible for me to avoid occasional error. I therefore concluded that I absolutely must find some competent person who, simply out of such interest and magnanimity as had been shown by Professor Ford, would review what I had written. And again I was the beneficiary of what seemed like providential good fortune.

Of all contemporary writing in the field of biology, I admire none more than that of J. T. Bonner of Princeton, as represented by his books, *Cells and Societies* (Princeton, 1955), *Size and Cycle* (Princeton, 1965), and *On Development* (Cambridge, Mass., 1974). I had already known of him as the editor of D'Arcy Thompson's masterpiece, *On Growth and Form* (abridged edition, Cambridge, England, 1971). Now, through the kind intermediation of a common friend, I entered into correspondence with him. The result was that he took part of his summer vacation in 1974, when he was busy with his own writing, to review and correct my Part Two. How can one ever be grateful enough for such generosity, which one finds so much more readily among the big minds than among the little in any field?

Professor Bonner did say that there were some points on which I would do well to consult a specialist in molecular biology, but I failed in such effort as I then made to find one who would respond.

In spite of Professors Ford and Bonner, it cannot be that there are no errors at all in Parts One or Two. I can only hope that such as remain are inconsequential in terms of the large picture I have undertaken to present. What is clear, however, is that any errors are my own, for neither of the scholars who came to my aid could have been expected to guarantee my final text in detail.

The problems posed for me by Part Three, on the evolution of mankind, were not so great as those posed by Parts One and Two. For one thing, I had been a graduate student in anthropology. And now again I studied a vast literature, undertaking to put myself in the position of being able to cite my authority for every statement that might be open to question. For the overall picture of the evolution of man, as distinct from specialized aspects of it, I relied particularly on two excellent books, *Mankind in the Making* by William Howells (revised edition, New York, 1967) and *The Emergence of Man* by J. E. Pfeiffer (London, 1973).

While it is possible to give a comprehensive and inclusive account of Relativity and quantum theory within limited space, as I have in Part One, it is hardly possible to do as much where the subject is the history of civilization, for here uniformity is lacking and (for reasons that will become apparent in the text) we find ourselves closer to chaos. Civilization does not obey a few simple laws of nature, and every manifestation of it is in some respects unique. Consequently, my account in Part Four, after several chapters of generalization, follows the procedure of describing what are hardly more than samples of the main civilizations to be distinguished in the general evolution of civilization. This includes, however, seven chapters on Chinese civilization, the history of which I know chiefly from C. P. FitzGerald's *China: A Short Cultural History* (New York, 1950), a notable book that I have read and reread with fascination ever since I first discovered it a quarter of a century ago. Professor FitzGerald himself had the generosity, for which I am warmly grateful, to read over these chapters and make suggestions that were embodied in a final revision. I must, however, take entire responsibility for the shortcomings that remain in them.

Parts Five and Six have entailed, for the most part, the presentation of my own thought rather than the reporting of established knowledge. It was necessary, however, that the two chapters on music in Part Five be monitored by someone with the technical knowledge I lacked. This was done for me by my friend William Lugg of Geneva in the conscientious fashion that is native to him. The corrections and suggestions he made brought improvements for which I feel the most grateful appreciation. Again, however, such faults as remain are necessarily mine.

The reader will see that the progression in this book is from the large toward the little, from the distant toward the here-and-now. Part One is concerned with the whole known universe, which is 20,000 million light-years across and 10,000 million years old. Part Two is confined to our single planet over a period of 4,000 million years. Part Three covers some 400 million years, Part Four some 6,000. We may say of Parts Five and Six that they deal with the present — and, indeed, they are cut short, with a certain abruptness, by the uncrossed threshold of the future.

The reader will also see that the book begins with straightforward description of the universe and of life on earth. As it progresses, however, and even before the end of Part One (e.g., Chapter XII), certain philosophical principles begin to emerge, seemingly of their own accord, with ever greater force — until, by the end, a whole philosophy has asserted itself. I cannot help feeling that this philosophy is not of my invention but implicit in the material.

This brings me back to the premise set forth in my first paragraph above, that the realm of being appears meaningful to the extent that we are able to achieve a comprehensive view. I have felt like one who, putting the meaningless bits of a picture-puzzle together, sees meaning gradually emerge of itself. (Who, for instance, at the outset of this undertaking, could have imagined that a continuous line would connect quantum mechanics with James Joyce's *Ulysses,* thereby illuminating the significance of the latter? Certainly I myself had nothing of the sort in mind; yet the connection is not bizarre in the context, as it is bound to seem when I refer to it so bluntly here.) Such is the outcome that has justified this undertaking and, I hope the reader will agree, validated the premise on which it is based.

ACKNOWLEDGEMENTS

I have spoken above of my debt to Messrs. Ford and Bonner, to Professor FitzGerald, and to Mr. Lugg.

When I embarked on the actual writing of this book, in 1971, I had long been conducting a seminar and giving an annual course of lectures at The Graduate Institute of International Studies in Geneva. My preoccupation with the book, however, became steadily more absorbing, and it was in recognition of this that in 1973 the Director of the Institute, Professor Jacques Freymond, acting on the basis of his usual sensitive insight, relieved me of the need to continue my annual series of lectures. By then it had become evident to me that, sooner or later, I must put myself in a position to give my full time to the book. Consequently, in 1974, when a successor had been found to assume the burden of the seminar, I retired from teaching completely, although continuing to enjoy the nominal status of a professor at the Institute. Moreover, the Institute undertook, in conjunction with a foundation grant, to act as sponsor of the book. All this has added to the debt of gratitude I owe Professor Freymond and the Institute, a debt which has been accumulating over the twenty years of our association.

I am most grateful to The Rockefeller Foundation for a grant in support of the work that I here present for the reader's consideration.

The publication of any book is a work of partnership between author and publisher. I here express my warm appreciation and acknowledge my particular obligation, for their important part in this enterprise, to Mr. Richard B. McAdoo, Mrs. Ruth K. Hapgood, and Mrs. Gail Stewart of Houghton Mifflin.

FINAL NOTICE TO THE READER UPON EMBARKATION

For most readers, the bulk of Part One and at least the first chapters of Part Two will not be easy reading, if only because they deal with unfamiliar worlds in terms of a logic that cannot be followed without careful attention. There are no like difficulties in the rest of the book.

The book may serve two purposes. Because it contains the material of a general education, it may be used simply for the purpose of promoting such an education. More importantly, the comprehensive philosophy that arises out of the material, in suggesting the direction of evolution, may give a meaning to our individual lives that they would otherwise lack. In fact, however, these two purposes are not alternative but complementary.

L.J.H.

Geneva, 1976

A Note on Numerical Notation

THE USE of our ordinary notation for such large numbers as are needed in physics and astronomy is too cumbersome. Therefore the custom is to use instead a system of notation that increases from one number to the next by a factor of 10 — i.e., 10, 10^2, 10^3, etc. The 1,000 of our ordinary notation is, in this notation, 10^3; 1,000,000 is 10^6. The superscript represents the number of zeros after the figure 1 in ordinary notation. The reader will find it convenient to acquire the habit of seeing 10^6 as a million, 10^9 as a thousand million (called a billion in the United States but not in Britain), 10^{12} as a million million.

To appreciate the magnitudes involved one should have it vividly in mind that each increase of one in the superscript increases the amount tenfold. The breadth of the universe known to us is 2×10^{10} light-years. A distance of 2×10^{11} light-years, although the figure that is multiplied by 2 is the next in the series, would accommodate ten such universes side by side. 2×10^{12} would accommodate a hundred. The magnitude of the difference between 10^{17} and 10^{18}, so small in its appearance as written, is beyond the imagination of man. 10^{17} is, after all, only one tenth of 10^{18}.

The same notation with a minus sign before the superscript represents division rather than multiplication and is used for such small quantities as the distances inside atoms. While 10^6 cm. is a million centimeters, 10^{-6} cm. is the millionth part of one centimeter — i.e., $\frac{1}{10^6}$ cm.

Because the units of the more convenient metric system are now slated to replace the miles, feet, inches, and pounds that have hitherto served the English-speaking world, I have used them throughout. For the benefit of readers who think in the traditional units, I here give the following factors of conversion:

1 kilometer = 0.62 miles	1 centimeter = 0.39 inches
1 meter = 3.28 feet or 39.27 inches	1 kilogram = 2.20 pounds

Contents

PART THREE: MIND

PART FOUR: CIVILIZATION

PART SIX: IMPLICATIONS

PART ONE

The Physical Universe

This theme of order and chaos . . . illustrates as clearly as anything can the complete revolution in our view of the world that has been brought about by the achievements of physical science in this century.

Briefly stated, the new view is a view of chaos beneath order — or, what is the same thing, of order imposed upon a deeper and more fundamental chaos. This is in startling contrast to the view developed and solidified in the three centuries from Kepler to Einstein, a view of order beneath chaos.

— *Kenneth W. Ford*

I

The Dwarf Flea

BECAUSE I WISH TO BEGIN in the simplest possible terms, I do so with the ancient tale of the five blind men and the elephant. Having heard that there was such a beast, the five decided to find out what it was like by examining a specimen in the zoo. The first, approaching the elephant with hands outstretched, got hold of its trunk, whereupon he reported that the elephant was like a great serpent; the second, getting hold of an ear, reported that it was like a leaf; the third, embracing a leg, said it was like a tree; the fourth, encountering its flank, said it was like a wall; and the fifth, grasping its tail, that it was like a rope.

One can draw more than one moral from this tale. The one I choose to draw here is that nothing has meaning except in terms of its context, its connection with something larger, so that the process of discovering truth is the process of extending one's knowledge.

The immediate does not exist in itself. It belongs to a larger whole, embracing larger dimensions of space and longer lapses of time. The larger whole, in turn, belongs to one still larger. The acquisition of knowledge by our kind, over the thousands of years since we began to accumulate it by making records, has been a process of enlargement. That process has brought us to the point where today we have some knowledge, at least, of what extends over such a distance that light, traveling at 300,000 kilometers per second, takes 2×10^{10} years to traverse it; which is also to say that it has brought us to the point where we have some knowledge, at least, of a lapse of time half that large.

As we have discovered only in this century, time and space are related as different dimensions of one four-dimensional whole. By the enlargement of our knowledge, then, to embrace such orders of spatial and temporal magnitude, we have discovered a previously unsuspected connection between space and time — just as the blind men might, by the enlargement of their knowledge, have discovered the connection between the elephant's trunk and its tail.

Imagine the case of some very small creature, say a dwarf flea, possessed of a scientific curiosity that impels it to examine its surroundings with a view to understanding the great world in which it finds itself. Since it is so small, its vision does not extend beyond half a dozen cells of the leaf on which it happens to be standing. This is the here-and-now to which it is confined, at least initially.

In the attempt to satisfy its scientific curiosity, it embarks on a study of the leaf-cells to which its vision is limited. We, with our larger vision, know that the poor flea will never be able to gain an understanding of what a leaf-cell is — its significance, its place in the realm of being — without understanding what a leaf is; that it will never be able to understand what a leaf is without understanding what a tree is; that it will never be able to understand what a tree is without understanding the evolution of vegetable life; and so on.

Is it not possible that our own inability to understand the cosmos we inhabit is due to the misfortune that our own vision, although larger than that of the flea, is still too restricted? Perhaps, if our vision could encompass 2×10^{11} light-years, instead of merely 2×10^{10}, many mysteries of being that now confront us would be resolved. I conclude that the only thing for us to do is to continue to enlarge our vision as much as we can. Then we shall see.

II

Orders of Magnitude

THE NATURAL MAN has only his five unaided senses for the perception of the physical world in which he finds himself. He has no telescope or microscope, no hearing aid, no radio or x-ray machine to tell him of the electromagnetic radiation outside the band of frequencies seen by his unaided eyes as light. In his experience of physical reality he is confined to orders of magnitude between the extremes of what is too small for him to detect and what is too large for him to comprehend, orders of magnitude that constitute an infinitesimal band in the entire scale of magnitudes that we have only recently come to know of.

The smallest distance he can distinguish with his unaided eye is about one tenth of a millimeter. If he set out to analyze a piece of matter into its progressively smaller components, that is where he would have to stop.

Scanning the night sky, the natural man might see a dim spot of light, what we know to be the spiral nebula in Andromeda. Even though he saw it, however, he would have no way of knowing that it was not a faint luminous cloud in the immediate vicinity of the earth but, rather, a galaxy 2 million light-years away. Therefore, the fact that he saw it would not enlarge the dimensions of the universe his consciousness inhabited, just as the fact that light from the sun reaching the eye of the flea would not enlarge the dimensions of the universe it knew. The natural man would still know only such distances as he was able to experience within the scale of dimensions proper to his earthly environment. The greatest such distance is the circumference of the earth, 40,000 kilometers; but even the conception of such a limited distance as this requires a developed capacity for abstraction. It belongs to the realm of book-learning, rather than to that of what is encompassed by our senses. We may say, then, that the natural man is confined by the limit of the distances he may traverse on foot, which are to be measured at the most in hundreds of kilometers. (On the scale of the universe it makes no difference whether we take 100 kilometers or 40,000 kilometers as the figure here.) So we may conclude that he is confined, spatially, within the limits of magnitude denoted by one tenth of a millimeter and some hundreds of kilometers.

The smallest time-span natural man experiences might be five thousandths of a second, supposing that he could not see an image, feel a touch, or hear a sound that manifested itself more briefly.

What is the largest?

The more primitive the man, the more he would tend to live in a narrow present. Span of memory or of anticipation, and degrees of consciousness, are not sharply definable; nor need they be, since we are here concerned only with orders of magnitude. I have seen a cock pigeon, five minutes after having nearly been killed by a falcon, courting a hen with such single-minded intensity as to leave no doubt that the event had already effectively faded from his memory. Before men had acquired the ability to keep records, they might have been consciously aware of one life-span, with some extension for the generation before and the generation after — say a hundred years in all. (Again, on the scale of the universe it makes no difference whether we say a hundred or a thousand years.) Even when past experience was handed down from generation to generation by word-of-mouth, it tended to merge, in men's minds, into a timeless background of legend. We may conclude, then, that the temporal span of natural man's awareness, in terms of orders of magnitude, is from five thousandths of a second to one century.

Until recently, our kind had no reason not to assume that the reality we knew within these confines was representative of all reality. We assumed that, if we could make ourselves small enough to move about in the realm of being whose order of magnitude was under one tenth of a millimeter, we would find that its basic constitution was just like that of the realm we did move about in. Like our own realm, that of the very small would be divided between matter and empty space, and the laws of nature that governed the behavior of the matter would be those we already knew. Just as two bodies cannot occupy the same space at the same time in our familiar world, so two bodies could not occupy the same space at the same time in the world too small for our perception. In that world, as in our familiar world, if a body was in one place at one moment and another a moment later, it must in the intervening time have moved from the first to the second along some continuous path that connected the two.

Nor did it occur to us that we could not assume the prevalence of the laws of nature, as we knew them within our own confines, in the realm of what we might think of as infinite space and infinite time. We assumed, for example, that in infinite space, as within the confines of the space we knew, a straight line, defined as the shortest distance between two points, could never return upon itself like a snake biting its tail. We assumed that Euclidean geometry, to the extent that it was valid on earth, was valid for the entire cosmos. We assumed that time was absolute, as we took it to be within our own confines, so that, during the time in which our earth aged a hundred years, everything else in the cosmos would also have aged a hundred years.

Only since the beginning of this century have we discovered that these assumptions are false. Until so recently we have been like fish confined to the oceanic depths to whom it had never occurred that water might not fill the entire space of the universe, and that therefore such rules as those defining the weight of objects and the resistance to their movement in water, or those governing the propagation of light in water, were not universal. Until now we have been like the blind man who thought that what he found to be like a rope was representative of the whole elephant.

If we think of a scale of magnitude from one tenth of the unit we call a fermi (which is 10^{-12} centimeter) to 2×10^{10} light-years (a light-year being 9.23×10^{12} kilometers), then the range of magnitudes within which we live our own little lives — from a tenth of a millimeter to the 40,000 kilometers of the earth's circumference — is an infinitesimal fraction of the whole, a point on the scale so small as to be virtually nothing. It is from our knowledge of only this point, however, that until the most recent times we have been deriving what we have assumed to be the laws of the entire universe.

From the time when we began to think about the universe, we assumed that our own place in it was central. The part we inhabited was the main part, across which sun and moon traveled like lanterns provided for its illumination, over which the stars had been arranged to form a canopy. This is to say that we thought in terms of earthly dimensions, familiar orders of magnitude, rather than of such dimensions as we now measure in light-years.

When our inherited religions tell us that the Creator, in creating the universe, had it in mind as a habitation for man, the conception of the universe to which they refer is that proper to the earlier time, when our knowledge of it was so much narrower. This applies as well to some philosophical visions that are widely acclaimed in our day, such as the vision set forth by Teilhard de Chardin in *Le Phéno-mène humain*. It applies to much of what may be called humanistic philosophy, the philosophy which tends to base itself on the premise that our particular species (uncompleted, perhaps, in its evolution) among all the species on a single planet orbiting what is only one among 10^{11} stars in only one galaxy among more than a thousand million scattered across space — that this single species of ours is the be-all and end-all of creation.

To those for whom life is worthwhile and the future hopeful only in terms of a universe in which our kind is central, it may seem like an act of pure negation to call attention, as I am doing, to the dimensions of the universe that we now know to exist. I would respond by making two points. One is that, when epistemological considerations are taken into account, the centrality of man, or the centrality of life on earth, remains a possibility. The other is that the enlargement of the physical universe we know is an enlargement in more senses than one. It is a liberation. It opens up possibilities that could hardly have been contemplated in the "world view" of a century ago.

III

The Problem of Knowing

OUR KNOWLEDGE OF THE WORLD reaches us through five senses. Such knowledge is not as direct or as sure as we necessarily assume it to be.

Although I may say that I see a rock, what impresses itself on my eyes is not the rock itself but light which I infer to be reflected from it. Although I touch the rock, what I experience is sensations in the nerve-endings of my fingers that I interpret as representing the same object as that from which the light was reflected. If the rock were a piece of cheese, I would also have the indirect evidence of smell and taste; if a bell, the evidence of hearing. While I have only indirect evidence, all of it fits together with a plausibility that is beautiful and satisfying. My respective senses, in the respective items of evidence they provide, confirm one another. I also have the confirmation of other beings like myself, whose independent existence I cannot prove but assume, and who seem, for the most part, to see what I see, feel what I feel. However, the indirectness of my knowledge remains. It depends on assumptions the validity of which I cannot prove — such as that what my senses conspire to tell me is essentially true, that what I take to be other beings like me exist and experience essentially what I experience, that the interpretation of sensory experience by my brain is a true interpretation.

We have no workable alternative to making these assumptions, since without them we could not conduct our lives. However, even though we accept what, on the basis of these assumptions, we regard as knowledge, we have to recognize that it has its equivocal aspects — as when others see the grass as green while I, being color-blind, do not. My only point here is that our knowledge of the world we know "directly" with our natural senses is not direct in the absolute meaning of the term, and not without an element of uncertainty. Let us, however, for working purposes, accept the evidence of our senses as directly received knowledge that we need not ordinarily question.

We can apply simple aids to our senses without basically altering this situation. When I apply a telescope or a microscope to my eye, I extend the range of size that it can perceive, without thereby adding any important element of indirectness or uncertainty to my observation. Suppose I go a step further, however, and depend on a photograph taken through the telescope or the microscope. The photographic apparatus may extend my vision, as when it registers for my vision the infrared radiation that is invisible to my naked eye. However, in addition to such account as I may have to take of any misrepresentations of reality caused by inadequacies in my eye, I shall now have to take account of any misrepresentations caused by inadequacies of the apparatus. Through the telescope the light rays themselves had reached my eye, but it is a representation of them I see in the photograph.

In general, the more elaborate the aids I use to supplement my senses, the greater the element of indirectness and, ultimately, of uncertainty. It is only by the development of such aids, however, that we can expand the range of magnitudes accessible to our knowing.

The resulting problem is especially vivid with respect to the realm of the very small. Let me exemplify this, in the first instance, by reference to the realm of small living organisms.

We can know a dog rather well because he belongs to our own order of magnitude. We are in two-way communication with him. The case is different with a microbe too small to be visible to our naked eyes, inhabiting a drop of water which is its entire universe. There is no way that we can make ourselves small enough to enter that universe. We can see the microbe in its universe only through the intervening agency of the microscope, and if we happened not to have the sense of sight, in addition to the other four, one wonders how we could ever know about its existence at all. (What may there not be in the universe of which we cannot know the existence because of sixth, seventh, or eighth senses that we lack?) It, for its part, cannot enter into our universe and know us. Even if it had the brain and the five senses of a dog there could hardly be meaningful communication between us.

With the aid of a microscope I can at least see the microbe with my own eyes, although I cannot hear, feel, taste, or smell it as an individual. An electron, however, is less than 10^{-14} the size of the microbe. No device can ever make it accessible to any of my senses. The nearest I can come to seeing one is to see the track it leaves in a bubble chamber, from which I infer its existence and something of its behavior. This is like inferring the existence of an airplane one cannot see from the contrail it leaves in its passage. One could not have as precise or sure an idea of the airplane, its structure and shape, its inner workings, as if one could see it "directly" — that is, by light reflected from its surface.

With smaller particles still, particles in the nucleus of the atom that may have a "lifetime" of only 3×10^{-14} second, the indirectness of our observation and the degree of our uncertainty become greater yet. We infer their existence by interpreting certain measurements in terms of what we understand to be certain laws of nature, or we infer it by phenomena that we cannot otherwise account for. Such a particle as a photon, the irreducible unit of light, is an abstract conception in our minds which we cannot properly visualize at all as a physical object like those familiar to us within our own order of magnitude. Whatever it may be, it is not a solid object like a golf ball. The word "particle," applied to it, had best be regarded as metaphorical. It represents the application to a quite different world of a vocabulary developed for the description of our own. We cannot even say it is a "thing," but we call it a "particle" because that is the traditional word, going back to the days when we thought matter was made up of atoms which were solid and too hard to cut.

In any ultimate accounting, no tenable argument can be made against Otto Frisch's statement that

> we should not ask what light *really* is. Particles and waves are both constructs of the human mind, designed to help us speak about the behaviour of light in different circumstances. With [Niels] Bohr we give up the naïve concept of reality, the idea that the world is made up of things, waiting for us to discover their nature. The world is made up by us, out of our experiences and the concepts we create to link them together.*

*

The assumption that our means of perception and interpretation represent the reality of an independently existing realm of being is only one of two unprovable assumptions that we necessarily make. The other is that, when we have the choice among alternative explanations of natural phenomena, each of which appears to be equally sound in logic, the simplest is to be taken as representing the truth. So we reject the old Ptolemaic view that the sun orbits the earth in favor of the Copernican view that the earth orbits the sun, not because we are necessarily unable to make a logical case for the former, but because, if we could make such a case, it would be one of

* *The Nature of Matter*, London, 1972, p. 105.

almost unimaginable complexity, while the case for the Copernican view is one of exceeding simplicity. Although we accept Newton's dictum that "truth is ever to be found in simplicity, and not in the multiplicity and confusion of things," we cannot be sure that it does not represent simply the unwarranted projection on nature of a preference that is merely human. However that may be, we have no choice but to make this unprovable assumption if our understanding of the world is not to crumble into chaos; for, if we did not make it, we would confront an unlimited number of possible explanations for every natural phenomenon, almost all of a complexity we could hardly cope with, and we could make no choice among them.

*

In terms of size we men stand roughly halfway between the smallest particle known to us and the distance of the most remote objects we have been able to detect. Nothing like the same indirectness and uncertainty afflict us in the observation of the very large as in that of the very small. A galaxy 10^9 light-years away radiates exactly the same kind of light as our sun, or as a glow-worm. We have evidence that its composition is the same as that of the galaxy to which our solar system belongs, that it is made up of suns like our own sun that produce light, as it does, by the fusion of hydrogen atoms like those in any glass of water.

Moreover, if we are small for the exploration of a world so large, this disability is not in itself as fundamental as that of being too large to enter the minuscule world at all.

What is a greater disability than our size is that the speed of communication throughout the entire universe, large and small, is limited to the speed of light, 300,000 kilometers per second. We see the most distant galaxy visible to us (by way of telescope and photographic apparatus) as it was 10^{10} years ago, when the light we now see left it; and if we want to see it here on earth as it is today we must wait another 10^{10} years. If Proxima Centauri, the star nearest to our solar system, should have a planetary satellite like our earth, supporting intelligent life like our own, any exchange of communications with that life would take four years each way. However, the statistical chances of the existence of other intelligent life in the universe appears to be such that the odds would be against finding it so nearby that the time for a message to go one way could be measured in less than two or three hundred years.* It follows that, even if we should someday succeed in populating planets circling

* See "The Search for Extraterrestrial Intelligence" by Carl Sagan and Frank Drake in *Scientific American*, May 1975, p. 83.

other stars like our sun, the problem of getting word back from the colonists would require a patience that would be almost the equivalent of total frustration.

Exploration of the very large has also an element of basic uncertainty, although it may not be as disturbing as the basic uncertainty we encounter in our exploration of the very small. It has confronted us with a world of four dimensions that we are incapable of visualizing, although we can define it in the abstract language of mathematics. A mathematical description of reality may not be uncertain on its own terms, but the impossibility of giving it meaning in terms that fit our experience of the sensible world leaves us in the position of someone whose questions are met with answers that, however true, cannot be translated into terms that have meaningful reality for him.

This is not a problem that troubles the layman only. Niels Bohr, who has as good a claim as anyone to be called the father of quantum theory (the body of theory that applies to the very small), constantly emphasized "the necessity of seeking a solid foundation for our lofty abstractions in some simple concrete aspect of the phenomena immediately accessible to observation." *

In any case, investigation of the very large, and of speeds up to the speed of light (which also occur in the realm of the very small), has shown, as has the investigation of the very small, that the common sense based on knowledge only of our own narrow range of magnitudes does not necessarily apply to the universe as a whole. It has shown that categories we have always thought of as independent of one another — such as energy and mass, time and space, gravitational force and inertial force (resistance to acceleration) — are related and may even be no more than different manifestations of the same thing. It has suggested that there is an order in the physical universe that far transcends, in its grandeur and integrity, those limited manifestations of it which we had, until recently, thought to be the whole thing.

*

It is only since the beginning of the present century that the expansion of our knowledge beyond its natural bounds, into the realms of the large and the small alike, has revealed the inapplicability to the universe as a whole of rules of common sense which we had thought to be universal. We may suppose that we are only at the beginning

* Léon Rosenfeld in Stefan Rozental (ed.), *Niels Bohr,* Amsterdam, 1967, p. 115. See also in ibid.: Werner Heisenberg, p. 98; Christian Møller and Mogens Pihl, pp. 251 and 256–257.

of an expanding process of discovery — that we are at the same stage in the discovery of the nature of the physical world that the Europeans were at in the discovery of America during the first two decades of the sixteenth century. We have discovered that the Newtonian conception of the order of nature, although it seemed to fit the universe known to us within limited orders of magnitude, does not fit the expanded universe to which our observation now extends. The beginnings of a new conception of order, that does fit it, have been provided in the form of Einstein's Theory of Relativity, part of which (Special Relativity) appears to have been confirmed beyond question (like a part of the American coastline mapped), much of which remains in the realm of plausible speculation. Insofar as it has been developed today, however, this new order is, indeed, just that. It satisfies the human need to bring order out of chaos.

The exploration of the very small has contributed no less importantly, it may be, to the discovery of a new order, its contribution taking the form of quantum mechanics. It has also, however, introduced elements that, as they are widely interpreted in our day, make for chaos. Recalling, however, the tale of the dwarf flea in Chapter I, we may find that intimations of chaos in the very small are not irreconcilable with indications of order in the very large.

The chief point is that, in the eighth decade of the twentieth century, physical science has produced nothing complete and finished. It is only at the beginning of a development that already represents an immense and revolutionary expansion of our knowledge and understanding. What our novel experience with the very large, the very fast, and the very small has done is to open up a new continent of possibilities.

IV

The World of the Very Large:

1. Time and Distance

COMMON SENSE is based on common experience, supported and elaborated by the logic we apply to the explanation of that experience. It is therefore limited by the limitations of that experience. To a species of fish confined in its range to the middle depths of the ocean it would be common sense that the whole universe was water.

Much of our own common sense represents the traditional limitation of our experience to the confines of the planet we inhabit. Within this limitation time is absolute: it passes at a fixed rate, so that a day or a year is the same length in Peking as in New York. Within this limitation every object is either stationary or in motion, and if in motion is so at a precisely measurable speed. Within this limitation a stick one meter long, whether in motion or not, will always measure the same distance.

We had always assumed that what was true on earth, and was therefore a matter of common sense to us, was universally true. A unit of time far away in universal space could be exactly matched to a unit of time on earth; "now" on earth would be the same "now" in the most distant galaxy, so that we could say of an event in the galaxy that it was simultaneous with an event on earth.

Newton himself never doubted this common sense. For example, he never doubted that an object in outer space must be either stationary or in motion, and, if in motion, at a speed measurable in absolute terms. He did recognize a practical dilemma here. On earth we know whether a wagon, say, is at rest or in motion by reference to the surface of the earth under it, which represents absolute rest for all practical purposes. If, however, the wagon were out in empty space, how would one know whether it was or was not in uniform motion? (Of course, if it were accelerating, we might expect that inertial force, which is the resistance to acceleration, would make itself felt; but, throughout this chapter, when I refer to motion I am referring only to uniform motion, which means an unchanging state of motion.) There would have to be some object outside the wagon itself, an object known to be stationary, by reference to which one could determine the wagon's motion or lack of it.

What we are picturing is the wagon alone in empty space: in all directions, to infinity, there is nothing. Our common language, however, plays a trick on us here. If we took the term "nothing" literally, there would not even be space, although we happen to be incapable of imagining such a situation. When, as children, some of us tried to imagine what was before the Creation, we pictured the total darkness of endless space, stretching back through endless time without change, and this was what we meant by "nothing." We could not imagine the absence of either space or time. In the same way, we refer to nothing as if it were something when, in describing a universe imagined to be empty, we say: "There is nothing" — for what we have in mind is space enduring in time, and this is something.

Thinking in such terms, it does not seem illogical to refer to space as being stationary. "Absolute space," Newton wrote, "in its own nature and without regard to anything external, remains always similar and immutable." While recognizing that there was no way of using space as a frame of reference by which to determine the motion or motionlessness of any object in it, he nevertheless assumed like everyone else that space was stationary, so that any object either did or did not have motion with respect to it, even though there could be no way of knowing whether it did. The common sense based on the limitations of our earthly experience told us that an object either was or was not in motion, and all of us, including Newton, applied that common sense to the entire realm of being.

After Newton, the concept of truly empty space in which the astral bodies circulated began to give increasing trouble. Nowhere, after all, was that space devoid of starlight, and it was everywhere, as well, the medium through which gravitational force was transmitted. Whatever light and force might be, they were not literally nothing. To meet the difficulty, the scientists of the nineteenth century decided that space must be filled with a substance so ethereal that it might appropriately be called "ether." It could not be seen, heard, smelled, or tasted. No direct evidence of its existence had been found, but the common sense of us earthbound mortals showed that it must exist as the medium for the transmission of gravitational force, of light waves, and of other electromagnetic radiation.

The ether also solved, in principle, the problem of finding an absolute frame of reference by which to measure motion, for it was itself presumed to be a motionless sea through which the astral bodies circulated like fish in the depths of a stagnant ocean. All that remained was to find out how one could measure one's passage through it.

A fish moving through still water might measure its motion by the rate at which the water seems to flow along its flanks, which is really the rate at which it is, itself, moving through the motionless water. Likewise, the movement of the earth through the ether should be measurable by the consequent flow of the ether, the "ether wind," which would also provide the empirical evidence of the ether's existence that was still lacking. The problem was how to detect and measure that wind. The solution seemed to lie in the fact that it was the medium through which light waves passed.

A ship moving through the ocean can obtain evidence of its own motion by measuring the speed with which waves pass it, especially if those waves move in a fixed direction and are uniform in their wavelength. (It should be recalled that a wave moving through water lifts and drops the surface of the water in its passage without taking the water along with it — that it is not the water itself traveling, but simply the wave being transmitted across it.) In the same way, the earth moving through the ether could obtain evidence of its own motion (and of the ether's existence) if those traveling with it could measure the speed with which light waves passed it. When the earth was moving directly toward the source of light waves that had a fixed wavelength and velocity, its own velocity would be added to theirs to give a certain relative velocity of earth to waves, while when it was moving in the same direction as the waves its own velocity would be subtracted from theirs to give a lower relative velocity.

By the 1880s the necessary technology for such measurements had been developed and the experiment to detect the "ether wind" was undertaken. The inexplicable result, in repeated trials, was to show that light always passed the measuring apparatus, on its earth platform, at exactly the same velocity, whatever the direction in which the apparatus was pointed. This result violated common sense. It was as if the ship found the waves passing it at the same rate whether it was moving with them or against them.

Einstein's great merit was that he had the boldness to interpret violations of common sense as proof that the common sense itself was false. He therefore abandoned it and took, instead, as a premise from which to derive the laws of nature, the constancy of the speed of light (300,000 kilometers per second) relative to any and all observers, no matter how different their respective states of motion might be. Thus an observer moving toward a star at 100,000 kilometers per second, and another moving away from it at 100,000

km.p.s., would each alike find the light from the star passing him at
300,000 km.p.s. Having accepted this violation of common sense as
a fundamental fact of nature, and as a point of departure for the
description of the physical universe, Einstein dropped the idea of
the ether as unnecessary.

The picture of the universe that resulted, when one extrapolated
from this fundamental fact, when one worked out its logical implications, was revolutionary. The implications overthrew a good part of
the common sense that had prevailed theretofore. They entailed
the abandonment of the idea of a stationary space on the basis of
which one could infer absolute motion or lack of it in the objects
scattered about in it. They entailed the abandonment of the idea
that there was any absolute frame of reference by which to measure
absolute motion. Instead, henceforth all motion or lack of it was
merely relative to whatever frame of reference was chosen, presumably as a matter of convenience.

*

Among the tenets of traditional common sense that fell victim to
Einstein's revolution were the idea of simultaneity, the idea of a
fixed rate of time throughout the universe, and the idea of absolute
distance (the idea that one and the same meter-stick, if it undergoes
no physical expansion or shrinkage, will measure the same distance
under all circumstances). These consequences can be demonstrated
by a couple of thought experiments involving up to four observers
in boundless space. In making them we must recall that, if there
were only one object in all space, it would be meaningless to ask
whether it was stationary or in a state of motion; and that, if there
were only two objects, and they were approaching each other or
receding from each other, it would be meaningless to ask whether
object A was stationary and object B moving, or A moving and B stationary, or both moving. The relative motion of one object to another is the only kind of motion there is.

Let us test, now, by a thought experiment, the commonsense assumption that an event in one part of the universe may be simultaneous with (may occur at the same instant as) another event in another part of the universe.

We suppose two observers in empty space, A and B, separated
from each other by a fixed distance of 144 million kilometers, which
is the distance light travels in eight minutes. Since they are not moving relative to each other, they occupy the same frame of reference,
which we will call Frame A/B. They communicate with each other
by radio signals, which are carried by electromagnetic waves that,

like all such waves, travel at 300,000 km.p.s. Both, knowing the fixed distance that separates them, know that the signals must take precisely eight minutes to cross that distance. Both have identical clocks that keep perfect time. Now they undertake, by a procedure already agreed on, to see whether their clocks are keeping the same time — that is to say, whether they are synchronized so that at any particular instance they have the same reading.

At the instant when A's clock reads 12, he dispatches the single word "twelve" to B, whose clock reads 12.08 when he receives it. B instantly dispatches the return message "twelve-eight" to A, whose clock reads 12.16 when he receives it. Both are now satisfied that their clocks are synchronized.

There is, however, a third observer, C, with a clock just like theirs, located roughly midway between them. He is not moving with them in their frame of reference A/B but has his own Frame C. A and B, regarding their frame as stationary, see him moving at 18 million kilometers per minute toward A and away from B. He himself, regarding his own frame as stationary, sees A moving toward him and B moving away from him, both at the same rate of 18 million kilometers per minute. He has observed the process of synchronizing clocks between A and B, but his interpretation of the result is different from theirs. This is the way he saw what happened.

When A's clock read 12, A signaled "twelve" to B. The signal traveled in eight minutes the 144 million kilometers to the point where B had been when the signal left A. Meanwhile, however, B had moved on, so that the signal did not catch up with him until he had gone a further 18 million kilometers, by which time nine minutes had elapsed. The fact that B's clock read 12.08 when he received the signal means, to C, that it was a minute behind A's clock, which at that instant read 12.09. B signaled back "twelve-eight," and the message took only seven minutes to reach A because the latter had advanced 18 million kilometers to meet it since it left B. Therefore, when A received B's message, "twelve-eight," his own clock read 12.16 (B's read 12.15).

From the point of view of Frame A/B, the two clocks were showing simultaneous instants of time. Both, for example, showed 12.08 simultaneously. From the point of view of Frame C, they were a minute apart, so that, when B's clock showed 12.08, A's showed 12.09.

Which was right?

If Frame A/B was at rest and Frame C in motion, A and B were right. If Frame C was at rest and A/B in motion, C was right. If both were in motion both were wrong.

We have already seen that, in a case like this, it is meaningless to

ask which was at rest and which in motion. Therefore it is meaningless to ask which was right. The conclusion is that there is no
absolute simultaneity in the universe between events separated in
space, that the appearance of simultaneity is merely a consequence
of the state of motion of the observer relative to the points at which
the apparently simultaneous events occur.

Because any such violation of common sense is difficult to grasp, I
here offer briefly a standard variation of the thought experiment I
have just described — in a form essentially the same as that in which
Einstein himself presented it.

Remaining exactly midway between A and B, and therefore in the
same frame of reference, is an observer called Inter-A/B. By
prearrangement, both A and B, having synchronized their clocks, set
off a light-flash at the instant that their clocks read 12.30. The two
flashes of light reach Inter-A/B at the same instant, since he is midway between their respective sources, so that he says they were simultaneous. (He, like A and B, assumes that their common frame
of reference is stationary.) It happens that our previously mentioned observer, C, was exactly opposite Inter-A/B at the instant
when, according to the latter's calculations, the two flashes were set
off. But C saw A's flash a minute before B's. Inter-A/B says this is
because C was moving toward A's flash and away from B's, so that
A's flash had less distance than B's to travel and therefore reached
him sooner. C claims, on the contrary, that B's flash was set off a
minute after A's, but, since Inter-A/B was moving toward it and
away from A's, A's flash had to travel a minute longer than B's
before reaching him, with the consequence that, although occurring
a minute apart, because the two flashes had different distances to
travel they reached him at the same instant.

Again we see that simultaneity is merely a function of the observer's relative movement.

The reason why we never before noticed that this was so is that it
becomes observable only over distances and in terms of velocities
greater than those familiar to us within the limits of our earthly
orders of magnitude. I have explained the impossibility of synchronizing clocks in any except an arbitrary and relative sense, and I
have explained the relativity of simultaneity, in terms of distances
measured in tens of millions of kilometers and velocities measured
in millions of kilometers per minute. The same situation would
prevail if the observers A and B had been standing only a hundred
meters apart on the surface of the earth, while C had been walking
from one to the other at three kilometers per hour. Since, however,
the light would still be traveling at 300,000 km.p.s., although over

such short distances and during time-lapses so small, the difference
between the A/B measurements and the C measurements would be
so infinitesimal as to be undetectable by any means ordinarily available to us. The concept of simultaneity therefore makes practical
sense within the limits of our natural magnitudes, and has become
part of our common sense, although it breaks down when tested in
terms of larger orders of magnitude.

Here is an example of how the enlargement of our knowledge,
simply in physical terms, has enlarged our understanding. Unless
we are sufficiently determined to remain physically and mentally
confined by our earthly orders of magnitude, and to retain our ancient ignorance, the day will surely come when the relativity of simultaneity will have become part of our corrected common sense.
Then people may wonder how their forebears could have believed
in absolute simultaneity (even though it is still the apparent experience of their everyday lives), just as some people today wonder how
our forebears could have believed that the earth was flat (even
though it still appears flat within the limits to which our everyday
lives are confined).

*

Einstein's proposition that the speed of light is the same for all observers, in addition to disproving our theretofore unquestioned idea
of simultaneity, had other implications equally revolutionary by the
test of our common sense. For, if it is impossible for observers in
different frames of reference to agree on simultaneity, it must also
be impossible for them to agree on measurements of distance or
measurements of time. Like the relativity of simultaneity, the relativity of distance and of time may be demonstrated by a thought experiment.

Imagine, now, two parallel measuring rods that, traveling along a
line parallel to their length, pass each other in space. Both are
marked off in kilometers, the kilometers on each being numbered
consecutively like the centimeters on a ruler. We shall call the two
rods P and Q. On each, two observers — PA and PB in the one
case, QA and QB in the other — are standing, separated from each
other by 144 million kilometers according to the markings on their
respective rods. PA and PB may be recognized as the observers
A and B of our earlier thought experiment, now with a measuring
rod under their feet.

By a pre-arranged procedure, PA and PB now undertake to check
the accuracy of rod Q. At the instant when both their clocks, having
already been synchronized by the procedure we know, read 12, each

notes the number of the mark that is opposite him on rod Q. If Q is accurate, according to PA and PB, then their readings of the respective numbers will show that the marks are 144 million kilometers apart. Instead, what the readings show is that they are 162 million kilometers apart. They therefore report to QA and QB that the kilometer-intervals on their rod are too short, since they give a reading of 162 million kilometers for a distance that is, in fact, only 144 million kilometers.

The situation as PA and PB see it

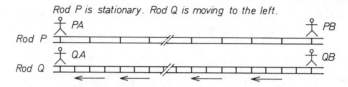

The situation as QA and QB see it

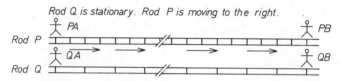

Each sees the kilometers on the other rod as too short

QA and QB, however, claim that PA and PB made a mistake in their measurement of the distance because they thought their clocks were showing the same time when, in fact, PB's clock was one minute behind PA's (for the reason that C gave in the other thought experiment). What had happened, according to QA and QB, was that, when PA's clock read 12 and he took down the number of the mark opposite him, PB's clock still read only 11.59. PB therefore waited another minute before making his reading, and in the course of that minute he moved 18 million kilometers farther on. These 18 million kilometers, added to the 144 million, had given PA and PB the mistaken total of 162 million kilometers.

Since the situation is symmetrical, as between the two measuring rods and the respective pairs of observers traveling with each, if QA and QB decided to test the accuracy of rod P, they would come to the conclusion that the intervals between the kilometer-marks on it were too short by a factor of 162 million divided by 144 million. The observers in either frame of reference, then, would note the same contraction of distance in the other frame of reference.

What this demonstrates is the contraction of an object, from the point of view of any observer relative to whom it is moving, a contraction that depends on its relative velocity. A rod laid out in the line of its relative motion and flying past an observer will seem to be shorter the greater its relative velocity, its apparent length approaching zero as it approaches the speed of light. The shrinkage, however, is only in the direction of motion, so that a bullet, for example, would appear shorter but not narrower (i.e., would change its shape to become stubbier).

Since time and distance share the same relativity, the phenomenon of contraction of distance with motion is matched by that of the dilation of time with motion. The Q observers say that the P clocks are running slow because they still show light taking eight minutes to traverse 144 million kilometers on measuring rod P despite the shrinkage those kilometers have undergone in consequence of the rod's contraction. The P observers say the same about the Q clocks.

According to Einstein's theory, which has now been amply proved by actual experiments with atomic particles in accelerators, uniform motion relative to an observer (a) contracts distance as velocity increases, and (b) slows down time — so that, as an object approaches the speed of light, its length (in the direction of motion) approaches zero, while its ever-retarded time approaches the stopping point.

No object, however, can surpass the speed of light because, as it approaches that speed its mass approaches infinity, and its mass (which in our common experience is its weight) is the measure of its resistance to acceleration. In other words, as it approaches the speed of light (and therefore approaches the total abolition of its length and the total stoppage of its time) its resistance to further acceleration approaches infinity.

The law of nature says, not that no object can move at the speed of light, but that no object can accelerate to the point of exceeding that speed. Such massless particles as photons and neutrinos are always in motion at exactly the speed of light.

*

The contraction of distance and the dilation of time have interesting implications for the possibilities of space-travel.

I mentioned in the last chapter that, since the nearest star, Proxima Centauri, is four light-years distant, no message from earth could reach it in less than four years. It was earth-years that I was referring to, years as measured in our own undilated time. In the same way, when I refer to the distance from earth to Proxima Centauri as being 42,539,000 million kilometers, I am referring to our own uncontracted kilometers.

Imagine, now, a space-traveler who passes our earth on his way to Proxima Centauri at a speed of 259,000 km.p.s. relative to us. By our earth time, it is going to take him over four years to reach the star, and we shall all be more than four years older when he does. Because of the dilation of time, however, he ages only half as fast and will be only two years older when he arrives.

We who remain on earth may say that it would take over 2 million years for a traveler in a space-ship to reach the great spiral nebula in Andromeda, so that anyone who was making the trip would be dead of old age before it had been well begun. Because of the dilation of time, however, a space-traveler passing the earth on his way to the nebula might be only ten years older when he got there — even though all of us would by then have been dead for over 2 million years.

Of course the space-traveler would not have measured the distance from earth to the nebula as being nearly as great as our measurement showed it to be; for in that case he would have found that to cover it in what he measured as ten years he would have had to move at many times the speed of light, which would have been impossible. Because of the contraction of distance, however, his measurement would have shown earth and the nebula as being not nearly so far apart as our measurement showed them to be.

While all this violates our common sense, and is therefore hard for us to grasp, if our minds get used to inhabiting the great reaches of space, and to thinking in terms of the velocities suitable to its distances, it will surely come to be part of what we may then call our corrected common sense — and, as such, not at all hard to grasp. An imaginary parallel may help to make this clear.

A hominid of a near-sighted species, incapable of seeing anything at a distance of more than five centimeters, would surely have difficulty in grasping the laws of perspective that govern the appearance of things over the far greater distances encompassed by our own vision. If, then, we told him that a man two meters tall appeared only one meter tall at a certain distance, that at a still greater distance he appeared only ten centimeters tall, and that he appeared progressively smaller with the increase of distance until he disappeared entirely — if we told him this, he would surely regard it as an extraordinary paradox that violated his common sense. However, if his own vision, then, were extended so that he could see as far as we did, he would soon become as accustomed as we are to such effects of perspective, which would consequently become part of what could properly be called his corrected common sense. It would be proper, then, to consider that he had grown in his understanding of reality. It would be proper to consider that he had made progress in going beyond the elephant's tail; and such progress would give hope of a day when at last he would know what an elephant was.

The World of the Very Large:

2. *Mass and Energy*

WHAT I GAVE AN ACCOUNT of in the last chapter was Einstein's Special Theory of Relativity, which is confined to relations among objects in uniform motion. Uniform motion, as opposed to accelerated motion, is distinguished as a special case of motion, and so Special Relativity is distinguished from General Relativity.

Here the word "accelerated" has a broader meaning than in our daily usage. An automobile is said to accelerate only if it increases its speed, not if it slows down, and not if it goes around a curve without changing its speed. In scientific usage, however, any change in an object's state of motion is acceleration.

According to Newton's First Law of Motion, "every body continues in a state of rest, or uniform motion in a straight line, unless it is compelled to change that state by forces impressed upon it." That law may be regarded as still holding good in Einstein's universe, albeit with qualifications of a secondary nature. The scientific distinction between uniform and accelerated motion, then, is the distinction between a body that, having no forces impressed upon it, continues in its state of motion, and a body that, under the impress of force, changes its state of motion — whether by slowing down, by speeding up, or by taking a new direction.

Because the General Theory deals with accelerated motion, it is necessarily concerned with the forces that are impressed upon objects. In the universe as a whole, excluding the very small, the chief such forces are those of gravity and electromagnetism.

In Newton's universe there had been another force as well, that of inertia.

According to Newton's Third Law of Motion, when two bodies interact, the forces exerted by each body on the other are equal and opposite. This is to say that, if two bodies, however unequal in weight, collide in space, the force of each on the other is the same (although the lighter body, less resistant than the heavier to an equal amount of force, will undergo a greater deflection from its course). If a feather drifts down from the sky to land on the desk in front of me, its pressure against the combination of the desk and the entire terrestrial globe under it is equaled by the counter-pressure that desk and globe exert against it. Newton's Third Law is one of the foundations of symmetry, equilibrium, and stability in the universe.

What holds me to the earth, and the earth to me, is what Newton first defined and measured as the force of gravitation. With respect to any particular object on the earth, we measure that force as its weight. My weight, for example, is 73 kilograms, as against the 5.44×10^{22} kilograms of the earth. It is the product of these two weights (the second assumed as a constant within our earthly confines) by which one would have to measure the force of mutual gravitational attraction between the earth and me, taking account of the fact that this force diminishes as the square of the distance between our respective centers of gravity. (On top of Mount Everest I weigh less than at its base — although not enough less to notice the difference.)

What we call weight in ordinary parlance is what is called mass in scientific parlance. In Newton's universe there were two kinds of mass. One was gravitational mass, which represented a body's force of attraction on other bodies. The other was inertial mass, which represented the resistance of any body to acceleration. Of the two bodies that collide in space, the lighter is deflected more than the heavier because its inertial mass is less, because it is less resistant to acceleration. A wagon of 400 kilograms at rest on a flat surface will require twice as much force (over a given time) to start it rolling at a certain speed as a wagon of 200 kilograms. Once rolling, it will require twice as much force (over a given time) to stop it as the 200-kilogram wagon rolling at the same speed. The heavier wagon will also require more force to deflect it from a straight line than the lighter wagon. This resistance to acceleration is what inertial mass represents.

By what seemed an extraordinary coincidence, in Newton's universe gravitational mass and inertial mass, although quite separate properties of matter, exactly matched each other. (The reason why, in a vacuum, a pebble dropped from a height fell to the ground with the same acceleration as a cannon-ball dropped from the same height, in spite of its lesser force of attraction to the earth, was that its relative resistance to acceleration was less by precisely the amount necessary to compensate for the difference in the forces of attraction. In other words, the difference in inertial mass exactly compensated for the difference in gravitational mass.) The measure of any object's gravitational mass was exactly equivalent, then, to the measure of its inertial mass. This was the extraordinary coincidence. Einstein, in his General Theory, explained it by saying that gravitation and inertia were one and the same thing.

As with the denial of simultaneity, the Principle of Equivalence, as Einstein's explanation is called, can be demonstrated by thought experiments. Imagine a large box without windows placed on the edge of a revolving merry-go-round in totally empty space. A man inside the box finds himself pressed against its outside wall by what we call centrifugal force. His tendency to continue his state of motion in a straight line is countered by the pressure of the wall as it deflects him from it. His weight presses him against the outside wall, which he regards as a floor, and he can measure that weight by standing on scales between him and it. Under the circumstances, the weight he measured would represent his inertial mass rather than his gravitational mass, for he is not in a gravitational field. But he cannot know this. Walking about on "the floor" of the box, there is no way for him to tell whether he is experiencing gravitational or inertial force, whether his box is resting on the surface of a planetary mass or being swung through empty space in a circle.

Einstein himself composed the best known thought experiment for demonstrating the equivalence of inertia and gravitation. Imagine a windowless elevator being towed through empty space at a constant rate of acceleration. If it were moving at a uniform rather than an accelerating rate, a passenger, sharing its uniform motion, would be weightless in obedience to Newton's First Law, floating in the space of its interior. Because of its constant acceleration, however, what he terms the floor of the elevator is constantly catching up with him, is pressing against him — although he might well think of himself, rather, as being pressed against it by his own weight.

Again, there is no way by which the passenger can make the distinction between inertial force and gravitational force. There is no way he can tell whether his elevator is moving through empty space at constant acceleration or is at rest on some planetary body. If, standing with his feet pressed to the floor, he lets go of a rubber ball that he was holding in his hand, the ball will move to the floor at a constantly accelerating rate and, bouncing against it, rebound toward his hand. There is no way that he can tell whether the ball is drawn to the floor by the gravitational attraction of a planetary body upon which the elevator is resting, or whether, when he lets it go, it simply continues in uniform motion until the accelerating floor catches up and hits it.

Imagine, now, a gunman in space who shoots at the elevator. The bullet, traveling in a straight line, pierces one wall, crosses the inside space, and goes out through the opposite wall. If the passenger made a photographic record of its path, that path, which was a straight line from the gunman's point of view, would appear to be curved "downward," toward the floor, on the photographs. For, while the bullet was crossing the interior, the whole elevator, together with the photographic apparatus, would have been moving "upward" at constant acceleration. The effect would have been the same whether the elevator moved "upward" or the bullet "downward." Again, the passenger could not tell whether the apparent curvature was due to gravitational attraction exerted on the bullet by a planetary mass with respect to which the elevator was at rest, or to the fact that the apparatus, together with the whole elevator, was moving at an accelerating rate transversely to its path.

Now imagine a ray of light in place of the bullet, and windows in opposite walls of the elevator through which it could pass. Like the path of the bullet, the path followed by the light would appear to the passenger to be curved, since the elevator would have moved across that path at an accelerating rate while the light traversed its interior. (Although the curvature would be imperceptible if the elevator moved at the usual speed of elevators, we have only to imagine it accelerating at the rate of, say, 100,000 km.p.s. every second to make the curve obvious.)

In Newton's universe light had no weight, it had no mass, it was not subject to gravitational attraction, and it always traveled in a straight line. If that belief was right, would it not follow that the apparent curvature of the light beam, as observed by the passenger, would betray the fact that he was in accelerated motion rather than at rest with respect to a planetary mass?

Einstein's answer was that light, as it manifests itself in reality, does have mass, and is indeed deflected, just like a bullet, by the force of gravitational attraction. To test this answer, observations were undertaken by the British in 1919 on a total eclipse of the sun that, by cutting off the blinding sunlight, made it possible to photograph stars that appeared close to its edge, their light having therefore to pass near to the sun on its way to the earth. The results satisfied the leading astronomers of Britain that the path of the light was indeed bent by the sun's gravitational attraction.

Here we see again how the exploration of the very large has upset our common sense, which had been based only on experience within the limitations of our own terrestrial order of magnitude. The weight of light does not manifest itself on a perceptible scale within that order.

*

At this point I resort to an analogy to prepare the reader for what follows. If, while keeping my eyes focused on some object, I try to give an account of what appears in the rest of my field of vision, I find that as I move out, in terms of mental concentration, from the center on which my eyes are focused what I see, while not fading, becomes increasingly indefinable in an indefinable way, and I cannot find any precise boundary to my field of vision simply because of the way definition is gradually lost from the center outward. My mental grasp of what shows in the field becomes less until I can no longer be quite sure I am seeing anything — without, at the same time, being quite sure I am not seeing something. There is a parallel between this experience and that of trying to grasp what, with respect to the physical world, is at the frontiers of our knowledge. By certain devices, we have come to know a good deal about what seems to be at the frontiers, but we cannot make a proper image of it.

The certain devices to which I refer are those of mathematics. Mathematics can give us quite definite information about what we cannot see or even picture in our imaginations. None of us, for example, could picture a five-dimensional world, but mathematics is capable of giving a precise account of such a world.

The information that mathematics may convey extends far into realms of what is unimaginable in terms of sensory experience. There are physicists who are relatively untroubled by this, whose capacity for living in a world that is almost completely abstract is such that the lack of connection between it and the world of sense impressions hardly makes it seem less real to them, if at all. Others, exemplified by Niels Bohr, may be competent to find their way about the world of mathematical abstractions but still feel a profound need to relate it, where possible, to a world that can be visualized.

The problem is frustrating for those of us to whom mathematics, except in its elementary forms, is an unknown language. But that language has, since Newton's day, been developing increasingly abstruse forms to the point where it is no longer possible for any physicist — or any mathematician, for that matter — to command all of it. One of the greatest of the mathematical physicists, P. A. M. Dirac, has written:

> It seems to be one of the fundamental features of nature that fundamental physical laws are described in terms of a mathematical theory of great beauty and power, needing quite a high standard of mathematics for one to understand it. You may wonder: Why is nature constructed along these lines? One can only answer that our present knowledge seems to show that na-

ture is so constructed. We simply have to accept it. One could perhaps describe the situation by saying that God is a mathematician of a very high order, and He used very advanced mathematics in constructing the universe. Our feeble attempts at mathematics enable us to understand a bit of the universe, and as we proceed to develop higher and higher mathematics we can hope to understand the universe better.*

As the twentieth century has passed, then, our comprehension of physical reality has moved beyond what we can visualize into a world of mathematical formulas — and in that mathematical world, which has become divorced altogether from what we can visualize, it has moved on to the frontiers of what the most advanced mathematicians among us can understand. Without taking too precise an account of possibilities, one could imagine that an intellectual prodigy might someday arise to reveal the ultimate secret of the universe, but to reveal it in the form of an equation so far beyond the understanding of all the rest of us that it left us none the wiser.

In the last chapter, what I described could still be taken quite literally. As one goes further in General Relativity and quantum theory, however, any description of nature in visualizable terms has increasingly to be regarded as more or less metaphorical.

*

In the last chapter I left a loose end that I now take up.

Physicists before the twentieth century had been troubled by the conception of space as being empty, a vacuum. How did the sun communicate its gravitational attractive force across a vacuum to seize the earth and hold it prisoner in an orbit? Such "action at a distance" violated their common sense.

Again, if electromagnetic radiation — for example, that of the light from the sun — was in the form of waves crossing empty space, what was it that waved? A wave, after all, is not a thing in itself but, rather, a form that matter assumes, which means that there has to be matter to assume it.

It seemed obvious, then, that there must be some unknown matter that filled space, and this unknown matter was given the name "ether."

With the acceptance of Einstein's Special Relativity, however, the concept of such a substance was discarded; and changing attitudes, including increasing confinement to mathematical abstraction, made the question of "action at a distance" seem irrelevant to the theoreti-

* "The Evolution of the Physicist's Picture of Nature," *Scientific American,* May 1963.

cal physicist's proper concerns. (God, one might say, from having been a mechanic in Newton's day, had become a mathematician.) Even so, it was hard to get away from the logic, based on the definition of the word "wave," that one could not have a wave of nothing. By this time, however, the concept of something called "field" had caught on. One referred to the earth as being in the gravitational field of the sun. Light rays, one said, were electromagnetic fields propagating as waves.

Ether had been regarded as simply a kind of matter — as atoms are matter or wood is matter — not operationally defined in terms such as force and energy. Field is so defined. It is "something" in the way that energy is "something," rather than in the way that matter is "something." *

There is not one field that fills space, one gathers, but many. For example, the sun is surrounded by its own gravitational field, which extends outward indefinitely from its center of gravity, diminishing in "strength" with the square of the distance. (One never talked about the "strength" of the ether.) This is one kind of field, a gravitational field. Again, if a coil of electrically charged wire is moved, it propagates around itself an electromagnetic field (made up of alternating electric and magnetic fields) that also extends outward indefinitely in all directions, diminishing in "strength" with the square of the distance. Electromagnetic fields propagate at the constant speed of light, 300,000 km.p.s., in the form of waves of fixed length (the wave-lengths between certain limits being visible as light).

All this suggests that "field" means something quite different from "ether," while still leaving the question of what it is that waves without an answer that our traditional common sense would find satisfactory. The fault, we must suppose, is with our traditional common sense.

The only possible answer to be given in the first instance is that the question, however relevant to the world of our traditional common sense, is irrelevant to the world we have now entered, which transcends that common sense. In the old commonsense world, at any particular point in the universe there had to be either matter or space, one or the other. Matter was something and space was nothing. Nothing doesn't vibrate, nothing doesn't wave. If there are waves or vibrations, then they must be waves or vibrations of matter.

When one thinks about it, however, one can see that this is too simple a view — that it is even too simple a view of the universe as it was known in Newton's day. Newton must have known that there

* For an answer to the question whether field is real, see Kenneth W. Ford, *Classical and Modern Physics*, Lexington (Mass.), 1972–1974, pp. 682–683.

was not one square millimeter of the known or visible universe without some light in it; but he could assume, as he did, that the light consisted of streams of particles moving at the high velocity we know (which had already been measured approximately), and the particles could be identified as matter while the intervals between them could be regarded as nothing through which they streamed.

There was also the gravitational force that somehow extended from one object in space to another, and it would have seemed absurd to say that it, too, consisted of particles. Newton simply accepted this challenge to common sense, however, as a mystery to which, amid all his other preoccupations, he was not prepared to give his attention.

A supplementary or supporting answer to the question of what it is that waves, or of what it is through which gravitational force is communicated, is that science is not required to answer it at all. The argument — which in the nineteenth century was supplied with a rationale in the form of Auguste Comte's positivistic philosophy — was that the business of science is to discover and describe *what,* not *how.* For example, a ray of light in a laboratory, after traversing a vacuum, passes through a pinhole in an opaque sheet to strike a screen. The spot of light on the screen has an outline that could be formed only by diffraction of the light as it passed through the hole, and only waves are subject to diffraction. Therefore the light consists of waves, and therefore what crossed the vacuum was waves. Science has answered the question, *what?*

But *how?,* you ask.

The answer is that it is not the business of science to say *how.*

The acceptability of this answer, I suggest, is a function of the fact that, for the time being at least, it is the best there is. If science were able to say *how* but refused to do so, it would not be acceptable.

Physics today has answers to many questions in the form of equations that tell *what* and provide a sound basis for the prediction of *what,* but do not tell *how.* Accepting this approach, as we must, we can see how such a question as what it is that waves is invalidated rather than answered.

The situation, however, is not quite as unsatisfactory as I have made it seem. Out of General Relativity and quantum theory, what might be called a picture of the universe does begin to emerge, even if it is still as hard to define as the images we see, so to speak, out of the corners of our eyes.

*

We may think of the entire universe as filled with energy, thereby abandoning the old conception of endless nothing in which bits of matter are scattered. Electromagnetism is energy, and it is continuous throughout the four dimensions of space-time.

The second step is to grasp the fact that energy and matter are simply different manifestations of the same thing. Analyzing matter down to its constituents in the smallest particles we have so far been able to identify, we can describe those invisible particles (which we will never be able to see) as irreducible units or quanta of energy more plausibly than we can describe them as the solid stuff that we call matter in the world of our own dimensions.

The property of matter that counts most, when it comes to the structure and behavior of the physical universe, is mass. Every bit of what we call matter, down to the smallest particles, has mass.* However, if mass, as a quantity, is a measure of matter, it is no less a measure of energy as well. Matter has mass; energy has mass. The precise formula that applies here is Einstein's equation, $e = mc^2$, which tells us that the energy of any object is equal to its mass multiplied by the square of "c," which is the constant speed of light. Turning the equation around, we have $m = \dfrac{e}{c^2}$. The conversion factor of mass to energy is c^2; the conversion factor of energy to mass is $\dfrac{1}{c^2}$.

The point is that energy converts to mass and mass to energy. This is tantamount to saying that matter *is* energy — in storage if one wishes so to regard it.

I have now made two points: (1) that the universe is filled continuously with energy; (2) that energy and matter are, ultimately, the same thing. A possible implication is that the universe is basically of uniform composition throughout, in the sense that it is a four-dimensional continuum of what we may call matter-energy. It is non-uniform in composition only to the extent that the matter-energy may be more intense in some parts than in others — or, cor-

---

* When we say that photons and neutrinos are massless particles we mean that they have no "rest-mass"; which is to say that their mass would be zero if they were at rest (which they never are). The only question, here, is of how we choose to define mass. A physicist who defines it as a property to be measured only as it would manifest itself in an object at rest relative to the observer, who does the measuring, says that photons and neutrinos have zero mass. Another physicist who defines it as a relativistic property — a quantity that varies with the state of motion of the object relative to the observer — would assign a positive mass to photons and neutrinos, which always move at the speed of light relative to any and every observer. Both physicists would agree that these particles, as they exist in reality, have momentum and are influenced by gravity. these being the two properties we associate with mass.

respondingly, that it may manifest itself differently at one location than at another.

In two-dimensional terms, and speaking quite metaphorically, we may picture a tablecloth that has, at scattered points, been gathered up into bunches from which wrinkles radiate in all directions. It is all the same material, but concentrated here and there, the effect of each concentration being to distort the area surrounding it. May we not say that the universe is all matter-energy, but concentrated here and there, the concentrations distorting the areas surrounding them? The sun is such a concentration, the earth a smaller one. The distortions by which they are surrounded are what we call their gravitational fields. At this point, and in these terms, the word "field" begins to have some meaning.

An electromagnetic field is also a disturbance in matter-energy. An excited atom, let us say, propagates a disturbance in the matter-energy around itself, like a stone dropped into still water. The propagating disturbance may at last reach my eye in the form of what I call light, if its wavelength is within certain limits; or it may reach my radio-antenna in the form of what I call radio-waves, if it is within other limits. In either case, it is electromagnetic radiation, and the area across which it is propagated is not empty space but space occupied by electromagnetic field.

Does it not look as if we may be at least beginning, now, to replace the traditional common sense, which was still unquestioned in Newton's day, with what we might call a new, or a corrected, or an enlarged common sense?

*

We have now done away with empty space, which is not to be found anywhere. The universe is one great ocean of matter-energy that takes the form of fields — gravitational fields, electromagnetic fields (which may some day prove to be all one). This conception is necessarily hard for us to grasp at the present stage in the development of our minds, if only because we have no vocabulary adapted to what is remote from our traditional experience. The inadequacy of our traditional vocabulary is part of the difficulty we are dealing with when we try to say what this ocean of a universe is full of — "radiation," "particles," "fields," "matter-energy." Nevertheless, the two questions of how there can be "action at a distance," and of what it is that waves, now begin to lose their point. Space is nowhere empty.

*

I have referred all along to gravitational "force" as if it were something that reached out from any mass of material to pull other bodies toward that mass. But gravitation, according to Einstein's Principle of Equivalence, is inertia — and inertia, according to Newton's First Law, is simply the resistance of an object to any change in its state of rest or of motion in a straight line.

The term "straight line," in this definition of inertia, is obsolete today. Newton's space was one of straight lines, but Einstein's is not. Newton's three-dimensional universe was Euclidean, its space cubic, its geometry rectilinear. In such a universe distances are measured in lines that are perceived to be straight. A straight line is the shortest distance between two points; it is the path followed by an object in uniform motion when no forces are impressed upon it. In such a universe, if the earth moves in a circle rather than a straight line it must be because the sun exerts a gravitational "force" in the form of a tug that pulls it away from the straight trajectory it would otherwise follow.

Einstein's universe, however, is not Euclidean, not cubic, not rectilinear. Unfortunately, we cannot picture this four-dimensional continuum; but we can grasp some of its features by pictorial similes, such as the following.

We are able to represent visually, in the form of a globe, the three-dimensional earth on which we live. Taking account of all three of the dimensions occupied by its convex surface, we can see how, on that surface, the shortest distance between two points takes the form of a curve. Suppose, however, that the limitation of our minds enabled us to visualize only two dimensions. In that case, the three dimensions of the earth's surface could be represented for us visually only by one of those two-dimensional projections that we are familiar with in flat maps. The reduction from the three dimensions of the convex reality to the two dimensions of the map necessarily involves some distortion. On Mercator's projection, for example, horizontal lengths are distorted so that they expand with distance from the equator, a meter along the 90th parallel of north latitude being, consequently, almost six times as long as a meter along the equator. Again, on the flat surface of Mercator's projection the shortest distance between two points, such as New York and London, shows as a curved rather than a straight line. This kind of distortion in the two-dimensional projection is what would reveal, to those of us with minds unable to visualize more than two dimensions, the curvature of the three-dimensional reality. So the distortions that manifest themselves in the three-dimensional projections of Einstein's four-dimensional universe, which are all our minds can visualize, are what reveal the curvature of the four-dimensional reality.*

The ocean of matter-energy, which is Einstein's four-dimensional universe, is non-uniform, for there are concentrations of the matter-energy that affect it in their vicinity as the bunching of the material of a tablecloth spreads wrinkles around the bunches. The matter-energy of this universe may be thought of as curved and convoluted, so that the shortest line between two points in it is not necessarily one that appears straight to us as projected upon the three-dimensional world of our minds. When the light from a star bends through the gravitational field of the sun on its way to the earth it is simply taking the shortest distance between two points in a four-dimensional space-time continuum that is locally shaped by the concentration of matter-energy called the sun. In these terms, what we are describing is inertial behavior. We can equally well say that the light is drawn closer to the sun by the sun's gravitational field, in which case we are describing Newton's "force" of gravitation. But it is all the same, for inertia and gravitation are the same.

*

The curvature of the universe, in Einstein's account of it, is such that, although unbounded, like the surface of the earth, it is, like the surface of the earth, finite. It curves to return upon itself, so that the light going out from a star will eventually return to it like a radio-wave encircling the earth.

Einstein's universe is harder to grasp than Newton's because it differs more widely from the world of our familiar experience. But it is basically simpler, for it has made single phenomena of what were considered quite separate and unrelated phenomena in Newton's universe. It has combined time and space; it has combined matter and energy; and it has combined gravitation with inertia. It is therefore less chaotic than Newton's universe, more orderly.

* For a beautiful exposition of this see J. J. Callahan, "The Curvature of Space in a Finite Universe," *Scientific American,* August 1976.

VI

The World of the Very Large:

3. Acceleration and Gravity

ACCELERATED MOTION, no less than uniform motion, is relative. If the accelerating elevator we imagined in the last chapter were the only object in an otherwise empty universe, its passenger would presumably not have the problem of determining whether he was experiencing the effect of inertial or of gravitational force. There would be nothing relative to which it was accelerating, and therefore, presumably, he would experience no force at all.

Suppose, now, that two elevators pass each other at an accelerating rate in what is otherwise empty space (as our traditional common sense conceives it). Each would be in a state of acceleration relative to the other, and the passenger in each would therefore experience a force of inertia or of gravitation — albeit so infinitesimal as to be imperceptible to ordinary human beings, the masses involved being so small. Nevertheless, we will suppose each passenger to be aware of the force and concerned to explain it.

If the two passengers, in their respective elevators, share our traditional common sense, it would be natural for each to suppose the other's elevator in a state of rest, his own in a state of acceleration that accounted for what he would regard as the inertial force he was experiencing.

The question each answered in this fashion would be a false question, however, for the reason that, if we accept the Principle of Equivalence, inertial force and gravitational force are names for what are merely different manifestations of the same thing.

To explain this we have to widen our conception of what determines the strength of a gravitational field.

Each elevator may be said, simply by its existence, to generate around itself a gravitational field the strength of which, proportional to its mass, diminishes with the square of the distance from its center of gravity. The two elevators, both at rest, would experience a mutual gravitational attraction proportional to their combined mass and inversely proportional to the square of the distance between them (measured from their respective centers of gravity). Our widened conception of the gravitational field comes when we add to this formulation that the strength of the combined gravitational field is greater in proportion to the relative acceleration between the two elevators. This being so, it makes no difference whether the passenger in either calls the force he feels inertial — attributing it to his own acceleration relative to the other elevator, regarded as being at rest — or, regarding his own elevator as being at rest, calls it gravitational, attributing it to the strengthening of the other's gravitational field in consequence of its acceleration relative to his own elevator. These are simply two different ways of looking at the same thing, using the word "inertia" in the one case, "gravitation" in the other.

Let me now add what is, for the purpose of this exposition, a final fact. Time dilation, which varies with the velocity of one frame of reference relative to an observer in another, also varies with the strength of the gravitational potential.* Just as a clock weighs more at sea-level than on the summit of Mount Everest, which is farther from the earth's center of gravity, so it runs slower at sea-level than on the summit of Mount Everest.

All this is introductory to the explanation of the so-called "twin paradox," which has been debated ever since Einstein published his Special Theory of Relativity.

*

We suppose a pair of twins, of whom Arthur remains on earth while Bernard leaves in a space-ship traveling at 259,000 km.p.s. At this speed, Arthur sees Bernard's clock as running only half as fast as his own, so that Bernard is aging only half as fast as he is. If both were twenty years old when they parted, Bernard is only thirty when Arthur is forty. This calculation, however, involves the arbitrary assumption by Arthur that he himself, remaining on earth, is at rest, that Bernard is the one in motion. Nothing in the Special Theory, however, makes it any less valid for Bernard to assume the contrary: that he himself has remained at rest in his space-ship while Arthur and the earth to which he is attached have moved off at 259,000 km.p.s. On this assumption, Bernard regards Arthur's clock as running at half-time, and regards Arthur as aging only half as fast as he is. It follows that, while Arthur regards Bernard as thiry years old and himself as forty, Bernard regards Arthur as thirty and himself as forty. It is logically impossible for both to be right. If they came

* In any gravitational field, the gravitational "potential" is relative to the distance from the center of gravity.

together again, face-to-face, each could not be younger than the other.

In the situation we have described, however, the distance between them is constantly widening and they do not come together again. If, now, in an effort to resolve the contradiction, they communicate with each other by radio across the light-years that separate them, the messages traveling back and forth at 300,000 km.p.s., it transpires that they cannot synchronize their clocks, they cannot agree on a common "now," and therefore they cannot agree on a common time-scale as a basis for deciding which, if either, is the younger. They would have to come together again before they could compare their clocks meaningfully to determine which, if either, registered the greater lapse of time.

Let us, then, bring them together again. Bernard relative to Arthur, or Arthur relative to Bernard, depending on the point of view, slows down to a stop, reverses his course, and returns back upon it at 259,000 km.p.s. — until he slows down and stops to join the other in their original common frame of reference. They then compare clocks, only to find that Bernard's has registered a shorter lapse of time since they parted from each other, that Bernard is therefore the younger of the two.

If, as we have supposed, the situation is symmetrical, so that what happens to Bernard's time from Arthur's point of view must happen as well to Arthur's time from Bernard's point of view, then there is no reason why, when the twins come together again and compare their clocks, it should transpire that Bernard's time has fallen behind Arthur's, not Arthur's behind Bernard's. What this unsymmetrical result shows is that the situation cannot be symmetrical after all.

In what respect, then, is it not symmetrical?

Our clue to the answer lies in a difference between what Arthur experiences and what Bernard experiences. When Bernard in his space-ship blasts off from the earth, when he and Arthur separate from each other, he feels what he identifies as a crushing inertial force that is not felt by Arthur. He feels himself pressed against the back of his seat in the space-ship as, according to his interpretation, it accelerates away from the stationary earth. While we may as properly say that the space-ship, with Bernard in it, remains *in situ*, that it is the earth with Arthur on it which accelerates away from the space-ship, Arthur does not experience the force associated with acceleration that Bernard does. Here is an asymmetry in the respective experiences of the two.

The same asymmetry of experience manifests itself when the space-ship speeding away from the earth (or the earth speeding away from the space-ship, or each speeding away from the other) slows down and at last reverses course (the space-ship back toward the earth, or the earth back toward the space-ship, or each back toward the other). It manifests itself still a third time when the space-ship slows down to come to a stop against the earth (or the earth slows down to come to a stop against the space-ship, or each slows down to join the other). In each of these cases, Bernard experiences the forces associated with change of speed while Arthur does not.

What is the essential difference between the respective situations of the two that accounts for this difference in their respective experiences?

Relativity theory, which we are not putting into question, tells us that it is as valid for us to regard the earth as accelerating away from the space-ship, then reversing course to return to the space-ship, and finally slowing down to join it, as to regard the space-ship as leaving an earth that is fixed in space and then returning to it. Let us, then, suppose that the space-ship with Bernard remains in place, while the earth with Arthur moves off and then returns. How, on the basis of such a supposition, do we account for the crushing force experienced three times by Bernard but never by Arthur?

We account for it by what is the one notable difference between the respective situations of the twins. When the earth with Arthur on it accelerates away from Bernard in his space-ship, the whole solar system, the whole Milky Way, and all the other galaxies of the universe accelerate with the earth and Arthur relative to Bernard's little space-ship. The crushing force that Bernard alone experiences is the gravitational force generated by the acceleration, with respect to the relatively infinitesimal mass of Bernard and his space-ship, of the total mass of all the matter in the universe. It is in this quantitative difference between the respective masses accelerating relative to each other that the basic asymmetry lies.

A simile may help make this clear. When a light bullet is fired from a heavy gun, the situation is symmetrical in that the force pushing the gun away from the bullet (causing it to recoil) is exactly equal to the force pushing the bullet away from the gun. However, because the mass of the gun is so much greater than that of the bullet, a flea (called Bernard) clinging to the bullet will experience that force as a flea (called Arthur) clinging to the gun will not.

In our interpretation of the thought experiment with the twins, Bernard experiences a degree of gravitational force that Arthur does not. The effect of gravitation, which only he of the two experiences in such a high degree (experiencing it three successive times) is to slow down his clock relative to Arthur's (he would see this as a speeding up of Arthur's clock relative to his own), causing Arthur to age faster than himself during the three periods of relative acceleration. This speeded-up process of Arthur's aging, during these periods, more than makes up for the retardation Bernard observes in the process during the periods when they are in uniform motion relative to each other — thereby leading him to expect what he later discovers to be the case, that Arthur will be older than he is when they come together again.

If all concerned had chosen to regard Bernard as accelerating relative to an Arthur who remained fixed in space, then the succession of different inertial frames of reference through which Bernard went during the three periods of his acceleration would be what accounted for Arthur's more rapid aging. Either way, there would be reason for the lesser age of Bernard when the two came together again.

*

One might be tempted to believe, on the basis of this thought experiment, that the distribution of the preponderant masses of the universe does establish something like a privileged frame of reference — a frame that, at least for all practical purposes, defines absolute rest. To be precise, we can regard the general distribution of mass throughout the universe as defining one frame of reference that is privileged in the sense that it provides, by its overwhelmingly preponderant mass, a frame of reference that may reasonably be regarded as representing rest and, therefore, as serving for the measurement of what may reasonably be regarded as the movement of all individual objects or clusters of objects that are in motion relative to it. This frame makes itself physically felt in the dragging influence it exerts on whatever accelerates relative to it, although it is without physical effect on anything that is in uniform motion relative to it.

We have a similar situation when an apple falls from its tree to the ground. In principle, the planet earth and the apple mutually attract each other with the same force of attraction, the earth moving toward the apple as the apple moves toward the earth. The basic situation is symmetrical. But the inertial mass of the earth, its resistance to acceleration, is so much greater than that of the apple as to make any movement of the earth toward the apple (relative to the rest of the universe) immeasurably small. For all practical purposes, we say that the apple falls to the earth, not that the earth falls to the apple or that both fall toward each other.

With some simplification one might regard all the galaxies as together representing one frame of reference. If, then, one pictures a space-ship traveling through the universe at a speed of 259,000 km.p.s., relative to the universal frame of reference, for all practical purposes we can say (and it is our habit to say) that the galactic universe is at rest, the space-ship in motion. To put the two frames on a basis of equality, saying that they are mutually moving past each other at the relative rate given, would seem as unrealistic as to say that the earth and the apple are in mutual movement toward each other, coming together at last at a point intermediate between the respective positions originally occupied by each.

Still, it is basic that gravitation, regarded as a force, is not unilateral, that it is not a force which works in one direction only, operating on one object and not the other in the interaction between the two. (This is Newton's Third Law, set forth on page 26, which is still accepted as one of the fundamental laws of nature.) In the same way, it is basic that there is no frame of reference representing an absolute state of rest in the universe, even though something like majority rule tends to disguise this — even though the preponderance of mass in the universe, by its preponderant gravitational influence, seems to provide an absolute basis for distinguishing between uniform and accelerated motion.

*

I should note in conclusion that not all physicists are untroubled by the logic on which General Relativity is based. There are some who claim, for example, that the thought experiment by which the twin paradox is resolved can be invalidated by extending the period of relative uniform motion to something approaching infinity, thereby extending the period of time during which, from Bernard's point of view, Arthur's clock is running slow, without extending the time during which, in consequence of acceleration, Arthur's clock, as seen by Bernard, is running fast. If, moreover, the curvature of the universe means that Bernard in his space-ship must eventually return to earth without any deviation from his uniform motion, once it is attained, then one can reduce the period of acceleration to an insignificant fraction of the total time.

A layman like myself, unable to judge these differences among the qualified professionals, has no choice but to suppose that the consensus of the overwhelming majority is valid — even though he knows how often, in the past, such a consensus has proved to be wrong. Few scientists, however, would disagree with the statement that Einstein's Relativity does not provide a final understanding of the universe any more than Newton's mechanics did. It can be expected, with the passage of time, to show points of weakness, points on which it cannot be reconciled with some increasing body of experimental evidence; just as Newton's mechanics eventually did. Then it, too, will have to be radically corrected by some still more developed theory.

VII

The World of the Very Small:

1. The Constitution of Matter

THE READER may note our inability to avoid discussing these matters in terms of conceptions that cannot represent the objective universe.

In the last chapter I referred to what the situation might be if, in a universe that otherwise consisted of empty space, there were only one material object — in this case, the elevator of the thought experiment. But the conception we have of what we call "empty space" must be quite foreign to the external reality we assume to exist. The external reality cannot be that of "nothing," of "emptiness," extended in three dimensions or four, with bits of matter scattered about it. What this conception represents is simply a way of thinking and a way of speaking that our kind developed to describe limited topical circumstances. For example, after the wine has been poured out of a wine bottle we say that the bottle is "empty," that there is "nothing" in it, even though we know that the visible wine was immediately relaced by invisible air. Presumably such terminology comes down to us from a time when we did assume that there was nothing in such regions of space as contained only what we could not see or feel by touching.

In a naïve view, the universe is indeed divided between "matter" and "nothing"; but this view and its associated terminology have become increasingly misleading in their application to our cosmic environment. Today it is more plausible to believe that what has extension in the four dimensions we know by our own direct experience is not "nothing" but, rather, something that we may call "matter-energy." Space and time, we may well believe, exist as functions or manifestations of this something, which gives the universe its dimensional character as its gaseous contents give a balloon its shape, holding its sides apart. We may suppose that the empty universe of our thought experiment, if it could be brought into existence, would immediately collapse. I repeat from an earlier chapter:

a literal signification of the word "nothing" would exclude, in addition to everything else, space and time as well.

Today we do best to think of the cosmic environment in which we find ourselves as a universal sea of matter-energy that manifests itself in various forms. What we refer to as an area where there is nothing, an area of empty space, still does have content, like the bottle that is full of air rather than wine. Such an area is full of matter-energy that simply manifests itself differently from the matter-energy that manifests itself as, say, the moon. Its manifestations, moreover, are no less measurable than those that take the form of the moon; for we can measure the strength of the gravitational field, and we can measure the strength of the electromagnetic fields, in areas of what old linguistic habit impels us to refer to, still, as empty space.

*

Confined to the ocean of matter-energy as we are, may we not be in the position of fish confined to the middle depths of our terrestrial seas? The fish, if capable of thought, would surely assume that their salt-water environment was the entire universe. The three dimensions of space we know, and the one of time, are but features of the particular ocean to which we are confined. What we cannot know is that there is not a wider universe beyond. Not knowing this, neither can we know that there may not await us an immortality constituted not by eternity in time, but by existence beyond space and time alike. Since, when it comes to ultimate matters, we are all as ignorant of what is not as of what is, all possibilities must be regarded as open.

*

In the naïve conceptual world we have inherited, what is so small as to be invisible simply duplicates, on its smaller scale, our own visible world. In the planetary model of the atom put forward by Rutherford in 1911, a model long since superseded, electrons orbited the nucleus as the planets orbit the sun. I remember indulging, once, in the fancy that those planetary electrons might support populations like those of the species on our earth, that the world of an electron might be identical with our own world, not even seeming smaller to its inhabitants in the absence of an opportunity for comparison.

One could extrapolate this line of imagination indefinitely because, if the world of the electron was identical with our own, except for size, then it must be composed of doubly infinitesimal planetary atoms with electrons supporting a doubly infinitesimal life — and so *ad infinitum.*   And one could extrapolate upward as well, imagining that our solar system was one atom in a larger world that supported populations of beings as much larger than ourselves as it was, itself, larger than our solar system — and so upward *ad infinitum.*

What might be wrong with this conception was first impressed on me, I believe, when I read that such a giant as the one described in the tale of "Jack and the Beanstalk" could not function in reality because, if he tried to walk, he would break his leg at the first step. With increasing size, it transpired, weight increases at a proportionately greater rate than the strength of the skeleton that supports it. Therefore, the bones of a man proportioned in every respect like myself, but ten times as tall, would not suppport his weight.

This was at least suggestive, if not conclusive.   The large-scale duplicate of me might do well on a planet with less gravitational mass, a situation in which I, myself, might do badly if, because of my smaller size, my own gravitational attachment to it was so slight that any current of air might carry me away.   Nevertheless, the fact that mass does not diminish with linear dimensions at a rate that would keep the relationship the same, together with other like facts, left little choice but to abandon the naïve assumption that reality as we know it in our own order of magnitude could be the same in other orders. The problem is that our minds, our concepts, and our consequent vocabulary have developed to fit only our own order of magnitude. The corresponding challenge, then, is to develop them from now on so that they will be suitable to those wider horizons, of which we have just become aware, that embrace other orders of magnitude.

We are facing this challenge for the first time in our own day. Perhaps it will take us thousands of years to meet it, by which time we may be facing other challenges beyond it.

*

Ever since the ancient Greeks first asked themselves what the basic composition of matter might be, common sense has assumed that it is composed of such stuff as we see with our eyes or feel with our fingers, although on a scale too small to be seen or felt by such big creatures as ourselves.   If one analyzed any piece of matter into ever smaller components, cutting it into ever finer bits, one would eventually arrive at an irreducible particle that could not be divided further — the atom of the ancient philosophers.   This atom, however, except for the property that made it indivisible, was regarded as having the same basic properties as other matter one could see.   It was hard and opaque, it had weight and a fixed shape.

This conception lies behind the word "particle," which is the traditional word we use to denote the most elementary forms to which we have been able, by logical theorizing and experiment, to reduce matter. The name "atom" itself became attached to a constituent of most matter on earth that was then found to consist of still more elementary particles — namely, electrons and nucleons. Now we have found that electrons and nucleons can, in turn, be transformed into quite a number of other elementary particles, including pions, kaons, neutrinos, and photons.

In a naïve view, these elementary particles would be visible to us as such if we could reduce ourselves to their scale. If, in this view, I could reduce myself from a height of 1.78 meters to a height of 10^{-15} meter, then I ought to be able to see electrons as bodies approximately my own size.

What, however, do we mean by "seeing"? Can we think of the electron as a star like our sun that radiates in all directions the light that, reaching our eyes, makes it visible? Or can we think of it as a body like the moon that is visible because it reflects into our eyes the light from some other source? What do we mean by light when we reduce it to the scale of the electron?

The smallest unit of light is the photon, which is listed with the electron as one of the elementary particles. Electrons do, on occasion, emit photons; but when one does so the photon emitted carries away an appreciable part of its energy. If, then, the emitted photon struck the miniature observer in the eye he would never be the same again. (Of course our imagining, here, is ridiculous, because the observer's eye, itself, would be far smaller than an electron, so that we would have to ask what it would be composed of and how it would function.) Light also manifests itself as waves in an electromagnetic field, but the shortest wavelength of visible light would be millions of times as long as the electron in the greatest dimension we could reasonably attribute to it. This suggests that the electron could no more reflect a wave of light than a grain of dust floating on the sea could turn back a comber — and, even if it could reflect such a wave, the eye of the miniature observer could not register it.

It is evident that visibility refers to a phenomenon associated with the order of magnitude in which we live our own natural lives, but that could not occur within the limits of the atomic order of magnitude. If we cannot see an electron, then, it is not simply because our eyesight is not good enough to see anything so small. The single photon that an electron emits, on rare occasions, could not make the electron visible as a material body. In a word, any entity that small is, by its nature, invisible. It is invisible in itself, and not because of defective vision in the would-be observer. The concept of visibility does not apply.

It is also inaudible in its activity, since it would be infinitesimal in proportion to the molecules of the atmosphere through which sound waves are propagated and to the waves themselves. Neither could it be felt with the fingers, tasted with the tongue, or smelled with the nose. It is invisible, inaudible, intangible, without taste, and without odor. In our common parlance we would not call such an entity "material."

On the other hand, electrons have mass, which is surely an attribute of matter. Because, in accordance with relativity theory, their mass is proportional to the energy of their motion (relative to the observer), what might be regarded as the intrinsic mass of these particles is referred to as their "rest-mass," their mass when they are motionless in the observer's frame of reference. The rest-mass of photons and neutrinos, however, is zero, so that they are often excluded from the category of "material" particles that have a positive rest-mass. On the other hand, even photons and neutrinos — which always travel at the speed of light in a vacuum (the speed-limit of the universe) because they have no resistance to acceleration — are said to spin. Can an immaterial entity spin?

While some of the elementary particles appear to be immortal in the sense that each survives forever unchanged unless it collides and interacts with another particle, others automatically disintegrate, after a certain average lifetime, into other elementary particles. Some of these average lifetimes are inconceivably short. The neutral sigma particle, for example, has an average lifetime of 10^{-20} second. That long after it has been brought to birth by some interaction among other particles, it disintegrates into a lambda particle and a photon. The lambda particle then distintegrates, after about 25×10^{-9} second, into a proton and a positive pion; the positive pion disintegrates, after about 26×10^{-7} second, into a positive muon and what is known as a muon's neutrino; the positive muon disintegrates, after a relatively long life of about two millionths of a second, into an electron, a muon's neutrino, and the so-called antiparticle of an electron's neutrino.

As for the pions — in certain situations their lives have such a short duration that, as seems likely, the basic natural law of the conservation of energy does not have time to take effect with them at all. It is as if there was no time to register their existence, together with the energy they represent, and under these circumstances the physicists refer to them as "virtual particles." Each of the protons in the nucleus of the atom is thought to be constantly surrounded by a cloud of virtual particles that are extinguished virtually as soon as they are born.

Moreover, although thirty or more "elementary particles" have been listed, it may be that they are merely different states of some one something; for a "particle" may "come apart" into other "particles," of which one may "come apart" into still other "particles," of which one may be identical with the original "particle."

It is evident that this world of the very small is fundamentally different from the familiar world for the description of which our vocabulary was designed. Consequently, when we try to describe it in that vocabulary, when we try to force it into the verbal categories of that vocabulary, we are almost sure to falsify it and so to mislead ourselves. What is the use of asking whether a photon is "material" or "immaterial"? It appears to be a partially definable entity, more or less distinguishable from its surroundings, which is involved in the constitution of matter as we know it on our own scale — which is involved, that is, in the constitution of what we may properly call "material." Perhaps it should be regarded not as a discrete entity in itself but as an aspect or a localized manifestation of the universal something we have called "matter-energy" — or of what we call "field." Perhaps our distinction between the one and the many does not apply throughout this other world, so that it may be dubious for us to refer to "one" photon or "one" pion as if photons or pions were subject to the same kind of accounting as pebbles in a box. We don't talk about "one" water; and what we generally mean by "water" is not one molecule of H_2O (which has none of the familiar properties of water, such as wetness or liquidity) but a sufficient aggregation of such molecules to be perceptible to our senses, in the form such an aggregation takes under certain conditions of temperature and atmospheric pressure. An elementary particle, by itself, can hardly represent what we have in mind when we refer to "matter," but in the aggregate such particles do. What is recognizably material, in the familiar sense, is what we get from the combination or accumulation of what is not recognizably material.

One cannot truly visualize what, by its nature, has no visible existence. We mistake reality, then, if we ask what a photon looks like. It has no "look." But we know what a stream of photons in their millions of millions looks like — at least, when they are between certain limits of energy — because we see such a stream as light.

*

It is a plausible belief that we can never know much about the world of the very small because it is so different from the world most directly accessible to our senses, and because we can apprehend it only through chains of cause and effect that lead from it to such remote final manifestations as clicking noises on a counter or oscillations of needles on dials. This is not the "seeing" that we would like to have as the basis for our "believing."

Experience suggests, however, that we must hesitate to define the limits of possibility for human knowledge. Some of the ancient Greeks thought man could never know what lay in the southern hemisphere because they supposed the equatorial belt too hot for him ever to cross. Little more than a century ago Auguste Comte said, what must have seemed unquestionable at the time, that the chemical composition of the stars was forever beyond the reach of human knowledge. But for many decades, now, we have known the chemical composition of stars, even those in remote galaxies, as well as we know the chemical composition of our own earth.

VIII

The World of the Very Small:

2. *Wavicles*

THE H$_2$O MOLECULE is our familiar water only in an aggregation large enough for us to see and feel. Except in such an aggregation it lacks wetness, liquidity, what we regard as the properties of water. In the same sense, the elementary particles show all the properties we associate with matter only in their combination and aggregation. We have no adequate name and no adequate description for what they are in themselves, for we lack a vocabulary and an associated conceptual complex suited to whatever constitutes reality on their scale.

This is not to say that they do not, like H$_2$O molecules, have an individual existence. It is merely to say that, assuming they do, we are limited in the conceptions we can form of their reality in that capacity.

Even the word "individuality," applied to them, had best be used in a qualified and sceptical sense. In a book entitled *What is History?*, E. H. Carr automatically applies to the submicroscopic realm the common sense that pertains to our own order of magnitude, writing: "no two geological formations, no two animals of the same species, and no two atoms are identical." If, however, there is any difference between, for example, one atom of the common hydrogen and another, we have no evidence for it.

A photon from the sun, entering the earth's atmosphere, is deflected by collision with the nucleus of an atom. In the interaction it loses some of its energy to the nucleus and flies off from the scene at an angle to its original course. This is one way of putting it. But we could equally well say that the photon was annihilated in the collision with the nucleus, which got rid of the surplus energy received from it by emitting a new photon with less energy than the original. The question this appears to raise is whether the photon that left the scene of the collision was the one that entered into it or a different one. Such a question, however, may well be irrelevant to reality if, as seems to be the case, there is no intrinsic difference between the photon that entered the collision and the one that emerged from it. If the one that emerged was in no way different, how can we ask whether it was a different photon? What do we mean by "different"? The question whether it is the same or different implies a distinction of individuality that may not exist in the world of the very small. It is not that we can never know whether it was the same photon or another, but that the question presumably has no meaning in terms of the photon's world. It assumes without warrant the applicability to that world of a distinction that applies only, perhaps, to the world with which the questioner is familiar.

One might say that, if there was a lapse of time, however small, during which there was no photon, then the photon that left the scene was a different one because it was a new one. But I could answer that a photon is simply a quantum of energy, that according to the law of the conservation of energy the energy represented by the incoming photon could not have disappeared. If, for an immeasurable instant, it took some other form, then it reverted to its original form at its departure. If a man gives me a check on his bank for one dollar, and the next day I repay him with a check on my bank for one dollar, it is meaningless to ask whether the dollar I paid back was the same one I had received or a different one. A dollar is simply a quantum of value. I do not know that a photon is not in the same category.

Even in our macroscopic world the identification of individuality may be nominal and arbitrary. This was pointed out by Heraclitus in his remark that "you cannot step twice into the same river, for fresh waters are ever flowing in." If, despite Heraclitus, it is possible for a person to step into the same river twice, is it the same person who does so the second time?

> Full fathom five thy father lies;
>   Of his bones are coral made:
> Those are pearls that were his eyes:
>   Nothing of him that doth fade,
>   But doth suffer a sea-change
>   Into something rich and strange.

Is it right to identify the bones as "thy father"?

A question to exercise our philosophical faculties concerns a pocket knife with many folding blades that, as they wear out over the years, are replaced one by one, and which finally has its handle replaced as well. Is it still the same knife? If not, when did it become a different one?

The reader will appreciate that these questions do not bear on ultimate reality so much as on the senses we choose to attribute to terms like "identity," and on the corresponding concepts in our minds. This is not to say, however, that they are either insignificant or irrelevant to the present context.

Individual distinction and the continuity of the distinction is something each of us feels in himself and apprehends in other human beings, so that each of us regards himself as the individual he was at birth, even though he has since changed beyond recognition. Each of us regards himself as differing from all others in his individuality.

This last, however, is a matter of degree. There is little doubt, for example, that the distinction of individuality is less marked among worker bees in a hive than among human beings in a city. It may be virtually imperceptible in a colony of microbes with the same genetic heritage.

I speculate that, the more complex an entity, in the sense of being composed of other entities — as I am composed of cells composed of atoms, etc., as the sun is composed of elementary particles — the less likely it is that identical counterparts could be found. Is it not our anthropomorphic tendency, then, that prompts us to ask whether the photon that emerges from an interaction is the same as the one that entered into it? When we were more primitive in our thinking we attributed human personality to everything in nature: the sun was Apollo, the north wind was Boreas, a particular river was the god Scamander. Perhaps we commit a like error when we attribute individuality to entities in the submicroscopic world. I daresay that, ten thousand years from now, we shall know better.

*

The reader should note that I have been using the concept of individuality in two senses. In the opening paragraphs of this chapter the sense was simply that of what is discrete, what has its own existence apart from its surroundings. I then referred to individual distinction in the sense of what may make one discrete entity different from all others, including those of its kind. Perhaps, however, even the basic concept of discreteness may be questioned in its application to the submicroscopic world.

In our own macroscopic world a particle is one thing, a wave another. In the submicroscopic world, however, there is no such thing as a particle in the literal sense of the word — no such thing as a pebble-like object measuring 10^{-13} centimeter. Whatever the properties of what we call an elementary particle, it is not hard, tangible, or potentially visible. One may at least question whether, in the submicroscopic world, there is such a thing as a wave in the literal sense of the word — although here the literal sense is more protean than in the case of particle, since it does not refer to an entity but to a certain kind of movement, since it refers to any kind of more-or-less regular oscillation, or to the form taken by what oscillates. We should bear all this in mind when we consider the question whether light is composed of particles or of waves (which, after all, must be waves of "field" or something else), and when we accept the best answer available as yet, that the entities of which it is composed are, at one and the same time, both particles and waves. More precisely formulated, this answer is that the ultimate constituents of light manifest, at one and the same time, features of behavior that (in our macroscopic world) we associate with particles, and features that we associate with waves. What would be impossible in our macroscopic world appears to be possible in the world of the very small, which is one more indication that the world of the very small must be fundamentally different.

Light certainly does manifest behavior that is proper to waves and impossible for particles as we conceive them. The notable example is that of the so-called interference effect.

Picture a sea wall and, parallel to it, a breakwater that bounds a port. Waves of regular wavelength (regular, that is, in the distance between crests), each extending from horizon to horizon, are coming in from the sea, each in turn to rise up against that part of the wall which is not sheltered by the breakwater. But where these waves touch the end of the breakwater they are broken and deflected from their original course. The result is two sets of waves crossing each other at an angle. There are the waves that, unaffected by the breakwater, continue on to the wall, and there are those deflected from it that move at an angle across the first set until they, too, splash up against the wall. Where a wave coming from the end of the breakwater reaches any particular point on the wall at the same time that one coming directly from the sea reaches it, the two reinforce each other to make a wave higher than either alone. But, where a wave from one set coincides, as it reaches the wall, with a trough of the other, wave and trough cancel each other out. All along the wall then, at any given moment (as a snapshot would show), there will be high waves at regular intervals, where the two sets reinforce each other, separated by intervals where they cancel each other out.

Light, in its wave-behavior, produces the same phenomenon. If, under circumstances permitting such observation, a light beam is projected onto a screen past the vertical edge of an intervening barrier that corresponds to the breakwater, the illuminated part of the screen, beyond the barrier's shadow, will show alternating vertical bands of light and dark. The evidence is that the light consists of waves, that those waves are broken into two sets where they touch the edge of the barrier, and that the two sets, alternately reinforcing and annulling each other, produce the alternate bands of light and dark on the screen.

What we call light is electromagnetic radiation of wavelengths that, in the entire spectrum of wavelengths from the longest to the shortest, extend only across a narrow band situated at just under 3×10^{-5} centimeter. All the other wavelengths, above and below that band alike, are invisible to us. The entire known spectrum, however, extends from about 3×10^{-22} centimeter, at one extreme, to some three thousand kilometers at the other. The shorter wavelengths in this spectrum, those of visible light or shorter, represent electromagnetic radiation that in some circumstances manifests the behavior of distinct and separate packets of energy rather than of waves. (A wavelength as long as a thousand kilometers might also manifest such behavior, but each packet would have so little energy as to defy detection.) It is in this role that such radiation is regarded as consisting of the particles called photons, particles that qualify by their behavior for full membership in the family of elementary particles, with which they collide and interact. Thus, when light or other electromagnetic radiation below a certain wavelength falls on a metal plate, electrons are knocked out of the plate in such a fashion as to show that they are being expelled by what can be regarded only as distinct particles like bullets. So it is that light consists of waves rather than particles in some of its manifestations, of particles rather than waves in others.

The wave-particle duality applies to all the constituents of matter. The particle nature of an electron is attested by the photograph of the linear track it leaves in a bubble chamber. It is attested by the fact that it has a precise mass, and that when it collides with another particle the two recoil from each other like billiard balls. The electron manifests itself as a discrete entity, so that we can count how many are included in each atom: one in a hydrogen atom, two in a helium atom, etc. However, if a single beam of electrons is directed past a barrier with a sharp edge at a screen that registers its arrival by glowing, the same alternating bands of light and dark will appear as in the case of the beam of light similarly directed. This shows that electrons, like photons, have a wave nature as well as a particle nature.

What is true of photons and electrons is true, as well, of all the other elementary particles, so-called; and it is therefore true of the combinations of elementary particles known as atoms, which also have their proper wavelengths and vibration periods.

*

The experimental evidence, in its totality, does not permit a choice between the identification of these entities as either particles or waves. Setting aside our common sense, on which we have learned not to rely, we have to identify them as both. The difference between particles and waves may, however, have implications for the question of individuality raised at the opening of this chapter. While a particle is clearly definable as a discrete entity — so that it is individual in this sense — a wave is not. A wave in water, for example, is simply a disturbance of the water, not a thing in itself.

If we think of what is another name for a wave, a vibration, we can see that it implies plurality. Anything that undergoes one displacement only, and then returns to its original position, can hardly be said to vibrate. Vibration is rhythmic, implying a regular sequence of displacements and returns. One wave, also, is simply one unit in what has rhythmic extension. A wave is either one in a series or it is not a wave at all; and this is so even if only because an initially produced wave produces a series by generating others. If the observer dampens the process, preventing its continuance beyond the initial wave, he has simply annulled the wave phenomenon at its birth.

Successive waves, moreover, have a continuity that a succession of particles cannot have. A single wave is hardly discrete. There is bound to be an arbitrary element in any attempt to say where one wave stops (where it is no more) and a different one begins. (Where does the disturbance of the water stop and another disturbance begin?)

I make this point, without knowing how great its significance may be, because our conceptual difficulties in the world of the very small appear to have some connection with our traditional way of thinking, going back to the ancient Greeks, by which we assume that matter, in its ultimate constitution, must consist of individual particles. Perhaps there is a continuous field of matter-energy throughout the universe in which, even at the level of the very small, what we sometimes regard as particles and sometimes as waves are simply disturbances — not detached, as such, from the universal whole.

The difficulties we have at present in reconciling waves and particles may be the consequence of the time-lag whereby our common sense is not able to keep up with our advancing knowledge. Today we can see that, on the one hand, the elephant is very like a particle, that on the other it is very like a wave. Ten thousand years from now, when we can see the elephant whole, our common sense will no longer find any contradiction.

IX

The World of the Very Small:

3. Rhythm and Harmony

ALL SPACE is filled with that vague something we call "field." The vagueness is reduced if we identify "field" with the less vague term, "energy"; for energy, because we experience it in our ordinary lives, belongs to the world of our common sense.

Energy (as we saw in Chapter V) may take the form of matter, while matter may be regarded as energy in storage. Therefore I have, in these speculations, referred to the physical universe as solidly filled with matter-energy, discernible as fields of measurable "strength" throughout what we used to regard as empty space. And I have referred to the theory that what we have always regarded as pieces of matter scattered about the empty space were really concentrations of matter-energy. The moon or a pebble, in this view, is a concentration of matter-energy.

Just as a pebble is essentially like the moon, only smaller, so we have traditionally thought of atomic and subatomic particles as being essentially like pebbles, only smaller. But we have seen, now, that this is inherently absurd, for such particles could not possibly have, even on their own scale, the attributes of tangibility or corporeality by which we identify the moon and the pebble alike as matter.

It seems less misleading, and our conceptual difficulty is less, if we refer to them as "quanta of energy." This implies energy distributed in concentrations of fixed quantity.

In this development of our vocabulary, may it not be useful to make a new distinction (albeit less than absolute) between matter and energy? The distinction is like the one we made at the beginning of the last chapter between H_2O and water as we commonly experience it: an aggregation of H_2O large enough to be apprehended directly by our senses is what we call water, and only such an aggregation has the attributes by which we commonly identify and define water. In the same way, quanta of energy in an aggregation sufficiently large and concentrated to be apprehended by us as tangible constitute what we call matter, and only such an aggregation has the attributes by which we commonly identify matter.

The picture of the universe at which we have now tentatively arrived is one of energy that solidly fills four-dimensional space-time. This energy is in constant vibration, vibration which is measurable, at every point, in terms of wavelength or frequency, and of amplitude. (Wavelength and frequency are alternative measures of the same thing because, assuming waves to travel at a fixed rate, the less the wavelength the greater the frequency with which they pass a given point, frequency therefore being inversely proportional to wavelength.) The energy manifests itself variously, but in one of its common manifestations it takes the form of minute concentrations, each of which appears to have a discrete existence — concentrations that we have decided to refer to as quanta of energy. These quanta combine variously in various aggregations that, on a large enough scale, are identified by us as matter.

To this layman, at least, such a picture of the universe (together with its associated vocabulary) makes it easier to grasp quantum theory and the operations of quantum mechanics.

*

Relativity theory represents one of the two great discoveries or advances of physics in the first quarter of the twentieth century. The other is represented by quantum theory.

Quantum theory began with the discovery in 1900 that, in the world of the very small, energy increases or decreases by quantum jumps rather than by the apparently unbroken continuity with which we are familiar in our macroscopic world. It rises or descends like a staircase, step by step, rather than like the unbroken slope of a ramp. It is as if the temperature of water could rise no less and no more than one degree centigrade at a time, so that, if one put a cup of water at 20° over a flame, the water would remain at 20° until enough heat had accumulated to lift it to 21°, a temperature to which it would then jump without passing through the intermediate temperatures — and so on, jumping always one degree at a time. Cooling off, the temperature would similarly come down in a succession of one-degree steps with pauses between

Consider a hydrogen atom, which consists of one proton as its nucleus and one electron that may be thought of as being in orbit around it. At the atom's minimum energy, the electron is said to be in its ground state. If, now, we undertake to raise the electron's energy, say by having photons collide with it, we shall find it cannot receive less than a minimum quantum of energy. It will not receive any energy less than the amount required to lift it from its ground state to its first excited state; in its first excited state it will not receive any energy less than what is required to lift it to its second excited state — and so on. If, in an excited state, it loses energy, it will lose it by the same step-like process in reverse — successively emitting, let us say, photons that represent the prescribed quanta of energy, until it has dropped, step by step, to its ground state.

In the old planetary model of the atom, what this meant was that the electron jumped to successively larger orbits as it received the prescribed doses of energy — but did so, somehow, without traversing the intermediate regions in which it was not allowed.

The quantization of energy is universal in the world of the very small (which is to say that it is universal for all orders of magnitude, since the large is composed of the very small, but negligible except on the scale of the very small). A photon, an electron, an atom, or a molecule can increase or decrease in its intrinsic energy only by quantum jumps.

This is incomprehensible to our common sense when we think of the very small as composed of particles, just as it is incomprehensible to our common sense that an electron could jump from one orbit to another without traversing the intervening space. It becomes comprehensible, however, when we think of the very small as waves or vibrations; for then it is precisely equivalent to our common experience of how, in music, the successive tones of the harmonic series are produced.

Imagine a flute with all the holes along its side closed so that, when the flutist breathes gently against the mouth-hole, it sounds its fundamental tone or lowest note, which is middle C, representing a vibrational frequency of 262 cycles per second. This is the flute's "ground state." If, now, the flutist imparts constantly more energy to the instrument, by gradually intensifying the stream of air from his lips, a time will come when the pitch abruptly jumps up one octave by a doubling of the frequency (524 instead of 262), and it will make this jump without traversing any of the intermediate frequencies. If the flutist continues gradually to increase the energy he imparts to the instrument, it will jump successively from the octave to the twelfth, to the fifteenth, to the seventeenth, to the nineteenth, and so on. The successive jumps represent the successive doubling, tripling, quadrupling, etc., of the fundamental frequency. So the pitch will rise by ever smaller quantum jumps.

What accounts for this particular succession of pitches, the harmonic series, is best illustrated by a stretched violin string (although the principle is the same, if harder to visualize, in the flute). When sounding its fundamental pitch, the string's vibration causes it to take the form of a single wave, its troughs corresponding to the fixed ends on either side, its crest in the middle. When sounding the octave, it takes the form of two waves, separated by a trough in the middle, its frequency being doubled as its wavelength is halved. When sounding the twelfth, it takes the form of three waves, separated by troughs at intervals of a third of the length, its frequency being tripled as the wavelength is reduced to a third. And so *ad infinitum*, at least in principle, although the quantum intervals quickly become so small, and the higher tones so faint, as at last to be imperceptible to the ear.

If one undertakes to feed energy at a smoothly increasing rate into a hydrogen atom, its energy will remain at the ground state until, at a certain point, it makes its first quantum jump to 10.2 electron volts higher, remaining in that state of energy until it makes its next jump to 12.1 ev. above the ground state, then to 12.8 ev., then to 13.1 ev., and so on. The intermediate states are impossible for it, just as the intermediate tones are impossible for the violin string.

The phenomenon is basically the same in the atom as in the violin. We might say it was exactly the same if the circular orbit of the electron around the nucleus, corresponding to the length of the violin string, remained, like the string, of fixed length. The electron's ground state, then, would correspond to the length of the electron's lowest orbit, and the succession of the electron's excited states, as increasing energy was communicated to it, would correspond to the successive divisions of its entire orbit by 2, 3, 4, etc., just as in the case of the violin string. In the case of the atom, however, the electron's orbit becomes larger for each successive state of increasing excitement — so that the situation is as if the violin string, at the same time that the number of divisions in which it vibrated increased (to 2, 3, 4, etc.), also increased in length. The ground state, represented by a wavelength corresponding to the length of the total orbit, would be followed by a first excited state that represented a wavelength corresponding to half the total length of an orbit four times as long, to be followed in turn by a still higher excited state corresponding to a wavelength one third the total length of an orbit nine times as long, etc.

As increasing energy is imparted to a flute by the breath of the flutist, the frequency with which the column of air it encloses vibrates (apprehended by our ears as the pitch of its sound) jumps successively from the number of its fundamental tone to double that number (the octave), to three times that number (the twelfth), to four times (the fifteenth), to five times (the seventeenth), and on up the harmonic series. In actual fact, the flute sounds all these tones at once, though with diminishing intensity, in its ground state; and all but those below the pitch of whatever excited state it may be in. This is to say that when, for example, its fundamental tone is played, the column of air vibrates, at one and the same time, in its entire length, in half its length, in a third, and so on. Just as a great oceanic wave may have small waves on its slopes that in turn have wavelets on their slopes that in turn have ripples, so the column of air (or the string, in the case of the violin) vibrates in the long and successively shorter lengths at the same time. (We call the tones that are thus produced above the fundamental its overtones or harmonics, and they are what give brilliance to instrumental sound.)

In the case of the atom's electron, too, the frequencies of its own harmonic series overlap, so to speak. As increasing energy is imparted to it (entailing successive enlargements of its orbit), it vibrates simultaneously at the frequency of its ground state and that of its first excited state, the vibration of the former weakening as that of the latter strengthens. So it goes up through its own harmonic series gradually, but without traversing any of the intermediate frequencies.

The Pythagoreans believed that the planets in their rhythmic rounds produced an inaudible music, what they called "the music of the spheres." If there is not, in fact, an inaudible music of the planetary spheres, there is, in a real sense, an inaudible music of the atoms. The harmonic series is a mathematically definable phenomenon that is one of the fundamental elements in all music. Precisely the same element pervades the world of the very small, even though it does not, in this case, manifest itself as sound. It is the same phenomenon; and it is, as we shall see, one of the bases of order in the universe.

The universe is everywhere filled with rhythm and harmony. Because, in a large view, rhythm and harmony are one, being the constituents of music, the universe is everywhere filled with music.

X

The World of the Very Small:
4. *The Quantum of Irreducibility*

So far in these chapters I have mentioned two facts that are elemental to physical being as we know it. One is the limit to the speed at which anything can move relative to any observer, designated by c (300,000 km.p.s.). This in itself sets the limits and establishes, in large measure, the design of the universe as we know it. It establishes or defines the relationship between time and space that makes the universe four-dimensional. It also establishes the relationship between energy and mass that constitutes the second elemental fact I have mentioned so far, the relationship defined by the formula $e = mc^2$. Just as c connects time and space in a four-dimensional continuum, so $e = mc^2$ connects energy and mass as different measures or different manifestations of what is basically one thing — thereby associating space, time, matter, and energy in one coherent relationship or design.

A third elemental fact is designated by the letter h, known as Planck's constant. It is the amount by which frequency must be multiplied to get the minimum quantity of energy proper to it. The formula is $e = hf$: the quantum of energy equals the frequency times h. Just as c is 300,000 km.p.s., so h is 663×10^{-25} of an erg second — an erg being the minuscule amount of energy needed to raise a milligram one centimeter.

Given such a low frequency as that of a clock's pendulum, one second, the minimum quantum of change in the pendulum's energy would be the fraction of an erg just mentioned (h multiplied by one). If the pendulum is allowed to slow down to a stop, its frequency remaining the same but its swings becoming shorter, it will do so in a succession of quantum jumps of this amount, an amount so small as to be undetectable. However, for electromagnetic radiation with a frequency of 10^{32}, the minimum quantum of change would be 15,000 ergs. If it lost energy, this is the minimum amount it could lose in one jump. Nor could it receive additions to its energy in smaller amounts. This is to say that it could increase or decrease its energy (represented by the amplitude of its vibrations) only in such an appreciable amount as it takes to lift 15 grams one centimeter — or by multiples of that amount.

If we think of the four-dimensional universe as consisting of energy in vibration — with various frequencies of which we know, as yet, neither an upward nor a downward limit — we must regard that energy as occurring in the discrete packets called quanta, albeit these packets range in size from the infinitesimal, in the world represented by the large orders of magnitude, to who knows what size in the world of the very small. These quanta may plausibly be identified with photons (as well as with other elementary particles), since photons (or other elementary particles) are what a particle ultimately absorbs or emits when it gains or loses energy.

For centuries we assumed that the realm of physical being consisted of space with pieces of matter scattered about it. Because we called the space nothing, there could be no question of analyzing it. But matter, being something, did lend itself to analysis. We assumed for centuries, then, that matter could be analyzed into ever smaller components, until an irreducible component called the atom was reached.

Today, however, we do better if we regard the realm of physical being as entirely filled with energy, which we call field and which, in certain of its configurations, takes the form of matter. The irreducible component, then, is not the atom but the quantum — and this may not seem so far from classical theory if we are right in identifying it with the photon and other elementary particles.

As energy is all one thing, however various in its manifestations, the measure of the irreducible quantum varies with the manifestations. Nevertheless, the fact remains that physical being, when analyzed, proves to consist of irreducible components, components of measurable quantity that, like the atoms of the ancients, can be divided or reduced no further.

The quanta are the building blocks of the universe. Take, for example, a particular atom at a particular moment, such an atom representing a measurable quantity of energy organized in a standard form. If that energy is to receive an addition, such an addition cannot be less than a prescribed minimum quantity. The smallest addition that can be made may be thought of as the smallest building block available. Again, if that energy is to be reduced, it cannot be reduced by less than a minimum amount — by the removal, so to speak, of less than one building block of the minimum size.

Another metaphoric way of putting this is to say that physical being is granular, made up of irreducible grains of energy that are constantly in process of being assembled or separated from one another. And, since this process takes place step by step, we may speculate that time, too, is granular, that there are irreducible quanta of time as well as of matter — that the entire four-dimensional universe, in fact, is granular. (Let the reader be warned that this last is the purest speculation.)

In the progress of human understanding we are, at this point, approaching one of the frontiers of what the human mind, in its present stage of development, can comprehend. The granularity of physical being appears to entail unexpected consequences that set limits to the possibility of knowledge. More than that, today these consequences are widely regarded as casting doubt on the whole conception of a universe governed by a rigid mechanism of cause and effect.

*

Photographs of the tracks they leave in a bubble chamber give evidence that there are single particles, each existing in itself as a discrete entity, each taking its own course through four-dimensional space-time. The velocity and the path of such a particle can be measured, and its course can be predicted, but only within certain limits of precision. Beyond these limits we cannot measure, at one and the same time, both its position and its velocity, although we can measure either alone. For the more precisely we measure its position, the more uncertain our measurement of its velocity must be; and the more precisely we measure its velocity, the more uncertain our measurement of its position must be. This is because its velocity can be measured only by determining how far it has traveled in an interval of time, and this requires that we know its position at the beginning and again at the end of the interval; while, if we measure its position, we can do so only by the mediation (between the particle and the recording device, whether an eye or a camera) of at least one photon that, being bounced off the particle or emitted from it, changes its velocity. (If, in the latter case, we try to correct for the influence of the photon, other factors of uncertainty enter in.)

Again, what applies to the very small applies in principle to the large as well. If, in order to observe the position at a given instant of a ball swinging at the end of a string, I shine a light on it, the stream of photons that constitutes the light will, by its pressure, change the ball's state of motion — but by an amount so small as to be neither measurable nor significant. A photon that ricochets from an electron, however, changes the electron's state of motion as a stone flung against the swinging ball would change the ball's state of motion.

Because we cannot, beyond certain limits of precision, determine both the position and the velocity of any single particle at a single instant, we cannot predict its future course beyond those limits; for the prediction of that course depends on knowledge of its position and its velocity alike. This is to say that our knowledge of the future of any single particle is bound to be uncertain. The degree of the uncertainty is defined by Planck's constant, h. The uncertainty of position and the uncertainty of momentum (which is related to velocity) vary inversely to each other, but the product of the two uncertainties can never be less than h. The irreducible quantum of energy, therefore, is also a quantum of irreducible uncertainty. The gap between allowable states of energy for any particle is related to the magnitude of the uncertainty that must be attributed to our knowledge of that particle's future. This is what is known as the Uncertainty Principle.

A measurable element of uncertainty in prediction has always had an important part in classical mechanics. However, unlike the uncertainty of the Uncertainty Principle associated with quantum mechanics, all that this traditional uncertainty represents is the necessary inadequacy of the information available to us limited human beings as a basis for prediction.

The laws of nature, as we have known them so far, are of two kinds. One, represented by the law that no object can be accelerated beyond the speed of light, is absolute. The other is a matter of probabilities, which is to say that it comprehends an element of uncertainty, however small. The element of uncertainty, as we have seen, tends to be inversely proportional to the order of magnitude to which it is applied.

Suppose I have a closed box divided into two equal compartments by a partition in the middle. One compartment is empty in the sense that it is a total vacuum, while the other contains countless millions of countless millions of gas molecules all dashing about and colliding with the walls and one another. If, now, I remove the partition, I can predict that, after an interval of time, say ten seconds, the molecules will be so evenly distributed over the entire interior of the box that half will be in what had been the one compartment and half in the other. That prediction, allowing for an insignificant margin of error, would be a matter of overwhelming probability, equivalent to certainty for all practical purposes, the quantity of molecules being so large — but still a matter of probability only. I can also predict that, in countless millions of countless million of millennia to come, there will never be a moment when all the molecules will again be in the half of the box they had been in before the removal of the partition. My prediction will, again, represent an overwhelming probability, tantamount to certainty, but still a probability only.

Suppose, now, that this thought experiment is performed with only two molecules instead of the quantity we have been imagining. In this case, the probability that, ten seconds after the removal of the partition, half the molecules will be in one half of the box, half in the other, will be only 50 percent; and the probability that, in the course of the many millennia we have imagined, all the molecules would never once find themselves together in the half of the box they had been in originally would, in fact, be an overwhelming improbability, tantamount to a certainty.

The probabilistic laws of nature, as opposed to the absolute ones, are also illustrated by radioactive decay. An atom of thorium-234 decays by emitting an electron, thereby being transmuted into an atom of the chemical element called protactinium. Consider, now, the question of how long after the atom of thorium comes into existence (by the decay of a uranium atom) it emits the electron that transmutes it.

No one can answer this question, referring as it does to one atom only. However, if the same question is asked about a lump of thorium-234 that is composed of countless millions of atoms, it can be answered with precision. In 24.1 days (to refine the figure no further) half the atoms in the lump will have been transmuted; in another 24.1 days, half the remaining atoms will have been transmuted; and so on until we are no longer dealing with the great quantities of atoms on which our relative precision depends.

The thorium atom's average half-life is 24.1 days, which means that where the quantity of thorium is large enough we can be sure that 50 percent will decay in a precisely defined time, the margin of error being negligible. The smaller the quantity, however, the greater the margin of error. With only one atom, the best one can do is to say that the probability of its decay in less than 24.1 days is 50 percent and the probability of its surviving longer is 50 percent. In fact, it is overwhelmingly unlikely that the single atom will decay within, say, one minute of 24.1 days. It may decay in less than half a second or not for a century.

The example I gave above of the molecules in a box illustrates classical uncertainty, which is fundamentally different from the quantum uncertainty illustrated by the decay of the thorium atom. Classical mechanics assumed that the position occupied by each of the millions of molecules in the box ten seconds (or a thousand years) after the removal of the partition was predetermined and therefore predictable in principle, its uncertainty in practice arising only from the fact that one would need, what one could not possibly have, complete knowledge of the mass, momentum, direction, and every other fact about every particle involved, and every fact about every environmental circumstance, and one would then have to make calculations beyond human possibility in order to realize it. Not the position of each particle, but only our knowledge of it, was uncertain. The case is quite different with the thorium atoms, for the instant when any particular atom will decay by emitting an electron is uncertain because undetermined in itself, because the time when it will decay simply has not been established in advance.

Under quantum mechanics, the uncertainty of the Uncertainty Principle is not simply a matter of insurmountable obstacles to the prediction in practice of what, because it is predetermined, is predictable in principle. It arises, rather, from the fact that the future is not predetermined — or not precisely predetermined. The uncertainty to which it refers is the uncertainty of predetermination. It is the uncertainty of what has not yet been decided — of what Nature herself, so to speak, has left open. Prediction cannot be more certain than the future is in itself. The quantum of uncertainty defined by h is inherent in being, a fundamental property of the physical world. It represents the ultimate limit of precision in the movements and interactions of objects. It is equivalent to an irreducible looseness or play in the mechanism of a watch.

*

I return, now, to the order of magnitude to which our experience had always been limited until, in our present, we have begun to extend our knowledge to the world of the very small. In the world of our familiar order of magnitude, and in the astronomical world, physical phenomena appear to conform to mechanical laws that make them predictable in absolute terms. We can, for example, fire a missile into space and, on the basis of its position and momentum at a given instant, predict its course without any appreciable uncertainty. We feel justified in saying that its course is predetermined, and that the physical world to which it belongs is a deterministic world. This general conclusion, like so much else, has always been a matter of our common sense.

Now, however, our exploration of the world of the very small has entailed a discovery that violates this common sense — the discovery that we cannot predict the course of an elementary particle, as we can that of the missile, because its course has not been determined.

Determinism has proved to be inapplicable to the world of the very small. And, if determinism is not applicable to the world of the very small, then neither can it be applicable to the larger worlds, composed as they are of the very small, even though the limits of its applicability to those larger worlds are, relatively, of such infinitesimal degree as to be imperceptible.*

* See, however, the first footnote on p. 75 below.

XI

The World of the Very Small:

5. *Indeterminacy*

WHEN WE EXPLORED the world of the very large, as it is explained by
the Theory of Relativity, we found that it did not conform to our
traditional common sense, according to which space and time were
absolute. It was clear, however, that the fault was with our common
sense. That common sense had been based only on experience limited to our familiar order of magnitude, and we had not been justified in applying it, as we had done without thinking, to the world
of the very large. All that the larger understanding represented by
Relativity required of us, then, was the revision of our common
sense, its enlargement to accommodate the larger world into which
our minds had at last moved.

The exploration of the very small, however, has now confronted
us with a challenge of an altogether more serious nature. For the
Uncertainty Principle goes beyond the violation of our traditional
common sense to discredit the fundamental logic on which our conception of an orderly universe is necessarily based.

The existence of any logical order implies that any configuration
of its elements is what it is for a reason, and that any event or any
evolution within it occurs for a reason. Everything must be the effect of antecedent causes, which in their turn are the effects of
causes antecedent to them. If a thorium atom emits an electron at a
particular moment there must have been a cause of its doing so at
that moment, and the cause in turn must have had other causes in
what is to be regarded as chains and networks of causation stretching back through all time past. In an ideal thought experiment one
could go back along the chains to some moment untold millions of
years before the emission of the electron. Every link in the chains
would be determined by all the preceding links and, in conjunction
with other links, would determine what followed. So the emission of
the electron at the particular moment would have been predetermined by the whole antecedent history. A mind capable of infinite

comprehension, knowing everything about every particle in the universe all those millions of years earlier, would have been able on the basis of that information to predict infallibly the emission of the electron at the precise moment when it occurred.

If this is repellent to us in its absolute determinism, implying a mechanism of cause and effect without any freedom, it remains true that we cannot logically conceive of an effect in the physical world that is not ineluctably determined in every particular by an immediately antecedent combination of causes, or of antecedent causes that are not themselves ineluctably determined by causes antecedent to them. We cannot logically conceive of any freedom at all in the mechanism because we cannot conceive that whatever supposed choice that freedom allowed, however small, would not itself be made in obedience to antecedent causes that predetermined it.

The logic of cause and effect is native to our minds. Its rigidity is, in principle, absolute; for even where it appears as if there is a range of alternatives, representing a degree of freedom from strict determinism, we are bound to ask why one is realized rather than any of the others, and to assume a determining cause. To be told, then, that there can be situations like this in which there is no cause, no reason, no explanation of what happened, is to be confronted with a realm of being to which the native uses of our minds do not apply, to which our sanity is irrelevant.

*

Especially when we confront ultimate questions of being, we find ourselves before contradictions that we cannot logically resolve. For example, after generations of debate we have at last given up the attempt to determine whether light consists of particles or waves, recognizing that each of what seem to be mutually contradictory concepts is alike supported by experimental evidence. In the same way, I cannot reconcile my subjective experience of exercising free will with the logic of cause and effect to which I have just referred. Such intellectual frustrations as these may be attributed to the fact that our knowledge comprehends only part of a reality that makes sense, ultimately, only in its entirety. We cannot reconcile our concept of the elephant as being like a rope, for which we have experimental evidence, with our concept of the elephant as being like a wall, for which we have equally good experimental evidence. Under such circumstances we must suppose that, as our vision continues to widen, concepts that now seem irreconcilably contradictory will be reconciled within the larger terms of more comprehensive concepts based on more comprehensive views. Then we shall see that there is no contradiction between light as particles and light as waves, no contradiction between the elephant as a rope and the elephant as a wall. We may already make a beginning in this direction, as we shall see in the next chapter, with the contradiction between the logic of cause and effect, on the one hand, and the Uncertainty Principle on the other.

Meanwhile, if only provisionally, we need a logical device by which we can accommodate in our thinking the contradictions we hope eventually to resolve within the framework of wider views.

Winston Churchill, in one of those passages that are as light-hearted as they are serious, once gave his own conclusion on the question of Free Will *vs.* Predestination:

> . . . namely — let the reader mark it — that they are identical.
> I have always loved butterflies. In Uganda I saw glorious but-terflies the colour of whose wings changed from the deepest russet brown to the most brilliant blue, according to the angle from which you saw them. In Brazil as everyone knows there are butterflies of this kind even larger and more vivid. The contrast is extreme. You could not conceive colour effects more violently opposed; but it is the same butterfly. The butterfly is the Fact — gleaming, fluttering, settling for an instant with wings fully spread to the sun, then vanishing in the shades of the forest. Whether you believe in Free Will or Predestination, all depends on the slanting glimpse you had of the colour of his wings — which are in fact at least two colours at the same time.*

The knowledgeable will recognize in this statement, set down in 1930 or earlier, the Principle of Complementarity formulated by Niels Bohr in 1927. That Principle has been defined as follows: "In quantum theory the situation is such that certain concepts, indis-pensable for a complete description, are in a sense contradictory to each other, the word complementarity expressing this peculiar kind of contrariety, where one member of such a pair of concepts is the complement of the other member but also sets a limit to its simulta-neous use." † So what is a wave from one angle is a particle from another. So, in a larger view than we can yet comprehend, the ques-tion of a distinction and a choice between determinism and indeter-minism may not arise at all.

In the next chapter we shall see whether we cannot make a first move, at least, in the direction of such a larger view.

---

* *A Roving Commission: My Early Life,* New York, 1930, p. 28.
† Oskar Klein in Stefan Rozental (ed.), *Niels Bohr,* Amsterdam, 1967, p. 91.

XII

The Underlying Chaos

THE UNCERTAINTY PRINCIPLE tells us that the course taken by a single particle is not precisely predetermined. This indeterminacy is associated with the world of the very small. When an electron is deflected from its course by collision with a photon, no one can predict precisely what its consequent course will be because that course has not been precisely determined; but when a billiard ball is struck by another billiard ball, no one doubts that its consequent course has been precisely determined and is, therefore, precisely predictable. The range of indeterminacy, significant on the scale of the electron, is imperceptible and therefore insignificant on the scale of the billiard ball.

Nevertheless, what applies to the world of the very small must be fundamental to the entire universe, which is simply a build-up of the very small. It is true that, in our own order of magnitude, the factor of uncertainty is so small as to be imperceptible and therefore insignificant * — but it is not imperceptible or insignificant if we allow its effects to accumulate over countless millions of millennia. If we imagine billiard balls that have been moving about the table and colliding with one another over such a span of time, then we must recognize that an observer at the beginning of it, who had knowledge of all the elements initially involved, could not have predicted precisely the position of every ball at the end of it, because the cumulative effect of even such infinitesimal uncertainties over such a span of time would have falsified his prediction. In the same way, the deviation of a projectile from a straight trajectory by only a millionth of a millimeter in 10,000 kilometers might be considered as no deviation at all over the distance of one kilometer; but over a

* A. S. Eddington calculated that the uncertainty in the position of an electron after one second, during which it might have traveled 10,000 miles (16,000 km.), would be three or four centimeters. For a particle 0.001 mm. in diameter, the uncertainty would be 0.002 mm. after a thousand years. (Cited by T. E. W. Schumann in *Weather*, Vol. V., no. 7, p. 249.)

sufficiently long distance that deviation would at last amount to 360°.*

The objective of philosophy and pure science is to discover progressively, by the progressive enlargement of our vision, the logical order that governs the universe. Because we cannot conceive of such an order except as one of strict cause and effect, in which every item is predetermined by antecedent causes that are predetermined, in turn, by their own antecedent causes, our logic requires us to equate indeterminism with chaos. Like the indeterminism itself, however, the chaos is a matter of degree. We may therefore say that the chaos is greatest relative to the elementary units out of which the great universe is composed. As these units combine in ever larger entities the chaos diminishes proportionately and the sway of order becomes ever more complete.

Referring to the new view of the physical world opened up by the advances in our knowledge since the beginning of this century, Kenneth Ford writes that it is "a view of chaos *beneath* order — or, what is the same thing, of order imposed upon a deeper and more fundamental chaos." † This new view is not without a certain resemblance to an old one. "In the beginning . . . the earth was without form and void." In the beginning, that is, there was only chaos. Then "the Spirit of God moved," and out of the chaos came an order. The resemblance between the old view and the new suggests that the idea of an underlying chaos, implicit in the Uncertainty Principle, should not be as strange or disturbing to us as it has been in the minds of many.

What confronts us here is a phenomenon that we have encountered before in these pages: the characteristics of physical being that we regard as fundamental are dependent on a minimum order of magnitude. The characteristics by which we identify matter — tangibility, visibility, audibility, taste, or odor — are not to be found in the elementary particles of which it is composed but only in their combination on a large enough scale. May we not say that the logi-

---

* Indeterminacy could also manifest itself abruptly in the world of the very large where the balance of probability between alternatives was equal. I cite the following imaginary example. "Suppose that ten million years hence a heavenly body passes so near to our earth that the moon is caught in unstable equilibrium between the earth and the unwelcome visitor from outer space, i.e. the chances are even for the moon to be retained by the earth or carried away in the train of the passing planet. At the critical moment the position of the planet relative to the earth as determined from its motion ten million years previously would be precisely known according to Newton's laws, but according to quantum mechanics it might be a fraction of a millimeter 'off' this position, and this slight discrepancy may make all the difference to the future history of the moon" (T. E. W. Schumann, op. cit.).

† *Basic Physics,* Waltham (Mass.), 1968, p. 931.

cal order of being, too, manifests itself only as one goes up the scale of magnitude from the very small?

If, descending the scale of magnitude, we progressively analyze being down to its smallest components of time or of space we find that, as we approach the extreme of ultimate granularity, we discover a condition representative of chaos. Going back up the scale, we find order emerging progressively from the underlying chaos as the ultimate grains combine in larger and larger combinations, until at last chaos has become imperceptible and only the overlying order remains in evidence.

The phenomenon this represents has always been so familiar in our daily life that one wonders why its centrality in human experience has not become a matter of common knowledge and acceptance. One example will suffice.

Suppose I draw a circle with pencil on paper, using compasses. Viewing that circle from a sufficient distance, so that I see it in the large, it appears to me to be a perfect circle. The closer and more detailed my view, however, the more likely I am to notice little imperfections, irregularities caused by the roughness of the paper or by lack of perfect steadiness in the hand that guided the instrument. If I take a magnifying glass to it I shall find it even more imperfect; and if, at last, I use a microscope, I shall no longer be able to see a circle at all, only a chaos of smudges on the paper. It is, however, out of the chaos of these smudges, representing the very small, that the order represented by the circle as a whole is built. The circle stands for the order that overlies chaos; the smudges stand for the chaos that underlies order.

My point is that the chaos implied by the Uncertainty Principle, in what it tells us about the very small, has a significance wider and more fundamental than has been appreciated. We shall see in Chapter XV how being, generally, is orderly in the large and disorderly in detail, how what applies to the circle applies no less to the sphericity of the earth or the moon. Recalling, then, the elephant of the fable with which these chapters opened, we shall find it not implausible to surmise that there is a perfect order of being which manifests its full perfection only on the scale of the whole.

XIII

Time

> If no one asks me what [time] is, I know;
> if called upon to explain, I know not.
>
> — *St. Augustine of Hippo*

THE CONCEPT OF TIME has always given us more difficulty than that of space.

In the world of our inherited common sense there are three spatial dimensions.* There is also what we have traditionally regarded as the independent phenomenon of time, a continuous passage of all being in an irreversible direction that does not belong to the order of phenomena represented by spatial directions but is, rather, *sui generis*.

In terms of our common sense we have always supposed time to have the same objective existence, independent of our own observation, as we have attributed to space. But the evidence for its objective existence has been more difficult to adduce than evidence for the objective existence of space. For space is present to us in its entirety, surrounding us and abiding our examination; while of time we have available for direct observation only the present, a continuously changing point that, lacking extension, exists conceptually only — as a point in space, lacking any dimensions, exists only conceptually. While space itself is hardly more vivid and fundamental to our common sense than time, yet the reality time has for us de-

---

* Our inherited common sense, however, has always been evolving, as the following statement exemplifies. "Before Newton, people looked on the world as being essentially two-dimensional — the two dimensions in which one can walk about — and the up-and-down dimension seemed to be something essentially different. Newton showed how one can look on the up-and-down direction as being symmetrical with the other two directions, by bringing in gravitational forces and showing how they take their place in physical theory. One can say that Newton enabled us to pass from a picture with two-dimensional symmetry to a picture with three-dimensional symmetry" (P. A. M. Dirac, "The Evolution of the Physicist's Picture of Nature," *Scientific American*, May 1963).

pends entirely on the special faculty of memory that is so highly developed in us, and that is extended by verbal records.

The more primitive human life is, and the more primitive life in
general is, the less this special faculty is developed. There may, for
all I know, be a valid sense in which the span of a butterfly's memory
is no greater than a microsecond, in which case a butterfly, no matter how developed its other faculties, might not be capable of the
conception of time. Accepting, as we are learning to do, the fact
that time is a fourth dimension of what we must now call space-time,
we might say that, where we are capable of knowing ourselves to inhabit a four-dimensional world, the butterfly, inhabiting that same
world, is capable of knowing it only in three dimensions. (It seems
to me plausible that, in the eyes of some being who knew everything,
say the omniscient God of Christian tradition, the difference between the inadequacy of our faculties and that of the butterfly's, for
the appreciation of what may be a myriad-dimensional world, would
be insignificant.)

To the extent that our knowledge of time depends directly on
memory it is a function of that subjective faculty. Memory is of what
we call the past; but to the past we add, by extrapolation, what we
call the future, a reality-to-be which, when realized, will immediately
become part of the past. If only because this is the nature of the faculty on which our knowledge of time depends, time presents itself to
our consciousness as having, unlike the spatial dimensions, a unique
direction. We are moved inexorably along it at a set pace, without
any possibility of reversing our course. We have traditionally assumed, moreover, that all being is so moved, although relativity
theory has now brought us to introduce some variability into the
measurements, at least, of the rate of movement as it manifests itself
in different frames of reference.

None of the three spatial dimensions has had, for our common
sense, quite the same independent reality as time. Each has been
simply a conceptual device by which we have described and measured a physical reality that is irreducibly three-dimensional. Except
in conceptual or mathematical terms, we have not been able to dis-
mantle that reality by detaching one or two of the dimensions from
any piece of it. (The line we imagine when we think of one dimension without the other two is an ideal line of the mind only; the surface we imagine when we think of two dimensions without the third
is an ideal surface of the mind only.) Mathematically, we can discuss
one or the other of the three dimensions as if it had separate physical reality, and the habitual device of measuring them separately has
accustomed us to regard them as if they had such reality in fact. If

only as a matter of custom, then, the purely mathematical conception involved in the contemplation of individual dimensions has come, at last, to give us no difficulty, although the physical reality remains that of an irreducibly three-dimensional space.

The conception of a measurable passage of time from past to future has had for us a reality separable from that of space. If we continue our progress in knowledge, however, and especially if we make ourselves increasingly at home in the great distances of the universe, it is going to seem increasingly obvious to us that space and time are inseparable altogether, that to measure the universe truly we must do so in terms of four axes — that to do so in terms of only three is as misleading as to measure the height of an object as it appears to be without correcting for the diminution of apparent height with distance.

Still, while we are coming to see with increasing ease that time and space are mutually interdependent parts of one irreducible whole that is four-dimensional, we do not see this automatically, as yet, but only by way of the kind of arithmetic set forth in Chapter IV.

To most of us the shortest distance between two points is still the straight line of Euclidean geometry, which is valid for two dimensions or three but not for the four dimensions of the larger reality we are familiarizing ourselves with today. We know today (or feel sure we know) that the shortest distance between two points must be traced through a four-dimensional reality; and that, when we do this, the habitual exclusion of the fourth dimension from the image we make in our minds will paradoxically make that shortest distance seem like a curving line in three-dimensional space — as when a ray of light from a star seems to bend through the gravitational field of the sun. (In the same way, the shortest distance between two points on our planet appears as a curved line on a two-dimensional projection, like Mercator's, which necessarily distorts it. See page 36 above.) At this point in our development, however, although we know the nature of four-dimensional reality, we are able to grasp it only as we grasp the images at some distance from the center of our field of vision.

In Chapter V I referred to the fact that the field of our vision, when we focus our eyes on a particular point, has no precise boundaries: its contents simply become less resolvable into realities with increasing distance from the center of focus, until we can no longer say what it is we see or whether we are seeing any reality at all. Mathematics today is capable of describing a cosmos of five or more dimensions. Perhaps there will someday be mathematicians who can, so to speak, see such a cosmos out of the corners of their eyes, and perhaps a day will come when the reality of such a cosmos (if such a cosmos should prove to be real) is a matter of common sense. However, without having been able to define boundaries to my own field of vision, I have to recognize that at this point what I think I see has such abstraction that I can no longer take it in (or hardly) as part of the furniture of reality in my mind.

*

We have always been able to postulate what we could not imagine. (So I can postulate a beginning to being, but without being able to exclude the question of what came before it.) Although the imagination of reality cannot accompany a postulate of logic that goes beyond a certain limit of abstraction, it is nevertheless drawn to such a postulate in the degree that its logic is persuasive, and so may catch up in time. Already the traditional conception of absolute time, like that of absolute space, is giving way in our imaginations. We are coming to the stage when it will seem only common sense that time slows down in proportion to velocity, just as it is common sense to us today that the image of an object diminishes with distance.

For us today, the question whether time had a beginning remains excessively abstract. However, the question whether it is confined, as it seems to be, to one direction — from an absolute past to an absolute future — has become meaningful. It arose irresistibly when Einstein defined time as a fourth dimension; for it is an apparent property of the other three dimensions, to which he equated it, that each exists simultaneously in its entire length, rather than being created and abolished point by point, so that one can move back and forth along each. (The simultaneity with which each exists throughout its length loses precision increasingly with distance, as we saw in Chapter IV, so that for the sake of precision I refer to this as an "apparent" property.) Moreover, when Einstein invalidated the commonsense conception of instantaneous simultaneity throughout three-dimensional space, at the same time that he showed time's measurement to vary with the relative motion of the measurer, it became plausible to ask whether the apparent fixity of its direction (or the apparent irreversibility of our passage through it) was, like the apparent simultaneity, merely another illusion of our discredited common sense.

Such objective evidence as we have supports our subjective impression, based on the faculty of memory, that time moves irresistibly and irreversibly in one direction only, even if at different rates for different states of relative motion. It is merely a popular misunderstanding that relativity theory has invalidated the idea of uni-directionality along with that of simultaneity.*

The available evidence for the uniqueness of time's direction, however, cannot be considered eternally valid. Moreover, it takes the form not of an absolute law of nature but of such a probabilistic law, based on large statistics, as I dealt with in Chapter X. I gave, there, the example of the box divided by a partition into two equal compartments, one containing millions of gas molecules, the other empty. Removal of the partition allows a natural process to get under way whereby what had been gathered together becomes increasingly scattered, until it becomes evenly distributed over the whole of the larger space to which it is now confined. The process of scattering, the increasing entropy of the collection of molecules (entropy being the term for the randomness of their distribution), marks the direction of time. If we saw all the molecules, starting from a state of equal distribution through the entire box, progressively gather together in one half of it, leaving the other half empty, we might think that time was going backwards, except that the time of which we were subjectively conscious would deny this.

Another example of the increasing entropy that marks the direction of time would be provided by putting a hot brick into a tub of cold water. The heat of the brick would tend to become evenly diffused through the entire system composed of brick, water, and tub until all were the same temperature. While the reverse process would be theoretically possible, its improbability would be virtually equivalent to impossibility.

Aside from our subjective consciousness of the direction of time, the increase of entropy is the only evidence we have of the single direction time takes in the world as we know it. It is the only objective evidence; but its probabilistic character, in itself, makes the reversal of time, as evidenced by decreasing entropy, less than a total impossibility in principle.

The irreversible increase of entropy occurs in all isolated systems that are quantitatively sufficient for what we may call statistical sig-

* We have already seen, in these pages, that what applies to the large orders of magnitude (where relativity is supreme) does not necessarily apply to the smallest (where the quantum reigns). The world of the very small provides no evidence to support the proposition that being can move only one way through time. If what we call particles do, indeed, seem to move only one way (our way), what we call antiparticles can be adequately explained as particles moving the other way. One may speculate that, just as progress upward through the orders of magnitude is marked by decreasing chaos and increasing order, so such progress is also marked by an increasing confinement to one direction through time (a conception difficult for us to grasp at this stage in the development of our understanding). Some cosmological theories, moreover, would be compatible with the model of a universe that swings back and forth through time like

nificance. Here again we see how most laws of nature in the world as we know it depend on such quantity as we can define only vaguely in terms of order of magnitude. So a molecule of H_2O is not water as we know it, but a large aggregation, properly organized, is. So an elementary particle is not matter as we know it, but a large enough aggregation, properly organized, is. So the movement of an elementary particle appears not to obey the logic of cause and effect, but the aggregation of such particles in an object the size of a billiard ball does. So the evidence for the direction of time does not show itself in a small quantity of material but does where the quantity is great enough. Again we see that chaos, in its degree, is to be associated with the world of the very small, and that this chaos is overlaid by order as one goes up the scale of magnitudes.

In the examples I gave of increasing entropy, the box and its contents in the one case, the brick, water, and tub in the other, were regarded as isolated systems — as though nothing existed outside them. The universe in its entirety is such a system, and it is in this truly and uniquely isolated system that increasing entropy gives objective evidence that time is moving in a fixed and irreversible direction.

This is not to say that entropy is increasing everywhere in the universe, for this is manifestly not so. When scattered molecules of H_2O distributed as a gas come together to form droplets of water, and the droplets come together to form drops of rain, the process is in the direction of decreasing entropy. When an organism grows from the germ in the egg-cell to become, at last, an elephant, the process, again, is in the direction of decreasing entropy. It is a process in which relatively random matter is increasingly gathered together in an organization that is not random. But neither the molecules of H_2O nor the growing elephant constitute isolated systems; and so the decreasing randomness they represent, their increasing organization, has no more significance, for the direction of time, than would the fact that many of the molecules in the box, having gone beyond the half in which they had originally been confined, returned to it.

It appears to be a fact that the universe as a whole is running down through the process of increasing entropy, that it is becoming increasingly less organized, that its order is becoming less, that it is

a pendulum, going one way up to a certain point, then reversing its course. An observer who was confined to only one direction might see it as alternately expanding and contracting; but what such an observer regarded as a process of contraction would appear as a process of expansion to an observer moving the other way through time, and *vice versa*.

therefore moving inexorably, by way of increasing disorder, toward a future in which all will be reduced, at last, to a universal chaos. Then, unimaginable as that may be to us, the very concept of time will become doubtful in that there will be no objective test of it, no further process of systematic change by which it might, in principle, be defined, be given direction, or be measured. (Neither, of course, would there be any subjective test, since conscious being as we know it could not exist.)

May we not say of time, then, as we have already said of space, that it is not an independent phenomenon, not a thing in itself? It is merely a function of a system in which the organization of matter-energy, however brought about to begin with, is undergoing dissolution. We have already seen that what we call space is a manifestation of matter-energy; now we see that time is too — as, indeed, its association with space as a fourth dimension of space-time would require. Space-time, we may conclude, is an irreducible manifestation of matter-energy.

So matter, energy, space, and time are interdependent aspects of one universal order.

XIV

One Realm of Being

IN THE FOUR-DIMENSIONAL GEOMETRY that we can describe mathematically but not visualize, the universe is unbounded but finite — like the surface of a sphere. It is composed of matter-energy in a variety of guises. There is field, manifesting itself throughout the whole extent of the universe in the phenomena of radiation and gravitation. Our senses do not directly record field, or any of the forms of radiation except that small band in the electromagnetic spectrum that our eyes register as light and that the sensory nerves in our skin may register as heat. Therefore we think of the universe as empty except for the scattered forms of what we call matter. These forms, in the large, are the galaxies, the stars of which the galaxies are composed, clouds of gaseous matter, comets, planets, and certain lesser objects.

The aim implicit in our continuing pursuit of knowledge is that of progressively discovering the unity in this variety of being. The great frustration of Einstein's career was in his failure to reduce the gravitational field and the electromagnetic field to one, but we must continue to hope for its accomplishment. He did succeed in reducing time and space, matter and energy, inertial mass and gravitational mass, to differing forms or manifestations of what was essentially one phenomenon in each case. And in the conception that the geometry of space-time is determined by the distribution of mass he implicitly established a unifying relationship between space-time and matter-energy.

It has properly been a cause of distress to the physicists who have been exploring the world of the very small that, over the past few decades, they have been discovering constantly more species of elementary particles without being able to reduce their increasing variety, without being able to make any apparent progress toward the discovery of one ultimate particle of which the many now known are merely manifestations; but they console themselves with the hope that this is no more than a passing stage in the long progress toward unity.

Let us return, now, to the unbounded universe as a whole. The material objects in it — stars, planets, etc. — may be regarded as disturbances in the continuous fields that extend everywhere, or as local concentrations of ubiquitous matter-energy. The stars, of which our sun is one, may be analyzed as gaseous concentrations of elementary particles and atomic nuclei. These stars are, in turn, gathered into the clusters we call galaxies. We surmise that there may be some ten thousand million galaxies scattered through the area over which our vision now extends. Our own galaxy, which is not untypical, contains some hundred thousand million stars.

Our knowledge of these stars depends primarily on the electromagnetic radiation that reaches us from them, secondarily on indications of their gravitational influence. Until recently, it was only by way of the excessively narrow portion of the entire electromagnetic spectrum visible to us as light that information about the contents of the universe reached us. This must have entailed an excessively partial view, representing the special limitations of our information-receiving apparatus more than the reality itself. In recent times, however, we have developed instruments to register the incoming radiation of shorter wavelengths (x-rays, gamma rays, and cosmic rays) and of the longer radio waves. We have thereby discovered the existence of quasars (quasi-stellar radio sources), entities too small to be galaxies and too intense in their radiation to be stars. We also surmise the possible existence of entities of such mass that their gravitational influence prevents the escape of any radiation to signal their presence to us directly, the so-called black holes. And who knows what else there may be of which the dwarf flea is not yet able to gain knowledge because its senses have evolved for the receipt only of such limited kinds of information as it needs for the conduct of its life in its own restricted locality?

*

> We had the sky, up there, all speckled with stars, and we used to lay on our backs and look up at them, and discuss about whether they was made, or only just happened.
>
> — *Huckleberry Finn*

When we look at the night sky, powdered and jeweled with points of light, the impression we have is of stillness and an eternal repose. In fact, the dynamism of the cosmos we see is on the scale of its temporal and spatial dimensions. Let alone the fact that all these points of light are nuclear fires from which high-energy radiation pours, the whole assemblage is expanding as if in an explosion on the same vast scale of space and time — an explosion in one infinitesimal instant of which the generations of our kind find themselves riding, inexplicably, on one planetary satellite of an incidental star in the accumulation of accumulations that extends across the unbounded universe. We know only that, in terms of time and space beyond the grasp of our provincial imaginations, all the galaxies are receding from us and from one another at astronomical velocities.

Like the ancient Greeks when they first tried to explain the basic nature of matter, all we can do as yet is to formulate hypotheses that we cannot test. Some Greeks said that the basic constituents of matter were earth, water, air, and fire; others that they were atoms which cohered by means of hooks. So we ourselves propound various hypothetical explanations of the universal expansion. Some say the universe began as an infinitely dense concentration of matter that exploded in consequence of the electromagnetic repulsion among its particles. Others say that the universe pulsates, expanding from a condition of concentration until, having attained a certain degree of diffusion, it falls back in on itself, only to expand again — and so *ad infinitum*. Others say that it is expanding eternally, but without thinning out because new matter is being constantly created throughout its extent. Still others say that it began as a diffuse cloud of particles and antiparticles, that as the cloud became more concentrated in consequence of gravitational attraction the increasing pressure of radiation resulting from the mutually annihilating collisions of particles and antiparticles overcame the gravitational attraction, initiating the expansion that is still going on.*

One may well ask how the theory that the universe as a whole is evolving in the direction of maximum entropy bears on these theories that seek to explain its history. There is no difficulty in formulating speculative answers — such as that the increasing entropy represents merely a transient and reversible phase in the history of the universe — but it is apparent that we have, as yet, insufficient grounds for more than such speculation.

*

We may now return from speculation at the outer boundaries of our present knowledge to what is central and fundamental.

* Most readers will recognize the first of the theories here listed as the so-called "big-bang" theory. The second is simply a logical extension of it. The third is the so-called "steady-state" theory. For the last, see "Antimatter and Cosmology" by Hannes Alfvén in *Scientific American*, April 1967.

Vast as the universe is in its four dimensions, it represents but a single order of being based on uniformity of composition and uniformity of the processes that go on throughout it. A star in some other galaxy, even though 6,000 million light-years away, is composed like our sun of hydrogen, helium, carbon, nitrogen, and other elements that we are at home with on our own little earth. All the stars are so composed. And in all of them the interactions of the elements are the same as in our sun, producing the same radiation (which is how we know it to be so). The laws of nature that prevail in our own little sphere prevail equally at the distance in space and time of the most remote star. The order that overlies chaos there is the order that overlies it here.

The universality of the single order is surely the most significant and hopeful fact about the realm of being. It is a fact that we have had no choice but to assume from the beginning, even though we did so on faith alone, because any alternative assumption would have implications of chaos that could not be contemplated simply because they would erase the distinction in principle between sanity and insanity on which we depend in our thinking and our living alike. It is of immeasurable importance, therefore, to have, as we do have, experimental confirmation.

If we find that, here and now, fire is hot and ice cold, we must assume that this is so on the other side of the mountain as well. If, then, empirical evidence should not confirm our assumption, we could not respond by simply discarding it. We would, rather, have to find a larger framework of logic within which the postulated uniformity of all being could be confirmed. We would have to find out why it was that conditions on one side of the mountain produced different consequences from conditions on the other, assuming that the same conditions would produce the same consequences on either side, that the laws of nature were everywhere the same. In a word, it would be impossible for us to accept the concept of a fragmented reality, a reality that was not basically uniform. It would be impossible for us to accept such a concept simply because we could not live with it. The progress of our kind in what ultimately counts, however, depends on confirmation, the kind of confirmation that comes when the spectral lines of light from the most distant galaxy show its composition to be the same as that of our own galaxy.

All man's basic science, all his artistic creation, even his social and political philosophy, have in their development been directed at the progressive realization, through comprehension, of a single logical order conceived as representing one universal realm of being in its ultimate reality.

The ancient Greeks, on the most partial geographical evidence only, supplemented by the occasional view of the earth's shadow on the moon, conceived the earth to be a sphere, the only shape that is symmetrical from every angle of three-dimensional space. They knew that, in the limited area of its surface with which they were familiar, the rays of the midday sun fell at a more perpendicular angle as one went southward, at a less perpendicular angle as one went northward; they knew that the climate became warmer southward, cooler northward; they formulated a logic by which they equated these two facts; and then they extrapolated from them, thereby adducing certain conclusions, which they were as yet unable to test empirically, with respect to the nature of the earth far beyond the limits of their own experience or the reports that had come to them from others. They postulated, as existing in one direction, a north-polar region of perpetual snow and ice, and in the other a torrid equatorial zone. Beyond that equatorial zone they postulated another hemisphere, the mirror-image of what they conceived to be a northern hemisphere, extending to a south-polar region of snow and ice like the north-polar region.

Why should they not have considered the possibility that the earth below the equator was jagged or flat or anything but hemispherical?

One way of answering this is to say that any such hypothesis would have offended their aesthetic sense, the same sense that prompted them to design temples expressive of harmony, of symmetry, of rhythm, of the regularity that order, as opposed to chaos, implies. This is to say that their science was not something apart from art — as science never is in its creative manifestations. In their scientific thinking they assumed an order in nature that represented the harmony on which their own aesthetic values were based. What their cosmology expressed was, at its foundation, what the Parthenon expressed. Nor did they need to rely only on their own aesthetic intuitions in this, for they had, by observation, already become aware of how much in nature tends toward the symmetrical. They knew the sun and the moon, and the perfect arcs they traced in the rhythmic repetitions of their passage across the skies; they knew the bilateral symmetry of birds and fishes, and the regularity of snow crystals or of ripples spreading rhythmically across water. The identity between the one great order of being and music was everywhere evident — in the flight of a bird, in the movement of the heavenly spheres.

Let us imagine that, having postulated a southern hemisphere to match and balance the northern in a single terrestrial harmony, they had then discovered by actual exploration that the world below the equator was of no definable shape at all but, rather, a jagged chaos of broken forms. Or let us suppose them to have found that the laws of nature familiar to them in the northern hemisphere did not apply in the southern — so that, for example, the area on which the rays of the midday sun fell most directly were the coldest. Is it not clear that, in such a situation, they could not have allowed themselves to conclude that there were no natural laws of universal sway, that the laws of nature were local ones only? In the situation I have described they would, rather, have been driven to discover another universal order to replace the order they had wrongly supposed, on the basis of their excessively local experience, to be universal. They would have been driven to discover new natural laws that would account equally for the disparate phenomena on the two sides of the equator respectively. Their aesthetic sense itself — as manifested in their architecture, in their sculpture, in their literature, and in their music — would have driven them to reject the implications of a universal chaos, and the role of their aesthetic perceptions would, in this respect, have been scientifically valid. It is only the small minds in science, the uncreative minds confined to analysis and quantification, that do not recognize the validity of the aesthetic test. Einstein was a great scientist because he had the artist's vision. The Theory of Relativity is, first of all, a work of art — although, where creativity is involved, the distinction between art and science is at best secondary.*

The mathematical physicist P. A. M. Dirac, one of the small group of creative scientists who produced the scientific revolution of our century, has written that "it is more important to have beauty in one's equations than to have them fit experiment. . . . It seems that if one is working from the point of view of getting beauty in one's equations, and if one has really a sound insight, one is on a sure line of progress." † This statement is eloquent in its implications for the nature of reality and the validity of our aesthetic intuitions.

If we had discovered that there seemed to be no uniformity between being as it manifested itself in our own world and as it manifested itself 6,000 million light-years away, that the laws of nature were different there from here, we could not have accepted the conclusion that this was so. We would then have had to set about the discovery of other uniformities and other laws of nature that embraced equally, in their application, the distant and the near alike.

It is not without a reassuring significance that, when the exploration of the southern hemisphere did at last take place, it confirmed the surmise of the Greeks, based on their imputation of harmony to

* For a fuller discussion of this point see Part Five, Chapter XII.
† "The Evolution of the Physicist's Picture of Nature," *Scientific American*, May 1963.

nature. And it is not without a like significance that the most distant parts of the cosmos, as we have now discovered, are made of the same stuff as our own corner of it, and are subject to the same laws.

In important respects our expanding exploration of the realm of being has supported us in our necessary belief that there is one harmonious order for all being. Where that exploration has confronted us with contradictions irresolvable for the moment, as in some of quantum theory today, we must look for new and more comprehensive principles or laws by which to resolve them.

What I have been saying here is that there is an accord, on which we have to rely, between the subjective logic that is native to our minds and the logic of the great external realm we inhabit. Increasingly, in modern times, this logic has taken a mathematical form for us. This gives particular point to a citation of Kenneth Ford with which I conclude this chapter. "Science," he writes, "rests basically upon man's awareness of an orderly world outside himself. Mathematics rests basically upon man's awareness of an orderly world within himself." * Ultimately, the two worlds are one.

* *Basic Physics,* Waltham (Mass.), 1968, p. 102.

XV

The Central Order

ALL THOUGHT is necessarily based on the premise that being is to be equated with an order of some sort. This is the irreducible premise on which the conduct of our lives, individual or collective, rests. A man who plows the soil in preparation for the spring planting is acting on the assumption of an order in nature — one that, in this case, involves the regular succession of the seasons. So is a man who, in implicit recognition of wave theory, tunes a violin. So is a woman who, in accordance with the Second Law of Thermodynamics, puts a kettle over a fire to boil water.

We have generally thought of this order as existing in a world of nature external to us as individuals, and not dependent on our observation. We have thought of it as existing before we were born, to continue after we die. In another view, which cannot be disproved, we have regarded it as we regard the content of our dreams. In still another but related view, the violinist who, sounding middle C, hears the harmonic overtones that accompany it, may argue, with a logic not to be disproved, that the series of sounds he hears is a product of his own faculties: what he hears is determined by the characteristics of his auricular apparatus, by the nature of his brain, and by the previous conditioning on which the response of his brain depends. The scientist who translates the sound into vibrations, which he analyzes as a series of frequencies representing an orderly numerical succession, may argue that he is thereby projecting upon the illusion of an external nature an order solely of his own conceiving. So I might say that, when I relate the harmonic series in music to the quantum series of an electron in orbit about a proton (as I did in Chapter IX), I am imposing on the illusion of an external nature an order that belongs to my own mind only.

As increasing numbers of people have come to live in urban communities that are the products of human artifice, so that they have been increasingly insulated from the pre-existing and underlying world of nature, and as the surface of the earth has been increasingly transformed by the impositions of human artifice, the view has spread that there is no order in being aside from what man creates.*

I admit my inability to know that anything exists outside myself, that my life is not just a dream; or to know that, if there is a world outside myself, my faculties report it to me truly. At least for working purposes, however, I assume the existence of an external world that bears a correspondence to the appearances presented to me through my faculties. The farmer who believes that any apparent order in nature is of his own creation may still make troublesome provision, in advance, against the unwelcome coming of winter; and the solipsist is unlikely to let his philosophy prevent him from coming in out of the rain.

Granting what I conceive to be the ultimate ignorance of us all, it remains true that the existence of an order of some sort — whether external, internal, or both — is the irreducible premise on which the conduct of our lives and the hopes of our future rest. A peculiarity of this order is that it exists for us in two forms. As we conceive or apprehend it in our minds it is perfect; as represented in external nature it is imperfect.

In the last chapter I cited the example of the ancient Greeks, who conceived the earth to be a sphere because such a shape corresponded with a conception of symmetrical harmony that they had in their minds and that they attributed to external nature. I called attention to the significance of the fact that empirical investigation subsequently proved them right. In what most of us would consider a pettifogging view, however, the empirical investigation did not prove them right. If a sphere is, as my dictionary says, "a round body of which the surface is at all points equidistant from the centre," † then the earth is not a sphere. For one thing, it has an irregular surface, what with its mountains and valleys, which varies in its distance from the center. And even if we overlooked the mountains and valleys, we would have to recognize that, in literal terms, it is a

---

* I find this view first suggested in Karl Marx's *Capital* (translation into English by Moore and Aveling, Moscow, 1961, Vol. I, pp. 177–178). It is represented today by philosophers who are associated, if only in the public mind, with the vague movement called existentialism. There is something of it in the disposition of Socrates to avert his eyes from the manifestations of external nature and, instead, to look inward for the discovery of truth. (See Plato's *Phaedo,* 10.) On the whole, however, I find it typical of urban philosophers who live their lives in a man-made environment, and there is reason to doubt that the minds of those who hold it have grasped the implications of the scientific revolution that, in our century, has revealed how immense is the cosmos and how insignificant, on its scale, is the speck of dust to which man is confined.

† *The Shorter Oxford English Dictionary,* Oxford, 1933.

spheroid that approaches but does not exactly correspond to the shape of a perfect sphere. Nevertheless, we are in the habit of referring to the earth as a sphere because implicit in all our thinking is a distinction between the perfect idea and the rendition of it in a physical reality that, as we have learned to take for granted, is in some degree imperfect. The shape of the earth approaches, without fully realizing, the perfect symmetry that the Greeks postulated for it in their minds. So the order within differs from the order without.

In Chapter XII we saw how a pencil-drawn circle, if seen in the large from a certain distance, appears perfect, but appears imperfect in the close-up, detailed view. If we could see the earth as a whole from the necessary distance, as we see the moon, its deviations from perfect sphericity would, as in the case of the moon, be too small for us to note or, if we did so, to regard as significant. It is only when we look close, taking account of relatively small differences of measurement, that we become aware of the irregularities — the mountains and valleys, the flattenings or the swellings of the surface here or there. It is only when we look close that we see the chaos which underlies the order.

Throughout these pages, so far, we have concerned ourselves sometimes with the very large, sometimes with the very small. There is a sense in which our exploration of the very large has given us a satisfaction that was wanting in our exploration of the very small. The Theory of Relativity, which we associate primarily with the very large, impresses us with its beauty as a work of art does.* On the other hand, quantum theory, which manifests itself appreciably only in the world of the very small, does not provide us with a like degree of aesthetic satisfaction; and in the Uncertainty Principle, associated with the granularity of the very small, it positively disturbs us in its denial of the perfect precision that our aesthetic satisfaction demands.

Is it not evident that what confronts us here is the contrast between the perfect world of our mental conceptions, which is represented without noticeable imperfection when physical being is looked at in the large, and the imperfect world of physical being as we find it to be when we examine it in close detail? The order tends to manifest itself in the accumulation of what, in detail, tends to manifest chaos. The order is built on an underlying chaos.

I suggest that the Uncertainty Principle gives us a clue, at least, to

* It also manifests itself when elementary particles, which we identify with the world of the very small, travel at high velocities, but appreciably only when they travel over distances that transcend the world of the very small.

the fundamental distinction between the perfect conception and its imperfect realization in empirical experience.

*

The irreducible premise of all our thinking is that being is to be equated with an order of some sort. The order is perfect in conception, and we may therefore think of the conception as primary, but its representation in the world of physical being always falls short of perfection.

We are bound to assume that the order is one order for all being, and this assumption tends to be confirmed by our ever increasing empirical knowledge. It transpires that the southern hemisphere is indeed a mirror image of the northern, as the Greeks had assumed — although this is so, not in detail, but only when viewed in the large. It transpires that the composition of a galaxy 6,000 million light-years away, and the processes that go on in it, are (again in the large) the same as the composition and the processes of our own galaxy. There is one order, then, which we may refer to henceforth as the central order, primary and perfect in conception, secondary and imperfect in realization.

We men are driven to comprehend the central order by progressively enlarging our understanding. This mission, as we may regard it, is realized in all our creative activities, in science, in art, and in social organization alike.* It is not a coincidence, then, that creative scientists from Pythagoras to Einstein have tended to be attracted to music, that music has tended to play a part in their lives and in their thinking.

Among the small group of creative scientists who brought about the scientific revolution of this century, Werner Heisenberg was not the least. He was seventeen years old in 1919, when his native Germany, having just been defeated in World War I, was in a state of intellectual and moral crisis that affected particularly the generation just coming of age. Basic values and basic conceptions of the order of being, which had been taken for granted by the older generation, were now discredited or put in question. It was in these circumstances of intellectual and moral chaos, and mental uncertainty, that the young Heisenberg attended a youth assembly at Prunn Castle in Bavaria. The purpose of the assembly was to discuss what sort of future the new generation might build. I here give Heisenberg's own account of what followed.

* The exemplification of this is provided in Part Five.

Prunn Castle stands sheer on a rock at the edge of the valley. The courtyard, with its central well, was teeming with people. Most of them were schoolboys, but there was a sprinkling of older boys who had suffered all the horrors of war at the front and had returned to a completely changed world. There were many speeches that day, full of the kind of pathos that would ring quite false today. We argued passionately about whether the fate of our own nation mattered more than that of all mankind; whether the death of those who had fallen for their country had become meaningless through defeat; whether youth had the right to fashion life according to its own values; whether inner truth was more important than all the old forms that had been shaping human life for centuries.

I myself was much too unsure to join in the debates, but I listened and once again thought a great deal about the meaning of "order." From the remarks of the speakers it was clear that different orders, however sincerely upheld, could clash, and that the result was the very opposite of order. This, I felt, was only possible because all these types of order were partial, mere fragments that had split off from the central order; they might not have lost their creative force, but they were no longer directed toward a unifying center. Its absence was brought home to me with increasingly painful intensity the longer I listened. I was suffering almost physically, but I was quite unable to discover a way toward the center through the thicket of conflicting opinions. Thus the hours ticked by, while more speeches were delivered and more disputes were born. The shadows in the courtyard grew longer, and finally the hot day gave way to slate-gray dusk and a moonlit night. The talk was still going on when, quite suddenly, a young violinist appeared on a balcony above the courtyard. There was a hush as, high above us, he struck up the first great D minor chords of Bach's Chaconne. All at once, and with utter certainty, I had found my link with the center. The moonlit Altmühl Valley below would have been reason enough for a romantic transfiguration; but that was not it. The clear phrases of the Chaconne touched me like a cool wind, breaking through the mist and revealing the towering structures beyond. There had always been a path to the central order in the language of music, in philosophy and in religion, today no less than in Plato's day and in Bach's. That I now knew from my own experience.*

This is the note on which I have wished to conclude Part One. What follows bridges the gap to Part Two.

*

* *Physics and Beyond* (trans. by A. J. Pomerans), New York, 1971, pp. 10–11.

The star we know best, our sun, is composed of certain elementary particles in various configurations. The untold millions of untold millions of other stars in the cosmos, in conformity with the central order, are composed of the same elementary particles in like configurations. Within the overall uniformity there is, however, a range of individual variety. Some stars are larger than our sun, some smaller; some hotter, some cooler; some younger, some older. We know our sun to be attended by planets in orbit around it. It would be a violation of statistical plausibility, associated with the logic of cause and effect, if millions of millions of other stars were not likewise attended by planets in orbit around them. (In fact, we have already discovered one star, known as Barnard's star, that is attended by a planet.)

We also know that intelligent life has developed on one of the sun's planets. Surely it is not believable, in combined terms of statistical probability and the logic of cause and effect, that intelligent life has not developed as well on many of the planets attending other stars across the immensity of space-time we know. As the Greeks could assume the sphericity of the earth, as we have been able to assume the elementary composition of the most distant stars, so we can assume the existence of intelligent life at other localities beside our own in the one vast realm of being, governed as it is by the central order.

It is, then, to the nature of life that we turn next.

PART TWO

Life

For all its backward eddies, the flow of a stream does correlate with the slope of the landscape. Yet if only small bits of the stream are seen at a time this may not be apparent.

— Charles Hartshorne

———————

I

The Place of Life on Earth

THE NUMBER OF STARS in as much of the universe as we have been able to observe is 10^{20}, of which one tenth (10^{19}) are thought to be attended by planets. Of these planets, some 10^{10} "would be like our Earth in almost all respects and, therefore, likely capable of supporting life." * Although life on earth is the only life for which we have evidence, our lack of evidence for its existence elsewhere, reflecting only the limitations on what is accessible to our observation, does not diminish the possibility of such existence. It simply means that if we speculate about it we must do so on the basis of logic alone — as we used to speculate, before we had the confirmation of evidence, that the far side of the moon was essentially like the side we could see. The basic uniformity of the universe is the foundation for this logic. The conditions that produced life on this planet must be expected to produce it wherever they exist, just as the conditions that produce heat must be expected to produce it wherever they exist.

Reference to life on earth may suggest that it is a superficial occurrence, like dust on a windowpane. In fact, however, it is an integral part of the earth's structure. The earth has what we believe to be a hard metallic core surrounded by molten iron, which is enclosed by a mineral mantle, which is covered by a crust that we call the lithosphere. In a schematic description, the oceans form a hydrosphere outside the lithosphere, and the atmosphere constitutes the outermost envelope. The use of the term biosphere to denote the mantle of life, which interpenetrates with the hydrosphere and the atmosphere, reflects the fact that this sphere, no less than the others, is an

* Sidney W. Fox, and Klaus Dose, *Molecular Evolution and the Origin of Life,* San Francisco, 1972, p. 318, citing Harlow Shapley, *View from a Distant Star,* New York, 1963. See also Hannes and Kerstin Alfvén, *Living on the Third Planet,* San Francisco, 1972, p. 167; and John C. Brandt, and Stephen P. Maran, *New Horizons in Astronomy,* San Francisco, 1972, pp. 435-436. A range of temperature and atmospheric pressure that allows water to exist in the liquid state is the chief determinant of a planet's ability to support life as we know it.

integral part of the planet. It may be thought of as the integument of the solid earth, between the lithosphere, which it has largely transformed, and the atmosphere, which is largely of its composing.

When the biosphere began to develop, the atmosphere was devoid of free oxygen. However, the carbon dioxide, which we suppose to have been abundantly present, may be said to have been breathed in by the first vegetable life to evolve, which converted it by photosynthesis into the oxygen which it then exhaled. So the primitive and proliferating vegetable life manufactured the oxygen that made possible the development of animal life, which reversed the process by inhaling oxygen and exhaling carbon dioxide. This reciprocal action between vegetable and animal life is the basis of today's biosphere and atmosphere alike. The extent to which the composition of the atmosphere is thus determined by the biosphere is indicated by estimates that in today's world all the carbon dioxide passes through the process of photosynthesis approximately every 350 years, all the oxygen every 2,000 years. Now our own species is, by its industrial processes, increasing the amount of carbon dioxide in the atmosphere, as well as changing the surface of the earth.

Since the lithosphere, like the atmosphere, has been profoundly modified by the activity of the biosphere, it follows that life is an intrinsic part of the planet as it is today, rather than something that merely dwells upon it.

*

The earth, together with the rest of the solar system, came into being 4,500 million years ago, presumably when a cloud of gases and other matter (débris from a star that had exploded) condensed to form it. Life had already begun upon it more than 3,000 million years ago.

Living matter is distinguished from non-living by the dynamism with which it multiplies, develops, and spreads itself. From primitive beginnings it has proliferated, at first slowly, but ever more rapidly with the passage of so many millions of years, until it has at last formed the dense and variegated biosphere of which we ourselves are part.

Throughout all these millions of years, life in all its forms has behaved as if it had one overriding purpose, that of its own survival and increase. In addition to adapting itself by evolution to changes in its local environments, it has constantly tended, by its proliferation, to overflow those environments, with the result that it has had to adapt itself to the new environments into which it has spilled. Thus organisms in an increasingly crowded body of water might acquire adaptations that allowed them, eventually, to emerge onto the relatively empty surrounding land; organisms inhabiting valleys might be driven up mountain slopes to become specialized at last, like the Eurasian snow finch, for life among the summits.

Since the tendency of populations to expand up to the capacity of their environments makes evolutionary development a competitive process, the particular forms of life, if they are to survive, must constantly improve their adaptations to the environments they inhabit, even though there should be no significant change in those environments. Otherwise, competing forms, becoming better adapted, might simply displace them — the result being, perhaps, their extinction. On the whole, this competitive adaptation, as well as the adaptation to environments that were not originally natural for life, has resulted in a progressive complexification of forms.

As life proliferates it not only adapts itself to the mundane environment in all its varieties, it also transforms it. Just as the composition of the earth's atmosphere is largely determined by the operations of the biosphere, so are the composition of the earth's waters and the character of the earth's surface. This process of creating an environment increasingly able to accommodate ever more varied and developed forms of life has been fundamental to that expansion of life on earth which has produced the present biosphere.

*

The result of the process of evolution over more than 3,000 million years is that the habitable areas of the earth (that is, virtually the whole earth except the interior of the Antarctic continent) have filled up, that the forms of life have become as varied as the environments they inhabit, and that they have become ever more elaborate in their attributes.

If the proliferation and spread of the life we know is to continue, we may expect that, having filled up the earth, it will next move out into space. Our kind is already developing the means to travel about the solar system, and even beyond. One possibility is that we might eventually populate Mars or Venus or Saturn's moon, Titan, having first done what was necessary to make them habitable. The atmosphere of Venus today, like the original atmosphere of earth, is composed overwhelmingly of carbon dioxide. There is no theoretical reason why we could not — perhaps by transplanting microorganisms from our own biosphere, perhaps by technological means — effect essentially the same adaptation of its atmosphere to human habitation that has already been effected on our native planet, but effect it much faster. We may even foresee the day when we spread beyond the solar system.*

* For various possibilities of this sort see pp. 498 and 631–632 below.

One can imagine this happening within the next hundred years. If, on the other hand, there should be a collapse of the civilization that supports our efforts in this direction, and another such interval as followed the fall of Rome, it might happen a couple of thousand years from now. Again, it may be that a great deal more evolution of our kind, or of a competing kind that replaced us, would have to take place first, so that the settlement of other objects in space by life coming from the earth might not occur for a million years or more. (In the long view, the difference between a hundred and a million years is insignificant.) The chief point is that today, a century after Auguste Comte said with such plausibility that we could never know the chemical composition of the stars, we have reason to believe that the settlement of other planets is not impossible. Indeed, we are already beginning to spill out beyond the earth.

Finally, there is the fact that the sun will burn itself out in a few thousand million years, and that the earth will be destroyed in its final flare-up. Surely it is not unrealistic today to contemplate the possibility that, when this doomsday comes, the life we represent will no longer be dependent for its survival on the particular star (a yellow dwarf) on which it still depends today.

The biosphere, as we know it today on earth, has created the conditions for its own survival. Whether it may now go on to create the conditions for its own elimination, in part or in whole, by transforming the environment too drastically and too suddenly, has become a valid question with the recent and revolutionary emergence of our own kind into a position of dominating power. Because we are already finding ourselves imprisoned on too small a sphere, a sphere that does not have room even for our own waste products, we have reason, today, to concentrate on the possibility of spreading beyond it.

II

The Origin of Life

IN PART ONE we saw how, out of the chaos represented by the elementary units of being in themselves, an ever increasing order emerges with their ever more elaborate combination; so that we found reason to think of order as being "imposed upon a deeper and more fundamental chaos." The ever more elaborate combination of the elements, resulting in an order progressively more complete, was also associated with increasing size, which suggested that the only complete and perfect order was represented by being as a whole, on the full scale of the universe. Being becomes meaningful to us, then, in the measure that we are able to enlarge our vision.

A metaphoric parallel for this association of meaning with the ever greater combination of elements meaningless in themselves is that of written language. The individual letters, lacking any logical meaning in themselves, combine to form syllables, the syllables to form words, and the words to form sentences that do have logical meaning. The logical meaning of the sentences, however, is incomplete, depending as it does on their association in paragraphs that combine to make chapters that combine to make, at last, one book — say Melville's *Moby Dick*. We are impressed by the grand meaning of *Moby Dick* as a whole, regarding the meaning of its chapters, its paragraphs, and its sentences (in this descending order) as progressively less complete, until we come down at last to the elemental chaos of its individual letters.

We shall see that this development of a meaningful order as we go from small to large applies as well to the category of being we call life.

We hardly know enough about what we call elementary particles in the atom even to say whether they are discrete entities in themselves that combine to make atoms as letters combine to make words. But we are justified in regarding atoms as such entities. It happens that some atoms fit together with others so that, when they encoun-

ter, they become locked together in molecules. Thus an ion of sodium,* lacking one electron (with its negative charge) to balance the
number of its protons (with their positive charges), will have a net
positive charge by which it is attracted, in mutuality, to an ion of
chlorine that, having one too many electrons, has a net negative
charge; since negative and positive mutually attract each other, the
two ions become locked together to form one molecule of sodium
chloride. Or two atoms of chlorine, each requiring 17 electrons to
balance its 17 protons, become locked together in a chlorine molecule by sharing two of the electrons on their peripheries where they
touch.

As far as we know, it is pure coincidence that most atoms are so
constructed as to lock together when they encounter one another,
thereby tending to agglomerate and form ever larger entities. This
structure of the atoms, however, is the basis on which order develops
out of chaos. The increasing combination of elements on which an
increasing order depends could never have gone beyond the scale of
the atom itself if it had not been for the peculiar structure that
causes atoms to combine in what are ultimately architectural structures embodying form, proportion, symmetry, and all the other elements of what we call design.

We cannot properly attribute any form to elementary particles.
Although we think of the atom as having the form of our solar system, with electrons in orbit about a nucleus, this is largely metaphorical. Presumably we come closer to the reality when we think of the
nucleus as surrounded by a cloud, without sharp outline, that manifests itself in pulsations. When we get to molecules, however, we
find that they do have their fixed forms. These forms become visi-
bly manifest to us, at second hand, when molecules or groups of
molecules with shapes that fit against each other join like so many
building blocks to become crystals — such as the cubic crystals of sodium chloride, such as the hexagonal ice crystals with their arbores-
cent forms that drift down from the sky as snowflakes. So, in the
progress from elementary particles to crystals, we see how order
arises out of what had been without form and void.

The crystal, however, whether snowflake or diamond, represents
the end of its particular line of development; for it is simply one
form multiplied, at best, to the limit of repeatability, incapable of intrinsic elaboration. Another and similar line of development, that
by which organic molecules combine, leads into the ever greater
elaboration of living forms that we know. It leads to the falcon

---

* An ion is an atom that, because its protons and electrons are not equal in number,
has a net electric charge. The word is also applied to charged molecules.

swooping from the sky in its long trajectory — not by gravity alone, like the snowflake, but by a self-contained volition of its own; it leads to the evening primrose that sends out scent signals, and to the moth that, receiving them, comes to fertilize it; it leads to mind and the consciousness of knowing in the reader of these words; and beyond that we cannot tell where it may lead.

*

The evolution of life on earth has, on the whole, been from small to large. Evolutionary progress has entailed an increase in complexity, and complexity an increase in size. The logic of this is not far to find. Beginnings are rudimentary, while improvements take the form of elaborations added on to the rudimentary. The first houses of primitive men had one room only; but with the passage of time they were improved by the addition of storage rooms, kitchens, bathrooms — the consequence being that they grew as they became more complex. So too, what begins as a one-celled organism acquires means of locomotion, devices for capturing food, faculties for the detection of light and sound. The result is that, in its evolution, it grows over the ages until it has become as much more complex and as much larger than its ancestors as, say, a butterfly, a fish, or a mountain goat.

This progression is represented in microcosm by the growth of the individual in the more evolved species of our present. A single spermatozoon is an independent cell of microscopic size. Moving about freely, it encounters an egg cell, also microscopic, and merges with it. What begins as one fertilized cell then proliferates into a growing complex of variously specialized and differentiated cells, constantly increasing in size as it grows in complexity until it has become a blue whale thirty meters long, comprising uncountable millions of millions of cells. All the apparatus that the blue whale acquires in the course of this development — a brain, eyes, digestive organs, flippers, etc. — could not possibly have been contained within the microscopic dimensions of the original cell. (But, as we shall see, the design for it all was contained within those dimensions.) The growth of an orchid or an oak would represent the same kind of development, symbolically re-enacting evolution itself. The higher or more developed forms of life that belong to our own order of magnitude could not exist in terms of a lesser order of magnitude.

In life, as in other aspects of being, the emergence of order from chaos tends to proceed from the small to the large. One approach to an understanding of living beings, then, is by the preliminary consideration of orders of magnitude.

The size of a proton (which constitutes the entire nucleus of the simplest atom) is 10^{-13} cm. across. An atom is a hundred thousand times larger, being 10^{-8} cm. across.* Atoms become interlocked to form molecules, the largest of which may comprise thousands of millions of atoms. The splitting and replication of such macro-molecules was what is thought to have produced the first living matter, which has since multiplied and covered the earth to constitute its biosphere.

Viruses are by far the smallest forms of living matter known today, some being no bigger than 10^{-6} cm. Bacteria, which come next in size, may be as small as 2×10^{-4} cm. by 10^{-4} cm. — that is, a hundred times the size of the smallest virus. In their length the smallest bacteria are 20,000 times the size of an atom, 2,000 million times that of a proton. These small bacteria are almost submicro-scopic, hardly to be seen through the most powerful optical micro-scope. Others, which may be as long as one two-hundredth of a cen-timeter, and correspondingly wide, are fully microscopic. The microscopic world also includes a variety of other life, such as algae and amoebas.

The naturally visible world begins with dimensions of about a hundredth of a centimeter. The mites that infest poultry will do as examples of the smallest visible life. Now that we have arrived at the visible world we can pass quickly up the scale through the variety of arachnids, insects, crustaceans, fungi, mosses, amphibians, reptiles, birds, mammals, herbs, woody plants, etc. Here in the visible world we have reached our own order of magnitude, the most developed order that we know in the realm of what we call living being.

*

> Just as there is no particular moment in an infant's or an embryo's life when we can say, "Mind has awakened," so in the world of life as a whole we cannot say, "Lo, here," or "Lo, there."
>
> — *J. Arthur Thomson*

We commonly think only of life as evolving, regarding inanimate matter as fixed. In a large view, however, this is not so. Just as the

---

* Protons and atoms are not solids with measurable dimensions. An atom, presum-ably, is more aptly compared to a cloud than to a billiard ball, although it is neither. What references to the size of atoms signify, then, is the distance from the center of one atom to the center of an adjacent atom when a known number are packed together in a molecule of measurable size. The measurements given for nuclear par-ticles are based on the distances over which they interact.

advent of the first mammals marks merely a stage in a process of evolution that had already been under way, so the advent of what we call life marks merely a stage in a process of evolution that had already been under way. The large view requires us to think of evolution as a continuous process that has been going on since before the earth itself came into being.

Moreover, the abrupt transitions suggested by such phrases as "the advent of the first mammals" correspond only crudely at best to the reality of evolution. Although mammals evolved from reptiles (the class Reptilia), there was no one reptile that on a fixed date gave birth to the first mammal. There was, rather, a branch of reptiles, at first imperceptible as such, that over countless generations became increasingly distinct from the other reptiles, until at last it might properly be regarded as representing a new and different class, the class Mammalia. In a manner of speaking we may say that a new class had been born; but there was no date of birth. Similarly, we must doubt that, in the evolution of organic molecules and their combination from simpler to more complex, there was any moment at which life was born. The distinction we have in our minds between living and non-living matter must have developed gradually (which is to say that it is not intrinsically a sharp or an absolute distinction, that it is more like the distinction between cold and hot).

There was a time, before the earth itself had been formed, when complex carbon compounds had already developed on chunks of solid matter in our evolving solar system. The earth is thought to have been built up in part out of these chunks, which were drawn together by gravitational attraction. At a certain stage, shallow pools of water and mudflats formed on its surface, providing an environment in which the molecules of these carbon compounds, becoming concentrated, combined to form still larger and more complex molecules. Where certain of these complex molecules existed in association with the necessary raw materials and with a source of energy to provide the necessary power, they proceeded automatically to replicate themselves and proliferate. In a developed form, this continuing replication and proliferation manifests itself in the replication and proliferation of organic cells, eventually of such complex organisms as ourselves.

III

From Molecule to Cell

SCIENTIFIC INQUIRY limits itself to seeking natural explanations, which is to say that it accepts only such explanations as remain within the observed operations of the laws of nature. Explanations that entail the intervention of a hidden hand from outside are excluded. The record of scientific progress so far justifies this exclusion. While we have, for example, gained in meteorological knowledge since the days of Homer, the gain owes nothing to those who explained thunder as the intervention of Zeus.

The question of how being began (if it had a beginning) lies outside the bounds of scientific inquiry. At the point where such inquiry starts, space, time, energy, and elementary particles already exist, whether in themselves or as different aspects of what is all one. Such inquiry, then, concerns itself with their properties, their relationships, and the consequences of their existence. Life must be regarded as one of those consequences. If there were no nuclear interactions that bound the elementary particles to one another there would be no atomic nuclei; if there were no electromagnetic interactions that drew electrons into association with atomic nuclei to make up atoms, and then bound the atoms to one another, there would be no molecules; if the molecules were not so constituted as to combine in a variety of aggregations distinguished by varied geometric forms, and if some of those forms did not have the faculties of feeding, growing, and reproducing, there would be no life.

Remaining within the bounds of science, we can base our definition of life exclusively on the properties, actual and potential, of the self-replicating complex of molecules. Some of us, subjectively aware of what life is in our own selves, would not consider that this purely scientific definition was adequate; for we experience intimations of something that lies beyond the bounds of scientific inquiry. But I shall not attempt to go beyond those bounds in these pages.

Even without going beyond them one can say that, just as the

Greek temple is more than an aggregation of stones, so each of us human beings is more than an aggregation of molecules. This is no less true of the eagle that rides the wind, the fish that darts through the pondweed, the butterfly that waves its patterned wings, or the crocus that spreads its petals to the sun. Matter, as it builds up from less to more, acquires form, and form represents the order that arises out of the original chaos.

Much of the scientific explanation offered for the origin and development of life appears to entail a haphazard succession of coincidences, representing chaos, that gradually assumes an ever more compelling direction. It is as if a lot of variously shaped stones tumbling down a mountainside, converging in channels as they fall, should come to rest at the bottom, one on top of another, in the shape of the Parthenon. Science must attempt to explain this by the operation of natural laws alone.

*

The uniformity of the universe is represented by the fact that its structures are all built up out of the same building blocks, the hundred or so chemical elements, all there are in the entire universe. These elements are the several kinds of atom, each defined by the number of electrons around its nucleus. The fact that most of them are attracted to one another and, when they come into contact, fit together like the pieces of a jigsaw puzzle is one basis of cosmic order.

The kinds of atom vary, so to speak, in their sociability. Helium atoms do not combine with any others, whether of their own or a different kind. At the other extreme is the carbon atom, which combines freely with a wide range of its fellow atoms — its own kind as well as those of hydrogen, oxygen, nitrogen, phosphorus, and others — in the largest molecular complexes known. The molecular structures that, in the course of evolution, have developed into living matter are all carbon compounds of this sort.

Such carbon compounds were evolving at large in the universe and may even have evolved into the rudiments of life before the earth was formed. The atmosphere of the earth during the first thousand million years of its existence contained molecules of methane (one atom of carbon to four of hydrogen, designated CH_4), of ammonia (nitrogen and hydrogen $= NH_3$), of water (H_2O), and of hydrogen. The energy of the ultraviolet radiation from the sun — not attenuated as today by filtration through oxygen in the upper atmosphere — tended to break up these molecules, with the result that the constituent atoms, set free and colliding with one another at ran-

dom, recombined occasionally to form the carbon compounds that
are the raw material of living matter. They recombined to form the
molecules called nucleotides, which are particular structural arrangements of carbon, hydrogen, nitrogen, oxygen, and phosphorus. The nucleotides became linked together in the chains
called nucleic acids, which began to replicate themselves and which
(as we shall see) became the agents for the production of those other
molecular chains, composed of amino acids, called proteins. When
this happened, something at least approaching living matter could
be said to exist on earth.

*

The basic uniformity of the material universe as a whole, constructed as it is out of some hundred elements only, is matched by
the basic uniformity of life as we know it. From the smallest bacterium to the blue whale, all life in its basic constitution consists of
only a few molecular compounds organized in cells.* A human
being is composed of some 10^{13} cells in association, but each cell is
the same in its essential composition as the single cell that constitutes
a paramecium or a diatom. Varied as life is, then, its variety is like
that of musical variations on a single theme.

There is no evidence left of how the self-replicating cell originated. As, in the aboriginal chaos, atoms combined to form molecules, and as molecules then combined to form self-replicating
chains, an increasingly evident evolution took an increasingly evident direction that, at some point, produced the living cell. The
fully developed cell is itself sufficiently complex to justify the simile
of a Parthenon resulting from the random piling up of stones that
have tumbled down a mountainside. The molecules are the
variously shaped stones, the cell is the Parthenon.

A fully developed cell † is bounded by a protein-lipid membrane
and has, like the stone inside a peach, a nucleus also enclosed by a
membrane. The nucleus is the central repository of the nucleic

* Viruses provide the only example of living matter that is not organized in cells. A
virus is basically nucleic acid in a protein container, like toothpaste in a tube. It cannot replicate itself until, the nucleic acid having been poured out of its container into
the cell of some living organism (the container left behind), the cellular machinery is
used to do so. This is to say that it has to appropriate from other living matter the indispensable cellular organization that it lacks itself. While it constitutes living matter
at its simplest, it should probably be regarded as representing not the most primitive
surviving form of life but a degenerate form. The earliest life could not have depended for its survival on parisitizing forms that had not yet developed. There are
scientists who hold that a virus is not a living being at all, if only because life, as they
define it, is cellular, and a virus is not.
† By this term I refer to the eukaryotic cells out of which all except the most primitive
cellular life is composed. In Chapter VII I shall deal with the distinction between
such cells and the primitive prokaryotic cells.

acids that govern the process of reproduction. Outside it the cell is filled with a jellylike protein, the cytoplasm, in which a variety of specialized organelles are distributed — organelles being to the cell what organs are to the body in the higher animals.

If cells were uniform in their composition, like globules of jelly, each might reproduce itself by simply breaking in two, the resultant divisions then absorbing nutrients from the environment to grow and divide again. Like the human body, however, a cell is a complex organism with specialized parts elaborately ordered in precise relations to one another and to the whole. Its replication therefore poses essentially the same problem as would the replication of an architectural structure like the Parthenon.

The first thing needed for the replication of the Parthenon would be a complete set of detailed information. There would have to be specifications for all the stones required, their respective sizes and shapes, their precise arrangements relative to one another for the formation of all the parts — for the formation of the stepped base, the inner chambers, porticos, and colonnades, the peristyle, the architrave, frieze, and cornice, the tiled roof, the fine detail of metopes, triglyphs, rain-spouts, etc. On the basis of this information the stones would then have to be provided from some quarry, each precisely cut and shaped to fit into the place for which it was destined. There would have to be just so many drums with their varying taper and their Doric fluting that, placed one upon the other in their prescribed places, constituted the columns of the peristyle — and so on for the whole building. Finally, again on the basis of the specific information, all these stones would have to be put in their proper places, with whatever expenditure of energy had to be provided, from some source prepared for the purpose.

The information needed for the replication of the Parthenon could take the form of blueprints, or it could be in written language. The information for the replication of the cell, contained in the nucleic acids that are stored in its nucleus, takes the form of a written language to be read as one reads lines of print in a book.

The basic information is that which specifies the particular proteins needed for the complete replication of the cell in all its parts.

How is this information written down?

*

All proteins are chains of amino-acid molecules, of which some twenty kinds are involved.* The sequence of these kinds in the

* Because the amino acids are joined together by peptide bonds, and because each loses a molecule of water in the process of such joining, it is more precise to refer to them as amino-acid residues. For the sake of terminological simplicity, however, I shall not do so in these pages.

chain determines the kind of protein that it constitutes. The number of possible sequences in which twenty amino acids may fall in a chain of a thousand is $2 \times 10^{1,000}$, so that the number of possible proteins may, for all practical purposes, be regarded as infinite. When a cell replicates itself, however, the replica it produces, if it is truly a replica, must be composed of the same proteins as in the original; which is to say that the variety of protein chains in the original must be duplicated in the replica by chains representing, respectively, the same sequences of amino-acid molecules. The function of arranging all this belongs to the nucleic acids, of which one kind is deoxyribonucleic acid, better known as DNA. It is the DNA in each cell that "knows" what proteins are needed, and that governs the replication accordingly.

The DNA is composed, as we have seen, of the molecules called nucleotides arranged in chains. Each unit of DNA is, in fact, composed of two chains tied to each other by connecting links at regular intervals — so that we may think of a DNA unit as a ladder: two uprights connected by a succession of rungs. The two uprights (which, in fact, curl about each other to form a double helix) are composed of alternating molecules of phosphate and a sugar. The rungs, which cross between the sugar molecules, are composed of two molecules each, one attached to each upright, linked where the two meet at the center by an atom of hydrogen. The molecules composing the rungs are of four kinds: adenine, guanine, thymine, and cytosine, hereafter referred to respectively as A, G, T, and C. These four letters stand for the alphabet of the language in which the information for the replication of the cell is written.

For the purpose of this exposition, let us divide the ladder in half, down the middle between the two uprights, simply removing the hydrogen bonds that, rung by rung, hold the two sides together. All the information stored in the ladder as a whole is complete in either of the halves, so that it will be simpler at this stage to examine just one half.

Each half-rung is one letter of the alphabet, either A, G, T, or C. In their succession they spell words, generally of three letters each, that denote, respectively, some twenty amino acids out of which proteins are composed. (The number of three-letter words in which the four letters of the DNA alphabet can be arranged is $4^3 = 64$, which is over three times as many as would be needed to denote the twenty principal amino acids.) AGA spells the amino acid called arginine, CAA spells leucine, GCA spells alanine — and so on for the remaining twenty. A single chain of DNA may contain some 500 million letters — that is to say, the four letters strung out in various sequences to this length, which is enough to make over 150 million three-letter words, each standing for one of the twenty amino acids. A DNA sentence with that many words could designate more different sequences of amino acids — more proteins, that is — than there are elementary particles in the whole universe. It follows that the four-letter alphabet of the DNA is more than sufficient to designate the various proteins needed for the replication of the cell.

The picture at this point is of the four letters following one another along the upright in an unbroken sequence of indefinite length — as if all the letters that constitute this book followed one another without any break to mark off words, paragraphs, or chapters. In fact, as we have seen, they are divided, for the most part, into three-letter words, each designating an amino acid.

I have remarked that all the information in the double chain or ladder is contained in either half of it — so that it is, in effect, repeated twice over. Given either half of the ladder, then, the other can be duplicated. It happens that a half-rung A can form a hydrogen bond only with a half-rung T, and *vice versa,* and that a half-rung G and a half-rung C can also bond only with each other. Therefore, knowledge of the sequence of letters (of half-rungs) in one half of the ladder reveals what the sequence in the other half must be, making possible its reconstruction if it has been lost. (Thus a sequence G, T, T, A, C on one side could be matched only by the sequence C, A, A, T, G on the other.)

In the simplest examples of organic reproduction, a cell divides into halves that each develops, then, into a complete replica of the original cell. The information for such replication must therefore be separately available to each half. The fact that each unit of DNA contains all this information twice makes this possible. Before the cell divides, the hydrogen bonds that hold together the two strands of the DNA chain give way, allowing one strand (which will then generate a duplicate of its lost companion) to accompany each half. So each half is provided with a full set of the information required for completing itself on the model of the original or parent cell.

*

Up to this point I have described only how the specifications of the various proteins needed for replication are recorded in the DNA. Directly or indirectly, however, the DNA contains all the detailed specifications for the reproduction of the most complicated organisms. This is to say that all the genetic characteristics of the most complicated organism are determined by the totality of the proteins, in their various combinations, that the DNA specifies.

Consider the microscopic cell that is the newly fertilized ovum of a human female. The DNA in its nucleus contains, implicit in the information on the required proteins, all the other information needed for the constitution of a human being — more information, surely, than is in all the books of all the libraries of the world. It has full information on the design of the skeleton and the composition of its bones; on the cardiovascular system; on the network of nerves and the convolutions of the brain; on the color and shape of the eyebrows, the construction of the gall bladder, the variety and location of the endocrine glands, etc. Here, surely, is the ultimate example of *multum in parvo*.

Add to the information on all the physical characteristics of the organism to be created the information on its proper behavioral characteristics.

Item. When a wood pigeon lands on the ground to feed, where other pigeons have not already settled, it remains alert for a moment as if to make sure that it is safe. Having apparently satisfied itself on this point, it raises and lowers its tail just once, whereupon it proceeds to walk about and feed. The information about this behavioral trait, manifested by all its progenitors through untold generations, was recorded, along with everything else, in the DNA which was packed into the nucleus of the mother pigeon's ovum.

Item. In many species of birds, individuals hatched in the spring embark on their first autumnal migration quite independently of older individuals who might otherwise show them the way. These young, who have never been away from the area in which they were hatched, may thus have to find their own way over ancestral routes or across thousands of miles of open sea to land on the other side. Not only the impulse to do this, together with its timing, but also the necessary geographical knowledge, and the knowledge of astronomy needed for navigation, must somehow have been written into the DNA of the maternal ovum.*

Item. The song of the song sparrow — its pattern, its melody, its

---

* The young of the Hudsonian godwit (*Limosa haemastica*), having been hatched and raised on nesting grounds in northwestern Canada, leave a month ahead of the adults on migration to their wintering grounds in southern South America. (See O. S. Pettingill, Jr., *Ornithology*, 4th ed., Minneapolis, pp. 295–296.) The shining cuckoo (*Chalcites lucidus*), hardly larger than a sparrow, after being raised in New Zealand by foster parents of another species that may not be migratory at all, migrates 2,500 miles across the open sea to the Solomon Islands and the Bismarck Archipelago. (See G. V. T. Matthews, *Bird Navigation*, 2nd ed., Cambridge, 1968, p. 2.) Geneticists are generally not disposed to accept the inheritance of memory, but in the cases cited here something that is, at least, rather like memory must be inherited.

phrasing, its timing, its pitch, the detailed order of its successive notes — is all written in DNA.*

> . . . the music of the moon
> Sleeps in the plain eggs of the nightingale.

* Song sparrows (*Melospiza melodia*) reared from the egg by canaries, without ever hearing the song of their own kind, will nevertheless sing it when they mature in a rendition indistinguishable from that of song sparrows reared in the wild by their natural parents. (See R. A. Hinde, *Animal Behavior,* 2nd ed., Tokyo, 1970, pp. 457–458.)

IV

Creativity within the Cell

WE HAVE SEEN how the information required for the replication of the cell is stored in the nucleic acids kept within its nucleus. That information specifies the proteins needed. It remains for the cell to manufacture them.

Beside the nucleic acid called deoxyribonucleic acid or DNA, there is another called ribonucleic acid or RNA that varies from it only in two minor points: its sugar molecule contains two oxygen atoms instead of one; and in place of the base thymine (T) it has a base called uracil (U) that differs from thymine only in having four rather than five carbon atoms. Where we read T on the DNA chain we have to read U on the RNA; but the U has the same selective affinity as the T for A.

RNA, known in this role as "messenger RNA," is what carries the information from the DNA in the nucleus to the points in the cell, outside the nucleus, where the specified proteins are to be manufactured. What happens is that the two halves of the DNA ladder separate from one end like a crocodile opening its jaws. An RNA chain then forms from loose nucleotides in the vicinity on one of the halves, just as when the DNA replicates itself. The order of the bases in the DNA is thus copied by the messenger RNA, whereupon it moves off, through the membrane surrounding the nucleus, to the outer part of the cell, where it finds one of the myriad organelles called ribosomes. The ribosomes are the sites where the proteins are produced according to the specifications delivered by the messenger RNA.

The next step is to assemble the various amino-acid molecules called for by the messenger RNA in order to link them together in the order specified. This is the function of what is called "transfer RNA." We may think of the transfer RNA as differing from the messenger RNA only in that it exists as relatively small molecules. Each such molecule, bearing the three-letter designation of one of the twenty amino acids, cruises about the cytoplasm (the substance that fills the cell outside the nucleus) until, having found an amino-acid molecule of the kind for which it is coded, it hooks onto it and tows it off to the ribosome.

We must picture a busy scene with many molecules of transfer RNA arriving together at the ribosome where the chain of messenger RNA awaits them, each with its proper amino acid in tow. Each finds its proper place along the chain of messenger RNA — an AGA molecule with its arginine positioning itself opposite the letters UCU (the letters complementary to AGA on the messenger RNA), a GCA molecule with its adanine stationing itself opposite the letters CGU, etc. When this step in the process is completed there are, for the moment, three parallel chains: (1) the chain of messenger RNA, (2) the chain of transfer RNA that has formed up along it in the order specified by it, and (3) the chain of amino acids carried by the transfer RNA, these amino acids having linked themselves together in the order in which they had been placed, the order specified by the messenger RNA. This last chain is the protein whose manufacture had been ordered in the first place by the DNA in the nucleus, the order having been delivered by the messenger RNA. This protein having now been manufactured, the molecules of transfer RNA detach themselves and go off to assemble the components of another protein for which the order, borne by another chain of messenger RNA, has come from the DNA in the nucleus.

I have now described the essential procedure by which proteins are manufactured, but to refine the picture let me add that the transfer RNA does not consist of just three-letter molecules, each attached to a single chain of alternate sugar and phosphate links. It consists of molecules some 77 letters long arranged, like the DNA, in a double helix. (But the DNA, as we have seen, may be 500 million letters long.) At one end of each double helix is the triplet ACC, which constitutes the hook for the amino acid to be taken in tow. At the other end is whatever triplet corresponds to the place of destination along the chain of messenger RNA (i.e., AGA, GCA, CGU, or any other of the combinations).

The reader will have in mind that all this busy movement of molecular groups to and fro requires a source of power, just as the movement of an automobile requires the source of power provided by the combustion (the oxidization) of gasoline.

Each cell contains organelles called mitochondria which are the generators of the necessary power. In each, molecules of sugar are decomposed to form molecules of carbon dioxide and of water (which is to say that they are burned or oxidized), with a consequent release of some of the energy contained in the original molecule. The process is the same process of oxidization as occurs when wood is burned in a fireplace. Here, however, the energy it produces, instead of being dissipated as heat, is stored by using it to raise certain storage molecules to a higher energy state, the molecules being those of adenosine triphosphate or ATP. The ATP molecules then cruise around the cell, supplying power where it is needed.

Earlier I had occasion to compare the fully developed cell, as a product of accidental molecular combinations, to a duplicate of the Parthenon produced by a rockslide. Perhaps it would have been more appropriate to compare it — with its many ribosomes, mitochondria, and other organelles — to a great manufacturing complex so produced. We must picture atoms, colliding with one another at random over millions of years, occasionally combining to form particular molecules that, colliding with one another from time to time over still further millions of years, occasionally combine into particular macromolecules (nucleic acids and proteins) — the whole process becoming more orderly with time and culminating in the complex, delicate, self-replicating organism that is a living cell. But the process continues beyond this culmination, and we have not yet seen the end of it.

V

Creativity
at the Molecular Level

ELEMENTARY PARTICLES combine to compose atoms, which compose molecules, which compose larger forms. In our minds we divide these larger forms into two categories, those that have life and those that do not. The snow crystal adrift in the air does not have life, but the diatom adrift in the ocean does.

We think of life as a property that invests certain compound forms of matter temporarily. Although the diatom as a whole is alive, if we take it apart we find no evidence that the molecules of which it is composed are any more alive than those of the snow crystal. Moreover, the diatom will die, which is to say that in due course it will be bereft of the life it had for a term, its body remaining as a lifeless form like the snow crystal. The reader will be aware of himself being, like the diatom, in temporary possession of the same ephemeral property, which he must at last lose.

Life is ephemeral only in relation to the particular forms that are invested with it at particular moments. The particular forms pass it on, generation after generation, to others that succeed them for a term, only to pass it on again. In this continuity through the generations it manifests itself by an apparently self-contained dynamism, a directional drive. It seems to be governed by the intrinsic purpose of perpetuating itself. In the actual history of life on earth, this self-perpetuation has entailed self-development, from the most primitive forms of 3,000 million years ago to the most advanced forms of today.*

We suppose that, as atoms originally combined to make molecules, and molecules to make more developed forms, a moment came when what had been lifeless took on the property of life. I doubt, however, that the distinction on which this is based, between what is without dynamism or drive and what is driven to perpetuate itself, is valid at the most primitive level. There may be something like a cre-

* See Chapter XX.

ative tendency in all being, in what we call lifeless matter as in what we call living matter. A drop of water has a certain form, which is imposed on it by the unequal electromagnetic tension among the molecules on its surface and those in its interior, by the pressure of the surrounding atmosphere, and by any gravitational attraction to which it may be subject.* That form is coherent and symmetrical, representative of a natural order. When the drop becomes enlarged to a certain point by the absorption of additional molecules (its volume increasing at twice the rate of its surface), it breaks apart into two drops, each with the same form as the original. No one suggests that this is self-perpetuation in the sense that the diatom's similar division is self-perpetuation, but there is a resemblance. In both cases a form is reproducing itself.

Perhaps we may say of the snow crystal that it, too, is governed by features of natural law that tend to its perpetuation. It is a symmetrical structure built up of water molecules in accordance with certain physico-mathematical principles. Where the environmental conditions that permitted its formation persist, it will tend to repair any broken part by the attraction of molecules to replace those lost.†

What is basic to being is the tendency of its elements to combine in forms or patterns that have coherence and symmetry, that represent a logical order. This seems to be a single progressive tendency to bring order out of chaos, which manifests itself in the formation of the crystal and the reproduction of the diatom alike.‡

On such grounds as this I would speculate that the property of matter we call life began to manifest itself some 3,500 million years

---

* Its constituent molecules are mutually attracted to their neighbors all around them by a weak electromagnetic force, but those on the surface are drawn inward, having no neighboring molecules on the outside to balance the attraction from the inside. This lack of equilibrium, by drawing the surface molecules into a tighter array, creates the surface tension to be found on any body of water. The layer of surface molecules is like a film that tends to shrink, just as the rubber surface of a child's inflated balloon tends to shrink. Since, of all possible shapes, a sphere has the smallest proportion of surface to volume, a water drop and a balloon alike tend, in the shrinkage of their respective surfaces, to assume a spherical shape.

† See D'Arcy Thompson, *On Growth and Form*, Cambridge (England), 1971, p. 170; and S. P. F. Humphreys-Owen, "Physical Principles underlying Inorganic Form," in L. L. Whyte, *Aspects of Form*, London, 1968, p. 15.

‡ Some writers (e.g., Harold F. Blum in *Time's Arrow and Evolution*, Princeton, 1968) insist on the tendency of the physical universe as a whole to maximize entropy, in accordance with the Second Law of Thermodynamics, concluding that it is progressing from order toward chaos. We cannot, however, make sensible statements about all being in all time; and even though the entropy of the universe as a whole is constantly increasing at present, as we must suppose, the evolution of our part of the universe at present — at least of the biosphere — appears to manifest the opposite tendency. (See Part One, Chapter XIII.) As evidence that a contrary view of what is happening to the universe as a whole can be upheld by persons who represent authority, see David Layzer, "The Arrow of Time," *Scientific American*, December 1975.

ago simply as a continuing intensification of a tendency somehow inherent in being as a whole. There is a continuous development between the pre-life that the snow crystal represents and the life that the reader represents. The crystal does not know in itself a drive to survive and to perpetuate what it represents, but the reader does know such a drive in himself. The difference can be defined in terms of a spectrum of intensity without drawing a categorical distinction at any point. (No one can say, "Lo, here," or "Lo, there.")

*

Just as the Greek temple is more than an aggregation of stones, so a living being is more than an aggregation of molecules. As, over hundreds of millions of years, some molecules under rare circumstances aggregate in certain ways, an element of coherent design enters into their association. Many organic molecules manifest what appears to be a spontaneous impulse to form symmetrical structures. In its simplest form, involving only molecules that are all of one kind, this architectonic tendency leads to the formation of crystals, whether quartz crystals or the crystals of frost on a windowpane. The same tendency operates on various organic molecules suspended in liquids — adrift, let us say, in shallow warm waters of the primitive earth. Their surfaces carry electric charges, positive and negative, that tend to bind them to one another when they come into contact. The molecules of the liquid environment (e.g., those of H_2O) are constantly breaking up the developing clusters of organic molecules by colliding with them. But the larger aggregations, such as the tangled chains of amino acids or of nucleotides, by their size and the combined strength of their electric charges, may achieve a solidity that resists the buffets of the small molecules. If the tendency of such aggregations is to hold together, if their mutual adherence represents somehow a creative disposition of nature, then size is an advantage. The aggregations grow by attracting loose molecules from the environment, and may in fact come to compete for such molecules. The structure of some aggregations, their formal design, may give them an advantage in such competition over other aggregations with more imperfect structures. So natural selection would get under way even at this primitive stage, favoring the proliferation of what may become, with time, increasingly harmonious and elaborate designs. The equivalent of the Parthenon may at last emerge, then, from the random collision of atoms and molecules, taking the form of the living cell.

VI

The Cell

THE HISTORY OF LIFE ON EARTH, if not of all being, is that of an architectonic tendency progressively realizing itself. We must assume, for purposes of scientific inquiry, that this tendency is inherent in physical being, as natural to it as the tendency of water to seek its own level. It manifests itself in the whorled forms of spiral nebulae and the spherical shape of stars and planets no less than in snow crystals and the molecular combinations that constitute diatoms and dolphins. Gravitation is one expression of it, electromagnetic attraction another. Here, however, we are concerned only with those manifestations that have led to the development of life.

In the shallow waters that came to constitute a broth of organic molecules on the surface of the primitive earth there developed, over hundreds of millions of years, the cell that is the basic unit of all autonomous living matter, whether in the form of a bacterium, an orchid, or a blue whale. A fully developed cell is a complex unit that, of its own impulsion, draws on its environment to provide for its growth and reproduction. Its complexity is that of a community, like a city-state, in which the division of labor is organized by the assignment of different tasks to different elements. One element in a city-state may be composed of farmers who, operating on the outskirts, provide the food. Particular neighborhoods may be occupied by artisans of various sorts: cobblers, weavers, metalsmiths, etc., who provide for various needs of the community as a whole. Other groups may furnish transport and communications, seeing to the exchange of goods and services, or to the dissemination of information. Still others may provide overall direction and coordination. Although one city-state may differ from another in its superficial topography or in particular arrangements, all are basically the same in the provisions they make and the way they make them.

Every fully developed cell is enclosed by a membrane like a boundary wall. It has a nucleus, comparable to a citadel, in which the

DNA that contains the basic information for its replication is stored. Outside the nucleus are organelles, such as mitochondria and chloroplasts, that engage in chemical activity for the production of the energy that enters into all the activities of the cell. Other organelles outside the nucleus include the countless ribosomes where the proteins needed by the cell for its metabolism and its replication are manufactured in accordance with the specifications contained in the DNA. A full description of any cell would have to list other organelles and specialized parts, all working together for the common purpose of the whole.

The cells of single-celled organisms — bacteria, algae, protozoa, etc. — are complete units of life in themselves, containing all the specialized devices they need in order to draw sustenance from the environment and to use that sustenance for their self-perpetuation and proliferation. At a more advanced stage of evolution, when cells combine to form multicellular organisms, they become specialized in different ways, losing their independence and joining in a common interdependence. What properly comes first, however, in any description, as in the history of life itself, is the independent cell that has within itself all it needs, together with the resources of its environment, to meet its own requirements.

The ultimate source of energy for all life today is the radiant energy of sunlight, of the photons or electromagnetic waves that pour upon the earth. The cells of vegetable life have organelles called chloroplasts that capture this energy and store it in the form of organic materials which are burned or oxidized as the energy is required. All other organisms, lacking the ability to capture the energy of the sunlight directly, acquire it by feeding on the organisms that do have the ability, or on others that, perhaps by several removes, have fed on them — so that the energy utilized by all has its original source in the sunlight.

However, the first organisms to represent recognizable life, over 3,000 million years ago, did not have the means to capture and store the energy of the sunlight. Their only source of energy was that of the organic molecules — sugars, fats, carbohydrates, proteins, nucleic acids — afloat in the shallow waters in which they had developed. By fragmenting these molecules and rearranging their parts, through the process known as fermentation, they released some of the energy that had held them together in their original configurations. This process of fermentation is still exemplified today by the cells of yeast, a primitive fungus, which break apart and arrange molecules of sugar (thereby constituting an exception to what was said in the last sentence of the preceding paragraph). By breaking

180 grams of sugar into 88 grams of carbon dioxide and 92 grams of alcohol, yeast releases 20,000 calories of energy (the energy that had held the 88 grams and the 92 grams together in one bundle) for its own use.* Fermentation, however, supplies energy only by using up the stock of organic materials in the environment, which accumulated only slowly on the primitive earth, and the first life, which depended on it, would therefore have come to an end when it had exhausted this stock.

Before that could happen, the evolving cells had developed the process of photosynthesis for capturing the constantly inflowing energy of solar radiation. (The impact of photons raises electrons to higher levels of energy; the electrons are then passed on to molecules which thereby have their own levels of energy raised, and which can therefore supply energy, as needed and where needed, for the activities of the cell by releasing the increments they have received.) From carbon dioxide and water the evolving cells, using the energy of sunlight, were at last able to manufacture their own sugar molecules to provide the fuel they needed — to provide, that is, the molecular matter in which the captured energy of the sunlight was stored. (Two hundred and sixty-four grams of carbon dioxide plus 108 grams of water, with the application of 700,000 calories of energy provided by sunlight, furnished 180 grams of sugar and 192 of oxygen.) Then, drawing as well on ammonia and nitrates in the atmosphere, they were able to manufacture other compounds that served them as fuel for the energy-releasing process of fermentation. This is to say that, with the energy of sunlight, they manufactured for themselves the fuels needed in the process of fermentation, rather than depending on the exhaustible stocks that had been accumulating so slowly over millions of years.

Fermentation, however, in addition to being inefficient, polluted the environment with its noxious waste products. We see here how, from its beginnings, life was transforming its environment, in some ways that were to prove deleterious and in others that would at last assure its future as it had not been assured at first. The most important product of photosynthesis proved to be free oxygen (O_2), of which the atmosphere had until then been almost or entirely devoid. (The cells kept the carbon in carbon dioxide, and released the oxygen.) Oxygen now provided the basis for replacing the process of fermentation with the more efficient one of respiration. Respiration is the process of oxidization, of incorporating free oxygen in compounds, that produces the energy released as heat in the burning of

* A masterly brief account of these matters is "The Origin of Life" by George Wald, *Scientific American*, August 1954.

wood or of any other substance susceptible to such a process. Respiration oxidizes sugar, for example, breaking it up in order to combine its carbon and hydrogen, respectively, with free oxygen to form carbon dioxide and water, thereby releasing energy. The organelles called mitochondria receive high-energy electrons from the sugar and transfer them to phosphate molecules that thereby have their own levels of energy raised, and the energized molecules (of adenosine triphosphate, called ATP) then carry the extra energy to where it is needed in the cell. From the same amount of sugar, respiration produces thirty-five times as much energy as fermentation, and its waste products have so far constituted no problem.*

In fact, the addition of free oxygen to the atmosphere made possible much of the development and proliferation of life that has since taken place. Until it occurred, life could not, one supposes, have emerged from the water, where it was sheltered from the ultraviolet rays of the sun that would have killed it. But the free oxygen added to the atmosphere, forming a layer of ozone (O_3) in its upper reaches, filtered out most of the ultraviolet radiation, preventing it from reaching the surface of the earth. So it was that life was able to emerge from the water and spread onto the dry land, where it proceeded to undergo the development we know.

* It may be that for the first time in our own day, in consequence of the industrial activities of our own species, there is beginning to be an excessive accumulation of carbon dioxide in the atmosphere. One can hardly know as yet, however, what significance this may have in a perspective of thousands of millions of years.

VII

Symbiosis

THERE ARE TWO WAYS in which the community that is a fully developed living cell might, in the course of evolution, have originated. One is by generating within itself, from its own resources, the organelles that belong to that community today. The other is by the mutual association of independent cells, some of them the ancestors of the present organelles, in what was at first a symbiotic relationship. We have reason to believe that such association accounts for at least some of the organelles in the developed cell, that it may account for its entire constitution. The developed cell may well be a community of primitive cells that, with the passage of time, became integrated into one another to form the complex unit we know today.

Symbiosis, which is the association of discrete organisms for their mutual benefit, plays a major role in the competitive process of natural selection by which life on earth has evolved and continues to evolve. Organisms struggling to survive and perpetuate themselves discover, in effect, that they can profit from association with one another in partnerships, and such partnerships may in time become indissoluble, the survival of the partners having come to depend on them. To begin with, the relationship may be of the loosest sort. So it is that gulls have come to be associated with the cities of men, where they find their food in the waste products of human activity and enjoy human protection in return for their contribution to urban sanitation. Some thousands of years ago a species of wild cat came into association with human communities, where its members were sheltered and fed, as their domestic descendents are today, in return for keeping down the population of rodents. Some communities of ants rear and cherish communities of aphids that, in return, secrete a substance on which the ants feed.

A physically closer association is that of the sea anemone which attaches itself to the shell of a hermit crab, thereby providing the crab with camouflage and the protection of its own stinging tentacles, obtaining in return the advantage of the crab's mobility together with the scraps left over from its feeding. Here, however, the association is still not so close that the partners cannot live apart from each other.

The case is different with the nitrogen-fixing bacteria that live inside the roots of leguminous plants, providing the plants with the nitrogen they need in the form of usable compounds, deriving their own nourishment from the plants in return. In at least one instance of this, the bacteria are transmitted through the seeds to successive generations of the plants. Here the association is permanent and indissoluble, each partner having become completely dependent on the other for its survival. Similarly, orchids normally depend for the germination and development of their seeds on fungi that, inhabiting both the seeds and the roots, live off of the orchids in turn. Any lichen, which we think of as a single species, consists in fact of a blue-green alga and a fungus joined in an inseparable association. Again — termites eat wood which, by themselves, they are incapable of digesting. For its digestion they rely on protozoa that, inhabiting their digestive tracts, break the wood down into a digestible sugar. We ourselves contain within our bodies a varied flora and fauna, on a microscopic scale, much of which contributes to our survival in return for living off of us.

Some deep-sea fish have luminous organs, to light up their environments or to attract prey, in which the light is supplied by luminescent bacteria contained within those organs as symbionts, and are able to turn the lights off or on at will by folds of skin that function like eyelids. The symbiont bacteria, in this case, are equivalent to the organelles that supply energy for single cells.

All this is to say that the concept of organisms as colonies, or as in part colonial, and the associated concept of the symbiotic relationship, represent the rule rather than the exception in the more advanced forms of living nature. What is true of multicellular organisms like termites, men, and deep-sea fishes may be no less true of single cells.

*

In Chapter VI I used the simile of the city-state to describe the fully developed cell, which in its economy may be regarded as a complex community operating on the basis of a division of labor among its variously specialized members. This communal cell, which is the basic unit of all but the most primitive life today, is so highly developed in itself that it must represent a notable advance, in terms of evolution, over the first cellular manifestations of life more than

3,000 million years ago. The first cells must have been quite different, and if we ask what they were like we may turn for evidence to the persistence of such cells into our present.

In the world of our present there are two sharply differentiated kinds of cell. There are the complex cells I have described, known as eukaryotic cells, and there are the primitively simple cells called prokaryotic. Prokaryotic cells are represented today almost exclusively by the blue-green algae and the bacteria, which must therefore be classed as representing the most primitive life that still exists.

It must be significant that there are no cells, today, intermediate between the prokaryotes and the eukaryotes, widely different as they are. One would think that, if the eukaryotes had evolved gradually from prokaryotes by the ordinary processes of natural selection, examples of intermediate forms would have survived, just as the prokaryotes themselves have survived. Instead, one has the impression of an evolutionary leap from prokaryotic to eukaryotic — and the transition may indeed have been something of a leap, perhaps the most important event in the history of life.

Prokaryotic cells are so small that they could be accommodated inside the much larger eukaryotic cells like beads in a bag, and they lack the well defined organelles of the latter. The function of a mitochondrium in a eukaryotic cell (see Chapter IV) tends to be carried on by the prokaryotic cell as a whole. The function of photosynthesis, carried on by the chloroplasts in a eukaryotic cell (see Chapter VI), tends to be carried on by the cell as a whole in the case of those prokaryotic cells that are photosynthesizing.

There is reason to believe that the mitochondria and the chloroplasts inside eukaryotic cells were originally independent organisms in themselves. What suggests this chiefly is the fact that each has its own DNA, in which information for its replication is encoded, just like a prokaryotic cell. Each has its own ribosomes for the manufacture of proteins it needs, and its own transfer RNA to gather and assemble the amino acids that enter into the composition of those proteins. In fact, each has what is required to reproduce itself largely on its own, and we know that some organelles do so reproduce themselves.

The implication here is that the mitochondria and the chloroplasts alike, as well as other organelles similarly equipped, originated as independent prokaryotic cells, thereafter entering into symbiotic relationships with other cells, coming at last to be fully integrated into the larger complexes. "It now seems certain," writes Lynn Margulis, "that mitochondria were once free-living bacteria that over a long period of time established a hereditary symbiosis with ancestral hosts that ultimately evolved into animal cells, plant cells and cells that fit neither of these categories. The same history evidently holds true for plastids [the category of organelles to which chloroplasts belong], which were originally free-living algae." *

Flagella and cilia, those hairlike appendages by which protozoa propel themselves through the water or, if they have a fixed attachment, create currents to carry food to themselves, are also organelles that probably were incorporated as independent organisms, originally, by way of symbiosis. In one case, indeed, what appear to be flagella and, as such, organelles of the protozoon cell, prove to be, rather, distinct organisms that have established a symbiotic relationship with it. The protozoon *Myxotricha paradoxa* is solidly covered with what were always regarded as flagella, fine hairs that by their whiplike action move it through the water, until it was discovered that each hair was in fact a distinct bacterium living as a symbiont on the protozoon's surface. Add to this (1) that each of these symbiotic bacteria is symbiotically associated with another species of symbiotic bacterium on the protozoon's surface, (2) that still other bacteria live symbiotically inside the same protozoon, and (3) that the protozoon, with its symbionts, is itself symbiont in the gut of a termite.

Another protozoon, *Paramecium bursaria,* contains within itself, in symbiotic association, cells of a green alga equipped with chloroplasts that carry out the vegetable process of photosynthesis for the animal host as well as for the vegetable symbionts to which they belong as organelles. This is to say that the chloroplasts in the alga capture the energy of the sunlight, a surplus of which the alga then supplies to the protozoon within which it resides. It is easy to imagine that the relationship between the chloroplasts and the alga was once like that which now exists between the alga and the protozoon.

A general conclusion may be drawn from all this. Traditionally we have thought of organic evolution as being progressive change proceeding separately at the twig-ends of the branching tree of life — proceeding separately, that is, in individual species. But all organisms, to a greater extent than we have commonly appreciated, are the products of evolving colonial associations, the association of organisms in communities that, with time, have become increasingly integrated, until the communities have themselves become organisms. Time and again, twig-ends that were remote from each other on the tree of life have joined and grown together (thereby rather spoiling the metaphoric picture of the tree with its simple branching).

* "Symbiosis and Evolution," *Scientific American,* August 1971, p. 52.

Elementary particles combine to make atoms, atoms to make molecules, molecules to make primitive organic cells, primitive organic cells to make developed organic cells, and developed organic cells (as we shall see) to make ever more highly organized forms of life —until in our own time, going from small to large, we come to human beings and blue whales.

VIII

Reproduction

THE CELL may conveniently be regarded as the unit of reproduction for all life, whether represented by a bacterium or a blue whale. Reproduction is going on continuously in all of us, since many of our body cells are constantly dividing to make replicas of themselves. And when a new human being is formed in the womb it begins as a single cell that multiplies in the same way as a diatom or an amoeba.

We should, however, be on our guard here. To say that the cell is the unit of reproduction for all life is simply to say that it is the basic unit of life, and this is a truth of convenience rather than one that is quite literal.* If the observer were bounded within a eukaryotic cell, he would see its organelles reproducing themselves, and so he might hesitate to call the cell as a whole the irreducible unit of reproduction. The fact remains, however, that aside from the equivocal case of viruses, all life is organized in cells, and when it reproduces itself it does so, ultimately, by the multiplication of these units — even though some organelles, which probably were cells in their own right to begin with, reproduce themselves at what, in their case, has become the subcellular level.

*

In Chapter III I gave an account of the DNA which, inhabiting the nucleus of the cell, contains the information for the reproduction of

* Some biologists, accepting the definition of life as cellular, consequently maintain that viruses, which are hardly more than batches of nucleic acids in protein containers, do not represent life, that they are not, in a word, living. But this seems farfetched to others, who see the viruses reproducing themselves by the replication of nucleic acids and the synthesis of proteins, albeit parasitically inside the cells of what are undoubtedly living organisms. Let the reader note that the question whether viruses do or do not represent life is a nominal one. It is the question of how we choose to apply the word "life." In any case, we must always expect this kind of difficulty in applying words, which are necessarily categorical (that being the nature of language), to a reality which is never quite categorical (that being the nature of reality). We have already supposed that, in the evolution out of which life originated, there was no one point at which what had been dead sprang to life. We have supposed that there was, rather, a gradual genesis.

the organism to which it belongs. It is double-stranded, each strand containing a full record of that information, so that the record can be duplicated by the separation of the strands and the formation on each of a new strand identical with the one from which it was separated.

The double strands of DNA are set in threadlike bodies, variously convoluted or coiled, called chromosomes. The process by which the chromosomes divide is the process by which the cell reproduces itself. It is, consequently, the basic process, called mitosis, by which life survives. First the DNA in each chromosome doubles itself by replication. Next each chromosome, which itself consists, now, of two parallel strands (each with its set of DNA), coils up into a more compact, rodlike body. At the same time, a sort of scaffolding, called the spindle, forms outside the nucleus that contains the chromosomes. Two small structures called centrioles, which we may think of as hooks, take up their respective positions at opposite ends of the cell — near its north pole and its south pole, so to speak — apparently connected with each other by exceedingly fine fibers. We may think of each fiber in the developing spindle as resembling a filament of spiderweb.

In a typical case the membrane enclosing the nucleus now dissolves, the nucleus disappearing as such. The chromosomes, freed from their confinement, move to a plane that constitutes a cross-section of the cell at what we may regard as its equator. Each chromosome now has attached to its two strands, respectively, two fibers that run respectively north and south to the centrioles that mark the opposite apexes of the spindle. The picture that presents itself at this point is that of a structure (like those made by tent caterpillars in the trees of eastern North America) composed of spiderwebbing that spreads from the apexes at the respective poles to the chromosomes at the plane of the equator. This is the spindle.

What happens next is that the two strands of the respective chromosomes appear to be pulled apart, each being drawn by its attached fiber toward the pole on its side. The result is two identical sets of chromosomes, with their identical assortments of DNA, at opposite ends of the cell, which now proceeds to divide into two cells at the plane of the equator. In each of the two cells that are the products of this division a nucleus forms to contain the chromosomes, and so the process of reproduction has been completed. By the same process, the two cells produce four, the four eight, and so on.

What I have now described in essence is the process of reproduction called mitosis as it has been observed chiefly in eukaryotic cells. In the primitive prokaryotic cells it is basically the same, if simpler.

(For example, in some bacteria there is only one chromosome, consisting of only one macromolecule of DNA, its ends joined to make a ring, the process of chromosomal replication consisting simply of the separation of the two strands that compose it and the consequent formation of two rings.) In animal cells the division takes place by the constriction of the original cell at the equator until the two halves separate. In plant cells it generally entails the formation of a partition across the original cell at the equator. There are countless variations in detail, but the basic uniformity remains.

I have confined myself, in this account, to the reproduction of the essential genetic material, in the form of chromosomes and their content of DNA, which is thereby passed on through the generations. However, when a cell divides, the new generations carry duplicates of all the parts that compose it, not of the chromosomes only. This presents no problem for parts that are present in large quantity and evenly distributed throughout the cell, as may be the case with such organelles as mitochondria and plastids (e.g., chloroplasts). Here the division of the cell automatically leaves an approximately equal number in the respective progeny. In other cases, organelles cluster in two groups, one on either side of the plane of cleavage, in preparation for the division of the cell. In some cases, the mitochondria become elongated and stretch across the plane of cleavage, with the result that they are divided by the division of the cells into halves that respectively develop new wholes, just as the halves of the cells themselves do.

In conclusion, let the reader recall that the process I have now described is not only the process by which unicellular organisms like diatoms and amoebas reproduce themselves. It is also the basic process by which human beings renew and reproduce themselves, in their parts and as whole individuals. Only, when they reproduce themselves as whole individuals a supplementary process, that of sexual combination (which we shall consider in Chapter XVI), intervenes with radical effect at one point in the basic process.

IX

Enzymes

IN CHAPTER III I said that the information contained in the DNA of an organism was no more than a catalogue of proteins. I also said that the DNA contained complete information for the reconstitution of the organism's structure and the re-enactment of its behavior. These two statements are reconciled by the fact that the organism's structure and behavior are predetermined by the combination of proteins prescribed in the DNA. The proteins are the executors of the inheritance recorded in the DNA. Accordingly, one set of proteins produces a bacillus, another a Douglas fir, another a nightingale.

The proteins, it has been said, are "the regulators of all the activities carried out by the living machine. To perform their regulatory function, proteins are endowed with specificity, the ability to distinguish among different molecules. This property, more than any other, is characteristic of the phenomenon of life itself, and the specificity of proteins is believed not only to permit the regulation of the multitude of cellular processes, but also to constitute the molecular basis of the differences that exist between individuals and between species." *

The proteins, of which one human cell may contain a hundred thousand kinds, constitute almost half the dry matter of an organism — half, that is, of the 30 percent that is not water. Most are structural, the materials out of which bone, cartilage, and skin in the advanced animals, for example, are made. However, those that count primarily for the realization of the genetic heritage are the enzymes. The enzymes initiate and carry on all the activities of an organism, including those of photosynthesis, of respiration, of digestion, and of manufacturing new organic materials. Each activity has its own enzyme or group of enzymes to carry it on, and each is carried on as it is because of those particular enzymes. It follows

* A. G. Loewy and Philip Siekevitz, *Cell Structure and Function,* 2nd ed., London/New York, 1970, p. 172.

that the list of enzymes produced in accordance with the specifications of the DNA predetermines the activities in which every part of the organism will engage, thereby predetermining how the organism will develop and what it will be. The enzymes in the single cell from which the reader grew, prescribed as they were by the DNA, are what caused that cell to develop into a human being rather than a butterfly or a sardine.

The enzymes are catalysts, performing the indispensable mediatory role in the chemical activities of organisms. A catalyst, although it changes what it acts upon, itself emerges from the action unchanged. (So the state of a minister performing a wedding ceremony remains the same after as before, although the state of those on whom he performs it is changed.)

In Chapter VI I mentioned that the organelles called chloroplasts, found in the cells of green plants, capture the energy of sunlight, which is then stored in various forms to provide the energy needed in all the processes of life; and that the organelles called mitochondria extract this energy from the organic materials in which it has been stored, transferring it to ATP molecules, which carry it about the cells for use wherever it is needed. All these processes of extraction, storage, and transfer are catalyzed by enzymes.

The energy of the photons that pour upon the earth from the sun is initially captured by molecules of chlorophyll in the chloroplasts. When photons strike a chlorophyll molecule they "excite" some of its electrons, raising them to higher levels of energy. In the absence of alternatives, these excited electrons would quickly fall back to their original level, shedding the extra energy in the form of departing photons that would make them momentarily luminescent. (In fact, chlorophyll extracted from cells in the laboratory will, under these circumstances, glow like any glow-worm.) This does not happen in nature, however, because of specialized enzymes that are at hand to prevent it. Each excited electron is immediately captured by a molecule of such an enzyme and detached from the chlorophyll, to be passed on from one molecule to another in a circle that returns it, at last, to its place in the chlorophyll. As the electron goes through the successive steps of its circular journey it gives up its extra energy in successive bits to the molecules along the way, until upon its return that energy has, by this succession of steps, dropped back to its original level. In other words, by the intervention of enzymes, the electron has been captured, has had its extra energy taken from it, and has then been returned to the place where it had been captured.*

What happens to the energy taken from the electron?

* The kidnapped electron, in these transfers, generally comes into association with a proton to form a hydrogen atom. (The common terminology, here, can be confus-

Part of it goes into the creation of adenosine triphosphate molecules (molecules of ATP) that carry it about the cell, discharging it at last where it is needed to provide power for some cellular activity. Specifically, the energy is converted into the binding energy whereby a third phosphate group is attached to a molecule of ADP (adenosine diphosphate rather than triphosphate). This ADP already has two phosphate groups, so that the attachment of a third, entailing an input of binding energy, changes it into the higher energy ATP molecule, which carries the added energy to where it is needed in the cell. The ATP then releases that energy by transferring the third phosphate group, with its binding energy, to an "acceptor" molecule, thereby reverting to its original state as a molecule of ADP.

However, it is only part of the solar energy captured by the chlorophyll that goes directly into the making of ATP. The rest goes into the making of the carbohydrate fuel in which the energy is stored until released by oxidation — perhaps through mitochondria in the cells, perhaps in the digestive system of an animal that has fed on the plant that made it, perhaps in a furnace that burns the fossilized plant-life called coal (in which it has been stored for hundreds of millions of years).

I shall not attempt to give an account of the sequence of events, still imperfectly known, by which a plant manufactures the carbohydrates within which the energy from the sun is stored. Suffice it to say that this sequence entails essentially the same catalytic process of passing electrons from one specialized enzyme to another, a process that ends by putting together atoms of carbon, hydrogen, and oxygen, thereby synthesizing carbohydrates in which the atoms are bound to one another by binding energy that is released when, at last, the carbohydrates are again broken down by oxidation in the course of respiration or burning.

When the carbohydrates are broken down inside organic cells, through the agency of mitochondria and by the process of respiration, their disintegration takes place step by step in a long sequence, each step catalyzed by an enzyme or a system of enzymes specifically designed for it, energy being extracted at each step to produce ATP molecules. In the course of this step-by-step breakdown, it appears,

---

ing, because a proton, when it is regarded as the nucleus of a hydrogen atom from which the electron has been stripped — i.e., of an ionized atom — is referred to, not as a proton but as a hydrogen ion, an ion being any atom that has an electric charge in consequence of the fact that the number of positively charged protons in the nucleus is not matched by the number of negatively charged electrons encircling it.) Consequently, what is transferred is generally a hydrogen atom; or one may say that electrons and hydrogen ions (H^+) are transferred. However, it is the electron, with its heightened energy, that counts in this transaction.

"electrons are extracted from the intermediates by enzymes and fed into a series of electron-carrier molecules, collectively called the respiratory chain. This chain of enzyme molecules is the final common pathway of all electrons removed from foodstuff molecules during biological oxidation. At the last link in the chain, the electrons combine with oxygen to form water. The breakdown of foodstuffs by respiration therefore in essence reverses the process of photosynthesis in which electrons are removed from water to form oxygen. Moreover, it is striking that the electron carriers in the respiratory chain bear many chemical similarities to those of the corresponding chain in photosynthesis." *

*

Not only do the enzymes provide the efficient means for carrying on all the activities of organisms, they also regulate those activities by turning them on or off as required. They decide, so to speak, when a particular operation is to be undertaken and when the time has come for it to be discontinued. It is this regulatory activity that determines how a cell will develop, and into what.

In Chapter III I described how a list of all the proteins needed by a cell is written down in its DNA, in the form of what are called genes, those groups of successive nucleotides (each equivalent to a letter of the alphabet) that spell out the different sequences of amino acids which constitute, respectively, the different proteins. Then, in Chapter IV, I gave an account of how this information is transcribed by messenger RNA and taken to the ribosomes, where the proteins are manufactured. Presumably, however, breakdown and chaos would ensue if the ribosomes were called upon to produce, constantly and indiscriminately, all the proteins listed in the DNA. Instead, what the messenger RNA communicates to the ribosomes at any particular time is simply a list of the proteins required at that time, omitting those not required. This means that, at any particular time, the genes in the DNA which denote the unrequired proteins must somehow be covered up, to be uncovered when a requirement for them arises.

How is this done?

The evidence indicates that for each set of genes in the DNA there is a specially designed molecule of protein called a repressor, itself the product of a particular gene existing only for the purpose, which attaches itself directly to the gene to be repressed, thereby putting it

* A. L. Lehninger, "How Cells Transform Energy," *Scientific American*, September 1961.

out of action. It continues to cover the gene until it receives a signal that the protein denoted by the gene is now needed. Such a signal often takes the form of a small molecule, called an inducer, which attaches itself to the repressor, altering the repressor's shape so that it becomes detached from the gene, thereby uncovering it.

Let me give a specific example. A bacterium, *Escherichia coli,* has a gene that denotes an enzyme whose sole function is to break down lactose into galactose and glucose, thereby releasing energy. As long as there is no lactose present, and consequently no need for the enzyme that breaks it down, a specific lac-repressor remains attached to the gene for this enzyme. When lactose arrives on the scene, however, it produces, by breakdown, a small molecule (an inducer) which proceeds to attach itself to the lac-repressor, thereby causing the lac-repressor to uncover the gene, which thereupon communicates to the ribosomes, through messenger RNA, the need that has now arisen for the enzyme's production. The production of the enzyme, thus inaugurated, continues until the lactose is exhausted, whereupon the lac-repressor, freed from the inducer molecule, again covers up the gene.*

In some cases an activity, when it has gone far enough, is turned off by a feedback mechanism. A special molecule is formed that goes back along the chain of catalyzed reactions to inhibit the process at its source.

*

It remains to account for the extreme specificity of enzymes, the apparent ability of each to pick out, from among innumerable molecules, those that belong to the precise species for which it was created and on which it has to act. The answer lies in the three-dimensional structure of the protein molecules that function as enzymes.

Up to this point I have referred to the proteins as if they were simply linear, chains of amino acid stretched out in one dimension only. In fact, each forms a more-or-less rigid globular structure, its chain weaving in and out of itself, the whole held to its precise shape by bonds that tie together links which may be distant from each other in the linear sequence.

We may think of an enzyme as a globular structure that has an irregular surface, with pits and clefts, bumps and knobs. One area on this surface, called the active site, is so designed in its irregularities

* I have taken this example and, indeed, my whole account of repressors and inducers from Mark Ptashne and Walter Gilbert, "Genetic Repressors," *Scientific American,* June 1970.

that it fits precisely the particular molecule or molecular complex, called the substrate, that it exists to engage. The enzyme and its substrate are made for each other as lock and key. This is what is thought to account for the specificity of each enzyme, its fine discrimination in attaching itself only to the particular kind of molecule it has to act upon.

An example is provided by an enzyme called lysozyme, composed of 129 amino acids in a chain that, entangled and cross-bound with itself, has a precise and rather rigid if irregular shape. Lysozyme exists to break a particular carbon-oxygen bond in a polysaccharide chain at a particular point in its sequence of links. A three-dimensional model of the lysozyme molecule shows a deep cleft. This is the active site into which the portion of the polysaccharide chain containing the carbon-oxygen bond fits.*

In addition to such mechanical binding between enzyme and substrate, there is presumably chemical binding, which holds two such partners together by the electromagnetic force that constitutes a chemical bond.

Multiply this example, and the example of the lac-repressor with its associated inducer, by many thousands, all different, and one begins to get an idea of what an elaborate and busy community a living cell is. This also suggests what, as a whole, is almost beyond imagining, how far the cell has evolved since it first came into existence, supposedly as a consequence of the combination of atoms to form molecules, and of molecules to form macromolecules, which combined in turn to form such associations as those between nucleic acids and proteins or those between enzymes and their substrates — associations mutually matched, in precise and intricate detail, over the whole range of their countless varieties. This is part of what one has in mind when one apprehends an architectonic tendency in nature.

* This is represented in diagrams on pages 217, 255, 256, and 257 of Loewy and Siekevitz, op. cit., and a detailed account of it is given in the accompanying text.

X

The Combination of Cells

WITH THE PASSAGE OF TIME, the elements of matter have combined to form ever larger and more elaborate structures, and at a certain stage some of these structures have come to life. We have already traced this process from elementary particles to the point where the single cell, which is the unit of life, has come into being. But the process does not stop here, for single cells then combine among themselves to form multicellular organisms, which in continuation of the process develop in size, in complexity, and in something difficult to define that we apprehend as the quality of life.

We have seen that unicellular organisms reproduce by division. Each chromosome, with its DNA, duplicates itself; the resulting twins are drawn, respectively, toward the opposite poles of the cell, which then divides at its equator. The product, in the most primitive forms of life, is two quite separate and mutually independent unicellular organisms where there had been only one before.

Suppose, now, that the two remain in physical touch with each other, perhaps merely by adherence of their surfaces. As they, in turn, multiply by division, and if the progeny in successive generations continue to hold together, the product will not necessarily be one multicellular organism, but it will at least be a tight colonial mass of unicellular organisms that looks like one.

In the development of such colonial complexes, a point may be reached at which the interdependence of the individual members, and the specialization of some of them, entailing structural differentiation and a division of labor, is such that the whole, if it is not one multicellular organism, appears to be at least intermediate between a colony of single cells and such an organism. One cannot say which it is.

There is a species of amoeba, *Dictyostelium discoideum*, known as "slime mold" in one of its manifestations, that reproduces by fission to engender unicellular progeny just like itself, separate and independent of one another. Under certain conditions, however, these individual amoebas will gather together in a solid mass, embracing perhaps hundreds of thousands, which has the form of a fat worm or a slug, which has a front end and a hind end, and which proceeds to move forward like a slug moving over a rock and leaving a slimy track behind it. The integration of these amoebas in the form of the slug goes so far that differentiation among them is manifested according to their place in the whole, those in the front third being larger than and chemically distinguishable from those in the posterior two thirds. A point comes when the slug, having come to a stop, proceeds to transform itself into a vertical structure with a disc for its base, a slender stalk held rigid by a cellulose cylinder that the amoebas manufacture, and a globular head balanced on top. (The delicacy of this form is that of a Venetian glass goblet.) Next, each of the cells that had formed the posterior two thirds of the slug encases itself in cellulose, so to remain until the time comes for it to undergo the process of fission by which a new generation of individual amoebas, altogether separate from one another, is produced.

Is the shaped mass of amoebas, whether slug or goblet, a colony of single cells, or is it one multicellular organism?

Not only is its outward behavior that of one organism, but it shows a differentiation and a division of labor among its constituent cells. The bees of a hive, however, also show differentiation and a division of labor, without thereby constituting what we regard as a single organism. Since the shaped mass represents only one stage in the amoeba's life-cycle, and since it takes no nourishment, its members having done all their feeding before assembling, biologists regard it as a temporary colony of amoebas, like a column of army ants.

Two mutually related groups of unicellular organisms, the flagellates and the ciliates, are so primitive that, as groups, they cannot be classified as either vegetable or animal. They may resemble the common ancestors of both kingdoms. (The reader will recall from Chapter VII that the flagella and cilia, which give these organisms their respective names, probably originated as independent organisms that first became associated with them by symbiosis.) The collar-flagellates, developing stems by which they fasten themselves to the bottom in the shallow waters they inhabit, divide at the tops of their stems to produce progeny that remain mutually attached like the florets of a daisy. In the absence of any communication among these cells, we say that they constitute a colony.

In the case of *Zoothamnium,* however, communication is not absent. The cells in their collectivity acquire the form of a tree with branches extending from a central trunk, individual cells appearing like blossoms along the branches. All are connected by contractile thread that runs from the tips of the branches and down the central trunk. Touch but one cell and the whole tree responds, drawing itself downward. On the other hand, each cell must feed itself, being unable to derive nourishment from its neighbors as it would if attached by some equivalent of an umbilical cord.

Perhaps the chief reason for calling the *Zoothamnium* complex a colony rather than an organism is the fact that each cell has to feed itself, using apparatus of its own to capture, engulf, and digest its organic food. But organisms with chlorophyll don't require organic food from outside or any equivalent of a mouth for engulfing it, for they use the energy of sunlight to produce their own organic nourishment, within themselves, by photosynthesis. Consider, then, the photosynthetic flagellate called *Volvox*. Its cells combine to form a hollow ball lined with jelly. The ball has an up side and a down side, and by the coordinated action of the flagella of its associated cells it spins on its axis, sometimes in one direction, sometimes in another. Because it lives by photosynthesis, the question of feeding does not arise any more than it arises in the case of a blade of grass; but otherwise there is no reason to regard the *Volvox* complex, more than the *Zoothamnium* complex, as an organism rather than a colony.

Sponges are composed largely of collar-flagellates, like those referred to three paragraphs back. These flagellates combine to form hollow, bulbous bodies, each with pores on the sides and an opening at one end. By all waving their flagella together, they set up a current that comes in through the many pores and goes out through the opening at the end. As the water flows past them, each on its own draws particles of organic nourishment from it.

Is this not the behavior of a cooperative colony, like that of bees in a hive, each of which still has to do its own eating?

A. S. Romer, who has referred to the aforementioned collar-flagellates and to *Volvox* as colonial, says, with reference to these sponges, that "we are not dealing here with a colony, but with a multicellular organism. . . ." "Were there no other cells in a sponge's body," he writes, "than this inner sheet of collar cells, we might still think of this structure as a colony. But although they are the most numerous, they are not the only kind present; we have in a sponge cell differentiation as well as multiplication. A series of flattened cells covers the outer surface of the sponge; the pores are lined and guarded by other types; still others form hard spicules of skeletal material which stiffen the bodies of many large sponges. These cells are not individuals; they are here parts of an organism, each contributing its share toward the maintenance and well-being of the

whole." * These other cells, however, although they cannot themselves draw the food-bearing water past themselves in a current, still
have to feed themselves from what it supplies. The individuals in
the beehive are also differentiated and specialized in their functions,
and some are fed by the food that others bring in, but we do not
therefore say that the hive is one organism.

Surely, in these borderline cases, the question whether a grouping
is a colony or one organism is nominal rather than real. One knows
what the reality is. The question is that of how we wish to use two
categorical terms, conceived as mutually exclusive alternatives, in
describing it. "The dividing line between colony and organism" according to J. T. Bonner, "is a gradual and tenuous one." †

*

Having considered slime molds, colonial flagellates, and sponges, let
us take one last example of combination among cells.

A fertilized egg cell, enclosed in the ovary of a flower, begins to
multiply in the usual way. The proliferating cells remain attached to
one another, and at an early stage they begin to develop differen-
tially. Those on the surface of what may now be referred to as an
embryo acquire the character of epidermal cells; those just beneath
them become cortex cells; those in the center become procambium
cells. The developed ovum with its embryo, now constituting a seed,
may lie dormant until environmental circumstances, such as moisture and a growing warmth in the soil on which it has fallen, waken
it to renewed development.

The embryo in the seed, awakened, proceeds to germinate, breaking through the seed-casing. The embryonic root, constantly growing by the multiplication of its cells, makes its way downward into
the soil, while at the other end a shoot rises into the air. Root and
shoot, continuing their development, branch and branch again.
New differentiation occurs in the proliferating cells, producing specialized varieties that form cambium, wood, bast, leaves, flowers.
With the passage of years, the fully developed product comes to
manifest itself as an apple tree, composed of millions of millions of
variously specialized cells bound in an association that we regard not
as a colony of organisms but as one organism.

We regard the apple tree as such because of the degree to which it
is integrated in all the aspects of its functioning. Water and salts, absorbed by its roots from the soil, are drawn upward through specialized pipe-like cells inside trunk and branches until they reach the

* *The Procession of Life*, London, 1968, pp. 34–35.
† *Cells and Societies*, Princeton, 1955, p. 104.

leaves, where by the agency of photosynthetic cells they are made to produce sugar, which then descends through other specialized cells to nourish the whole tree in all its living parts.

Atoms combine to form molecules, molecules combine to form cells, and cells combine in ever more elaborate associations to form apple trees or porpoises, apes or orchids. After 3,500 million years of a continuing evolution they combine to form even such a pitiful phenomenon as the poor scholar who, sitting in his study like Faust, tries to comprehend it all.

XI

Differentiation

EVERY ORGANISM, whether a bacterium or a tree, an amoeba or an antelope, is the product of a single cell that divides to reproduce itself. In its set of genes, in the written language of its DNA, the cell contains complete information on the organism's structure, its functioning, and its behavioral responses to the environment — information which it passes on unchanged to each of the proliferating cells, which in their turn pass it on to the successive generations of cells. It follows that, barring accidents, all the amoebas of any generation are genetically identical with the ancestral amoeba and with one another. Generation after generation, the genetically unchanged organism is reproduced, and each reproduction contains exactly the same genetic information for its further duplication.

What is true of the amoeba is true, as well, of the cells that constitute such a multicellular organism as an apple tree or an antelope, all of them produced by the division of an original egg cell. Each of the countless cells that compose the antelope contains a full set of genes, copied from that in the egg cell, which is to say that each holds the information needed to reproduce the entire organism in every detail. In the nucleus of just one cell of the follicle of one hair of the reader's head is all the information that had been contained in the original egg cell from which he developed, including the information on the structure of his pancreas, the shape of his nose, the age at which he should undergo puberty, and his innate capacity for logical thought.

In the genetic process as I have described it, excluding accidents, cells reproduce themselves through the ages in identical copies. If, then, this process were all, if environmental factors could be excluded, there would be no differentiation and no evolution. Every amoeba, for as long as the species survived, would be identical with every other amoeba since the first; the egg cell of the antelope would, in the process of its successive divisions, produce only exact copies of itself, rather than the array of increasingly differentiated and specialized cells — nerve cells, blood cells, etc. — that it does in fact produce as it develops from the egg to the fully formed adult (which is to say that it would not produce an antelope).

However, one cannot imagine the absence of environmental factors, and the absurdity of even postulating it is patent. Although we may, for the sake of heuristic convenience, talk of genetic factors as if they were distinct and separable from environmental factors, they have their expression and are realized only by interaction with environmental factors. The elementary particle does not exist in and of itself, but is part of a field; the atom is a bundle of mass-energy interacting with what is around it, and could not otherwise be a bundle of mass-energy; the single cell has its micro-environment, the micro-environment its macro-environment; and all organisms are in part the products of interaction with the radiation that fills the four dimensions of space-time to the uttermost bounds of the universe. Nothing is separable from the total environment. In this sense, the universe is one seamless whole.

The fertilized egg cell of the apple tree, reproducing itself by division, does so in the tight enclosure of an ovary, which imposes differentiation on the multiplying cells according to their different positions in that enclosure, or according to how they are placed in relation to one another. The differentiation then proceeds to increase by its own dynamics, first in the embryo and then in the growing tree. Cells differently placed develop differently, those in the interior in certain ways, those at the periphery in other ways.

We saw in Chapter IX what the basic mechanics of cellular differentiation appear to be. While every cell in a multicellular organism has the complete set of genes originally contained in the fertilized egg from which it developed, the activity or inactivity of particular genes in that set is selectively determined by environmental circumstances. Genes for the manufacture of particular proteins go into production when environmental circumstances call for those proteins, remaining out of production otherwise. Cells in different positions, and therefore subject to different environmental influences, develop differently on that account.

When I have said, in these pages, that the DNA in the nucleus of a cell contains all the information for making a complete duplicate of the organism to which it belongs, the role of environmental factors has been tacitly understood. Down to the least detail of reproduction or development, however, the environment is no less essential than the genes. Although the DNA of a mammal contains complete information for the construction of its skeleton, the skeleton will not be constructed unless the environment contains materials for the manufacture of bones. A fish growing up in an environment deficient in certain minerals needed for its growth will be smaller than another of its kind that has grown up in an adequately supplied environment. The color of my skin is the product of sunlight in my environment as well as of the genetic heritage that predetermined how it would react to sunlight. The DNA in the germ cell of the apple tree contains full information on how it is to grow and branch, but it will not complete the prescribed process of growing and branching if, having germinated deep in a cave, it lacks light to provide the energy for growth after the initial stages; and, in fact, every individual, in growing and branching, will take a form different from that of every other individual of its species, if only because environmental circumstances are not the same for any two. DNA determines the song the nightingale will sing under normal environmental circumstances only. It is true that, in the development of each individual, inheritance comes first. (Another genetic inheritance might have made a mouse of me, which is more than another environment could have done.) In terms of the whole, however, genetic heritages have developed to fit pre-existing environments. Environmental factors may exist without genetic factors, but not genetic without environmental. If the point is obvious, once made, it is easily overlooked and, in any case, needs to be given prominence in all our thinking about development and evolution.

The interior of a fertilized frog's egg does not constitute a uniform environment. For one thing, most of its yolk is concentrated at what we may think of as its south pole, diminishing toward the north pole. When this polarized cell has divided twice longitudinally, the four resulting divisions are alike in size and shape, like those of an apple cut into quarters. The third cleavage, however, which is latitudinal, occurs north of the equator, so that the four southern divisions that result are larger than the four northern, and somewhat different in shape. Differentiation, based on position in the complex, has begun, to become more marked as the process continues, increased environmental differences giving rise to increased differentiation.

As the cells continue to divide and redivide they take the form, collectively, of a rubber ball, one spherical layer of cells enclosing a hollow. They now begin to move about this structure. A cleft appears through which cells flow into the interior, and the whole tends to fold inward in various ways until there are three layers, and at one point an opening like a mouth. It is clear that the cells of each layer, and those along the lip of the opening, are respectively subject to different environmental circumstances. Responding to these different circumstances, they begin to assume various shapes and to become specialized in various ways. The embryo, which will some day be a frog, is developing.

XII

Specialization

ALL ORGANISMS that belong to orders of magnitude above the microscopic are readily separable into a vegetable kingdom and an animal kingdom.* From the speedwell that sparkles in the grass to the big tree of the California mountains, from the aphid to the whale, these are the largest of living beings because the most elaborately organized, and the most elaborately organized because the most developed. They have come the farthest along the ever branching pathways of evolution from the growing aggregations of molecules that, some 3,500 million years ago, began to show unmistakable signs of life.

The cells of multicellular plants differ from animal cells in having rigid walls of cellulose and in being cemented to one another, so that they cannot either change their shapes like amoebas or move through their own ranks like the cells that migrate over the embryo of the frog to find new points of attachment. The stem and branches of the plant, like a structure raised by piling brick on brick, grow all one way, not changing their growing forms in themselves but adding onto them. Moreover, unlike animals, they stop growing only when they die. While the structure of their reproductive organs, known as flowers in the highest plants, may be specialized and elaborate to a degree, the most developed plants are still far simpler in structure, in organization, and in functioning than the most developed animals. Complex and delicate as an orchid is, its inherent limitations contrast with the wide possibilities open to any bird or mammal. It has no nervous system, therefore no brain, and it cannot go on journeys, being rooted for life to the spot where it was born. When, in primitive times, the two kingdoms separated by branching from a common stock, the animal kingdom took a direction that opened upon wider vistas. If life on earth ever populates other planets, it will be by the realization of possibilities that only animal life possesses.

* For an exception, see page 192 below.

This is also to say that cellular differentiation and specialization have gone further in the animal than in the vegetable kingdom. There is nothing in plant tissues as elaborate and versatile as the muscle tissues of animals, and no specialization as extreme as that represented by the nerve cells which, among their other functions, command the action of the muscles. In what follows, then, I shall indicate how far the differentiation and specialization of cells have gone since they began, which means that I shall confine myself to describing developments in the animal kingdom.

RED BLOOD CELLS

We saw in Chapter X that there is no absolute distinction between a single multicellular organism, on the one hand, and a colony of unicellular organisms on the other. Just as we regard the stones of the Parthenon as constituting one structure, so we regard the cells of an antelope as constituting one organism. A more precise observation of the antelope, however, might bring us to see in the status and behavior of some of its cells implications of the independence we associate with individual bees in a hive.

If, under a microscope, one observes sperm cells swimming freely in a soup of antelope semen, each propelling itself by the lashings of its flagellum, they appear as so many discrete individuals in a colony rather than as the building blocks of a larger individual. Each sperm, so far from being an integral part of one antelope, is a messenger appointed to deliver a genetic message from one antelope to another. In order to do so it has to move out of the one into the other, perhaps to end its days by fusing with an almost equally independent egg cell awaiting it inside the second antelope. The very fact that it lives part of its life inside one individual and part inside another shows that it is not integral to either. (This applies as well to the pollen cell of a flowering plant.)

I have so far referred to all cells as self-reproducing by division, but the sperm is an exception. (The antelope is the sperm's only way of making more sperm.*) Another exception is the mammalian red blood cell, which has some of the sperm's independence and is as narrowly specialized. It lacks the nucleus that, in other cells, contains the basic genetic information (so that it also constitutes an exception to my statement that all the cells of any organism contain complete information for its reproduction). Precisely because it lacks a nucleus, which is indispensable to any cell's maintenance over the long run, it remains alive only a few months. Just as the antelope's sperm cells, having short lives and being unable to reproduce

* "The hen," said Samuel Butler, "is the egg's way of making another egg."

themselves directly, are constantly replaced by new ones being constantly produced in the antelope's testes, so its red blood cells are constantly replaced by new ones being produced in the marrow of its bones.

Although the red blood cell, unlike the sperm, does not propel itself, it too is without attachment to the organism inside which it passes its life, being carried about that organism by the liquid stream which circulates endlessly through its system of pipes. If the role of the sperm is to carry information from one organism to another, that of the red blood cell is to transport chemical substances within the organism to which it is confined. The untold millions of living cells in the tissues of a mammal all need a constant supply of oxygen for their respiration, a process which produces carbon dioxide as a waste product. The red blood cells, after picking up the oxygen molecules in the lungs, into which they have been drawn from the atmosphere, carry them through the arteries and capillaries to all the tissues of the body, where they deliver them, picking up in exchange molecules of carbon dioxide which they carry back to the lungs for discharge by exhalation. (In the human body, the total length of the capillaries alone is some 95,000 kilometers, and no cell of the body tissues is more than one one-hundredth of a centimeter from a capillary.)

The degree of specialization for this function is manifested by the fact that the mature mammalian cells lack not only a nucleus but also mitochondria, ribosomes, and other organelles, their internal space being occupied instead by hemoglobin molecules. (In their formative stages they do have such organelles as ribosomes for the production of the hemoglobin that will replace them.)

Every hemoglobin molecule, of which one red blood cell contains some 280 million, is itself composed of some 10,000 atoms arranged to form four chains, each consisting of 140 amino acids in an established order. The key element in the structure of each chain is the so-called heme group, an atom of iron surrounded by atoms of nitrogen, carbon, and hydrogen like a king surrounded by courtiers. In the lungs, each of the hemoglobin molecule's four heme groups combines with a molecule of free oxygen (that makes 1,120 million oxygen molecules per cell for a full load), which it carries to the tissues whose constituent cells need it for their respiration. Having delivered this cargo, the red blood cell then picks up the cargo of carbon dioxide which it carries back to the lungs for disposal.

By entering into the detail of the hemoglobin molecule's three-dimensional structure, and of the processes by which it takes on oxygen molecules at one point in order to release them at another, as if it knew what it was doing, one could elaborate this account to show one extreme to which cells have gone in their differentiation for specialized roles.* Suffice it here, however, to add only that the oxygen molecules delivered by the red blood cells are received and stored, pending their use for respiration by the tissues, in molecules of myoglobin, each of which is the counterpart of a single hemoglobin chain with one heme group to combine temporarily with one oxygen molecule.

The red blood cell, then, is one product of the differentiation and progressive specialization that accompany the repeated division of a multicellular organism's single egg cell.

MUSCLE CELLS

Through the process of respiration, the oxygen delivered to the tissues by the red blood cells breaks down sugar molecules, combining with the respective products of the breakdown, carbon and hydrogen, to form carbon dioxide and water. This leaves a residue of energy which is transferred, in the form of high-energy electrons, to the mitochondria inside each cell. As I recounted in Chapter IX, the mitochondria, in their turn, transfer it to molecules of adenosine diphosphate (ADP), thereby empowering their conversion into the higher energy molecules of adenosine triphosphate (ATP), which carry the added energy to wherever it is needed inside the cell.

When an animal uses its muscles, the energy consumed within each cell of muscular tissue is borne to the points of consumption by ATP molecules, which obtain it from mitochondria, which obtain it from sugar molecules broken down by oxygen, which is delivered by red blood cells, which pick it up in the lungs, which draw it in from the atmosphere. A man running as fast as he can soon finds difficulty in maintaining the supply of energy needed for such intense and continued muscular exertion. The expansion of his lungs at each inhalation, and the rate of alternating inhalation and exhalation, are increased to the limit of possibility so as to provide the greatest possible supply of oxygen to the red cells in the blood, the flow of which is accelerated by the increased pumping of the heart. (In other words, he puffs hard and his heart pounds within him.) Even so, his muscles begin to ache as the energy required exceeds the rate of supply by the ATP molecules. The supply of oxygen to oxidate the sugar becomes exhausted — so that the runner at last collapses and "blacks out," his whole organism, including his brain,

* For more detailed accounts see M. F. Perutz, "The Hemoglobin Molecule," *Scientific American*, November 1964; and J. T. Bonner, *Cells and Societies*, Princeton, 1955, Chap. 19.

suffering from the deficiency of oxygen that has resulted from a muscular effort greater than the supply could sustain.

The long narrow cell of a muscle is like a tube, with threads called fibrils that run through it. Each fibril is composed of short filaments gathered together in successive sheaves along its length. There are two kinds of filament, one thick, the other thin. Sheaves of thick filaments alternate with sheaves of thin ones throughout the length of each fibril — as if bundles of steel rods alternated with bundles of wires. The sheaves overlap, the ends of the thin filaments of one sheaf being interspersed with the ends of the thick filaments of the adjacent sheaf, so that each sheaf interpenetrates its respective neighbors at each end. The contraction of the cell is produced by an increase in the overlap, and when all the cells in a muscle contract the muscle as a whole contracts.

How is the increase in the overlap produced?

The thick filaments are composed of chainlike myosin molecules stretched out in straight lines but in staggered array (which is to say that their ends do not lie together), each having at one end a projection, which we may think of as a hook, that makes an angle with its axis. Consequently, the thick filaments, instead of being smooth, are roughened by a multitude of projecting hooks along most of their length. The increase in the overlap between the sheaves, which causes the contraction, is produced by the action of these hooks, which catch hold of the overlapping thin filaments from adjacent sheaves, on either side, and pull them inward. The pulling takes the form of successive tugs, as if the thin filaments were being pulled along by a hand-over-hand process. Each hook, having caught hold of a thin filament, tugs it by swiveling or leaning backward, so to speak, then lets go to gain another hold farther along and, swiveling again, tugs it still farther.

While the thick filaments are composed basically of the hooked myosin molecules, the thin ones are composed basically of bead-shaped actin molecules in two intertwined chains like chains of pearls. When an order comes from the organism's central nervous system for the muscle to contract, each myosin hook on the thick filaments binds to an actin bead on a thin filament, tugs it in the direction of greater overlap, lets go in order to bind to another bead farther along, tugs it in turn, lets go in order to bind to still another bead still farther along — and so on until the contraction has gone far enough, the order having been fulfilled.

Each myosin hook, otherwise inert, is activated when an ATP molecule binds to it, providing the energy for just one tug. In about a thousandth of a second after the ATP molecule has surrendered that energy, it is replaced by another ATP molecule which, binding to the hook, provides the energy for another tug — and so for one tug after another, each requiring the contribution of a new ATP molecule.

What is it, inside the cell, that starts this process, prompting the ATP molecules to bind to the hook, thereby causing the hooks to bind to the actin molecules?

The process is started by the release of calcium ions from special storage vesicles into the fluid surrounding the filaments. (How many millions of years, one may ask, did it take for the random process of mutation and natural selection to arrive at the device of such vesicles to hold such ions designed to activate such molecules to tug such filaments?) Their presence in the fluid is normally required in order that the ATP molecules activate the hooks by binding to them. A fraction of a second after the ions have been released from their storage to set the process off, they are recalled to storage by a special pump in the cell, thereby stopping it.*

If the release of the calcium ions within each cell is the immediate occasion for its contraction, what is it that occasions their release?

Their release is prompted by a signal that reaches the muscle cell from outside, traveling along a pathway of nerve cells. If my finger comes into contact with a hot stove, a signal travels from it along such a pathway to the muscles of my upper arm, where vesicles in millions of muscle cells respond by releasing clouds of calcium ions, whereupon countless ATP molecules bind to countless myosin molecules, each of which thereupon binds to an actin molecule. As a succession of ATP molecules deliver up their respective quotas of energy, each myosin molecule tugs an actin molecule, releases it, binds to a new one, tugs it in turn, etc. The result is that my arm muscles contract and my finger is drawn away from the stove in one smooth movement that occupies a fraction of a second. But so much has happened in that fraction of a second that to tell it all would take hours.

The muscle cells that I have just described, specialized as they are, are not fundamentally different from the basic cell that constitutes a diatom or an amoeba. Each has a nucleus (sometimes more than one) that contains, in the DNA of its chromosomes, information for the complete reconstitution of the organism to which it belongs, whether an antelope or a man. Each has mitochondria, ribosomes, and all the other standard organelles that, in their activity, make the

---

* The reader will find a more detailed and less simplified account of this process in J. M. Murray and Annemarie Weber, "The Cooperative Action of Muscle Proteins," *Scientific American*, February 1974.

life of the cell like that of a city. The features required by its specialization, such as the thick and thin filaments, are simply additional to
the basic features. In this it illustrates the fact that, throughout the
realm of living being, as throughout the realm of non-living being,
variety develops on a foundation of uniformity. The muscle cells
and the red blood cells of the individual organism are, after all, the
progeny, by repeated division, of one and the same egg cell. They
are bits of one cell that broke and broke again as it grew.

NERVE CELLS

What applies to the muscle cells applies as well to the nerve cells. A
nerve cell has the shape of a globular body with one or several limbs.
The resemblance of its body to an amoeba is unmistakable. It has a
nucleus, ribosomes, mitochondria, and the other standard organelles
of the animal cell (lysosomes, Golgi apparatuses, endoplasmic re-
ticulums, etc.) which I have not had occasion to mention in the summary accounts that I am providing in these pages.

Unlike an amoeba, however, the fully developed nerve cell does
not divide, and there is no alternative means for its reproduction
within the organism to which it belongs, such as that provided by the
testes in the case of the sperm cell and by the bone marrow in the
case of the red blood cell (these two kinds of cell being distinguished
by their lack of attachment to the organism from which they spring).
On the other hand, unlike sperm or red blood cells, the nerve cell
lives out the lifetime of the organism, and when injured it may in
some measure be able to repair itself.

The specialization of the nerve cell is represented chiefly by its
principal limb. Called the axon, it is a fine fiber which may, in man,
be a meter or more long. (If there are 95,000 kilometers of capillaries in the human body, I suppose there may be as many kilometers of axons.) Electrical disturbances travel through it as electric
signals travel through a telephone wire, but by a different mode.
The signals in a telephone wire are carried by a continuous flow of
electric current, which is to say by a directional movement of free
electrons. In an axon the traveling electrical disturbances represent
a local change in electric potential that moves from one end to the
other.

What is electric potential?

If there is a difference of voltage between the matter on one side
of a membrane and that on the other, the difference is called the
electric potential. It is described in terms of positive and negative,
the higher voltage being regarded as positive, the lower as negative.

When the axon is not in use to transmit a signal the fluid of its interior, enclosed by the cellular membrane, is negative (lower in voltage) by contrast with the fluid surrounding it, which is therefore positive. The form taken by a signal is that of an electrical impulse produced by a local reversal of this potential, which travels the length of the axon. At the point where the impulse is at any particular instant, the interior is positive (higher in voltage) by contrast with the exterior, which is therefore negative. The point of reversal is what moves through the axon — moving at speeds that may exceed 360 kilometers per hour (100 meters per second).

The potential of the resting axon results from a chemical difference between the fluid outside, with its higher voltage, and the fluid inside; and the reversal of potential results from an exchange of chemical substances across the more-or-less permeable membrane. The substances are various ions — that is to say, atoms with a negative charge in consequence of having more electrons than protons, or with a positive charge in consequence of having fewer electrons than protons. (Here the terms "negative" and "positive" have an absolute meaning by contrast with the relative meaning associated with a difference in potential, where less positive is considered negative in relation to more positive.) In the case of the resting axon, the principal ion on the outside is that of sodium, whereas the principal ion on the inside is that of potassium. Together with certain other ions on either side, the proportions are such as to account for the positive condition (the greater voltage) outside, the negative condition inside.

It happens that there is constant leakage through the membrane in both directions. While sodium ions leak in from outside, however, a "pump" forces them out again, replacing them with potassium ions that it draws in from outside (but which tend to leak out again). The nature of the pump is not known, but it may be an enzyme, each molecule of which picks up a sodium ion inside the cell, carries it out through the membrane, releases it, and returns with a potassium ion. The pump thus maintains the potential that characterizes the resting state.

If, now, the sodium ions entering from outside are allowed to increase inside, they reduce the difference in voltage, and this reduction progressively facilitates the entrance of more sodium ions, until suddenly the gates are opened wide, so to speak, and sodium ions flood in, reversing the potential. Such an event, in itself, opens the gates of the membrane immediately ahead of the point at which it occurs, thereby propagating itself forward; while immediately behind that point the membrane again becomes relatively impermeable to inflowing sodium ions but, for the instant, opens the gates to

outflowing potassium ions. The result is that, as the reversal of potential moves forward, the original potential is restored behind it.
The moving point representing the momentary reversal of potential
is the signal that the axon exists to transmit. In practice, it may
transmit a succession of such signals as pulses that may follow one
another at intervals to be measured in milliseconds (one millisecond
being one thousandth of a second).

Such a signal, which may have to be communicated from one end
of a blue whale to another, generally passes through a chainlike
series of nerve cells placed end to end but not quite touching, so that
there are gaps between them.

How are these gaps bridged?

When the signal reaches the far end of an axon it prompts certain
vesicles at that end to release a chemical substance which diffuses
across the gap to the cell beyond. This substance excites the cell
beyond, thereby starting a reversal of potential that travels down its
length to the next gap, where the process is repeated.

When my finger touches a hot stove an impulse is set off in a
receptor nerve cell at that point. This impulse runs through a series
of axons, crossing the gaps, to some point in my cranium or in my
spinal column, where it is communicated across a gap to one or
more motor nerve cells, which proceed to send a like impulse down
similar pathways to the muscles of my arm. When it reaches these
muscles, as it does along many pathways, it crosses the gaps between
the nerve cells and the muscle cells by the same intermediation of a
chemical substance as in the case of the gaps between nerve cells.
Vesicles in the muscle cells are thereby prompted to release calcium
ions, which prompt ATP molecules to bind to myosin molecules,
which bind successively to successions of actin molecules, tugging at
them to shorten the muscles. So my finger is drawn away from the
stove in what looks like one simple movement.

There is no point on the living surface of my body that is not thick
with receptor nerve cells, all connected by a network of pathways
with motor nerve cells inside my skull and backbone, which are connected by another network with every cell of every muscle in my
body. When I touch the stove, the signal that is set off thereby
travels simultaneously through many pathways, so that it would
make no difference if it were blocked along any particular pathway.

The coast-to-coast telephone network of the United States is rudimentary compared to the electrical communication system inside the
wee body of a mouse. When we see how alert the mouse is, how
quickly it reacts to the least indication of danger, we have an example of the speed and effectiveness with which that system works.

When we watch a flying goshawk thread its way at high speed through a forest, seeing and avoiding every branch in its path, tilting to slip through openings, swerving and dodging by rapidly adjusting wings and tail, we have a like example. The countless millions of ions of sodium, potassium, and calcium in the goshawk's millions of cells must be in a constant state of orchestrated movement, while ATP molecules in immeasurable numbers are built up by mitochondria and broken down again to supply the needed power. Simply to describe what goes on in the process whereby it receives through its eyes, and interprets in its brain, the images that confront it in its course would require volumes.

A man's brain — like that of mouse or goshawk but larger — is a packed mass of specialized nerve cells to be numbered in thousands of millions, every one where it is and functioning as it does on the basis of some design written into the DNA. These cells are even capable of assimilating abstract information and storing it in what is called memory, but no one knows how. The operation of such a brain is beyond its own comprehension.

A disembodied mind of three or four thousand million years ago, observing the random collision and the occasional mutual adherence of molecules in shallow water, could hardly have predicted that these undirected events — acquiring a cumulative character, taking a direction of their own, manifesting the architectonic tendency of matter on an ever increasing scale — would someday lead to this.

XIII

The Unity of Life

PRESUMABLY the first cellular life (one dare not say the first life of all, for we must doubt that life had an absolute beginning) was microscopic and limited by the rudimentary simplicity of its constitution. The first cell that we might have considered recognizable as such (viewing it by way of an electron microscope) must have consisted of a membrane enclosing strands of nucleic acid, strands of protein, and one or more enzymes for extracting energy from the organic molecules that jostled against it, fermenting them upon contact as an acid eats metal. Such a cell was a speck of mixed chemicals that, by absorbing energy from its environment, tended to grow, splitting at intervals in the course of its growth as a raindrop splits when it gets too large.

Jumping 3,000 million years to our present, we confront the consequences of this growth in the goshawk, the mouse, and the man. My purpose in the last chapter was to suggest how far matters have gone in the course of these years. But I could not begin to describe, in the few pages I allowed myself, the degree of elaboration that has been reached. A reader who has not studied these matters could hardly imagine what would have been entailed if, for example, I had undertaken to describe nothing more than the multitudinous steps and channels — through the specially patterned tissues that constitute the corneas, the pupils, and the lenses of the goshawk's paired eyes, through their vitreous bodies, through the receptor nerves of their retinas differentiated as rods and cones (which carry electrochemical impulses set off by photons), through the ganglion cells, through the bundles and across the gaps of the axons that constitute the optic nerves, and through the complex of brain cells — a lay reader, I say, could hardly imagine what would have been entailed if I had undertaken to describe nothing more than the steps and channels through which the goshawk registered the presence of a twig just ahead in the path of its flight.*

* Darwin, who could not have known how complex the whole visual apparatus really

The complexity, however, has developed on a foundation of simplicity that remains. Just as all the stars in all the galaxies are made of the same few elements that we know on our earth, so all the forms of life we see about us today are made of the same few substances in various combinations. "Organisms as apparently dissimilar as men and molds have almost identical nucleic acids and have similarly identical enzyme systems for utilizing the energy stored in foodstuffs. Their proteins are made up of the same twenty amino acid units." * The complexity, therefore, is composed rather than basic, secondary rather than elemental. It represents the composition of an ever more extensive and elaborate order out of the chaos that was in the beginning.

There is evidence that all life on earth is descended from one common ancestor, which we may think of as the first cell (or the first association of molecules that we would be prepared to recognize as a cell).† That cell has lived, now, for over 3,000 million years, growing and splitting all the time. It lives still, and we individuals are but broken-off pieces of it.

There are two lines of descent in one, distinguished from each other as microcosm and macrocosm. I, an individual, am descended directly from a single egg cell that grew and split, as it is still doing. This is the microcosmic line, its temporal span measured in years. The macrocosmic line, best measured in terms of geological time, goes back to the primordial first cell of all. Because the lesser line recapitulates the greater, it is true in a fundamental sense that ontogeny recapitulates phylogeny.‡

---

was, nevertheless wrote: "To suppose that the eye with all its inimitable contrivances for adjusting the focus to different distances, for admitting different amounts of light, and for the correction of spherical and chromatic aberration, could have been formed by natural selection, seems, I freely confess, absurd in the highest degree" (*The Origin of Species*, 6th ed., New York/London, 1915, Chap. VI, 223–224). Note that he wrote "seems," not "is."

* Lynn Margulis, "Symbiosis and Evolution," *Scientific American*, August 1971.

† When amino acids form out of their atomic constituents they may equally well have a left-handed or a right-handed configuration. If today's life represented a variety of origins, one would expect its amino acids to fall equally into the two categories. In fact, they are virtually all left-handed. "The many similarities in the key constituents of most diverse organisms (e.g., the two varieties of nucleic acids, DNA and RNA, and energy-storing compounds such as adenosine triphosphate) argue against a polyphyletic origin" (Theodosius Dobzhansky, *Genetics of the Evolutionary Process*, New York/London, 1970, p. 7).

‡ The history of the individual, from egg to adult, recapitulates the history of the kind. This formulation is known as Haeckel's Law after the German follower of Darwin. By one of those semi-rational movements of intellectual fashion, however, Haeckel's Law has fallen into disrepute on the grounds that it is not literally true, not true in detail. (One can see that it should have been called Haeckel's Rule, a term which would have implied no more than that it was true in a general way.) The social

As the primordial cell grew and split, again and again — the one becoming many while remaining one — a progressive differentiation manifested itself in a growing variety. This process, whereby descendants went separate ways, was occasionally complemented by a contrary process of association and combination. So the original cell, in its perpetuation, became elaborated not only by differentiation but also by the symbiotic combination of its own varieties, which came together as organelles within the bounds of one cellular membrane. In the single egg cell of speedwell or pine, of aphid or antelope, the primitive association of a few chemical substances at last evolved into the bustling city we know, with its RNA molecules foraging for amino acids, with its Golgi apparatus producing and packaging a variety of chemicals, with its mitochondria combining phosphate molecules to invest them with energy, with its ATP molecules transporting the energy to where it is needed for respiration — and, in the nucleus, with the chains of DNA replicating themselves in the splitting chromosomes to provide for the continued reproduction of the cell that had its gradual origin in a pool of warm water over 3,000 million years ago. Nevertheless, the egg cell is generalized by contrast with the products of its own growth and splitting (in the microcosmic line), represented by the finished goshawk, the mouse, and the man. From the generalized egg cell came the red blood cells, muscle cells, and nerve cells in which we see the ultimate development, so far, of differentiation and specialization.

Differentiation has proceeded steadily since the first cell began splitting — as it does still today. Association and combination of primitive prokaryotic cells to make the advanced eukaryotic cell opened new possibilities for the spread and elaboration of order that had been the direction taken by life from the beginning. But the independent single cell, however elaborate it became in itself, was still limited in its self-contained possibilities.

For one thing, it could not well have achieved the size associated with the development of the most advanced life existing today. Size, in many objects animate and inanimate, is limited by a simple rule of geometry. When a body grows, while retaining its shape, its surface

---

pressure to reject Haeckel's Law has been harmful, however, in closing an important door to understanding. For it is not only revealing of taxonomic relationships based on heredity, it represents a large ontological truth.

A more complicated but a scientifically acceptable statement of the relationship between the development of the individual and the evolutionary history of its kind is to be found in *Embryos and Ancestors* by Gavin de Beer, 3rd ed., London, 1958, especially Chapter I.

increases as the square of its linear dimensions, its volume increases as the square of its surface or the cube of its linear dimensions. (This, so far from being abstruse, is represented by the banal fact that a square is one of its sides squared, a cube is that side cubed.) If you increase the size of a box by doubling its length, breadth, and height, or double the diameter of a sphere, or make a cathedral or a blue whale larger by twice its length, breadth, and height, you thereby quadruple the surface of each and increase its volume eightfold. A room with windows just large enough to provide sufficient light will no longer have large enough windows if you increase its size, for the space to be lighted will have increased twice as much as the window openings through which it is lighted. If it is heated or cooled through its surfaces the same problem will arise. If a cell is oxygenated through its membrane, the oxygen supply will tend to become insufficient as it grows. This might be dealt with by infolding the cell surfaces or pleating or wrinkling them to increase their area, or by adding pits or protuberances. Beyond a certain point, however, such devices would prove increasingly inadequate and impracticable. What is involved, after all, is more than just the doubling or squaring or cubing referred to above. All the advanced forms of life belong to an altogether different order of magnitude from the unicellular organisms one sees through a microscope. How many times would one have to double the linear dimensions of a paramecium to make a man, octupling its volume each time?

The relationship of weight to linear dimensions or surface is like that of volume. It increases faster. This is why a mosquito can stand on threadlike limbs while an elephant needs pillars for its support. Enlarge the mosquito until its weight equals that of the elephant and its legs will buckle under it.

A raindrop breaks into two when it has grown to a certain size because its surface tension can no longer contain a volume and weight of water that has increased as the square of its surface. The rule of geometry that thus limits its size, causing it to break beyond a certain point, presumably is what has tended to limit the size of living cells, causing them to split, normally, when they have doubled in linear growth. The problems of nourishing and of eliminating the wastes of a larger volume through a proportionately lesser surface become too great.*

---

* The record size attained by a single cell today is that of the ostrich egg; but it is a special case, if only because it contains at the outset, stored in its yolk, all the nourishment needed for the fulfillment of its role in housing the growing embryo, and its construction is porous enough to allow access to all its parts of oxygen from the outside. Even so, it might become unworkable if it grew any larger because of the problem of exchanging oxygen and moisture with its environment, or of keeping its interior heated during incubation. Moreover, it cannot fly or gallop.

The limitation of size is not the only factor limiting the possibilities of unicellular development. Specialization of organs, members, and tissues in the higher forms of life, whether plant or animal, has been largely associated with the development of specialized cells in the ontogenetic or microcosmic line of descent. The egg cell of bird or man is generalized, but as it grows and splits in successive generations it differentiates and specializes progressively to produce red blood cells, muscle cells, nerve cells, etc. At the same time, the animal develops a vascular system through which its blood flows, including a muscular pump; it develops a skeleton of jointed bones with cartilage, ligaments, and muscles to articulate them; it develops distinct parts like the head, the torso, and the limbs, arms or legs, wings or flippers.

Such a specialization implies a division of the whole body into parts that show a degree of separation to which the internal configuration of the single cell — even in its most elaborate form, with organelles that have their own membranes — appears not to lend itself as well as the association of separate and differentiated cells in a multicellular organism.

What I have written in the paragraphs immediately above is more a matter of plausible speculation than of absolute knowledge, since we can never know what adaptations to development the single cell might have made if there had not been a better alternative. In any case, one can see that immense new possibilities opened up when colonial associations of single cells first developed into multicellular organisms.* So the progressive increase in size and elaboration of organisms over the hundreds of millions of years entailed the addition of ontogenetic to phylogenetic development, of the microcosmic to the macrocosmic descent, of multicellular to unicellular life.

*

In that lonely masterpiece, *On Growth and Form*, D'Arcy Thompson wrote: "The biologist, as well as the philosopher, learns to recognize that the whole is not merely the sum of its parts." By way of conclusion to this chapter on the unity of life I cannot do better than to present his application of this to the elaborated organisms that all descended from the single cell of 3,000 million years ago:

> A bridge was once upon a time a loose heap of pillars and
> rods and rivets of steel. But the identity of these is lost, just as if

* It may be that such colonial associations of the present as those of termites or men will, 500 million years from now, have developed into superorganisms or their equivalent, and that this will open up still greater possibilities to earthly life, which by that time may have become extraterrestrial. For a more specific account of how this might happen see footnote on p. 498.

they were fused into a solid mass, when once the bridge is built; their separate functions are only to be recognised and analysed in so far as we can analyse the stresses, the tensions and the pressures, which affect this part of the structure or that; and these forces are not themselves separate entities, but are the resultants of an analysis of the whole field of force. Moreover, when the bridge is broken it is no longer a bridge, and all its strength is gone.

As we analyse a thing into its parts or into its properties, we tend to magnify these, to exaggerate their apparent independence, and to hide from ourselves (at least for a time) the essential integrity and individuality of the composite whole. We divide the body into its organs, the skeleton into its bones, as in very much the same fashion we make a subjective analysis of the mind, according to the teachings of psychology, into component factors: but we know very well that judgment and knowledge, courage or gentleness, love or fear, have no separate existence, but are somehow mere manifestations, or imaginary coefficients, of a most complex integral. And likewise, as biologists, we may go so far as to say that even the bones themselves are only in a limited and even a deceptive sense, separate and individual things. The skeleton begins as a *continuum,* and a *continuum* it remains all life long. The things that link bone with bone, cartilage, ligaments, membranes, are fashioned out of the same primordial tissue, and come into being *pari passu* with the bones themselves. The entire fabric has its soft parts and its hard, its rigid and its flexible parts; but until we disrupt and dismember its bony, gristly and fibrous parts one from another, it exists simply as a "skeleton," as one integral and individual whole.*

"We analyse to destroy," said Wordsworth. The creative act is that of seeing the whole within which, alone, the parts represent an order and have meaning.

* D'Arcy Thompson, *On Growth and Form,* abridged ed. by J. T. Bonner, Cambridge (England), 1971, pp. 262–263. (I have here reversed the order of two paragraphs in the original.)

XIV

Mutation

IF WE SUPPOSE only one origin for life, and a first cell that produces only identical copies of itself, which in turn produce only identical copies through the generations, then cells identical with the original would still be the only life on earth. (But such life would long ago have expired of starvation, having used up the store of organic molecules on which it fed by fermentation.)

Variation is the condition precedent for evolution, since without variation there are no alternatives to what was in the beginning. The variation, however, must be in the genetic material, in the instructions for replication written in DNA. If, by virtue of a favorable environment, a particular cell should be more vigorous than its fellows, this variation, not manifesting itself as a change in the genetic code, could not be passed on to its progeny, which would continue to be made on the original model.

Since variation in the genes is what constitutes the condition precedent of evolution, such variation must have taken place ever since evolution began. In Chapter III I gave an account of how a strand of DNA, consisting of a particular succession of nucleotides designated A, G, T, and C, replicates itself. Loose nucleotides come together and, binding to their complementary nucleotides on the chain, form a complementary chain. Normally, an A binds only to a T, a G only to a C. When a third chain is formed, complementary to the second, it is naturally identical with the first, Ts binding to As, Cs to Gs. Sometimes it will happen, however, that an atom on one of the nucleotides gets displaced from its usual position, perhaps by the impact of ultraviolet radiation or x-rays. If a T is so deformed, it may pair with a C instead of the A that constitutes its natural partner; or a G, so deformed, may pair with a T rather than a C. This is as if a typographical error occurred in copying the chain, changing one word in the genetic code. Perhaps ATG becomes CTG, resulting in a different gene that calls for the production of a different protein and, consequently, produces a variation in the organism that is created in accordance with the instructions written into the DNA. So a mutation has occurred, with the result, perhaps, that a fruit fly is born with white eyes rather than the normal red ones.

The mutation is in the genes, and the somatic change (the change in the body) is its manifestation, which is therefore secondary. The manifestation cannot reproduce itself. However, the original gene having been replaced by a mutant, it is the mutant that will thereafter be copied in successive replications, if they take place at all, thus producing the secondary somatic change (say white eyes instead of red) in succeeding generations.

We must picture the putative first cell on earth growing and dividing to produce successive generations of proliferating progeny genetically identical with itself. Then an accident occurs to one of the descendants. A photon of ultraviolet light, penetrating the cellular membrane, displaces an atom from one of the nucleotides, which is therefore copied wrong. When the cell to which it belongs divides, the result is two cells that, in addition to containing copies of the accidentally changed nucleic acid rather than of the original, are somatically different in that they are formed in response to accidentally altered genetic instructions. Perhaps a change in the protein of which the membrane is composed makes it stronger, or perhaps the enzyme that ferments the organic molecules with which it comes into contact has been changed into one that is more efficient in its performance. The change is incorporated permanently in one line of descent represented by the mutant cell. Now, as a consequence of this variation, there are two kinds of cells constituting two genetically different lines of descent: the line of those that, not having undergone change, represent the original cell, and the line of those that were changed by the accidental mutation. The first branching of the tree of life has occurred.

If the manifestation of the mutation in the cells that are affected by it proves disadvantageous, the mutant line may be expected to die out, leaving all as before. If on the other hand it confers an advantage, the mutant line, as its numbers proliferate, may be able to compete so successfuly with the unchanged line for a limited food supply or for room in the most favorable environmental locations that it eliminates the original line, taking its place.

Call the original line A and the mutant B. The advantage enjoyed by B may lead it to pre-empt the food supply and the favorable environmental locations, thereby bringing about the extinction of A.

Another possibility is that A will be confined to a marginal environment in which it proves able to survive as well as or better than B.

A third possibility is that the change brought about by the mutation in B enables it to spread into adjacent areas in which environmental circumstances exclude A. In this case, perhaps, both lines survive, but in different environmental niches.

Let us be specific. The original cell (A) had developed (on the earth of three to four thousand million years ago) in the mud at the bottom of pools of water at a certain optimum depth. Below that depth, we shall suppose, conditions of temperature and pressure, or a reduced supply of organic molecules for fermentation, made its perpetuation and survival increasingly difficult. Above that depth it was excessively exposed to the ultraviolet radiation that, in the absence of atmospheric oxygen, poured unfiltered upon the surface of the earth and its waters, but was filtered by the water in proportion to its depth.* Perhaps the stronger membrane we have attributed to the cells of line B, being more opaque, makes them more resistant to ultraviolet radiation. This enables them to proliferate in shallower waters, from which the cells of A are excluded. There is now a difference in distribution. A occupies deeper waters, where it can hold its own against B or even have an advantage, while B occupies shallower waters where A could not survive. Life has begun not only to evolve but also to spread.

In lines A and B alike, mutations continue to happen, typographical errors occur in the replication of the nucleic acids. Most are disadvantageous, with the consequence that the cells embodying them die out, leaving all as before. Some mutations, however, confer an advantage in terms of the environment. The A cells, driven to greater depths by their inability to compete with B cells at lesser depths, are benefited by mutations that make them better adapted to the greater depths, so that new lines embodying such mutations proliferate, replacing or displacing the old lines. The B cells are benefited by mutations (producing, let us say, more opaque membranes) that make them better adapted to shallow water, consequently producing new lines. By this process, continued over thousands of millions of years and supplemented by more elaborate devices of differentiation, ever more diverse forms of life will spread ever more widely — until in our own day we find fish eleven kilometers below the surface of the sea and spiders almost seven kilometers above it in the Himalayas (not to mention men in outer space).

*

* The harmful effects of ultraviolet radiation in a case like this would be produced by an increased rate of mutation, the majority of mutations being harmful. Ultraviolet light does not have this effect on large multicellular organisms like ourselves because it does not penetrate to the sex cells, sperm or egg. But x-rays and other ionizing radiation (radiation that strips electrons from atoms) do have this effect.

We should at this point make explicit, in terms of vocabulary, a distinction fundamental to the process of evolution. There are two distinct and mutually interacting entities involved. One is the genotype, which is the total store of genetic information written on the strands of nucleic acid lodged in the chromosomes. The other is the phenotype, which is the complete organism produced in accordance with that information. Mutation occurs only in the genotype. In speaking loosely we may say that the white eyes of a normally red-eyed fly constitute a mutation; but in precise fact what they constitute is the manifestation in the phenotype of a mutation in the genotype.

Natural selection, however, which determines the course of evolution, is never exercised directly on the genotype, but only on the phenotype that results from it.* A mutation is a change in the lettering on the DNA that is neither good nor bad in itself. That change in lettering causes a change in the organism (the phenotype) whose heredity it is transmitting. The change in the phenotype, too, is not good or bad in itself, but only in terms of a particular environment.† A mutation that has given me a darker skin, which is more effective in filtering out ultraviolet radiation, may be advantageous if I live on top of a mountain in the tropics, where such radiation is excessive, but harmful if I live on a cloud-capped island in the Arctic Ocean, where it is insufficient. Here we have a parallel to the specialized adaptation for different environments that we imagined with reference to the immediate descendants of the original cell: line A adapted to deeper, line B to shallower water. In any case, the mutation is only in the genotype, while the testing by natural selection is only of its phenotypic manifestation. Since the genotype is reproduced in successive generations through the agency of the phenotype only, a mutation that, in its manifestation, is harmful to the phenotype tends to be eliminated by decreasing the chance that the phenotype will be able to reproduce the genotype with its mutation by reproducing itself.

* A mutation may prove not to be viable in terms of the operations of organelles at the intracellular level — may, indeed, prove not to be viable at the molecular level — and so be eliminated by natural selection before it has a chance to manifest itself in the phenotype. Here it is the cell (or one organelle or one molecular combination) that plays the testing role of the phenotype. The a priori logic of this has been well argued by Lancelot Law Whyte in his Internal Factors in Evolution, London, 1965.
† A mutation that impaired the functioning of the human heart, although it might not be linked to the external environment, would be linked to the internal environment. When we consider environment in its totality, we do well to bear in mind the environment interior to any organism, to which its internal parts must be adapted, as well as the environment outside.

XV

Recombination

As the original cell proliferated, the occasional typographical error that we call mutation engendered ever more lines of descent. These lines, themselves branching and branching again, diverged ever more widely to produce, at last, the range of living beings that we know today.

Although mutation was the only agency of differentiation at first, differentiation itself made possible a secondary agency, that of recombination. Two genotypes, each with its own individual set of genes, would be combined to make a third that consisted of genes from each. No new genes are created by such combination, but since every phenotype is the manifestation of a particular combination of genes, a new combination produces a new phenotype that, under certain circumstances, might engender a new line of descent which diverged from the ancestral one. So the differentiation and expansion of life is the product of recombination as well as mutation.

The process of recombination we are familiar with is that of all the higher plants and animals, entailing two sexes, the production by each of a sexual cell (sperm or pollen in the male, egg in the female) that encloses certain particulars of a genetic heritage, and the merger of the two cells to produce the one fertilized egg, containing the genetic particulars of the two together, which develops into a new phenotype by repeated division. But this is not the only mode of recombination.

Let me give an example of recombination in the most rudimentary life that exists today. I mentioned on page 110 that a virus consists of little more than nucleic acids in a protein container. A virus cannot reproduce itself out of its own resources because it has no raw materials or reproductive equipment, no spare nucleotides and amino acids of its own, no ribosomes or ATP molecules to provide the energy required to put them together. Therefore, in order to

reproduce itself it has to inject itself — to inject, at least, the batch of
nucleic acids that constitutes the entire contents of its protein container — into some organic cell that does have what is needed for
reproduction (leaving its container outside). The batch of nucleic
acids then reproduces itself by using the cell's nucleotides, amino
acids, ATP, ribosomes, etc. If two viruses happen to invade the
same cell at the same time, the two batches of nucleic acids get mixed
together, so that many of the progeny proliferating inside the cell
will be the products of recombination.

Another example. When the batch of nucleic acids pours itself
out of its protein container into a bacterial cell it commonly proceeds
to reproduce itself in the form of new viral particles (nucleic acids in
protein containers), using the cell's resources for reproduction, until
the victimized cell bursts and the new viruses spill out to invade
other cells and produce still newer generations inside them. Sometimes, however, the batch of DNA that is poured from its protein
container into a bacterial cell, instead of proceeding immediately
with the production of new viral particles, attaches itself to the bacterial chromosome, thereby becoming continuous with the bacterium's
own DNA. When the bacterium reproduces itself by fission, generation after generation, the viral DNA is reproduced along with the
bacterial DNA.

A time may come, however, when the DNA descended from the
virus becomes virulent, producing viral particles that burst open the
bacterial cell, spill out, and proceed to infect other bacterial cells in
order to reproduce themselves further. When that happens the
viral particles may carry along with them some of the bacterial DNA
from the host they have killed by their proliferation, DNA which
gets deposited in the bacteria that they then proceed to invade. If
they remain latent inside their new bacterial hosts, allowing them to
live, the latter will reproduce a recombined strain of bacteria. So,
through the agency of viruses, recombination is effected between
bacteria.

Bacteria may, however, effect recombination on their own, without the intervention of viruses. In the case of some species it may
happen that two bacteria come into contact with each other, a connection is formed, and a chromosome from one enters the other,
after which the two part.

It may also happen, at least in the laboratory, that DNA molecules
from one strain of bacteria, perhaps released from cells that have
died, seep through the membrane of a bacterium that represents a
slightly different strain, to add themselves on to the DNA already
there, so transforming the genetic heritage of the bacterium that re-

ceives them. Again, genetic change has been brought about by recombination.

A protozoan, *Euplotes,* belonging to an altogether more advanced form of life than the bacteria, effects recombination by a kind of sexual mating. Two individual cells become joined together by a passageway through which a temporary fusion of their respective nuclei is effected. When the two separate again, reproduction has not taken place but recombination has. The nucleus of each now contains genes from both, so that the combined heritage will be transmitted to the new generations which each produces by splitting.

*

Judging only by such scientific evidence as we have, the primary role in the origin of life and its subsequent evolution is played by accident. (This is not to say that either the origin of life or a particular course of evolution was, in itself, an accident that might equally well not have happened. The selection for survival among accidental mutations is based on criteria that predetermine evolution in greater or lesser measure. See Chapter XXI.) Accidental collisions among certain atoms produced molecules, accidental collisions among certain molecules produced macromolecules, and certain macromolecules came into contact with organic molecules that, because of the chemical materials involved, fermented upon such contact, their lost energy going to the macromolecules that had collided with them. At some point, complexes of macromolecules, nourished by the fermentation of organic molecules, began replicating themselves by an accident, or a series of accidents. Accidental mutations in the course of replication gave rise to variety, and once that had happened natural selection among varieties was inevitable.*

Although the process of evolution needed nothing more than the occurrence of mutations to provide new varieties for natural selection to operate on, it would have been a far slower process than it has been if there had been no other means for the production of such varieties.

One can see that the first recombinations, like every other initial event in the origin and evolution of life from chaotic antecedents, must also have been accidental. Some nucleic acid, accidentally escaped from one cell, seeped into another; or two cells, pushed up against each other, merged as a consequence of contact, with the

---

* I say inevitable because, given all the circumstances, natural selection represents an *a priori* and inescapable logic. It is more than just the best explanation we have been able to think of for the evolutionary developments we have observed. In the absence of any observation at all, we would still have been justified in postulating it.

result that a strand of DNA from one became linked to a strand from the other. Such combinations could diversify the genetic content and multiply the variety of organisms faster than mutation alone could do so — leading to the day when there would be organisms like ourselves, each individual with a genotype consisting of hundreds of millions of genes, and no two genotypes quite alike (identical twins excepted). Where recombined varieties were favored by natural selection, recombination itself was thereby favored. And so, over the millions of years, its effectuation became ever more established and ever more elaborate. From an accidental seepage of DNA, this evolution led to the mating behavior of demoiselle cranes and sea lions, based on a complex process of specialization and association at the cellular level. Unlike mutation, which continued to be accidental, recombination came to be programmed. Recombination by sexual conjugation, as manifested in all the higher forms of life today, is an elaborate, precise, ritualistic, and purposeful process.

XVI

The Mortality of the Individual and
the Immortality of Species

IN AN ADVANCED MULTICELLULAR ORGANISM like a pheasant an egg cell, by repeated division, produces a hen pheasant containing egg cells that, by repeated division, produce other hen pheasants containing egg cells that divide to produce still other hen pheasants. (For the sake of simplicity I omit, at this stage, the sperm-containing cock pheasant.) So we may think of reproduction in pheasants as proceeding by the alternation of hen and egg.

For purposes of comparison, the amoeba may be regarded as an egg that reproduces itself directly, without the intermediation of a hen. It divides like an egg cell to produce more amoebas, which divide to produce still more.

There are various ways in which we can interpret these processes of generation, and in what follows I allow myself to be in some measure playful with various possible concepts — such playfulness representing an exercise that has a serious purpose.

*

Might we not generalize Samuel Butler's teasing remark, that the hen is the egg's way of making another egg, by saying that the phenotype is the genotype's way of making another genotype?

The egg, however, is merely the repository of the genotype, not the genotype itself. Neither is the DNA inside the nucleus of the egg the genotype itself. The genotype has no physical existence any more than a poem or a play by Shakespeare has physical existence. It is language, and the DNA is simply the ink in which it is written.

As for the phenotype, it is the physical realization of the genotype as the performance of a play is the physical realization of its script. And just as the play is permanent while each performance is passing, so the genotype has an immortality lacking in the succession of mortal phenotypes.

In the evolution of the past 3,000 million years what has evolved has been the genotype, its evolution having been outwardly manifested in the phenotypes that have succeeded one another generation after generation. The script written in DNA has undergone a continual revision on the basis of successive performances, and that revision has made it ever more complex and voluminous.

When we observe evolution, however, what we see is only the succession of phenotypes, not the changing genotype of which they are the manifestations. We see the incarnations of the Logos, of the Word that was in the beginning, but not the Logos itself. We see the performance, not the script. Therefore we tend to assume that evolution is simply of phenotypes, that inheritance is direct from parent to child. (In the old formulation, it was the blood of the parents that passed to the children, and recombination was the mixing of blood.) If, however, each of us did in fact inherit his genetic characteristics directly from either or both of his parents, how could one explain blue eyes in the child of parents who were both brown-eyed? Or, since they presumably had the same inheritance, how could one explain the common phenomenon of two brothers, one brown-eyed, the other blue-eyed?

I could say that, for advanced multicellular organisms like ourselves (and pheasants) there are two lines of inheritance, the phylogenetic and the ontogenetic. Each must be seen in its own proper perspective. For an ample view of the phylogenetic line, in the case of man or pheasant, one ought to have a perspective that spanned centuries at least, but preferably thousands of centuries. For a complete view of the ontogenetic line, however, years will do, or months, or (in the case of house flies) days.

When we contemplate the phylogenetic line, phenotypes, which live such a short time in any case, are properly regarded as secondary. (The play is primary, the transient performances by which it is tested secondary.) Inheritance is through the gametes (sperm cell or egg cell), and the successive generations of phenotypes may properly be regarded as their containers — equivalent to the virus's protein container. Two gametes combine to produce a fertilized egg cell from which a new generation of gametes arises (together with their containers). The gametes of the new generation repeat the process — and so, generation after generation, the genotype is perpetuated. The mortality of the individual pays for the immortality of the species.

Taking the long phylogenetic perspective, and putting the matter as I have, it seems not implausible that the hen is the egg's way of making another egg.

In the shorter perspective proper to ontogeny, however, the fully developed phenotype is everything, the gamete appearing as an insignificant part of it. Not only is the phenotype longer lived than the gamete, it is immensely bigger and more developed. The gamete is microscopic, on the same scale as the amoeba, and no further developed, while the phenotype is millions of millions of times larger, and much greater in the complexity of its organization as well. In the case of man we have, by contrast with the gamete, a phenotype with a mind, a phenotype that knows sorrow and suffering, a phenotype that comprehends the perspective proper to phylogeny, a phenotype able to take the measure of space that is twenty thousand million light-years across, a phenotype capable of apprehending principles of order in the universe. Surely this is something more than the virus's protein container!

I invoke, here, Niels Bohr's Principle of Complementarity (see Part One, Chapter XI). The table on which I am writing is, in one perspective, solid matter. In another it may be regarded as empty space with atomic particles dashing about in it. The two perspectives are equally valid and mutually complementary. What I have called the phylogenetic perspective and the ontogenetic perspective are also equally valid and mutually complementary. My own opinion is that, in the largest view, life is all of one piece, the distinction between hen and egg is without significance, and the question of which has priority does not arise.

*

In terms of my immediate descent from one fertilized egg cell that divided again and again, the process that produced me was exactly the same process of mitosis (described in Chapter VIII) that produces a colony of amoebas, such as a slime mold, from one ancestral amoeba. Like the ancestral amoeba, the egg cell had, in addition to such other organelles as ribosomes and mitochondria, a nucleus that enclosed the chromosomes that incorporated the DNA that contained my genotype in the form of written information. First the chromosomes duplicated themselves, including their strands of DNA, by splitting throughout their length. The identical chromosome twins thus produced then formed up, respectively, on opposite sides of the cell's equator, one of each pair on what we may call the northern side, the other on the southern. The nuclear membrane by which they had been contained dissolved, the spindle formed, and the two identical sets of chromosomes were drawn away from each other, up into the northern hemisphere and down into the southern respectively. Two new nuclei now formed, one in each hemisphere, to enclose each set. That done, the whole cell split at the equator, becoming two cells. In each of the two, under the direction of its DNA, all the organelles in the original were replicated, making the two complete copies of their common ancestor. The two then divided in the same fashion to make four, the four to make eight — and so on until all the 10^{13} cells that compose me had been engendered, every one of them containing a full complement of chromosomes and associated genes. (Each of the red blood cells, even, had such a complement until, in the course of its development, its nucleus dissolved to make room for hemoglobin.) There was only one exception. Each gamete, for a reason that will become apparent, had only half the full complement.

Although it is not directly relevant to my theme, I should not overlook one distinct difference between the process of descent by division in the amoeba and the process of descent from the egg cell that was my direct ancestor. As that egg cell divided and redivided, the products of its division, cohering rather than separating like amoebas, began increasingly to differentiate, becoming specialized for certain functions within the cohering complex of what was developing as one multicellular organism. The specialized cells of various tissues began to emerge as distinct and to find their respective places in the whole. Bone cells emerged to form bones, and from the marrow of the bones red blood cells were engendered. Muscle cells, with their bundles of fibrils, nerve cells with their axons and dendrites, proliferated and proceeded to combine in complex ways. So the elaborate phenotype that writes these lines was produced, and at a certain stage endowed with gametes out of which the next generation would grow. However, although this process of differentiation, specialization, and association represents an important difference between my ontogenetic descent and an amoeba's descent, a difference in which I rejoice, it is still a secondary difference.

What I have now described is my immediate or ontogenetic descent — the expiring line of descent that we may think of as a branch or a loop, in each generation, on the never expiring main line of phylogenetic descent. How about this phylogenetic line, which goes on forever from the fertilized egg cell of one generation to that of the next by way of the transient phenotype?

Reproduction in the ontogenetic line is basically primitive, involving no recombination. In the phylogenetic line, however, recombination occurs in every generation, and there is no reproduction without it. A diagrammatic representation would have to show, not straight lines radiating again and again, without ever crossing, as in the case of ontogenetic descent or that of the amoeba, but a network with three lines radiating from every knot. Two lines join at a knot to produce a third, which a generation further on makes a knot with a second of its generation to produce a third, which another generation on makes a knot with a second of its generation — and so on, as far as we know, forever.*

At every knot two gametes combine. A sperm cell, with its content of genes (the text of the DNA), combines with and is absorbed into an egg cell with its content of genes, producing a fertilized egg cell that has exactly twice as many genes as were in either gamete. If each of the gametes had had a full complement of genes (comprising two sets of instructions, so to speak), then the fertilized egg cell, and all the cells descended from it by mitosis, would have had twice the number of genes (comprising four sets of instructions) that were proper to them. Therefore, each of the gametes had only half the number of genes (comprising only one set of instructions) that make up a full complement.

Only half of my father's genes (one set of instructions), and only half of my mother's (another set), entered into the egg cell from which I am descended by mitosis. This means that half the genetic inheritance represented in each of my parents did not come to me at all, and this in turn explains why the assumption that two brothers have the same inheritance is false. It is possible in principle, however unlikely in practice, that my brother inherited from our common parents all the genes that I did not inherit, and only those genes, in which case we would have no common heritage and would not be related to each other at all — not even in the degree of distant cousins. No wonder if he should have blue eyes where I have brown.

Each of us inherited two full sets of genes (two sets of instructions), one from each parent, each set embodying all the information needed to make a complete human being. Each separate set had, *inter alia,* certain genes for eye-color. Although eye-color in human beings happens to be polygenic (produced by a combination of genes rather than by one alone), let us suppose that it is the product of one special gene for eye-color alone — thereby simplifying the reality, for the purpose of exemplification, without falsifying it. My father, then, had two genes for eye-color of which I inherited only one, as I inherited only one of my mother's two genes for eye-color; and each of my children has inherited from me only one of my two genes for

---

* Recombination in each generation, whereby an individual's ancestors are twice as many for every generation back, means that the number of the reader's ancestors twenty centuries ago was roughly 2^{80}, a figure that exceeds by many times the number of human beings who have ever lived. But the reader will not need me to explain this paradox.

eye-color, either the one that I myself inherited from my father or the one I inherited from my mother. Although my brother and I had inherited the same gene for eye-color from one of our parents, if we inherited different ones from the other parent the different combination that resulted would suffice to account for the fact that we differed in eye-color.

I have referred to a full set of genes as comprising a full set of instructions, and to a full complement as comprising two full sets of genes (i.e., two sets of instructions). It follows that the division of the genes to provide only half of a full complement (i.e., one set of instructions) for each gamete is not a random division. If the genes of each cell were, like so many pebbles, all in one loose heap which was stirred and then divided into two equal parts, the fertilized egg cell might receive no gene at all for eye-color. Perhaps it would receive too many genes for making teeth and not enough to make a tongue. In fact, however, the genes (or combinations of genes) for every item in the phenotype that requires genetic coding come to it in multiples of two. When the total number of genes is halved to furnish a gamete, one gene (or combination) for each item is contributed to it, the other being withheld. So it is that there are two corresponding sets of genes in each cell, each set coding for a complete phenotype, and one of the two sets is passed on complete to the gamete.

So far from coming in loose or random batches of DNA, the genes are all neatly packaged in chromosomes of various sizes and shapes, some long and some short, some straight and some bent. In a bacterium there is only one chromosome, but in the cells of all sexually reproducing organisms the standard number is necessarily even, since it was produced by the combination of two equal sets and will have to divide again into two equal parts for the production of gametes. So it is that every chromosome has its double, making two sets of chromosomes in every cell (gametes excepted). A human cell has 46 chromosomes, constituted by two sets of 23 each. The two sets are homologous, each chromosome in one having its homologue in the other.

Every human cell with 46 chromosomes has (in our simplified model) two genes for eye-color, which are, respectively, at corresponding points on two homologous chromosomes — and so with all the other genes. When the process of mitosis takes place and the chromosomes divide for the production of new cells, all 46 divide just once, thereby providing two identical sets of 46 each for the two progeny cells of the one progenitor. An additional process of division must take place, however, when the gametes, which are to have only 23 chromosomes apiece, are to be produced. This additional process, which usually takes place before mitosis, is as follows.

(1) Each chromosome comes together with its homologue so that the two lie side-by-side. Each has already prepared for mitosis to the extent that it has already split into two parallel strands, called chromatids (which, in mitosis, will be drawn toward opposite poles of the cell to form, respectively, the two separate sets of chromosomes around which the two progeny cells will be formed by the splitting of the one parent cell). So the chromosomes that lie side-by-side in homologous pairs each consists of two chromatids.

(2) Now a crossing-over or exchange of parts takes place between the two chromosomes of each pair, segments of a chromatid belonging to one changing places with the equivalent segments of a chromatid belonging to the other. When this exchange of parts has taken place, however, the chromosomes, each consisting of two chromatids, are still lying side-by-side in their homologous pairs.

(3) The exchange of parts having been completed, the pairs now separate into two sets of 23, each set containing only one of every type of chromosome instead of the two that had been associated, to begin with, as homologues in the cell's one set. Here, then, are the makings of two cells with only 23 chromosomes apiece. But each chromosome consists of two strands of chromatids, on the basis of which the second division, the mitotic division, takes place, the final product being four cells, each with half the normal complement of chromosomes, 23 instead of 46. These are the gametes, either egg cells or sperm cells. Later, when a sperm, incorporating 23 chromosomes, merges with an egg, also incorporating 23 chromosomes, the product will be the fertilized egg cell, with 46 chromosomes, that proceeds to replicate itself by division and redivision through the process of mitosis.

Note that at stage 2 of the process just described recombination has taken place. Let us suppose that one chromosome of set A, which we shall designate A_x, contains both a gene for blue eyes (in our simplified model) and another for curly hair. Its homologue in set B, B_x, contains a gene for brown eyes and another for straight hair. If this is so, the two traits, being on one chromosome, are linked: hair-form goes with eye-color. In the absence of internal recombination, generation after generation of blue eyes might invariably go with curly hair, brown eyes with straight. Behold, however, what happens by virtue of internal recombination. When chromosomes A and B lie alongside each other and mate, so to speak, exchanging corresponding segments of chromatid, their respective genes for eye-color may exchange places while the genes for

hair-form are not exchanged. The consequence of this partial exchange is that blue eyes are now associated with straight hair, brown
eyes with curly hair. So genetic variety, for natural selection to work
on, has been promoted by a random recombination even before the
second recombination in which the 23 chromosomes of one parent
are combined with the 23 of the other in the fertilized egg cell from
which their progeny is to develop.

Recombination may also be effected by the re-assortment of whole
chromosomes.

*

One key question remains. If the progeny receives genes for brown
eyes from one parent and genes for blue eyes from the other, are we
to expect that its eyes will be a blend of the two colors, which might
make them a rather dark green? This, as we know, is not what happens. Normally, human eyes can be classified as either blue (including gray) or brown, never as a blend of the two. The explanation is
that brown eyes are dominant, blue eyes recessive — which is to say
that, where genes for each color are present, the brown prevails,
suppressing the blue entirely. Only where both sets of genes are for
blue do blue eyes result. The possession of blue eyes means that
both sets of genes were coded for blue; while the possession of
brown eyes means that both may have been coded for brown or that
one was coded for brown and the other for blue.

This explanation, however, only raises a new question, for one
would wish to know the mechanics by which the genes for brown
nullify the genes for blue in determining the eye-color of the phenotype.

Let us take the classic case, that of the breeding experiments by
which Gregor Mendel discovered the basic laws of genetics. He took
two varieties of pea, one that had produced only purple flowers for
generations, the other that had produced only white flowers, and he
crossed them. The first generation of progeny turned out to be all
purple flowered. He then bred these purple flowered peas of the
first generation with each other, the result being that, in the second
generation (the grandchildren), there tended to be one white-
flowered pea for every three that had purple flowers.

We know the explanation in the terms I have already set forth.
Purple was dominant, white recessive. Each of the original purple-
flowered parents, having been bred true for generations, had two
genes for purple, which we may designate p_1/p_2. Each of the white-
flowered parents had two genes for white, w_1/w_2. Consequently, the
crosses of the first generation all had one p and one w; and, since p

was dominant over w, all were purple-flowered. However, when these p/w's were bred among themselves, the result in terms of statistical probabilities was three plants that included at least one p to one with two w's and no p. (The eight possible combinations were p_1/p_2, p_2/p_1, p_1/w_1, p_2/w_1, p_1/w_2, p_2/w_2, w_1/w_2, and w_2/w_1. Thus only two out of the eight would be white-flowered.)

What are the mechanics of dominance in this case?

The gene for purple is coded for the production of an enzyme that catalyzes the synthesis of a purple pigment. One such gene produces enough of the enzyme to synthesize all the pigment needed, so that p/w flowers are as purple as p/p's, and only w/w's are white because, in their case, none of the enzyme is produced at all.

This case is exceptional in its neatness. In the case of other plants the p/w combination might produce flowers of an intermediate pink because one p synthesized enough of the enzyme for a faint purple but not enough for the deep purple produced by the p/p combination. To take another example — when an African black is crossed with a European white, the mulatto children are intermediate in skin-pigmentation, the b/w combination producing less pigmentation than the b/b. The reason why I preferred the example of the peas for the explanation of dominance was that its neatness was not quite matched by the example of eye-color in human beings. Although a person with one combination of genes for brown eyes and one for blue will have brown eyes, they are likely not to be as dark as those of one who has both combinations coded for brown, because the latter is likely to have more brown pigment than the former.

To this one should add that most genetic traits in the phenotype are produced by more or less elaborate combinations of many genes. Variously linked groups of genes may be involved. When one of two brothers is tall and the other short (although both have been brought up in the same environmental conditions, including equal nourishment), it is unlikely that this is the consequence of two alternative genes for stature, one coded for tall and the other for short. What is more likely is that it is the consequence of a combination of genes which produce a variety of enzymes that bear on a variety of factors.

As usual, the basic situation is simple, essentially the same in an amoeba as in a man. What evolution over 3,000 million years has done is to combine the simple elements in ways that are ever more complex.

XVII

The Categories of
an Uncategorical Reality

IN THE LAST CHAPTER I invoked the Principle of Complementarity to justify the equal validity of concepts that seem mutually opposed. It was first applied by Niels Bohr to the apparently opposed concepts of electromagnetic radiation as particles and as waves. Here I apply it to examples of one reality viewed in different perspectives, or to different partial views of one reality, and since I expect to be doing so throughout the remainder of this work I shall pause here, if only briefly, to exemplify and expound it.

Item. In one perspective my writing table is solid matter, in another it is almost empty space. Both perspectives are equally valid.

Item. The water of the chemist is H_2O, a molecule that has none of the wetness or other properties we associate with water under common circumstances; but we and the chemist are both right, water is and is not wet.

Item. Two photographs of one mountain, showing it from the north and the south respectively, appear to represent two different realities, whereas they are equally valid and complementary views of one reality.

Item. Two painters set up their easels side by side to paint the same landscape. One is interested in its fine detail, which he depicts precisely, showing the individual leaves on the trees and the blades of grass. He conceives of himself as representing on canvas what he knows to be really there. The other, who uses a broad brush, conceives of himself as representing only what he sees, which is light reflected from masses of foliage, or from fields of grass, in which details blend and are lost. Although their two paintings seem to represent different realities, both may be equally true to the one reality.

Item. General de Gaulle regarded France as an idea which great men had occasionally embodied. A sociologist regards France as a complex of social relationships among various groups. It is both.

Item. The open ocean does not seem flat to the swimmer, and the waves that tower over him seem immense, while from the airplane passing high overhead the waves appear as wrinkles on a flat surface. The ocean is and is not flat, depending on one's perspective.

Item. English and Americans seem quite different to an observer whose view does not extend beyond the two nations, but in a global view that includes Hottentots and Eskimos they seem alike. The apparent contradiction is not between true and false: English and Americans are and are not alike.

Different perspectives are equally valid in the sense that none are false. They may differ, however, in their value where the objective is understanding. The swimmer's view of the sea entails a more intimate experience of it than the view from the airplane, but the latter offers a more comprehensive understanding; just as my view of the earth offers a more comprehensive understanding than the earthworm's. One would wish to know the sea and the earth in terms of both perspectives; but the comprehensive understanding, which does not exclude intimate knowledge, represents the greater achievement. We humans are, after all, earthworms who have learned to fly.

One may think of a watch as an assemblage of bits and pieces, or one may regard it as a whole within which the bits and pieces have lost their separate identities. (One may think of a cell as a whole within which the organelles, the molecules, the atoms, and the atomic particles have lost their separate identities.) Darwin was inspired by a vision of evolution in which life was essentially one, and it was to confirm and support this vision that he studied such matters as the structure of orchids and the habits of earthworms. Another biologist, trained exclusively for analytical research, would be apt to regard the bits and pieces of biological reality as primary, and to persuade himself that only the inductive approach, from the little to the large, was properly scientific.

At the end of Chapter XIII I quoted D'Arcy Thompson's statement of the holistic as opposed to the analytical approach. Let me here quote Theodosius Dobzhansky in the same sense.

> Contrary to the views of early geneticists, the organism is not an aggregate of "unit" traits or characters or qualities. Traits, characters, and qualities are not biological units; they are abstractions, words, semantic devices that a student needs in order to describe and communicate the results of his observations. A trait has no adaptive significance in isolation from the whole developmental pattern that an organism exhibits at a certain stage of its life cycle. . . .*

*

* *Genetics of the Evolutionary Process*, New York/London, 1970, p. 64.

In terms of what has always been the normal perspective for us humans, the concept that every living being belongs to one or another of distinct species has been virtually self-evident. This normal perspective depends, however, on confinement to the limited temporal scale on which one measures lifetimes, and to the spatial limits of the immediate country one inhabits. For example, anyone who passed his life in eighteenth-century England, like the author of *The Natural History of Selborne*, Gilbert White, could see for himself that every bird, every beast, and every plant belonged to a distinct and readily identifiable species. The jackdaws would constitute one such species, the cuckoos another, the hedgehogs another. Every orchid he saw, and every oak, clearly had its own species to which it belonged.

An observer thus limited in time and space would, in addition, be confirmed by traditional authority. White, who was a churchman, presumably did not doubt the passage in Genesis which reports that "God made the beast of the earth after his kind, and cattle after their kind, and every thing that creepeth upon the earth after his kind"; that he made in like fashion the fish of the sea, and the fowl of the air, and "every plant of the field before it was in the earth, and every herb of the field before it grew." And when Adam, at the behest of the Lord, gave names to all cattle and to the fowl of the air, and to every beast of the field, it would have been clear that what he gave them was the names of their respective kinds, their species names.

If White, himself, had been entrusted by the Lord with the naming of the species that he knew in the time and place to which he was confined he would hardly have had any difficulty in distinguishing them. He could not, for example, have doubted that the herring gull was one species, the lesser black-backed gull another. He would have noticed that the former had a light gray mantle (the upper surfaces of the wings connected across the back) and pink feet, while the latter had an almost black mantle and yellow feet. Within the limits to which his vision extended there would have been no intermediate specimens to obscure the distinction, and he might have concluded from the fact that there was no interbreeding between the two kinds that they themselves recognized their separateness.

Suppose, however, that his geographical horizons had been enlarged to span the area from the Arctic Circle to the Tropic of Capricorn and from England to Russia. He would have found that, as he traveled southward or eastward, he came across specimens that he could not readily assign to one or the other species. In the Mediterranean he would have discovered that what he had taken for herring gulls at first, because they had light gray mantles, had yellow feet instead of pink. (At that point he might have pondered whether the Lord would expect him to name two species of herring gull, one pink-footed and the other yellow-footed, or two species of lesser black-backed gull, one black-mantled and one gray-mantled.) Proceeding farther south or east he would have found that the mantles of the yellow-footed herring gulls, as he might have decided to call them, gradually became darker, until at last he was compelled to recognize that the birds were closer to what, if he had been back home, he would have called lesser black-backed gulls. (At that point he might have pondered whether the Lord would expect him to name only one species, the lesser black-backed herring gull, its mantle varying from black to light gray, its feet either pink or yellow — a species, moreover, the various forms of which had been found to interbreed at certain places.)

If Gilbert White, visiting Massachusetts, had seen there a bunting called the song sparrow, and if he had then sailed around the Horn to California, he would have found in California a similar bunting that he might well have set down as a distinct species. But if he had crossed the continent directly he would have found a continuous gradation of intermediate forms between the two — and how, in that case, could he have made the distinction?

I shall not multiply examples. The fact is that the concept of species, which mankind has accepted as self-evident from the beginning, no longer seems self-evident and, indeed, tends to break down completely as we enlarge our spatial horizons.

As long as Gilbert White remained in England and confined to the present he would have had no trouble in distinguishing the herring gull and the lesser black-backed gull as two distinct species. Suppose, however, that, although remaining in England, he had had English specimens to examine from every century going back over tens of millennia. He would have found that, as he traced them back in time, the difference between the two became less, until it disappeared entirely in what, despite Genesis, he had to recognize as a common ancestor. (If he thought that what the Lord had created was the common ancestor he had only to continue backward in time, perhaps until he came to a prokaryotic cell that was his own ancestor as well as that of all other life on earth, gulls included.)

If, then, he could break immemorial habits of thought, he would have recognized that the concept of species is, in the largest view, no more than an invention of heuristic convenience for marking off segments on a continuum as one marks off degrees centigrade on a thermometer.

A century later Darwin, having traveled widely in time and space, wrote in a book which he nevertheless entitled *The Origin of Species:*

> I look at the term species as one arbitrarily given, for the sake of convenience, to a set of individuals closely resembling each other, and . . . it does not essentially differ from the term variety, which is given to less distinct and more fluctuating forms. The term variety, again, in comparison with more individual differences, is also applied arbitrarily, for convenience' sake.*

To paraphrase Dobzhansky: Species are not biological units; they are abstractions, words, semantic devices that a student needs in order to describe and communicate the results of his observations.

Even at the birth of the modern theory of evolution by natural selection, the father of that theory found himself embarrassed by the traditional concept of species as the fundamental categories of life, separate and distinct from each other. This concept still prevails today, and indeed is indispensable, but it is valid in the limited traditional perspective only. (It is valid as the concept of overwhelming waves is valid to the swimmer although not to the observer in the airplane.) When I do what Gilbert White did, observe the present-day behavior of birds and mammals where I live, there can be no question of my not thinking in terms of species. The behavior I observe so close up is not the behavior of some abstraction called "life on earth" or "bird-life" but of, say, the willow tit, a species that in this limited perspective is quite separate and distinct.†

It was Darwin's generation that first developed the larger perspective by adopting the higher standpoint from which one could view the whole globe and its history. In this larger perspective, which was in addition to the smaller rather than in replacement of it, species disappeared altogether as fundamental categories. Darwin, even as he named his book *The Origin of Species,* saw this and was troubled by it.

Students of evolution and genetics have been troubled by it ever since. Consequently, there has been a developing tendency on their part to think in terms of populations rather than species, a popula-

---

* 6th ed., New York/London, 1915, p. 51.
† I should qualify this by saying that, even in this limited perspective, the concept of species becomes difficult or impossible of application in certain cases. This is especially true of the plant kingdom. There is no difficulty in applying the concept to song thrushes or mistle thrushes, but it is virtually inapplicable to some of the asters of North America and some of the gentians of Europe.

tion being defined as an aggregate of interbreeding individuals. When we think in terms of populations the difficulties posed by the concept of species, when viewed in the large perspective, disappear. It no longer makes any difference whether the willow tit of Europe and the black-capped chickadee of North America are one species or not. They constitute two separate populations of interbreeding individuals, and the question whether the European individuals would interbreed freely with the American individuals if geography allowed becomes academic. What counts is that, whatever the reason, they do not interbreed, and because they do not interbreed they constitute two separate and distinct lines of descent.

It may be that the song sparrows of Massachusetts and those of California are so different that, even if geography allowed, they would not interbreed. But the question whether they would or would not is academic in view of the fact that they belong to one population of interbreeding individuals, so that they could exchange genes across the continent by way of the intermediate forms. The Massachusetts and California birds do interbreed, although only indirectly. If the intermediate forms died out there would be no more such interbreeding, and then there would *ipso facto* be two populations where there had been only one.

The concept of distinct breeding populations is made meaningful by the associated concept of gene pools. The gene pool is to the population what the genotype is to the phenotype. All the genes in the pool are accessible to the entire population, which in this sense makes it a common pool from which they all derive what is basically a common heritage. The common heritage is what evolution works on.

As always, however, one must qualify in applying categorical concepts to an uncategorical reality. Populations, too, may be uncertain of definition, as where there is limited interbreeding, perhaps only occasional, between what one would otherwise regard categorically as two populations. The metaphor of the uniform gene pool with fixed shores is also too simple and categorical. The dark song sparrow of the wooded New England countryside does, after all, have a different genotype from that of the pale song sparrow found in Southwestern deserts.* This is not because the genes which provide for the relatively heavy pigmentation of the New England birds are not available through intermediate varieties to the Southwestern birds, but because such pigmentation constitutes a disadvantage against the desert background (making the birds too conspicuous to

---

* It is also true that every individual song sparrow has a somewhat different genotype from that of every other individual (identical twins excepted).

predators), so that this genetic trait, even if inherited by one or some of the Southwestern birds, would be unlikely to spread or even survive among them. The song sparrows constitute one population, which varies in a continuous gradation from east to west. This phenotypic variation, however, is only the outward and visible manifestation of a genotypic variation. The gradual variation in the population from east to west represents a gradual variation in the gene pool.

A case like this reveals a situation more complex and subtle than is implied by the metaphor of the pool. So we are ever driven toward the conclusion that no category will match reality except that of life as a whole. But even this will not match it, for we must doubt whether there is a sharp division between life and non-life. In the largest view, I daresay, all being is the only category that holds.

The concept of the population or the gene pool, like that of species, is an abstraction, a nominal device that a student needs in order to describe and communicate the results of his observations. As such, however, it is more serviceable in the larger perspective than the concept of species, which is, however, more serviceable in the close-up perspective.

*

Must we not say of our other traditional categories what we have said of species, that they are artificial devices of convenience which can be applied only in terms of a view that is partial rather than whole?

For countless generations we have been brought up to believe that all life is divided into two kingdoms, plant and animal respectively. As long as we took account of the visible world only, this was a matter of common sense because self-evident. On a day in 1674, however, Anthony van Leeuwenhoek, peering through a homemade microscope, became the first man to see the bacteria and the protozoa that represented a hitherto unsuspected realm of life.*

When we found ourselves having to take account of the teeming life in this subliminal realm, it was natural that we should undertake to assign its respective forms to one or the other of the two kingdoms into which, we still believed, all life was divided. The attempt to do so, however, encountered frustrating difficulties, for the dis-

* Although this day marked one of the notable stages in the expansion of human knowledge, Leeuwenhoek's discovery went unregarded for over a century. Perhaps the people of the time found it hard to take seriously the existence of life on such a scale, not being able to relate it in their minds to the life that the Lord had created during the seven days chronicled in Genesis. It violated the common sense of the times as the very small in the realm of physics violates our own common sense.

tinction between plant and animal turned out not to be consistently obvious in this Lilliputian world. The microscopic flagellates, for example, propel themselves through water by the action of their flagella. Since such mobility is a defining characteristic of animals in the visible world, distinguishing them from plants, one would on that account assign them to the animal kingdom. But some live by photosynthesis, like any herb, and this has always been a defining characteristic of plants, distinguishing them from animals. Situations like this must at last bring one to the conclusion that the concept of the two kingdoms, so applicable in the narrower perspective, is not applicable in a perspective that embraces the whole.

Shall we, then, have three kingdoms, adding to the traditional two a third called the kingdom of the protists (from the Greek for "the very first")? This solution has widespread acceptance today, but entails the embarrassment of lumping together in one kingdom organisms as different as paramecia, mushrooms, and seaweeds that are over thirty meters long.

Another solution has been to add two more kingdoms, rather than just one: the kingdom of the lower protists, confined to the organisms with prokaryotic cells (i.e., bacteria and blue-green algae), and the kingdom of the higher protists, including all the other algae, the fungi, and the protozoa. Or the fungi may be given a kingdom to themselves, making three additional kingdoms for a total of five. These attempted solutions, however, still leave paramecia and seaweeds sharing a common kingdom, while separating blue-green algae from green algae as roses are separated from dormice. What these failures signify is that, by enlarging our view, we have come up against the fact that life as a whole, seen in its entirety, is not divided into kingdoms any more than it is divided into species.

We need not here put the other categories into which we have customarily divided living organisms, those intermediate between kingdom and species, to the same proof. Applied to life as a whole they have no more natural validity than any filing system.*

All I am saying here is that life in its totality, including its extension in time, is one. It is one by what appears to be the common descent of all its forms. In schematic terms we may put it that the tree

---

* Even the smallest category, that of the individual, is often arbitrary or equivocal. One could write a volume on this, but I shall offer only one example, that of any ground-covering plant, like the English ivy (*Hedera helix*), the branching stems of which run in all directions, putting down roots at intervals, until an acre or more of ground is covered by it. Is it all one individual? If we say it is, and if I then cut through the stems between the points of rooting, a procedure that will cause no death, have I thereby transformed one individual into a multitude — and, if I have, in what does their individuality consist, or what is its significance? We humans are too

of life is all one tree. But to say this is not to say that it does not have distinct branches. As one ascends the tree from the beginning (3,500 million years ago) one finds that at some stage it has produced two great branches, one vegetable and the other animal. These two, once they have sprung from the basal trunk, represent the principal lines of evolutionary development. But they are still not the whole tree, not even in our own day, for there remain all the forms of microscopic life, and other primitive forms such as seaweeds and fungi, numerically far exceeding the highly developed plants and animals; and this more primitive life is a major element in today's biosphere. The two branches are real. The vegetable kingdom and the animal kingdom are real as the species mistle thrush and the species song thrush are real.

Simply as a matter of convenience, any filing system or other system of classification that embraces a wide diversity needs to be hierarchical, its categories broken down into successively lesser categories. This, however, is not only a matter of convenience in classifying the multitudinous forms of life. Because, for the most part, the process of evolution itself has been one of branching and rebranching, any system of classification must be hierarchical in order to reflect the reality. The branches on the tree of life are real, and the principal ones are self-evident, so that it would be patently absurd to associate an orchid with an oyster in one group, a lily with an elephant in another, and an aphid with an albatross in a third.

Because the major divisions among the advanced organisms of the visible world are self-evident, a system of classification which developed in the days when the authority for the origin of species was Genesis has proved serviceable, still, since the authority of Darwinism took its place. Although widening geographical horizons may reduce or eliminate the categorical distinction between the herring gull and the lesser black-backed, they do not affect the much greater distinction between birds and mammals, or between mammals and fish. These branchings of the animal branch of the tree of life took place so long ago that the separations between them in our present are wide and unmistakable. One would have to go back tens or hundreds of millions of years before one found intermediate forms that filled in or obscured these separations — that is to say, before the branches came close to their mutual joining.

For a reason that I surmise to be clear and simple, but that eludes me, the classification of the vegetable kingdom, at all levels, presents

ready to attribute to all other species the individuality of which we are so poignantly aware in ourselves.

far greater difficulties than that of the animal. Consequently, it has never been possible to establish a system of classification for it that has the general acceptance given to the system for the classification of animal life. The animal kingdom, according to this system, is divided into phyla (e.g., chordates), which are divided into subphyla (e.g., vertebrates), which are divided into classes (e.g., birds), which are divided into orders (e.g., Charadriiformes), which are divided into families (e.g., Laridae), which are divided into genera (e.g., *Larus*), which are divided into species (e.g., *argentatus*), which are divided into subspecies or races or varieties (e.g., *smithsonianus*). The race of the herring gull that occurs in eastern North America is *smithsonianus*, its species *argentatus*, its genus *Larus*. While one calls it "the herring gull" in the vernacular, in scientific nomenclature one identifies it by genus, species, and subspecies as "*Larus argentatus smithsonianus*." (The English race of the lesser black-backed gull is *Larus fuscus graellsii*.) It belongs to the family Laridae of the order Charadriiformes of the class Aves of the subphylum Vertebrata of the phylum Chordata of the animal kingdom. (The author of these lines, scientifically unidentified as to subspecies or race, belongs to the species *sapiens* of the genus *Homo* of the class Mammalia of the subphylum Vertebrata, etc.)

This provides an excellent filing system and, more than that, within the limits of what we know or surmise about the lines of descent, it suggests what the phylogenetic relationships are.

As yet we have no more than a partial view of being. We are able to explore it only as a flea explores an elephant, in terms of a perspective that shows separate parts rather than the whole. Because language is categorical, as reality is not, even if we could see the whole we would still be able to describe it in words only by the application of nominal categories that would not fit its uncategorical reality. As it is, however, we still see clearly only some parts, and it is upon them that our categories are imposed in much of what follows.

XVIII

Our Most Primitive
Contemporaries

ONE REASON why we tend still to divide all living nature between a
plant kingdom and an animal kingdom is that, by old custom, all
students of living nature tend to be divided between the disciplines
of botany and zoology. Two separate systems of authority require
two separate kingdoms. This has led to a somewhat arbitrary division of jurisdiction in what might otherwise be disputed territory.
So it is that, by common agreement, the algae and fungi have been
given to the botanists, the protozoa to the zoologists. The agreement is not perfect, because both are disposed to claim the flagellates that are grouped together as the euglenophytes, but by and
large it is a practical agreement that works. What we should understand, however, is that it is not much more than this, as botanists and
zoologists alike recognize. It is an arrangement of convenience. Let
me, by way of illustration, quote a botanist, Theodore Delevoryas, on
the place of what are called the fungi in the scheme of things:

> There seems little doubt that at least some of the fungi either
> had algal ancestors or evolved from the same kind of ancestors
> as did some algae. On the other hand, there is good evidence
> that not all fungi had the same ancestry and that at least some
> had origins among protozoans. As with the algae, it is probably
> erroneous to refer to the "fungi" as a group of naturally related
> plants. It would be better to regard them as plants or plantlike
> organisms grouped together only because of certain superfi-
> cially similar features.*

The ancestry of our own kind goes back more than 3,000 million
years to the first life on earth; but so does the ancestry of any bacterium. The difference is that our line has gone further in the same
length of time. We therefore do better to judge what life on earth

* *Plant Diversification*, New York/London, 1966, p. 33.

was 3,000 million years ago by the bacterium than by the mammal. This is the basis for saying that the bacterium represents primitive life.*

In the rest of this chapter I mean simply to sample the primitive life of our own day for what it suggests about the early stages of evolution.

*

A virus is a particle of what I shall call living matter that may be smaller than one millionth of a centimeter across. Since the shortest wavelength of visible light is still about a hundred times as long as this, light simply goes past it without being reflected, so that the virus could not be seen even in the most powerful optical microscope one could imagine. Yet it reproduces itself on the basis of a genotype that is subject to mutation, and sometimes does so (as we saw in Chapter XV) by recombination.

Each kind of virus, in order to reproduce, must become attached in a certain way to a particular point on whatever species of cell its kind parasitizes. By means of an enzyme, it then dissolves the cell wall at the point of attachment, making a hole through which its DNA flows into the cell, leaving its protein container outside.

Here we have what most of us would call life, but devoid of many attributes we expect life to have. A virus has no organs or organelles in the familiar sense of either term. One can hardly say that it divides to reproduce itself. It has no built-in source of stored energy, such as ATP molecules. It has no metabolism, for it does not breathe, feed, or excrete. The whole virus in its protein container is simply a quantity of chemical substances like a test-tube full of water, although on an infinitesimal scale and moved by a dynamism of self-replication that seems magical because we do not really know what drives it. Like the water-filled test-tube, it is altogether insensible. Although it reproduces itself, it can feel no urge to do so any more than a growing snowflake can feel an urge to grow.

Most biologists identify the viral particles as living beings, but by tacit agreement do not include them in any of the categories they have devised for the classification of life. Viruses belong to no kingdom, are not named by genus and species, and on the diagrammatic tree of life are not to be found at all. Where, after all, would one put them? One can hardly imagine how they came into being. Were they cells that lost their cellular attributes in consequence of

* The oldest fossils so far discovered are of bacteria and other prokaryotes, some resembling the blue-green algae of our present, that lived well over 3,000 million years ago. See E. S. Barghoorn, "The Oldest Fossils," *Scientific American*, May 1971.

the parasitic dependence into which they fell? Are they fallen angels?

Except for viruses one would say, or in spite of viruses one does say, that all life is cellular; and if one is ordering it in a system of classification, from most primitive to most developed, one must begin with the most primitive single cells, the prokaryotic cells, disregarding the viruses. This means that one must begin with bacteria and blue-green algae, for the cells of virtually all other organisms are eukaryotic.

The smallest bacterium has about forty times the width and eighty times the length of a small virus, which makes it just large enough to be seen through a powerful optical microscope. The smallest blue-green alga has about four times the width and the length of the smallest bacterium, which makes it equal to a middle-sized bacterium or to the mitochondrium of a eukaryotic cell.

These prokaryotic organisms are highly developed and elaborate by comparison with viruses. As W. R. Sistrom has pointed out, however, "almost the only thing a bacterium does is to make another bacterium. It does not make cells of different sorts, nor does it do much mechanical work, make seeds and flowers, or walk and talk." * The gap in degree of development between the virus and the bacterium is matched by the gap between the bacterium and the reader.

The nuclei of bacteria are not separated by membranes from the cells in which they occur, and each consists of just one macromolecule of DNA. A bacterial cell contains no mitochondria, if only because, being about the same size as a mitochondrium, it would not have room for one. The whole cell appears to perform the function of the mitochondrium in charging ATP molecules, as if it were itself a mitochondrium — and indeed, as we saw in Chapter VII, the mitochondria of the much larger eukaryotic cells presumably originated as bacteria that entered into symbiotic association with the other contents of such cells. May we not say flatly that a bacterium is, in fact, a mitochondrium, whatever else it may also be?

Bacteria that engage in photosynthesis have no chloroplasts, the photosynthetic function being carried out more or less over the cell at large. Again, the chloroplasts of eukaryotic cells presumably originated as bacteria, or as algae, that entered into symbiotic association with them. May we not say that the original chloroplast was a photosynthetic bacterium or a blue-green alga?

Unlike viruses but like ourselves, bacteria engage in the life-processes subsumed under the heading of metabolism. Some ferment organic matter; most extract energy from organic matter by

* *Microbial Life,* New York/London, 1969, p. 18.

respiration; some utilize the energy of sunlight to convert inorganic into organic matter. Bacteria are the prime agents in the rotting or decay (i.e., the chemical breakdown) of living matter that has died, thereby restoring to the atmosphere in the form of carbon dioxide the carbon that had been locked into it. Partly, however, in consequence of their smallness, which entails such a large proportion of surface to volume, they absorb their nourishment through the membranes that enclose them, without any need for the equivalent of a mouth.

Although many bacteria have flagella by means of which they swim about actively, their flagella do not have the internal structure of the flagella in eukaryotic cells (including human sperm). Since a bacterium has nothing equivalent to muscles, nothing equivalent to nerves for the transmission of commands, and nothing equivalent to a brain as a directing center that sends out commands, no one knows by what mechanism the flagella operate. Certainly a bacterium does not move by decision and volition any more than a falling snowflake does. (Apparatus for decision-making requires more room than a bacterium affords.) It must be as insensible as a snowflake, being equally devoid of sensory organs. It responds to heat and cold, but only as a snowflake does, without feeling them. Even if there were not such a difference of size between us, we would find that we could not enter into communication with a bacterium as a fellow member of the community we call life.

On the other hand, the bacterial cell is like the cells of our own bodies in the sense that proteins are manufactured on the organelles called ribosomes, of which there may be some ten thousand per cell, through the agency of messenger RNA (which conveys the genetic code from the nucleic DNA) and transfer RNA (which assembles the amino acids). Moreover, it reproduces, just as a human cell does, by mitotic division. So we are all one life after all.

*

Among the most primitive eukaryotic organisms are the unicellular algae, which live by photosynthesis and commonly have flagella by which they propel themselves. Some have what is called an "eyespot," sensitive to light. Although such sensitivity cannot be that of a nervous system, it foreshadows the eye of the goshawk.

Chlamydomonas is a genus of unicellular green algae that occasionally reproduces itself by sexual means as an alternative to simple mitotic division. In such a case, the two progeny cells resulting from a simple division function as gametes. They constitute two mating types (the equivalent of male and female), each fusing with another of complementary mating type to form what is the equivalent of a fertilized egg cell, from which new generations are then produced. The reproductive procedures of orchids in the present must have evolved from some such procedure in the past.

In some algae the proliferating cells resulting from division remain attached to one another, forming long filaments. In some the filaments branch, prefiguring the heather and the oak. The cells of what is called sea lettuce, algae of the genus *Ulva,* form a sinuous frond two cells thick. The group of so-called brown algae include the seaweeds, kelps, and sargassum weed, some growing for over thirty meters along the floors of shallow waters.

I have already mentioned in these pages the microscopic unicellular algae called diatoms. Each encased in a glassy wall of silica, they are in their myriads like snow crystals of varied, elaborate, and symmetrical shapes. Other algae are encased in walls of cellulose that, in their rigidity, prefigure the cellular walls of all the advanced plants, enabling great trees to stand erect without the internal skeletons they would need if their cells were as flesh. Together with the flagellated algae, the diatoms constitute the principal element in the pastures of the sea that, directly or indirectly, support all its life; for the wide expanses of the deep sea bear no multicellular vegetation. They compose the marine equivalent of grasslands on which small animals — such crustaceans as the krill — graze, to be grazed upon in turn by fish, by seals, by penguins, by dolphins, and by the great whales with slatted mouths.

Other algae form scums on still pools, or in the rain forests and cloud forests coat the dripping boles with green.

*

The term "fungus" lumps together, if only for convenience, a variety of organisms which include those microscopic kinds that produce mildew on books left in damp cellars, yeast, mushrooms, and the bracket fungi attached to forest trees. Lacking chlorophyll, they cannot manufacture their own organic nourishment, and they also lack the attributes that enable animals to go in search of the organisms on which they graze or prey. Some are saprophytic — which is to say that they live on organic material in solution or, like many bacteria, live on organic material that has died, promoting its chemical decomposition. For the rest, however, they live in dependence on other living organisms, by parasitism or symbiosis.

*

The protozoa are one-celled organisms, widely varied, that traditional thinking has assigned to the animal kingdom. Indeed, the functioning and behavior of many species represent animal function and behavior in rudimentary form. Thus one may, without being excessively fanciful, regard the common amoeba found in pond water, *Amoeba proteus,* as a predatory hunter. It moves about freely over a surface. It responds to external stimuli, perhaps being repelled by some inert object but being attracted by such prey as a bacterium, which it will proceed to catch. It reacts to light. This is to suggest that it has something in its composition that does for the nervous system in higher animals. (Whatever this is, it is hardly a rudimentary nervous system, although it may have some properties of such a system; and some predatory plants, like the Venus's flytrap, although they cannot go a-hunting like the amoeba, have similar reactions to external stimuli.) Perhaps one could even say, on the basis of the amoeba's capacity for being attracted or repelled, that we have here in its most rudimentary form the capacity of higher animals for likes and dislikes.

The amoeba progresses by extending itself at any point along its surface, and then flowing into the extension. When *Amoeba proteus,* which is about a quarter of a millimeter across, encounters a bacterium (which might be three hundredths of a millimeter long), it produces two extensions like arms that embrace and engulf it for digestion. The amoeba also forms bubbles in its interior which, when filled with water, move to the surface and discharge it. What all this represents is the basic series of animal functions — hunting, capturing, eating, excreting — without any specialized organs for the purpose. The amoeba has no legs or flagella, but can extend its body at any point for locomotion. It has no jaws for capturing prey, but can form them anywhere on its surface. It has no stomach for digestion, but performs the function anywhere in its interior. It has no outlet for excretion, but can excrete from any point on its surface. And all these functions without organs, including nervous functions, are performed within the limits of one cell.

In Chapter X we saw how the amoebas of one species are attracted to one another, in consequence of which they form elaborately functioning societies called slime molds. It is not too much to say, then, that in amoebas we see the rudiments of human life.

Another protozoan, the paramecium, may be regarded as representing the highest development of the unicellular life that the amoeba represents in a more primitive form. Unlike the amoeba, it is confined by a firm casing that prevents it from changing its shape. It has cilia all over its surface that operate in synchronous waves to propel it as if they were oars, their movements being coordinated by filaments that connect them at their bases and that correspond to a network of nerves. It has a mouth lined with cilia that sweep its prey — bacteria, algae, or other protozoa — into a gullet, and on to what corresponds to a stomach for digestion. Undigested food is excreted through an anal opening.

While paramecia reproduce by simple binary fission, like amoebas, two individuals sometimes come together and mate, combining their respective genotypes.

The paramecium, then, represents about as far as a single cell can go in the development of specialized organs for special functions. The next step in development must be that of multicellular animal life, a development that leads to the mole and the eagle, the mouse, the mountain goat, and the man.

XIX

Mutual Evolution

IN ONE VIEW, evolution is the process by which particular forms of life become increasingly well adapted to their environmental circumstances. Since the circumstances are those of a crowded biosphere, they include all the other forms of life by which any particular form is surrounded. So the various forms interact, evolving in relation to one another.

The most obvious kind of interaction is competition. The falcons that live off of the pigeons they are able to catch, and the pigeons that survive only by escaping capture, alike tend to develop greater speed in the course of an evolution that is therefore mutual. Such interaction is generally beneficial, simply by the test of survival, to both parties. The speed of the pigeons tends to eliminate the weaker falcons, which cannot catch them, leaving only the stronger to perpetuate the species. Reciprocally, by capturing chiefly the weaker pigeons the falcons preserve the genetic strength of the stock on which they prey, as well as eliminating diseased individuals before they infect the others.

In the mutual evolution of two apparently opposed species, an equilibrium on which both depend may develop. If the everglade kite, which lives exclusively on snails of the genus *Pomacea*, should become so effective in its predation that it exterminated the snails, it might thereby bring about its own extinction by destroying its food supply. If the snails should become so effective in escaping capture that they proliferated out of control, the result might be a destruction of their own food supply that threatened their own extinction.

The two examples I have given so far are of interacting species that are overtly in conflict. In the interaction of individuals, which is the only visible interaction, if one wins the other loses, and it is only on the phylogenetic time-scale that both species benefit. Quite a different kind of relationship is represented by the association between the yellow-billed oxpecker of Africa and the rhinoceros. The oxpecker, by feeding on the ticks that attach themselves to the hide of the rhinoceros in order to suck its blood, benefits the rhinoceros as well as itself. The feet and tail of the bird, together with other parts, have become adapted in the course of evolution to exploring the hide of the mammal. Although it may be that the mammal in its evolution has acquired some degree of dependence on the bird, as well as a tolerant behavior toward it, in this case we must suppose that the adaptive evolution is more in the bird than in the mammal.

Certain ants raise and care for aphids that, in return, secrete a substance on which they feed. Many flowering plants produce nectar to attract and feed the flying insects that fertilize them in return. All such cases are the products of mutual evolution by which two species become increasingly well adapted to each other.

Every lichen is a mutual association between a fungus and a blue-green alga. The fungus lives on nourishment that the alga produces by photosynthesis, and may, in return, provide favorable growing conditions for the alga. Here the physical association is so intimate that the two appear to constitute one organism. Such intimacy, like that of the ants and the aphids, can only be the product of mutual evolution over a long time.

This process of mutual evolution is also illustrated by leguminous plants and the nitrogen-fixing bacteria that, living inside their roots, are transmitted to successive generations through their seeds. The plants harbor the bacteria which provide them with the nitrogen they need.

Orchids are able to produce an enormous number of seeds (as many as 3 million per plant) because the seeds are so small. Because the seeds are so small, however, they lack room for the storage of the food on which the embryo depends in the early stages of its growth. The consequent lack of a proper food supply may be what makes necessary the presence of certain enzymes that can be supplied only by a fungus which lives in the roots of the orchid and infects the surface on which it grows. If an orchid seed lands on a surface devoid of the fungus it does not germinate properly. This association between orchid and fungus, each depending on the other, must also be the product of mutual evolution.

I offer these examples simply to suggest the variety of associations among utterly disparate species that have been produced by evolution. Our vocabulary provides a limited number of terms to denote the kinds of association, but the kinds are not as distinct or as categorical as the terms imply. Where one animal species lives off another, but is neither physically bound to it nor exclusively dependent on it, as in the case of the falcon and the pigeon, the relationship is simply that of predator and prey. Where the two are in constant physical contact, and the dependence of the one on the other is total, as in the case of the tapeworm that inhabits the intestine of the vertebrate from which it takes food, we call the relationship parasitic. For the case of the tick that lives on the rhinoceros, which in some ways is intermediate between the two cases just cited, we have no special word. Where one species depends on the provision made by another, as the house sparrow depends on the environment created by man, we call the relationship commensal — which is to say that, in metaphoric terms, the dependent species obtains its food at the dining-table of its host, like one who gathers leftovers from a feast. For a loose relationship of mutual service — as in the case of the ox-pecker and the rhinoceros, or that of the nectar-producing lily and the butterfly that fertilizes it — we again have no term. But if the relationship is physically intimate and indissoluble, and the mutual dependence total — as in the case of the bacterium that, living in the roots of the alfalfa plant, provides it with nitrogen — we call it symbiotic.

There are gradations here, including gradations of intimacy. Because the intimacy is generally a product of evolution, the greater intimacy may imply a longer or more complete course of evolution. In the case of the mutually beneficial association that we call symbiosis, two distinct species may evolve reciprocally so as to fit each other ever more closely until, perhaps, they end by becoming one. Because this may not be the least significant kind of association, either for the past or for the future evolution of life, I shall concentrate upon it in the remainder of this chapter.

*

In Chapter VII I referred to the distinction between the primitive prokaryotic cells, represented in today's world by the bacteria and the blue-green algae, and the much larger, more developed, and more elaborate eukaryotic cells with their variety of organelles. The whole of a bacterial cell functions as if it were a mitochondrium, producing ATP molecules for the supply of the energy it requires, and since it averages about the size of the mitochondria in eukaryotic cells it is logical to surmise that these latter, which have their own DNA for their own reproduction, are basically bacteria that by symbiotic association came to live within the eukaryotic cells, for which they now provide packaged energy — just as the protozoa that live in the intestines of termites provide what the termites need in order to digest the food on which they live, just as the bacteria that live in the alfalfa roots provide the nitrogen that the alfalfa plant needs.

In the same way, the cells of blue-green algae may be equated with the chloroplasts of eukaryotic cells, thereby suggesting that chloroplasts, which have their own DNA for their own reproduction, are basically blue-green algae that, by symbiotic association, came to live within the eukaryotic cells, for which they performed the function of photosynthesis.

If it is true that mitochondria and chloroplasts originated as independent organisms — independendent species, if one wishes — that became parts of the larger eukaryotic complexes by symbiosis, the process of their assimilation has at last gone so far that we are able to regard them, today, not as distinct organisms living in symbiotic association with other distinct organisms, but simply as organs of the organism to which they belong. In that case, a process of mutual evolution between unrelated species has produced a merging rather than a separation of branches on the tree of life.

May we not, then, envisage at least the possibility of a day, perhaps hundreds of millions of years hence, when the mutual evolution of blue-green algae and fungi associated as lichens has led to a like merger? May we not, as well, envisage at least the possibility of a day when the mutual evolution of termites and the protozoan symbionts in their digestive tracts has led to such a merger?

If such organelles as mitochondria and chloroplasts are indeed products of what was originally a symbiotic association, we may regard them as representing the complete merger of separate species to form new ones. In the cases of the termites and the protozoa, of the alfalfa and the bacteria, and of the orchids and fungi, the species remain distinct but cohabit in great intimacy and interdependence, one symbiont passing much or all of its life inside the other. Here, on this larger scale, and presumably on the basis of less time for evolution, the process of merger has not gone as far as in the case of mitochondria and chloroplasts. If we continue up the scale to larger and still more developed organisms, on both sides of their association, the intimacy of symbiotic relations becomes less, until at last we confront quasi-symbiotic or commensal relations, relations in which the process of mutual association has, at best, not gone beyond the most rudimentary stage. Yet one might be able to trace something at least suggesting a continuous gradation, from the mitochondrium in the cell, which goes back to the origin of eukaryotic cells a thousand million years ago, to the association of men and the gulls that scavenge in their cities, which goes back a century.

The mutually beneficial association of highly developed species belonging to our own order of magnitude is represented by the insects and the flowering plants that supply them with food in return for being fertilized by their agency. Such associations, like those between tick-eating birds and tick-infested mammals, are rarely exclusive between two species. The flowering plant that supplies food for insects, which fertilize it in return, does not usually supply it for one species of insect only, and the insect that fertilizes it usually fertilizes other plants as well. But there may, nevertheless, be total mutual dependence between a group of plant species, however large, and a group of insect species.

I wish I could, at this point, present the entire text of Darwin's *The Various Contrivances by which Orchids are Fertilized by Insects* for the examples it gives of how far evolution has gone since life first began to develop from an accidental association of molecules. Instead, I shall confine myself to a few examples.

Most orchids have one petal, larger and showier than the others, called the labellum, which has the general shape and position of a man's tongue projecting outward and downward from his open mouth. It is a landing platform for the flying insects on which the orchid depends for cross-fertilization — for the fertilization of one flower, that is, by pollen transported from another. Typically, the open mouth behind this tongue leads into a closed throat, the nectary, which is in effect a thin vase, looking like a spur from outside, that contains nectar. An insect of the right kind lands on the labellum, attracted by its bright colors and by the odor of the nectar. It pushes its proboscis and head into the nectary to suck up the nectar. Because of the construction of the flower, proboscis and head are guided so as to touch a cuplike organ, called the rostellum, that ruptures at the touch. By rupturing it exposes two viscid discs in such a way that they adhere to the insect's head. The two discs form the bases for two stalks, each with a clublike mass of mutually adhering pollen grains at the top, so that the insect now appears to have horns.

The viscid discs, which had retained their stickiness only because they were immersed in the liquid of the cuplike rostellum, now set like cement, thereby fastening the horns firmly to the insect's head. The insect, having sucked up the nectar, flies off with its horns to land on the labellum of another flower, so as to obtain some more nectar.

The passage from one flower to another generally takes some thirty seconds. In that thirty seconds, the horns, which had stood vertically on their respective discs like the stems of goblets on their bases, bend forward and downward through almost ninety degrees.

Consequently, the two clublike masses of pollen occupy quite a different position relative to the insect's head and proboscis when it reaches the second flower. In their new position, the pollen masses come into contact with the sticky stigma (the female organ) of the second flower, to which some of the pollen grains adhere when the insect withdraws its head and proboscis. So the male element of one flower is deposited on the female element of another and cross-fertilization is achieved at the expense of two drinks for the insect.

The variations on this basic performance are wide-ranging and as numerous as the species of orchids, which are countless, and of their respective insect partners. What I have described as the two horns may be both on one disc, which may wrap itself around the proboscis of the insect rather than sticking to its head, thereby causing the horns to diverge laterally, instead of bending forward, to match the entirely different position of the stigma in another species.

In the case of the species that Darwin identifies as *Catasetum saccatum*, there is no nectar but there is succulent tissue in a partly covered bowl formed by the labellum, to be entered only from a small opening above. The insect cannot enter without touching the tip of a long dangling appendage from the anther overhead, which acts as a trigger. When this trigger is touched the rostellum ruptures and the one viscid disc, which supports a stalk that has two pollen masses at its end, is projected like an arrow from a bow to land, viscid end first, at just the right point on the insect's thorax. The force of the projection is such that, if the arrow is not intercepted by the insect's body, it will fly to a distance of two or three feet.

In all these cases, be it noted, plant and insect have evolved to fit each other with some precision. One may say quite properly, depending on the case, that the nectary has been designed to fit the insect's proboscis, the insect's proboscis to fit the nectary. The evolution of plant and insect has been mutual.

In another orchid, fertilized by bees, the insect is directed to a slippery chute, down which it slides helplessly on its back, only to pick up two pollen masses with their attendant apparatus at the bottom.

The flower of another orchid, *Ophrys speculum*, has evolved to resemble the female of a certain insect species, *Scolia ciliata*, in odor as well as appearance. Here the attraction is not nectar. Succumbing to another attraction, the male insect tries to copulate with the flower, thereby achieving the mating, not of his own kind but of the orchid. He carries the pollen masses away with him to the next flower with which he tries to copulate.

I shall give one more example, this time of a case in which each of a particular genus of plant and a particular genus of insect is wholly dependent on the other for its own reproduction and, consequently, survival. Such partnerships exist between species of the plant genus *Yucca* and species of insects known as yucca moths (*Tegeticula* and *Parategeticula*). In each case, the female moth has a special organ developed from the mouth-parts, which other moths lack, for collecting the yucca's pollen. The yucca produces flowers that are open for only a brief time, and not always every year. The female of the moth can do her part only when she is ready to lay eggs, which must be at the time when the yucca flowers are open. She then uses her special organ to collect a ball of pollen from one yucca flower, which she carries to another yucca flower. At the second flower, using a specialized ovipositor, she inserts one or more eggs into the ovaries. She then climbs up the pistil (in many but not in all cases) and places the pollen ball on the stigma, thereby fertilizing the flower. The seeds that, in consequence of this fertilization, are produced where the eggs were laid, are the only food on which the larvae hatched from the eggs can live, but each larva consumes only a few seeds, and a sufficient number are formed to reproduce the plant as well as feed the larvae.

There are years when no yuccas bloom at all over as wide an area as the moths can travel, but the moths escape consequent extirpation because, when that happens, their larvae continue for another year in the chrysalis, changing into moths only when the yuccas bloom again.*

*

In Chapter XII I described certain mechanisms of animal life that represented its most extreme evolution up to our present — the red blood cells, the muscles, the nerves — and I referred to the combined action of these mechanisms whereby, for example, a goshawk is able to avoid every branch and twig as it shoots through the forest canopy in pursuit of its winged prey. In conclusion, I wrote that a disembodied mind of three or four thousand million years ago, observing the random collision and the occasional mutual adherence of molecules in shallow water, could hardly have predicted that these undirected events — acquiring a cumulative character, taking a direction of their own, manifesting the architectonic tendency of matter on an ever increasing scale — would someday lead to this.

Let us consider, now, the course of mutual and complementary

* I am grateful to Professor Jerry A. Powell of the University of California, Berkeley, for going over this and the preceding paragraph in their original form and making some necessary corrections. See J. A. Powell and R. A. Mackie, "Biological Interrelationships of Moths and Yucca Whipplei" in *University of California Publications in Entomology*, Berkeley and Los Angeles, 1966.

evolution by which the yucca and the moth, each evolving separately at first, began to evolve in complementarity until, becoming increasingly adapted to each other, each came at last to play an indispensable role in the reproduction of the other.

Imagine the moth's ancestor, a primitive insect crawling among the stalks of a primitive vegetation; and the yucca's ancestor, a primitive plant that produced reproductive cells of two mating types, to be distinguished as male and female. The insect may have found food of some sort on the reproductive organs of the plant, where the male cells were produced. Or perhaps what it found was shelter, protection from the weather or from predators — perhaps also a good place to deposit its eggs. Crawling from one plant to another, it sometimes carried along some of the male cells, the pollen grains, caught in the hairs of its body, and they were brushed off against the female parts of the second plant. Cross-fertilization resulted, with its genetic advantage of recombination.

By natural selection over hundreds of thousands of years, then, the reproductive organs of the plant developed so as to attract the insect. They became showy, and they emanated the odor of the nectar with which they came to reward the insects that were drawn to them. At some stage, the insect developed wings to fly, rather than crawl, from one flower to another. At some stage it developed the habit of cleaning itself by gathering into a ball the pollen with which its hair was dusted, carrying the ball along with it in flight because of some obscure satisfaction it afforded. Perhaps the satisfaction was one of taste, or the pollen stimulated its digestive activity. Perhaps it also came to constitute a reserve food supply, or the medium on which a reserve food supply grew, so that the insect acquired the habit of leaving it at the flowers where it fed. In any case, where the insect acquired this habit the plants reproduced themselves more abundantly and more effectively than elsewhere, thereby providing conditions beneficial to the insect in its struggle for survival — and so, by indirection, the individual insects in which the habit was well developed were favored by natural selection over those in which it was not developed, or not as well developed. The same process favored the development in the insect of a special organ between the jaws for the collection of pollen, natural selection favoring any genetic strain that produced in the phenotype a more effective structure for the purpose.

At first the female of the insect laid her eggs at the place on the flower where she deposited the pollen ball, which was also the place where the seeds of the plant, on which her larvae would feed, developed. With time, however, the ovary of the plant, in which the seeds developed, became increasingly separated from what became the stigma, where the pollen had to be placed if it was to perform its function, until stigma and ovary had become separated by the length of what was now a pistil. At first, as this separation began, the insect began to have to force an access for herself into the ovarian chamber, and as the problem of forcing such access increased she began to develop a special organ for the purpose by the same interaction between genotype and phenotype as I have described in connection with the special organ for gathering pollen. This led, at last, to the present circumstances in which the female moth gathers a ball of pollen on one flower, flies to the base of another flower's pistil, cuts an access hole in it, lays her eggs inside, and then climbs the pistil to deposit the ball of pollen on the stigma.*

To return to the beginning, the larvae of the primitive insect, satisfying their hunger on whatever lay at hand, began to relish the seeds of the plant, which thereby came to constitute an added attraction for the insect that provided the plant with such a valuable service. Therefore, by natural selection the seeds of the plant became adapted to the needs of the larvae, and a surplus came to be produced for the purpose.

The process of mutual adaptation came to manifest itself in the respective structures of both parties, in their behavior, in the timing of the events that marked their respective annual cycles. The plant developed showy flowers and a fragrance to attract the insect, and eventually came to provide special shelter for its eggs as well as food for its young. By something like this process of mutual adaptation, the plant became today's yucca, the insect today's yucca moth. (Perhaps someday the plants will have grown into a communal complex within which the moths pass their lives.)

We must assume that it was in some such way that the present partnership between the yucca and the yucca moth — or between the bee and the orchid, or between the ant and the aphid — developed. This is the explanation at which we arrive when, beginning at our present and looking backward, we imagine what the antecedents must have been. But if, as a disembodied mind, we stood at the other end, at the beginning of life, looking forward, we

* I know of no agency other than natural selection, as basically conceived by Darwin, that accounts for evolution. I therefore evoke no other cause of evolution, in addition to natural selection, even in cases where the explanation offered by natural selection tends to strain credulity. But I do believe that our knowledge of the evolution of life is still far from complete, and when the most plausible possible account of an evolutionary development, confining itself to Darwinian selection, is still less plausible than one could wish, my disposition is to face the fact in terms of our residual ignorance, and so to keep an open mind for what new theoretical insights the future may bring.

might well be impressed by how overwhelming the odds were against the development of the macromolecules of the time into the present partnership of the yucca and the yucca moth.

In the following two chapters which conclude Part Two, taken together, I shall consider the question of how we must understand the occurrence in fact of what seems so overwhelmingly improbable.

XX

The Vital Drive

THE MOST IMPORTANT FACTOR in evolution receives little attention in the literature of evolution, if only because there is so little one can say about it. Another reason for not laboring it may be the fact that, rightly or wrongly, it seems to have implications of the doctrine called "vitalism," associated principally with the philosophy of Henri Bergson. Bergson, in his *L'Évolution créatrice*, published in 1907, postulated an *"élan vital,"* a creative drive in all living being by which he accounted for its evolution in the direction of constant self-improvement. This notion, unscientific in itself, has the status of a heresy among biological scientists, so that in their writings they are at constant pains to dissociate themselves from it.

Since I am about to tread on delicate ground, I must take care not to be misunderstood. It is proper that Bergson's concept of an *élan vital,* in itself, should be no less unacceptable to science than the traditional concept of the soul. Just as biologists are unable to locate and examine the soul, so they are unable to discover the source and the mechanism of Bergson's *élan vital.* Without such circumstantial information, the postulation of a mysterious driving force that accounts for evolution simply begs the question, as one would beg the question by postulating a mysterious impulsion that was said to account for the growth of plants.

It is not untrue, however, to say that the growth of plants is caused by an impulsion. Only if one stops there does one beg the question of what causes their growth. If one goes on to tell how the impulsion is powered by radiant energy from the sun through the process of photosynthesis, then it is no longer begged. The fault of vitalism is not that it postulates a vital drive that does not exist, for such a drive clearly does exist. The fault is in not going on to explain it. Left unexplained, it is given the status of a mystery — like the soul, or the will of God — and although such mysteries have their place in the curious discipline of religious doctrine they have no place in science.

What, then, is the vital drive, defined in such circumstantial terms as are proper to science?

It is the impulsion manifested by all the forms of life to survive and to perpetuate their kind. This it is that drives the evolution of living organisms.

We see how, in the first place, the structure and behavior of every individual organism appears designed to encompass its own survival, to avert its own death. There is only one class of exceptions to this, consisting of the exceptions that must be made by every individual, in its behavior, to ensure the perpetuation of its kind — for the survival of the individual is secondary to the survival of its kind, although to nothing else.

Let me give an example. Everything a particular female eider duck does, with certain exceptions, may be explained in terms of a purpose to survive, to avert death. She seeks food, avoids predators, defends herself when attacked, etc. The exceptions manifest themselves in the spring of the year, when she leaves the relative safety of the sea to venture inland, where dangers unknown at sea await her, where she is excessively vulnerable to such predators at stoats, foxes, hawks, and owls. In the midst of an open grassy field she lays a clutch of eggs and sits on them, night and day, to keep them warm. Now she risks her own life for the sake of the eggs and the ducklings that, in due course, hatch from them. If one comes upon her on her nest, one can often put one's hand on her before she will move to expose the hope of the future that she guards. (This means that, if one were so inclined, one could seize her to make a meal of her.) And when she does move it will be to a distance of only some three meters, where she will flap about and make as much commotion as possible to distract one's attention from her treasure to herself. She will try to lead away the fox in the same fashion, risking her own life to bring about the survival of her kind. This surely represents something like a purpose in nature, and an impulsion to realize it. That purpose and the associated impulsion are represented as well, if less dramatically, by an amoeba or a pine tree, by a bacterium or a blue-green alga. One is tempted to call it the basic characteristic of all life, distinguishing it from what is not life, from sticks and stones — or, for that matter, from the eider after death.

I have said that the vital drive, of which I have now given an example, is aimed primarily at the perpetuation of the kind, secondarily at the survival of the individual. But the perpetuation of the kind, while it requires the survival of the individual for a time, depends on the mortality of the individual, depends on there being a term to its life. If there is to be evolutionary progress, the kind must be constantly renewed at the expense of the individual, by its re-placement.* The renewal of the kind, generation after generation, is not indiscriminate. It is the selective renewal of what best fits the kind to its environment, and the purging (through the death of the individual) of whatever tends to unfit it. Those of the eider's duck-lings that survive to reproduce in their turn will tend to be the ones that represent those features inherited from their forebears (from the gene pool) that contribute most to survival in the particular envi-ronment, not those that represent features inimical to such survival. Natural selection means renewal with improvements, which entails the replacement of the old by the new, generation after generation.

All forms of life, then, are driven by an impulsion to perpetuate themselves, which in all the circumstances, notably including those of competition, generally requires constant improvement.

Everything I have just said is, surely, in keeping with biological orthodoxy. Does it not, however, make vitalists of us all?

The real grounds for objection to the philosophical vitalism repre-sented by Bergson are that it is content to regard the *élan vital* as something like a mysterious spiritual force. I, myself, am not willing to remove it from the sphere accessible to scientific inquiry by regarding it as such. To say that it is a spiritual force, except in the context of some body of religious beliefs which I do not hold, would be to say nothing. In the present state of our knowledge we must try to explain it in terms of natural selection alone.

When the first organisms or proto-organisms began to develop and to compete with one another, those that behaved in such a way as best to promote their own perpetuation were favored by natural selection, thereby causing the vital drive to evolve progressively in its intensity. This appears to be the best explanation we can give.

Is it not, however, a circular explanation, according to which the impulsion that drives evolution, and on which evolution may there-fore be thought to depend, is itself the product of evolution?

I think not, for it is possible to imagine evolution through natural selection occurring even in the absence of any such impulsion.

Let us imagine certain molecular combinations that, purely as a matter of the mechanisms described by physics (i.e., the interaction of particles), grow to a certain size at which they break into two equal parts, each of which repeats the process. This is to say that these combinations form and proliferate according to the laws of nature that govern any combination of molecules, whether raindrops or salt crystals. The limiting capacity of the environment imposes a limita-tion on the proliferation. If, among the proliferating molecular

* See J. T. Bonner, *On Development*, Cambridge (Mass.), 1974, p. 16.

combinations, some varieties are more apt than others to increase their numbers by proliferation, they will do so at the expense of the others, which will consequently tend to disappear — in what we cannot properly, however, call the competition among them.

We cannot properly call it competition, at this early stage, because competition implies purpose and consequent striving; and these molecular combinations are just as incapable of purpose and striving as raindrops or crystals of salt. It would be ridiculous to suppose that they somehow cared to increase and therefore strove to do so.

The fact remains that, even in the absence of purpose or any drive at all, natural selection has begun to operate. We have supposed that there is variety among the proliferating molecular combinations. Those varieties best adapted to increase through proliferation are constantly taking the place of the others. This is an open-ended directional process entailing selection for whatever characteristics favor increase, even though there is still no volition or drive of any sort on the part of the combinations themselves.

Eventually, in this process, we might recognize that the variety among the combinations had begun to manifest itself in differences of what we might call behavior. Those that behaved in certain ways would be more likely to survive than those that behaved in other ways. As certain kinds of behavior, if we may call it that, became more marked, they would begin to seem increasingly purposeful, until at last one could no longer doubt that purpose was implicit in them. So, after some four thousand million years, the process of natural selection, which had begun without a driving purpose, would lead to the eider purposefully defending her eggs with her life. Although evolution did not, in the first instance, depend on a drive, it generated a drive as it progressed.

I offer this hypothetical explanation as the best we can give in the present state of our knowledge. It is surely insufficient, as any explanation of anything must suffer from an ultimate insufficiency as long as we cannot explain the fact of being itself, the fact that there is something (space, time, matter, energy) rather than nothing. But insufficiency is a matter of more or less. Let us hope that, with a continuing growth of our knowledge, the insufficiency of our hypothetical explanations will become less.

In this exposition we have arrived, now, at the outermost boundaries of biological science, beyond which is the realm of religion (in the formal aspects of which I cannot believe) or of metaphysics (a term that I do not necessarily use in the pejorative sense common today). When I postulate the development of order out of chaos I already have one foot in metaphysics.

I am also, at this point, exposing myself to the suspicion that I believe in teleology, a term that has the same pejorative connotations as the term metaphysics in our day. But I do not here offer a teleological explanation of the tendency for order to emerge from chaos. This is to say that I do not attribute the tendency to a pre-existing purpose, which there might or might not have been. Given the active drive to self-perpetuation that I have discussed in this chapter, the tendency for order to replace chaos can be explained by a natural process of screening, which is passive rather than active, which is known as natural selection, and which I describe, albeit in metaphorical terms, in the chapter that, following this one, concludes Part Two.

XXI

The Selection of Order

IMAGINE A BLIND CHILD who has at hand an unlimited supply of wooden squares, each marked with a letter of the alphabet. If the child picks up these squares at random and places them in line one after another, what are the chances that it will produce the exact sequence of letters represented by Milton's *Paradise Lost?*

Let us say there are 500,000 letters in *Paradise Lost.* The number of different sequences of 500,000 in which the 26 letters of the alphabet can be laid out is $26^{500,000}$. Therefore, when the child has laid out 500,000 squares, one after the other, the chances are only 1 in $26^{500,000}$ that they will spell out *Paradise Lost.*

The magnitude of the improbability, here, is unimaginable, but there are ways in which we can get a notion of it. Suppose that the child has, against odds of $26^{499,999}$, laid out the first 499,999 letters of the poem, so that it has only one letter to go. The chances are still 26 to 1 against its completing the poem by the right letter. If, against odds of $26^{499,998}$, it has laid out all but the last two letters, the chances are 26^2 (i.e., 676) to 1 against its completing the poem. If it has laid out all but the last three, the chances are 26^3 (17,576) to 1 against success. If it has laid out all but the last four, the chances are 456,975 to 1 against it; if all but the last five, 11,881,350 to 1 against it. Let the reader extrapolate this, letter by letter, for the remaining 499,995.

The odds against producing *Paradise Lost* in this fashion are tantamount to infinity. If, against such odds, the child did succeed in spelling out *Paradise Lost,* we could be altogether sure that trickery had been involved, for odds so adverse are equivalent to impossibility.*

Let us, however, modify the game by setting certain limits. Sup-

---

* The odds would be equally against whatever sequence of 500,000 letters the child laid out. What is equivalent to impossibility is to guess in advance what the sequence of letters will be.

pose that only sequences of letters that spell words in Milton's vocabulary endure, that all letters not belonging to such words vanish. It follows that now, as the child adds letter to letter, it writes out a sequence of words. If, then, there are 5,000 words in Milton's vocabulary, and *Paradise Lost* consists of 90,000 words, the odds are still only 1 in $5,000^{90,000}$ that the child will spell out the poem. These are immensely better odds than those we have been dealing with, but still tantamount to impossibility.

Now let us set another limit. Any word not forming part of a phrase that makes sense vanishes. Therefore, as the child adds letter to letter it spells out a sequence of phrases, each of which makes sense in itself.

Now a third limit: any phrase that does not form part of a paragraph that makes sense vanishes. And a fourth: any paragraph that does not form part of a larger grouping that makes sense vanishes. Continue to set additional limits along this line. By the imposition of these limits we progressively reduce the odds, until at last we have ensured that the sequence of 500,000 letters will constitute a literary whole that makes sense as such. This literary whole may not be *Paradise Lost,* but it must resemble it in being meaningful; for anything that was not meaningful would have been eliminated by what we may consider the equivalent of natural selection.

The parallel to natural selection is imperfect. I daresay I could make it less so if I postulated the condition that *Paradise Lost* was one of rather few possible sequences of 500,000 letters that would make sense. I would be going too far in the direction of determinism, however, if I held it to be the only such sequence that would make sense, so that with enough time the child would be bound to write it out verbatim.

Elementary particles combine to make atoms as letters combine to make words; atoms combine to make molecules as words combine to make phrases; molecules combine to make macromolecules as phrases combine to make paragraphs; macromolecules associate with one another to make cells as paragraphs do to make chapters. The final result of such a process, extrapolated, is bound to be a single, complete, universal order.

The evolution of being is based on a process of natural selection that prefers order to chaos. Although organic molecules have been combining for three or four thousand million years now, only those combinations that have made sense, in terms of order as opposed to chaos, have survived. The others, which are the overwhelming majority, have vanished. Moreover, those that have made more sense have displaced those that have made less sense, and the latter have vanished in consequence. By this process a progressive and expanding order has been emerging from an original chaos. The process is incomplete as yet, but it has already led, *inter alia,* to the orchid and the goshawk. It has already led to mind and the consciousness of knowing in our species.

The process continues — to what end, no one knows.

PART THREE

Mind

The world was made to be inhabited by beasts, but studied and contemplated by man. . . . Without this, the world is still as though it had not been, or as it was before the sixth day, when as yet there was not a creature that could conceive or say there was a world.

— *Sir Thomas Browne*

I

The Origin of Mind

THE PHYSICAL UNIVERSE of which we have become aware consists of thousands of millions of galaxies, among which our own has no distinction. Our sun is only one among some hundred million stars that constitute this galaxy, and our earth one of nine planets that circle it. There is nothing central about our position, but it is the only standpoint we have for viewing the universal environment in which we find ourselves.

The question why the universe is at all, why there is space or time or being, is beyond the range of our faculties, even that of imagination. Nor can we pretend that we understand the reality of the universe in any ultimate sense. We are the prisoners of our own limited faculties for observation as well as of the standpoint in time and space to which we are confined. Within these limits we do the best we can, assuming a logical external order to which the logic of our minds corresponds.

Knowing the existence of space-time and matter-energy as a fact, we have no reason to believe that life is implicit in it. We can plausibly imagine a universe without life, one in which lifeless planets circle about the stars that are clustered in galaxies. The emergence of life, then, appears almost as extraordinary as the fact of being itself. If we imagine a disembodied consciousness observing the earth of 4,500 million years ago, we may well wonder how it could have believed even in the possibility that the association of quanta, the elementary units of matter, in ever larger combinations would eventuate in life as we know it today.

Our earth is as one mote in clouds of dust scattered over unimaginable distances. The logic of our minds, reflecting an order that we find in this universe of motes, makes it implausible that the phenomenon of life should have manifested itself on our mote only. We have discovered that the universe is basically uniform, all the stars in all the galaxies being composed of the same hundred or so elements, and all governed by the same laws of nature. If, then, there is life on our mote there must be life on others as well.

*

In Part One we reviewed what we have already discovered of the physical universe at large, its constitution, its composition, and the laws by which it is governed. In Part Two we reviewed what we have so far discovered about the emergence and development on our own mote of the life that has come to cover its surface. Atoms, resulting from the combination of quanta, combined to form molecules, which combined to form macromolecules, which at some stage began to engage in a process of self-replication that provided the basis for a progressive evolution governed by natural selection. About 1,500 million years after the formation of the earth, recognizable life began to proliferate over its surface, constantly evolving larger and more complex forms.

From our point of view, then, there are two great facts: one is the inexplicable fact of being itself, the other the unexpectable emergence of a progressively evolving life within the framework of being. To these two we may now add a third: the progressive emergence of mind within the framework of life.

Rather than attempt a definition of mind at this point, I shall rely largely on the implicit definition provided by context in what follows.* Associated with mind, however, is consciousness, the awareness of one's own living existence and of an environment in which one's existence occurs.

The basic characteristic of life is self-replication. A macromolecule of DNA replicates itself; a virus replicates itself; a bacterium replicates itself. We have no grounds for attributing any consciousness to the macromolecule, the virus, or the bacterium. They have no sense organs or nerves, let alone brains. How, then, could a bacterium, any more than a raindrop, feel anything? It lacks the means of experiencing any sensation at all. Yet a bacterium may be capable of moving (of its own volition, one would say, except that it can have no volition), and will draw back from a potentially deleterious contact (from an unpleasant contact, one might say, except that it has no organ through which to experience unpleasantness). The amoeba appears to hunt its food, moving through the medium it inhabits until it encounters a food-particle which it proceeds to engulf; but we cannot say that it hunts deliberately, for it has no organ of deliberation, or that it feels hunger, or that it enjoys satisfaction when it captures its prey. When a paramecium, propelling itself by means

* I first undertake to define it explicitly on p. 272 below.

of cilia, catches and eats a bacterium, how can either it or the bacterium have any consciousness of the event? Consciousness, which we know in ourselves, requires a complex nervous system centered in something like a brain, and the unicellular creatures referred to above have no nervous system at all, nor any special organ for experiencing or registering what we call sensations, like the sensation of touch or hearing. It is hard to escape the conclusion that a paramecium or a diatom can have no more "awareness" than a grain of sand or a speck of dust. (Words like "awareness" and "consciousness" have come into being to denote our own experience, and it is a question how far we may properly go in attributing such experience to other forms of life.)

This is equally true of all plant-life, the most advanced no less than the most primitive. The great oak and the little diatom alike manifest the impulsion of all organisms to survive and perpetuate their kind; but the impulsion can have no conscious component, there can be no "desire" or "intention" or "will" to survive on their part. Nor may we suppose that, when the woodman applies his axe to the oak, cutting through its trunk in successive strokes, it suffers pain or dismay or has any consciousness of the experience at all, any more than a rock under the blows of a sledge-hammer.

The crocus in an Alpine pasture opens its petals at the touch of the sun's radiance, closing them again when an intervening cloud cuts it off. We say the crocus performs these movements, but this is wrong if it implies deliberate action. The petals spread or close, presumably, as a strip of lifeless paper curls in the presence of moisture.

Touch a leaf of the sensitive plant (*Mimosa pudica*) with a needle, and it reacts abruptly. It collapses, the leaflets closing in on themselves. But the sensitivity of the sensitive plant is not to pain, as in the case of the higher animals, for it has no physiological apparatus to serve as a medium of awareness, painful or otherwise.

Since our common concern here is with the evolution of awareness, consciousness, mind (as we know them in ourselves), we hardly need bother with any unicellular life, or with the plant kingdom as a whole. This evolutionary development appears to be confined to the animal kingdom, and then only beyond the point at which it began to form ever larger and more complex multicellular organisms.

The problem of understanding that we face here has already been anticipated in Part Two (see Chapter XX, entitled "The Vital Drive"). There we saw how every form of life, down to the most primitive, manifested an impulsion to survive and perpetuate its kind — this being the driving force, so to speak, of evolution. Speculating about the origin and development of this impulsion, we imagined molecular combinations "that, purely as a matter of the mechanisms described by physics (i.e., the interaction of particles), grow to a certain size at which they break into two equal parts, each of which repeats the process." If various molecular combinations are thus proliferating in an environment of limited capacity, those that persist and proliferate most effectively will tend to pre-empt that environment, causing the others to disappear. Something like a continuing competition has been set off in which natural selection, simply by a mechanical logic, favors the survival of those combinations best adapted to persisting and increasing in whatever the circumstances may be. This goes on without purpose or any consciousness at all on the part of the varieties that are tending (but not intending) to pre-empt the environment and thereby exclude one another. So a progressive process is inaugurated that leads to the eider duck, which in its behavior appears to manifest something like a conscious purpose to perpetuate her kind in opposition to competing kinds of which she is, one gathers, aware. Consciousness has been born.

*

Everything in evolution is gradual when seen close up. Viewing the process in a distant perspective that embraces thousands of millions of years we may say that mammals suddenly appeared on the scene 150 million years ago; but this does not mean that at a particular moment an ancestral member of the class Reptilia gave birth to the first representative of the class Mammalia. It means that a branch of reptiles diverged so widely, over a span of tens of millions of years, that it had at last to be considered a distinct class altogether.

I have supposed that life originated gradually in the same way, that there was not a particular macromolecule, without life, that split to produce two macromolecules that did have life. What I have here applied speculatively to the origin of life applies as well to the origin of consciousness and, eventually, mind. There was no moment when consciousness was born, or another when mind was born. (Mind, I surmise, is still only in the process of being born today, for it seems still to have an uncertain place in our local realm of being, and to manifest itself only incompletely. In any case, we know that it is very new.)

I said above that, from our point of view, there are two great facts, one the fact of being itself, the other the emergence of an evolving life within the framework of being. To this I added a third, the emergence of mind in the course of the evolution of life. But we are still too close to this third fact to understand its significance. Our position may be equivalent to that of the disembodied observer on the earth of three thousand million years ago. By that time bacteria were present, differing so distinctly from inert matter that they would have been recognizable as life. But what grounds would the observer have had for attaching to the emergence of what they represented the importance we attach to it today? He could not have known that this life, so insignificant at first, would develop as it since has. He could not have foreseen what would give it importance *ex post facto.*

When I say that the emergence of mind in the last million years may be as important as the emergence of life 3,500 million years ago, I can do so only in terms of speculation, since I cannot know to what it may lead. But in itself it is revolutionary — as the original emergence of life was, in itself, revolutionary.

Our present vocabulary is inadequate to describe the phenomenon. The word "awareness" may be used for the earliest stage in the development that leads to mind. It is hard to see how a bacterium, lacking the necessary organs, could be aware of its environment or of its own existence any more than a grain of pollen (which is also alive). Perhaps there was already a rudimentary capacity for the sensation we call "feeling" in primitive coelenterates, the ancestors of today's jellyfish. We may think of them as reacting to the chemical effects of contact with their environments in a way that was like awareness of touch, withdrawing from what was in some rudimentary way disagreeable, although without experiencing the sensation of touch as we know it. (The terms "experience" and "sensation of touch," which are relevant to us, would have been irrelevant to them.)

By the time evolution had produced such flatworms as the planarians we can use the term "awareness" with confidence; for they have "a developed nervous system, which here consists of a pair of lengthwise cords, and a pair of swellings for a brain of sorts in the head." * They also have eyes for the detection of light.

Let the reader trace the development of awareness in imagination, now, from the flatworm to the eider duck. It is hard to say what goes on in a duck's brain, but the eider has the means of seeing herself, so to speak, as an entity distinct from an environment which she perceives in circumstantial detail. Sitting on her eggs, she is aware not only of what is in the environment but also of what may be, alert with eyes and ears to detect dangers that she merely apprehends.

* A. S. Romer, *The Procession of Life*, London, 1968, p. 55.

Here, however loosely, we may use the word "consciousness" to denote a more developed form of awareness.

But the eider, we suppose, is not capable of the introspection we
call "self-consciousness." For an example of such introspective consciousness I quote from Kipling's *Kim*.

> "Now am I alone — all alone," he thought. "In all India is no
> one so alone as I! If I die today, who shall bring the news —
> and to whom? . . . — I, Kim. . . .
> "Who is Kim — Kim — Kim?"
> He squatted in a corner of the clanging waiting-room, rapt
> from all other thoughts; hands folded in lap, and pupils con-
> tracted to pin-points. In a minute — in another half second —
> he felt he would arrive at the solution of the tremendous
> puzzle. . . .*

This represents an advance on the flatworm, albeit one achieved by
imperceptible gradations over the millions of millennia of evolution.

Where there is such self-consciousness there is already the faculty
we call "mind." This faculty is associated with one species only, and
that one is our own.

* Rudyard Kipling, *Kim*, New York, 1901, pp. 241–242.

II

The Evolution That Led to Man:

1. The Rise of the Vertebrates

THE FLATWORMS, invertebrates with rudimentary brains, emerged in the evolutionary progress some 400 million years ago.* The first vertebrates emerged about the same time, in the form of little jawless fish that sucked their food from mud bottoms. Because the skeletons of the vertebrates were internal, by contrast with the external skeletons of such invertebrates as insects and crustaceans (e.g., the lobster), it would transpire that they were particularly suited to achieve large size in the course of their evolution. Large size, in turn, would make possible developments that could not have been realized on the scale to which life had been confined during its first 3,000 million years.

The fish, in far more developed forms than their jawless precursors, would come to fill all the waters of the earth with their varieties. One of their branches, the lobe-fins, would develop lungs, together with fleshy fins that were reinforced by bones and could therefore serve for feet. Presumably because they inhabited fresh water that was liable to dry up, they were under pressure to develop the means of surviving out of water. In developing those means, some 350 million years ago, they came to constitute a new class, Amphibia. The amphibians were not only the first animals to take to the land, they were also the first of the four-limbed animals that have since come to constitute all the higher orders.

Just as the salamander (a contemporary amphibian) has the basic form of the lizard (a contemporary reptile), so the first amphibians to rise above the waters — some looking like tadpoles with feet, some shaped like stubby alligators — prefigured their descendants, the

* Most accounts of evolution divide the past into eras (e.g., the Paleozoic, the Mesozoic, the Cenozoic), subdivided into periods (e.g., the Jurassic), subdivided for the last two periods into epochs (e.g., the Pleistocene). Because precise dates for these divisions are not known, and the divisions themselves are not sharp, the figures I give should be regarded as loose indications merely, like orders of magnitude in astronomy.

reptiles, which would be the first four-footed creatures to be completely adapted to dry land. Some of these early amphibians constitute the evolutionary line that connects the fish, which were confined to the water, with the reptiles, which were fully at home only on land. It is almost certain that all land vertebrates, in fact, are descended from these primitive amphibians. They are the common ancestors of lizards and crocodiles, of ostriches and hummingbirds, of bats and men.

*

Although the primitive amphibians were fish that had come up out of the water, undergoing transformation in the process, they came only halfway, so to speak. For the females had to return to lay their masses of eggs in the water like any fish; the males had to return to discharge the sperm that would fertilize those eggs; and the progeny, just like fish, would hatch into the water at an early stage of their embryonic development, those that survived growing up in the ancestral environment as tadpoles still do today. It was, then, only in the later stages of their individual lives that the amphibians could live out of the water, although this enabled them, unlike fish, to disperse overland from pond to pond. They left the water in each generation, however, only to return to it.

The change from amphibian to reptile came with the advent of a new kind of egg, what we might call a land egg rather than a water egg. Unlike the fish or amphibian egg, which was hardly more than a globule of jelly enclosing the germ, it provided within itself all the conditions that the embryo needed for its development. It provided a packaged internal environment adapted to that development, including a watery medium to replace that of ponds and watercourses, and enough stored food to support development past the early tadpole stage, as we may call it, to the point where the growing organism would be better able to fend for itself when it emerged into the external world. This would lead to the day when goslings would peck their way out of large hard-shelled eggs, already clothed in down and with eyes open, to run about and feed themselves. It would lead to the day when the infant antelope would spend an appreciable part of its youth in its mother's womb, not emerging until it was already able to follow her about on its own four feet. Perhaps we may say that it would foreshadow a day when bees would provide for themselves the enclosed environment of the hive, and men would provide for themselves the largely enclosed environment of the city, in which they might respectively pass their lives.

We may plausibly believe that the development of the new egg, like the development of the lung and of feet, was primarily a response to the tendency of the ponds in which eggs had traditionally been laid to dry up.

The so-called Age of Reptiles began some 200 million years ago, to last almost 150 million years. Up to 70 million years ago, then, a variety of reptiles flourished, some the size of lizards, others approaching thirty meters in length. Some dinosaurs may have weighed 45,000 kilograms and stood nine meters tall. Some swam in the oceans and some flew through the air, including one with a wingspread of over fifteen meters. Almost all this wealth of reptilian diversity disappears, however, at the end of the age of reptilian dominance, leaving only the crocodilians, the turtles, the lizards, and the snakes to persist as the representatives of a minor class into our present.

Since the Age of Reptiles, which ended some 70 million years ago, the dominant vertebrates on land have been the birds and the mammals. They are distinguished from the reptiles, the amphibians, and all other classes by the fact that they maintain their own fixed internal temperature, whatever the temperature of their surroundings may be. (They are "warm-blooded," as we put it unscientifically, by contrast with the "cold-blooded" fish, reptiles, insects, etc.) This adds to that relative independence of environmental circumstances toward which evolution appears to have been progressing. It allows a species like the puma to be at home from Alaska to Patagonia, from sea-level in the tropics to the Andean snows, remaining active at all seasons.

Heat, which is simply kinetic energy, is necessary for activity of any sort. By maintaining their own internal temperatures, birds and mammals are able to sustain a high level of activity in spite of low temperatures in the surrounding air or water. Animals that cannot do this become torpid as, with the reduction of external temperature, their own falls. So it is that lizards must go into hibernation when winter comes, while even such tiny birds as tits and kinglets, wrapped in their feathery insulation and with bodies like furnaces, maintain full activity through a winter in the spruce forests of northern Scandinavia. So it is that the polar bear thrives under conditions that would kill a dinosaur.

It is significant that birds and mammals, respectively descended from quite different branches of "cold-blooded" reptiles, evolved "warm blood" independently of each other, and by means of the same devices. When evolution was ready for this development it occurred simultaneously in two separate lines. (Birds and mammals also evolved, quite independently of each other, the system of blood circulation, exclusive to them, whereby the deoxygenated blood returning to the lungs is kept apart from the oxygenated blood flowing out from the lungs.)

Presumably the birds evolved some 150 million years ago from early reptiles that had taken to running on their hind legs, thereby leaving their forelimbs free to specialize as wings. Wings proved to have conspicuous advantages, although the alternative development of the forelimbs into hands ultimately proved, in one line of mammals, to have even greater advantages. (If only the amphibians, like the insects, had had six limbs instead of four, their descendents might, like the angels of Christian art, have developed both wings and hands together. Perhaps on some other planetary speck in the wide universe such creatures have in fact evolved.)

Just as the reptiles appear to have descended from early and primitive amphibians, rather than from the more evolved amphibians that followed them, so the birds and mammals, the two most advanced classes so far, appear alike to have descended from early rather than late reptiles. But where the birds evolved from reptiles that had risen on their hind legs the mammals evolved from others that specialized in the development of a quadrupedal efficiency lacking in their amphibian forebears. (Their upper legs, instead of continuing to stick out from the body to the elbow or knee joints, as in an alligator, were drawn in against the body, the elbows and knees pointing backward and forward, respectively, rather than outward.) The first mammals appeared about the same time as the first birds, say 150 million years ago.

For many millions of years the mammals were few, they were as small as mice or rats, and they were inconspicuous by contrast with the great reptiles that dominated the landscape. If their consciousness had been capable of it, they would surely have suffered from a sense of their relative inferiority; and it seems unlikely that the hypothetical disembodied consciousness, already evoked in these pages, would have foreseen to what an extent the future was theirs. For 80 million years they hardly showed their promise, but they were steadily developing the brain that would, in our own day, become the seat of what I have referred to as mind — presumably because, physically vulnerable as they were, they had to rely on their wits to save them from the overbearing reptiles. The simultaneously evolving birds, we may note, were to be second only to the mammals in the development of brains.

The mammals also developed a process of keeping the developing foetus within the mother's body, by which it was protected and nourished, rather than in an egg that had been ejected from the body, until it was at last ready to come out into the world; and even then the mother's body continued to provide it with nourishment through mammary glands.

All these devices, we should recall, were the product of natural selection acting on self-replicating combinations of molecules that were composed of particles interacting in accordance with the laws of quantum physics.

*

Some 70 million years ago the Age of the Reptiles came to an end as the greatest of the reptiles, failing to cope with a changing environment, disappeared from the earth.

The immense herbivorous dinosaurs must have depended on swamps, in which their bodies got some support from water, for they were too big to get about on land otherwise. They must also have depended on mild and relatively unchanging atmospheric temperatures the year around. The upheaval of mountains, however, and cooling climates over much of the earth, may have radically reduced these conditions for their survival, bringing the accentuated contrast between summer and winter that characterizes our temperate zones today.

The primitive little mammals of that time, many resembling the present-day shrews and moles, had no such dependence on these special conditions. And the disappearance of the great reptiles left the land largely to them among the four-footed creatures. Maintaining their own temperature, they lacked the reptilian vulnerability to climatic changes and meteorological stringencies, against which they could also protect their young by the devices we have seen. Moreover, like the birds they had better brains than their forebears. The end of the Age of Reptiles, then, coincided with the opening of the Age of Mammals. (Perhaps we should call it the Age of Mammals and Birds.) Relieved of the competition and predation of the great reptiles, the new class underwent an efflorescence, producing the widest variety of new forms to occupy, along with the birds, most of the large environmental niches of the land, from underground to treetop, from swamp to mountain-peak, from rain forest to desert, from the equatorial to the polar regions. They even took to the air in the form of bats, and returned to the ancestral sea as porpoises, dolphins, and whales, not to mention the amphibious seals.

Our disembodied observer, watching this constant radiation and proliferation of mammalian lines from, say, 70 million to 10 million years ago, might have speculated that the future lay with the elephants, or perhaps with the great carnivores. In fact we now know that his choice should have lighted on some exceedingly inconspicuous creatures rather like shrews, although arboreal, perhaps best represented today by the tree shrews of Southeast Asia. They were the first primates.

Again, as in the case of the first mammals among the lordly reptiles, we see the meek inheriting the earth.

III

The Evolution That Led to Man:

2. *The Rise of the Primates*

In our mind's eye we should retain the entire picture of the evolution that has so far led to man and the emergence of mind.

The earth came into being 4,500 million years ago. Well before 3,000 million B.P. (Before the Present), microscopic cells similar to the bacteria and blue-green algae of our day were already proliferating on its surface. By 2,000 million B.P. they had begun to diversify through the process of what was still an exceedingly slow evolution by natural selection. At a point halfway between that time and our present, 1,000 million B.P., eukaryotic cells had come into being. By the dynamics of their reproduction, through combination and recombination, evolution now began to advance at an accelerating pace, diversifying, radiating in its divisions and subdivisions. Life began to be something more than an invisible seasoning of warm broth, an occasional discoloration of the water, or a scum on its surface.

By 500 million B.P. there were animal organisms, visible (if there had been any observer with eyes like ours) as individuals or organized colonies, attached to shallow bottoms and filtering food from the waters; there were sponges and spongelike animals; there were small molluscs of a primitive sort; there were basic gastropods from which the slugs and snails of our own day would stem; and there may have been arachnids ancestral to our own horseshoe crabs and spiders. But all this developing life was confined, still, to the water, the land remaining bare.

A hundred million years later, about 400 million B.P., the flatworms with their rudimentary brains appeared, as well as the first vertebrates. By 350 million B.P. the first amphibians were emerging from the water. By 200 million B.P. the Age of Reptiles had begun, to continue until 70 million B.P., when the Age of Mammals (and Birds) succeeded it. This was at a point in time 99 percent of the way from the beginning of the earth to our present, 98 percent of the way from the first signs of life on the fossil record to our present. But evolution had been accelerating. Its progress over the 150 million years from the first mammals to the emergence of modern man, only one or two million years ago, has been spectacular by comparison with earlier progress. And in the last million years — more precisely, in the last 10,000 years, and especially in the last 500 — the face of the earth has been transformed by our own newly arrived species.

We may plausibly believe that, after 3,500 million years of evolution, we stand, today, at the point of the emergence of mind, in the process that began (to the extent that there are any beginnings) with the self-replication of large molecules.

*

Life, like the elephant of the fable, is basically indivisible. (Indeed, we cannot logically escape the conclusion that being itself is indivisible.) We may trace the evolution of a particular line, isolated like an elephant's tail for heuristic purposes, but it is life as a whole that evolves, so that a comprehensive understanding would require us to see it as the single entity it is, having parts only as a human body has parts. There is a sort of universal symbiosis, indirect if not direct. Animals could not have come into being if the evolution of the first organisms had not resulted in the device of photosynthesis, by which the oxygen they breathe was added to the environment; and photosynthesizing plants could not have evolved if animal metabolism had not maintained the supply of carbon dioxide they need. Primates, as we know them, could not have evolved in the absence of the trees that emerged in the evolution of plant life, for their basic evolution represented an adaptation to arboreal living.*

We may think of our shrewlike arboreal ancestor as growing larger, in the course of its evolution, and at some stage developing grasping hands. A small enough mammal can cling to bark with its claws, like a squirrel, but as it gets larger its weight increases at roughly four times the rate of its linear dimensions, until a point is reached at which, to support itself, it had better be able to embrace branches with hands or their equivalent.

Animals that run and leap through the branches of the forest canopy need good eyes, preferably with stereoscopic vision, to judge distances; but they can dispense with the acute sense of smell needed by those that move over the ground. So our arboreal ancestors developed a special dependence on vision, by contrast with such mammals as dogs and rodents, in which there was a preferential develop-

* Life "is like a grain of mustard seed, which a man took, and cast into his garden; and it grew, and waxed a great tree; and the fowls of the air lodged in the branches of it."

ment of smell. (Birds flying through mazes of branch and twig, like the goshawk today, or locating food across long stretches of open space, developed the same reliance on sight rather than smell.)

For animals the size of even the smallest birds and mammals, arboreal life requires the services of a developed brain. Anyone who has looked up to watch a spider monkey scampering and leaping through the confusion of leafy branches high overhead can appreciate how rapidly and accurately it must exercise the remarkably free movement of its four limbs, and all the other parts of its body, separately but in coordination, doing so largely on the basis of the evidence constantly provided by its eyes. This is something different from merely swimming like a paramecium or crawling like a beetle. It requires a directing brain that interprets the kaleidoscopic evidence of the eyes and orders the coordinated movements of all the parts of the body accordingly. No wonder that primates, even apart from man, have the largest and most developed brains among the mammals.*

For those who dwell in the trees, the scene is complex, requiring a complex brain for the interpretation of what the eyes and ears register. The safety of a bird or primate in the treetops requires that it be alert in interpreting all the moving lights and shadows, and the constant, multifarious sounds; and such alertness is akin to curiosity. Therefore, the high development of curiosity that we find in birds and mammals generally is particularly marked in the primates. This curiosity ("the curiosity of a monkey") is what, in the course of evolution, leads to the emergence of mind in modern man. What had been a condition of survival for the primitive primate has become, at last, the curiosity that moves its descendant to inquire into the structure of the universe, the origin of life, and the nature of his own ancestry.

*

The first primates, 70 million years ago, were probably bundles of fur that lived in the forest trees on an insect diet. Forty million years later, one branch of their descendants had become sufficiently distinct so that we may properly identify it as a suborder, the Anthropoidea or higher primates (as distinct from the Prosimii or lower

---

* In general, the larger a brain the more advanced its development. But its proportion to body size must be taken into account. The brain of an elephant had better be larger than that of a mouse because it has more body to control (more nerve-endings, more muscle-fibers, etc.). While the brain of a sperm whale is larger than that of a man, it is smaller in proportion to the body, and therefore less developed in spite of its absolute size. On the other hand, some small New World monkeys have larger brains for their size than man. Even if a flea's brain were half its body it would presumably be less developed than a man's. There is a limit to the faculties that can be packed into the dimensions of a speck of dust.

primates like the tree shrew). Continued branching eventually produced the family of New World monkeys, the marmoset family, and
the family of Old World monkeys. It also produced the family of
apes, Pongidae, and the family Hominidae, to which modern man
belongs. The Pongidae and Hominidae, confined to the Old World
until the recent spread of our own species, are associated together in
a superfamily, Hominoidea, which today consists of four species of
ape (gibbon, orangutan, gorilla, and chimpanzee) and only one species of man, the other Hominidae having become extinct.*

I here follow the custom of confining the vernacular term "man"
to members of the genus *Homo*. In this usage, members of other
genera, like *Australopithecus*, are often referred to as "man-apes,"
having been more like the apes than are the members of our own
more evolved genus. Extinct species of *Homo* are distinguished from
sapiens, the sole surviving species of the present, as the "primitive
men" who preceded "modern man" — the latter being represented
by the reader of these lines, whether he be an Australian aborigine,
an Eskimo, a Hottentot, a Nordic, or even a Neanderthal.

To sum up, the order Primates, originating some 70 million years
ago, branched to form the suborders Prosimii and Anthropoidea
some 50 million years ago; the Anthropoidea branched to form,
among others, the superfamily Hominoidea, which branched to
form the families Pongidae and Hominidae; the Hominidae
branched to form, *inter alia*, the genus *Homo* (all the members of
which are called "man"), which branched to produce a number of
species, of which *sapiens* is the only one to have survived into the
present.†

Our information on evolution from the original primates of 70
million B.P. to ourselves is sparse because it depends so largely on a
fossil record that consists of occasional bone fragments, their separation in time perhaps amounting to tens of millions of years for which
the record is blank. To reconstruct our evolutionary history on this
basis is like trying to recapture a picture from the few remaining
pieces of a picture-puzzle when no two of them fit together. It is
worse, for any particular fossil may consist of no more than a tooth
or a fragment of skull, not enough to tell, for example, whether the

---

* For the system of classification on which these paragraphs are based see page
191 above.
† It is just as well that only *sapiens* has survived, for otherwise we might be faced with
the problem of whether "human rights" applied to the genus as a whole or only to the
one species that was our own. An earlier generation might have had to decide
whether the other species had immortal souls. (In our own time there were some
who doubted whether the native Tasmanians, any more than chimpanzees, had immortal souls.)

individual to whom it belonged walked upright or on all fours. Conjecture, based on judgements of plausibility, must play its part.

The first apes of which we have remains date from about 40 million B.P. Perhaps three feet tall, they probably swung from branch to branch in the lovely method of locomotion, called brachiation, that distinguishes contemporary gibbons and orangutans. (It is like music in its rhythmic harmony.) Just as they were vastly larger than the first primates, so, with continued growth, some of their descendants may have attained a size that made it more convenient to move about on the ground — like the gorilla today, which stands partly upright but walks on all fours.

Meanwhile, the continuing upheaval of the land to form mountain-ranges reduced the relative uniformity of climate and habitat that had prevailed during the Age of Reptiles. Not only was there the greater seasonal variation in prevailing temperatures, which increased the advantages of maintaining, like the mammals and birds, an independent internal temperature, mountain-ranges, by screening prevailing winds, reduced rainfall in their lee, and where rainfall was reduced the continuous forest tended to give way to those grasslands, interrupted by clumps of brush and trees, called savannas.

At this point I cite a situation that represents direct personal observation. Adjacent to my home on the Lake of Geneva is a marsh of some three acres inhabited by the species of waterfowl called common gallinule in America, moorhen in Britain. A series of successful breeding seasons and protection from human hunting have caused an increase in its numbers beyond what the marsh can support. Especially in winter, now, individuals are increasingly driven by hunger to go searching for food beyond the bounds of their marshy habitat. As never used to be the case, they explore our lawn, coming up the hill to the shrubbery around our house, and year by year they become more familiar with a new habitat which is not native to them. If this should continue long enough, it would surely entail evolutionary adaptations to life on uplands, away from marshes. Eventually there might be a new species, "the upland gallinule," distinct from the moorhen of the marshes. Or, if the marshes should all dry up, the descendants of the present moorhens, having escaped in time, might be exclusively upland birds, perhaps no longer able to swim.

May we not plausibly imagine our ancestors, forest primates that had already descended from the trees to pass most of their daylight hours on the ground — may we not imagine them adventuring out along the edges of the new savannas that were forming? They would have found different food there, and this in time might have changed their food habits. Having been largely herbivorous, although not exclusively, they might have increased the proportion of animal food in their diet. There would have been insects like our grasshoppers, there would have been lizards, there would have been rodents. In time, they might have become increasingly adapted to the savannas, so that they no longer had to remain along the edges of the forests, to retreat into them at night or at any sign of danger as the moorhens retreat into the marsh.

What would such adaptation entail?

While still in the forest, these anthropoids had moved over the ground on all fours, albeit repeatedly rearing up on their hind legs to look about. In the forest they did not have to move fast, for they lived largely on vegetable matter and they would not, in any case, have had to catch their prey by extended chases. When alarmed by the approach of a predator they would have taken to the trees.

On the open savanna, however, they would have frequent occasion to move fast while remaining in a position to see over the grass through which they were moving. The distinctive gait of our own species is far better adapted to such requirements than that of gorilla or chimpanzee.

Man, today, is the only creature that walks fully upright (if one leaves out the equivocal case of birds). His usual method of locomotion is a stride, which has no parallel among the apes. It is based on the fully upright position and consists of allowing the body's main weight to fall constantly forward while the legs move smoothly under it to keep up. This is quite different from the shuffle of a brown bear upreared on its hind legs, but bent at the knees and hips, which places one foot forward at a time, shifting its weight to the new position, after which it moves the other foot forward, each step being a separate maneuver. A gorilla or chimpanzee, when it rears up, momentarily refraining from the use of its front limbs for support or propulsion, moves in the same way, one step at a time, with something approaching a full stop between.

By an act of plausible imagining we have now peopled the savannas with upright apelike creatures, which tend to walk and run as we do, which live by hunting and gathering. They are hominids — members of the family of man, the Hominidae — and we have fossil evidence of their existence.

*

When the ancestors of today's apes and those of today's men separated, perhaps 30 million years ago, it may be because the former remained committed to a forest life, swinging themselves arm after arm through the branches, while the latter took to the ground, adopting the bipedal locomotion that, as it became increasingly efficient, extended their range out over the grasslands.

The early hominids must still have been rather stooped in their posture, knees bent and leaning forward from the hips; but they became more fully upright with time. I remarked above that they became upright because they wanted to see over the tall grass as they moved through it, but this is conjecture that has much against it. Presumably they might, like today's baboons, have made themselves at home in the grasslands while remaining on all fours. Like baboons (or squirrels, for that matter), they could always have freed their hands for other uses by sitting down. One is tempted to believe that they needed to be free to carry things in their hands, perhaps in their arms. What is certain is that, with the freeing of their forelimbs, they did come to carry things, food and babies, eventually weapons and tools, while the apes continued to swing by their arms through the trees.

The difficulty is only in knowing how the upright position and bipedalism got started. Once the hands began to be freed they developed uses that called for the increase of their freedom. The hominids became dependent on them for carrying food. As hind feet lost the ability to grasp objects, infants could no longer cling to their mothers by all four extremities, the way an infant baboon clings to its mother's fur, so that the mothers had to hold them in their arms. It was advantageous to be able to wave broken branches at threatening predators or at one another, as chimpanzees sometimes do today, or to strike an opponent with a stick, a tactic not unknown among chimpanzees that might, in time, have become common among the increasingly upright. With the development of weapons and tools, which began by the use of sticks and stones, the dependence on the freedom of the forelimbs would have become ever greater, thereby determining the course of natural selection.

J. E. Pfeiffer refers to further advantages as by-products of the upright position. "Walking erect resulted in a continuous and more panoramic view of the savanna, an increased ability to see things coming and to detect and anticipate danger. Looking ahead from an elevated position may also have extended the sense of the future." * This was the beginning of that progressive enlargement of man's world, in space and time alike, which was to lead to the Theory of Relativity. It would also be represented by men who would someday view the earth from airplanes miles above its surface — who would, indeed, view it from the moon.

* J. E. Pfeiffer, *The Emergence of Man*, London, 1973, p. 51.

IV

The Coming of Man

WE NOTED IN PART TWO (Chapter XVII) that the categories by which we classify organisms for heuristic purposes are not categorical in nature, if we regard nature as the single whole in time and space that it is. Biologists may agree that the differences between two related groups, and the similarities within each, justify their representation as two genera; but the two groups diverged gradually in the course of evolution, and the question when their divergence had become great enough to justify the naming of two genera is, at best, a matter of arbitrary rules of nomenclature. Consequently, taxonomists commonly have difficulty agreeing about the application of generic designations, and there are frequent changes of mind resulting in revisions.

If this is the case with organisms alive today and available for comprehensive study, the uncertainty must be even greater in giving generic names to extinct forms of which only a few teeth or bone fragments, millions of years old, remain. Consequently, we should not regard the various genera by which the remains of man's forerunners are identified as signifying more than they do. Such generic names as *Aegyptopithecus, Sinanthropus,* and *Dryopithecus* are tentative attempts at working out a taxonomic arrangement rather than revelations of categories found as such in nature. This applies equally to hominoid species and races, to such formulations as *Telanthropus capensis* and *Homo erectus modjokertensis.*

Although the division of a part of the Anthropoidae into two branches — the Pongidae, leading to modern apes, and the Hominidae, leading to modern men — may have occurred as much as thirty million years ago, the earliest hominid known so far is *Ramapithecus punjabicus,* of which only some jaws and teeth, dating back ten million years, remain. William Howells writes that "there is no concrete evidence as to how *Ramapithecus* may have stood or walked, but the short face and front teeth imply that the hands had more work to do in feeding than they have in chimpanzees or gorillas." * The logic of this is that small canine teeth and a flat face, such as we have, limit the possibilities of picking up matter with the mouth and of biting, and therefore imply a greater dependence on hands.

Ramapithecus was followed by *Australopithecus,* a more developed hominid of which the earliest remains may be 4 million years old. There appear to have been at least two species, one about four and the other about five feet tall. They walked upright, or virtually so, and they shaped simple tools of stone and, presumably, of bone and wood as well. We must picture little bands of them traveling or resting on the savannas. They lacked the domed head of modern man, with the great vault of the skull extending from the eyebrows to the overhang of the occiput above the back of the neck. Instead, they had only a small brain-case behind a large face with a mouth that projected forward as in chimpanzees. (The brain of *Australopithecus* was little larger than that of modern apes, by contrast with our own brain.) They would surely have been slender, like modern men, without the great barrel-chested breadth of gorillas. With legs and feet much like ours, they might have run fast over the savannas, although they lacked our proficiency in walking with a smooth arm-swinging stride. They did not wear clothes, and presumably they had dark hairy bodies like most apes and monkeys today. They may have grunted, cooed, whispered, shouted, smacked their lips, or made clicking sounds, but although they were probably better at oral communication than today's apes, they can hardly have had any such developed language as we have.

These creatures (I had almost said "people") may have been our ancestors, but there is reason to believe that *Australopithecus* was on the scene when the first representatives of *Homo* evolved, and may have co-existed with them in parts of Africa. Indeed, *Australopithecus* may not antedate *Homo* by much. If *Homo* did not evolve from *Australopithecus,* however, it must have evolved from something similar, some upright creature that lived in bands roaming the open country in search of roots, berries, grains, and small animals. Like *Australopithecus,* it must have taken refuge from predators in trees at night.

The transition from "man-apes" (such as *Australopithecus*) to "men" (*Homo*) was gradual, so that no one could say at what precise point it had been accomplished. About all that can safely be said of the first "men," according to Professor Howells, is that they "had achieved a skeleton which cannot be distinguished from our own, as far as we know, and were all about as big in the body as we are. Also, they

* William Howells, *Mankind in the Making,* New York, 1967, p. 135.

show a definite reduction in the size of the molar teeth compared to
the australopiths, as well as a diminution of the jaw, and so eventually of the face. Certainly their brains soon became larger. And
they were making tools as far back as we can trace them, and were
surely beginning to speak as well; we cannot tell if the man-apes had
any ability at all to speak." *

Although it has been customary, until recently, to classify the first
"men," according to their fossil remains, as belonging to various
genera, I here follow the latest tendency, which is to lump them all
as *Homo*. This has a semantic convenience, for it means that anything we call "human" is *Homo,* and whatever is not *Homo* is not
"human."

Until now, if anyone asked how long "man" had been in existence,
the answer was: about a million years. This is to say that we have
found remains of *Homo* going back that far, by contrast with the
remains of *Australopithecus,* which go back 4 million years. Recently,
however, a claim has been made that certain fossil finds in Tanzania
represent remains of *Homo* 1.75 million years old; even more recently a claim has been made that certain fossil finds in Kenya represent remains of *Homo* 2.6 million years old; and most recently a
claim has been made that certain fossil finds in Ethiopia represent
Homo remains some 4 million years old. I can only say that, evolution being as gradual and uncategorical as it is, we must not expect
exact datings, and that in the perspective of 3,000 million years it
makes little difference.

Although we may call the men of one to four million years ago
Homo, they were definitely not *sapiens,* and it is convenient to group
their remains under the designation *Homo erectus.* The first remains
of such men to be discovered, in Java in 1890, were formerly identified as belonging to *Pithecanthropus erectus* or Java Man, and a later
discovery in China was identified as *Sinanthropus pekinensis* or Peking
Man. Java Man appears to have been in the same size-range as European man today. While he stood quite erect, he had a large face
with great and still rather projecting jaws, and an immensely thick
skull. His cranial capacity was in the vicinity of 900 cubic centimeters, compared with about 394 cc. for a chimpanzee, 508 cc. for
Australopithecus, and 1,450 cc. for modern man. Peking Man, although much like Java Man in other respects, had a cranial capacity
of some 1,100 cc., and was more like modern man in his jaws and
teeth as well.

We have now got so close to our present that we have to count in
tens of thousands of years rather than in millions. Beginning at

* Howells, op. cit., p. 139.

some undefined point in time, perhaps 70,000 years ago, Neanderthal Man appeared on the scene. As we shall see in Chapter IX, he represents the beginning of civilized man in the sense that he went in for religious observances, which suggests an intellectual capacity for abstract concepts. It also suggests that he must have had the kind of spoken language we have, if less refined and subtle. Indeed, his brain was as large as ours, although presumably rather different, for his skull was low-browed and bun-shaped rather than domed. His face was most of his head, chinless and not flattened to the extent that ours is. "The Neanderthals," writes Professor Howells, "must have been short in stature, but powerful and bear-like. . . ." *
They inhabited Europe, the Middle East, and central Asia until roughly 35,000 B.P., when they disappeared, perhaps because they were unable to compete with or defend themselves against men of our own kind, who were replacing them.

"Men of our own kind," I say, meaning our direct ancestors; for we appear not to be descended from Neanderthal. We may call Neanderthal *Homo neanderthalis,* as has been common in the past, or we may follow the newer tendency and call him *Homo sapiens* (of the subspecies or race *neanderthalis*). In the latter case, he is simply one among the races of modern men that became extinct, as the Tasmanians became extinct within living memory.

The Neanderthal men disappeared rather suddenly 35,000 years ago, to the best of our knowledge, being replaced by what we can refer to as "ourselves." At this point in time, we ourselves have at last arrived on the scene and are about to demonstrate that life, all along, had a potentiality of which it gave no sign when it first began over 3,000 million years ago.†

* Howells, op. cit., pp. 192–193.
† By "ourselves" I mean our kind as it is in the twentieth century. However, since this includes African Pygmies, Eskimos, Nordics, and Australian aborigines, a certain breadth must be attributed to the term. It is as hard to apply the classical concept of races or subspecies to contemporary men as it is to apply it to domestic dogs, although the "breeds" of the latter vary from the Russian wolfhound to the Mexican hairless (two forms that are unlikely ever to have interbred). There are, moreover, reasons why we must be cautious of multiplying or emphasizing distinctions within the concept of a humanity which we have traditionally regarded as being one by virtue of a unique distinction that we may call "soul" or "human dignity" — a distinction related to mind, surely — that requires us to emphasize what we all have in common.

V

The Evolution of Brains

WHAT WE PROPERLY REGARD as the chief distinction of our own species is its brain. Like everything else in modern man, it is the product of a continuous evolution, going back, in this case, to some such rudimentary organization of nerves as is found in the head of a planarian.* Its development from this rudimentary level is associated with the vertebrates, partly because only they have grown large enough to provide the necessary room.

It is a notable fact that the development of the brain in birds and mammals sets these two classes off from all others and provides common ground between them. Because of the intellectual capacity they have in common, a man can enter into relations of mutual understanding and cooperation with a chimpanzee, an elephant, a dog, a dolphin — all of them fellow mammals. He can engage in reciprocal communication with any of them, as when a man asks a dog to fetch something or a dog suggests to a man that they go for a walk together.

Essentially the same mutual relationship is possible between men and birds, as anyone who has kept a pet crow or parrot knows. But we cannot enjoy it with reptiles, amphibians, or fish. A man and a lizard cannot communicate back and forth, holding what are in effect conversations, as a man and a bear can, or a man and a swan. This is because the development of the brain in birds and mammals is of a distinctly higher order than its development in other classes of vertebrates.†

* See p. 223 above.
† I don't know what species outside these two classes would have the most highly developed brain — perhaps, since size counts, an iguana or a Galapagos tortoise — and it is at least conceivable to me that there are reptiles which would meet the test of intellectual capacity I have here posed at least as well as, say, a mole. Perhaps the relations an Indian snake-charmer has with his performing cobra appear more intimate than any he could have with a mole, but I suspect that this would be an illusion consequent on the fact that the mole is slow-moving and, unlike the snake, unadapted to a habitat in which a man can meet it. Even though there were such a case, how-

It is significant that this development occurred quite independently in birds and mammals respectively, but at the same point in the history of the evolution of life — i.e., 150 million years ago. We may confidently attribute it to particular new requirements, arising in the relations between organism and environment, that imposed themselves on the process of natural selection, thereby determining that evolution would be in this direction. We may say, as I already have, that flight in birds, or such a necessity as that of leaping from branch to branch in mammals, caused natural selection to favor a brain equal to the task of coordinating all the sensations and movements that such operations entail. Without doubting this, however, I incline to believe that there is more to the matter.

Let me present a parallel case, that of the development of internal temperature control, which took place only in birds and mammals, and which occurred independently in each but at the same point in the history of evolution. Climatological changes undoubtedly favored the development, through natural selection, of such temperature control. But I suggest that, at earlier stages in the evolution of life, like climatological changes would not have caused it to occur.

To take an extreme example: before the advent of multicellular organisms such temperature control could not have developed. For one thing, unicellular organisms have too much surface in proportion to volume. For another, such insulation as is provided by feathers or fur requires the multiplication of cells. For still another, the basic equipment to be adapted, by evolution, for the production of heat or the reduction of temperature was lacking. Any adaptation of the organisms to such climatological severities at an earlier stage of evolution would therefore have had to take a different form (such as periods of dormancy) from that of internal temperature control.

To say this is to say that such temperature control could not evolve until life had reached a stage of overall development at which it was at last possible. What I suggest now — and this is my main point — is that, when life reached that stage, the development of temperature control became not only possible but virtually inevitable. We must consider that, under any circumstances in which environmental temperatures vary in a marked degree, internal temperature control is advantageous; and natural selection favors whatever is advantageous. So it is not an accidental coincidence that, although the class Aves and the class Mammalia each developed temperature con-

---

ever, it would be exceptional and would therefore not alter the basic fact of the gap in intellectual capacity between birds and mammals, on the one hand, and all the remaining forms of life on the other.

trol independently for itself, they developed it at the same time. The time had come when life was at last ready for it.

Internal temperature control tends to be a categorical condition: either an organism has it, as a bird does, or lacks it, like a fish or a lizard. An advanced brain is more a matter of degree. But there was a surge in the development of this organ, independently in birds and mammals at the same time, such as tends to make a change in degree a change in kind. The advanced development of the brain manifested by birds and mammals alike is advantageous simply in terms of the general environment they inhabit, aside from any special new features in that environment; and so, I suggest, it was virtually inevitable once it had become possible.

A second revolutionary development of the brain occurred some 150 million years after the first, associated with the emergence of modern man, and it may still be going on. I daresay it, too, had a certain inevitability.

We are not required to choose, here, between alternative explanations: (1) that temperature control or the modern brain developed because of specific environmental changes that imposed specific new requirements, or (2) that the reason it developed was that life had evolved to the point where it had become possible. The two explanations are equally valid and mutually complementary.

There are philosophical implications here, of the most fundamental kind, to which I call attention. What is implied is that evolution is a realization of potentialities inherent in life from the beginning, so that, barring accidents, it has a certain inevitability in its direction. A parallel is that of a newborn infant, which will predictably develop into a man with basic specifications that are known in advance, barring only such accidents as might prematurely cut off its life or leave it in an abnormal condition. When we come to deal with human history we shall have occasion to speculate about whether what happens in the evolution of civilization does not also have a certain inevitability.

So the process of evolution, in itself, represents the order that arises out of an original chaos.

The Beginning of Human Culture

UP TO THIS POINT we have been concerned with the emergence of modern man as one among other biological organisms. From here on, our concern will be with the evolution of human culture as well.

Human culture entails an adaptation of elements in the environment to human needs. The simplest example is the use of natural objects as tools. This is not quite confined to man. In the Galapagos Islands there is a finch, *Camarhynchus pallidus,* that picks up a twig and, holding it in its bill, uses it to dislodge insects that have taken refuge under the bark of trees where it cannot otherwise reach them.

A chimpanzee will use a twig to catch the termites on which it feeds, licking it first, then poking it into a termite hill and withdrawing it with termites stuck to its slimy surface. By contrast with the Galapagos finch, however, the chimpanzee may be said to manufacture its tool, for it pulls off any leaves or side-shoots on the twig it plans to use, trimming it carefully. This is essentially what a man does when he shapes the handle of an axe.

Australopithecus collected rocks, such collections having been found among the fossilized remains of his living-sites, some brought from miles away. We don't know what he did with them, but it would hardly have been beyond his ingenuity to put them to such simple uses as that of cracking nuts. (A herring gull or a hooded crow, with much less brain, will drop clams from a height to break them open.) One can imagine a man-ape knocking some sharp protuberance off a rock he was using so that it would not cut into the palm of his hand. One can imagine him rubbing it up to make it more comfortable to the hand.

If you strike one rock against another, perhaps just in play, you may chip pieces off it, and if the rock is flint the pieces are likely to have the shape of long flakes. So you may learn in time how to produce a sharp edge that proves useful. There is no reason to think that the man-apes carried this process far, but the hominids who succeeded them did. The results of their handiwork have survived, and there is evidence that they came to take artistic satisfaction in it.

The man-apes presumably used their fingers to dig for edible roots, but because the ground was excessively hard in places they would have been apt to discover the usefulness of sticks for digging. At some stage they would have begun to shape their digging sticks, perhaps using sharpened flints to give them pointed ends. Once a hominid had taken the trouble to shape a digging stick he would be more likely to keep it for further use, carrying it along on foraging expeditions, regarding it as a personal possession. (The making of tools must have given birth to the idea of property.) And once the hominids began carrying sticks with them they would surely have found them useful for all sorts of purposes, for striking at a poisonous snake, for knocking down fruit that would otherwise be beyond reach, for threatening a potential predator, perhaps for whacking an opponent over the head. They might also have found that the horns of dead antelopes came in handy for digging, and so picked them up as useful property when they came across them. What with one thing or another, they were becoming tool users, even tool makers, and as such were beginning to treasure up possessions.

The brain has to reach a certain stage of development before an organism will shape a tool. The Galapagos finch, intent on dislodging a particular insect at a particular moment, picks up a twig in its natural state, dropping it once the insect has been dislodged. In doing this it has no occasion to think beyond the moment, and indeed its brain would be incapable of the foresight needed. But the chimpanzee, preparing a probe to catch termites, plans ahead. Chimpanzees "do not always find a promising termite hill and then proceed to make a probe. They make the probe first, anticipating a meal of termites, although neither termites nor termite hills are in sight. . . . So these apes seem to have the basic concept of a tool as something to be shaped for a situation that has not yet materialized. . . ." *

*

We are concerned, in these chapters, with something called mind, associated with the most developed brains produced by evolution so

* J. E. Pfeiffer, *The Emergence of Man*, London, 1973, pp. 50–51. Note that the chimpanzee, being quadrupedal in its locomotion, had to carry the probe in its mouth, and this might be a reason for not carrying it as long or as far as otherwise. See also R. A. Hinde, *Animal Behavior*, 2nd ed., Tokyo, 1970, pp. 449–450.

far. One attribute of mind is its ability to comprehend what extends beyond the here-and-now. We may suppose that an earthworm, an oyster, or a butterfly has no awareness of anything beyond the sensations it experiences at the moment when it experiences them. It cannot remember yesterday, or anticipate tomorrow, or picture in imagination what is not present to its senses. It lives exclusively in the here-and-now.

Surely this applies, if in somewhat lesser degree, even to those relatively advanced organisms, birds. As I mentioned earlier, I have seen a cock pigeon ardently courting a hen five minutes after having almost been killed by a falcon — five minutes, indeed, after having been stunned by flying into a roof in its effort to escape. Apparently no impression of the experience remained in its consciousness five minutes later.

We must be careful here. I, who am often puzzled to know how my fellow men see the world we share in common, knowing only that they apparently do not see it quite as I do, cannot really tell how a bird sees it. But there is evidence that is at least suggestive, as in the case I have just cited; and simply on the basis of the structure of a bird's brain we may properly feel assured that it does not have a memory equal to our own.

We also have reason to believe that a bird lacks our ability to anticipate the future. But this is not always obvious in birds' behavior. While it is still only mid-afternoon, the Alpine choughs that have been feeding in the valleys take off for their roosting places among the high peaks many miles away, allowing themselves time to get to quarters before the fall of night. We say this is conditioned behavior of an automatic kind, not thoughtful, or that it represents an inherited pattern of behavior; but it is nevertheless such an anticipation of the future as would, one supposes, be beyond lower forms of life.

The black tern flies south to warm countries in autumn without consciously anticipating the winter that it has never experienced. We must suppose that it does so in response to an impulse the sense of which is unknown to it (but not to us).

A crow builds a nest by a like impulse, not thinking of the eggs for which it is being made; and later hatches the eggs without any appreciation of the fact that, since all the living crows must die, they have to be replaced by new generations if their kind is to survive.

However, even if we supposed that the crow built its nest because it wanted to produce progeny that it already saw in imagination, we could hardly credit it with a knowledge of the world before its own time, or a concern with what changes might occur in times to come. Our species, by contrast, has in its recent development reached a point where we can take account of thousands of millions of years, and measure distances in a like number of light-years.

As yet, it is not every representative of *Homo sapiens* who, like the reader of these pages, thinks in such large terms; but the farmer who, while it is still summer, builds a barn to shelter his cattle when winter comes, and who visits the graves of his parents on the anniversaries of their birth — such a farmer is manifesting the capacity for living beyond the here and the now that is a prime characteristic of what we call mind, and that is not manifested by any other species.

However, the chimpanzee that prepares a probe first, and then sets off to find a termite hill, is showing at least the rudiments of the capacity that allows us to plan for months and years ahead.

*

When an aberrant line of reptiles first developed wings, giving rise to the class Aves, the use of wings itself brought new requirements for natural selection to meet. It brought a requirement for better eyesight, and for a brain that could act quickly to coordinate multitudes of passing sensory impressions and muscular actions. The improved eyesight and the more developed brain, in their turn, made possible a better use of the wings in the form of swifter or more agile flight, which in turn called for still better eyesight and a still more developed brain. So a reciprocating evolution got under way (although, indeed, something like it had already long been under way), improvement in the efficiency of the wings, in this case, promoting improvements in the brain that, in turn, allowed further improvement in the wings.

When certain primates began to depend on tools, such dependence influenced the direction of their biological evolution. Their hands, originally evolved for clinging to branches, must have tended to become constantly more apt for the manipulation of instruments. (Perhaps our own ability to operate each finger independently of the others, as in playing the piano — which is not developed in our toes — represents the influence that the use of tools has had on the evolution of the hominid hand.) Above all, the dependence on tools must have caused natural selection to favor the development of certain aptitudes in the brain. Forethought would have been one such aptitude, since the manufacture of a tool must generally be undertaken in advance of the occasions for its use. The need to think beyond the moment would also have tended to favor memory, for the memory of circumstances in which a tool would have been useful may be what prompts its manufacture. (Perhaps the chimpanzee prepares his probe in anticipation of another visit to termite hills that he remembers from past visits.)

Finally, the manufacture and use of tools require the kind of intelligence that comprehends cause and effect. The hominid who chips away at a lump of flint, knocking off flakes, knows in advance that the effect of such trimming will be to give it a sharp edge, and knows in advance what a sharp edge can do. Since the relationship between cause and effect generally takes time to manifest itself, its appreciation is in itself associated with the ability to live beyond the immediate.

As tools became more elaborate, embodying an ever increasing element of artifice, the requirements that the brain was called on to meet would have increased, causing natural selection to produce ever more intelligent hominids who, by virtue of their developing intelligence, were able to produce ever more elaborate tools — and not only tools but clothing and shelter and a widening variety of amenities.

The point I am making is that, with the advent of culture, represented by the resort to artificial devices, biological and cultural evolution proceed by mutual interaction. Hand and brain combine to produce tools; the growing use of ever more elaborate tools and other artificial devices influences, in turn, the evolution of hand and brain — indeed, of the whole organism. When, for instance, man becomes a farmer rather than a hunter, the requirements of agriculture will promote the development by natural selection of bodily and mental aptitudes different from those he had had. A stocky if slow-moving body may be best for the man who works with a spade, while a slender, long-limbed body is best for the man who hunts with bow-and-arrow or with spear. Certainly the ability to plan is even more important for the farmer than for the hunter. So the whole cultural complex, as it develops, influences the direction of organic evolution.

From this point on, then, it will be well to think of human evolution as advancing along two lines on a basis of reciprocal action (although in the largest view all is one). Organic and cultural evolution advance in mutuality.

When this begins, with the first use of unshaped rocks or sticks by man-apes, the process of reciprocation is so slow as hardly to be perceptible except over periods of tens of thousands of years. But with the constant development of culture, the cultural factors in evolution become ever more prominent, thereby tending toward a constant speeding up of the whole process — for cultural evolution is not inherently limited in its pace as genetic evolution is (there can be no genetic change at all in less than one generation, and even then it can hardly spread through a population in less than many generations). So it is that what one sees today is an increasingly rapid cultural evolution of mankind that draws the slower process of biological evolution after it.

Not just man, but life itself, has entered a new phase.

VII

The Beginning of Human Society

A MONKEY COPES WITH PREDATORS by its agility in escaping through the mazes of the forest it inhabits. A gorilla deters them by its size and power, which are particularly effective inside the jungle of forest trees, where a leopard, for example, cannot maneuver freely.

On the open plain, mammalian predators are more likely to hunt in packs, like wild dogs, or in small groups, like lions. The relatively unarmed mammals on which they prey had better be small enough to hide in the grass or in burrows, or fleet of foot like antelopes, or as big as elephants (which, along with their size, have feet to trample and tusks to tear). If they have none of these advantages, their only recourse is to come together in bands organized for a common defence, like baboons.

The first primates to venture out onto the savannas must have been in somewhat the position of present-day baboons. They were not small enough to hide, or large enough to intimidate, or fleet enough to outrun the great predators that hunted over the open plain. Consequently, they must have been compelled to develop a degree of social organization, involving cooperation and discipline, that had been unnecessary in the labyrinth of the forest.

A monkey alone in the forest can survive, but a baboon alone on the savanna cannot. He will quickly be found by a predator that he can neither escape nor resist. His only security, then, is to be in the midst of a community organized for a common defence.

There are groves of trees scattered about the savannas, and it is in the branches of such a grove that a troop of East African baboons, perhaps numbering eighty individuals, will spend the night. When morning comes it sets out on a foraging expedition across the open grassland, but in formation. The mothers with infants, accompanied by young juveniles and older males, are in the center of the formation; younger adults of both sexes surround them; adult males tend to form an outer ring. Any predators are likely to be deterred by a line of male baboons, with fangs bared, that confronts them as they consider whether to attack. These outer males are not defending themselves, primarily, but the community.

Such close association of baboons, because it gives rise to tensions between individuals that may lead to excessive quarreling, requires the maintenance of discipline. Adult males interfere to stop the quarreling of others, and the dominant male in a troop occasionally has to assert his authority over other adult males. A degree of order must be kept if the troop is to be held together as an effective organization for mutual defence, and this requires policing by those best able to discharge the responsibility.*

As the first primates to do so ventured ever farther out on the savannas they must have developed some like social organization, for they could not otherwise have survived in the open. The man-apes must have traveled in troops, they must have set guards, they must have taken special measures for the protection of mothers and infants, and they must have attended to the maintenance of discipline. Because they were upright, however, with a capacity for using their hands to provide and manipulate tools, they were to go beyond the baboons in this and associated developments.

*

The primate order is basically vegetarian, and so were our ancestors while they still inhabited the forest. When they emerged from it, however, their new life on the savannas must have entailed an increasing dependence on meat; for the savannas, rich in animal life and in grasses, were poor in nuts and fruit. They would surely have caught grasshoppers and lizards, as Australian aborigines still do. They would have taken birds' eggs, fledglings, and any injured birds or small mammals they found. Fossil remains show that they came in time to depend increasingly on catching larger game, which provided a more ample diet if also a greater challenge. So the vulnerable vegetarians from the forest themselves became predators on an ever larger scale.

An experienced hunter in open country today can run down and catch with his bare hands hares, small antelopes, even pheasants. Although a hare can run faster than a man, a man who knows its ways can, by anticipating its changes of course, close in on it by shortcuts. Moreover, after its initial sprint a hare generally "freezes," trying to escape detection by immobility, and while this

---

* For this account of social organization among the baboons I have relied on Pfeiffer, op. cit., chiefly pp. 85–90 and 254–271, M. D. Sahlins, "The Origin of Society," *Scientific American*, September 1960; and S. L. Washburn and Irven DeVore, "The Social Life of Baboons," *Scientific American*, June 1961.

may succeed with predators that can recognize as life only what moves, it is less apt to put an intelligent hominid off the track. As to any ground bird with habits like those of a pheasant, when pursued it quickly exhausts itself by successive flights, each shorter than the last, until the pursuer can put his hands upon it.

The man-apes of 4 million years ago, still not altogether upright, may have matched us more closely in running than in walking ability. Even if they were inferior in both, however, their evolutionary adaptation to open country would, over the millennia, have increased their fleetness of foot. As they evolved increasingly for life in the open, the proportion of insects and lizards in their diet must have diminished while the proportion of mammals, up to the size of small antelopes, rose.

Although their teeth and fingers would have been adequate for skinning a hare to get at its flesh, they would not have served to tear away the tougher skin of an antelope. Consequently, the systematic hunting of game that large, even if it did not have to await the invention of weapons, must have depended on the development of sharp-edged tools for cutting and skinning.

With the passage of the millennia they would also have learned to organize themselves for the collective hunting required by larger game. We know how wolves and other carnivores cooperate to bring down prey that would be beyond the capacity of one alone. The developing hominids, undoubtedly, also came to cooperate in ambushing prospective prey, in cutting it off from escape, or in attacking it from more than one side at a time. So, having begun by organizing themselves for defence against predation, they must have gone on to organize themselves for predation itself.

What was notable about the early hominids (as about their descendants) was how poorly furnished they were by nature for fighting, either to defend themselves or to overcome the resistance of their prey. Having developed as vegetarians primarily, they lacked the tearing claws or penetrating fangs of the great carnivores; presumably because they had originally inhabited the forests, they lacked the swiftness of foot by which such ungulates as zebras and wild asses were able to survive; and they were not clothed in such armor as protects armadilloes. These natural deficiencies were to be made good, in time, by organization and artifice, the artifice consisting of manufactured tools, weapons, and protective devices. There would be spears, slingshots, bows-and-arrows, shields — eventually firearms. In a word, the deficiencies would be made good by a cultural evolution that was closely associated with the evolution of the brain.

*

Nothing is more notable in the emergence of man than the development of his brain, how far it went how quickly. From *Australopithecus* to *Homo erectus* the hominid brain almost doubled in size. One has the impression of such a development as causes a flower, long prepared, to open overnight.

I have already observed that the size of organisms is a precondition for the development of a brain. An insect, limited in size by its structure, could not develop a brain capable of memory, let alone abstract thought. The limitation that flight imposes on the size of flying birds precludes the development of a brain like modern man's, which occupies some 1,400 cc. of space within the organism. The large reptiles of 200 million years ago failed to develop it, as they failed to develop internal temperature control, and the reptiles that remain today, like the fishes and amphibians, show no promise of doing so. That leaves the mammals. The largest mammals, elephants and whales, have brains that exceed by orders of magnitude those of any non-mammalian forms of life — in their capabilities as in their size.*

Even if elephants or whales had the brains needed for making tools, they would find themselves in the position of armless men if they tried to make them. It is not the brain alone but the combination of hand and brain, together with the eye, that enters into primate tool-making. In any case, elephants and whales, being less helpless before the challenges of the environment than the early hominids, have had no like need to make up for natural deficiencies by artifice. So it is that the most spectacular development of the mammalian brain has been in the primate line that leads to modern man.

A direct consequence of this development has been the enlargement of the head that holds the brain. This has entailed a widening of the female pelvis to make room for the enlarged head in the process of birth, thereby creating a separation between the legs that is lacking in the male. This separation, because it impairs the female's ability in running and leaping, has made for a differentiation between the respective roles of male and female, perhaps most markedly so in the days when our ancestors lived largely by hunting. Because hunting required speed and agility, it was necessarily reserved for males.

There is reason to think that the role of the male as hunter, re-

* The elephant's reputation for memory has a basis in reality (see Pfeiffer, op. cit., pp. 297–298), and the humpback whale indulges in vocal performances, equivalent to song in birds, that quite exceed the capacity of any bird's brain (see Charles Hartshorne, *Born to Sing: An Interpretation and World Survey of Bird Song*, Bloomington, 1973, p. 31).

flected in the course of natural selection, increased the sexual differentiation on which it was based. The female did not have to be as
big and strong as the male, nor to have his judgement in timing and
the estimation of distances, the more so because she could rely on
him for protection as well as for meat.

The size of the human brain at birth was only one of the factors
that entered into the progressive differentiation, alike in bodily
structure and in role, between male and female. The increasing
dependence of the species on the effectiveness of its brain required,
in addition to the brain itself, its training by means of the process we
call learning. The human brain is able to divide twenty-one by
seven, but not until it has been trained to do so, and such training
cannot normally be completed in less than the first six years of life.
It is also able to derive square roots, but the training to do this would
require more than the first six years. Today, the production of a
trained physicist normally takes over twenty years. As the demands
made on the brain in the course of evolution increased, the learning
process lengthened. As the learning process lengthened, the period
of juvenile dependence on parental care lengthened with it. A monkey is independent of such care within a year, but a human infant at
one year old is still helpless. The progressive lengthening of the
period of juvenile dependence, manifested in physiological as well as
mental development, required the maternal parent to concentrate
on the care of her progeny, not for a few weeks or months but for
years. This made her, in turn, more dependent on permanent protection and provision by the male. Here was one basis for permanent mating and the development of the family within the larger
social organization of a band.

While the female hominid could hardly have gone hunting with
the male, if only because she had to attend constantly to her children, she could forage for roots and other vegetable food, taking the
children along. Here we have the basis of a society organized for
hunting and gathering in terms of a division of labor, like the societies of Australian aborigines or African Bushmen today, the men
being hunters, the women gatherers. However, if the men of a
troop are to go off in one direction every morning, and the women
in another, there must be a home base at which they reunite in the
evening. A troop of baboons, organized chiefly for gathering, can
move all together and find a new place of encampment every evening, but a troop based on such a division of labor as requires the
dispersal of its members must have a fixed center which is home.
And if a society possessed of the growing hominid skills has a home,
it will be disposed to do some rearranging in it — if only, to begin

with, pushing a rock out of the way or removing a litter of dead branches. The evolving hominids will be constantly improving the facilities of the natural environment, until someday it will no longer be the natural environment at all.* Here the artifice that will eventually blossom into civilization begins to go beyond the making of tools.

The hominid division of labor also implies a development of sharing. It will not do for the men to eat their prey upon the spot as soon as they have killed it, or for the women to eat the roots and berries they find as they find them; for the consequence would be that the men ate only meat, the women and children only vegetable food. Therefore, the men must bring their kill and the women the fruit of their gathering back to the home base, where all sit down together for a mixed meal of meat, vegetables, and fruit. Such sharing, which requires planning and organization, is exclusively human.

*

The organized activities of a company of baboons are sufficiently simple to require no more than a few simple means of communication among its members. There must be some warning signal, perhaps a particular kind of grunt, by which one member alerts the others to danger. There are bodily attitudes, facial expressions, or sounds whereby one threatens another, or responds to a threat by appeasement. There are the gestures and sounds connected with courtship, and those by which adults impose obedience on the young. When a troop, leaving the grove in which it has passed the night, sets out on a foraging expedition, it may be that a dominant male starts the proceeding and gives the direction by simply setting forth himself, to be followed by the others as school-children follow their teacher. Natural selection has prevented any such extreme of noncomformist individualism as would cause members to take the directions they might severally prefer if the choice were theirs, in disregard of leadership or consensus.

As the activities of a society become more complex, however, requiring coordination of dispersed undertakings by various subgroups within it, the requirements that the means of communication have to meet increase. If, at dawn, the men are to go off in one direction and the women in another, it may be important for the two groups to be able to agree on where they shall come together again, if only because they have to change their home base from time to time. If some are to go one way in quest of stones to make new

* It will be the environment represented by a penthouse apartment in Manhattan.

tools, while others are to explore a certain riverbed in search of birds' eggs or frogs, and others still are to go somewhere else in the hope of ambushing a young buffalo from a herd discovered the day before — if there is to be a division of labor at this level of complexity, involving different activities by different groups, activities that vary from day to day, then a few grunts, posturings, or facial expressions will no longer suffice. So all the developments we have been discussing in this and the previous chapter lead to the necessary development of language — of such language as is known to the primitive hunters and gatherers of our own day.

Like almost everything else in evolution, language as we practice it was not a sudden invention. It was a gradual elaboration, imperceptible over the generations, of the devices by which all the higher animals carry on communication within the membership of their own kind. In the case of man alone, it would grow beyond the practical requirements of daily intercourse to accommodate abstract thought. And this would become the principal foundation of what I have called mind.

Over the thousands of millions of years, atoms had combined to form molecules, molecules to form cells, and cells to form ever larger and more elaborate organisms. Out of an underlying chaos, these combinations of elementary particles seem to have formed themselves. When at last they began to speak in the language of men a threshold was crossed. Mind had been born.

VIII

Promethean Man

THROUGHOUT THE AGE OF REPTILES the climate had been mild over most of the earth, intermediate between excessive heat and excessive cold, with little difference between seasons. Then it began to be more marked in its seasonal variations. Between a million and half a million years ago, the earth began to go through a series of glacial periods, lasting tens of thousands of years, separated by interglacial periods that lasted up to hundreds of thousands of years.* (We may be in such an interglacial period today.) Ice-caps like those that still remain on Greenland and the Antarctic continent spread, during the periods of glaciation, to cover a large part of the northern hemisphere, including the region of the Great Lakes, the British Isles, and such mountainous areas farther south as the Alps and the Caucasus.

The extremes of climatic variability represented by the alternating glacial and interglacial periods called for adaptations beyond the capacity of many forms of life, which consequently became extinct. The genus *Homo*, however, although it must have suffered, not only continued its progress but appears to have thriven on adversity. This can only be because it had already reached the stage at which genetic adaptation was being supplemented by ever more elaborate cultural adaptation. Human artifice could, increasingly, provide insulation against a hostile environment.

When the series of glaciations began, perhaps 500,000 to 600,000 years ago, members of the genus *Homo* appear to have spread from East Africa to what is now the south of France. By the time of the last glacial period so far, some 70,000 years ago, Neanderthal man was enduring it in what is now France, Belgium, and Germany.

He could surely not have survived in snow and ice and blizzard if he had not already gone well beyond the beginning stage in the cul-

* We don't know just when this was and the dating of the glaciations is a matter of diverse estimates by different authorities.

tural evolution of his kind. Indeed, the rigors of the environment must have forced the pace of his cultural evolution and the associated development of his brain. He endured because he clothed himself in the hairy or furry skins of the animals he killed with his increasingly effective weapons, and housed himself in caves from which he excluded the most extreme manifestations of the elements. Above all, he endured because he had mastered the use of fire for the provision of warmth and protection.

*

Although men have thought of fire as a substance, like earth or water, and although it has had the name of a substance in all languages, and although we still speak of it as if it were a substance, it is nothing of the sort. It is not matter at all but, rather, the manifestation of a certain chemical activity going on in matter. It is energy given off in the form of light and heat during the process called oxidation.

To those who think of it as a substance it must appear to have magical properties, for mere friction may cause it to spring out of nothing, after which it may die away into nothing again. Nor is it subject, like earth and water, to measure; for a single spark may grow with the utmost rapidity to engulf a forest, while as much as engulfs a forest may dwindle to a spark and then disappear altogether.

For those who think of it as a substance, it not only has these magical properties but has them in association with a unique power to inflict pain and destruction. A spark may become a prairie fire, bringing death to all animals that are unable to outdistance it in the rapidity of its spread, and where it has passed it leaves only a blackened desert. Therefore it arouses terror and is avoided by all living creatures that have mobility and the sensory means to detect it at a distance.

All the higher animals in a state of nature must feel this fear of fire.* For fire, although it appears to be living, cannot be seized, cannot be driven back, cannot be overcome by any strength. Man, too, must have known this fear. But a time came when, mastering it, he also learned to master its hitherto unmasterable cause. He must have acquired some familiarity with the ways of fire, how it depends on fuel to keep alive, dying when fuel is denied it; how it is baffled

---

* A primitive primate, the Philippine tarsier, is said to pick up hot embers left from camp-fires (Pfeiffer, op. cit., pp. 148–149). How few are the statements one can make to which there are no exceptions! But a rule is not necessarily invalidated by exceptions.

by moisture, diminishing with a hissing sound among wet leaves, succumbing to heavy rain. And, at the same time that such observations may have lessened his terror, he presumably had occasion to appreciate the fact that fire has its good side as well as its bad. Under control, it might be used to supply the warmth on which survival depends — for men may die of either extreme, of ice as well as of fire. And, finally, it provided light in the darkness.

The mastery of fire was not as gradual a process as the mastery of tool-craft. Although it could hardly have been achieved overnight, one can still imagine an individual human who was the first to hold aloft a burning branch. One can imagine that it became a kind of sport to do so. There was daredevilry for young men in going about among their fellows with a branch that had fire at its far end. They might threaten one another with such branches in play, and if they could do that they could equally well threaten the saber-toothed tiger, who would be baffled, who would flatten his ears to his head and make off. A tiger that had a flaming brand hurled at it might be wary of ever again attacking men.

Once men began to handle burning sticks they would quickly learn how to control fire — how to transfer it from stick to stick, how to keep it alive by feeding, how to keep it within appointed limits by clearing the surrounding ground of anything it might catch hold of in its greed. Their chief concern would have been to keep it going once they had it, and to acquire it again when they had lost it. Naturally occurring fire is not common away from the cones of live volcanoes. It arises, perhaps only briefly, among dead trees struck by lightning, or falling rocks may strike sparks in dry grass, or there may be spontaneous combustion in deposits of coal or shale-oil. The time would come when men were able to make fire by striking sparks deliberately, or by rubbing wood until the friction made it hot enough to light tinder. The important thing at first, however, must have been not to let fire go out. It was a sort of capricious god that had to be fed as did men, and fuel began to take on some of the importance of food. All this required planning, and the association of cause and affect.

With cold winters upon them, the men who had mastered fire would have achieved a superiority to all the other animals, like that of gods. It is here that human supremacy truly begins.

Until he had the help of fire man could not make a home for himself in caves, for they were already occupied by beasts of greater power than himself, such as bears and hyenas. Men cornered in a cave, moreover, might be easy prey for such wildcats as the saber-toothed tiger. The earliest clear evidence of man's use of fire is in a cave of southern France, which has the charred remains of a number of hearths going back, apparently, to some 750,000 years ago. So, at about the time when the series of successive glaciations began, man in western Europe acquired the means of dispossessing the other cave dwellers, to make his own hearth and home in the quarters from which he had evicted them.

Until men brought fire into their service they had never had the use of any physical power except that of their own muscles. With the mastery of fire they added power from the environment in the form of energy released by chemical reactions. For the best part of a million years that energy was used only in its raw form as heat and light. It was used to communicate warmth to the human body, and in time it was used for cooking. (A piece of raw meat fallen accidentally among the embers would have made for the discovery of cooking, or a piece of frozen meat thawed out before the fire might have done the same.) It was certainly used to cow predators, making them keep their distance. And with this use must have begun that remarkable awe of man, since compounded by his resort to missiles that strike from a distance, an awe which seems to have become incorporated into the genetic constitution of virtually all wild birds and mammals. For even the greatest wildcats, and other beasts more powerful than naked man, will avoid him and run from him, though the littlest birds and beasts, which also fear him, will move about fearlessly among the horses or cattle that, in themselves, are conspicuously bigger and stronger.

The time would come, although still far away, when the energy of fire would be used in converted form: for example, as steam-pressure to move pistons and turn wheels. Water power and wind power would someday be added to it as environmental energy that man would bring into his own use. Finally, a form of power that manifests itself naturally in the sun, but nowhere on earth, would also be added, the nuclear energy released, not by chemical reactions but by reactions within the nucleus of the atom.

*

Up to this point we have followed man's descent from that first vertebrate, the little jawless fish of 400 million years ago, through the amphibians and reptiles to the arboreal creature, rather like a shrew, that was the first primate; and from this first primate through the man-apes, *Ramapithecus* and *Australopithecus*. The evolution it represents over its 400 million years is ever accelerating, as it had been for the 3,000 million years that preceded it, as it will continue to be, as it still is today. At the point where man (defined as the genus *Homo*) emerges, that evolution is marked by the sudden growth of the brain, which had begun (e.g., in the flatworm) merely as a nerve center to receive sensations from the immediate environment and communicate responses to the parts of the body concerned.

As far as we have gone in this review (i.e., up to about 600,000 years ago), the evolution of the brain has been purely utilitarian. It has enabled the evolving hominids to make tools and weapons, to organize society on the basis of planning for mutual advantage, to divide their labor and share its products, to bring fire into their service. They now live in caves, wear clothes, manufacture a variety of implements, cook their food, and apparently are able, by organized conspiracy, to hunt down and kill even such beasts as the rhinoceros and the woolly mammoth. At night they sit in a circle around the campfire, which, in addition to keeping off predators, provides warmth and a flickering visibility. Perhaps the changing images made by the flames and the shadows on the rock stimulate their imagination in ways we have all experienced.

Now, at this key point, the developing brain begins to be used for a purpose that can no longer be defined as strictly utilitarian. It suddenly takes on a life of its own, creating its own world of abstractions. It begins to liberate itself from the here-and-now, not just for the purpose of exploring other actualities elsewhere but so as to create worlds of the imagination in which the chaos of the here-and-now may be resolved into some kind of order.

The brain that has taken on a life of its own in this sense has acquired the attribute we call mind.

IX

Imagination

WE SEE in every domain of experience that the particles of being are meaningless by themselves, that mutually unassociated particulars, each standing alone, represent chaos. If we examine the letters in the preceding sentence one by one, each as an entity in itself, we find no meaning in them. If we examine the words one by one, we find that, although the letters of which they are composed gain some significance, chaos remains as long as each word, regarded separately, is thereby deprived of context. Even the sentence as a whole needs a framework of thought to be meaningful — such a framework as I began establishing in Part One, Chapter I. The reader who has comprehended this framework knows what I mean, now, when I say that order arises out of an underlying chaos.

However, when one begins to establish associations among particulars in one's mind one begins to move in the direction of increasing abstraction. If I refer to a particular man I am not referring to an abstraction; but if I refer to five men as a committee I am; and if I refer to the French nation (the nation of Frenchmen) I am carrying abstraction still further in the degree of its removal from particulars; and I am carrying it further still when, as I have been doing right along, I refer to "man."

An earthworm is incapable of abstraction because, having no more than the rudiments of a brain, it is limited to the immediate here-and-now. It cannot in its consciousness put one experience together with another such experience, and so arrive at an abstraction, because it has no memory within which to retain experiences while it puts them together. Birds do have a capacity to remember, but, as we saw in Chapter VI, it is limited. An elephant, confronted by a man it last saw ten years before, may react in such a way as to suggest that it retains the memory of him, but here the term "memory" is, perhaps, being used in a special sense.

What we mean by "memory," using the term loosely, may be simply a kind of conditioning. The pigeon that has been attacked by the falcon may not "remember" the experience five minutes later, but it has been conditioned so that the next time it sees a falcon it will show a fear born of the experience it does not "remember." The experience has left an impression, but the impression does not manifest itself in the bird's consciousness as a direct memory of the experience. Perhaps the elephant's "memory" of the man it has not seen for ten years represents merely a like conditioning.

The distinction I am making here entails the faculty of imagination. A man who is attacked by a bull, as the pigeon was attacked by the falcon, can later reproduce the experience in his imagination, so that when he returns home he is able to tell his wife about it in circumstantial detail. I can evoke in my imagination the image of a person I have not seen for ten years so as to give a description of him, but whether such a feat is possible for the elephant, or possible in more than rudimentary terms, I don't know.*

*

I have said that, with the advent of man, a threshold has been crossed, mind has been born. Consequently, man behaves like no other animal.

No other animal tends to the ill or injured of its kind, let alone to the dead. If one in a troop of baboons, or one in a pack of wolves, or one in a herd of elephants, being injured or ill, cannot keep up with the others, it falls behind, disregarded, to meet the death that presumably awaits it. A dog knows death in its experience of particular corpses — whether of a hare it has killed, of another dog, or of its dead master over whom it may stand guard in uncomprehending distress — but can have no notion of death in the abstract. It cannot ponder the difference between being and non-being. It is not even aware of the fact of its own incomprehension, which consists of its inability to answer a question it could not have asked. Indeed, the very fact that so abstract a question cannot occur to it represents the limits within which its consciousness is confined. (Since we ourselves can think only in words, the dog would have to have language like ours before it could engage in such question and answer. Abstractions are nominal in the sense that they are associated with words.)

---

* I am here presenting in categorical terms, for the purpose of exposition, a distinction that I suppose not to be categorical in fact. Perhaps the elephant did retain a vague and faint image of the man during the ten years, an image which may occasionally have appeared to it in its dreams. Presumably elephants do dream (since we have reason to believe that dogs dream), and dreaming represents imagination. The faculty of imagination may be more developed or less, and with it the capacity for remembering in imagination.

I cannot say that the dog does not transcend the immediate here-and-now, since it may go in search of human help for a dead master. But this is still the exercise of the brain within those limits of the particular and the utilitarian that the mind of man has transcended.

Neanderthal man not only buried his dead but did so to the accompaniment of ritualistic observances. The corpse was carefully laid in the grave dug for it, with tools at its hand in case of need, and apparently with the roasted meat of cattle to appease hunger on some journey of the dead. Around the head of one grave six pairs of ibex horns were fixed in the earth, presumably to serve the purpose of a gravestone. The fossilized remains of pollen in another case suggest that the corpse was laid on a bed of flowers, accompanied by a woven wreath, and that probably flowers were scattered on top of the grave. I cannot improve on Professor Pfeiffer's interpretation, which I here cite:

> Neanderthal man invented, or at least formalized, illusion when he invented burial. The belief in an afterlife says in effect that death is not what it seems; that it represents an apparent ending only, an ending only as far as the evidence of the senses is concerned; and that in this case, the crude evidence of the senses is wrong. Reality involves not observed and observable "facts" but an abstraction, the idea that death is actually a passage from one world to another. In this respect the burial ceremonies of prehistoric hunters expressed the kind of thinking used today to develop theories about the structure of the atomic nucleus or the expanding universe.*

We see in the Neanderthal burial all science and all poetry, for both are the products of the imagination that engenders abstractions. As the above quotation notes its relevance to science, so the following suggests its relevance to poetry:

> And as imagination bodies forth
> The forms of things unknown, the poet's pen
> Turns them to shapes, and gives to airy nothing
> A local habitation and a name.†

When our vision, extending ever further beyond the here-and-now, has at last reached a certain extent, we begin to wonder what came before and what comes after these little lives of ours that we know directly. The lives we know directly, as experience of the

* J. E. Pfeiffer, *The Emergence of Man*, London, 1973, pp. 171–172.
† Shakespeare, *A Midsummer Night's Dream*, V, 1, 14–17.

here-and-now, represent chaos in the absence of a context. So our imagination bodies forth the form of things unknown out of a need to resolve the chaos, to discover order.

Now, for the first time since life began, it has evolved to the point where its most advanced organisms have at last become conscious of a world that extends, not just beyond the here-and-now, but across the horizon into the realm of what is unknown. They have become aware that the scene on which they find themselves existed before they came, that death will remove them from it in due course, and that it will remain after their removal as before their arrival. Evolution has progressed to the point where the most advanced representatives of life hold in imagination a wide world that, in addition to dwarfing them, exists quite independently of them, so that they feel themselves strangers in it.* They have become aware of inhabiting only temporarily an alien world, and of being, so to speak, under the imminent and final jurisdiction of death, which may take them away at any moment, either transporting them to a realm of which no one has any direct knowledge or simply returning them to nothingness.

Knowledge of the fact of the unknown, in itself, makes for an anxiety that is perpetual. A dog may experience anxiety when his master fails to come home at an expected hour; but such anxiety, being contingent on circumstances belonging to the here-and-now, is passing. It is not like the permanent state of anxiety in which the dog would live if conscious of the fact that death, existing as an abstraction in his imagination, might come at any moment to strike his master or himself, and that it was, in any case, inevitable.

Evolving life, in the form of man, has at last come to bear the burden of the knowledge of infinity.

Men, having become conscious of inhabiting this world only temporarily, are yet without direct knowledge of what came before or what will come after. Their limited faculties, like the eyes of a blind man, present only nothingness when they try to apprehend what lies beyond this world's horizons. But nothingness, if accepted as the context of life, would leave life without meaning, like a lone word on an otherwise blank page.

If our minds are to retain the sanity we associate with sense, as opposed to nonsense, if we are to escape from chaos, then we must assume that the context of the being we know is some order, even if we don't know what that order is. Most of us have to fill the vacuum of ignorance, however, with something more specific than the postulation of an order accepted as unknown. We are moved to fill it with

* This sense of a separation between oneself and the world, which is the basis of self-consciousness, will lead to Kim's question: "Who is Kim?" It will also lead A. E. Housman to refer to himself as "a stranger and afraid/In a world I never made."

a particular imagined order that we believe in, perhaps, only on the basis of tradition and faith. So the apparently capricious death of a cherished child, which might otherwise seem to represent chaos, may be explained as the summons of an unseen deity to life in an afterworld, where we will join it when our own time comes. We people the realm of ignorance with imagined deities, thus bodying forth the forms of things unknown. In default of anything better, we create an imaginary order to hold back chaos. Or, as opportunity serves, we create progressively the expanding scientific order that, as far as we can make it go (and there will always be a beyond from which it is excluded), accommodates what we are able to observe, directly or indirectly, through our senses.

As the realm of science has widened, the world of the mythologizing imagination has had to give way or adapt itself. Men could imagine that the summit of Mount Olympus was the abode of gods only until, having at last climbed up to it, they had seen for themselves. They could imagine that the God of Genesis had created the earth and all its species in six days — but only until, having uncovered the geological and paleontological evidence, they saw that it could not have been literally so.

*

"Here-and-now" is not an exact term, if only because, in common usage, each of its components is conceived of as having some undefined extension. (A point in either time or space, defined as dimensionless, is no more than a mathematical concept without physical being.) When I refer to the present, using the term "now," I may mean the present minute or the present year, depending on the context. If I say of someone that he lives only in the "here-and-now" I may mean that on any particular day his mind is completely preoccupied by what he has to do that day. "Here-and-now," although imprecise in both cases, is more limited for an earthworm than for a farmer who, surveying his land from a hilltop, decides on the next task to be undertaken, whether to plow the field at the foot of the hill or to cut the hay on its slope.

Perhaps, when I have referred in these pages to the increasing capacity of evolving life to live beyond the here-and-now, I should have referred to its capacity to live in an ever wider here-and-now. With some variability depending on context, however, there are limits to how far the term can be stretched. Stretching it to these limits, it can still not be made to include, for any one of us, the world before we were born or any afterlife in which we may believe or about which we may speculate.

For hundreds of millions of years consciousness had been developing among the forms of life that represented the vanguard of evolution, and with it an ever broadening awareness of the environment that, in each case, constituted its here-and-now. Always, however, the horizon of what was directly accessible to testing, through the medium of the senses, confined it. This is the horizon that, with the advent of mind, was at last transcended; and its transcendence was what opened up the vistas of infinity.

The mythology of the Greeks or of Genesis was, presumably, beyond the imaginative capacity of Neanderthal man, as was the formal science of historic times. But he had become aware of abstract death, and so of an unknown world beyond the one that was physically accessible. In him, imagination had at last gone off the edge of the knowable world into what lies beyond. There can be no other explanation of the fact that he buried his dead in such a way as to equip them for a journey on which, as he must have imagined, they were destined to embark.

X

The Advent of Modern Man

I CONCLUDED CHAPTER IV with the statement that the Neanderthal men disappeared rather suddenly 35,000 years ago, being replaced by men like the present-day Caucasians. The newcomers were the so-called Cro-Magnon men. "These people," William Howells writes, "were Europeans, the forerunners, and at least partly the ancestors, of the people who live there today. There can be no doubt that they were members of the White, or Caucasoid, racial stock, because the features of their skulls and facial skeletons all have that stamp. The one actual painting of a man so far known . . . gives us a White man . . . with black hair and a black beard." *

In Cro-Magnon, certain tendencies in hominid evolution appear to achieve their fulfillment. The face, with its jaws and teeth, has been retracted and diminished to the point where it is no more than what is needed by a creature that, after cooking its meat, lifts it to the mouth, rather than eating it as a dog eats a carcass lying on the ground. At the same time, the skull, with a thinner wall, has become domed over a high forehead, providing a better designed case for the enlarged brain. While Neanderthal's brain was about as large, it may have been somewhat less advanced, housed as it was in a bun-shaped cranium; and this makes more plausible the supposition that Neanderthal disappeared because he could not hold his own against the newly arrived Cro-Magnon.

With the arrival of Cro-Magnon various advances in utilitarian technology occur, represented by a harpoon with backward-pointing barbs, a spear-thrower, the bow-and-arrow, bone needles for sewing. But the technology now begins to go markedly beyond the utilitarian to achieve what has artistic value in itself — as when a woman of our time, having made a dress for the utilitarian purpose of keeping herself warm, decorates it with embroidery. Some of these people produced thin stone blades in the shape of laurel leaves too deli-

* *Mankind in the Making*, New York, 1967, pp. 208–209.

cate for use, as if the demonstration of fine craftsmanship was a sufficient end in itself.

We must think increasingly, now, of people living like the primitive peoples of our own era — say the pre-agricultural Indians of North America before the coming of the white man — in temporary settlements with shelters of various kinds, using language as we do, elaborating mythologies, engaging in ceremonies or rituals; but nomadic in greater or lesser degree, following the animal herds, visiting salmon runs in season to trap fish. Although we refer to them as "Cro-Magnon man" at the time of their arrival on the scene, the fact that they are, in effect, ourselves, is reason for dropping the term at this point and referring to them as "prehistoric man" — until, some 6,000 years ago, they develop a written language and begin to keep records, thereby inaugurating what we call history.

(These people have come a long way from the tree-shrew, let alone the first organic cell; but by an evolution imperceptible from century to century and unbroken in its continuity. If, in any one generation, the question where this evolution was going had been asked, the only possible response would have been that a much larger temporal perspective was needed before an answer could even be suggested. This is still the only possible response.)

*

The period we are now dealing with runs from 33,000 to about 6,000 B.P. It is the period of the fourth and latest glaciation so far, and of its retreat. At its mid-point, say 20,000 B.P., the North Sea, the English Channel, and the Irish Sea do not exist, so that there are no British Isles or any peninsula where Denmark now is. The Scandinavian ice-sheet, however, covers what is today Denmark, Scotland, northern England, and most of Ireland. Another ice-sheet covers most of what is Switzerland.

The prehistoric men who concern us here — the most highly developed primates, the vanguard of evolution — must be living in something approaching Arctic conditions, on the cold and largely treeless expanses of what is now southern France and northern Spain. What keeps them there is the abundance of big game, herds of reindeer, of horses, of wild cattle, in addition to woolly mammoths, woolly rhinoceroses, ibexes, wild boars, and other beasts great or small. They clothe themselves in skins and furs against the cold out-of-doors, depending on fire to keep them warm indoors, in the caves or in the shelters they make at the foot of cliffs. They pit their own conspiratorial cleverness against the genetically inherited defences of the beasts on which they prey, trapping them, ambushing them, wounding, weakening, and killing the greatest of them by arrows or spear-thrusts from all sides, harpooning them. (Is not the Spanish bullfight of today a ritualistic re-enactment of their own hunting 20,000 years ago?) The people are few and the beasts many, so that there is generally an abundance of meat, like that on the great plains of East Africa today. The people operate on the basis of an organized division of labor, sharing the food that the hunters bring in; they have leisure for craftsmanship; they know death and have ideas about what it signifies; they know anxiety and in their anxiety think constantly of powers outside themselves that can confer or withhold success in hunting. Their own mythological imagination creates most of the world they live in, filling out the relatively small part they know directly, completing the vision of a single order of being.

For the first time, now, there is a clear separation between the beasts of the earth and human beings, who in the language of recent times have souls as the beasts do not. It is the separation figuratively represented in the first chapter of Genesis, where men have "dominion over the fish of the sea, and over the fowl of the air, and over the cattle, and over all the earth, and over every creeping thing that creepeth upon the earth."

After about 12,000 B.P., the climate became warmer, the ice-sheets melted back (flooding the lowlands east and south of Britain with melt-water), and the great herds of beasts diminished or, like the reindeer, retreated northward. Conditions became ripe for the invention of agriculture; agricultural communities would learn how to keep written records; and history, in the midst of which we find ourselves today, would begin.

*

Evolution by natural selection, as it has manifested itself for 3,000 million years, is directed entirely by pragmatic considerations, being governed by utilitarian criteria only. Operating among varieties, whether of form or behavior, it selects those that are the most practical, that work best in the particular environment in which they respectively occur. It follows that the criteria of the selection that resulted in the peacock's tail could hardly have been altogether the same as those that would have governed a jury of art connoisseurs. The peacock's tail is beautiful because it represents an order, in the form of a harmonious design, but the order it represents must have emerged from the process of natural selection by meeting criteria that were utilitarian rather than directly aesthetic. Again, the nightingale's song is beautiful because it represents an order, but the order it represents responded not to the principles of musicology in themselves but to the practical demands of the environment. So we must believe, in the present state of our knowledge; and if such belief presents any difficulty we must seek to resolve it by determining what it is that constitutes beauty in our eyes, by accounting for aesthetic standards, rather than by questioning the utilitarian basis of natural selection.

Like the peacock's tail and the nightingale's song, the aptitudes and inclinations we associate with mind, while we suppose them to be utilitarian in origin, are not obviously so. At the most primitive level of evolution the question of beauty hardly arises at all. At that level, a cell with a relatively opaque outer membrane might be selected for the protection it affords against ultraviolet radiation, and we would not regard it as more beautiful than its more primitive predecessor, or as beautiful at all. The same may be true even at an advanced level; for the thickness of the hide that protects the rhinoceros, the hedgehog's habit of curling up in the presence of a predator, the skunk's way of discharging an obnoxious liquid — these are characteristics that appear to respond to purely utilitarian criteria, and we are not tempted to seek any further explanation of them.

How about Neanderthal man's habit of decorating the graves of his dead? If we insist that it is ultimately the product of a natural selection that is no more than utilitarian, we have to admit that it is not as obviously so as in the cases I have just cited.

The advent of mind seems, at least, to have introduced something new. We get the impression that mind seeks order for its own sake rather than for the sake of some practical advantage associated with it. Not only is it moved to seek order in nature, it imagines order beyond what it is able to find in nature. And it does not only imagine order but, having done so, proceeds to represent it — in myths, in the graphic arts, in music and poetry, in dancing and ritual. Mind, in a word, is creative in itself. It creates an imagined order, which may correspond more or less, or not at all, to external reality, whether the order be that of *Prometheus Bound,* that of *The Divine Comedy* or *The Tempest,* that of a Chinese temple or a Gothic cathedral, that of Bach's Chaconne (see Part One, Chapter XV) or More's *Utopia* or Einstein's Relativity. Perhaps we could now define mind as a creative faculty produced by natural selection which is attracted to order, which seeks it or creates it.

A reindeer, like a peacock's tail, represents a certain manifestation of order to the questing mind. It has bilateral symmetry, one branched antler balancing the other, one side doubling the other. It moves with a rhythm that could be rendered in music. This appeals to our aesthetic sense, which is our appreciation of the order for which mind has an affinity. It appealed specifically to the aesthetic sense of prehistoric man, as we know from the remains of his cultural activity.

Before coming to prehistoric man's representations of this appeal, however, let us make a distinction, if only for heuristic purposes, without getting ourselves into a muddle over the question whether that distinction is real or not. Let us distinguish the order from any particular animal that embodies it. We may say in crude terms that an artist, on the basis of this distinction, has a choice between painting the animal and painting the order, between painting the portrait of a particular individual among the reindeer, with whatever individual departures from the norm it may show (the broken tip of an antler, the bare skin where some hair has been rubbed off), and painting the perfect reindeer of the normative imagination as a more accurate representation of the order.

The remains of prehistoric man in Europe — of what, on his initial appearance, we call Cro-Magnon man — include the first major examples that have come down to us of artistic creation. I refer to the mural paintings, some over 30,000 years old, on the walls of caves in northern Spain and southern France. The best of these paintings are so advanced in conception and accomplished in rendition that it is not ludicrous to compare them to Michelangelo's murals in the Sistine Chapel. Although not equal to Michelangelo's work, they represent the same eye for line, for form, and for movement, and the same kind of skill in rendition, practiced under circumstances of greater difficulty and more limited opportunity. They are, in fact, so far from primitive in character that, for many decades after their discovery in the nineteenth century, they were thought to be the work of modern men with professional training. There must have been a millennial tradition of painting and engraving behind them, although lost to us. They are far from the beginnings of art.

These cave-paintings are found, for the most part, in the total darkness of interior chambers or in the long tunnels by which these chambers are reached, decorating the walls and the ceilings. The artists must have painted them by firelight, from memory and imagination rather than from models. There are engravings incised in the stone and bas-reliefs, as well as paintings done with manganese paints in black, ocher, red, and yellow. For the most part they are representations of the great mammals with which and on which these people lived: woolly mammoths, rhinoceroses, wild oxen, bison, bears, horses, red deer, reindeer, wild boars, and ibex such as one still sees in the Alps. Human figures are relatively rare, but there are scenes of hunting, and animals are occasionally shown wounded, pierced by spears or arrows.

Judging by the art of primitive peoples in our own time, these representations must have had a ritualistic significance, in the context of a mythology based on a belief in supernatural powers that might side with the hunters or against them, that had to be solicited or appeased. There was sorcery or magic in making these imitations of one's prey on the cave walls. I venture to think, however, that we must understand the artistic impulse behind these works at a deeper level.

The artist was representing the beautiful in the sense I have here given the term. This is clear from his work in itself. He was abstracting the beautiful from nature and making it a fixture of his environment. I said above that the reindeer represents an order, for it has symmetry of form and there is music in its rhythmic movement. But the unsophisticated eye is hardly aware of these qualities in the natural reality itself until it has been shown them in the artist's representation. The animal embodies an order that was not seen until the artist painted it.*

Add to this that the artist fixes what is fleeting. The curve of a bison's horn changes with the angle presented to the beholder's eye, disappearing as the beast turns its head. The reindeer leaps in the trajectory of an arc that is gone as it takes the next step. But, in the artist's rendition, the arc outlives the life of the beholder, perhaps surviving for tens of thousands of years on a cave wall. What had the duration of the twinkling of an eye has been made permanent. As in the case of Keats's Grecian Urn, the mortal has assumed the dignity of immortality, which is an attribute of divinity.

This is the magic of mind, which apprehends and seeks to fix forever the order that it thinks it sees in nature.

* In Part Five I shall be dealing more fully with the significance of art, and this is my excuse for dealing less fully with it here.

XI

Man's Increasing Mastery
of the Earth

EVEN AS RECENTLY as 30,000 years ago man was not yet conspicuous by his numbers on the face of the earth, his entire population amounting to no more, perhaps, than the population of New York City today. The disembodied observer whom I have previously invoked in these pages, surveying southern France at the time, would have noted the various species of ungulates, some in great herds. Among the animals that preyed on them he would have noted wild dogs of various species and great wildcats, but only occasional bands of the primate, man. The relatively few men were without the natural armament of the other predators; and the observer might well have overlooked the implications for the future of such facts as that they alone wore clothes, constructed traps, manufactured weapons (including missiles and missile-launchers), and commanded the use of fire. He might not have foreseen that they would "be fruitful, and multiply, and replenish the earth, and subdue it: and have dominion over the fish of the sea, and over the fowl of the air, and over every living thing that moveth upon the earth."

The white Europeans that had appeared in southern France were far from being the only men on earth. In addition to any Neanderthal remnants of 30,000 years ago, there were men in Africa, presumably black-skinned, and there were men here and there in the expanses of Asia, many of whom must have had the Mongolian features we know today. The groups of men were scattered so sparsely over such immeasurable distances, however, that they were as unlikely to meet as ships in the wide ocean when they are few. This separation was what allowed the development of such distinct races as, in more crowded times, would begin to intermingle and blend.

Because the various men had hands, and because they had certain aptitudes that went with their peculiarly developed brains, they were beginning to multiply and spread over the earth.

During the successive glaciations, when the oceans were partly depleted to form the ice-sheets, a plain more than a thousand miles wide extended between what are now Siberia and Alaska. Occasional groups of nomads, coming from the west or the south, followed the herds of ungulates into Siberia and, simply continuing eastward, entered North America without knowing, any more than the herds they followed, that they had ventured into what their successors would regard as another hemisphere. The groups that wandered into the Western Hemisphere from time to time — perhaps beginning as much as 100,000 years ago, and almost surely not later than 40,000 years ago — were of various origins, and they tended to become lost in the boundless expanses of the New World, some drifting eastward, generation after generation, until brought up against the shores of the Atlantic, others moving southward until, at last, the uttermost wanderers reached Tierra del Fuego and the Horn. Long after the beginning of history in the Old World, however, even as late as 1492, they had only begun to occupy North America, their total numbers north of Mexico amounting, probably, to no more than a million and a half — fewer than now populate the little island of Manhattan on any weekday. It is only in the last century that the occupation of North America has been completed.

Although the original infiltration of North America by prehistoric men occurred during the periods of glaciation, the plain now flooded by the Bering Sea, together with much of western Alaska, must have been relatively ice-free because relatively free from precipitation, the winds passing over to deposit their burden of moisture beyond. So the reindeer, the wild horses, the wild sheep, and other ungulates grazed their way across what must have been tundra, followed by the men who lived upon their numbers.*

Man spread from the mainland of Asia not only to the New World but also to Australia. The present aboriginal population of Australia is racially distinct from the peoples of Asia or other continents. While it is composed of the most primitive peoples to have survived into modern times, they could have arrived only from across the sea in boats of their own making, whether canoes or rafts; and the Australian wild dog, called dingo, must have accompanied them in the

---

* Contrary to the popular impression, there is no such thing as an American Indian race. Separate groups representing separate genetic stocks from different regions of the Old World entered the New World separately from time to time. Many of the American Indians belong to the Mongolian race. Others (e.g., the Crow and Blackfoot) appear to be of the same stock as present-day Tibetans, which is to say that they are basically Caucasian, like the bulk of the people who were later to come to the New World across the Atlantic. Nor do the many Indian languages stem, like the Indo-European languages, from a common stock.

capacity of a domestic animal, for Australia and its surrounding islands have been separated from the rest of the world by water for some seventy-five million years, and no carnivores ever reached it by themselves. The racial distinction of the Australian aborigines argues a long history in Australia, while their mastery of navigation before coming argues a more recent arrival. In fact, we don't know when they arrived.

*

I might have said, in the last sentence but one, that the argument for a recent arrival of the aborigines in Australia was based not only on the mastery of navigation required, but also on the fact that they had taken to the domestication of animals, as witness the dogs they brought with them. We associate the domestication of animals with the beginning of agriculture (i.e., the domestication of plants) as marking the stage at which man had at last advanced to a point where he no longer had to live as a savage wanderer, hunting in packs like the wolves, but could settle down to build the foundations of civilization. This is true only if we identify the domestication of animals with animal husbandry as practiced in historical times.

In itself, however, the domestication of animals was not a sudden or an ingenious invention, such as the bow-and-arrow must have been. Under conditions that occur naturally, some animals simply associate themselves with man of their own accord and assume the status of domesticity. These are the commensal animals, the animals that have settled down to live on the crumbs from his table. The house mouse, where it is not persecuted, will become so tame that it takes food from the hand. The wild chipmunk will enter houses and sit under the dining table at meal times, waiting for fallen crumbs or alms. We may suppose that the cave-dwellers, when they brought home meat, were attended by wild dogs, such as the jackal, which, if tolerated, may have entered the caves and waited for the discarded bones to which remnants of meat or marrow clung, or for scraps held out to them.

One may plausibly imagine, as well, wild dogs that, having gradually become associated with man as scavengers, helped him find game or, by their superior sense of smell, warned him of any dangerous predators lurking in the vicinity. If the caves of men were infested with rodents, as they may well have been, the men might have welcomed the presence of small wild cats that would have come in for warmth and shelter as well as for rodents. The domestication of animals by man would initially amount, in such cases, to little more than his acceptance of their intrusion. I venture to think that 70,000 years ago Neanderthal man was attended by some mammals and some birds in a commensal relationship, perhaps half domesticated. Cowbirds wait on cattle for the insects they stir up as they graze, and it may be that even the man-apes of 4 million years ago were so attended.

We must bear in mind that the fear of man characteristic of virtually all wild animals today has resulted from his development of missile weapons, especially firearms. There is reason to think that, even a thousand years ago, there was no such fear of him.

The eiders that nest on the coasts of Iceland and Norway are protected by the local communities of men and even supplied with artificial nesting sites for the sake of the eiderdown taken from their nests to stuff cushions. These are wild ducks, but because of the way they are cherished by man they have become tame, behaving in his presence like his own domestic fowl. Goosanders, provided with nesting boxes and cherished for their eggs in Scandinavia, have become equally tame. It would be an easy step to pen the ducks of either species and control their breeding. (This is not done because, since they live on fish or shellfish, there would be a problem of feeding them in captivity, so that it is better to let them wander and forage for themselves, even going south in winter with the assurance that they will return for another nesting season in association with man.)

Again, a sort of maternalistic impulse, which may already have existed in the earliest humans, might have prompted them to rescue and raise orphaned young of wild mammals or birds. Eventually, the young of wild pigs might have been kept and raised in enclosures for their meat, the young of wild goats for their milk. Wild horses and cattle might also have been brought into domesticity by the raising of their young. In any case, it is no great wonder if, even several tens of thousands of years ago, the ancestors of the Australian aborigines had already entered into relations of domesticity with a dog closely related to some of our own domestic species. While the status of the dingo in Australia today is that of a wild carnivore, like the coyote in western North America, any that are captured as puppies and raised by men are, unlike the coyote, as domestic as any domestic dog. Adaptation to domesticity appears to be part of their genetic heritage.

Still again, the hunters who lived on the herds of wild reindeer might naturally, at a certain stage, begin to herd them, directing their movements, eventually caring for orphaned young, protecting herds from predators (perhaps with the help of dogs), even concerning themselves with the problem of winter pasture or winter feed. At what stage could one say that the reindeer had become domestic animals?

We may surely assume that the domestication of plants also came about, if not of itself, by a natural progression. The primitive gatherers of vegetable food, once they had achieved their unique capacity for looking beyond the immediate present, would begin to tend their sources of supply. If the reader of these lines were in the habit of gathering fruit from a particular patch of wild blackberries, he would almost automatically be disposed, in the course of his picking, to pull out any honeysuckle vines he saw that were tending to choke or shade out the blackberry plants. No doubt weeding was the beginning of agriculture.

Again, if there was a field of wild wheat on which primitive men depended for food, they might, by weeding, defend it against the invasion of other plants; and from doing this to clearing out competing plants on the margin of the field, so that the wheat could spread, would be but a step. From such clearing of the ground to transplantation would be another step — and so on to the point where they were deliberately seeding the cleared ground. At what stage could it be said that man was at last practicing agriculture?

*

Certain innovations appear to be almost inevitable when evolution has reached the point at which they become feasible. So the control of body temperature, making it largely independent of environmental temperature, occurred simultaneously but separately in birds and mammals, vertebrate evolution having reached the point at which this advantageous innovation had at last become possible. So the development of the brain for certain mental aptitudes — well beyond those of fish, amphibians, or reptiles — appeared at the same time, but independently, in birds and mammals. (See pages 227 and 243 above.)

We may plausibly believe that agriculture and the domestication of animals occurred when it did (gradually in the perspective of 10,000 years, but suddenly in that of 3,000 million) because life, in its evolution, had reached that point. This is supported by the fact that the inhabitants of the New World appear to have developed agriculture and the domestication of animals quite independently of the same developments by the inhabitants of the Old World, but at about the same time.*

* The best evidence is that the plants and animals domesticated in the New World are all descended from wild progenitors that did not occur in the Old World.

The immediately antecedent cause of the development of agriculture was the development of the brain so as to endow it with imagination — with the aptitude for remembering the past and anticipating the future ("If winter comes, can spring be far behind?"). The emergence of this aptitude may itself have had a certain inevitability. The evolution of life, which may have begun in a relatively haphazard fashion, which was for a long time slow and uncertain, accelerates and appears to become increasingly determined in its direction as it progresses — until at last each development implies the one that follows it.

However that may be, man's development of agriculture, including the domestication of animals, was bound to have far-reaching consequences for himself in particular, for life on earth in general.

XII

Language

MEN DID NOT necessarily have to await the development of agriculture before abandoning their nomadic life to form permanent settlements. Indeed, such exploitation of a local environment as leads to
agriculture was more likely to develop where people had already
settled down. If it is true that a community does not abandon the
site where it has planted grain, leaving the grain unharvested, it is
also true that it does not plant grain where it intends to move on
before the time for harvesting.

Even without agriculture, increased skill in gathering, hunting,
trapping, and fishing makes it less necessary for a community to
move constantly from one locality to another, tempting it to remain
and settle in any locality that is particularly favorable to occupation
the year around. Such pre-agricultural settlements appear to have
existed in the Middle East between 5,000 and 10,000 B.C. One can
easily imagine that those who lived in them permanently took more
pains than those who were merely passing through a locality to arrange the features of the local environment, to make paths and
clearings, to identify themselves with particular herds of wild goats
in the vicinity, to protect and maintain the fields that were productive of wild vegetable foods, and so to drift into agricultural usages.*

Just as the spread of life from the water to the land became inevitable once the development of the amniotic egg (the egg that is a
package enclosed by a membrane) had made it possible, just as the
proliferation of life in regions of extreme heat and cold became inevitable once the development of internal temperature control had
opened up that possibility, just as the manufacture of artifacts and

* I engage in some simplification here, for there are intermediate conditions between
nomadism and settlement. A community may, for example, move back and forth between summer and winter quarters in an established fashion, as those who tend cattle
in the Alps move with them to higher pastures in summer, descending again in winter. We would not call these nomads, but others whom we would identify as such are
apt to have regular annual rounds.

the mastery of fire became inevitable once the brain and hand had reached a point of development that allowed it, so now the constant progress of evolution, having at last produced the conditions precedent, made it inevitable that men would settle into fixed communities and embark on the practice of agriculture. One proof is that, as I have already mentioned, this step was taken independently at about the same time in the Old World and the New. There is reason to believe that, even within the confines of the Old World, it was taken independently at more than one point — in the Middle East, in southeastern Asia, and perhaps elsewhere as well. Such steps in the evolution of life occur as if they had been programmed. Just as a growing infant, whether in South America, in Scandinavia, in Africa, or in southeastern Asia, having reached the age of two years, begins to walk erect, so life on earth, having reached a certain stage of development that seems to have been implicit in its evolution all along, emerges from the water onto dry land, or organizes itself into societies based on the division of labor.

So it is that primates of the genus *Homo,* having reached a certain stage, settled down and took to the practice of agriculture. At a later stage they would build vast urban conglomerations, practice advanced industrial skills, and develop such abilities and resources as would enable them to visit the moon. At a still later stage, if later stages there are to be, life will go on to do — who knows what?

The division of labor, developing ever more fully with the evolution of human society, released individual men and women for activities other than the primary ones of foraging, fighting, and renewing their kind. Among all other animals except the social insects, an adult that cannot provide for itself will normally starve to death, even though the other members of its group are enjoying plenty. A disabled tiger cannot expect its mate to bring it food. But the queen in a hive of honey bees never has to forage for herself, being fed by worker bees in return for her own contribution to the political economy of the hive.

Men, later than the social insects, have followed them in such division of labor. While some gather food, others perform other tasks, and a general exchange is maintained. There is a like division of labor in a band of baboons, a division between the sexes, or between old males and young, but with a difference. The adult male who guards the community against predators still has to forage for himself.

In the human community, since the advent of *Homo sapiens,* the division of labor releases some individuals for activities, identified with the uses of the mind, that do not bear on the primary functions of foraging, fighting, or renewing the kind — that do not, in fact, bear on any utilitarian purpose except such as may be engendered in imagination. Even among the Neanderthals there may well have been individuals, supported by the community, whose special function was to organize and preside over such ceremonial observances as were thought to be required in connection with birth, mating, and the burial of the dead. Among our own Cro-Magnon ancestors the division of labor made it possible for some to cultivate and practice, as specialists, the art of the engraver or the painter, thereby fulfilling some communal purpose associated with needs of the mind that are not easy to define at this early stage in its evolution.

The chief difference between modern man and all other forms of life is represented by his capacity and disposition to comprehend, in his consciousness, unlimited space and time beyond the here-and-now. He is, consequently, curious about his forebears and concerned with his posterity.

As long as 300,000 years ago, nomads were building huts at stations of temporary sojourn on the north shore of the Mediterranean near the present city of Nice. The huts sheltered them for some days or weeks only before they moved on to new pastures. Each year for eleven years they returned to the site in season, but on each return had to build anew; for it was beyond their capacity, and presumably beyond their conception, to build what would last from one year to the next. Less than 300,000 years later men would be building for their posterity when they themselves had passed away, preferring to wood as a building material, where they had the choice, the more costly but less perishable stone. They would be concerned to know of their ancestors, to whom they looked for the heritage of such wisdom as they had, and they would seek a sort of immortality for themselves by leaving messages and memorabilia for their descendants — thereby satisfying the need that is satisfied in the author of these lines when he thinks that they will remain, still speaking with his voice, after he, in his corporeal person, is no more. (This is the principal theme of the sonnets that were composed four hundred years ago by one who represented the highest development of mind.) Those who built the Parthenon were addressing themselves to their posterity, for they would not otherwise have built in stone. But the Parthenon exists only in its unique manifestation, which has shown itself vulnerable where "broils root out the work of masonry." Written language escapes this vulnerability, redeeming men, within the measure of the possible, from their natural condition as "the fools of time"; for words may survive the voice that speaks them or the material on which they are written, being susceptible of storage in memory or endless recordation and rerecordation. The Parthenon is as perishable as the stone of which it is made, but a sonnet will outlive any single memory in which it is stored or any piece of paper on which it is written.

> Now with the drops of this most balmy time
> My love looks fresh, and Death to me subscribes,
> Since, spite of him, I'll live in this poor rime,
> While he insults o'er dull and speechless tribes.

The "dull and speechless" tribes were the only ones that lived, as yet, 300,000 years ago, at a time when evolution was already pregnant with mind.

*

The indispensable vehicle of mind is language, from which it is inseparable. We think in words. The "dull and speechless tribes" are dull because speechless in the sense that their vocabulary is limited. A crow has a vocabulary that, in its entirety, may consist of little more than one sound to warn of danger, another to express the allied emotions of fear and anger, another to communicate a general inclination toward sociability with others of its kind, and perhaps another for expressing and inspiring a sense of mutual intimacy between two birds in the mating relationship. Such a vocabulary is relevant to nothing beyond the here-and-now. The danger call cannot speak of yesterday's danger or warn of tomorrow's. One might say without absurdity that a crow could not think of tomorrow at all, if only because it had no word for it; or that, if its mental development had reached the point where it was potentially able to think of tomorrow, it could not realize that potentiality without expanding its vocabulary.

I do not suppose that the development of human language as we know it — a development that is part of the evolution of life on earth — responded initially to any need to consider such questions as the immortality of the soul. It responded, rather, to the utilitarian requirements of mutual planning among the members of societies that were based on the division of labor. One can imagine that a group of men preparing to set out on an overnight hunting expedition would have to agree among themselves on its duration, as well as to inform those left behind of when they meant to be back. To do this they would find ways of expressing the alternation of daylight and darkness or the rising and setting of the sun. For longer periods they would find ways of expressing the cycles of the moon, or the cycle of the year which entails the succession of the seasons. (We are still so close to these origins that the word "month," among others, betrays them.) They would then find it expedient to count months or years on their ten fingers, and eventually by multiples of ten, thereby expanding the span of time that could be comprehended.

The new vocabulary, however, would in itself open up possibilities beyond the requirements that had called it into being. Where there is a vocabulary for denoting extended spans of time, as well as a word for birth and another for death, with life-span thereby implied, the possibility of formulating certain questions, theretofore excluded, will have been opened for the mind that has become capable of long-range and abstract thinking. We may be sure that the ceremonial burial of the dead among Neanderthal men represented an already advanced development of such language. A priest who presided over the Neanderthal burial 35,000 years ago would necessarily have had something in common with Shakespeare. So it is that, if the utilitarian came first, the abstract and non-utilitarian followed hard upon it.

*

In Part One I had occasion to observe that there is a logic of the mind which matches the logic that we assume to exist independently in the realm of external being. This logic of the mind is language.

Any language, whether the specialized language of mathematics or a vernacular language like Chinese or English, is a system of logic in itself. The vernacular language, which is what concerns us here, has its taxonomic logic, for it divides the world of experience into categories and subcategories denoted by its nouns and verbs — denoted, indeed, by all its terms. It has its logic of cause and effect, as when the poet says that, unlike the poor and speechless tribes, over whom death prevails, he, himself, will live in his rhyme. Its grammar is a logic imposed as a discipline on the ordering of its terms. Even in its musical manifestations — the harmony, the rhythm, and the balance that are produced by particular sequences into which its terms are ordered — it represents the emergence of a logical order from an initial chaos.

The emergence of mind and of language in the course of evolution are but two aspects of the same development, which is the progressive emergence from the underlying chaos of a logic, internal to living beings, that must be supposed to match the logic external to them.

Our concern in Part Three, which I now bring to an end, has been

with the emergence of mind, exclusively associated with man, in the
long evolution of life on earth. It is with the birth of language that
mind itself may be said to be born.

However, even after men had begun to settle down in agricultural
communities based on a division of labor that gave increasing scope
for mind — even after this their language long remained, still, a
spoken language only. It is not until the spoken language begins to
be written as well that we emerge from what we call prehistory into
the historical times that are the subject of Part Four.

PART FOUR

Civilization

Most animals — as, for instance, bees, spiders and beavers — have a kind of art peculiar to themselves; but each race of animals has no more than one art, and this one has had no first inventor among the race. Man, on the other hand, has an infinity of different arts which were not born with his race, and of which the glory is his own.

— *Fontenelle*

I

The Direction of Evolution and
the Dynamics of Acceleration

IN THE SHORT VIEW, evolution is the process by which particular
varieties of life, in their successive generations, become adapted to
the immediate environmental circumstances that occur in a state of
nature. In the long view, however, it is, rather, the process by which
life becomes increasingly independent of any such environmental
circumstances at all. Thus the advent of the amniotic egg, 200 million years ago, by packaging the liquid environment on which embryos depend, allowed life to emerge from the water onto dry land.
The advent of internal temperature control, 150 million years ago,
allowed life to achieve a certain independence of the temperature in
its immediate surroundings, whether of air or water — so that the
variations in temperature, whether diurnal or annual, became a matter of relative indifference, thereby making it possible for a species
like the puma to inhabit arctic and tropical regions alike.*

When men learned to command fire, when they began to clothe
themselves, and when they began to build ever more elaborate shelters, they were simply representing the long-range progress of evolution in the direction, not of adapting life to the natural environment, but of making it more independent of that environment.
This progress has so far been carried to the point where our kind
lives in air-conditioned apartments — which embody alike the principle of the amniotic egg and that of internal temperature control —
and, in a packaged environment of its own provision, has been able
to extend its range as far as the moon.

If we understand that this is the direction taken by evolution over
the past 3,000 million years, we may plausibly imagine possibilities
for the future of life, in interplanetary space and beyond, that we
shall have occasion to consider in later chapters.

*

* See pp. 226–227.

In the long perspective we see that some of the principal natural processes known to us appear to obey a rule of acceleration.

Item. Stellar and planetary bodies are formed by the condensation of clouds of dust under the influence of gravitational attraction. While the particles and clouds are still widely scattered the process is slow; but as they draw together their mutual attraction increases inversely to the square of the distance that separates them, so that the process is self-accelerating by its nature and could not be otherwise.

Item. In the apparent explosion of the universe that is now occurring, its galaxies recede from one another at an accelerating rate, the outermost receding the fastest because they have been accelerating the longest.

The first life of 3,500 million years ago consisted of prokaryotic cells that reproduced only by splitting, so that the progeny of each were identical twins. No choices were presented for natural selection except where an occasional mutation occurred. A relative uniformity prevailed, and because natural selection had little to work on the progress of evolution was so slow as to be imperceptible over millions of years. Two thousand million years (more than half the time since life began) may have passed before the first eukaryotic cells opened the way, by their more complex and varied organization, for new possibilities and an increasing pace of evolution.

Returning again to the beginning of life, we see that the earth's surface and its atmosphere had to be transformed before conditions were provided for the development of the higher forms of life as known to us. The process of photosynthesis in the population of microscopic prokaryotes, limited as it must have been, had to supply the entire atmospheric envelope of the earth with oxygen before any life was possible outside the water, before any animal life at all was possible. This, in itself, might have retarded by one or two thousand million years an advance beyond the prokaryotic level represented by bacteria and blue-green algae.

After 2,500 million years of evolution (that is, only about 1,000 million years ago), when a propitious environment had at last been created, the development of sexual reproduction, entailing recombination in addition to mutation, increased the range and rapidity of the variation on which natural selection operated, thereby accelerating the pace of evolution. So the very process of evolution, creating new and ever larger possibilities for itself, is self-accelerating, like that whereby the stars and planets are formed. The development of the amniotic egg, a package containing within itself the watery environment and other provision needed by the embryo, allowed life to escape from the watery external environment and generate on dry land. The development of internal temperature control opened

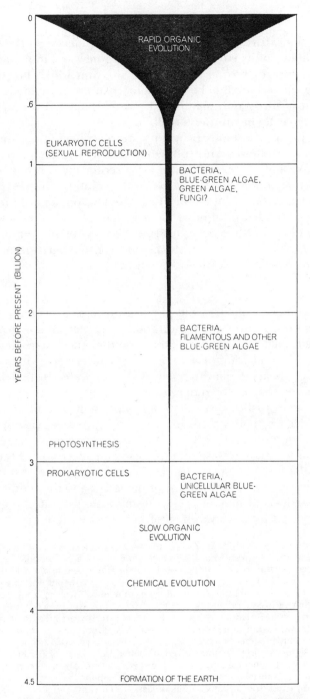

The above diagram has been adapted by permission of *Scientific American* from one that illustrates "The Oldest Fossils" by Elso S. Barghoorn, copyright © 1971, in its issue of May 1971.

another door, further freeing life from dependence on the immediate conditions of its environment, enabling new and more developed forms to spread into parts of the earth from which life had previously been excluded. The development of the brain made possible the flight of birds and, manifested as mind, opened up possibilities that have hardly begun to be realized as yet.

So evolution, constantly providing improved conditions for its own advance, has followed an exponential course of acceleration over at least 3,500 million years. In the most recent times it has begun to provide the conditions for a cultural evolution that increasingly drives the genetic evolution on which the development of life has exclusively depended until now. So it is that, at last in our own short day, the whole earth is being transformed, by the life that invests it, at a rate that makes its transformation conspicuous within a small part of the reader's lifetime or my own.*

*

In Part One we examined the physical universe in its temporal-spatial extension, on the one hand, and in the elements of which it is composed, such as quanta and atoms, on the other. The elements of which it is composed appear to be forever invariable, while in its extension it appears, from the point of view provided by our own local frame of reference, to undergo such change as is represented by what we take to be its accelerating expansion in our time. To a greater degree than we readily recognize, however, it approaches the status of a metaphysical entity in the conception we entertain of it. For, as we strive toward an ultimate comprehension of the whole, or toward a fuller comprehension of either space-time or quanta, we sustain an increasing impression of being close to the borderline between physics and metaphysics. In any case, with all the qualifications required by the awareness of our ultimate ignorance, we may

---

* The rate at which life proliferates is implicitly exponential. It "multiplies." Therefore it repeatedly manifests what I have called the rule of acceleration. For example, until this century the collared dove, a bird of Asia Minor, had not spread beyond the Turkish Straits. In 1912 it first appeared in Belgrade; in 1930 it was spreading over southern Hungary; in 1943 it was at the gates of Vienna; in 1957 it was first seen in Geneva (where I lived then and do now); by 1974 it had spread over most of Europe and had arrived in Iceland. As I write, less than sixteen years after the first one was seen in Geneva, I count thirty outside my window. From none at all, it has in a few years (within my lifetime) become one of the abundant birds of Europe.

What is significant in this example is that some development of the European environment or some genetic adaptation in the species — perhaps both together — must suddenly have removed an obstacle to an implicitly exponential proliferation that had been held in check for perhaps a million years. So it is that, in accordance with the rule of acceleration, the evolution of the biosphere can manifest sudden developments that, on the evolutionary scale of time, are nothing less than explosions.

plausibly regard the physical universe as being basically invariable, even if it should manifest such rhythmic and regular changes as are represented equally by the oscillation of particular atoms or the hypothesis of an alternately expanding and contracting universe. It is not basically different today from what it was many thousands of millions of years ago.

In Part Two we examined the emergence of life on our own planet, and its ever accelerating evolution, over a span of three and a half thousand million years to the present, from insensible bits of matter on a microscopic scale to the range of organisms, constantly more varied, elaborate, and profuse, that, having at last covered and transformed its surface, have just begun, apparently, to expand into the surrounding space.

In Part Three we examined the emergence of mind, which has occurred so recently that we are no more able to comprehend its significance than we would have been able, as disembodied observers, to comprehend the significance of the emergence of life when the first few prokaryotic cells had appeared somewhere on earth three and a half thousand million years ago. The advent of mind, however, has entailed a cultural evolution that increasingly supplements and directs the evolution recorded in the genes. This cultural evolution, itself accelerating, is so recent that it does not begin to come into prominence until some 10,000 years ago. In that time, however, it has brought about the accelerating transformation of the earth that our crude observation is at last able to register in terms of mere decades.

We have seen, in the course of this survey, how the association of elementary particles to constitute atoms, of atoms to constitute molecules, and of molecules to constitute ever larger organisms has represented the progressive development of order from an initial or underlying chaos. At last we come to mind, which we have tentatively defined as "a creative faculty produced by natural selection which is attracted to order, which seeks it or creates it." * Mind is moved to seek order in nature, and to imagine order beyond what it is able to find in nature.

When men begin to organize themselves as large-scale and established societies — whether tribes or city-states or nation-states or civilizations — the forms of those societies, including their structures and their modes of operation alike, are based on normative orders produced, not by nature directly but by mind.

The fact that the societies of men are based on normative orders produced in the minds of the men concerned is demonstrated by

* See p. 272.

contrasting them with the societies of the social insects (or of any other non-human animals, whether howler monkeys or musk-oxen, wolves or baboons, penquins or porpoises, corals or slime molds). A hive of honeybees represents a normative order, based on the division of labor, that resembles, at least superficially, a busy human society composed of peasants, merchants, soldiers, etc. — each class with its own function in the economy of the whole. But bees, with their minute and correspondingly limited brains, entirely lack the powers of imagination and conceptualization that distinguish the exclusively human faculty called mind. Therefore their society is not of their own design or devising.

How, then, did it come into being?

Presumably the primitive association among the ancestors of the honeybees was as loose as that among the non-social species of bees today, based on the distinction between two classes only, undifferentiated males and undifferentiated females. We may suppose that, as in the case of house flies today, after a male and female, casually encountering each other, had mated, the female would go off by herself to lay her eggs at some unprepared point. Natural selection, however, tended to favor the occasional female that, on the basis of her genotype, provided the protection of what at last came to be a nest for her eggs (as each female among the non-social bees does today); and in time, when all were building nests, it favored those individuals that, by genetic heritage, tended to build their nests together, thus forming colonies. As the colonies, by natural selection, became ever more integrated and elaborate, such selection came to favor varieties that tended to develop specialization and a division of labor among increasingly specialized groups in each population; and this would in time lead to the emergence of such distinct castes as drones, workers, and queens. This is to say that everything about the beehive today, given the basic environmental factors, has been genetically determined by the relatively slow process of Darwinian evolution. The form of that society, including its structure and mode of operation alike, has over the aeons come to be recorded — not in the minds of the individual bees, for they have no minds, but in their genes. Today, each individual bee in the society of the hive performs its role, in accordance with the common genetic heritage, as automatically as an amoeba ingests a particle of food in its path, as automatically as a moth weaves a cocoon, not knowing what end it serves in doing so.

Because the design of the apian society is set forth only in the genes, and so transferred as a whole to each successive generation, it is, as a human society is not, basically invariable. An individual queen bee, taken from a hive in Tierra del Fuego and released in Siberia, will build a nest in which she will lay eggs that will produce a population, divided into castes, that will organize itself into a society identical, in its structure and mode of operation, with the hive in Tierra del Fuego from which the queen had been taken — and will do this even though the queen had died after having laid the eggs from which they had hatched posthumously. So it is that there is no perceptible difference between the design of a society of a particular species in North America and that of a society of the same species in India or Australia; nor, we may be sure, between the design of a society today and that of an ancestral society a thousand years ago. Because the design is not a product of the mind, with its free-ranging imagination, but is genetically fixed, it does not vary except imperceptibly over the spans of time by which the operations of genetic evolution are normally to be measured.

Periclean Athens was also a society based on a division of labor represented by several clearly defined classes of its population. One class grew food, another purveyed it, another constructed walls and buildings, and still another (which would have been superfluous in the beehive) consisted of teachers who trained the young to play their roles in carrying on the life of the city. But the design of this human society, in its structure and its mode of operation, was certainly not registered in the genes of its human inhabitants as the design of the beehive was registered in the genes of the bees.

If, to engage in a thought experiment, one had taken a number of fertilized ova from Athenian women and, by artificial gestation and rearing in the absence of other human beings, had produced from them a population in some uninhabited part of Australia, the population so produced, even though it had had all the means at hand, would not have proceeded to build a replica of Athens in the new location. Indeed, it would hardly have known how to make provision for the organization of any kind of society at all, or for the production of food, or for the building of shelters. By contrast with the bees in Siberia, it would have been without a design for living; because the design of the parent generation, represented by Athens, had been in the minds of the parents rather than in their DNA. It had, in a word, been a cultural rather than a genetic heritage. A cultural heritage, which has its seat in the mind rather than in the genes, may be transmitted from generation to generation by teaching, but is not, like the genetic heritage, susceptible of automatic transmittal through the physical process of generation.*

* I have already made the point in these pages that no distinctions in living nature are literally categorical (i.e., without intermediate states) except from certain limited

The distinction between genetic and cultural is basic to everything that follows in these pages. It is a distinction that, expressed in various other terms, has been prominent in speculative discourse at least since Aristotle, who was concerned, in his *Politics,* with determining what form of society is "natural" for men as the society of the hive is natural for honeybees (concluding naïvely, as we can now see, that it was the city-state). Beginning with Thomas Hobbes, if not earlier, thinkers have assumed or pretended that there was a state of nature from which men departed when they became civilized. The distinction has also taken the form of the contrast between "nature" and "art" that has exercised philosophers for centuries.* But neither Aristotle nor Hobbes nor Rousseau nor John Stuart Mill had the knowledge of genetics that enables us to relate that contrast to the distinction between what is registered in the genes and what is registered in the mind — although some thinkers vaguely suggested the relationship when they distinguished what is "instinctive" from what is learned.

The beehive is a natural society, while Periclean Athens was an artificial society — artificial in that it was a creation of the mind, just as a wagon, a ship, a piece of sculpture, or a musical composition is a creation of the mind. An artificial society lacks the stability, the relative unchangeability of a natural society. Thus the design of the beehive, a natural society, is bound to be transmitted, complete and in detail, from one generation to another of bees through thousands of generations, and that without any perceptible change. For each example of that design is merely the equivalent of the phenotype that necessarily has to represent what is a fixed genotype. No change in the phenotype can affect the genotype, which changes only over the relatively long periods of time required for the operation of natural selection. Our use of the term "Periclean Athens," however, in itself represents the fact that we are referring to a particular society that did not endure beyond the lifetime of one man (and, in fact, not even that long). The failure of what we call "Peri-

---

points of view. The design for living represented by the beehive is genetically inherited rather than learned. We have already seen (p. 115) that the song of the song sparrow, too, is genetically inherited, without need of learning. But chaffinches (*Fringilla coelebs*) that have never heard the song of their kind sing only a simplified version of it, not singing the full song until they have learned it by hearing others sing it. (See R. A. Hinde, *Animal Behavior,* 2nd ed., Tokyo, 1970, p. 452.) Birds that have never seen a nest of their kind may go through the motions of building such a nest, but presumably are able to complete one only if they have at least a memory of having seen an example. (See A. L. Thomson [ed.], *A New Dictionary of Birds,* London, 1964, p. 528.) So it is that learning tends to play at least a secondary role in the design for living of all the higher vertebrates.

* See the essay entitled "Art" by Sidney Colvin in *Encyclopaedia Britannica,* 11th ed.

clean Athens" in the Peloponnesian War caused the design for living
that it represented to be widely discredited in the minds of its inhabitants, so that it was radically altered by the deliberate operations of
mind — after which it underwent a succession of such alterations,
some forms (e.g., "the Athens of the Thirty Tyrants") lasting less
than a year.

*

The civilizations of men are not like what we might call the civilizations of bees or of termites because they are free rather than genetically fixed in their designs. This freedom makes for relative chaos
in the short run. (It is still too early to say what it makes for in the
long run.) We do know, however, that it entails a process of selection, based on workability, that is not, like genetic selection, inherently limited in its pace. Therefore it tends increasingly to out-
strip genetic selection — even, as we shall see, to replace it.

We have here made a distinction between a design for living that
is written in the mind and one that is written in the genes. Within
the limited time-spans by which we measure human history, the latter is generally established and invariable, the former unfixed. A civilization (to use this term for what has its basis in the mind) is like an
experiment proceeding by trial and error, so that its forms and features are repeatedly being abandoned in favor of new forms and
features. Where there are successes, they are transitory; where
there are failures, they are followed by new beginnings; so that over
the millennia ruins accumulate upon ruins. We must hope that, as
with any process of trial and error, this constant failure and renewal
will lead to something better at last — will lead to a conclusion that
justifies it, to a stabilized order within which life has become consistently meaningful and rewarding. We must hope that it will lead to
enlargement — in the several senses of the term that are all one.*
But in our own time we can have no assurance of the future, only
the hope and the striving.

> Our little systems have their day;
>   They have their day and cease to be. . . .
>
> We have but faith: we cannot know;
>   For knowledge is of things we see; . . .

* See Part One, Chapter I above.

II

Normative Thinking

A CIVILIZATION EXISTS first of all in the mind, and only secondarily in its directly observable forms. So the sentence I have just written existed in my mind before I set it down on paper; so the statue of Athena on the Acropolis existed in the mind of Phidias before he cast it in bronze; so the constitution of Athens in the sixth century B.C. existed in Solon's mind before it was codified and put into operation.

If, then, a civilization inhabits the mind first of all, in what form does it do so?

Imagine a child brought up in nineteenth-century England. It will learn one language, which it will assume to be the natural language of mankind. In the absence of broader experience, it will assume that men speak English by nature, as dogs bark. And it will make the same assumption about all the features of the society in which it finds itself, which is the only one it knows. It will not distinguish, as we have, between the natural society of the beehive and the artificial society of a human civilization because it cannot tell that the latter, as known to it, is any less natural than the former.

We may identify the terms in which the child's mind is formed as those of normative thinking. The established customs and relationships of the society in which it is brought up become fixed in its mind as norms, so that any departures from them would seem abnormal.

Being brought up in nineteenth-century England, the child is likely to regard the division of society into classes as representing nature's norm no less than does the division of the bees into queens, workers, and drones. Because the society in which it finds itself is relatively stable, it will tend to assume that the customary relationship between the sexes, or between parents and children, or between masters and servants, is what God or nature intended for mankind.

When this child does get to the point of broadening its experience beyond nineteenth-century England, it will be inclined to do so in terms of the normative thinking that represents order and security to it. When it discovers that, outside England, in a place called Africa, there are little people called pygmies who run about naked and chatter in what seems gibberish, it may conclude that nature made Englishmen and barbarians as, within England, it made masters and servants.

If the child is among the minority that is given an advanced and cosmopolitan education, it may at last discover (perhaps reluctantly, obscurely, and only in part) that human civilizations are not like the societies of bees and termites. If it reaches the ultimate sophistication associated with the reader of these lines, it will largely replace the parochialism of its normative thinking with the conceptions of cultural relativism. It will learn to accept the fact that the norms of nineteenth-century England are not the norms of mankind, and it may even go so far as to doubt that there are any norms for mankind.* It will recognize that there is a Chinese civilization that must be regarded as no less valid, in normative terms, than the English (or as equally invalid); and that the norms of one century, whether in England or China, are not the norms of another. It will learn that civilization is basically artificial, that it is improvised and makeshift, that it is unstable, that it is subject to constant trial and error, and that it breaks down repeatedly, only to rise again in a new form on the ruins of the old. Those who reached this degree of sophistication in nineteenth-century England, however, were only a quantitatively insignificant minority.

Associated with the normative thinking that is the basis of civilization is the concept of legitimacy. To the degree that the civilization of nineteenth-century England was stable, it was so because the mass of its population accepted its forms, its modes, its organization, and its procedures as legitimate, regarding departures from them as illegitimate. The basis of the distinction between legitimate and illegitimate is the distinction between what is proper and what is improper in terms of what God or nature intended. The first two paragraphs of the American Declaration of Independence, too familiar to require repeating here, base the establishment of a new and independent American society on "the Laws of Nature and of Nature's

---

* This, however, would be going too far. There are, after all, forms and modes of behavior as natural to men as the organization of the hive is to bees. The construction of the human body, for example, among all the races of mankind alike, leaves no doubt that the natural mode of progression for the species is upright on its hind limbs, rather than on "all fours" like the ungulates.

God," thereby investing it with the sanction of legitimacy as representing the norm, not of a particular society, but of nature itself.

Broadly speaking, we know how the bees' design for living is written in the genes, and we have here raised the question how the design for living of a particular human civilization is written in the mind. The answer is that it is written in the terms of normative thinking, which defines propriety and impropriety, legitimacy and illegitimacy. But normative thinking, being so largely artificial, is unstable as the DNA is not, and therefore civilizations are unstable.

Having noted that a civilization exists first of all in the mind, as a complex of artificial norms, and having illustrated this by a hypothetical example, that of a child brought up in nineteenth-century England, we should now note that this primary existence is in what we may call a collective mind. The set of norms that constituted the primary terms of the civilization represented by Victorian England existed alike in the minds of all the millions of individuals who constituted the Victorian society, giving them a common language in a metaphoric as well as in a literal sense. Not only did they have a common language in which to talk with one another, they also had common values, common attitudes, common customs, common modes of behavior. When a child was born, when a couple was to be mated for life, when there was a death — in each such circumstance there were prescribed forms of personal behavior for those involved, and a prescribed ceremony. When there was a quarrel between two persons, there were prescribed procedures for resolving it, perhaps entailing such agencies as courts of law. The farmers who produced food delivered it up to certain persons who, in turn, delivered it to the consumers — all on established terms of exchange and according to modes of procedure that represented the norms of behavior by which the common mind was governed. Buildings were designed in accordance with canons of taste that, again, existed as norms in the common mind. But the norms, unlike those of the bees, were largely artificial rather than natural.

To any person who had lived only within this society, knowing it as it was at a given time and knowing nothing else, it represented what the beehive is to the bee, not an artifice but nature's immutable norm. Such a person could hardly imagine a different society of men, or would imagine it only as an exercise in phantasy. On the other side of the world, however, in imperial China, he would have found an altogether different society with altogether different norms; and if he could have jumped forward a century, say to the England of 1975, he would have found a substantially different society from that of the England in which he had been brought up. These differences in space and time would have represented differences in the normative concepts of the common mind — whether that of imperial China or that of twentieth-century England.

*

There is another respect, beside the lack of universality and stability, in which a society that represents a human civilization differs from a hive of bees. While the beehive and the human society alike represent a design for living based on a set of norms, the bees can know nothing of their own design for living because they have no minds in which the norms of their own behavior can dwell as concepts. They enact those norms blindly, automatically, not knowing of any large pattern by which their lives are regulated. It is only we humans who, being possessed of minds, comprehend that pattern and the norms associated with it. If, however, the bees did have minds, then a discrepancy might arise between the norms of their behavior as concepts in their minds, on the one hand, and the enactment of those norms in practice, on the other; and such a discrepancy would engender inner conflicts or psychological tensions from which the bees are free because, in fact, they do not have minds.

The norms associated with a human society exist in two forms: they exist in the mind, often as ideals, and they exist in their practical realization. Generally there is a discrepancy, more or less great, between the two. This discrepancy contributes to the instability of a civilization by contrast with the stability of the beehive.

A simple example is that of the norm which was supposed to govern relations between the sexes in Victorian England. According to it, sexual intimacy occurred only between married persons, being illegitimate in any other circumstances. This, however, called for such an "unnatural" constraint on human behavior, such a denial of a natural appetite, that the actual practice could not be universally or even generally governed by it. In this case, the discrepancy between what was a normative ideal and the actual practice was excessive, imposing great psychological strains on those who were torn between the norm, which represented propriety, and their natural needs, which were improper by the criterion of the norm.* The result was a rebellion against this norm in the twentieth century, and various efforts to substitute another and more realizable norm for it. So the discrepancy between the norm in the mind and general practice contributes, in its degree, to the instability of civilized society by contrast with the stability of the apian society.

*

* There is no more poignant expression of an insurmountable discrepancy between norm and practice, in this domain, than Tolstoy's Introduction to his *Kreutzer Sonata*.

I conclude these two first chapters by calling attention to a problem that I shall have occasion to treat more fully in Part Six.

The norms that constitute a civilization in its basic or primary aspect exist as custom in the collective mind of the society that represents it — i.e., exist as customary attitudes and customary modes of behavior. It is as such that they are passed on from generation to generation through the process of learning, which proceeds by the imitation of the attitudes and behavior that the child sees all about it, and by its acceptance of precepts impressed upon it. But customs, by definition, must have a certain extension in time. To resort to the *reductio ad absurdum,* there can be no custom of an hour's duration. The customary norms of civilization have always persisted, not only over the generations, but over the centuries, even though they were undergoing gradual modification.

With the constant acceleration of evolution, however, we have at last reached a point at which old norms become obsolete faster than new norms can become established in custom. Most of the people in the world today confront the problem, as they grow older, that many of the norms to which they were brought up are losing or have lost their authority, their legitimacy — which is to say, their character as norms. What is or has been normative to the older generation is not so to the younger. Severe strains are thereby set up, in the minds of individuals and in the cohesion of society alike. The civilization tends to come apart because new norms cannot become established as fast as old ones have to be abandoned. Here I merely call attention to the fact that, in the second half of the twentieth century, the acceleration of evolution has reached this point.

III

The Emergence of Civilization

AT THE END OF CHAPTER V, Part Three, I suggested that "evolution is a realization of potentialities inherent in life from the beginning, so that, barring accidents, it has a certain inevitability in its direction." At one stage, means would evolve whereby life was enabled to emerge from the water onto the land (i.e., the amniotic egg); at another, the advent of internal temperature control (independently in birds and mammals) would still further extend the ability of life to cope with various and changing environments; at still another, the brain would develop independently in birds and mammals alike. As the evolution of life continued, increasingly spearheaded by our own species, the first human domestication of plants and animals would occur simultaneously at scattered points around the globe. So, with the emergence and increasing dominance of mind, civilizations would begin to appear separately and simultaneously around the eastern Mediterranean, in the Far East, and in the New World (where the Mayan-Aztec civilization and the civilization associated with the Incas of Peru appear to have arisen about the same time, but independently of each other).

If we define civilization as we have so far, simply as the expression of a normative order registered in the common mind, then Neanderthal man was already civilized when he buried his dead with ceremonial observances that represented such an order. For his burial rites were purely artificial expressions of an order that the mind had created for itself, rather than of an order specified in the genes. If he had been responding only to what was specified in his genes — which is to say, if he had been acting naturally rather than artificially — he would simply have abandoned his dead, when they died, leaving them to be devoured by scavengers or to rot. Common usage, however, would not classify the Neanderthals as civilized men; nor does it classify even the Australian aborigines of our day as such, although their lives are dominated by the artifices we have here identified with civilization.

We may bridge this gap between our original definition of what constitutes civilization, on the one hand, and common usage, on the other, by saying that the artificial life, representing the creation of the mind, has to reach an advanced degree of development before we would, in common usage, identify it as civilized. We can, however, be more specific than this.

One effect of civilization, which we may regard as its principal effect in the long run, is to make men independent, in whatever degree, of the natural environment — to isolate them from it, to insulate them against it, to withdraw them into an artificial environment.* In the large view, this is the continuation of an evolution that began with the amniotic egg and continued with the development of internal temperature control. Although Neanderthal man undertook to protect his dead from the operations of the natural environment, in accordance with a mythological order of his own creation, he was still largely exposed to that environment in his daily life. His detachment from direct exposure to it may have been limited to what could be achieved by clothing himself in animal skins and using fire against the cold. The Australian aborigines of our own day are similarly exposed to the elements.

Contrast this with the life that one may plausibly imagine one of my readers to be living — in a penthouse, sealed against the unconditioned outer atmosphere, on top of an apartment building in Manhattan, the air in which he is bathed having been processed by air-conditioning machinery, the light by which he reads having been artificially generated, his food having been modified until it bears only a remote resemblance or none to anything in nature. He has been removed from the natural environment almost as completely as an astronaut in a space-ship.

As we saw in Chapter XII of Part Three, long before Neanderthal man disappeared, as long as 300,000 years ago, men were already building crude temporary huts on the shore of the Mediterranean. But we know almost nothing about them or their successors until some 6,000 years ago. It is at this point that civilization, which has been slowly developing here and there in the world for so many millennia, at last enters upon a sort of efflorescence, altering the natural landscape, leaving ruins and records for the contemplation of posterity.

Because the language in which we think, and consequently our habits of thought, are necessarily categorical, we have constantly to remind ourselves that reality is not. There was no instant at which life began, no instant at which mind was born. A newly fertilized

* See p. 289 above.

human ovum is not a person, nor is it, as yet, when it has split into two, four, or eight cells; and although there will come a time when all would agree that it had become a person, there will never have been a particular instant before which it had not been one but after which it had. So it is with civilization, and as an exercise of the imagination, at least, we can conceive of an historian living 10,000 years from now who found it plausible, in terms of his longer perspective, to say that civilization came to birth in the twenty-first century of our era.

*

A notable advance in cultural evolution occurred with the invention of written language, which greatly promoted the ability of men to "send word" across great distances, not only in space but also in time, for it enabled them to address, in their own words, those who would not be born until long after their own death. It contributed to the acceleration of cultural evolution by enshrining, in written form, the accumulated knowledge that provides a point of departure for the further enlargement of knowledge in each generation.

Before writing, there had been oral tradition, often committed to memory and so passed on from generation to generation verbatim; and there had been the knowledge that the young learned by imitation or by whatever procedures of education were in use. But the limitations of any alternative to writing are clear. Knowledge that is at once abstract, precise, and abstruse must lose its precision, at least, in oral transmission. (The knowledge represented by quantum theory and quantum mechanics, for example, would be too readily lost again if it could not be written down.) And there is a limit to how much the best memory can hold. The knowledge contained in a great encyclopedia is accessible to me as it would not be under the limitations of merely oral transmission.

No less important is the fact that our most advanced thinking can be done effectively and reliably only on paper. The thought we set down in writing thereby reveals defects that would otherwise escape correction. (This, surely, is the experience of every writer who undertakes to put in writing theories that, until then, he has merely spun in his head or expounded orally.)

I have, in these pages, albeit speculatively, attributed to the emergence of mind the same importance as we attach to the emergence of life. Mind is the creative faculty that seeks for an order in nature or creates an imagined order. It is the faculty by which we overcome chaos. The effectiveness of its operation — which depends entirely on language, since we think in words — was vastly extended by the invention and development of writing. So, since civilization is the expression of mind, its own development was correspondingly accelerated.*

*

Just as spoken language presumably began with the crude simplicity of warning cries or grunts to express emotion, developing by continuous elaboration and refinement until it had achieved a Shakespearian sophistication, so written language, as we know it today, must have developed in the same way from primitive beginnings. The marking of a trail through the woods by scoring the bark of trees along the way might be regarded as written language at its crudest. It bears a resemblance to the established practice of dogs, who mark their trails by leaving scent-signals on trees. But the dogs are acting naturally, in accordance with behavior that represents a prescription in their genes, whereas the men are acting artificially, in accordance with behavior conceived in their minds.

We may assume that, in the first stages of its development, written language had nothing to do with spoken language. It consisted of pictographs (which are conventional drawings that represent objects) and ideograms (which stand for ideas). Thus ╳⟶ might denote what an Englishman would call a "fish," what a Frenchman would call a "poisson," denoting the thing itself rather than any word for it; and so it would represent written language unrelated to spoken language.

A fish is a physical object, but sleep is a condition in which a physical object may find itself, a condition of which we have an idea in our minds. At an early stage of written language this idea might be represented by the conventional drawing for man, but placed horizontally rather than vertically — and with time it might by simplification become nothing more than a horizontal line (like the one that introduces this phrase), which would stand for what an Englishman calls "sleep," what a Frenchman calls "sommeil." As the sign for fish is a pictograph, so the sign I have imagined for sleep is an ideogram. The numerals in all written Indo-European languages are ideograms. Thus the figure 3 stands, not for a word, but for what in written English corresponding to spoken English is "three," or for what in written German corresponding to spoken German is "drei."

The advantage of such written language as this is that the barriers

---

* We may plausibly suppose that we live at a time when the possibilities of mind are only beginning to be realized. Perhaps there will, in the future, be other inventions that, like writing, enable it to extend its operations. Some speculate that this is what the invention of electronic digital computers in our day represents, but it is too early to know.

which prevent effective communication between the speakers of different languages don't exist for it. The figure 3 is read with equal ease by the speakers of all modern European languages, although they have different words for it. The limitations of such written language, however, are great, for it constitutes a language, apart from the spoken language, that lacks the flexibility, the range of expression, and the shades of meaning that distinguish spoken language. Let the reader but consider how he would render Plato's *Apology,* The Song of Solomon, The Gospel According to St. John, the 13th chapter of The First Epistle to the Corinthians, Tennyson's "In Memoriam," Darwin's *The Origin of Species,* or, for that matter, the text he is reading now — let him but consider how he would render these in pictographs and ideograms.

The great advance in the development of written language was the one whereby it became a counterpart of spoken language. One can only surmise how this occurred. Presumably the kind of verbal play represented by puns was involved. Thus what had originally been the pictograph for a fish might, by a conventional modification, become the written symbol of dish; so what had originally been the pictograph for a seal (the animal) might become the written symbol for a seal (the stamp used to authenticate documents); so what had been the pictograph for cat might come to stand for the spoken syllable "cat" in such words as "catalogue," "hecatomb," and "delicate." Written language would thereby become syllabic and finally alphabetic, denoting the actual sounds of spoken language.

One would be tempted to say that written language made possible what, in common usage, we call civilization. But the civilization presided over by the Incas of Peru, which was elaborate, had no written language, and other civilizations (e.g., the Mayan-Aztec) have had written languages that served for little more than numeration and the composition of calendars. One may properly doubt, however, that the early civilizations of which this was true could ever have reached the advanced stage of modern civilizations without means for putting spoken language into writing.

Although the advent of written language, in the course of evolution, may not coincide precisely with the advent of civilization, it marks, rather sharply, an important distinction in our knowledge of the past, the distinction between the prehistoric and the historical period. For the times before records were kept in writing we know relatively little of what human beings were up to, by contrast with our knowledge of what they have been up to ever since.

From this point on, then, we shall be concerned with history.

IV

The Period of Multiple Civilizations

UP TO NOW I have sometimes referred to civilization in generic terms, sometimes to specific civilizations, such as the Mayan-Aztec. The fact that civilization emerged independently at different places around the globe, when the evolution of life had reached that point, explains why there were, to begin with, a number of specific civilizations, distinct from one another and, for the most part, unaware of one another's existence. The civilizations that grew up in the area from the Nile Valley to Mesopotamia and the civilization that was developing in east Asia knew nothing of each other; nor, at a later date, did either the Greco-Roman or the Chinese civilization know anything of the Mayan-Aztec civilization or the civilization under the Incas in Peru, which in turn knew nothing of them. Indeed, the Mayan-Aztec and the Inca civilizations appear to have known nothing of each other. The civilizations were separated by space. In between them the world was either empty of humanity or sparsely populated by men who had not yet reached the stage of civilization.

The differences among civilizations — each with its own languages, its own norms of behavior, and its own modes of cultural expression — have been the rule ever since civilization began, even to our own day. It makes vivid the basic distinction between the society of the beehive, which is everywhere the same, being prescribed by the genes, and the societies of men, which are largely unprescribed, representing the relatively free creations of their own minds. It is only in our own day, when human populations have filled up the spaces between civilizations, and when the means of transport and communication have freed men from narrow territorial confinement, that we begin to see the emergence of one worldwide civilization into which the separate traditional civilizations are being absorbed.

We may plausibly suppose that, to an historian living in A.D. 5,000, the period from 4000 B.C. to A.D. 2000 will be regarded as the period of multiple civilizations. It will be regarded as the period before the separated groups of mankind, each with its own culture and developing civilization, coalesced to form a single civilization embracing a worldwide society of man. The image that comes to mind is that of the mangrove tree, like a Tree of Life turned upside-down, in which multiple roots spring from the soil to join above-ground in a single trunk.

At this point, then, we may attempt to define more narrowly than we have so far what constituted a civilization during the six thousand years after about 4000 B.C., the passing period of multiple civilizations. The problem is to distinguish what constitutes the unity of a civilization from its internal diversity and from the protean manifestations of its evolution in time. I quote here the definition by the late Robert Redfield, which takes account of this diversity and this continuous transformation alike.

> A civilization is a great culture; it is also a compound culture; rural people and townspeople are apart, different but traditionally interconnected. The rural people characteristically become peasantry, living in small communities that maintain local ways of life more or less coherent and in the main orally transmitted, like those of primitive peoples. But peasants depend in important part on the moral and ideational authority of intellectual elites, characteristically resident outside of the villages in towns, shrine-centers, temples, or monasteries. The peasant communities, local yet alike, together form a stratum, an "estate," within the civilized society; with respect or suspicion peasants look to the city man, the mandarin, pundit or imam, the priest, or the philosopher. Yet the content of their thought depends on these cultivators and modifiers of tradition, as the cultivated speculations and reflections of the intellectual class arise out of the unconsidered traditions of the illiterate. A civilization is an interaction of many little local cultures and a "high culture" (a "great tradition") that is considered, developed, and eventually written down by thinkers and teachers, with time to create works of the mind, connected with religious or philosophical institutions.*

Redfield's definition of civilization, insofar as I have quoted it, is incomplete to the extent that it omits, except by implication, the material aspects of a civilization as distinct from what he calls its ideational aspects. Both enter into the constitution of any civilization and tend to be interdependent. Since, however, a civilization is basically a product of mind, we may properly give priority to the ideational aspect.

The psychological condition denoted by the word "anxiety" consti-

* *Collier's Encyclopedia,* 1970, Vol. 6, p. 483.

tutes the soil out of which civilization grows; and anxiety, in turn, is the price our kind has to pay for its unique possession of the aptitude called mind. Mind, as we saw in Part Three, Chapter IX, liberates its possessors from imprisonment in the here-and-now. This liberation, however, makes them aware, as they could not otherwise have been, of an unknown world beyond the horizon of the known, extending alike in space and in time. It makes them aware of being surrounded by a darkness, full of unknown dangers, out of which unforeseen disaster may strike at any moment. It makes them aware of the fact that death waits for all, including themselves and those whom they cherish; but they cannot know at what moment it will carry off a particular victim, or what, if anything, may await the victim so carried off into the darkness. The consequence is that all men, unlike other species, live in a constant state of anxiety, which drives them alike to create bodies of religious belief and to build walled cities.

Imagination fills the darkness with elements of fear and hope; but hope is merely the complement and counterpart of fear, which comes first. So it is that religion and defence have together constituted a basis for the development of civilization.

*

A civilization is a design for living based on a complex of norms enshrined in custom. Although its inhabitants, because they have been brought up to it, may enjoy the illusion that it is natural, it is in fact an artifact, the free creation of the mind.

By what process is this artifact produced, and how is it maintained over the generations?

The basic requirement of any society is to come to terms with its environment. If it exists in an area of snow and ice, it will have to devise ways of protecting itself against the weather and supplying itself with food under the circumstances of such an environment. With time, these ways become enshrined in custom as norms. But they are not fixed, as are the ways by which the social insects, through natural selection, have come to terms with their environments. They are not spelled out in the DNA of every individual but imposed upon the individuals of each successive generation by exemplification and training. What this represents is the necessary concern of every society to perpetuate, by means that must themselves be largely artificial, its own artificial design, which depends for its survival on the maintenance of tradition. Because the design has been devised over generations to meet the challenge of an environment that is implicitly hostile (as every environment is), the physical and the psychological security of those who live according to it depend on such perpetuation.

What is artificial, however, cannot, as such, have the same normative authority over men's minds as what is natural. The apian way of life is right for the bees because it is the only possible one for them — because, in the common figure of speech, it is what nature intended for them. But the worldly reader of these lines would surely find it hard to make a like statement about any of the ways of life known to civilized human beings, saying that the traditional Chinese way of life, or the way of life exemplified by American industrial society, or the Aztec way of life is what nature intended for men. Nevertheless, those who give their allegiance to the design of a particular civilization, and who therefore wish to see it perpetuated, must be tempted to believe and to maintain that its norms, so far from being no more than improvisations of the human mind, represent what nature intended for men, just as the norms of the hive represent what nature intended for bees. They will try to show that its marriage customs, its traditional family organization, its division of labor among classes or castes, and every other basic aspect of its design represent some such propriety; for, even though this is not so, it must be felt to be so if a civilization is to retain its legitimacy and so to elicit the willing conformity on which its survival depends.*

If, however, the term "nature" is used only in its narrow and scientific sense, the sense in which it is distinguished from the supernatural, then its authority will hardly suffice to legitimate a human civilization. Ultimate authority dwells in the darkness beyond the known world. That is why the authors of the American Declaration of Independence invoked, not nature alone, but "Nature and Nature's God." In traditional Western civilization, the ultimate authority invoked for the legitimation of its norms has been God's will.†

Religion, then, has served from the beginning, not only to fill the vacuum of ignorance, but in doing so to give men the assurance they need that the normative order to which they are committed by the

---

* The Communist Manifesto, issued by Karl Marx and Friedrich Engels in 1848, was designed to evoke a like normative authority for their project of a classless society about to be born, for it presented a vision of a history that, by nature, had all along been moving toward this predestined end.

† "Because there is nothing greater on earth, after God, than the sovereign princes, and because they are established by him as his lieutenants, to rule over other men, it is necessary to have regard for their status, so as to respect and obey their majesty in all obedience, and to speak for them in honorable terms: for whoever shows contempt for his sovereign prince shows contempt for God, of whom he is the image on earth." (Translated from Jean Bodin, Les six livres de la République, Paris, 1579, pp. 154–155.)

accident of birth, whatever it may be, is the one and only proper order. It has provided that authority, in men's minds, for every civilization. (If it does not entirely do so for the author and his readers in the second half of the twentieth century, this is partly because they have risen above their own civilization to a world view that embraces many civilizations in time and in space. The situation was not the same for Jean Bodin.)

Because religion has played such a basic role from the beginning in the development of the civilizations that have appeared over the past five or six millennia, any history of how they have developed may well begin with it.

V

The Role of Religion

PRIMITIVE HUNTERS, in the anxiety with which they confront the unknown, have always been concerned not to antagonize the powers with which they have, in their imaginations, peopled it. These powers have generally been thought of as invisible personalities, which manifest in themselves the human emotions of greed, jealousy, and anger, which may take offense or, if won over, grant favor. The hunter performs whatever rites he thinks will win them over — including the ceremonial offer of sacrifices that represent a sort of bribery — because, if they oppose him or simply fail to favor him, his hunting will be unsuccessful. This typifies a widespread if primitive form of religion, which supports the artificial norms that, in primitive societies, may constitute the rudiments of a civilization.

In early agricultural societies a like anxiety is associated with the need to gain the assistance or to avoid the opposition of the unseen powers if the soil is to yield a good harvest. These powers, which may originally have been conceived as merely localized spirits, perhaps attached to particular features of the landscape or associated with particular species of animals, tend to be ennobled or enlarged by the myth-making proclivities of the mind, as civilization develops, until they have come to constitute a society of deities, the gods and goddesses of such a pantheon as was associated with the civilization of ancient Egypt or with the Hellenic civilization represented by Homer. The success or failure of Greeks or Trojans in *The Iliad* depends on the favor or opposition of the several gods or goddesses who oversee the affairs of men from their lofty abode on Mount Olympus; and it is only the hostility of the sea-god Poseidon that prevents Odysseus from returning to his home and family — until at last the goddess Athena, who has taken his side, wins favor for him in the Council of the Gods.

With the passage of the centuries, such religions tend to evolve, by way of ambiguous phases, from polytheistic to monotheistic. The

Old Testment and the New, taken together, embrace the history of such a development. In its most primitive passages, the Bible tells of demonic spirits that lodge themselves inside individual human bodies and have, if possible, to be exorcised. In the first five books of the Old Testament, known as the Pentateuch, the Jewish nation is represented as having its own national god, Yahweh, to which it owes an exclusive allegiance, but who is only one among a number of rival gods. Beginning with Isaiah 44:6, however, he proclaims himself, for the first time, the only god there is. In the books that follow, as in the first chapter of Genesis, there is generally only one God, who created the universe, who is all-powerful and without any rival; but other supernatural personalities do come into account, such as Satan, in The Book of Job, who provokes God into a demonstration of his power that would not have been necessary if he had been more powerful.

The New Testament takes its departure from the increasingly pronounced monotheism of the Old; but demons make their appearance in it, and among the archangels who should be the servants of God is one who, having fallen, is his opponent and rival — namely, the same Satan who cunningly incited God to torture Job, and who now, less successfully, tempts the Son of God. Commentators and controversialists have for centuries seen implications of polytheism in the Holy Trinity; and the way in which simple people worship the Virgin Mary or particular saints may be difficult to distinguish from the practices of a polytheistic religion.

It is evident that, whether or not man was created by God in his own image, the gods have been created by man in man's image. The deities I have cited here are all human in their susceptibility to frustration, in their capriciousness, in their partialities, in their mistaken expectations and consequent disappointments, in their doubts and anxieties.*

At a late stage, however, in the historical evolution I am tracing, the one supreme deity of monotheism tends to lose his human character and to become increasingly abstract. Traditionally, the supreme God of the Bible has been thought of as a bearded patriarch, such as Michelangelo depicted on the ceiling of the Sistine Chapel; and it has been supposed that his abode was somewhere in the sky above, which had not yet become accessible to human exploration. The more advanced theologians and clergymen of modern times,

---

* In the moving 18th chapter of Genesis, a weary and travel-stained Yahweh, received by Abraham and Sarah as their house-guest, is advised by Abraham on what to do if reports of sin in Sodom and Gomorrah should prove true. Here, surely, Abraham is distinctly superior to Yahweh in his moral sophistication. See the discussion of this in my *Men and Nations*, Princeton, 1962, Section 14, pp. 52–54 and 151–157.

however, regard such conceptions as figurative, like similes resorted to for pedagogical purposes, holding that, in fact, no physical form may literally be attributed to God, who cannot properly be thought of in such terms. God, in the most extreme version of this view, is merely a term for the abstract divinity that most of us apprehend in our minds as an element of being.

This identification of God as an abstraction does not, however, represent simply the last stage of a dying religious tradition. It has been associated with the most sophisticated minds for some two thousand years in the West, and for longer elsewhere; witness not only the pantheism of Spinoza in the seventeenth century, but also the first verse of The Gospel According to St. John, which was probably composed in the first century after Christ: "In the beginning was the Word, and the Word was with God, and the Word was God." *

What chiefly concerns us here, however, are the respective bodies of ethics associated with Judaism, Christianity, and all the other great religions, which in their turn are respectively associated with the several civilizations of mankind. Leviticus, Numbers, and Deuteronomy, in the Old Testament, consist largely of rules of conduct (including the Ten Commandments) dictated by Yahweh to Moses for him to communicate to the Jewish nation. They are remarkable for their detailed completeness, prescribing the conduct to be observed in virtually every kind of individual and social activity, setting forth precisely the punishments to be inflicted in the various circumstances of possible infringement.

Again, the Sermon on the Mount consists almost entirely of rules of conduct, albeit at a more abstract and elevated level. All these listings of laws, ordinances, and rules of conduct represent the attribution of divine authority to the norms of the civilization that produced them. They represent the need to legitimize the artifice.

*

It will be seen that neither Judaism nor Christianity is one coherent religion with one body of belief, but that each is a complex of beliefs which vary from primitive to sophisticated — e.g., from a belief in many gods with human attributes to a belief in some abstract and

---

* This reflects the Platonic view that ideas are the only authentic realities, physical phenomena being imperfect copies of them. It also represents the view already expressed in these pages that the conception in the mind — equated with "the Word" (the Logos), since the activity of the mind is inseparable from language — precedes the creation that is its expression as the image in the sculptor's mind precedes his carving. See the opening paragraph of Chapter II above.

dimly apprehended principle of divinity. The same may be said of other great religions or religious traditions.

Just as Judaism or Christianity is an imagined ordering of the unknown, which provides a putative basis of authority for certain norms of human conduct, so Hinduism, which originated some 4,000 years ago in the Indus Valley and the Indian subcontinent, is also an imagined ordering of the unknown; but a different ordering which provides a different basis for different norms, the difference between the one religion and the other corresponding to the difference between one civilization and another. This difference, in turn, represents the variety and instability of artificial society, by contrast with the uniformity and stability of a natural society like that of the bees.

Just as the Judeo-Christian tradition entails a tension between polytheistic and monotheistic tendencies, so does the Hindu tradition, albeit in a different way. Its pantheon is composed of Vishnu (who has various avatars or manifestations, the god Krishna being one of them), Siva, and hundreds of lesser gods and goddesses, including merely local deities. These are all, like Poseidon or Yahweh, gods with human attributes. Their polytheistic variety, however, is secondary to a grand pantheistic conception, that of one eternal, ubiquitous, universal, and never-changing spirit called Brahman. Every god is but a manifestation of Brahman — as, in a sense, is the individual soul of every human being. Brahman represents divinity at a level of abstraction almost beyond human apprehension, such as that of Spinoza's pantheistic God or the God of the opening words of The Gospel According to St. John.

Again, as in the case of the Judeo-Christian tradition, Hinduism provides the necessary authority, in the minds of men, for the artificial norms of a particular civilization. The Hindu scriptures (which consist of such Sanskrit classics as the Vedas, the Upanishads, and the Maahbarata epic to which the Bhagavad-Gita belongs) include an account of a supernatural origin for the caste-system that constitutes the very basis of Hindu society.

Every Hindu belongs by birth to one or the other of thousands of castes into which the society is divided as definitively as genera are divided into species. There can be no intermarriage among them, or any escape from one's own caste during one's lifetime. The castes form a hierarchy, with the Brahmins (typically priests and scholars) on top, the menial Sudras (including the untouchables) at the bottom. There is a superficial resemblance, here, to the natural division of bees into queens, drones, and workers — and, indeed, the caste divisions must seem no less natural to a devout Hindu. The respective occupations of each caste are prescribed, as are the respective occupations of the three apian divisions — although in the latter case the prescription is genetic.

The Hindu religion, through its scriptures, also prescribes the conduct proper to mankind generally, and to the members of each caste in particular, as well as the rites to accompany birth, marriage, death, and the various religious celebrations that come at their appointed times in the annual round. Obedience to all these norms of conduct is rewarded, and disobedience punished, by the fate of the individual in the successive lives he expects to lead as a consequence of his reincarnation after each death. By the rightness or wrongness of his conduct, he may in the course of successive reincarnations rise to godhead or sink to the level of a bug that is squashed under the foot of an untouchable. The more sophisticated Hindus, however, look forward to an ultimate release, earned by right conduct, from this otherwise interminable succession of reincarnations, and so to losing their individual identities through union with the universal and changeless Brahman.

Hinduism, then, provides another illustration of the point that the whole structure of any civilized society is an invention of the mind rather than a genetic endowment, so that it can prevail and survive only insofar as its members are persuaded that it represents, more than a natural dispensation, a supernatural providence. It is the plight of mankind, at the present stage in the development of life on earth, that this must be so.

*

No one can survey the basic beliefs underlying the various and variable civilizations of mankind without being impressed by the difficulty, based on their variability, of formulating generalizations applicable to all. All seem, indeed, to have begun with the belief in many spirits, demons, or limited gods whose favorable disposition was to be won or kept by various rites, including sacrifices. All seem to have produced as well, at some stage of their development, the concept of a universal spirit, or at least of one supreme god, such as the Allah of Islam. Such bodies of religious belief have served to legitimize the norms of civilized societies in the eyes of their members.

It must be said, however, that secular authority, as well as religious, has demonstrated its equal power to serve this function. Confucianism provides the classic example.

The history of China, as a monarchical society under a succession of dynasties, begins to emerge from the darkness of prehistory into historical visibility in the centuries between 2000 and 1500 B.C. As in other early agricultural societies, perhaps without exception, the first Chinese divinities were fertility gods, gods of the soil and gods of the crops, as well as spirits of the rivers and mountains. A cosmography appears also to have prevailed from the beginning, however, that is metaphysical rather than theological. It has been based on a universal dualism between two complementary principles, the Yin and the Yang, the former representing the Earth (as well as the dark, the negative, the female, etc.), the latter representing the sky or Heaven (as well as the light, the positive, the male, etc.). Heaven and Earth were regarded as supreme deities. Heaven, as the term implies, was a realm or a high and remote power, not to be thought of as a person like the Yahweh depicted by Michelangelo on the ceiling of the Sistine Chapel. This abstract philosophical conception provided the foundation for a political system that, whether or not it can be said to remain in being today, has endured 3,000 years. According to it, the ruler, known as the Son of Heaven or as the Emperor until our time, ruled by the Mandate of Heaven, which he retained only as long as he practiced right conduct; and he alone was responsible for keeping, by his conduct and the rites he performed, the good will of Heaven on behalf of the entire society over which he presided — a society regarded as, in principle, worldwide.

The concept of the ruler as the Son of Heaven, and the associated emphasis on good conduct, were in harmony with early ancestor worship and an emphasis on the virtue of loyalty, especially that of the son to the father, but in connection with various hierarchical and family ties as well. Here, to put it perhaps too crudely, is a body of belief dominated by principles rather than by gods. (Alongside it, the Homeric religion appears as one dominated by gods without principles.)

In any case, this system of broad principles — involving the Yin and the Yang, Earth and Heaven, and the rule that depended on the Mandate of Heaven — remained the unquestioned conceptual framework within which ethical norms were determined or disputed for three millennia. It constituted the framework of Confucianism, as well as of all competing doctrines that pretended to prescribe human conduct.

The point I am making here is that secular authority, as well as religious, has served to legitimize the norms of a civilized and therefore artificial society. Confucius, who lived from c. 551 to 479 B.C., was not the prophet or even the preacher of any religion, nor did he concern himself with unworldly or otherworldly matters. He was, no more nor less than Thomas Hobbes or Rousseau, a political philosopher, and his preoccupying concern with ethics was a concern with the kind of conduct that made possible the effective functioning of society. He was concerned exclusively with norms of conduct, such as are set forth in the sayings traditionally ascribed to him. Confucianism, then, is not a religion but an ethical system that takes the form of a body of rules to govern the conduct of one's life. Yet the authority of Confucius and Confucianism has had the same efficacity in legitimizing norms of behavior as the authority of Christ and Christianity, of Mohammed and Mohammedanism.

What is central, here, is human psychology, manifested in what the members of a society are ready to accept as ultimate authority for the norms on which their society is based. What they are ready to accept is a name and an associated doctrinal complex, even though it does not pretend to speak for the otherwise unknown world of the supernatural, the world that extends beyond the directly knowable here-and-now. The members of a society can become absolute believers in Confucianism as they can in Christianity, in Marxism as in Mohammedanism, accepting the authority of the secular prophet no less than that of the religious as ultimate and infallible.

Neither Confucius nor Marx, however, nor the bodies of belief associated with their respective names, ever pretended to represent the world beyond the directly knowable, the world of the supernatural, although this is the world I have cited as the supposed source of the authority that legitimizes the norms of a civilization. It is evident, then, that I shall have to modify the point I have made.

*

The prophet Mohammed has never been considered a god rather than a man. His utterances, however, as set forth in the Koran, are considered as representing the thought or the will of the one God, which must necessarily be infallible. What counts, in terms of authority over the human mind, is not whether Mohammed was a god or a man, but, rather, his supposed infallibility, whether in his own right or by derivation from God. Mohammed died thirteen centuries ago, so that what remains of him, beside the writings, is merely a memory that, passed on from generation to generation, has acquired the attributes of myth, in consequence of which he is a mythical as well as an historical person. As such, he might qualify in his own right for the worship of the true believer. The word of Mohammed, regarded as infallible, might be accepted as final authority even without the primary attribution to God.

Surrounded as we all are by the unknown, and consequently ridden by uncertainty and anxiety, we need to believe in some source of infallible knowledge to which we can look for assured answers to the questions for which we do not, ourselves, have answers. In fact, our need is not so much for the answers themselves as for the assurance that, however ignorant of them we happen to be, there is someone who does know them. So a child still young enough for such credulity is comforted by the assumption that, even though it does not itself know the explanation of many things, its parents do. There is, I think, a general need among us for someone who fills the role of the all-knowing father. We will find him in a mythical figure of our own common creation if we cannot find him otherwise; and, having found him, our own security of mind depends on untroubled faith in his ultimate wisdom.

The Mosaic law, as set forth in the Pentateuch, represents an unquestionable body of norms to the true believer because it comes, by way of Moses, from Yahweh himself, and Yahweh is a god. But the true believer could accept it as such, even without Yahweh, simply by believing that Moses was a godlike hero, representative of perfection and infallibility in himself. The line between heroes and gods — between Heracles and Apollo, between Abraham and Yahweh — is not sharp.

Our need is for mythic personages, whether we call them gods or heroes. Confucius was such a personage, and Mao Tse-tung has become one in our day (thus exemplifying the fact that the myth can be brought into being even during the lifetime of the man about whom it forms). Karl Marx was another such personage, whose myth began to be cultivated from the moment of his death.*

So it is that Confucius and Confucianism or Marx and Marxism play the same role as Christ and Christianity or Mohammed and Mohammedanism in providing the authority we need for the organization of our necessarily artificial societies, and for our own personal conduct within them.

It seems a prediction worth risking that, at the point where we now stand in history — the point at which one worldwide civilization is replacing the multiple civilizations of the past 10,000 years — the theological religions of the past, having become outdated, will be replaced by secular religions (also called ideologies) — specifically by a Marxism that is not one body of belief but that undergoes constant transformation and differentiation, as all the great religions have in the past.

* See my "Marx: His Death and Resurrection," *Encounter,* January 1970.

VI

Cities

IN ITS PHYSICAL ASPECTS, the development of civilized society was almost everywhere inseparable from the development of cities.*

At this point we again confront the philosophical problem of definition, which arises out of the fact that, while language is categorical, reality is not. In the long progress from the man-apes there is no point at which modern man is born, no point at which religion comes into being, no point at which civilization is invented — and there is no first city. Encampments develop into what may at last be called towns, towns into what may at last be called cities — and cities, perhaps, into what may at last be called something else. What we are concerned with here is the seamless reality, not the linguistic categories that we make use of for purposes of thought and exposition only.

Under these circumstances, a vague definition is more realistic than a precise one. What I mean by a city is "a community of substantial size and population density that shelters a variety of nonagricultural specialists, including a literate élite." † Such communities began to develop at about the same time in Mesopotamia (c. 3500 B.C.), the Nile Valley (c. 3100 B.C.), the Indus Valley (c. 2500 B.C.), and the valley of the Yellow River in China (c. 1500 B.C.). They began to develop quite independently in Middle America about the time of Christ. In the perspective of millions of years, this is tantamount to simultaneity.

Before such cities could develop, agriculture had not only to reach the point at which permanent settlement could replace nomadism; it also had to reach the point at which the production of surplus food

---

* The "almost" in this sentence is to take account of those who would define the term "civilized" broadly enough to include the Polynesians of old, whose culture was determined by its oceanic and insular setting. But there can be no categorical distinction between a pre-civilized culture and a civilization.

† Gideon Sjoberg, "The Origin and Evolution of Cities," *Scientific American,* September 1965. The virtue of this definition is in the vagueness of the adjective "substantial."

made a sophisticated division of labor possible by freeing many members of society from the need to produce their own. Such a division of labor requires organization for the collection, storing, and distribution of the food produced by some for all; this organization, in turn, makes its own demands, and these demands, in their turn, require further organization. So all developments contain the seed of further developments, perhaps in accelerating sequence.

In any society there must be a directing authority; and in all societies until recent times that authority has been intimately identified with an official body of religious belief. This is to say that civilized societies have tended to be theocracies, polities in which the ruler was also the high priest, the intermediary between ordinary mortals and divinity — like Moses or the Emperor of China.

It is no accident that the appearance of the first cities coincides with the invention of writing, because even the organization of primitive urban societies requires that written records be kept —records of laws, of regulations, of transactions, of the calendrical round associated with agriculture and religious feasts. And any society that engages in trading, on the basis of the division of labor, depends on some skill in counting and recorded arithmetic. Even the pre-urban or quasi-urban society under the Incas of Peru, although it had no true written language, used knotted cords for purposes of inventory.*

The development of cities also made for the division of society into classes. The government presided over by the ruler, with its ministers and magistrates, is bound to constitute an élite, if only because of the authority associated with it, an élite that demands to be served and fed by other elements of the society, lower in rank because of this servile or subordinate function. Almost until our own day, literacy in any society has been the property of a privileged minority only, and this in itself has tended to set that minority above the illiterate majority. Finally, those who engage in the more artificial professions, as distinct from the production of food, manifesting more specialized skills and being more "civilized" by virtue of their remoteness from the soil that the farmer tills, enjoy the standing this gives them as representatives of the higher achievements of civilization.

In this evolution of civilization, we must not look for simple cause-and-effect relationships. We can say, for example, that the development of writing made the more elaborate organization of society

---

* The combination of primitiveness in some respects and extensive organization in others may mark the Peruvian society as a borderline case, or may be taken to reflect the ambiguity of reality in terms of our logical categories. The reality it represents contradicts some of the generalizations one would otherwise have made with less hesitation.

possible; but the organization of society, in the degree of its elaboration, tended to force the development of the writing skill it required. The growth of civilization generates its own dynamics: social organization elicits the skills that require or make possible more elaborate organization that, in turn, requires still more developed and varied skills.

From the beginning, this reciprocating cultural evolution has entailed the kind of geographical concentration that defines a city. Poor subsistence farmers may be scattered; but when farmers produce a surplus of food that they exchange for goods and services provided by artisans, then the geographical distance over which the exchanges take place makes a difference. Those who are constantly engaged with one another in the organization, the regulation, and the performance of these exchanges must be in daily if not hourly touch with one another. The consequent requirements of propinquity are met by the development of the city.

Typically, the élite classes, with their retainers, live at the center of the city. The various artisans who serve them tend to have their shops in what we may think of schematically as a circle around the center. The lower classes who perform menial or peripheral functions tend to live in an outer circle, beyond which are the dwellings of the farmers who till the land.

This kind of concentration, in itself, stimulates the intellectual development on which the progress of civilization depends. If the literate and relatively educated élite are constantly together in the city, they are bound to be engaged in a virtually continuous process of discourse that, by means of dialectical progression, leads to ever more refined and sophisticated uses of the mind. They stimulate one another reciprocally. (The classic example, perhaps more ideal than typical, is provided by Plato's dialogues.) Similarly, association among the artisans tends to stimulate the progress of their respective arts.

Finally, the city meets the basic need for a common defence. We must picture the situation that prevailed for thousands of years. Those who settled down and developed a prosperity based on agriculture were liable to be attacked, because of their prosperity, by plundering bands of nomads living at the level of mere subsistence. Farmers, artisans, and others who lived scattered in geographical isolation, would be wholly vulnerable to such attacks. One solution was, in the first place, to come together in fortified cities; in the second place, to organize a common defence, perhaps involving, at last, the specialization associated with a professional army.

All these developments, as I say, tended to move forward together, reinforcing one another in their common progress, which was of an unparalleled rapidity in terms of the scale of millions of years to which we have become accustomed in these pages.

*

From the earliest stage, civilization has been associated with the development of cities, which we have habitually thought of as points on a map. But the influence of any city radiates as it grows in wealth and power, so that it tends to dominate ever wider areas — this radiation leading, in some cases, from the confined city-state to the universal empire of which Rome provides at once the classic and the most extreme example.

For many centuries, a small city with its surrounding fields — such as may still be seen in the independent city-state of San Marino, covering 60 square kilometers, and with a population of under 20,000 crowded on top of an acropolis in its midst — a city or city-state of this sort might have been economically and culturally self-sufficient. As it prospered, however, its inhabitants would have been disposed to reach out for the tempting products of regions beyond its frontiers. If, for example, it occupied an upland site, they might have sought the fruits of more or less distant lowlands. This might result in colonization of the lowlands, or in trade with populations already occupying them. Such a process of expansion might lead to the establishment of daughter settlements that might themselves grow to be cities, and to the development of trade-routes. It might also lead to the military conquest of an ever wider area. All this, like the radiating process of biological evolution that we examined in Part Two, might entail a constant complexification of society over an ever wider area, with increasing specialization and an ever more elaborate division of labor, resulting in new challenges to organizing skills and new demands on technology. Where expanding societies come into contact with other societies, conflict is implicit; and so such expansion might lead to military requirements that could radically affect the organization of society and the direction of its cultural development. (We remember, at a somewhat later stage, Persia, Athens and Sparta, Macedonia and Rome.)

It was by some such process, different in each case, that the civilizations of Egypt and the Middle East, of India, of China, and of Middle America developed. They developed from cities of which, in the case of the area from the Nile to the Tigris, the names still persist in our common memory (and in some instances the cities themselves): Memphis and Thebes in Egypt, Nineveh and Babylon in Mesopotamia, Damascus and Jersualem in ancient Syria.

*

The development of cities and the development of civilization have been associated from the beginning as aspects of a single development. The development of cities, which is more susceptible of measurement than the development of civilization, has, like the evolution of life to which it belongs, been accelerating at an exponential rate — until it appears to be reaching a point of imminent culmination in our present.

If the population of San Marino today is under 20,000, it seems unlikely that the population of Athens in the fifth century B.C. was as much as 40,000 (although in terms of the orders of magnitude that concern us here it makes little difference whether it was 20,000 or 80,000). We are told that the population of ancient Rome, at its largest, may have exceeded 300,000.* (The population of Rome in 1964 was over two and a half million.) We may say, then, that the largest city up to some 2,000 years ago had a population of some 300,000. Certainly the bulk of the world's population at that time lived on the natural earth, or in settlements and villages that were no more than occasional points on certain limited areas of its surface.

The development of modern cities — exemplified by London, Paris, Bologna, mediaeval Rome — began some 800 years ago in Europe and has continued ever since at an exponential rate. What has been entailed has been not only the transformation of what used to be called cities into the extended urban agglomerations of our day, which may cover, as in the case of London, over 1,600 square kilometers, but also the inclusion of an ever larger proportion of mankind in such agglomerations. This combined process has now become so rapid as to be striking within the lifetime of one man, and notable even in a single decade. It has become so rapid that the writer of these lines must expect that the urbanization of the world and mankind will have advanced measurably by the time they are put into print.

The following figures are taken from Kingsley Davis's Introduction to *Cities*.† In 1970 the number of cities of a hundred thousand or more inhabitants was about 1,725, and was increasing at about 2.5 percent per annum. The average population of such a city had risen from 422,000 in 1950 to 501,000 in 1970. (The largest urban conglomeration in 1973, that of New York City and its urban extensions, had a population of 16.5 million.) In 1900, only an estimated 5.5 percent of the world's rapidly increasing population lived in cit-

* Sjoberg, op. cit.
† Subtitled *Their Origin, Growth and Human Impact* (Readings from *Scientific American*), San Francisco, 1973.

ies of a hundred thousand or more. By 1950 the figure was 16.2 percent, and by 1970 it was 23.7 percent. Barring a catastrophe, it will be substantially higher by the time these words are in print.

The continuation of this kind of growth would rapidly lead to the point where the normal habitat of man, the world over, was the city. But the city, as we know it today, does not represent the environment to which mankind is genetically adapted. It is the product of a cultural evolution that, engendered by genetic evolution at a certain stage, has accelerated to the point where it has, in its pace, completely outstripped genetic evolution. In the great cities, genetic evolution, which in any case manifests itself only over generations, hardly counts anymore, not so much because of its slowness as because natural selection, if it has not been eliminated by medical skills and other provision for the protection of the weak, is no longer based on criteria that make for survival.*

As we have seen (pages 249–250), genetic and cultural evolution are but recriprocating aspects of one comprehensive process, which is the evolution of life on earth. Increasingly, cultural evolution has set the pace for genetic evolution, and at last is outrunning it completely.

The situation that exists in our own day is to be understood only in the context of the whole. For the first 2,000 million years, the progress of evolution did not go beyond the prokaryotic cell. Some 500 million years later, the process of evolution was accelerated by the development of the sexual reproduction that made recombination possible. That was only a thousand million years ago. Four hundred million years ago, the first vertebrate appeared. A hundred million years ago, or less, the birds and mammals replaced the reptiles as the dominant vertebrates. The first primates may have appeared 70 million years ago, the first anthropoids perhaps 50 million years ago, the first apes 40 million years ago, the first hominids perhaps 20 million years ago, the first representatives of the genus *Homo* perhaps 2 million years ago, the first modern man about 70,000 years ago, and the first cities about 5,000 years ago. Modern urban conglomerations began to develop some 800 years ago. At last we have got to the point where evolution is changing the face of the earth as much in a decade as it once did in millions of years. In our day, at last, the exponential curve of evolution approaches the vertical.

* "Any selective factors at work in city populations now come almost exclusively from differential birth rates, and these evidently favor carelessness and incompetence — traits that are peculiarly inappropriate for city existence." Kingsley Davis, op. cit., p. 5.

All this is occurring on one speck of dust that is revolving about one point of fire that is one of 100,000 million such points in a galaxy that is one of 1,000 million such galaxies scattered across 20,000 million light-years of space in a universe of matter-energy in which time and distance vary with the circumstances of the observer.

VII

The Taxonomy of Civilization

THE HISTORY OF CIVILIZED MANKIND has, up to now, been a history of
what we commonly regard as distinct civilizations. But when we try
to define the distinctness of each in terms of its geographical and
temporal boundaries we run into difficulties. Moving out from what
we regard as the geographical center of a particular civilization, we
see how it becomes increasingly modified the farther we go; and if
we follow its evolution we see how it is transformed with the passage
of time. We cannot be sure where one civilization ends and another
begins. This difficulty may lead us to conclude, at last, that we are
trying to impose too categorical an order, of our own imagining, on
a reality that is not so categorical. Perhaps we are still too close to
the underlying chaos to see the order that a larger perspective would
reveal.

Let me offer a somewhat extreme example of the problem that
confronts us. There was a civilization, called the civilization of Ancient Greece, which we associate with the Athens of the fifth century
B.C. An outpost of this civilization at the time was the Greek city of
Byzantium on the Bosporus, at the entrance to the Black Sea. In the
centuries that followed, Byzantium flourished (under the name of
Constantinople) and we find ourselves identifying it as the center of
what we call Byzantine civilization, a civilization that we regard as a
Greek branch or offshoot of the Roman civilization into which the
civilization of Ancient Greece was transformed or absorbed. Then,
in the fifteenth century after Christ, Ivan the Great, the first Russian
ruler to adopt the Roman title of Caesar or Czar, claimed to be the
heir to this Byzantine branch of the Roman civilization that is commonly regarded as a continuation and development of the civilization of Ancient Greece. But no one would identify the Muscovite
civilization over which Ivan presided with the civilization of the
Athens over which Pericles presided, although it is possible for the
historian of civilization to draw a continuous line between them,
however tenuous it may become at some points. When did one civi-

lization cease and another begin? Where are the geographical boundaries of the one or the other?

Everyone agrees in recognizing a civilization that arose in the valley of the Indus River, that spread over the Indian subcontinent, and that engendered the religion or the complex of religious beliefs called Buddhism. Everyone agrees, as well, in recognizing a separate Chinese civilization in which Buddhism, having spread from the Indian subcontinent, flourished more luxuriantly than in the land of its origin. But Buddhism was in constant process of transformation, so that the later Buddhism of China was not the same as the earlier Buddhism of India.

One might say that there was a distinct Indian civilization, a distinct Chinese civilization, a distinct Korean civilization, and a distinct Japanese civilization; but most of us would find it more realistic to regard the civilization in Korea and the civilization in Japan as no more than branches or offshoots of Chinese civilization, as subspecies rather than as distinct species in themselves.

We commonly speak of a Western civilization, but we subdivide it in various ways and are unsure of its boundaries in space or time. Does it go back so far as to include the "Classical" civilization of Ancient Greece and Rome? Or does it not come into being until about A.D. 1000, perhaps as the heir of the Classical civilization, after the period of chaos that followed the fall of Rome?

The reader will recognize here the problem of taxonomy to which we addressed ourselves in Part Two, Chapter XVII, the problem of imposing categorical distinctions, if only for heuristic purposes, on an uncategorical reality. So it is that we distinguish the birds from the reptiles, even though, in a close-up view, there is no one point on the line of evolution at which a particular pair of reptiles engendered the first bird.

*

The key to the puzzle I have been describing lies in the choice of mutually complementary perspectives that we considered at the beginning of Chapter XVII of Part Two. When, in the course of evolution, birds began to branch off from the reptilian line, a contemporary observer would have been too close to what was happening to see it for what it was. We are, similarly, too close to the first 6,000 years of civilization to make associations and distinctions that might be revealed in a larger perspective. To quote Charles Francis Atkinson: "It is, in history as in science, impossible to draw a curve through a mass of plotted observations when they are looked at closely and almost individually."

The relevance of this metaphor is indicated by the fact that it occurs in the Translator's Preface to the English edition of Oswald Spengler's *Decline of the West.* Spengler — like St. Paul, like Mohammed, like Dante, like Karl Marx — was captivated by a mythic vision of the world that we must regard as being neither entirely true nor altogether false.

> I see [he wrote] . . . the drama of *a number* of mighty Cultures [what I have here called "civilizations"], each springing with primitive strength from the soil of a mother-region to which it remains firmly bound throughout its whole life-cycle; each stamping its material, its mankind, in *its own* image; each having *its own* idea, *its own* passions, *its own* life, will and feelings, *its own* death. . . . Each Culture has its own new possibilities of self-expression which arise, ripen, decay, and never return. . . . These cultures, sublimated life-essences, grow with the same superb aimlessness as the flowers of the field. . . . I see world-history as a picture of endless formations and transformations, of the marvelous waxing and waning of organic forms.*

Others beside Spengler have had the impression of particular civilizations that rise and fall. In the early eighteenth century, Giambattista Vico had the vision of one civilization after another rising out of barbarism only to decline into it again. (His younger contemporary, Edward Gibbon, wrote the biography of a civilization in the process of such a decline.) At the end of the nineteenth century, in *The Law of Civilization and Decay,* Brooks Adams struggled painfully to bring to birth a theory according to which societies or civilizations go through a standard cycle of rise and decline. In Spengler's epic vision, civilizations were organisms that went through the same life-history as all advanced organisms, that of birth, youth, maturity, old age, and death. (He also put it that they had their spring, summer, autumn, and winter.) Finally, Spengler's younger contemporary, Arnold Toynbee, devised an elaborate theory of civilizations that might be independent or that might, alternatively, have "affiliations" among themselves.

What is significant in its bearing on our theme here is that these philosophers of history — like, indeed, all historians who take a sufficiently comprehensive view of world history — while they assume the existence of distinct civilizations, do not join in any general agreement on their specific identification. Thus, Spengler, who presents the most compelling vision of all, identifies some eight or ten civilizations that have lived since history began, including the

* Oswald Spengler, *The Decline of the West,* Vol. I, New York, 1927, pp. 21–22.

Mesopotamian or Babylonian (beginning c. 3000 B.C.), the Egyptian (beginning c. 2900 B.C.), the Indian (beginning c. 1500 B.C.), the Chinese (beginning c. 1300 B.C.), the Classical (beginning c. 1100 B.C.), the Arabian (beginning about the time of Christ), the Mayan-Aztec (beginning c. 613 B.C.), and the Western (beginning c. A.D. 900).* Toynbee, on the other hand, identifies twenty-six civilizations (including the "arrested" civilizations of Polynesians, Eskimos, post-agricultural Nomads of the steppe, Osmanlis, and Spartans), all of which have now broken down except our own.

The attempts made so far to discover and define a pattern of separate civilizations, each of which enacts a standard life-history from birth to death, a cycle of rise and fall, have all been so imperfect in their results as to provoke the denial of any pattern at all. "I can see only one emergency following upon another, as wave follows upon wave," wrote the historian H. A. L. Fisher, "only one great fact with respect to which, since it is unique, there can be no generalizations . . . the play of the contingent and the unforeseen." † This other extreme represented by Fisher, however, not only constitutes such a denial of meaning as makes the continuing pursuit of knowledge virtually pointless, but in itself is not less implausible than the visionary extremes to which it stands opposed. The ascent from barbarism, culminating in a civilized order of high attainments, and the subsequent decline of such an order, has been repeatedly enacted. Societies more or less coherent in language and culture have been inspired to produce works of art, including those of statecraft, only to lose their inspiration with time, declining into the disorder out of which they had arisen, the disorder in which the life of the society may again be nothing more than "one emergency following upon another," the disorder in which full freedom is restored at last to "the play of the contingent and the unforeseen." Certainly there was an inspiration, first manifesting itself clearly and powerfully in Homeric times, that led up to the statecraft of Pericles, the construc-

---

* Because Spengler treats some of the civilizations fully and others only by passing allusions I cannot be certain, without completely rereading his dense thousand pages (forty-eight years after I first read them), exactly how many civilizations he identifies. The fact that he makes only one glancing reference (in less than a sentence) to the Peruvian civilization under the Incas shows that he was not pretending to give a full list.

It should be noted that he used the term "culture" for what I have here called "civilization," confining the latter term to the period when the life has gone out of the organism but it remains in being, still, as the dead tree remains standing in the forest. I have not given his terminal dates because they do not represent the disappearance of the organism but simply the loss of its vitality.

† Quoted by Geoffrey Barraclough in *History in a Changing World*, Oxford, 1956, pp. 222–223.

tions in stone of Phidias, the dramas of Euripides, the philosophy of Plato, and the historical vision of Thucydides; nor is the Parthenon adequately accounted for by attributing it to the free play of "the contingent and the unforeseen." Certainly there was a new inspiration of the same kind that, many centuries later, produced the great Gothic cathedrals, which cannot be accounted for otherwise. We are not justified in saying that no pattern, no order exists, simply because we can see it, at best, only so imperfectly. The fact of distinct civilizations seems to me equally undeniable, for the civilizations of the New World are distinct from those of the Old, and the civilization of China during the Han Empire is distinct from the civilization of Rome under the Antonines. The one thing that is sure is that civilization is, in its measure, a transcendence of chaos, that the history of civilized mankind is not entirely without form, and void, however inchoate it may still be.

*

We understand civilization best, I surmise, if we regard it as still inchoate, as merely the germ of the embryo of what awaits a realization we cannot foresee.

The prime fact about civilization is that it represents the undertaking of mind to embark on an artificial progress of its own, departing from the natural progress represented by genetic evolution. As such it is a process of invention subject to the initial uncertainties of trial and error — uncertainties that in the short run make for chaos. A society is inspired by a mythical order of the imagination by which it explains the unknown, by which it fills the vacuum of ignorance. That order implies a way of life which governs the organization of the society and the behavior of individuals within it. It expresses itself in ceremony, inspires statecraft, engenders artistic production, lifting the level of human life above its natural or animal origins, mastering in its measure the original chaos. In this creative process of transcendence, however, it tends to make itself obsolete; for to the increasingly civilized people it produces it comes to seem increasingly naïve. By virtue of their greater sophistication they are unable to believe in it as their simpler-minded forebears had. The Homeric religion, which inspired the Greek civilization, had in large measure lost its credibility, and consequently its power to inspire, for the Greeks of Plato's day.* As the artificial order of the mind consequently lost its authority and its power to inspire, the society was increasingly beset by the chaos that we associate with its decline.

There are periods of creative inspiration followed by periods in

* See Plato's *Republic*, Book II, 377–381.

which inspiration is lost, when creation is replaced by such makeshift construction as is addressed only to the contingent, the unforeseen, the emergency of every day. So civilization declines and falls, as the Roman civilization declined and fell — to be followed by what?

It may be followed by a sort of static or lifeless continuation, like the thousand years of Byzantium, symbolized by the dead tree that remains standing in the forest. Or it may be followed by a decline into barbarism and chaos, as in western Europe during that period from about the year 400 to 1000, known as the Dark Ages, which followed the fall of Rome.

What I have described here are the dynamics of civilization. A body of beliefs and attitudes develops somehow; it gives a society coherence and inspires it to achieve the expression — in its organization, in its artistic and literary monuments, in its science — of an order that imposes itself on the underlying chaos. But the order is, in its particularities at least, artificial and arbitrary, without basis in the laws of nature, and this makes it fragile, its authority open to question. The inevitable imperfections of its working, moreover, manifesting themselves in what appear as injustices to many members of the society, eventually produce a loss of belief accompanied by a spreading alienation and revolt (such as we see among ourselves in our day). Increasingly, the society is held together and the order maintained by the bribery of bread and circuses or the impositions of force. By this time, however, its inspiration is gone and, if the society continues in being for a time, it does so only as the dead tree remains standing.

It is a convenient oversimplification to regard these civilizations as distinct individuals. But they bear upon one another in various ways, exerting and receiving influences, learning from one another as our Western civilization learned mathematics from what Spengler called the Arabic civilization. Indeed, they seem at times to flow into one another. And when they die they may leave a heritage by which later civilizations profit, thereby providing a basis for progress over the millennia. The growth of the natural sciences, since the days of the pre-Socratic philosophers, appears to offer one example. The replacement of the Roman by the Arabic system of numeration appears to offer another, for it is hard to believe that the mathematics of any future civilization, having access to this improvement, would again utilize a system as awkward and limited as the Roman. Nor is it a foregone conclusion that any great civilization of the future will return to the belief that the earth is the center of a universe created 6,000 years ago.

It is a matter of convenience, and the acknowledgement of what is at least a half-truth, to regard civilizations as individuals. If there is a difficulty in agreeing on the identity of particular ones, that may be because we are dealing with something similar to a complex composed of wheels within wheels. Not only are there the cultural influences that extend beyond boundaries, but there are the subcultures, such as the Italian subculture of city-states in the Renaissance, such as the Korean or the Japanese subcultures. We face, here, the old problem of taxonomy, of categorizing an uncategorical reality.

*

When, after all the chapters in which we have seen the emergence of order from an underlying chaos, we come to our own history, the history of civilized man, we seem to find order disintegrating once more into what represents at least an approach to chaos — the approach to chaos described by H. A. L. Fisher. But we must suppose this to be because we are, in fact, reverting to the close-up perspective of the very small. Where we had been dealing with the combinations formed by untold millions of millions of elementary particles, where we had been dealing with galaxies 10,000 million light-years away in time and space, where we had been dealing with the evolution of life over 3,500 million years, we are now dealing in mere centuries, and in vague entities called civilizations that no one numbers in more than two figures. As we have approached the here-and-now our perspective has necessarily narrowed; and, in accordance with the holistic principle set forth in the first chapter of Part One, as the perspective narrows meaning is lost.

The resort to a *reductio ad absurdum* will make this clear. There would be no use in the historian's writing an account of the history, over the centuries, of a particular square meter in Paris, or an account of one minute in the history of the world. No meaning, no sense, no element of sanity could be found in a view so narrow. Perhaps a mere 6,000 years, which is the time that has elapsed since civilization began, is too short to be meaningful. Perhaps ten civilizations so far, or twenty-six, constitute too small a sample. Perhaps we shall not be able to see meaning in the phenomenon of civilization, as a product of that new attribute of life called mind, until another million years have passed and the development of civilization has gone beyond its embryonic beginnings.

How, then, does one give a meaningful account of world history since it began some 6,000 years ago?

In my own view, which is subjective and ill-defined, there have been two lines of traditional civilization that represent human achievement at its highest, the Western and the Chinese. The Western tradition, which is not unbroken, has its origin in a broad region around the eastern Mediterranean. In the beginning it is excessively inchoate and disparate, including the Mesopotamian and Egyptian civilizations. It continues with the Classical civilization of Greece and Rome (which Spengler long ago taught me to see as all one). And after a lapse of a few centuries it rises again in western Europe on the ruins of the past, a new civilization quite different from the old (as the Cathedral of Chartres is different from the Parthenon), but fertilized by its remains and not unimpressed by its forms — a civilization that, even in its decline, has spread around the world, plausibly foreshadowing a time to come when one civilization will prevail permanently over the whole earth.

I shall in like fashion attempt to deal with a Chinese tradition that, if it is now in decline, appears to have maintained a coherence and continuity over the millennia that is unmatched in the Western tradition.

In the long run, which might mean a million years from now, we shall see that the history I here summarize is not something apart from the evolution of life on earth over the thousands of millions of years; but we cannot see it now, any more than our ancestors could see that man was not separate from the animal kingdom, any more than the disembodied observer of 3,000 million years ago would have been able to see that the prokaryotic cell would eventuate in mind. I embark on the chaos with as much detachment as possible, in the hope that some implications, at least, of a larger evolution may become apparent.

VIII

Genesis

WE IDENTIFY the beginning of history with the advent of writing and the consequent maintenance of records; and we identify the beginning of civilization with such complex social organization as requires formal institutions of government and law, entailing urban centralization. Since what we identify with the beginning of history and what we identify with the beginning of civilization occur together, being interrelated, history begins with civilization.

By about 4000 B.C., the development of life over millions of millennia had at last reached the stage at which civilization was ready to appear here and there all around the earth — as the first spring flowers suddenly emerge and unfold over a wide area when the ground has at last been prepared by the development of the season. Its first appearance was virtually simultaneous at widely scattered points: in Mesopotamia, in the Nile Valley, in the valley of the Indus, in China, in Central America, and in Peru.

The first civilizations grew out of the practice of agriculture, which, as we have seen, appears to have developed as early as anywhere in the area east of the Mediterranean, where wheat and barley grew wild, where sheep, goats, and pigs were native. What initially forced the artificial improvisations of civilization was the practice of agriculture under particular circumstances that required an especially high degree of social organization. Such circumstances exist wherever drainage and irrigation are necessary, as was the case in Mesopotamia, the Nile Valley, the Indus Valley, and the Yellow River Valley alike.

The Mesopotamia of 4000 B.C., where civilization first developed, was open land under grass. Two rivers, the Tigris and the Euphrates, run some 800 kilometers from the Anatolian plateau of Asia Minor and the northeast corner of the Mediterranean to the head of the Persian Gulf. Between them they water the broad alluvial valley of Mesopotamia, bounded by the mountain-ramparts of Persia to the northeast and the Arabian desert to the southwest. The banks of these rivers must originally have been marshy in many places, and there must have been lagoons. Such rain as fell on this great valley, then as now, did so chiefly during the cool winters, while the summers were dry as well as hot. In addition to determining the growing season, this made agriculture dependent on the waters of the two rivers, which would not have been enough at some times and places, too much at others. With the prehistoric development of extensive cultivation, the cultivators would have hit upon the device of digging ditches for the drainage of excessively marshy places, and canals to carry water to others that needed it.

This kind of situation, the world over, in addition to requiring social organization, entails social conflict. The farmers downstream may feel themselves at the mercy of those upstream who, receiving the life-giving water first, can divert it for their own use without regard for the effect on those farther down. In any case, drainage of marshes and lagoons may require cooperation, voluntary or compelled, over a wide area. Arrangements have to be made and enforced by means that must entail a measure of conflict and imposition.

Moreover, any great river valley draws peoples as well as waters into its bed, becoming an avenue of human flow and human expansion in which diverse peoples coming from different directions collide and conflict. The first peoples to settle in the Tigris-Euphrates Valley would have learned that they had constantly to cope with others of strange speech and custom — nomadic horsemen, herdsmen, eventually traders — who, in their wanderings, would be drawn down the mountain-slopes to the east, from the shores of the Mediterranean and the Anatolian plateau upstream, from the Persian Gulf downstream, from the arid lands to the west, many of them savage, warlike, and hungry. If those who had already settled and built villages were to survive they would have to organize for war as well as for the peaceful conduct of an agriculture that required the cooperative construction and maintenance of waterworks. All this would make constantly increasing demands on the faculty of mind (its capacity for anticipating and preparing), demands for the establishment of government and laws, demands for a written language to keep the necessary records, demands for such construction as is represented by walled cities.

So it is that, even before the dawn of history, those who inhabited Mesopotamia were far from being one people with one language. In fact, their diversity was so notable, and such a source of troubles, that they themselves felt the need to account for it, which they did by the legend of the Tower of Babel, familiar to us from Genesis 11. God, alarmed by the fact that, as one people having all one language, they were cooperating to build a tower by which to reach his Heaven, confounded their language so that, lacking a common speech, they would no longer be able to continue their cooperation. So they left off building the tower. The site of their failure was on the banks of the lower Euphrates.

The uncompleted Tower of Babel symbolizes what civilization has been ever since, for the unfinished work remains unfinished still today. In the few thousand years that are all we have had since civilization began, we have not yet succeeded in creating an order by which to transcend the chaos of its beginnings. One attempt after another has shown promise, only to fail at last.

*

Among the varied peoples who had entered Mesopotamia before the dawn of history were the Sumerians, to whom we must accord the distinction of being the first to create a civilization. They came from no one knows where. Both legend and circumstantial evidence suggest that they came by sea, from far away, to land and settle at the head of the Persian Gulf. Some authorities are more inclined to believe that they came across the Persian plateau from the shores of the Caspian Sea. They were physically distinct from the Semitic peoples who were to be their successors. (We know quite well what they looked like because they were to portray themselves in sculpture and mosaics.) Their language, which was to be preserved by those successors as a dead but honored language, as we preserve Latin, shows no relationship to any other known language. They established themselves in domination over the aboriginal inhabitants of the lower valley, cultivated the soil, built villages to begin with and, eventually, walled towns that constituted, respectively, the capitals of city-states, each at the center of an area of farmland irrigated by systems of canals that required constant and careful upkeep. Above all, having settled down and embarked on the construction of the first civilization, they proceeded to distinguish themselves further by being the first to invent writing. Both civilization and the art of writing were to prove contagious.

We may think of this inauguration of civilization and history as taking place some centuries before 3000 B.C., by which time it was at an advanced stage.

The writing invented by the Sumerians began with pictographs, but it quickly developed into the cuneiform writing that was to spread all over the Middle East and be used for a variety of languages. It consisted of a few wedge-shaped marks, in various arrangements, made by a three-angled reed stylus on clay tablets.* At first each combination stood for a particular word, but at the last each had come to stand for a syllable, so that the writing repeated the spoken language syllable by syllable. In its development, therefore, it came just short of the alphabetical writing exemplified by this sentence. What counts is that it represented the sounds of spoken language rather than what the sounds stood for, thereby enshrining the spoken language as pictographic and ideogramic writing could not. Since logic depends on words, rather than directly on the things and ideas that words represent, this made it a far more sophisticated instrument of thought — made it, in fact, a written system of logic in itself.

When civilization and history began, they were based on the institution known as the city-state — an area of farmland surrounding an urban center. The city-states of Sumeria — Ur, Eridu, Uruk, Lagash, Umma, and Nippur — were not essentially different from the Greek city-states of 2,500 years later, from the Italian city-states of 4,500 years later, or from the San Marino of today. Only in our own time, as civilization appears to be at the beginning of a vast new development, has this basic institution at last become obsolete.

Those of us who belong to Western civilization can trace an unbroken line of tradition from the first foundation of any civilization, in lower Mesopotamia, to the civilization in which we have been brought up. The legendary Garden of Eden, in which man is said to have begun his career, was considered to lie in the lower Euphrates. The Sumerian city of Ur is the city in which, according to Genesis 11, Abraham was born — the city from which he went forth with his wife, Sarah, to found a new nation in the land of Canaan. Sumeria as a whole was the scene of the flood that is memorialized in the story of Noah and the Ark.† As we have seen, the site of the Tower of Babel was just up the river.

* Because I have found no mention of it in the literature, I call attention to the fact that sedges, in cross-section, are solid and three-angled, while reeds are hollow and round. This suggests that the original stylus was a sedge rather than, as is generally said, a reed.

† "At Ur, digging against the northern margin of the Al 'Ubaid town, the excavators came upon a bed of clean silt eleven feet thick which had been deposited by a flood whose waters had broken against the obstruction of the town mound. Below the silt were the remains of houses which those waters had destroyed in their first onset. Mesopotamia is a land of floods, but in all its later history there is no record of such a flood as this; for that heaped silt to form, there must have been twenty or twenty-five feet of water, which would have covered the whole of the delta between the Iraqi desert and the foothills of Elam, and from Hillah, which is Babylon, to the Persian Gulf. This can be none other than the Deluge which was the subject of the most famous of Babylonian legends, the Hebrew version of which is familiar to us all in the story of Noah's Flood" (*Ur: The First Phases* by Leonard Woolley, London, 1946, pp. 12–13). I should add that Professor Woolley's conclusion is not universally shared by the authorities.

So it is that every schoolchild who is taught the Bible stories today, whether in South Africa or Alaska, is learning Sumerian history. He is inheriting a tradition, literary and historical, that goes back more than 5,000 years to the founding of the first civilization.

Today we stand as on a mountain-divide from which, looking back, we can see the entire history of our past, all the way to the dim point where two rivers, coming from afar, at last pour their waters into the sea.

IX

Civilization Spreads
in Mesopotamia

IN SUMERIA AND BEYOND, as its civilization spread up the valley, the basic political unit was the city-state, each consisting of a walled city presiding over a wide extent of surrounding agricultural land. The city of Uruk may have had a population as large as 50,000. Because stone and wood were lacking in the valley, these cities were built of bricks formed in molds from local clay.

The first monumental architecture arose in these cities. One form that it took was that of the so-called ziggurats, pyramidal towers square in plan and rising by a series of setbacks, the successive stages leading, generally by way of spiral ramps, to a temple on top of each that was the abode of the local god. The legend of the Tower of Babel suggests how the builders were moved by an aspiration to achieve ever greater heights — aiming, perhaps, at some point of ultimate transcendence. It is such aspiration as this that, ever since, has characterized the building of one civilization after another, each of which has ultimately failed.

In the course of time, the monumental architecture also took the form of palaces that were like cities in themselves, each constituting the center of authority over the activities of the swarming population that, within the new social order of the city-state, carried on the new work of civilization.

Within the city walls a busy urban life developed. Craftsmen worked in copper, bronze, and iron from the first. Ultimately there were goldsmiths (Benvenuto Cellinis in Ur as in Florence 4,000 years later), silversmiths, and other artists who produced jewelry, jeweled ornaments, and ornamented implements of elaborate design and fine workmanship. They may have had their workshops in narrow streets adjacent to the palace, where their clientele resided. Presumably each craft was associated with particular families, its skills being handed down from father to son. Craftsmen who had no sons apt for the task may have taken apprentices.

In the Sumerian city-states there was constant business to be carried on for the maintenance of the economic life of the state and its security against rivals. Implements of peace and war had to be manufactured, wool had to be spun and cloth woven. Boats had to be built for transport on the rivers, the canals, and the sea itself, as well as wagons made of wood imported from abroad. Bricks had to be baked, the construction and maintenance of buildings had to be attended to. Sanitation must have been a problem that required the making and enforcement of regulations. A water-supply had to be provided and maintained, in some cases by means of aqueducts. There was internal trading (albeit without money as yet), and external trading by transport along the rivers and canals, along the seacoasts and overland to distant places. Religious ceremonies had to be ordained and supervised. The stars had to be observed and a calendar kept. Provision had to be made for burials and the rites accompanying them. Taxes had to be levied and collected. Quarrels had to be settled, justice administered. Military defence or preparation for military expeditions required constant attention and sometimes made overriding demands. The skills of measurement and mathematics had to be exercised and developed. And, since all this activity entailed the keeping of records, there had to be scribes to set them down on clay tablets that would then be baked and perhaps stored away. Prayers, poems, and traditional tales also began to be set down. In time, great libraries would be founded to house the thousands and tens of thousands of tablets on which all was recorded. History was accumulating material for the historians.

The result of all these developments was that for the first time an urban population leading an urban life was brought into being. The city people were like a different breed from the country people. These craftsmen, artisans, builders, temple servants, scribes, traders, magistrates, housewives, slaves, prostitutes, and storytellers had withdrawn from the natural environment of land, water, and sky to live out their lives in an artificial structure of walls and streets and tenements. It was, like a beehive, full of activity. Within it, people were crowded and jostled, so that they became quicker and more nervous in their behavior. The artificial new environment exercised their minds by constantly confronting them with problems of unprecedented complexity and urgency. The density of population that kept them in constant contact with one another increased intellectual stimulation, promoting an articulateness hitherto unknown. There was constant discussion that involved the exchange and development of ideas — and undoubtedly an increase in mere chatter, in talk as a pastime. People became more competitive. Fashions — in thought, in language, in manners, in dress — became important.

*

As we have seen, what is primary in any civilization, the foundation on which everything else rests, is a mythical explanation of being, an order of the conceptualizing imagination that transfigures the chaos of raw experience at the same time that it fills the vacuum of ignorance. Such a mythology is the basis for the normative thinking on which any society depends for the definition of propriety in individual or collective behavior. As the Christian myth, for example, emphasized the chastity of divine personages — of the Virgin Mary, of Jesus, of the saints — so the traditional Christian society, from that of feudal times to that of Victorian England, has associated virginity with an exalted virtue (generally unattainable for ordinary mortals) and has branded sexual intercourse outside of marriage as improper. The norm, as Karl Marx pointed out, has been the Holy Family of Joseph, Mary, and the infant Jesus. Again, the Hindu myth of a hierarchy among the gods provides the normative basis for a society divided into castes, in which every caste has its own norm of behavior.

All this is preliminary to noting that the normative basis for the organization of Mesopotamian society was the Mesopotamian religion, which originated with the Sumerians who founded the civilization. Like all primitive religions it was polytheistic, representing a hierarchical society of greater and lesser gods who presided over the destiny of human communities and individuals. None of the Mesopotamian gods were either omniscient or omnipotent, and all were intensely human in their moodiness and the capriciousness of their behavior. In these respects they constituted the normative model for human conduct. We might put it that men had created gods in their own image as a way of defining the norms for the organization of their society and the behavior of the various elements that composed it, whether groups or individuals.

Each city-state had its own particular god, a member of the general pantheon, who was its real ruler. But when a divinity governs a society he often does so through an agent rather than directly, as Yahweh governed the Jews through Moses. So each city-state was under the direct rule of a king who was merely the lieutenant or deputy of its god, answerable to him as Moses was answerable to Yahweh, as the Emperor of China was answerable to Heaven.

The same religion [writes Leonard Woolley] prevailed throughout the whole land, but each state had one of the common pantheon for its particular patron deity, and that deity was the real king, the earthly ruler being content to entitle himself "the tenant farmer of the god." When two city-states engaged in war, as they often did, usually on the ground of landmarks displaced or of disputes about water rights, it was the god who led his forces to battle. When one city was so far successful in war that its ruler could claim overlordship over all his neighbours and his house could be ranked by the annalists as one of the "dynasties" of Sumer, then the god of that city became the principal god of the Sumerian pantheon.*

Although the hierarchical society of the gods had, at any particular moment, a principal god, it had no supreme god. Divine authority resided in the assembly of the gods, to which the principal god owed his position and before which he was responsible. (This was the norm, but norms are often violated, and it might happen that the principal god, attempting to make himself supreme, would succeed for a term.) Knowing the government of the divine society, we thereby know how the human societies were governed. In each city-state, normally, the king owed his position to the assembly, in which the supreme power resided.

Perhaps we can say that the pluralism and diffusion of authority within each city-state were matched by the relations among the city-states, regarded as constituting the larger society of a nation or civilization, as the Greek city-states constituted an Hellenic society or civilization. Such a constitution of society, like any other constitution, has an inherent instability. Within the assemblies of men or gods, or among city-states, there is constant competition for power; and in such competition a particularly energetic and able individual or state will sometimes achieve supremacy in violation of the pluralistic norm. This happened in Mesopotamian history and in modern European history alike; but, as in the case of Napoleon and Napoleonic France, it represented a departure from the norm. Finally, as happens with every civilization, all ends in an empire that becomes overextended, and in subsequent breakdown. Up to now, the record made by civilizations has shown them to be mortal.

The normative basis of the Mesopotamian civilization was reinforced by those written codes of law that, if only in their relative importance, constitute a peculiarity of the ancient Middle Eastern civilizations that is part of our own heritage. From an early stage there were thousands of written compilations of laws and regulations to govern every aspect of social activity. The name of one king after another is associated with a code of laws as the name of Napoleon is associated with the Napoleonic Code. There was the Code of Hammurabi, who was King of Babylonia around 1700 B.C. Finally, we have the compendia of legal regulations contained in four books of the Old Testament — Exodus, Leviticus, Numbers, and Deu-

* Ur: The First Phases, London, 1946, p.18.

teronomy — through which the Sumerians' original emphasis on law has been transmitted to Western civilization, coming down to our own times. While all civilizations must have bodies of law, those outside this tradition have not given the same prominence to law as a rigid, detailed, and comprehensive body of prescriptions for human conduct, to be followed literally.

The role of law in Mesopotamian civilization provided a restriction on the freedom of kings, in addition to those provided by their answerability in principle to the gods and the human assemblies alike. Government was supposed to be of laws rather than of men.

Throughout the youth of a civilization, and indeed until it loses its inspiration in old age, it is sustained in its works by the reality that its governing mythology has for those who belong to it. As far back as Neanderthal man, such a mythology has generally presented the picture of another world that the individual enters after he passes through the portals of death by which he leaves this world. The belief of the Mesopotamians in such an other world is revealed by their burial customs. The dead were buried, as the Neanderthal dead had been, with provisions that would be useful to them on the journey they were about to make or in the world to which they were going: food, drink, weapons, and personal ornaments. In the case of royal personages, who could not be expected to travel or to enter the other world without a retinue, they were accompanied into their tombs by the still living: intimate attendants, household servants, musicians, dancing women, soldiers, and even (as Leonard Woolley tells us) "the chariot drawn by oxen or by asses, with the drivers, the grooms and the animals." Presumably all this company entered the underground tomb at the appropriate point in the funeral service, and took the positions respectively assigned to them, after which each drank a narcotic from a little cup and went to sleep, having no doubt that all would wake up together in the realm beyond. In the grave of Queen Shub-ad at Ur, a girl musician was found (5,000 years after her burial) with her fingers still on the strings of her lyre, her music merely interrupted.

*

By 3000 B.C. the first civilization had been well founded and history had been inaugurated in an area of roughly 250 square kilometers where the Tigris and Euphrates empty into the Persian Gulf. Above the region inhabited by the Sumerians, but still in lower Mesopotamia, was a different people, Semites by virtue of the fact that, unlike the Sumerians, they spoke a Semitic language. In time, the Sumerians (but not the heritage they left behind) would disappear, and civilization throughout the Middle East, from the frontiers of Persia to those of Egypt, would be carried on largely by Semitic peoples, Jews and Arabs, until our own day.*

The Sumerians were able to maintain a position of military superiority and consequent political ascendancy over the Semitic people just up the valley from them for some eight centuries, during which the Semites acquired the Sumerian civilization, including the art of writing. Then, about 2300 B.C., a military leader, equivalent to Alexander the Great and Napoleon in later ages, rose among the Semites and embarked on a career of unlimited conquest. Because Sargon I, as he is known in history, established his capital in the city of Agad on the Euphrates, about a hundred and sixty kilometers north of Sumeria, the people whom he led came to be known as Akkadians and their home country as Akkadia. But the Akkadian civilization was a continuation of the Sumerian, with the Sumerians no longer in a position of dominance. In over half a century of rule, Sargon conquered the whole of Mesopotamia, from the Persian Gulf to the Anatolian plateau and the Mediterranean, as well as the southwestern part of what was to be Persia, thereby establishing the first great centralized empire of history. In doing so he spread civilization (which is to say Sumerian or Mesopotamian civilization) to all the conquered territories.

As might have been expected, this overextended empire collapsed after a couple of centuries, unable to hold back the barbarians along its borders, who were attracted by the wealth it contained. The consequence was a period of confusion and instability. A Semitic people from the west, called the Amorites (familiar to readers of the Old Testament as inhabitants of the land of Canaan), entered Mesopotamia in a series of successive migrations and, becoming dominant, established the Kingdom of Babylonia, embracing Sumeria and Akkadia, with its capital at Babylon on the Euphrates. The Amorites acquired the civilization of the land they now came to dominate, so that the Babylonian civilization is a continuation, still, of the one civilization founded by the Sumerians.

From the nineteenth to the sixteenth century the Babylonian kings maintained their rule. The greatest of them was Hammurabi (c. 1700 B.C.), a military conqueror and brilliant administrator whom we may think of as a combination of Julius and Augustus Caesar. Ham-

---

* Between them, demagogues and some bad scholars have, over the past century, spread the impression that "Aryan" and "Semitic" designate distinct races, and that "Semitic" means Jewish. But the terms, strictly speaking, refer to linguistic groups, and the Arabs are one with the Jews in being Semitic. The Babylonians, Assyrians, Phoenicians, and other peoples of the past were also Semitic — all descended, according to legend, from Shem, who was one of Noah's three sons.

murabi united the whole of Mesopotamia under the sway of Babylon and proceeded to prepare a new code of laws, to which we have already referred, suitable to the diversity of peoples, Sumerian and Semitic, associated together under one rule. By now the Mesopotamian civilization was at least 1,500 years old and in the ripeness of its age.

There was movement of peoples all over the Middle East in these times, with relative stability only in the old Sumer-Akkadia, now become Babylonia and ruled from Babylon. Alien peoples, some Semitic and some Aryan, flowed into the area from one side or another, creating confusion especially in the outlying lands of Palestine, Syria, and Anatolia. At last Babylonia itself could hold no longer, and about 1500 B.C. its capital was sacked by a people from the north called the Hittites.

There were other invaders, but as always the uncivilized conquerors were conquered by the civilization of the vanquished, which they proceeded to carry on. Aryan invaders, for example, ended by adopting the Semitic language in place of their own. So it was that Babylonia, slain, continued to live.

In the fourteenth century B.C., however, the country of the Assyrians, above Babylonia, with its capital at Nineveh on the Tigris, began its rise to dominance in Mesopotamia. The ensuing struggle between the Babylonians and the Assyrians was basically another conflict between the civilized and the outer barbarian; but when the Assyrian king captured Babylon late in the thirteenth century he assumed the ancient title of King of Sumer-Akkadia, thereby tacitly acknowledging that the millennial civilization of Sumeria had once again conquered its conqueror.

The empire of Sargon I had been merely ephemeral, like that of Alexander in a later age, but the Assyrian Empire that now arose on the basis of the traditional Mesopotamian civilization was like the Roman Empire that arose on the basis of the traditional Greek civilization. Its ascent was gradual, covering a period of centuries, and was marked by temporary breakdowns of one sort or another. At last in the eighth century it captured the cities of the Israelites and, finally reaching its greatest extension in the seventh century, conquered Egypt, which by then had long enjoyed an autonomous civilization of its own.

Now, however, the Assyrian Empire suffered the doom of all implicitly unlimited empires, its spirit brutalized by the requirements of extreme militarization, its frontiers overextended, its strength exhausted. In 612 B.C. Nineveh fell before the combined onslaught of Babylonians from the south, rising up against intolerable oppression, of Medes from the east, and of Scythians from the vicinity of the Black Sea.

Babylonia then enjoyed a brief revival, like the display of the setting sun. Under Nebuchadnezzar, who reigned from 605 to 562 B.C., the Jews were conquered and condemned to the Babylonian Captivity.* At the same time, Nebuchadnezzar created the Hanging Gardens of Babylon to astound the world with the final flare-up of an expiring civilization. When, in 539 B.C., Cyrus the Great of Persia overcame a Babylon that lacked the strength to resist him, one could conclude that the Mesopotamian civilization — of which the hopeful Sumerian dawn had taken place 3,000 years earlier, but which had long been no more than a whited sepulcher, full of dead men's bones — had at last come to its end.

---

* This was the occasion for what, setting aside its ending (which I do not give here), is one of the most moving statements in the traditional literature of any people: "By the rivers of Babylon, there we sat down, yea, we wept, when we remembered Zion. We hanged our harps upon the willows in the midst thereof. For there they that carried us away captive required of us a song; and they that wasted us required of us mirth, saying, Sing us one of the songs of Zion. How shall we sing the Lord's song in a strange land? If I forget thee, O Jerusalem, let my right hand forget her cunning. If I do not remember thee, let my tongue cleave to the roof of my mouth; if I prefer not Jerusalem above my chief joy." Such statements as this remind us of what is easily forgotten in such a summary account, that history is about the sufferings of human beings. See also The Book of Daniel in the Old Testament.

X

What Lives beyond Death

CIVILIZATIONS PASS AWAY, and with them the achievements of their political and military leaders. What remains for succeeding civilizations are the achievements associated with science, literature, and the arts.

The Mesopotamians must be regarded as the founders of mathematics, a field of the mind's activity in which they showed themselves superior to the members of the other early civilizations. This is testimony to their capacity for abstraction, which is exclusively a property of mind and one of its principal distinctions. Perhaps a chimpanzee could distinguish between two apples and three, noting that one was missing where there had been three, but it takes the mind of man to deal with two and three as nouns rather than adjectives — that is, as abstract concepts without embodiment in concrete objects like apples.

Mathematics defines relationships among quantities abstractly conceived, and in so doing provides logical procedures for determining those relationships — as when it defines the relationship between the length of a right-angle triangle's longest side and that of its remaining perimeter, thereby providing a procedure for determining the one, in the case of any particular triangle, on the basis of knowing the other.

Mathematics arises out of the need to measure — that is, to determine quantities by some procedure of calculation. Perhaps I need command no procedure of calculation to distinguish the difference between a set of two apples and a set of three alongside it, but the case is different if the one set contains 299 and the other 300 apples. In that case it would be well for me to have a language for counting each set separately and then comparing the results. Furthermore, having done so, it may be convenient for me to be able to determine that one set contains 0.33 percent more apples than the other, if only because it provides me with a logical basis on which to charge that much more for the larger set.

The Mesopotamians, as farmers, were under the necessity of measuring time and temporal relations as well as space and spatial relations, since their planting and harvesting had to be matched to the seasons of the year. The measurement of time on such a scale requires the ability to live beyond the here-and-now. If I undertake to count the number of days in the year it must be on the basis of comprehending that much time in my imagination. Moreover, the measurement of temporal relations in terms of the natural units of time on this planet — the day, the month, and the year — poses problems that are not to be solved except by procedures that allow one to divide them into fractional parts.

This would not be so if, let us say, the lunar month were precisely thirty days long and the year precisely twelve months long. The difficulty arises out of the fact that these basic units of temporal measurement, which are inescapably determined by the movements of the heavenly bodies, do not fit into each other without leaving fractional remainders. The length of the year is the time it takes for the sun to move (from the standpoint of the observer who regards the earth as a fixed frame of reference) from its lowest noontime elevation above the horizon (around December 22 in the northern hemisphere) to its highest (six months later) and back again. The length of the lunar month is determined by the time it takes the moon to go through a complete cycle, from one new moon to the next. The length of the day is determined by the time it takes (from the standpoint of the earthbound observer) for the sun to go around the earth once. One cannot, however, accurately relate these three units of measurement to one another except by the use of fractions: for the lunar month is 29.53 days long, and the number of such months in the year is 12.37, while the number of days in the year is 365.29.

To measure the number of days in the year, one must, to begin with, choose one that is identifiable in its annual recurrence — such as the day of the winter solstice, when the noonday sun is at its lowest. We may assume that the early Sumerians were not able to identify such a day with any assurance, lacking the skills to determine precisely the moment of the solar noon, or the precise elevation of the sun above the horizon at that moment. To count the number of days in the year they would also have had to devise, quite deliberately, some system of keeping the record, such as making a mark on a tree every day and counting the marks when a year was thought to have passed. Lacking the skills that were later to be developed (in Mesopotamia itself, and largely by the Babylonians), their count was, of necessity, impressionistic to a degree. Under the circumstances, the figure they arrived at was 360 (5.29 days off).

They must have been constantly driven, however, to devise means for more accurate determination of these relations among the natural units of time that they had no choice but to adopt. Since the annual activities of agriculture — preparing the ground, sowing, and harvesting — had to be closely correlated with the annual cycle of the seasons, the count of 360 days to the year was bound to prove unsatisfactory in a very short time. For if they fixed on, say, the tenth day of each year to plant barley, they would, in fact, be planting it 5.29 days earlier every year — 53 days earlier every ten years. Under such circumstances, one can see how the Mesopotamians were driven to develop the mathematical skills that came to distinguish them.*

So it was that, going back to Sumerian days, they laid the foundations for the development of mathematics ever since by inventing the device of place-value notation. This is the kind of notation represented by our own practice of assigning ten times the value of any particular digit, in a number composed of two or more, for every successive place in the sequence from right to left. (Thus, in the number 22, the 2 at the left is assigned ten times the value of the 2 at the right; although in the Mesopotamian system, which was sexagesimal rather than decimal, the 2 at the left would have sixty times the value of the 2 at the right.) Once this kind of notation has been invented, it is but one step to add places to the right, separated by a mark equivalent to our decimal point, every one of which is expotentially less as one goes from left to right (e.g., 22.22 in our notation). Before their civilization came to an end, the Mesopotamian mathematicians had reached this point.

More than this, before their civilization came to an end the Mesopotamians, with their capacity for abstraction, had already laid the foundations of algebra and were solving linear equations (e.g., $2 + x = 4$) and quadratic equations (e.g., $2 + x^2 = 4$).†

*

* Note that, while almost all life lives by the seasons, it is only man who has to have such recourse to artificial methods of measuring the passage of the year. In a migratory bird, for example, the annual cycle of change in the daily period of daylight produces physiological changes that, at the right stage, arouse in it the impulse to migrate. It is only because man's practice of agriculture is not a behavioral trait directly based on genetic endowment, as is the bird's practice of migration, that he has to resort to the artifices of measurement in order to know when to sow and when to reap. For him, mind has to make do for what, in the bird, we loosely call instinct.
† It is interesting to note that, until well into the present millennium, the greatest mathematicians were representative of the Middle Eastern civilizations, from the Sumerians through the Saracens. It may be that people living in environments typified by that of the Arabian Peninsula, depending on the sun and stars for navigation across featureless wastes of drifting sand, and ever conscious of the immensity of the night sky, tend to develop alike a particular interest in astronomy and a particular capacity for geometrical abstraction. The Mesopotamian empires did, after all, comprise large areas of sand beneath stars.

The development of mathematics among the Mesopotamians appears to have responded chiefly to the need of an accurate calendar, and the only basis for an accurate calendar is the changing positions, through the annual cycle, of the sun, the moon, the planets, and the stars. They did not know these great and little lights for what we now know them to be, but they did know that, all together, they constituted a clock. So they taught themselves to read the clock as such. This required them to equate the movements of its various indicators, chief of which were the sun and the moon — much as a savage who came upon one of our manufactured clocks for the first time might teach himself, by keeping records of their respective movements, the relationship between the minute hand and the hour hand, albeit without knowing what made them move. So they learned to keep time and, in doing so, founded the science of astronomy.

One has the impression that the Mesopotamian civilization, more than some others, was dominated by an awareness of time's passage. Surely the astronomy of the Mesopotamians is not unrelated to the words of the Preacher in Ecclesiastes, who represented the Mesopotamian heritage:

> One generation passeth away, and another generation cometh: but the earth abideth for ever.
>
> The sun also ariseth, and the sun goeth down, and hasteth to his place where he arose. . . .
>
> To every thing there is a season, and a time to every purpose under the heaven:
>
> A time to be born, and a time to die; a time to plant and a time to pluck up that which is planted.

Here time is described by describing its several rhythms in language that is itself rhythmic, with one rhythm inside another like the rhythm of the days within that of the years, and that of the years within that of the generations. So the Preacher was enshrining in language an order that he saw in the underlying chaos.

*

Having departed from the state of nature, in which the conduct of life is genetically determined and mindless, man is under the necessity of creating, in its place, a world of his own. Any world that one society of men or another creates, in response to this necessity, is a normative world of the mind. It constitutes a model for the behavior, individual or collective, of the society that created it and lives under its authority. Such a world, which is the basis of every civilization, represents an imagined order that may correspond more or less well, more or less badly, to the true order of nature, which is so largely unknown. It resolves the chaos that would make sanity and the conduct of life impossible — the chaos that has threatened us all ever since, in the course of evolution, the development of mind led us to depart from the state of nature and provide for ourselves.

Among the earliest civilizations, the imagined order is represented by myths that are, in the beginning, told out loud, and so handed down from generation to generation, until at last they are put into writing, often in the form of epics that report the deeds of gods or heroes who symbolize various aspects of being, good or evil.

According to the Mesopotamian myth of the Creation, in the beginning was Chaos, personified by the goddess Tiamat. As what was formless began, somehow, to take form, she undertook to destroy it — to destroy, that is, the emerging order. But a god called Marduk managed to kill her and to create, from her dead body, the heavens above and the earth below.* Marduk (or Ea, the god of wisdom, according to some accounts) then moistened some earth with his blood and, out of the resulting clay, created men to serve him and the other gods. The time came, however, when he and the other gods, dissatisfied with the men they had created, undertook to destroy them and their works in a great deluge. But one man called Shamash-napishtim had built an ark, within which he took refuge with his wife; and as the waters subsided his ark came to rest on a mountain called Nisir, from which he dispatched a dove to reconnoiter. Then he and his wife earned the good will of the gods by bribing them with sacrifices, and so mankind escaped utter extermination.

If this myth of the ark is obviously to be identified with its counterpart in Genesis, other Mesopotamian myths are no less obviously to be identified with the Greek myths of Persephone's descent into Hades, and the wooing of Adonis by Aphrodite. All these myths represent conceptual elements that, in one form or another, have characterized civilization in the West to our own day. The story of Persephone's descent into Hades and her return, like its Mesopotamian predecessor, the story of Ishtar's descent into the underworld and her return, represents the annual blighting of life at the end of autumn and its annual resurrection in spring. It represents the recurring seasons, "a time to plant and a time to pluck up

* The reader will note that the theme of what is, perhaps, the oldest piece of literature in the world is the same as that of the book he is reading at this moment.

that which is planted." It represents the same order in nature that we, today, explain by the annual movement of the earth around the sun on an axis tilted away from the perpendicular. (If the latter explanation is more plausible to us, one may surmise that it would have been less plausible to the Sumerians.)

Mesopotamian literature also contains prayers and psalms in which men stand humbly before the unknown, acknowledging their own ignorance and helplessness, pleading for rescue from the evils that surround them, asking to be uplifted. Even today, there must be many beside the author of these lines who identify themselves wholeheartedly with the Mesopotamian psalmist in his appeal to an unknown divinity, whether god or goddess he knew not:

> How long, my god,
> How long, my goddess, until thy face be turned to me?
> How long, known and unknown god, until the anger of thy
>   heart be appeased?
> Mankind is perverted, and has no judgment;
> Of all men who are alive, who knows anything?
> They do not know whether they do good or evil.
> O Lord, do not cast aside thy servant;
> He is cast into the mire; take his hand! *

Finally, Mesopotamia produced its great epic, *The Epic of Gilgamesh*, as Greece produced *The Iliad* and *The Odyssey*, as Anglo-Saxon England produced *Beowulf*, as mediaeval Europe produced the *Chanson de Roland* and the *Nibelungenlied*. Gilgamesh is the folk hero, part god and part man, who with his Herculean companion, Enkidu, lives and suffers, despairs and triumphs, on a scale that, while it arouses pity and awe, glorifies the human experience as known to us ordinary mortals. It lifts heroism and suffering above the level of the commonplace. Like the other epics mentioned above, it is a whole literature in itself, embracing a variety of originally separate folk-tales that must have been handed down from mouth to mouth, from generation to generation, since far back in prehistoric times.

*

The examples of graphic art left by the Mesopotamians show the ubiquity and prominence of animals in the world they had made for themselves. There was, for one thing, the heritage of the hunter's attitude, which goes back to the cave-paintings of 25,000 years earlier. In the beginning, men were attendants on herds of wild ani-

---

* From G. Maspero, *The Dawn of Civilization: Egypt and Chaldea*, London, 1897, p. 51; quoted by Will Durant in *Our Oriental Heritage*, New York, 1942, p. 242.

mals that must have quite outnumbered them, and later they were to
be attendants on domestic animals, as in peasant communities in the
Alps to this day, where the men, cultivating their beasts and the hay
to feed them, almost seem the servants of the animals on which they
live.

Until well into the first millennium B.C., lions must have occurred
throughout the Middle East and North Africa, as well as in the
Balkan Peninsula, and everywhere they appear to have been
regarded as symbols of nobility, so that they are commonly represented in sculpture from as early as 3000 B.C. in Sumeria to at least
as late as the fifth century B.C. in Greece (on the Acropolis in Athens). Wild cattle, the aurochs and the European bison, were presumably among the prey of lions and men alike. The great soaring
birds, vultures and eagles, must have been even commoner then
than they are now, often filling the sky.

The entrance to the temple at Al 'Ubaid near the Sumerian city of
Ur, built by a king of Ur about 3000 B.C., was flanked by life-size figures of lions made of copper that had been hammered over a
wooden core, with inlaid eyes and teeth that may have been of lapis
lazuli or shell. A frieze that ran around the wall showed, in white
shell against a background of black shale, a line of cattle moving in
stately procession, one after the other, as if to music. They represent an order emerging from the anarchy of life, the same rhythmic
mode and pastoral peace, the same frozen music, as on the Grecian
Urn described by Keats.

> Who are these coming to the sacrifice?
> To what green altar, O mysterious priest,
> Lead'st thou that heifer lowing at the skies,
> And all her silken flanks with garlands drest?

Over the entrance to the temple, a stylized bronze eagle with a
lion's head, wings outspread, had a talon on each of two antlered
stags that, back to back, faced away from the center, the three forming a symmetrical tableau. The worshipper who entered the temple,
between flanking lions and beneath the tableau (having already ad-
justed his step, perhaps, to the rhythm of the procession of cattle),
must have felt the influence of a harmony missing in the market-
place below.

The Sumerians' representations of themselves are less impressive.
The men, as represented, were clothed, for the most part, only from
the waist down, in long flounced skirts. They were tubby, made of
flesh rather than muscle, many with hairless heads like balls, their
foreheads low, their noses beaked. The total impression is one of

childlike simplicity. Yet these were not only mathematicians and harp-players, administrators and farmers, tradesmen and artisans. They were also, as they depicted themselves, warriors who rode crude wooden chariots, each with four solid wheels, into battle. Their conquering armies ranged over the whole of Mesopotamia, as far as Anatolia and the Mediterranean.

At feasts to celebrate victory — one of which is represented in a mosaic of shell, lapis lazuli, and red sandstone on the so-called Standard of Ur — the harp was played, presumably as an accompaniment to song or chant. Perhaps the trials of Gilgamesh were recounted at royal banquets in the same fashion as, according to *The Odyssey*, the minstrel recounted the tribulations of the Achaeans in the palace of King Alcinous.

The refined aesthetic sense and delicate craftsmanship of the Sumerians is revealed by the ornaments they made for personal wear: beech leaves of the thinnest gold, their veins incised, loosely pendent from chains of lapis-lazuli beads; a gold dagger with a lapis-lazuli hilt in a gold sheath of intricate design; a sculptured gold helmet. The people who produced these objects of artifice were lifting themselves above the world of the beasts to a world of their own creation.

The Semitic peoples who conquered the Sumerians about 2300 B.C., in taking over their civilization continued their artistic tradition. But inspiration is, by its nature, evanescent, and the quality of artistic production began to decline as, after so many centuries, the original inspiration was gradually lost. The worlds men create, in place of the natural world from which they have departed, do not last. Achievement seems to defeat itself; for the realization of hope never matches the dream it had been before its realization, and the struggle for the continuance or constant repetition of what has already been achieved no longer seems worthwhile.

As we have seen, under the Assyrians the Mesopotamian civilization became militarized and brutalized. The bas-reliefs in stone that have come down to us were made to memorialize the exploits of the king in war or the hunt. They show these Semitic people as quite different from their Sumerian predecessors: tall, muscular, angular, the men long-haired and with heavy beards that seem to have been artificially waved. They wear heavy robes, they hold themselves stiffly, and all look exactly alike.

What is notable, by contrast, is the depiction of animals in these bas-reliefs: the horses that pull the chariots, and the hunted lions, which generally have a vitality and even a grace that is lacking in the human figures.

The Assyrians conquered an empire, but their finest creation was the Dying Lioness of Nineveh, a bas-relief of a lioness pierced by three arrows. Her hindquarters have been paralyzed so that she drags them along the ground after her while she forces herself forward still on her forefeet, her ears flattened to her head and her mouth open in a final roar. She is at once terrible and pitiful. Dating from the middle of the seventh century B.C., she may be taken as the symbol of a civilization in the final agony of death.

XI

Egypt

From the mouths of the Tigris and Euphrates, at the head of the Persian Gulf, westward to the mouth of the Nile, is some 1,700 kilometers. The Mesopotamian Valley, extending northwest from the Persian Gulf, is about 1,000 kilometers long, which is about the length of the Nile Valley from the river's mouth southward to the first cataract at Assuan. Between the two valleys are Palestine, Syria, and northern Arabia. In a large view, this is all one region, over which a variety of nomadic peoples were wandering in late prehistoric and early historical times, while agriculture was taking root and spreading here or there, but chiefly in the two valleys. It follows that Mesopotamia and the Nile Valley were not isolated from each other. Trade goods would have passed across the intervening distance, as would inventions and cultural developments of one sort or another.

We have seen how the first civilization developed in Mesopotamia under the Sumerians; but another was developing at the same time in the Nile Valley, and the temporal priority of the former is so little, perhaps a few centuries, as to be insignificant. Although these two civilizations were so close to each other in space and time alike, and although they had many elements in common, and although they would exert reciprocal influences on each other, they were quite distinct.

In Mesopotamia and the Nile Valley alike, the early practitioners of agriculture confronted the same challenge: that of artificially directing the river waters to where they were needed. In both cases, the development of irrigation — involving the construction of networks of canals with dikes and sluice-gates — required coordination and, consequently, political unification over an extended area.

The problem posed by the thread of water which was the Nile was stark and simple by comparison with that posed by the skein of Mesopotamian waters; for the Nile, throughout the part of its length that concerned the Egyptians, receives no replenishment by tributaries or rain, but diminishes progressively in its course as it evaporates or seeps into the earth. It runs northward across the desert sands through a trough with stone walls that is only a few kilometers across for much of the distance. The society and civilization that we refer to as Ancient Egypt was strung out along this trough, which was the river valley in the desert.

From late July to late October the monsoon rains of tropical Africa and the melting snows of the Ethiopian highlands caused the waters to flood, filling the valley and thereby covering all the agricultural land available. Crops were planted as soon as they had subsided (but on soil that had to be irrigated because it would receive no rain), to be harvested before they rose again. Each year, when the waters had subsided, what remained in the alluvial basin was their deposit of a fresh coating of silt, which renewed the land even as it covered up old landmarks. This is to say that once a year the past was wiped out dramatically; and once a year life made a new start on virgin soil. This gave the Egyptians, like the Mesopotamians, a vivid consciousness of the revolution of the seasons, as well as making it natural for them to think in the normative terms of death and resurrection. It also caused them to preoccupy themselves with the establishment of a calendar, toward which end they took particular note of the seasonal changes in the daily course that the sun followed from one horizon to the other.

The Nile Valley from Assuan north was more isolated and self-contained than Mesopotamia, for it was guarded by desert on either side, and on the south by cataracts. The only ready entrance, therefore, was from the north and, as within a long and narrow vase, all travel was necessarily north and south. Like a narrow vase, however, it opened out at the top, the last 160 kilometers of the river, in its northward flow, branching and spreading over a wide delta before emptying into the Mediterranean. Early Egyptian history is based on a distinction between Upper Egypt, in the south, and Lower Egypt, which is largely the delta at the northern end of the long river.

Before the development of agriculture required extensive works of irrigation, people had lived along this waterway in small self-governing communities. As the development of an agricultural civilization caused them to be increasingly involved with one another over an ever wider area, local confederations developed, at last, into two kingdoms, one of Upper Egypt, to the south, and the other of Lower Egypt, to the north. Because both were, so to speak, in the one geographical vase which was the Nile Valley, it was natural that they should be combined, as they were at the beginning of history, into the single Kingdom of Egypt under the rule of its successive pharaohs.

The geographical unity represented by this artery, and the fact that all communication was through it alone, both facilitated and required a strongly centralized and therefore an authoritarian rule. It would not do to have the artery blocked by local jurisdictions, or to allow a prodigal use of the diminishing water by those who lived upstream to deprive those farther down of what they needed. Consequently, from the beginning, the pharaohs were not, like the Sumerian kings, rulers who were but the local tenant farmers of whatever gods might be, and limited by a body of customary or codified law. They were themselves gods, above the law, and absolute owners of the land. (This explains, surely, why there was never such a concern with law in Egypt as in Mesopotamia or among the Jews. No doubt, if the Sumerians or the Jews had lived in the Nile Valley, and the Egyptians in Mesopotamia or Palestine, their positions would have been reversed.)

*

All we can say of the people who founded Egyptian civilization is that they were of white but non-Arabic stock, that they had probably entered the Nile Valley from the north, and that they spoke a language not unrelated to those classified as Semitic. In prehistoric times, before they had become one people, their scattered communities presented a certain diversity of culture and religious belief. By about 3500 B.C. the process of coalescence appears to have produced the two kingdoms of Upper and Lower Egypt. The conquest of one by the other then led to the establishment of a dual kingdom (like the arrangement whereby England and Scotland were brought together in the United Kingdom), with a new capital at Memphis, near the frontier between the two. This is thought to have occurred about 3200 B.C., and the oldest examples of Egyptian writing are thought to date from 3000 B.C. Therefore, accepting the fact that we must in some degree be arbitrary about such matters, we may take these dates as marking alike the transition from pre-history to history and the beginning of the Egyptian civilization.

As the beginning of civilization in Mesopotamia is marked by the construction of ziggurats, so the beginning of civilization in Egypt is marked by the construction of pyramids. But the ziggurats, being of clay, have disappeared, while the pyramids, being of stone, remain. The first pyramid, which was also the first example in the world of monumental architecture in stone, was constructed about 2780 B.C.

at Sakkara (near the ancient capital, Memphis, or near present-day Cairo) by the first architect of historical record, Imhotep, for the Pharaoh Zoer. It was followed by other pyramids, culminating in the Great Pyramid built for the Pharaoh Khufu (or Cheops) about 2650 B.C. This latter is 147 meters high (about the height of a forty-story office-building in one of our cities) and 230 meters to a side.*

Unlike the ziggurats, which were temples in the midst of architectural compounds serving as centers of worship, the pyramids were royal tombs in the midst of necropolises, stations of departure from this life to the next. The reason for mentioning them at this point is that they show how far social organization had already developed at this early stage.

The Great Pyramid was constructed mostly of limestone blocks, quarried locally, and of some granite blocks that had to be brought 800 kilometers down the river from Assuan. The blocks have been described as immense, some 6 meters long. They had to be lifted by muscular power alone to heights of well over a hundred meters, and when in place they were fitted together with absolute precision. Presumably, a bureaucratic organization under the pharaoh directed the activities of engineers and of thousands of laborers who had to be housed, clothed, and fed over the decades required for the completion of the work. (This, in itself, entailed the imagination that projects itself beyond the here-and-now.) Herodotus, viewing the pyramids and discussing them with the local Egyptians, had no doubt that they were constructed by forced labor under circumstances of pitiless tyranny, and this is not implausible.† But he and the Egyptians he talked to were living 2,200 years later, nearer our own time than that of Khufu. For all we or they could know, the construction of the pyramids was welcomed by those who participated as an acceptable means of earning a living, or as army service is welcomed by many among us. Whatever the case, an elaborate organization would have been required, operating over a wide area, if only for the logistics involved, including administrators, accountants, and keepers of records.

Even without the pyramids, such bureaucratic organization would have been required for the government of such a centralized and authoritarian society extending over so great a distance. The pharaohs, lavish as they were in their expenditures, depended on

---

* The accuracy of the builders was such "that the four sides of the base have only a mean error of six-tenths of an inch in length and 12 seconds in angle from a perfect square" (W. M. Flinders Petrie in *Encyclopaedia Britannica*, 11th ed., 1910–1911, Vol. 22, p. 684).

† *The Histories of Herodotus of Halicarnassus*, trans. by Harry Carter, Oxford University Press: The World's Classics, London, 1962, pp. 141–144 (Book II, Chap. 123).

taxes levied in kind, for money had not been invented. This meant that tax collectors had to go from farm to farm, from household to household, in Upper Egypt and in Lower Egypt, collecting taxes in agricultural or other produce of one sort or another, which then had to be transported, sorted, stored in warehouses, and disbursed as payment to those who served the state, whether as laborers or ministers. And all had to be accounted for, as it came in or went out, on rolls of papyrus which then had to be filed away in accordance with a filing system that must have been elaborated by careful thought. It is no wonder that one of the most honored professions in ancient Egypt was that of the scribe, whose image has come down to us across the millennia in statues that seem speaking likenesses — sitting cross-legged with writing-tablet in lap and pen in hand.

One can hardly doubt that such a civilization as the Egyptian would not have been possible without the invention of writing. The first Egyptian writing, called hieroglyphic, was entirely pictographic — e.g., a conventional picture of a woman denoting woman, a conventional picture of a jar denoting jar. These pictures also came to denote the consonants associated with the spoken words for the objects they respectively represented. The hieroglyphic writing was always reserved, however, for such formal uses as inscriptions on the walls of tombs or temples.

A less cumbersome form of writing, the hieratic, developed out of the hieroglyphic. Its symbols were abstract and cursive, as in our own handwriting, having lost the directly representational character of pictographs. Some were signs for words, some were signs for consonants (there were none for vowels), and some, called determinatives, served to eliminate ambiguity where a preceding sign had alternative significations. It was this system that was used by the scribes, sitting cross-legged and writing with a stylus on the paper called papyrus, which was made from river-reeds pasted together to form a scroll.

However clumsy this system may seem to us, with our alphabetical writing, it was what made Egyptian civilization possible, as cuneiform made Mesopotamian civilization possible.

*

As with all the first civilizations, at least in their early stages, the Egyptian society was a dual society of gods and men. The deities, gods and goddesses, were simply men and women of more heroic mold, occupying a higher sphere and endowed with superior powers. In the lower and visible sphere the society was administered by priests who owed their authority to their special knowledge of the higher and invisible sphere, which they represented in the lower.

The pharaoh belonged to both spheres, was alike god and man.

In the beginning, there had been only gods of the cities, as among the Sumerians. But as the local communities joined to form confederations, the confederations to form two kingdoms, and the kingdoms to form one realm of Egypt, certain local gods gained an ascendency over their rivals until they had extended their sway to the entire realm. Thus Horus, having been a god of the Upper Kingdom only (and presumably less than that in his origins), became identified with the single and universal rule of his counterpart, the pharaoh. The successive pharaohs commonly added the god's name to their own, or their own to his, thereby symbolically transcending the final duality between the higher and the lower. The difference was that Sesostris or Thutmose was mortal, while Horus went on forever. (The desire for immortality, however, was strong among the Egyptians, and the mortality of the pharaoh entailed no more than his departure from this world to continue his life in another.)

There continued to be local gods, but there were also certain cosmic gods, not always clearly separable from the local ones, such as a sun god, Re, an earth god, Geb, and a sky goddess, Nut, who was alike Geb's wife and his sister in a society that was not averse to incest. All played their roles in a shifting mythology that reproduced human conflict, human success and failure, and human suffering on a higher plane.

This is the nature of religion in the early stages of civilization. People project themselves and their knowledge of themselves on imagined beings who live the same lives on a more heroic scale, thereby ennobling what might otherwise be merely sordid. We human beings, having acquired minds that have caused us to depart from the state of nature, need to be consoled for our lives.

One example will do. Osiris, the god, had originally been a mortal king whose brother Set, out of jealousy, had murdered him, had dismembered his corpse, and had finished by casting its separated members into the Nile. His loyal wife Isis, however, had retrieved the widely scattered members and brought them together, whereupon Osiris was restored to life as a ruler in the other world. There remained, however, an infant heir to Osiris's earthly throne, Horus, the son he had had by Isis. Now Set, having eliminated Osiris, turned his attention to Horus, thereby forcing Isis to flee with him in her arms to the marshes of the delta (presumably to the bulrushes that would later shelter the infant Moses). So Horus survived and grew up to overcome the wicked Set and, assuming his father's throne, restore the normative order, the order of the world as it should be.

The popularity of Osiris, Isis, and Horus among the ancient Egyptians must have reflected the comfort it was for individuals who had unjustly suffered frustration and defeat to identify themselves with these heroic beings, who had suffered like experiences only to rise above them at last to eternal fame.

The particular popularity of Osiris, above that of any other god, may be attributed to the fact that, like Jesus, he symbolized death and resurrection. For the Egyptians, like the Sumerians, and like the Christians after them, believed in a renewal of life beyond death, in which renewed life the justice that had failed them on this earth would be done by the dispensation of reward and punishment. Certainly the pharaohs and the members of their families were considered as embarking on a journey to a new world when they died, and were consequently supplied in their graves with what they might require on the journey and with such possessions as they might wish to have with them in their new life. Their earthly bodies were also preserved for them, to the extent that it could be done, by mummification or by replication on their coffins.*

*

It is customary to divide Egyptian history into an Old Kingdom (2780–2280 B.C.), a Middle Kingdom (2133–1780 B.C.) and a New Kingdom (1574–1085 B.C.), with so-called Intermediate Periods between them, and a final Period of Decline from 1085 B.C. to the receivership established by Alexander the Great in 332 B.C.

The pharaohs of the Old Kingdom, in addition to spending the resources of the Egyptian nation on those tombs for themselves of which the pyramids are the most impressive, sent military or trading expeditions northeast into Palestine, south into Nubia, and southeast to the African shore of the Gulf of Aden beyond the mouth of the Red Sea. The bureaucratic evils associated with overcentralization,

---

* I confess myself baffled that some peoples have believed in life after death and been intensely preoccupied by the prospects it provided, while others appear not to have thought about the matter at all. The Sumerians believed in it, as have the Christians, but the Jews, who were so close to the Mesopotamian civilization of the Sumerians, on the one hand, and to the Christian religion that developed out of their own, on the other, have not. (The problem of injustice, as presented in Job, exists only because there is no afterworld in which the injustices of this world might be redeemed.) Perhaps a pastoral people, whose flocks remain alive through the winter, is less inclined than an agricultural people, whose crops undergo annual death and rebirth, to believe in death and resurrection; but I cannot think this a valid or, at least, a sufficient explanation. For one thing, the early Christians were a pastoral people like the Jews — were, in fact, the Jews. It is true that the last books of the Old Testament and the Apocrypha (e.g., Daniel 12:2–3) refer to survival after death, but in terms that define it only vaguely if at all. The Greeks, too, conceived of a shadowy half-life for what Homer called "the strengthless dead" that was hardly life at all, but simply a fading away.

and the imposition of taxes by which tyranny supports itself and buys glory, aroused rebellion against the pharaohs, and a separatism that, after five hundred years, caused the Old Kingdom to fall apart. (What an infinitude of fears and sufferings, experienced by individuals of flesh-and-blood not unlike the reader and the writer of these lines, is summed up in one sentence!)

What followed was a period of chaos that made the Egyptians long for the days of old. For now, in the words of K. C. Seele, "brother was striving against brother, plunderers were abroad in the land, foreigners were infiltrating the Delta, burial monuments were being violated, the cults of the gods were neglected, hunger prevailed among princes, and former beggars were possessors of wealth." * (As Hobbes pointed out, the one condition that is more intolerable than tyranny is anarchy.)

With the re-establishment of unity by conquest, and the consequent founding of the Middle Kingdom about 2133 B.C., Egyptian power and trade again extended to Palestine, and even beyond it into Syria, as well as up-river to Nubia. An immense system of irrigation was constructed (and is still in use), whereby the flood-waters of the Nile were retained in a desert reservoir, southwest of Memphis, to irrigate the land after the annual flood had subsided and the annual drought begun. At the end of three or four centuries, however, the Middle Kingdom decayed in its turn, and suffered the fate of the Old Kingdom, leading to the Second Intermediate Period, in which the Asiatic nomads called Hyksos overran the delta and extended their sway up the river. The Hyksos, although they conquered much of Egypt, were in some measure absorbed by it, adopting the Egyptian religion and Egyptian ways, just as the Mongolian nomads who, at a later date, were to conquer China in similar fashion would become Chinese. The greatest contribution of the Hyksos to the Egyptian civilization is thought to have been their introduction of the horse.

About 1574 B.C., a succession of energetic pharaohs drove the Hyksos out of Egypt and founded the New Kingdom. The pharaohs now became great military conquerors — like the Mesopotamian, Nebuchadnezzar, like the Persian, Cyrus, like the first Caesars who ruled in Rome. They planted the Egyptian standard as far away as the banks of the Euphrates. They erected vast buildings and made displays of unparalleled magnificence, moved by the same impulse, no doubt, as moved Nebuchadnezzar to build the Hanging Gardens of Babylon for the astonishment of mankind.

This, however, was the sunset of the Egyptian civilization, wherein

* *Collier's Encyclopedia*, 1970, Vol. 8, p. 659.

it expended its remaining forces in one last display. When the display was over and the forces had been expended, the conquered peoples of Asia rose up in revolt against an overextended empire. Soon the barbarians were pouring into it from all sides — even Libyans from the deserts to the west. They came to occupy posts of administration, and about 590 B.C. a Libyan became pharaoh. There was increasing confusion, and degeneration into chaos, until in 332 B.C. Egypt succumbed, finally, to conquest by that Macedonian pupil of Aristotle, Alexander the Great.

By that time the first two civilizations in the history of life on earth — which had begun with prokaryotic cells three and a half thousand million years earlier — had spent themselves and expired, leaving ruins on which their successors would build.

XII

Egypt's Contribution to Civilization

THE GEOGRAPHY OF EGYPT, as we have seen, required the centralization of political authority over a wide area. The centralization of authority meant the concentration of power, and with the concentration of power went the concentration of wealth. So the geography of Egypt explains the scale of the pyramids.

Even the pharaohs of the Old Kingdom, who constructed the pyramids, were gods, as the little kings of Sumeria were not. They commanded relatively unlimited resources, not only in the goods of this world but in the labor and the skills of a subject population. Therefore they built large and wrought lavishly. Not only could they afford what would have been pretentiousness in mere men, their role required it.

Among the human resources at the disposition of the pharaohs were skilled engineers, who could plan and direct the construction of far-flung irrigation works, of canals from the Nile to the Red Sea, and of pyramids as remarkable for their geometrical conformity as for their size. All this required a certain mathematical ability, which in turn required a manageable system of numeration. Distances and angles had to be measured exactly — and so did time, for the making of a calendar. (But time is measured, in the first instance, by measuring distances and angles in the sky.) The Egyptians, however, devised no system of numeration as sophisticated as the Mesopotamian, with its place-value notation and its consequent capacity to deal with fractions. Their system was essentially like the Roman system of a later age, and anybody who tries to divide MCLXI by XIV will see the difficulties it poses. Moreover, it enabled them to deal with fractions, those remainders produced by the process of division, only in the most cumbersome fashion — as we would if our notation allowed only 1 to be used as a numerator, requiring that different fractions be shown by differences in their respective denominators (so that $\frac{2}{7}$ would have to be written $\frac{1}{6} + \frac{1}{9} + \frac{1}{126}$). If the pharaohs had had to make do with fewer mathematicians, a more efficient system of numeration would have been needed to achieve the same results.

In devising a calendar the Egyptians reconciled lunar and solar reckoning by making the year consist of twelve months, each thirty days long, and adding five additional days at the end of the twelfth month to make a year of 365 days. This meant that they got two days ahead every seven years; but, while they recognized this, the conservatism of a priestly society restrained them from doing anything about it. (After the Macedonian conquest, Ptolemy III, in 238 B.C., decreed that one day should be added every four years, which is the system still in effect among us — except that we have reduced the inaccuracy to 26 seconds per year by omitting the added day when the occasion for it falls in a century year that is not divisible by 400.) *

While there are abundant remains of Egyptian literature in the form of inscriptions on walls and papyri, or later copies of Egyptian originals, there is no epic that represented the civilization or constituted a classic on which its members were brought up, like the Epic of Gilgamesh in the Mesopotamian civilization or the Homeric epics in Greece and Rome. There are magical texts to help the dead enter upon the life to come, there are stories of adventure and romance that were presumably told at gatherings by professional story-tellers, there are love poems that evoke in our minds The Song of Solomon, there are collections of wise sayings like the Biblical Proverbs, there are religious poems like the Biblical Psalms, and such tales as those of Osiris, Isis, Horus, and Set must have existed in many forms. All this may be equal to the ancient Jewish literature, but it has not come down to our own times in the form and with the force of an Old Testament.

The architectural and artistic remains of the Egyptians have made more of an impression on their successors. The architecture impresses, perhaps too much, by its sheer physical magnitude, by the fact of so much stone transported, cut, and placed over such an extent of length, breadth, and height. The pharaohs, one judges, were less concerned to honor a divinity above them than to arouse in others an awe of their own divinity. The architecture of rulers who assume the status of gods is likely to be at the same time greater and lesser than that of rulers who do not so exalt themselves, as the

---

* Because the earth is accelerating in its repeated voyage around the sun, the length of the solar year is decreasing by about half a second per century, a point worth mentioning because it shows what progress in measurement has been made since the days of the Sumerians.

Pantheon in Rome is at once greater and lesser than the Parthenon.

The best architecture is that of the Old Kingdom. The pyramids, which were not repeated in later times, show simplicity as well as mass. They are rectilinear and Euclidean. The Temple of the Sphinx has a simple post-and-lintel construction in which the upright and the horizontal parts are, alike, square-cut blocks of red granite. It is in this Egypt of the Old Kingdom that columnar architecture originates. Among the remains of buildings around the first pyramid, which Imhotep built for the Pharaoh Zoser at Sakkara about 2780 B.C., are slender columns that represent, stylized in stone, sheaves of papyrus reeds bound together near the top. They manifest the greatest delicacy and grace to be found in Egyptian monumental architecture, which became ever heavier with time and pretentiousness.

By the time of the New Kingdom (which is the last kingdom), tombs and temples were being hollowed out of the cliffs that bounded the Nile Valley, and provided with extensive approaches from the light outdoors to the mysterious darkness within by way of ramps rising to successive terraces bounded by colonnades. On two obelisks erected before the extensive complex of temples at Karnak in Upper Egypt by Queen Hatshepsut (a female pharaoh, ruling about 1500 B.C., who assumed the regalia of a man and is represented in statuary with a beard), she had inscribed for the consideration of the posterity to which we belong:

> You who after long years shall see these monuments, who shall speak of what I have done, you will say, "We do not know, we do not know how they can have made a whole mountain of gold." . . . To guild them I have given gold measured by the bushel, as though it were sacks of grain, . . . for I knew that Karnak is the celestial horizon of the earth.*

Here at Karnak we still have the columns of Imhotep — shafts capped by stylized flowers of papyrus or lotus, open or closed — but immense, grown heavy with age, and crowded together as if the intention had been to diminish space. The pharaohs here seem to be saying, with Shelley's Ozymandias: "Look on my works, ye Mighty, and despair!" The whole of Notre-Dame de Paris could be stored in one chamber of the great temple at Karnak, yet the former, viewed from inside, seems the more spacious of the two.

As in the case of the Assyrian bas-reliefs (see pages 356–357), the

---

* Quoted by Will Durant, *Our Oriental Heritage*, New York, 1942, p. 143, from J. H. Breasted, *Ancient Records of Egypt*, Chicago, 1906, Vol. 2, p. 131. Cf. Shakespeare's Sonnet LV.

human body as represented in Egyptian sculpture and painting is rigid in pose, standing or sitting four-square like a pyramid, without flexibility in its balance or subtlety in its lines. Apparently such stiffness of corporeal attitude was associated with dignity, so that it is most marked in pharaohs and their queens. In the case of the sculpture in the round, which was designed to be seen from in front (one does not walk around an Egyptian statue), the chief interest is in the head, and the faces often show a sensitivity in the carving that, in the best examples, brings out not only serenity of expression but individual character. Presumably because the sculptor could be more relaxed when he was portraying ordinary rather than deified people, the finest examples are the portraits of commoners. Surely one of the outstanding works of portrait sculpture in the history of art is the statue in the Cairo Museum, carved in wood, of one who was an overseer of labor, dubbed (perhaps as an affectionate joke) "Sheik-el-Beled" or Mayor-of-the-Village. It would be hard to find any other head in the history of portraiture that so combined authority and serene good humor, although we have all known heads like that in real life. Another example of such accomplishment, also from the Old Kingdom, is the seated scribe in the Louvre, whose face is beautiful in its combination of intelligence and alertness. He seems as one taking dictation, waiting with pen poised for the next word. A third example of this quality in portrayal is the Old Kingdom bust of Prince Ankh-haf in the Boston Museum of Fine Arts. It seems to represent the ultimate refinement of intelligence as it shows in the human face. Those who are less than gods can afford to put intelligence before power.

There are other examples of Old Kingdom sculpture in stone that, in spite of their stiffness of pose, are beautiful in the subtlety with which the surfaces of the bodies are modeled, the outstanding examples being the diorite statue of the Pharaoh Khafre (also written Chephren) in the Cairo Museum, and that of the Pharaoh Menkoure and his queen in the Boston Museum of Fine Arts. This latter is curiously moving in its pose as well, for the queen has one arm about the pharaoh's waist, and the other arm reaching across her body so that the hand can rest affectionately on his near arm. The consequence is that the couple is human in spite of majesty.

There is nothing to equal these works after the Old Kingdom. Certainly the great stone figures of Rameses II in front of the cave temple of Abu Dimbel, erected in the days of the New Kingdom, being ten or twelve times as large as life, are famous for their size rather than their quality. An exception to everything said here must be made, however, for the New Kingdom head of Queen Nefretete in the State Museum of Berlin, carved in limestone and painted, which surely owes its appeal to the lovely balance of the head on the long neck, like a flower on its stalk.*

The Egyptians were given to covering surfaces with images or hieroglyphs, generally in horizontal or vertical rows. Originally they did so in shallow bas-reliefs, which represented the art of drawing rather than sculpture, and were often embellished with paint. At last, however, they painted directly on flat surfaces as well. Many of these works decorated the insides of tombs, providing images of the common life that might, one supposes, make the dead feel more at home in the life to come. The later pharaohs, especially, like the Mesopotamian kings, had their military triumphs recorded in bas-relief and painting.

Of the two subjects, everyday life and military exploits, the former is the more honest and appealing to those of us who are not pharaohs. There is something particularly moving about genre scenes in the art of any civilization, whether recorded by an artist of 2500 B.C. or by Pieter Bruegel the Elder over four thousand years later The lives of common men have a greater reality for most of us than the lives of gods. Bruegel's peasants, bringing their oxen in from the fields, would have felt a kinship with the two Egyptians of the Old Kingdom bas-relief, one leading an ox by a cord attached to a ring in its nose, the other following to slap its rump.† The painting on a chest in the Cairo Museum of Ikhnaton's successor, Tutenkhamon, in his chariot, vanquishing his enemies, represents a lesser or a less enduring reality. One recalls Roy Campbell's sonnet, "The Serf":

> . . . But as the turf divides
> I see in the slow progress of his strides
> Over the toppled clods and falling flowers,
> The timeless, surly patience of the serf
> That moves the nearest to the naked earth
> And ploughs down palaces, and thrones, and towers.

Like the Mesopotamians, the Egyptians had not mastered the art of representing the third dimension of depth on a flat surface by

* She was the wife of the Pharaoh Ikhnaton, who himself was an exception. He tried to abolish the whole traditional and rotten structure of the society that had come under his rule by inheritance, and to substitute a basic monotheism for the state religion. He insisted that art should imitate nature literally, warts and all. One admires his non-conformity but is appalled by the *hubris* that went with it. It is a tragic paradox that he hastened the decline and fall of the Egyptian civilization.
† Illustrated in *Encyclopaedia Britannica*, 11th ed., Cambridge, 1910, Vol. 9, plate III, opposite p. 66.

reproducing the illusions of perspective in nature. Where many figures are included in one scene, those supposed to be farther away
are likely to be represented higher up but no smaller; and if there is
a pharaoh present he is twice as large as anyone else solely by virtue
of his importance. Three-dimensional space — for the Mesopotamians and the Greeks, as well as for the Egyptians — was not a reality in and of itself, as it was for Chinese landscape painters, and as
it has been for a civilization that first framed such space inside the
Gothic cathedral and then defined it in Newton's mechanics.

Like the Mesopotamians, the Egyptians were surrounded by animals in the world they inhabited. They identified them with the
gods, many of which had their forms rather than human shape.
Horus was generally a falcon, Hather was a cow, and the god who
represented wisdom, Thoth, was a baboon (which, indeed, was probably the most intelligent of the wild animals that inhabited Egypt).
Where the animal forms were simply the clothing of divinity, they
tended to be stylized in their representation. But the animals which
were no more than animals, like the ox referred to above, were
represented realistically. There is a wall painting in Thebes that
shows a hunting scene in which two menials are holding some live
ducks by the wings brought together over their backs. The human
figures are stiff and awkward; but few bird painters of our day are
able to observe birds as well as the painter of these struggling ducks,
let alone to achieve such lifelike reality. To anyone who knows
birds, they are immediately recognizable as pintail (*Anas acuta*), a
species that breeds in northern Europe and still winters in Egypt
(where, no doubt, it is still hunted). They are more enduring, if not
also more glorious, than the Tutenkhamons of this world.

A bas-relief of about 2400 B.C., in the tomb of Ti at Sakkara,
shows a man wading across a stream with a calf on his shoulders.
The calf, in terror, has turned its head back toward its mother,
which follows after, head stretched toward it and mouth open with
such expressiveness that, in imagination, one hears her call and feels
her anxiety. This, more than the colossal representations of Rameses II, justifies the art of Egypt.

In the final reckoning, it is not Nebuchadnezzar but the anguish
of a wounded lioness, not Rameses but the anxiety of a cow for her
calf, that is seen to have achieved immortality.

XIII

India

FROM THE MOUTHS of the Tigris and Euphrates rivers, at the head of the Persian Gulf, westward to the mouth of the Nile is some 1,700 kilometers. From the mouths of the Tigris and Euphrates eastward (and a bit south) to the mouth of the Indus River is 1,900 kilometers. We may think of the first civilization as beginning in the Tigris-Euphrates Valley about 3500 B.C., of the second as beginning in the Nile Valley about 3000 B.C., and of the third as beginning in the Indus Valley about 2500 B.C.

Essentially the same environmental conditions existed in the Indus Valley as in the other two. There was the watercourse on which the life of agricultural man depended, which dominated his thinking by its seasonal changes, with its life-giving waters at some seasons and its occasional death-dealing floods. On one side lay the mountains that rose to the Persian plateau, and on the other lay the Indian desert.

We do not know for certain the identity of the people who founded this third civilization. In the highlands to the west there had been pastoral wanderers who had finally settled down to form villages in upland valleys, where they sometimes constructed stone dams to control the natural flow of water. They were potters as well as metallurgists, and by 3000 B.C. they were using the potter's wheel, as the Sumerians had begun to do somewhat earlier. Given the setting of a great river-valley, people like this were just ready for the take-off into history and civilization.

There were also peoples at the same stage of evolution in the Indus Valley itself, and indeed such peoples were scattered about the map from Asia Minor and Libya to India.

The impulse for the take-off must have come in large measure from Sumeria, for there were, from the first, trade exchanges between the Sumerians and the founders of the new civilization. The new civilization was not, however, an extension of the Sumerian, for it had its own distinct identity. It met the criterion for the passage from pre-history to history by having a written language, but we have not been able to decipher it and, since spoken language is ephemeral, we don't know what these people spoke at all. The writing is syllabic and partially pictographic, with no resemblance to Mesopotamian or Egyptian writing. To the extent, then, that this civilization wrote its own history in inscriptions on stone seals, on pottery, and on tablets of copper, we are unable to read it.

This Indus civilization (which is also called the Harappan civilization) is known chiefly from two ruined cities: Mohenjo-daro (which is estimated to have had a population of 40,000), some 320 kilometers up the river as the crow flies, and Harappa, on a branch of the river about 800 kilometers from its mouth. But it covered a substantially larger area than either the Mesopotamian or the Egyptian civilization, for it extended to the foothills of the Himalayas north of what is now Delhi, and southeast along the coast for some 600 kilometers to the present city of Baroda, as well as westward along the shore of the Arabian Sea.

A distinctive characteristic of this civilization, exemplified by the ruins of Mohenjo-daro and Harappa, is the centralized planning and organization of which the remains give evidence. By contrast with the Mesopotamian cities, the Indus cities were laid out in rectangular blocks separated by streets that crossed one another at right angles. There were communal granaries and the equivalent of barracks for workmen; there were standardized weights and measures represented by uniform series of stone weights; and there were carefully maintained wells and drains. What all this suggests is a society under something like military discipline; but there is a dearth of military paraphernalia, whether defensive outworks or weapons. Moreover, the lack of palaces and royal tombs indicates that these cities were not, like the Sumerian, ruled by kings. The best guess, therefore, is that they were theocratic societies, like the society of Tibet until the middle of the present century — in other words, that they were ruled by a hierarchical priesthood.

One feature that seems to prefigure Hindu civilization is the existence of bathing tanks for the ritual bathing that has always been a Hindu practice.

This Indus civilization did not have the chance, after its flourishing, to decay gradually over the centuries like the Mesopotamian, the Egyptian, and the Graeco-Roman civilizations. As the civilization under the Incas of Peru was killed by the conquering Spaniards, so this civilization appears to have been abruptly ended by conquerors coming from the northwest. It had already been decisively weakened, however, probably by natural disasters. There are indications that the Indus Valley was subject to geological catastrophes resulting in floods. Earthquakes, by damming the river, may have accounted for the repeated flooding of Mohenjo-daro. After each flood, the city was rebuilt upon its ruins, always at a higher level. But the struggle to keep going was doomed, and well before their conquest the cities and their civilization, for whatever reason, had already undergone considerable decay.

Having been founded about 2500 B.C., their final end a thousand years later was no less catastropic than a flood. Unburied skeletons of men, women, and children in Mohenjo-daro, some with sword-cuts on their skulls, show that its population was massacred. (We are called upon to imagine the terror and agony, for themselves and their families, of human beings essentially like us.) Other cities suffered a like fate at the same time. Nothing is certain in our knowledge here, but literary tradition combines with other evidence to indicate that those who did the massacring, about the year 1500 B.C., may well have been the still primitive Aryans, coming in successive waves from the northwest, who would later be associated with the Vedic writings belonging to the Hindu civilization.

All we know of the Indus religion is what we can conclude from the fact that the dead were buried with their property, presumably put there to accompany them into another life. Such literature as they may have produced we cannot read. The Indus artists made square seals of soapstone, showing in negative relief (for stamping positive reliefs out of clay) lovely and intricate designs with animals and inscriptions. There is some crude stone sculpture in the round, including the lifelike head of a man who seems to be looking down and about to speak, his eyes half closed in a fashion foreign to Mesopotamian or Egyptian representations of the human head. Finally, there are bronze and copper artifacts, together with ornaments of gold, of silver, and of glazed pottery.

*

There was an Indus or Harappian civilization from 2500 to 1500 B.C., when it succumbed to successive disasters at its center, in the valley of its origin. In a long view, however, the decline and fall of civilization in this one region was but an episode in the burgeoning and spread of civilization across the northern half of India and, eventually, over the entire subcontinent. In the millennium after 1500 B.C., the civilization that arose over most of the subcontinent was what we identify as the Hindu civilization, associated with the Vedas as Judeo-Christian civilization, if one may call it that, is associated with the books of the Bible.

Once we have entered the second half of the second millennium

B.C. (1500 to 1000), the history of civilization is no longer confined to, or even centered on a river-valley here or there. It has overflowed the valleys. It is beginning to spread all around the Mediterranean, where it is represented by the Achaeans at the siege of Troy, and where the Phoenicians are about to carry it through the Straits of Gibraltar. It is spreading all over southwestern Asia, including Persia. It is spreading across India to the Bay of Bengal. Over much of this distance (8,000 kilometers from Gibraltar to the Bay of Bengal), ships propelled by oars or with sails raised to the wind are plying the coasts; merchants, explorers, and adventurers of one sort or another have inaugurated international trade and travel. Such isolation as that in which the Sumerian civilization developed is no longer to be found except half a world away, where the Yellow River runs down to the Yellow Sea. (Here another civilization is beginning entirely on its own, while in the rest of the world the inarticulateness of pre-history still prevails — but not for long.)

Over the Indian subcontinent, which is what concerns us here, civilization is in constant flux, without the kind of social and political coherence to be found in the Nile Valley. Boundaries, spatial and temporal, are lacking or indistinct. For the most part, there is no one rule over the area, and the stages of development vary. To this day, however, we can best understand society and civilization in India if we divide the subcontinent into two parts. Northern India, then, would be that part north of a line (let us say from Baroda to Calcutta) that excludes the projecting peninsula proper; while southern India would be the peninsula, to which we may add the island of Ceylon. Northern India, south of the Himalayas, is a great alluvial plain which is drained westward into the Arabian Sea by the Indus and its tributaries, eastward into the Bay of Bengal by the Ganges. The Vindhya mountain-range, running eastward from Baroda, marks the boundary, such as it is, between it and peninsular India.

By the time civilization was beginning, from the Nile to the Indus, a degree of racial intermingling had already occurred on the subcontinent. The people of southern India, however, were, on the whole, darker-skinned, those of northern India lighter-skinned. By the time civilization was well under way, a clearer difference had come to distinguish the southern from the northern peoples — for the speech of the former belonged to the Dravidian family of languages (represented by the Tamil of southern India today), while that of the latter belonged to the Indo-European family (represented by Sanskrit in Vedic times, and by the language in which this text is written today).

We don't know where the people who founded the Indus civiliza-

tion came from or what language they spoke. By 1500 B.C. their civilization was terminated by the Aryans who entered the area from
the northwest. They came in successive waves and, being blocked
by the boundary of the Vindhya mountains, spread across the plain
to the whole of northern India, up the Indus and down the Ganges
to the Bay of Bengal. They belonged to the white or Caucasian race,
they spoke an Indo-European language, and their culture was similar to that of the Medes and the Persians who, coming from the general vicinity of the Caspian Sea, were about to spread over the Persian plateau. They appear to have displaced the people who spoke
Dravidian in northern India, thereby contributing to the ethnic and
cultural distinction between north and south.

The name Aryan, applied to these people, identifies them as having a language belonging to a broad group (the Indo-European) that
includes the Sanskrit of their classical literature, as well as Greek and
Latin. Sanskrit is represented today by Hindi, Urdu, Punjabi, and a
number of other languages, which are related to it as French, Spanish, and Italian are related to Latin.

In their primitive state, when they first came into India, these
Aryans did not yet possess the art of writing, so that their literature
was oral only, carried in memory to be recited from generation to
generation. They appear not to have acquired writing until the
ninth or eighth century B.C., when they imported from the west a
Semitic form of writing which they applied, in due course, to
Sanskrit, not enshrining their literature in writing before the time
when, on the shores of the Aegean, *The Iliad* and *The Odyssey* were
being so enshrined.

Just as the English word "gospel" originally meant good tidings, so
the Sanskrit word "veda" (akin to the Latin "video") meant wisdom
(an English word indirectly derived from the Latin and therefore
related to the Sanskrit). Like the Bible, the Vedas are not one work
but the literature of a people, embracing its accumulated wisdom (or
illusions). And just as we know about the life of the ancient Jews
from the books of the Old Testament, so we know about the life of
the first Hindus, as we must now call them, from the Rig-Veda, a
collection of hymns and psalms that was already a part of the heritage of these people by 1500 B.C., when Mohenjo-daro fell before
them.*

*

* In reading these chapters on civilization the reader should have in mind how reality
is distorted by our traditional distinction between a continent called Europe and
another called Asia. In terms of physical geography it does not exist at all. If it exists
in terms of ethnic geography, then India ought to be included in Europe.

The body of beliefs and attitudes, the world outlook, called Hinduism has its original and basic expression in the Vedas as Christianity has its original and basic expression in the New Testament. If one judges it by the most sophisticated passages in the Vedas, one cannot avoid the conclusion that no body of religious belief in the history of mankind has achieved a higher level of philosophical sophistication. There is, to begin with, a basic agnosticism, which accepts the total incomprehensibility of the fact that there is being at all. Being must have preceded the existence of the gods, according to one hymn, and perhaps the highest of the gods, even if he was the creator, does not know how it came about.*

There is also the monism (or holism, the term for it that has so far been used in these pages) that is basic to Hinduism, and that has its most thoughtful expression in those philosophical books of the Vedic literature called the Upanishads. Ultimately, the many is one. We may say that there are three thousand and three gods, or three hundred and three, or thirty-three, or six, or two — but when we get to the bottom of things there is only one.

Schopenhauer and Emerson were among the Western thinkers who were impressed by the Upanishads, and the latter wrote a poem, called "Brahma," of which I quote one verse:

> They reckon ill who leave me out;
> When me they fly, I am the wings;
> I am the doubter and the doubt,
> And I the hymn the Brahmin sings.

All this is simple, but on the level of Spinoza rather than of Genesis.

The other overriding aspect of Hinduism is the view, not only that the things of this world have no value, and not only that there is no value in the realization of our desires (which only those who have realized them can appreciate), but that our existence as individuals is such that we should look forward to escaping from it. The repeated reincarnation in successive lives, which Hinduism assumes, is merely a series of punishments, and the idea is to lose one's individual self entirely, at last, by absorption into the universal whole.

One would give much to know the process by which a savage people, the Aryans who in the second millennium B.C. entered India from the west, came to carry the process of thought so far, or how they came to achieve such a refined and subtle philosophical sensibility. It is as if a Voltaire had arisen among the wild Indians of Patagonia to shape their view of the world. What disenchanting expe-

* See citation by Will Durant in *Our Oriental Heritage*, New York, 1942, p. 409.

riences they must have suffered, and what occasions for unrelenting thought they must have had, generation after generation, to arrive at a view of the world so comprehensive, so detached, and so devoid of illusion! To this day, they must still be regarded as representing mind at its best.

*

When religion reaches the degree of philosophical subtlety I have described, its elements of faith and inspiration tend to become attenuated. It is but a step from saying that all being is God to saying that there is no God; but a step from agnosticism to atheism; but a step from scepticism to cynicism; but a step from the subtle disputations of the doctors to the refined nihilism of the Preacher in Ecclesiastes. These steps, moreover, are more likely to be taken where the corruption of a priestly establishment, playing on the gullibility of the ignorant, provokes a reaction.

Such was the case in Vedic India: on the one hand, the refinement of the most advanced thought, on the other, the corruption of priests who enriched themselves by selling salvation. Consequently, by the middle of the first millennium B.C., a whole literature of materialism and hedonism had grown up to undermine the authority of the Vedas and the Upanishads (just as, in the West, a whole literature grew up in the eighteenth and nineteenth centuries of our era to undermine the authority of the Bible). Over and over again, in the India of the sixth century B.C., literary works were saying, in almost identical terms, what Omar Khayyām would be saying in twelfth-century Persia, what Edward FitzGerald would be translating for nineteenth-century England:

> Ah, make the most of what we yet may spend,
> Before we too into the Dust descend;
>   Dust into Dust, and under Dust, to lie,
> Sans Wine, sans Song, sans Singer, and — sans End!

We may assume, however, that no great society or civilization can be without a body of religious or ideological belief. Just as Marxism, in the nineteenth and twentieth centuries, arose in the West to fill the vacuum left by the loss of faith in Christianity, providing a secular and atheistic religion to take its place, so Jainism and Buddhism arose in India about the middle of the first millennium B.C.

Jainism originally taught that there was no god, and that what is represented as human knowledge, rather than being absolute, is relative to the time and place and circumstances of those who speak for it. (The tale of the blind men and the elephant, which I cited in the first paragraph of the first chapter of Part One, is a Jain story by which the Jainist teachers explained the relativity of knowledge.) It also taught the dualism of mind (or soul) and matter, attributing both even to sticks and stones. Finally, it took the traditional Hindu view that one's own life is a burden to be got rid of, and so it approved of suicide. Its ethics entailed an extreme asceticism, and care not to kill even the most minute of living things (oneself excepted). Its appeal was to those who reacted against everything associated with the Hindu priestly establishment, as well as against the luxury and corruption of the life around them.

Every body of religious or ideological belief is associated with the name of one man as its founder, however little it may come to represent his teachings. The founder of Jainism, known as Mahavira, was born in northeastern India in the middle of the sixth century B.C. To the best of our knowledge, it was also in the middle of the sixth century B.C., and also in northeastern India, that the founder of Buddhism was born. His name was Siddhartha, of the clan of Gautama, and it is by the latter name that he is generally known (or as Gautama Buddha, or just as Buddha). He was a philosopher, like Socrates, claiming no divinity for himself or any knowledge of divinity. The traditional literature of what he taught has come down to us, but we have no firm knowledge of him. According to the literature, he was not only agnostic but, by his ironical references to the supposed existence of a god or gods, perhaps also atheistic in the tendency of his mind. There was no world of the supernatural for him. As in the case of Socrates (also a master of irony), as in the case of Confucius (the latter his contemporary, and the former not far from it), he was concerned only with ethics, with the way people ought to conduct their lives. Like Mahavira in all this, he was against the luxury and corruption of his times, and against what the Hindu priesthood had come to stand for. But he had the Hindu view of life as an unmitigated evil, he assumed its perpetuation by reincarnation, and he shared the view that one's aim must be to escape from it at last by the merger of one's individual identity into the whole, into what the Buddhists call Nirvana. Finally, his ethics consisted, like those of Mahavira, in the rejection of desire and a refusal to cater to the appetites. He taught that, in human relations, one should cultivate peace, returning good for evil. His teachings in this respect were like those of Jesus.

Buddhism, which began as a philosophy, has since, and to our own day, been cultivated as a religion, albeit a religion without a god. Important in India, it was to spread to China, Korea, and

Japan, becoming transmuted with time and distance — as all bodies of belief become transmuted, indeed, to the point where their nominal founders would no longer recognize them.*

*

So far, I have outlined the history of civilization between the Mediterranean Sea and the Bay of Bengal from its beginnings to the middle of the first millennium B.C. By this time, civilization and history had also got under way in the valley of the Yellow River, 3,200 kilometers northeast of the Bay of Bengal.

* Cf. Part Two, Chapter 5 ("The Grand Inquisitor") of Dostoyevsky's *The Brothers Karamazov.* Karl Marx, toward the end of his life, wrote to his son-in-law, Paul Lafargue: "What is certain is that I am not a Marxist" (quoted by T. B. Bottomore in *Karl Marx: Early Writings,* London, 1963, p. xiii, footnote).

XIV

China

As we distinguish between north India and south India, so we distinguish between north China and south China. North China is identified with the Yellow River, which flows from the highlands north of Tibet westward, by a deeply indented course, to empty at last into the bay that is enclosed by the Shantung Peninsula on one side, the Korean Peninsula on the other. South China is identified with the Yangtze River, which flows from the southeastern corner of Tibet to empty into the East China Sea at what is now Shanghai — and also, still farther south, with the basin of the West River, which empties into the South China Sea near what is now Canton. The original development of the Chinese civilization, and its center for millennia thereafter, was north China.

Although there is no reliable basis for assigning a date to the beginning of the Chinese civilization, we may safely place it between 2000 and 1500 B.C., with the establishment of the Hsia Dynasty, for which there is convincing traditional evidence. The place of its beginning is hundreds of kilometers up the Yellow River, in what is now southern Shansi province, although the Hsia Dynasty would at last extend its rule to the river's mouth.

The legendary founder of the Hsia Dynasty, whose historical reality is a matter of speculation, was the Emperor Yü. His fame in legend is "as regulator of the floods which had covered the whole empire, almost to the tops of the highest hills. At this task he had laboured for thirteen years, so assiduously that he did not once enter his own house until all was finished, although in the course of his labours he thrice passed the door and heard the cries of his children. His devotion to duty has remained the classic example. Yü's labours extended to all parts of China, and there are few rivers whose course he did not alter or enlarge in his work of draining the country." *

* C. P. FitzGerald, *China: A Short Cultural History,* New York, 1950, p. 14. In the account of Chinese civilization that follows I rely heavily on this example of historical scholarship and historical writing at their best.

This legend, like the Mesopotamian and Biblical legend of the flood, speaks for itself. The waters of the Yellow River, like those of the Tigris and Euphrates, the Nile, and the Indus, had to be controlled by the farmers who settled down to practice agriculture in its valley. The river flows through a region that has only a sparse rainfall for most of the year, when it carries relatively little water, but is subject to torrential rains in summer, when it may flood. The construction, maintenance, and operation of waterworks for flood-control and irrigation required social organization under centralized direction. According to the legend, this was what Yü provided, and in providing it he not only founded the Hsia Dynasty, he inaugurated the Chinese civilization. The traditional literature gives the date of this as 1989 B.C.

All the circumstances indicate that this Chinese civilization, like the Sumerian, originated of itself, without any contribution from outside. Those who brought it into being knew nothing of three other civilizations that had already got started in parts of the world with which they had no communication, direct or indirect.* The evolution of man from a sort of tree shrew had reached the point where he was ready to embark on civilization, in China as in Sumeria, with the consequence that civilization began in both places independently and, in the long view, simultaneously.

The history of China is the history of successive dynasties that successively decay until, in each case, a strong man sweeps the old one away to found a new one in its place. The Hsia Dynasty was replaced in 1557 B.C. (according to tradition) by the Shang Dynasty, the existence of which is attested by archaeology as well as legend; and the Shang Dynasty was replaced by the Chou in 1050 B.C. (according to tradition). By this time a loose feudal empire had been built up over a wide area. Within it much of south China had the colonial status it would continue to have throughout most of Chinese history.

The archaeological evidence that confirmed the legendary accounts of the Shang Dynasty was found at the site of an ancient city, Yin Hsü, which had been the Shang capital until it was destroyed by the flooding of the Yellow River. It took the form of what may, in a loose sense, be called archives: collections of bones and tortoise shells

---

* It is true that a bronze implement of the same form as one common in prehistoric Europe, the so-called socketed celt, is found among archaeological remains in the Yellow River Valley, from which we conclude that the model for it found its way, presumably in the baggage of prehistoric traders, across Siberia to China; but it was not known in Egypt, Mesopotamia, or India. There are also ceramics that seem to connect prehistoric China with prehistoric Europe. Such tenuous and indirect communication with prehistoric peoples in Europe as this represents would have counted for little more than nothing, at best, in the creation of Chinese civilization.

bearing inscriptions. The early Chinese used to inform themselves of what the future held by addressing questions to the spirits of their ancestors in the form of such inscriptions. They then heated the inscribed shells or bones until they cracked, reading the ancestral answers by the shapes the cracks took. The answers were sometimes inscribed, then, alongside the questions. The names of many of the Shang rulers, as formerly known only from the traditional and semi-legendary literature, were found on these oracle bones as identifying those who were making the appeals to the ancestral wisdom.

These Shang inscriptions, dating from the second millennium B.C., were set down, not in some lost script of the past like cuneiform, but in the Chinese writing that has come down to our own day; and, albeit the forms of the written characters are archaic, they represent, even in this early period, a degree of development from an initially simple pictographic and ideographic writing that must have taken a good many centuries. If, then, we say that Chinese civilization originated about 2000 B.C., we may plausibly speculate that Chinese writing originated about the same time.

The Chinese language is basically so different from the languages of the West as to confirm the conclusion that the cultural developments leading to civilization in eastern Asia were quite independent of those leading to civilization in western Asia and Europe. Its root words are monosyllabic, and otherwise identical monosyllables are distinguished, in the spoken language, by differences of intonation: i.e., high pitch, pitch rising from middle to high, pitch falling from high to low, pitch rising from low to middle.

As for the written language, its evolution from the original pictographic forms (e.g., a stylized image of a tree to denote tree) and ideographic forms (e.g., three parallel lines to denote three) led to characters that denote particular words of the spoken language in themselves, rather than images or ideas, but did not go beyond that, as in the West, to acquire syllabic and, at last, alphabetic characters. The consequence has been a written language that differs from the spoken language, and that is pronounced differently in the different dialects of the spoken language (as our Arabic numeral 3 is pronounced differently in Spanish, English, German, etc.). The situation is rather like what prevailed in Europe during the early Middle Ages, when the written language was Latin but the spoken languages were the emerging French, Spanish, Italian, etc. Taking all these linguistic differences between East and West into account, one could believe that the respective cultures had developed on different planets in space.

*

The tombs of Shang rulers have been found to contain fine bronzes, jades, and animal sculptures in stone. More than that, however, the skeletons of human attendants, as well as the remains of horses and chariots, have been found buried in association with them. Here is the closest possible parallel, harking back to Neanderthal man, with the royal tombs of Sumeria (see page 345) and those of the Egyptian pharaohs. The same belief in a journey of the dead to another world, in which they would wish to be accompanied by possessions and attendants, prevailed in the valley of the Yellow River as in Mesopotamia and the valley of the Nile. We must conclude that it is associated with this particular stage in the evolution of man, whether on one side of the earth or the other. Shang burials, like Sumerian burials, entailed human sacrifices.

Such burials were associated with the ancestor worship so prominent in Chinese religion — as represented, for example, by the oracle bones. Not only must provision be made for the departure of the dead from this world, provision must also be made by their male descendants, in perpetuity, to keep them alive in the afterworld by appropriate rites and sacrifices, without which they must finally fade into nothingness. (There is an extraordinary parallel, here, with the situation described in Book Eleven of *The Odyssey,* where Odysseus descends into the underworld to solicit information about the future from the spirits of the dead, his mother included, to whom he offers, in return, the blood of a lamb, as well as milk, honey, wine, and barley meal, all of which they seize upon eagerly for the renewal of their strength.) The spirits of the ancestors, once established in Heaven, have power to reward their descendants for these sustaining services, not only by answering their questions but by attending to their welfare.

The ancient Chinese, like all other peoples at the earliest stage of cultural development, also believed in local divinities associated with natural features in their environments, chiefly rivers and streams; in fertility gods; and in such other deities as a god of the soil and a god of the grain, both of whom were deified heroes — rather like Heracles, one supposes, or Persephone in Greek mythology.

So much for what primitive Chinese religious beliefs had in common with those of other peoples at the same stage of development.

What appears distinctive in Chinese belief is the concept of a normative order that depends, for its successful functioning, on an harmonious balance among its elements. These elements are basically dual, represented by the doctrine of the Yin and the Yang, which is itself symbolized by the diagrammatic circle that is equally divided into a dark half and a light half by a tight S-curve. The Yin and the

Yang are, respectively, the negative and the positive, the female and the male, the dark and the light. The earth is feminine, dark, identified with the Yin; the sky is masculine, light, and identified with the Yang. The sky is Heaven, the Supreme Ancestor, a sort of male divinity above all others — as, in Hindu theology, Brahma is above all others. Earth as a whole, extending under Heaven and dependent on it, is a female counterpart of Heaven.

This duality may plausibly be equated with the basic environmental situation in which the agricultural communities of the Yellow River struggled to survive through the four seasons of the year, year after year. When Heaven supplied the vernal rainfall, Earth flourished and the crops grew; but when Heaven withheld it Earth became barren and the crops failed, so that the people starved. When Heaven supplied too much rain in midsummer, the growing crops were washed away by floods, again with the result that the people starved. Such catastrophes, resulting in famine, have throughout the millennia occurred every four or five years in parts of China if not in the whole. Men have prospered only when the forces of nature, symbolized by the Yin and the Yang, are in harmonious balance.

For the Chinese, then, everything has traditionally depended on how Heaven is disposed toward the human society that lives upon Earth, which feeds it in return for its labor, but only when the relationship with Heaven is harmonious, when the balance of elements, the balance of forces, is in good order.

In the more individualistic societies of the West, the conclusion to be drawn from such a situation might have been that the people, severally and as a whole, should avoid such behavior as might be expected to antagonize the all-powerful, however identified. (So Yahweh's anger was kindled against those communities in which misbehavior was general, as in the case of Sodom and Gomorrah.) In China, by contrast, the maintenance of the harmonious relationship with Heaven depended on one man alone, the emperor, known as the Son of Heaven. His primary mission and obligation was not that of ruling the society but that of performing, throughout the annual round, the rites and sacrifices that, by propitiating Heaven, maintained the harmonious relationship between it and Earth on which the entire society depended. The emperor had to maintain the normative situation, which was one of balance between the Yin and the Yang; just as, in a family, the welfare of the children depended, *inter alia*, on a normative equilibrium between the male and female parents, who complemented each other as the Yang and the Yin within the circle of the whole.

It was not enough, however, that the Son of Heaven should properly perform all the rites and sacrifices. He had also to represent moral virtue, in himself and in his conduct alike. "Heaven," as C. P. FitzGerald puts it, "could not be served by a tyrant or a debauchee, the sacrifices of such a ruler would be of no avail, the divine harmony would be upset, prodigies and catastrophes would manifest the wrath of Heaven." *

What followed was that the mission of the emperor could be accomplished only by one who had the approval of Heaven, so that the authority by which an emperor held office as such was the so-called Mandate of Heaven. If he should fall into misconduct he would lose the Mandate. Then he would find himself replaced by some rebel against his rule who, by making good his rebellion, showed that the Mandate had been transferred to him (for otherwise he would not have been successful). So rebellion was justified only *ex post facto*, by its success if it succeeded, and so decayed dynasties were supplanted by adventurers who would have been usurpers if it had not been for the doctrine of the Mandate of Heaven, by which they were legitimized.

*

The Hsia Dynasty, known to us only through a traditional body of legend, was founded in 1989 B.C., according to tradition. Also according to tradition, the Mandate of Heaven passed from it to the Shang Dynasty in 1557 B.C., and from the Shang to the Chou Dynasty in 1050 B.C. By this time, as we have seen, a loose feudal empire had been built up over a wide area. This empire was based on a distinction fundamental to Chinese civilization throughout its history. There was an innermost group of states, on both sides of the Yellow River, that were truly Chinese in their culture and were consequently regarded as constituting "the Middle Kingdom." The outlying states, to the degree that they had not yet become culturally sinified, belonged to the category of "outer barbarians." (Through the nineteenth century of our era, and perhaps to this day, the distinction would persist in the minds of the Chinese — the British, the French, and other Western peoples, for example, being classified as outer barbarians, however civilized they might be, since their civilization was not the Chinese civilization.) It would be the fate of the Middle Kingdom to be conquered, time and again, by outer barbarians — who would then become Chinese, however, by the absorption of Chinese culture. In this way, at least until modern times, China has always conquered her conquerors.

* FitzGerald, op. cit., p. 40.

The Chinese Feudal Age is considered to have begun in 841 B.C. (the first authenticated date of Chinese history), when the Chou ruler was driven from his capital by a revolt of his oppressed subjects, a regency being established in his place. It ended in 221 B.C. with the conquest of the Middle Kingdom and its feudal dependencies by outer barbarians from the east.

Under the feudal system, the Chou ruler, the Son of Heaven, was supreme over the world that lay beneath Heaven. In theory, if not always in practice, the rulers of the states outside his royal domain, whether belonging to the Middle Kingdom or the outer barbarians, were his vassals, owing him homage and paying him tribute. They depended on him, if for nothing else, for the maintenance of the harmony between Heaven and Earth on which the prosperity of all depended.

This was the normative situation, representing the world as it should be. In 770 B.C., however, the Chou capital was captured and sacked by barbarians from the north, so that the Son of Heaven had to abandon the dynastic homeland and establish a new capital farther east. The consequent decline of the Chou Dynasty's power led to the establishment of hegemony by a succession of powerful vassals who, as such, were usurping the authority of the Son of Heaven. So a sharp difference arose between the normative situation and the actual situation.

Over the period of more than six centuries, from 841 to 221 B.C., the Chinese population was increasing and the Chinese space was filling up. At the beginning, the several states of what was a sort of feudal confederation had been separated from one another, in considerable measure, by areas of wilderness in which primitive barbarians lived. With the passage of time, however, the wilderness was increasingly squeezed out and the organized states began to press directly upon one another. (This represents an evolution that, on the scale of the whole world, would culminate in the twentieth century of our era.) The result was increasing rivalry expressing itself in increasingly intense warfare among the states. So the Feudal Age gradually became what is known to history as the Period of the Warring States. It became a time of troubles, such as every civilization knows in the course of its history, during which the normative order was increasingly submerged in a mounting chaos.

The decline into anarchy was gradual but progressive, and it could have but one end; for the proliferation of chaos always leads, at last, to the forcible imposition of a single rule by whatever power is strong enough to impose it. In 256 B.C., the Son of Heaven was despoiled of his possessions and the Chou Dynasty brought to an end. In 222 B.C., the ruler of Ch'in, a barbarian state to the west, completed the military conquest of the entire Chinese realm, after which he proceeded to set himself up as the first Emperor of China, thereby founding the historic Chinese Empire — which was to endure, as such, until the Revolution of 1911, when the Republic of China was set up in its place.*

* The term "emperor" cannot properly be used for the topmost Chinese feudal lords before this time, except as legendary rulers like Yü, founder of the legendary Hsia Dynasty, are graced with the title. Any historical ruler before 221 B.C. is better called "king."

The Mind in China

WE HAVE NOW EXAMINED the emergence of four separate civilizations from the virgin soil of pre-history; and we have seen how each, in its beginnings, was associated with a complex of religious beliefs that represented a normative order. However, when the social order fails notably to correspond in practice to the normative order, when the gap between the actual and the normative becomes too conspicuous — perhaps because the social order is crumbling — then thoughtful minds are impelled to think hard about beliefs that had previously been taken for granted. So it is that a time of troubles is apt to beget philosophy. Athenian philosophy, in the classic example, burgeoned after the Athenian social order had broken down as a consequence of defeat in the Peloponnesian War. An intense experience of disaster and disorder in India must surely account for the philosophy represented by the Upanishads and by the teachings attributed to Gautama Buddha, for it so clearly responded to the loss of illusions.

Until about the middle of the eighth century B.C., Chinese society had been organized in accordance with a certain complex of religious beliefs. The keystone in the arch, alike of the religious order and of the social order that corresponded to it, had been the supremacy of the Son of Heaven. In the Period of the Warring States the social order gradually succumbed to an increasing anarchy, out of which came the flowering of Chinese philosophy in what is known, with some poetic licence, as "the Hundred Schools." The great names of Chinese philosophy all belong to this Period of the Warring States and the Hundred Schools.

The term philosophy is so broad that its use in this context might, without qualification, be misleading. The philosophers produced by a time of troubles tend to focus their attention on the branch of philosophy called ethics. Their primary concern is with the conduct of life, by the individual or by the social group as a whole, whether that group be the family or the state. The pre-Socratic philosophers were concerned with the nature of being — with space and time and the structure of matter — but Socrates, the first philosopher of the time of troubles in Greece, was concerned with what constitutes the good life, and with what constitutes the good society within which such a life might be lived. Ethics cannot be separated entirely from a concern with the nature of being (such as led Socrates to his so-called Theory of Ideas), since the good life should, presumably, be in harmony with it; but its focus is on human conduct and the attitudes associated with human conduct. To the extent that the philosopher is concerned with how the good society should be organized (e.g., Socrates in Plato's *Republic*), he is a political philosopher.

Both Mahavira, the founder of Jainism, and Gautama Buddha were wholly preoccupied with ethics, with the way one should live one's life and, by association, with the attitudes of mind one should cultivate. This was equally true of Confucius, and every other philosopher of the Hundred Schools in China.*

The philosophers of the Hundred Schools tended to be more closely associated with statesmanship, with the actual governance of society, than the philosophers of any other time and place. They made their careers at the courts of feudal states as advisers to the lords they respectively served, and when any was dissatisfied with his career in the service of a particular lord he might remove to another state or enter the service of a new master.

Confucius, for example, was not only a teacher like Socrates,† surrounded by a little band of disciples wherever he went, he was also a minor official in his native state of Lu until, becoming dissatisfied with the violation of principle by those who constituted its government, he left to wander about the other states of China for thirteen years, trying to find a lord who would listen to his teaching and follow his advice. He was, in fact, the first of such ambulating professional sages, who went from court to court with their prescriptions for dealing with the ills of a crumbling social order.

The prescription of Confucius was essentially simple. It was to re-

---

* Gautama Buddha was born about 563 B.C., Confucius about 551 B.C., Mahavira perhaps in 549 B.C. (although some say 599 B.C.), and Socrates about 470 B.C. The list of such philosophers, all concerned with ethics and born within a century and a half of one another, could be lengthened — and not only by the swarms of Sophists or their equivalents who made their careers alongside the philosophers of authentic vision. Perhaps Jesus and Zoroaster, although requiring some expansion of the period, and although identified more with religion than with philosophy, should not be altogether excluded from it. One may speculate that the groping new civilization being developed by the descendants of the tree shrew had reached the stage at which an intense philosophical preoccupation with ethics was in order, just as the resort to agriculture and urbanization had been in order at earlier stages.

† Socrates denied that he was a teacher, and it is true that his formal method was simply to ask questions. This, however, is a Socratic quibble — the kind of quibble that made his teaching the more effective.

turn to the tried and true ways of a past that, in the light of the disordered present, was regarded as the Golden Age in which harmony had prevailed between father and son, between ruler and ruled, between Heaven and Earth — between every thing and everything else. This harmony had been maintained by respect for the normative order on the part of all who participated in it, high or low, but chiefly on the part of the rulers, and the consequent performance of all the established rites and observances. For Confucius, the world as it should be was a world of formality in which everyone knew his place and adhered to the role prescribed for that place; so that all relationships were harmonious, producing peace and prosperity for all and for each. If he had lived to read *Hamlet* he would have understood quite well what was rotten in the State of Denmark; * and, in fact, he abandoned his native state of Lu to embark on his wanderings when a usurping minister forced its lord into exile. To him, the realm of being was like a work of art, the harmony of which depends on all its respective parts being in their right places.

In the Confucian view of the world as it should be, the variety of relationships in which people stood to one another were all defined according to their variety. They might be relationships of obedience, or of loyalty, or of love, or of benevolence. Another school of this time, the Mohist, founded by Mo Tzu (500 to 420 B.C.), prescribed only one relationship, that of love. Everyone should properly love everyone else, in which case there would be one worldwide society without divisions, and no wars.

The Mohists could not have advocated the universal rule of love if they had not taken a favorable view of the possibilities inherent in human nature; for it would be idle to advocate the adoption of such a rule by beasts of prey. Other schools of philosophy, observing the predatory practices that went with power and the competition for power, took a wholly cynical view of human nature and its possibilities. The school of Yang Chu, concluding that all efforts to achieve general peace and happiness were hopeless, adopted the nihilism we have associated with the Preacher in Ecclesiastes and the self-regarding hedonism we have associated with Omar Khayyām. Finally, the Legists (or Legalists), regarding all men as dangerous beasts, advocated that they be kept under the restraint of a rigid legal code enforced by the brute power of an all-powerful state.

Let the reader note that these various attitudes and prescriptions relative to the conduct of life have arisen in most civilizations. The traditionalist prescriptions of Confucius, although they have a poetic

* See Part Five, Chapter V below.

flavor that is all their own, have much in common with the prescriptions of traditionalists everywhere who have wished to return to a normative order that they associate in their minds with an idealized past. The Mohist advocacy of universal love is represented in the West by the Christian sect best known as the Quakers. The Legist identification of security with an all-powerful and authoritarian state has its counterpart in Hobbes's *Leviathan;* and, indeed, it has for centuries represented the assumption on which the political organization of Russia has been based, that men are destructive creatures who must be restrained by the ruthless power of the state.

None of the schools so far described can be regarded as metaphysical. They are primarily pragmatic, even if only in negative terms, concerned with what will and what will not work. The case is rather different with Taoism, the legendary founder of which was Lao Tzu, said to have lived in the sixth century B.C. It based itself on the view that there was some order of nature according to which the universe was governed — namely, the Tao, which is generally translated as the Way. Just as one must, in Christian theology, discover what the will of God is, and then accord one's own will with it, so each of us must discover the Tao for himself, and then conduct his life in accordance with it.*

Taoism, which was individualistic in the extreme, took an utterly cynical view of society, which should be governed with no other objective than that of keeping the mass of the people mindless, contented, and docile. Regarding society as worthless, it held in contempt such putative social virtues as benevolence and righteousness. It was quietest, preferring inaction to action. Wisdom, which was regarded as the property only of enlightened individuals, would lead any such individual to renounce society, escaping from it in his mind if not physically as well. What this represented was the impulse toward withdrawal that always arises in times of social breakdown and hopelessness, impelling the individual to retire from the world so as to lead the life of solitary contemplation, perhaps in a monastic retreat, perhaps as a hermit. He can find the Tao by himself and for himself, where the ruck of mortals in society, confined to the level of the common mind, cannot.

The Taoists, then, tended to turn their backs on the world and to look inward. Although this meant that they solved no practical

---

* What began as a metaphysical philosophy was, centuries later, to become a religion. The Tao came to be regarded as the equivalent of the *Logos* — cf. the opening words of The Gospel According to St. John: "In the beginning was the" *Logos.* (See *The Tao of Painting* by Mai-Mai Sze, New York, 1963, p. 15.) Another parallel with Taoism is to be found in the Western doctrine of natural law, regarded as the rule or the way that God or Nature intended.

problems, except for themselves, their introspective contemplations did lead to a high level of sophistication in philosophy, in literature, and in painting — exemplified, *inter alia,* by the views of the Taoist philosopher of the third century B.C., Chuang Tzu. One well known sample, in which he refers to himself by a special personal name as Chuang Chou, will serve as illustration:

> Once Chuang Chou dreamed that he was a butterfly, flying about enjoying itself. It did not know that it was Chuang Chou. Suddenly he awoke, and veritably was Chuang Chou again. I do not know whether it was Chuang Chou dreaming that he was a butterfly, or whether now I am a butterfly dreaming that I am Chuang Chou.*

I cite this for the purpose of calling attention to a new development in the evolution of mind. The tree shrew would not have been capable of thinking in these terms — nor, one suspects, would Neanderthal man. Here mind has at last become reflective in the sense of being self-conscious.

*

When the Ch'in ruler, by military conquest, had at last made himself master of all China in 221 B.C., he declared himself the first universal emperor, under the name of Shih Huang Ti, and proceeded to replace the traditional feudal system, which had crumbled into chaos, by an undivided order under the single and absolute authority vested in him and his successors. His destruction of the ancient feudal nobility, although total, proved to be not enough in itself. Traditional thinking had to be obliterated so as to eliminate from the minds of the emperor's subjects the concept of a golden age in the past — naturally identified with the feudal system, since no other system was known — to the principles and practices of which society should return. This required the destruction of all the historical literature and, especially, of the literature that was based on the normative ideas of the Confucian school. What ensued was the notorious Burning of the Books. In 214 B.C., by order of the emperor, the scholars of China were required to take all books to the magistrates to be burned, the only exceptions being for books dealing with medicine, divination, and agriculture. According to the emperor's decree, those who dared to discuss and comment on the Chinese classics were to be put to death and their bodies exposed in the

---

* Translation by Yu-lan Fung, Shanghai, 1931, quoted in FitzGerald, op. cit., p. 86. Cf. quotation from Kipling on p. 224.

market-place. Those who praised ancient institutions in order to decry the new régime were to be exterminated with all the members of their families. Any who did not have their books burned within thirty days were to be branded and sent to forced labor on the Great Wall, which was among the immense public works instituted by the new state.

The burning of the books and the suppression of the traditional teaching destroyed perhaps a preponderant part of the classical literature forever, and appeared at the time to have been successful in eliminating the traditional normative ideas from the minds of the Chinese. However, a seed stock, from which it would be regenerated, survived the suppression of thought. Some books were saved from the general destruction, bricked up in walls or otherwise concealed by courageous individuals. After the dynasty and its fury had passed, they were brought out of hiding and a labor, long and great and partially successful, was undertaken to reconstruct the Confucian canon and its literature. Confucianism, unsuccessful in the time of Confucius and then persecuted, at last became the official philosophy of China, enduring as such for over nineteen centuries, when it again became the object of persecution.

In Chinese history there have been two totalitarian revolutions designed to create an entirely new society by completely replacing the ideological contents of men's minds. The first occurred in the third century B.C., the second in the twentieth century of our era.

The political philosophy with which the Emperor Shih Huang Ti identified his regime was Legism, which represented his principles and his practice. But Legism, while it would live on into the twentieth century of our era, would never again have the standing it had had under the first emperor.

The totalitarian tyranny of the first emperor aroused a popular discontent that culminated in rebellion after his death in 210 B.C. The final consequence of the rebellion was the accession to the imperial throne four years later, under the Mandate of Heaven, of the peasant Liu Pang, who founded the Han Dynasty that would preside over the grandeur of the Han Empire (206 B.C. to A.D. 220). The Han emperors, and those of the succeeding dynasties for some twenty centuries, would then make use of an evolved or adapted Confucianism to support the loyalty of their subjects to themselves. But the feudal system, which had disintegrated of itself before it had been replaced, would never be restored. From 221 B.C. to the present, the Chinese civilization has been under a centralized rule based on an official ideology.

XVI

The Expansion of China

A CERTAIN PATTERN of rise and decline tends to repeat itself in the history of civilizations. Each arises in some restricted geographical area. Inspired by a complex of religious or ideological beliefs that constitutes a normative vision to be realized, it thrives and spreads, at first, by a sort of cultural contagion. A time comes, however, when its initial impulse weakens or is spent, when it begins to disintegrate. The increasing anarchy that ensues is generally resolved, at last, by the organization of a centralized state based largely on military force. (Greece, in the classic example, is followed by the Rome of the Caesars.) This state expands imperially over a wide area, but in so doing tends to become overextended. At the same time, the barbarians around its frontiers, having acquired its civilized skills by contact with it, increase in their relative strength and begin to pour in from all sides until they have at last overwhelmed it. Although the barbarians acquire much of the civilization they have conquered, and seek to perpetuate it, a period of cultural extinction and darkness is likely to ensue — until, perhaps, the inspiration of a new normative vision leads to the rise of a new civilization.

This pattern of rise and decline is imprecise, so that its individual manifestations are not so rigid in their mutual similarity as one is tempted to make them appear. Surely, however, the general correspondence can be seen repeatedly in the history of civilization.

Roughly speaking, the Han Empire was bounded by an oceanic shoreline to the east and the south, and by the mountains that rise to the Tibetan plateau or that separate Burma and Indochina on the southwest. Only to the north and northwest did it lack a natural frontier for defence against barbarian invasion. This accounts for the Great Wall that was constructed by the first Chinese Emperor, Shih Huang Ti, in the third century B.C.

The nomadic barbarians who ranged over the wide realms north of the Great Wall and westward across central Asia to the Caspian

Sea — across the present Mongolia, Sinkiang, Turkestan, Kazakhis-
tan — were various and presumably of blood (of genes, to be precise) that had long been in process of mixture. The historians provide them with nominal identities, referring to them as "Turkic"
peoples, or as "Tungusic," or as "Tartars"; but this does little to help
us visualize their racial configurations. Turkic peoples, invading
Asia Minor from the east, gave their name to Turkey, but they may
have been of largely Mongolian blood that then became diffused
and lost, over the centuries, in the Caucasian blood of the conquered. It was Turkic peoples who pressed against the northwestern boundaries of China and the Great Wall, century after century.

The specific people against whom the Chinese first erected the
Wall are generally considered to have been at least a branch of the
people known as the Huns in the West — those warriors on horseback who, under Attila, sacked the cities of the Roman Empire in the
fifth century of our era, the people who are still commemorated in
the name of Hungary as the Turkic people in general are commemorated in the name of Turkey. The hordes of Hsiung Nu, to give
them their Chinese name, posed the chief external threat to the Han
Empire, providing the occasion for building the Wall.

In 138 B.C., the Emperor Wu, having heard reports of a people,
the Ta Yüeh Chi, living in central Asia on the other side of the
Hsiung Nu, dispatched a certain Chang Ch'ien as his ambassador to
seek their alliance. Ten years later, after an adventurous journey
through unknown lands and among strange peoples, Chang Ch'ien
found the Ta Yüeh Chi (who were what the West knows as Scythians) in the region south of the Aral Sea and east of the Caspian. To
him, the important fact was that they declined to join China against
the Hsiung Nu. To the historian of 2,000 years later, the important
fact is that China, in the person of Chang Ch'ien, had now reached
out so far as to establish a contact, however tenuous, with the Hellenistic civilization that had its center in Greece. For the lands occupied by the Ta Yüeh Chi had been conquered, two centuries before, by Alexander the Great, who had left superfluous kingdoms
behind him on his retirement. They are only some 1,300 kilometers
from Mesopotamia, to the west, from the valley of the Indus to the
south, but 5,000 kilometers from the valley of the Yellow River to
the east. They are on the borders of Persia.

After this, Chinese embassies to these regions were frequent. In
the period between 48 and 32 B.C., a Chinese commander entered
into alliance with Hermaeus, a Greek king, whom he installed as a
Chinese vassal in the rulership of a part of the Kabul valley that lies

in what is now Pakistan. In A.D. 73, a certain Pan Chao was dispatched to the west on a mission like that of Chang Ch'ien two centuries earlier. In A.D. 97, he led an army that, unopposed, extended the Chinese Empire to the shores of the Caspian Sea. Across that sea and the land of Armenia beyond were the frontiers of the Roman Empire. A century later, by which time the Roman frontiers would have been pushed to the western shores of the Caspian, the Chinese frontiers would have been drawn back from its eastern shores. In the case of both empires, the extension to the Caspian was too great to last.

From the eastern shore of the Caspian, Pan Chao sent an envoy to report on the world beyond, but the envoy was discouraged by the Parthians from advancing beyond the eastern shore of the Black Sea. His report, and those of merchants who made their way to China across central Asia or by way of India and the sea, gave the Chinese some vague knowledge of the Roman Empire, of Byzantium, and later of an emperor whom they called An Tun, whom we call Marcus Aurelius Antoninus.

This kind of expansion of civilization would one day fill up the world. Already the process had gone far beyond its beginning at the mouth of the Tigris and Euphrates rivers three or four thousand years earlier.

*

Any empire tends to press outward against its own frontiers, expanding where it finds little or no resistance until, perhaps, it has expanded over an area too wide to govern.

The desire of the Emperor Wu to open connections with India — which would remain frustrated by the impassability of Burma's mountains and its valleys infested by savages — moved him to expand his realm southward beyond the Yangtze River until, by 110 B.C., it extended to the south coast and the Gulf of Tonkin as far west as the present frontier of Vietnam.

Two years earlier, in an effort to outflank the Hsiung Nu (the Huns) from the east, he had added northern Korea to his Empire. Since the Korean Peninsula is to be regarded as a bridge between China and the arc of islands that today constitutes Japan, this extension resulted in the communication of the Chinese civilization to the inhabitants of these islands, who would in centuries to come develop their own version of it.

Now, however, internal weakness, like heart disease in an individual, was manifesting itself increasingly at the center of the Han Empire. In accordance with the normative vision on which it was based, the Empire was under the absolute rule of the Son of Heaven, who had the obligation of representing by his own conduct the virtues on which the realm depended for Heaven's grace. The reality, however, diverged more and more widely. The exalted standing of the Emperor caused him to be cut off from direct communication even with the ministers of his government, and from knowledge of the world beyond the palace gates. He tended to live his entire life among the ladies of the court and their attendant eunuchs, who alone had direct access to him. These feminine or emasculated courtiers, his only source of information and advice, misinformed him and misadvised him according to their own interests, which depended on the intrigues of the competing aspirants to power among which they were numbered. When it happened, time and again, that the hazards of succession by birth filled the imperial throne by an infant or young child, the power of the intriguing eunuchs, especially, became supreme. They used their power to enrich themselves by the sale of offices, privileges, and favor over the entire realm, until the entire realm began to sink under the weight of corruption and its corollary, incompetence. So the actual situation diverged increasingly from the normative, the imperial establishment lost its moral authority, disaffection spread, and an ever more active opposition grew throughout the empire. Confucius would have understood.

At last, in A.D. 189, the Army entered the imperial palace, massacred the eunuchs, and abducted the emperor. Puppet emperors were set up in succession to maintain the nominal rule of the Han Dynasty; but the Empire broke into three kingdoms, and in A.D. 220, when the last Han emperor, the puppet of a general, abdicated in favor of the general's son, even the nominal survival of the Dynasty was over.

Amid the increasing anarchy that followed, a succession of dynasties were proclaimed only to be overthrown. Then the rivals for the throne began to call in the Hsiung Nu and other Turkic barbarians for the support of their rival claims. In A.D. 311 the Hsiung Nu (the same people who, as the Huns under Attila, would invade the Roman Empire in the following century) captured the Han capital of Lo Yang, which they sacked and burned. The north of China became a battleground of rival barbarians.

C. P. FitzGerald has summed up the aftermath of the Han Empire's decline and fall:

> The period of exactly four hundred years which divides the collapse of the first strong centralised empire, the Han, from

the restoration of unity at the foundation of the Sui dynasty, is the age which in China most nearly approaches the character of the "Dark Ages" of European history. The causes were alike. The collapse of the world empire of the Han was followed, as in the west after the fall of Rome, by barbarian invasions, which, though less destructive in China, overthrew the centralised state and checked the cultural development of the eastern world. In China the consequences of the collapse and the barbarian invasions were by no means so serious as in the west. The memory of the past was never lost. The language and literature of the Han dynasty continued to be spoken and read, the continuity of Chinese civilisation was not irremediably impaired. In the southern empire, which escaped the Tartars [i.e., the Turkic barbarians], the traditions and culture of the Han period were kept alive, while even in the north, the Chinese proved too virile to be transformed by the Tartar conquest; on the contrary, they absorbed their conquerors and assimilated them into the body of the Chinese nation.*

Although we must resist the temptation to carry these parallels too far, we should not fail to take note of the resemblance between the rise and fall of the Classical civilization in the West and that of the first Chinese civilization.

In the Hellenic world of c. 900 B.C., we have first the period of feudalism represented by Homer, and later the decline into anarchy that begins with the Peloponnesian War. In the Chinese world of the Chou Dynasty, from c. 1100 B.C. to 220 B.C., we have first the period of feudalism and later the Period of the Warring States.

In the Mediterranean world of 50 B.C. to c. A.D. 400, we have the spread and dominance of the Roman Empire, followed by the barbarian anarchy of the Dark Ages, which lasts some five hundred years. In the Far Eastern world of 220 B.C. to c. A.D. 300, we have the spread and dominance of the Han Empire, followed by a period of barbarian anarchy that lasts some four hundred years.

I conclude this chapter by the notation: *da capo* to end of first paragraph.

* FitzGerald, op. cit., p. 249.

XVII

Chinese Cultural Remains

IN PART Two, Chapter XVII, we saw how all taxonomy, because it imposes categories on an uncategorical reality, must in some measure be arbitrary. What is true for the ordering of biological forms by genera and species is not less true for such attempts as have been made to distinguish civilizations as individually distinct organisms.* In a God's-eye perspective that embraced all being, alike in the large and in detail, all being would prove to be one and indivisible. But the perspectives among which we, ourselves, may make choice are limited, and in any case we need to categorize for heuristic purposes. Under such circumstances, our objective must be to minimize the arbitrariness of our categories, making them correspond as nearly as possible to the reality on which they are imposed.

I find it plausible to distinguish a Classical civilization that begins in Homeric times and ends with the fall of Rome, and another civilization, which we call Western civilization, that begins about A.D. 1000 and continues to our present. Similarly, I find it plausible to distinguish an earlier Chinese civilization, which begins about 1500 B.C. and ends with the fall of the Han Empire, from a later Chinese civilization that begins toward the end of the sixth century after Christ and continues into modern times — even though the break between the two is not as sharp as the break between the two civilizations in the West.

One has only to take account of the influence of Greek architecture, Greek philosophy, and the Greek language on the later civilization of the West to appreciate the fact of a heritage that constitutes an element of continuity between them (albeit interrupted for a few centuries). The like element of continuity between the two Chinese civilizations is even greater, as exemplified by the continuity of the language and the persistence of certain normative concepts associated with the Confucian tradition.

* See Chapter VII above.

In Chapter VII I gave it as my own view that two lines of traditional civilization represented human achievement at its highest, the Western and the Chinese. If one judged the Chinese tradition only by the remains of the first civilization, however, one would not come to this conclusion. The highest achievements of China, insofar as a stranger to the language and the culture can judge, are manifested chiefly by the remains of the second.

No doubt a principal reason for this is the extent to which the cultural monuments of the first Chinese civilization are unknown because they have failed to survive. One could make a case for it that the Burning of the Books in 214 B.C. was the greatest cultural disaster in the history of mind on earth. It was as if all the works of Greek literature and philosophy, from Homer to Epicurus and Zeno, had been burned, leaving only some fragments that were mostly incoherent. Such painstaking research as was pursued for many centuries after, in an effort to recover what was recoverable, recovered little by comparison with what remains forever lost.

Neither have the early Chinese monuments of the visual arts fared well. The environments in which the Mesopotamian and Egyptian cultures developed were dry and included large areas of desert inimical to the organisms of decay, so that even wood and paper might survive for 5,000 years into our present. And the great examples of Egyptian architecture, from an early stage, were of stone. But the humid climate of the Indus River and the Yellow River ensured decay, which repeated floods often anticipated by their destruction; while the buildings of ancient China were made not of stone but of wood or unbaked bricks, so that there are no remains of them at all — except indirectly, as they were occasionally depicted on vessels of pottery or bronze.

In Chapter XV we noted the development of philosophical thought, associated with the so-called Hundred Schools, in the Period of the Warring States. From this high peak, philosophy declined. Taoism degenerated into a crude religion associated with superstitious cults and the practice of magic. Local deities enlarged their domains by becoming fashionable, other deities were invented and promoted to support ulterior purposes of a political nature. A new polytheism, embracing a multitude of local cults, enjoyed high patronage. (Something rather similar happened, as well, in the Rome of the Caesars.)

The literary activity that flourished most successfully under the Han Empire was the one most appropriate to a civilization that has a past rather than a future, the recording of history. After the Burning of the Books, the supreme task of scholarship was to recover as much of the record as possible, and the challenge this posed produced a tradition of disciplined research and objective presentation which would, in our own day, merit the highest honor we can bestow on humanistic scholarship, that of calling it scientific. The same logic that requires the world to execrate the Emperor of China for the Burning of the Books also requires it to acknowledge an immeasurable debt to the historians who came after to deal with the damage.

These scholar historians, as well as doing what could be done for the accurate restoration and perpetuation of the historical record, also rescued and restored in considerable degree the classical poetry of the feudal period, much of which has, in English translation, a delicacy, a charm, and a sensitivity to elements of the scenic environment, viewed as *tableaux,* that is in keeping with Chinese brush-painting of later times.* The civilization of the Han Empire, however, was not distinguished for its poetry.

The objects of art that have survived the ravages of flood waters or decay are chiefly bronze artifacts, jade carvings, broken pieces of decorated pottery, and bas-reliefs in stone that represent legendary scenes in flat silhouette. Much of this material shows influences from central and western Asia. Judging by it alone, one would conclude that it did not equal the highest achievements of Egyptian, Mesopotamian, or Graeco-Roman art — if it were not for the exception of a bronze statuette, now in Peking, of a horse running like a bird flying, only one foot momentarily touching the ground.†

---

* The spirit of this poetry, if one judges by the translations, is well represented by the citation of Chuang Tzu on page 394; except that the latter, which is prose, lacks the pictorial element so prominent in the former.
† I have omitted any account at all of the mathematics and the calendrical system developed by the first Chinese civilization because they do not represent an evolution of mankind that goes beyond what had already been achieved by the Mesopotamians.

XVIII

Civilization in the New World

WHEN, IN ITS EVOLUTION, mankind had reached the point where it was ready to embark on civilization, it did so at separate points around the globe. In the preceding chapters we have seen how particular civilizations came into being independently in Mesopotamia, in Egypt, in the Indus Valley, and in the valley of the Yellow River. These four may be regarded as original civilizations in the sense that they did not grow out of previous civilizations or their remains.

The same may be said of two other civilizations, both in the New World: the Mayan-Aztec and the Peruvian. Our inadequate knowledge and the uncertainty of definition do not allow us to date their beginnings with any precision, so it seems best to say merely that they were at least in the bud during the centuries just before and after Christ. The Mayan-Aztec went through a classical phase (identified with the Maya) in the area south of Yucatán, followed by a militaristic imperial phase (identified with the Aztecs) that was centered in the Valley of Mexico. There is less certainty about the history of the Peruvian civilization, but it appears also to have had its classical phase, followed by an imperial phase under the rule of those potentates, the Incas, who had their capital in the Andean city of Cusco.

Because our primary concern is with the general development of civilization on earth, after millions of years of human evolution, of the evolution of mind, we need do no more than glance at these two civilizations, for they are marginal to the general development. The history of both was cut off by conquest from overseas; both were superseded in the New World by the civilization of the Old World that had conquered them. They had extraordinary features, however, which one would like to memorialize for their own sake, and it may be permissible merely to mention in passing what some of these were.

*

Item. Unlike the four Old World civilizations, the Mayan-Aztec did not originate in a river-valley where the distribution of water had to be artificially controlled to provide drainage and irrigation. Instead, it originated in tropical rain forest where ample water was found in deep wells formed by openings in the limestone substructure. (The Peruvian civilization, by contrast, may have originated at the mouths of rivers that flow from the Andes to the Pacific, moving constantly upstream because competition for the scarce supply of water impelled communities to migrate to points above their neighbors — until it had become an Andean civilization.)

Item. The birth of the Mayan-Aztec civilization cannot be identified with the organization of life in cities, in the sense that such identification may be made for the birth of the Old World civilizations; for the so-called cities of the Maya were centers of religious ceremonial rather than places of habitation, the people living, rather, in small settlements scattered about the surrounding countryside.

Item. The Peruvian civilization, unlike the Mayan-Aztec or the four civilizations of the Old World, did not depend on the invention of writing. Although records had to be kept, they were kept by an extraordinary makeshift in the absence of any written language at all. They took the form of bundles of colored strings with knots tied in them, the information contained by each being held in the mind of an official "rememberer" who, consequently, could report what it was for each of the bundles in his charge. One wonders why the ingenuity that produced such a system did not produce at least a primitive form of pictographic writing and of written numerals.

Item. The usefulness of the wheel in all the Old World civilizations, from the beginning, has been such that one must also wonder why it was never realized in the New World. It could not be said to have been unknown, because among the Mayan-Aztec peoples it was used on children's toys.

Item. On the other hand, the astronomy and mathematics of the Mayan-Aztec civilization was such as to produce a calendar more accurate than that of the Mesopotamian or any other Old World civilization, and made possible the accurate prediction of eclipses (which must have strengthened the authority of the priests who engaged in it). The written language that allowed of such mathematical calculations and records as were required by Mayan-Aztec astronomy was never developed, however, to the point where it would have made a written literature possible.

Item. Although the Incaic peoples were without writing or the wheel, they constructed, in addition to remarkable roads and bridges (including suspension bridges high above gorges), walls of cyclopean masonry that required them to move and put into place stones thirty tons in weight, and they cut the stones with the greatest accuracy. This, as a *tour de force,* exceeds the construction of the Egyptian pyramids.

Item. One may confidently say that the Maya were second to none of the six original civilizations in artistic production. At their ceremonial centers in the rain forest they erected steep pyramids topped by temples that were, in turn, crowned by high sculptured roofcombs. They also erected palaces with colonnades and towers.* The best stone sculpture of the Maya, whether bas-relief or in the round, certainly equals and, to my mind, exceeds anything produced in the Old World before the days of classical Greece. I need cite only the head of a maize god from Copán in the Fogg Museum of Harvard, which in its inwardness has almost a philosophical quality, epitomizing mind in its reflective aspect. I conclude by simply mentioning the ceramic statuettes of the Maya and the Peruvians alike, sometimes in the form of jugs, that represent simple human beings engaged in banal activities. We see ourselves in them, as we see ourselves in an Egyptian leading his cow to pasture.

*

We may close this account of the first six civilizations by noting that the coming of civilization had been prepared for thousands or millions of years beforehand — but, when it came, it came like a flower opening overnight, or like so many flowers opening overnight the world around.

* Many of the sites — such as Tikál, Uaxactún, Yaxchilán, and Piedras Negras —were, at least until recent years, inaccessible except if one mounted an expedition (as I once did) to visit them by muleback or dugout canoe. I have described the ruins at these and other sites in my *River of Ruins* (New York, 1941) and in my *Transcaribbean* (New York, 1936).

XIX

Civilization in the Aegean

THE SLOW EMERGENCE, development, and expansion of life on earth
has led to the recent emergence of mind, which, in our present, has
been leading to the sudden emergence of civilization. In the distant
view we are taking of the emergence of civilization, as if from another planet, we shall from here on be concerned only with two
main lines of development, one in what we call the West, the other
in the Far East. At the point we have reached in this account, the
first four Old World civilizations have run their course and now constitute, if only in their remains, a foundation on which the new ones
will arise.

We have seen how civilization began in Mesopotamia and in the
Nile Valley about 3000 B.C. By 2000 B.C. it had become more or less
continuous in the lands around the eastern end of the Mediterranean,
from Egypt to the eastern shore of the Aegean Sea. Now it would
spread to the islands of the Aegean and the Balkan peninsula, where
it would take the form of the rise of the Graeco-Roman civilization.

The Aegean Sea, lying between Asia Minor and the Balkan peninsula, is bounded on the south by the long horizontal island of Crete.
The first blossoming of what we properly regard as a new civilization
took place on this island, beginning about 2000 B.C. In our nomenclature we make this Cretan beginning a distinct civilization in itself,
calling it the Minoan civilization; and indeed its remains are distinctive. It was soon to become associated and even identified, however,
with the slightly later development of the so-called Mycenaean civilization on the Greek mainland, the civilization that is most familiar to
us as the Achaean civilization celebrated by Homer in *The Iliad* and
The Odyssey. This Mycenaean or Achaean or Homeric civilization
may, in turn, be thought of as representing the first age of the
Graeco-Roman civilization, equivalent to the feudal age of our own
civilization that was followed by the Renaissance and modern times.*

* The reader will appreciate that there is nothing scientific about the taxonomy of civilizations. The same confusion prevails here as in the traditional taxonomy of races,

During the third and second millennia B.C. there were great movements of peoples throughout the area west of the Caspian, and the result may have been the occupation of Crete by refugees from the Biblical lands to the east. Or perhaps the successive invasions of the Balkan peninsula from the north, which were to be such a decisive feature of the second millennium B.C., had already begun, driving refugees south to Crete, by 2000 B.C.

The advantages of Crete as a land of refuge were notable. A fertile island some 260 kilometers long, it provided military security for its inhabitants to the extent that they developed the maritime power necessary to dominate the surrounding seas. Because the Minoans did develop such power, their cities, unlike those of mainland Greece, could remain unwalled and unfortified, their land could escape the ravages of war, and they did not need to be constantly organized for military defence. This meant that they could concentrate their resources and their skills on the enjoyments of life; and, indeed, their art represents a relaxation and gaiety that provide a contrast to such grim preoccupations as are represented in, for example, the Assyrian bas-reliefs.

The necessity of cultivating the skills required to venture out upon the seas led to the development of a flourishing maritime commerce, with its economic benefits and, above all, its gift of such cosmopolitanism, acquired by contact with a variety of peoples, as stimulates cultural development. Crete was the first maritime civilization, anticipating Athens, Carthage, and ultimately Great Britain.

We don't know what language the people of Crete spoke at the time that Minoan civilization was beginning to develop. Either they had imported or they had invented for themselves a pictographic script that was to develop into a so-called linear script in which the individual symbols stood for syllables of the spoken language. The script called Linear B, associated with the height of their civilization in the middle of the second millennium B.C., is found as well in the Mycenaean remains on mainland Greece, and its decipherment has proved, to the satisfaction of most scholars, that the language for which it was used was an early form of Greek. It is this, chiefly, that has resulted in our association of the Minoan with the Mycenaean civilization as the beginning or forerunner of the classic Greek civilization.

---

which has for centuries allowed us to talk about the Caucasian, Mongolian, and Negro "races" into which the human "race" is divided, and to divide the Caucasian "race," for example, into "races" called Jewish or Nordic or Alpine. Such imprecision, however, is preferable to any alternative pretence to be more precise in one's account of reality than the reality is known to be in itself.

The association of the Minoan culture with Greek civilization is also supported by the Greek legend of Theseus and the Minotaur. According to it, Minos, King of Crete, required of Athens an annual tribute of seven youths and seven maidens whom he fed to a monster called the Minotaur, which was kept imprisoned at the center of a labyrinth. Theseus, son of the Athenian king, having enlisted as one of the seven youths, put an end to this situation with the help of Ariadne, daughter of Minos, by finding his way to the center of the labyrinth, slaying the monster, and then finding his way out again by following a thread that Ariadne had given him to unfold as he went in. We may plausibly suppose that this tale represents a time when cities of the Greek mainland were tributary to a Minoan ruler at Knossos, the Cretan capital. The elaborate plan of the Minoan palace at Knossos, known to us from its present ruins, suggests a basis for the conception of the labyrinth wherein the Minotaur was kept. With perhaps as many as a thousand rooms, with communications through any number of corridors and courts, it was a city in itself, and one in which a stranger might easily get lost.

Minoan civilization arose about 2000 B.C., represented by palaces at Knossos and other sites. The palaces and much of the civilization associated with them were destroyed about 1700 B.C. by a cataclysm of some sort; but larger palaces, now visible in their partially restored ruins, were then built to replace the old ones and the entire civilization, reborn, reached its apogee in the succeeding period. Then another disaster, perhaps an orgy of vandalism by conquering invaders, wrecked it again about 1450 B.C., leaving the ruins known today.

The palace of Knossos was elegant rather than designed to overpower by the immensity of the elements that entered into its construction. Ceilings were not high, chambers were not large, and columns were small. Flowing water was supplied to it by aqueducts and circulated by a system of drains that serviced toilets and carried off the sewage. The columns were all of wood, tapering from top to bottom, with large capitals shaped like cushions. Wood was also combined with cut stone in the construction, providing a binding useful in case of earthquake. Good taste is evident throughout.

The elegance of the civilization is even better represented by the frescoes and the statuettes in pottery or ivory, which show exceedingly slender, wasp-waisted boys and girls, often engaged in dancing or in acrobatics indistinguishable from dancing, refined in their features, in their hairdressing, and in the fashions of their clothes. The artists were concerned with movement, not only in depicting people but also in representing bulls, goats, boars, dogs, or dolphins. The movement they showed has always the quality of music, so that one can almost hear its sound as an accompaniment to the visual scene. (It is typical that the carving on a steatite vase, representing a company of harvesters evidently marching to the harvest, their tools over their shoulders, shows their mouths open in song — but the actual music, like that suggested on Keats's Grecian Urn, must remain forever unheard.) Moreover, the moving bodies, whether of people or animals, seem to be levitated, as if they were progressing through slowly flowing water that made them weightless. The Minoans were the first to represent running animals with all four feet off the ground.

*

The period of dominant Minoan influence was followed by one of dominant Mycenaean influence, the term Mycenaean here denoting the rougher and more warlike people of the mainland, who were represented by Homer in his account of how they besieged Troy and suffered a variety of disasters in the aftermath of their success.* Homer's Agamemnon had his seat at the military citadel of Mycenae, in the northeast corner of the Peloponnesus, where one may still admire its ruins, as Homer's Nestor had his seat at the military citadel of "sandy Pylos," on the western coast of the Peloponnesus, and as Homer's Odysseus had his seat and citadel on an offshore island that bore the name of the present Ithaca. These half-savage warlords, leaders of primitive tribal communities, living largely by military adventurism and pillage, gradually came together in such relations of mutual obligation as characterize any feudal system. We know them first in the legendary account of what was, nevertheless, an historical episode, the siege of Troy at the northeast corner of the Aegean, under the leadership of Agamemnon, perhaps a couple of centuries after the fall of the overly refined Cretan civilization, for which their ancestors may have been responsible.

---

* Thucydides, the first truly sophisticated historian, and since unsurpassed in his sophistication, wrote: "Before the Trojan war there is no indication of any common action in Greece, nor indeed of the name being given to the country as a whole; it went by the names of the different tribes. The best proof of this is furnished by Homer. Born long after the Trojan war, he nowhere calls all the Greeks by that name: in his poems they are called Danaans, Argives, and Achaeans. He does not even use the term 'barbarian,' probably because the Greeks had not yet been marked off from the rest of the world by one distinctive appellation. It appears therefore that the several Greek communities, comprising not only those who first acquired the name, city by city, as they came to understand each other, but also those who assumed it afterwards as the name of the whole people, were before the Trojan war prevented by their want of strength and the absence of mutual intercourse from collective action. Indeed, they could not unite for this expedition till they had gained increased familiarity with the sea" (*The History of the Peloponnesian War*, trans. by R. W. Livingstone, London, 1943, pp. 34-35).

We first hear of these so-called Mycenaeans (Danaans, Argives, or Achaeans) as savage warriors. However, like the Turkic barbarians who came into contact with Chinese civilization, they appear to have acquired from the Minoans the rudiments of a common culture, which would burgeon over the centuries to become the classical civilization that would reach its height in the Periclean Athens to which Thucydides belonged, and which would in time give the Roman barbarians the basis of such culture as they, in their turn, would acquire.

*

During the second millennium B.C. various tribes, coming down from the north, entered the Balkan peninsula, attempting to settle here or there, being displaced in conflict with one another. They were in some measure culturally diverse, Achaeans, Arcadians, Aeolians, and Ionians having their respective distinctions and, as Thucydides pointed out, not yet constituting one Greek or Hellenic people.* The last of the invading tribes, the Dorians, arriving about 1100 B.C., caused the Achaeans (in the generations of those who came after Agamemnon, Menelaus, Nestor, Achilles, Odysseus, *et alia*) to flee to the northwest, the Ionians and Aeolians to scatter over the islands of the Aegean and the coast of Asia Minor.

Allowing for all the elements of fiction, and for the fact that it was set down in writing by a poet of later times, Homer's *Odyssey* still gives us a vivid picture of what we may call Mycenaean or, more broadly, Achaean civilization. It was divided into scattered small societies, each under a warrior chieftain who (e.g. Odysseus) lived with his family and retainers in a crude palace, perhaps with dirt floors, or in a fortified stone castle. (We may still visit the small but massive castle of Agamemnon at Mycenae, with its cyclopean masonry and the sculptured lions over its entrance gate.) A chieftain like Odysseus might plow his own land, or himself engage in the physical labor of constructing his palace. The basic wealth of the people (as in the case of Job in the Old Testament) was in cattle, sheep, pigs, etc. What is striking in the account given by Homer, however, is the importance that primitive warrior peoples, living in such crude circumstances, attached to the amenities of life and skilled craftsmanship. Feasting, as is understandable, was important. Grapes were cultivated for the production of wine to be drunk at the feasts. Even more important, however, were the wrought stone bowls for mixing the wine, the gold or silver goblets, the

* See footnote on the preceding page. When they did become all one people they called themselves Hellenes. Our term "Greek" is derived from the Latin appellation later used by the Romans.

bronze tripods. Illiterate as these people must have been, for the most part, poetry was cultivated among them, being chanted at feasts, to the accompaniment of the lyre, by minstrels such as the blind Demodocus of *The Odyssey*, who had got by heart the dramatic poetry into which the story of the siege of Troy and the homecoming of the heroes had been cast. I myself find it tempting to believe that the description of the insular Phaeacians, masters of seacraft, contains at least the remembrance of a memory of the peaceable, wealthy, and excessively refined Minoans, also masters of seacraft. There is something of a social gap between the rough Achaeans and the ancient aristocracy of the Phaeacians, who keep a certain distance from ordinary mortals and are closer to the gods. So the parvenu Mycenaeans must have thought of the Minoans.

A cultural burgeoning took place at Mycenae and other mainland sites in the period immediately after the catastrophic destruction in Crete, which we date about 1450 B.C. Some of the treasures of metalwork and jewelry found in the Mycenaean tombs are, if not entirely Minoan in style, variations of Minoan. This is exemplified by the two gold cups from Vafio (near Menelaus's Sparta), now in the National Museum at Athens, that show in relief lively scenes of men trying to capture and tie down vigorously resisting bulls, surely among the greatest works of small-scale art in the brief history of our kind. Such works suggest that we should be referring to a Minoan-Mycenaean civilization, or an Aegean civilization, rather than merely to a Minoan civilization that represented the period from its early growth to full development in Crete.

We may think of the Aegean civilization as beginning in Crete c. 2000 B.C. and continuing to be centered there until the catastrophe of c. 1450 B.C., which is followed by the period of Achaean ascendency later memorialized by Homer. The siege of Troy probably took place between 1300 and 1200 B.C. About 1100 B.C. the Greek-speaking Dorians came down from the north, scattered the Greek-speaking Achaeans, Arcadians, Aeolians, and Ionians who had preceded them, and established themselves in the Peloponnesus. The disturbance they created must have caused a break in cultural development, so that the years from the beginning of the eleventh to the eighth century B.C. (probably the century in which the Homeric epics were written down) are years of which little knowledge is available to us. Then the classical Greek civilization began to arise with the creation of city-states and the emergence of the notion that there was one Greek nation surrounded by foreigners.

XX

The Rise of Greece

And the Lord said, Behold, the people is
one, and they have all one language; . . .
and now nothing will be restrained from
them, which they have imagined to do.

— *Genesis, 11:6*

IF ONE PLACES ONESELF in imagination upon the pinnacle of Greek
achievement — represented by the polity of Pericles, the Parthenon,
the historical work of Thucydides, the drama of Euripides, and the
philosophy of Plato — then the prospect ahead is not heartening inasmuch as there is no way forward that is not down. If, however,
one places oneself in the Greece of Homer, when the nation is
beginning to realize itself in its own conception, then the prospect of
an upward way is clear ahead.

The primitive Greeks of the mainland, having the example of
what the Minoans had achieved, knew that there was something better than the savage anarchy in which they lived their own lives. (So
it would also be in the days of Charlemagne, when the remembered
example would be a semi-mythical Rome.) The Greece of Homer's
day, still without a name, was constituted by little more than the occasional fortified citadels of warrior chieftains, each with his retainers and a small supporting population that worked the soil and
kept the herds. There were tribal differences among them, and in
any case even such a tenuous and imperfect unity as a few chieftains
might manage to maintain among themselves for ten years in order
to lay a common siege to Troy, as described by Homer, must have
been exceptional. (After all, the theme of *The Iliad* is the disunity of
the Greeks.) There was hardly enough security to make it worthwhile for the Achaeans and the others to invest heavily in the future,
as the Athenians were to do under Pericles when he directed the reconstruction of Athens after the Persians had so largely destroyed it.

Two things happened after the Dorian invasions of c. 1100 B.C. One was the dispersal of Greek-speaking peoples over the whole inland ocean from the Straits of Gibraltar to the eastern end of the Black Sea, making the peninsula of Greece the center of a maritime empire, economic and cultural, albeit not political. The other was that the various divisions of Greek-speaking peoples, finding themselves having to do with Phoenicians, Egyptians, Philistines, Scythians, and a variety of other peoples whose languages were "barbarian," began to think of themselves as a Greek nation.

*

Out of matter came life, and out of life mind. Civilization, the beginnings of which we have undertaken to describe, is a manifestation of mind.

Going back to Neanderthal man, say 50,000 years ago, we saw how he was moved to fill the vacuum of ignorance by an imagined mythology that told of a life after death.* This, however, was a creation of the poetic imagination only. More specifically, it was part of an official religion, which is to say that a priestly élite presented it to the common mind as knowledge that, having been revealed to it by a supernatural power or powers, was not to be questioned.

There is a distinction between such "revealed knowledge" and the knowledge that is based on a process of reasoning from observation. In the one case, questioning is excluded, while in the other it is the basis of the process by which knowledge is attained. If "revealed knowledge" is the business of priests, the other kind of knowledge is the business of philosophers and scientists.†

Until the Greeks, the vacuum of ignorance had always been filled by one or another of official religions. The beginning of philosophy, identified with the Greeks, marks a notable advance in the evolution of mind. It is worth asking, therefore, how it came about.

When a society lives in isolation, knowing only its own culture, it hardly has occasion to question the tenets of that culture — represented, let us say, by its one revealed religion. The case is otherwise where a multitude of different societies, with different cultures and different beliefs, jostle one another. Where Jews live alongside of Christians in friendly intercourse, it must occur to the occasional Jew that if he had been born into the family of his Christian neighbor, he would believe in the redemption of mankind by

* Part Three, Chapter IX above.
† One misses, here, the old usage of the term "natural philosophy," which embraced alike what we now distinguish, respectively, as philosophy and science. Thales of Miletus, Ptolemy, Copernicus, Galileo, Newton, and Einstein were all, in the old usage, philosophers, practicing natural philosophy.

Jesus; and it must occur to the occasional Christian that if he had been born into the family of his Jewish neighbor, he would not believe in the redemption. It might then occur to either of them that where belief depends on the accident of birth, it may be questioned.

Increasingly, after 1000 B.C., the Mediterranean was one cosmopolitan market-place in which Greeks were trading with Egyptians, Israelites, Phoenicians, Philistines, Hittites — and how many others? Already they had got some of the elements of their religious mythology from Persia, the Middle East, and other centers of early culture. Moreover, in their expansion across the length of the inland sea, by the establishment of colonies from the Caucasus to the Iberian coast, the integrity of their own inherited religious beliefs must have been impaired: the Greeks in Colchis (at the eastern end of the Black Sea) would have given prime importance to some deities, those in Massilia (at the mouth of the Rhône) to others. If we regard Greek civilization as including the Minoan, then it was the world's first maritime civilization, and maritime civilizations are cosmopolitan as land-locked civilizations are not.*

The increasingly wide and varied world of the Greeks who lived from 1000 to 500 B.C., then, tended to liberate them from intellectual bondage to any priesthood or body of religious dogma, freeing them for indulgence in intellectual speculation.

Merely to have the freedom to speculate, however, is not in itself an incentive to speculation. That incentive, I suggest, is in the mind's need to bring out of chaos the order on which it depends for its sanity. Any such order depends on the possibility of assembling in one coherent structure the separate particulars of experience. It depends, to revert to our metaphor, on the possibility of assembling the letters that have meaning only in the context of a word, the words that have meaning only in the context of a sentence, and so on.

*

The first philosopher on record was Thales of Miletus, who lived from c. 640 to 546 B.C. on the Aegean coast of Asia Minor. He was a natural philosopher in the old sense of the term, which is to say that he was concerned with the nature of physical being, rather than with ethics or social and political propriety as Gautama Buddha and Mahavira in India, as Confucius in China, would be a few years later. It is the tradition of physical science, down

* The Phoenicians, who were as widely dispersed a nation, never enjoyed independence and a national power structure long enough to found a distinct civilization of their own.

to Niels Bohr and Werner Heisenberg in our own day, that stems from him.

Thales, looking about him, experienced a diversity of unrelated particulars out of which physical being appeared to be composed. Earth was one thing, wood another, flesh still another. Just as physicists of the twentieth century have been concerned to discover one elementary particle out of which all matter is composed, so Thales was concerned to reduce all matter to one substance, and that substance, he thought, must be water.

Again, he was confronted with the sharp distinction, in experience, between what is non-living and what is living. Reflecting on this, he came to the conclusion that this distinction was one of appearance only, that in reality all matter is invested with the attribute of life.*

What we should note is that, if natural philosophy begins with Thales, it begins as monism, the doctrine that, behind the diversity of all being, there is unity. In his attempt to resolve the superficial chaos of experience the philosopher seeks to discover the one in the many.

A pupil of Thales, Anaximander, postulated an indefinite substance filling space, which temporarily takes the various forms of physical being we know — e.g., fire, water, earth. This is not essentially different from our own view that all the varieties of physical being are but the different forms in which matter-energy manifests itself.

To Heraclitus of Ephesus, who was born in 530 B.C., all the varieties of matter were forms provisionally taken by fire, which was the one eternal substance. He was impressed by the observation that everything is constantly changing, so that one cannot step into the same river twice. He was also impressed by the observation that everything exists in terms of contraries: life and death, good and evil, heat and cold are what they are relative to each other, so that opposites are, in fact, one and inseparable. There is a rightness about the whole of being (what the author of the Fourth Gospel would call the Logos) that is not to be found in its parts.

*

Of the founders of philosophy before Socrates I shall here mention only one more. Before coming to Pythagoras, however, I call attention to a distinction of which we must take account if we are to avoid confusion. I have said that philosophy begins with Thales of Miletus, and I have said that his entire concern was with the nature of

* See p. 107 above, where we at least approach the same conclusion.

the physical universe. But the Mesopotamians, more than 2,000 years before Thales, had begun to develop the study of astronomy in connection with the making of calendars. How, then, can one suggest that Thales was the first to concern himself with the nature of the physical universe?

The answer is that there is a world of difference between the observation of natural phenomena merely for the sake of practical application of the knowledge thereby gained, as when one counts the number of days in the year so as to have a basis for organizing agricultural activities, and speculation that aims at understanding for its own sake, representing the need to fill the vacuum of ignorance. This is the distinction that justifies us in calling Thales a philosopher when it would not occur to us to apply the epithet to the Mesopotamians who made a calendar on the basis of their astronomical observations. The Mesopotamian astronomers were concerned with appearances, and it mattered not to them whether the stars were holes in a canopy or spheres in space; but Thales was concerned with the reality behind appearances.

Pythagoras, who lived in the sixth century B.C., may be accounted the founder of mathematics in a sense different from that in which we attributed the foundation of mathematics to the Sumerians who lived some 3,000 years earlier and were concerned only with measurement. The Egyptians, too, had developed geometry thousands of years earlier, but only for the construction of their pyramids. They were engineers who, as such, were not concerned with understanding for its own sake, while he was a philosopher who, as such, had no other concern. He surmised that one way of explaining reality was by measurable relationships, relationships of proportion, that accorded with logically definable natural laws and could be expressed in numerical terms. Every aspect of music, for example, can be described in such terms, for music does obey mathematical laws (as we shall see in Part Five, Chapter IX) and may therefore be regarded as simply one expression of the mathematics that govern and explain the universe. The same may be said for the orbits of the planets and the trajectories of the stars, which also obey mathematical laws. (This associates music with the planets and stars.) As a matter of the natural order, the sum of the angles of any triangle is always half that of the angle swept out by a straight line, pivoting on one end, that makes one complete revolution to return to its original position. The order that stands opposed to chaos is a mathematical order.

*

The significance of this early Greek thought is less in the conclusions it reached than in the process by which it reached them. It is not enough to say that the process was one of reasoning, for reasoning had been practiced since mind began. It was a process that took its departure from an initial scepticism applied to whatever was presented as knowledge handed down from some high authority not to be questioned, and that then proceeded by rational speculation along dialectical lines. Speculation along dialectical lines is the process by which a proposed explanation of observed phenomena is put forward tentatively for a critical examination that leads to a revised explanation that, subjected to critical examination in its turn, is further revised — and so on. This philosophical procedure, first systematically practiced by the Greeks, is what has led, in the intervening twenty-five centuries, to quantum theory, to the Theory of Relativity, and to the replacement by Darwinism of the explanation of the origin of species given in Genesis.

This same process, which the Greeks applied to the investigation of the physical universe, they would in time apply, as well, to the problems of ethics and political philosophy.

The development of their social organization from Mycenaean times onward impelled the Greeks to preoccupy themselves with the question of what constituted justice in the organization of the state. At first, warrior chieftains like Agamemnon, largely by virtue of their ability, were leaders of primitive communities centered on such strongholds as those of Mycenae, Tiryns, Pylos, and Sparta. This represented the feudal system that has generally existed at a certain stage of social development, whereby people enter into the service of a strong man in return for his protection. The position of leadership tends to become hereditary, and where that is established an organized society may properly be called a monarchy. We refer to Odysseus as king of Ithaca, to Menelaus as king of Sparta, to Theseus first as prince and then as king of Athens in succession to his father, Aegeus.

However, as a primitive monarchical community grows, as it achieves military security (thereby lessening its dependence on one warrior chieftain), as economic activity expands and a well-to-do middle class comes into being, and as the amenities of life begin to be cultivated at levels below the summit of the social pyramid, the primitive monarchical system tends to become obsolete. The aristocracy, originally composed of the monarch's relatives, becomes unruly where the king by inheritance is unable to command its respect. The growing middle class, constantly increasing in wealth and sophistication, is no longer willing to practice the subservience of the serf. Eventually, the masses of common people, discovering the potential power of the many against the few, assert their claim to be heard in the government of the state.

The question that constantly arises and constantly takes new forms, in such an evolution of society, is that of justice. The rising middle class comes to feel it unjust that all power should be in the hands of an increasingly useless king or an idle aristocracy. The rising demos comes to regard it as unjust that society should be organized for the exclusive benefit of a privileged few who dispose of economic power.

The question of justice belongs to the domain of ethics, more particularly to the field of political philosophy. It is no wonder, then, that the Greeks began to apply the dialectical process to the question of what constitutes the proper organization of society as well as to the inquiry into the nature of being. What is generally considered to be the greatest of Plato's dialogues, *The Republic*, begins with the question of what constitutes justice, and goes on to speculate about what would constitute the best organization of society.

However, just as, in the development of mathematics and science, the practical problems presented themselves for resolution first, the pursuit of knowledge for its own sake coming later, so it was in the development of political thought. Solon came before Plato.

The evolution of the Athenian state provides the best example. According to legend (which may be taken to represent essential truth), Theseus was the strong man (the warrior chieftain), who won the independence of Athens (from Minos, King of Knossos) and, as a fighter, justified his suzerainty over the Athenians by protecting them from external attack. With increasing security, however, there was less justification for the suzerainty of his successors, with the consequence that the "first families" rose to power, replacing the monarchy by an oligarchy.

With economic expansion through the growth of maritime trade, a class of traders, professional men, craftsmen, and free laborers developed, and made its claim (in the name of justice) to participate in the government of the state. This led to a sort of social war and a corresponding constitutional crisis, which was resolved early in the sixth century by the reforms of Solon. He established equal justice under the law to the extent of making the laws applicable without distinction to all except slaves, to the rulers as well as the ruled, to the rich and poor alike.* One effect of his reforms was to weaken

* The institution of slavery must, by its nature, always represent an exception to equal justice under the law, since those who are private property do not, *ipso facto*, have the same legal standing as those who are free. Solon claimed to have given the Athenians, not the best laws but, rather, the best they were capable of receiving.

the oligarchy and to promote plutocracy in its place by diminishing the importance of birth relative to wealth. We may regard this as the rise of the middle class.

The reforms of Solon, although just and necessary, were de-stabilizing. They replaced what had the authority of tradition with what was more reasonable but lacked that authority.* Consequently, in Athens and in other Greek cities that underwent like reforms, there followed a period of tyrannies, so-called, in which individual dictators, represented by Pisistratus in Athens, used conspiratorial and demagogic means to necessary ends, imposing their own con-trived authority upon the simple and the ignorant, buying the sup-port of others by concessions to their interests. Pisistratus advanced the process of reform begun under Solon by distributing land to the poor. He stimulated the cultural life that was to bring Athens a unique renown. All in all, it would be hard either to approve or regret his dictatorship.†

The process of reform, entailing the ever increasing democratiza-tion of Athens, continued after Pisistratus to reach an optimum, if not a culmination, under Pericles (490–429 B.C.) a century later. The basic governing body, now, was the Assembly, consisting of all the citizens (i.e., some 43,000 free men of Athenian nationality in a much larger population including all women, those workers who were not free, and the resident aliens). Solon is reported to have told the Athenians: "Each of you individually treads like a fox, but collectively you are geese." The successors of Pericles would dis-cover how responsive such a mob was to the meretricious appeals of demagogy, and Plato has given an example in *The Apology,* his ac-count of the condemnation of Socrates by the Athenian Assembly. The final judgement of this decline into mass democracy was given by Thucydides, who in his *History of the Peloponnesian War* reported how the vulnerability of the many to the wiles of demagogues, each having as his first concern the achievement of personal power through popularity, produced disastrous errors of policy and the consequent ruin of Athens.

Successful civilizations may tend to an increasing egalitarianism, which represents a valid ideal of justice in itself, but, beyond a cer-

---

* There is a sense in which all political reforms are bound to fail in the end, because there are no good ways to govern a state, only some that are less evil than others; and in circumstances like this the authority of reason would not be enough, unless we were all Solons. Political reform is always necessary but, in its measure, always de-stabilizing.

† One who has seen politics close up may be allowed to observe that they are always a matter of necessary evil, which at best is directed to good ends and kept within the limits of the necessary.

tain point, becomes unworkable, if only for the reason that Solon stated so bluntly. The Graeco-Roman civilization would not again rise to the level of achievement represented by Athens at the time of its fall.

XXI

The Greek Contribution

THROUGHOUT THESE PAGES we have described or assumed a constant evolution from lower to higher by criteria that we all accept. Birds and mammals represent a higher form of life than bacteria; the first men represented an advance over the first primates; modern man is an improvement on Neanderthal man; the civilization of the Greeks in the fifth century B.C. was more developed than the civilization of the Sumerians 3,000 years earlier.

However, as we have advanced in our account of life on earth we have been dealing with progressively shorter periods of time, thereby progressively narrowing our perspective, coming closer up to our material. When we examined the development of eukaryotic cells out of their prokaryotic forerunners we did so in terms of thousands of millions of years. By the time we had come to the emergence of the man-apes we had already reduced our perspective to a few million years. With the appearance of man, we began to count in hundreds of thousands of years, and with the beginning of civilization we have been measuring time in mere centuries. Now, at last, we have arrived at such a close-up view that we find ourselves referring to particular years — e.g., 490 B.C. as the year in which Pericles was born.

What confronts us here is the normal illusion of perspective, but applied to time rather than space. What is distant seems less than what is near. Out of my window, as I write, I see a mountain thirty kilometers away, but only in its mass, without detail; while on a mere bush ten meters away, which fills my field of vision as fully as the mountain, I see the individual leaves. A century lasted as long, and may have been as crowded with events, a thousand million years ago as today; but at its distance from our present it is too short a time to be distinguished at all, while the century in which we live lasts longer than we do and is full of events that are conspicuous.

Even though the evolution of life has been accelerating since the beginning, so that changes of such magnitude that they once required hundreds of millions of years may now occur in decades, we have constantly to remind ourselves that we are now dealing in periods of time that may be too short to show the progress of evolution. As yet, civilization is only some five or six thousand years old. We can already see a definite progress from the civilization of Sumeria in 3500 B.C. to that of Greece in 500 B.C., but it is not in every respect that we can see a progress from that of Greece in 500 B.C. to our own civilization in A.D. 2000. Science has certainly made progress in these 2,500 years, but we may plausibly doubt that there has been any progress at all in, say, sculpture, that any sculpture produced since the time of the ancient Greeks is better than the best of theirs. Even with the acceleration of evolution, it may be that anything less than a million years of civilization affords too limited a perspective.

*

Some of the activities of mind tend to be progressive because the moving present is able to build on what the past has already achieved, starting always from the highest point already reached. This is particularly true of the natural sciences, which we may think of as having begun with Thales. As long as the knowledge accumulated in the two and a half millennia since he lived is not lost (by some equivalent of the Chinese Burning of the Books), we shall know, as the people of his time could not, that the basis of all matter is not water but something more fundamental, at the subatomic level. We shall know, as he did not, that the earth is a sphere orbiting the sun, which is but one star among innumerable others scattered across distances of which he had no conception.

As much cannot be said for the arts, where the level of achievement is not subject to such testing as is applicable to natural science. No one can say of sculpture as of science that, building on the ever accumulating achievement of the past, it tends to continue upward to constantly higher levels of achievement. The sculpture on the cathedral of Chartres is different from that on the Parthenon of seventeen centuries earlier, but not to be compared with it as better or worse (although one can say with confidence that the standing male nudes of the Greek sculptors who lived in the sixth century B.C. are not as good as those of the Greeks who lived in the fifth century B.C., since here we are dealing with one continuous tradition).

What, then, shall we say of philosophy, particularly of such philosophy (i.e., metaphysics) as is concerned with what is presumed to be the basic logic of being — represented by Pythagoras, Plato,

Descartes, Kant, and Hegel? * Is it progressive like science, or, like the arts, not necessarily so?

Such philosophy is not unrelated to the discoveries of natural science, although it goes beyond them. Since Einstein, for example, a philosopher can no longer base it on such untroubled confidence as Descartes had in the three-dimensional universe of our common sense; and, since Darwin, he can no longer base it on the assumption that each species of life is the product of special creation. It is clear that, while metaphysics may have made no notable advance since Plato, its nature is such as to allow it, nevertheless, to progress on the basis of what has gone before. (In any field of the mind's activity there are periods of sterility or even of retrogression, and this might be true of the period from the fourth century B.C. to our present, a period that will seem brief in the perspective of, say, 50,000 years.)

I observed in the last chapter that one of the distinctions of Greek thought was the speculative and dialectical process by which it reached its conclusions. This process is associated with the philosophical activity of Socrates (c. 470–399 B.C.) as reported by his disciple Plato (c. 427–347 B.C.), and since our only consequential knowledge of Socrates as a philosopher is as the chief exponent, in Plato's writings, of the thinking with which Plato associates himself, the thinking of the one may be regarded as that of the other and, for the most part, identified as Platonic.

No one speculates about questions to which he believes he already has the answer. Consequently, the awareness of one's own ignorance is a condition precedent of speculation. Such an awareness was fundamental to the mind of Socrates. When told that the Delphic oracle had said he was the wisest, which is to say the most knowledgeable man alive, he could account for this only by supposing that the oracle had singled him out, not for any erudition, but as the only man who knew his own ignorance. The measure of the intellectual sophistication that this knowledge of his own ignorance represented is suggested by the fact that the other professors in the Greece of his time (the so-called Sophists), and most of those since his time, have been in the habit of expressing themselves as pundits who, having already achieved knowledge, communicate it to the ignorant or the unenlightened.

In Plato's *Republic*, Socrates compares the condition of men to that of a company inhabiting a cavern, with their backs to the source of light and their eyes immovably fixed on the opposite wall that re-

---

* These names all belong to civilizations of the West because in other civilizations there has been no philosophy in the sense referred to here. The same may be said of natural science from Thales and Aristotle to Einstein and Darwin.

flects it. Various figures, constituting reality, move unseen against the light behind their backs, casting shadows on the wall before them. In their ignorance of their own ignorance, the men in the cave take the shadows for the reality.

This allegory of the cave, which is carried further than I have here reported, represents, like the knowledge of one's own ignorance, a philosophical sophistication not to be found before the classical civilization of Greece, and perhaps not again until, in the Europe of the eighteenth century, Hume and Kant represented it. In Plato one has something of Kant's sophistication twenty-three centuries earlier.

The knowledge of our universal human ignorance represents a liberation from the putative knowledge which men have always accepted at the hands of a pretended authority. It sets men free to exercise their faculty of reason speculatively, to follow wherever the argument leads. The actual reasoning practiced by Socrates on this principle, as reported in Plato's dialogues, is often undistinguished and, to a later age that looks back on it, faulty. Mankind has since progressed in its practice, if only by having learned the distinction, unknown to Socrates, between what is real and categories that are nominal. The achievement of the Greeks, however, chiefly identified with Plato, is in their adoption of the process of reasoning, freely exercised, in place of presumed higher authority as the way to an ever greater understanding.

The name of Plato, in addition to being associated with the inauguration of a new attitude and a new method in the history of mind, is associated with the vision of a duality in which ideas or mental images are distinguished from their counterparts in the world of material reality, the former having a perfection that is necessarily lacking in the latter.

To take the simplest possible example, let us say that I have in my mind the idea of a straight line, defined as extension in only one dimension and, therefore, in only one direction. If I undertake to represent this idea in the world of material reality, with pencil on paper, my rendition is bound to be imperfect, for my pencil-line, however thin, will have width (i.e., a second dimension) as well as length, and a careful examination would show at least slight waverings in its straightness that constitute changes in direction.

Note that, while there is only one idea of a straight line, there may be any number of representations in the material world, all more or less imperfect. Note also that the idea is primary and its representations secondary, since the latter are attempted renditions of the former.

This Platonic duality is the basis of what I have, in these pages, called normative thinking. The idea of the straight line is a normative idea that I may try, with greater or less success, to realize in the world of tangible reality.

I can explain all the products of human creativity by this duality. When Praxiteles carved his Hermes, he had in his mind a normative idea of the human body that he was undertaking to realize and to fix in stone. When Solon formulated a constitution for Athens, he had in his mind a normative idea of the state, the realization of which he sought to achieve, albeit within the limits of what, in his judgement, the Athenians of his day were capable of realizing.

Plato, through the mouth of Socrates in his dialogues, carried this so-called theory of ideas further than I have in my presentation of it here; but we can recognize its validity within the limited terms of my presentation without going beyond those terms as he did. I have applied it here only to the human act of creation, exemplified by Praxiteles and Solon. But Plato held that all of material nature, as it would exist even if there were no men, consists only of imperfect copies of an aggregation of perfect ideas that constitute basic reality, as the shadows on the wall of the cave are imperfect copies of realities that themselves remain unseen. Moreover, he also applied the theory to categories that most of us, today, would consider nominal rather than real — such categories as that of the good, the beautiful, etc. Socrates held that there was an idea of the good, or an idea of the beautiful, that existed independently of the human mind as one of the building blocks, so to speak, of Creation itself. We are free to disregard this, however, while still accepting the basic duality, in human experience, between normative ideas and their material representations or enactments.

*

Plato's philosophy explains Greek art, for his theory of ideas, which represents the basic outlook of the civilization to which he belonged, was expressed in works of art no less than in his own writings. I have already given the example of Praxiteles, who was representing an ideal of man (a normative idea) in stone, attempting to make the invisible visible. This is an entirely different kind of undertaking from that of portraiture, where the purpose is not to represent the idea of man, or even a type, but, rather, one individual in his unique individuality. There have come down to us, if only in Roman copies made later, a portrait in stone of the Athenian statesman Themistocles and another of Plato himself that clearly belong to a basically different kind of sculpture from that of the Hermes or of the Aphrodite of Melos in the Louvre (better known as the Venus de

Milo). But the great works of sculpture, if they bear names at all, bear the names of gods rather than mortals, and no one supposes that the gods sat for them. The Aphrodite of Melos is not a particular individual, the bodily imperfections of which an honest portraitist would have felt obliged to represent, but a normative idea of woman. By contrast, the sculptor who carved a portrait head of Socrates faithfully represented his physical ugliness — the bulbous head with a flat face and an excessively flattened nose. Its value to us is merely in its satisfaction of our curiosity about what Socrates looked like, or what a particular Greek of his time might have looked like. But the Hermes and the Aphrodite, being representations of ideas, are expressions of philosophy in stone.

The same may be said of a Greek temple like the Parthenon. Is this not a representation in stone of an idea or complex of ideas identified with the Pythagorean view of a harmony that arises out of numerical relationships? There is a rhythmic harmony in the Parthenon that justifies one in regarding it as music made visible.*

The same may be said of the Parthenon frieze, a continuous strip of bas-relief, about a meter wide, that runs around the outside walls of the Parthenon, within its colonnade. It represents a procession of men on horseback, of chariots with their charioteers, of youths and girls bearing offerings, of elders, and of cattle being led to the sacrifice — all converging on the group of gods whom the occasion is honoring. If only because it represents human beings and animals moving forward together, it may be compared with such works as the Sumerian frieze around the temple of Al 'Ubaid and the Egyptian bas-relief at Sakkara.† However, while these represented earthly scenes in a way that we find moving, the Parthenon frieze, in addition, lifts us up to the level of divinity. In it, the imperfect evokes the perfect. It is a frozen pageant moving to the rhythm of an unheard music that lacks the imperfection of such music as we might hear.

This frieze is the ultimate accomplishment of its kind, so that, if there is to be sculpture afterwards, it had better be of another kind. It is at once Pythagorean and Platonic.‡

*

Historical writing, whether as an art or a science, begins with the great age of Greece, some 3,000 years after the beginning of civilization and the concurrent invention of writing. The first historian is

* See pp. 576–577 below.
† See p. 355 and p. 372 respectively.
‡ For a fuller account of the frieze, see pp. 577–578 below.

Herodotus of Halicarnassus on the coast of Asia Minor, since he was born some twenty or thirty years before Thucydides of Athens (c. 460–c. 400 B.C.). I venture to offer what can only be a personal opinion, although not without wide acceptance, that the work of Thucydides, his *History of the Peloponnesian War*, has never been surpassed in its kind, just as the Parthenon frieze has never been surpassed in its kind. There has since been historical writing that is different in kind, as the cathedral of Chartres is different from the Parthenon, but none that can be accounted better. Not only did Thucydides adopt the critical approach that was to be developed especially by Western historians of the nineteenth century, he had an insight into human nature, under circumstances of political and social conflict, that has been equaled by no other historian, and that stands comparison with Shakespeare's insights.

The single work that constitutes the entire production of Thucydides, without being any the less a work of historical scholarship on that account, belongs to the domain of dramatic literature as well. Like Shakespeare, he had the tragic view of life, the vision of an essentially noble character doomed to defeat by the operation of inner weaknesses. As it was with Hamlet, Macbeth, and Lear, so it was with Athens.*

Indeed, one might say that the Athens of Thucydides, in addition to being associated with the birth of history, is to be identified with the birth of tragic drama. The *Prometheus Bound* of Aeschylus (525–456 B.C.) remains almost the type specimen of the literature that recounts the tragedy of a noble character doomed to destruction — although here, as in the case of the other Greek dramatists, the evil that brings about the hero's downfall comes from without rather than from within. (It is a paradox that, in respect to this, Thucydides is to be associated rather with Shakespeare than with the Athenian dramatists of his times.)

Fully to appreciate the power of the Athenian drama, one should read the account Thucydides gives of the cold-blooded cruelty with which the Athenians, brutalized by too long and intense an experience of warfare, destroyed the captured and helpless population of Melos — one should read this before reading *The Trojan Women* by Euripides (c. 485–406 B.C.), for the drama of the destruction of the captured and helpless Trojan population by the brutalized Achaeans, presented in the latter, was written immediately after the event chronicled by Thucydides, and was, in fact, a compassionate protest against it.

* For what may be considered as an extrapolation of these comments, see the Appendix of my *Civilization and Foreign Policy*, New York, 1955, entitled "A Message from Thucydides."

The third of the great dramatists of fifth-century Athens was Sophocles (c. 496–406 B.C.), whose accounts of the victimization by circumstances of Oedipus remain among the monuments of dramatic literature. In his *Antigone* he upheld a concept of overriding natural law, with respect to the conduct of human life, that corresponds to the original Chinese conception of the Tao.*

*

The reader will have observed that, implicit in this account, there is a disposition not to take our nominal categories as more than the heuristic conveniences they are. (If it had not been for this disposition, I would not have included Thucydides with the Greek dramatists under the heading of "tragic drama," as well as associating him with Herodotus, whom he resembles less, under the heading of "history.") Ever since the term "natural philosophy" has lapsed, we distinguish the field of "philosophy" categorically from that of "science," including in the latter, and thereby excluding from the former, such thinkers as Kepler, not to mention those successors of Thales and Heraclitus, Newton, Einstein, and Niels Bohr. I have, perhaps, gone too far, in the looseness of my adherence to the established categories, by associating Plato with the Greek sculptors because of their common concern for the relationship between the normative idea and its representations in the sensible world; and it might have been more correct, if not more proper, for me to follow my account of the philosopher Plato by that of his pupil, Aristotle.

Aristotle (384–322 B.C.) was, certainly, a philosopher as Plato was, formulating theories in the fields of metaphysics, logic, ethics, and political philosophy, as well as making contributions to aesthetics that have not since been surpassed. He lacked, however, the single coherent and comprehensive philosophical vision of Plato, and one could, without being dogmatic about it, make the argument that his prime distinction was in the field of science. He was the first notable researcher in the modern scientific sense of the term, the first to engage systematically in empirical investigation (which Einstein, for example, never did). He was a collector and cataloguer of information, whether on the structure of the reproductive organs in mammals or on the various constitutions of states; and as a cataloguer he may be regarded as the father of taxonomy. Where Plato was interested primarily in what he conceived to be the perfect ideas imperfectly represented by the many copies we perceive through our senses, Aristotle was interested primarily in the many copies, regarding the ideas as merely generalizations derived from them. Where

* See p. 393 above.

Plato put the one ahead of the many, Aristotle put the many ahead of the one.

The names I have cited in this chapter represent one of the pinnacles reached in the rise and fall of human civilizations so far. In the centuries that immediately followed, while there would still be distinguished contributions to culture, those contributions were virtually bound to represent a decline from a level of achievement so high.*

---

* The reader cannot be more poignantly aware than I am of how much has been omitted in carrying out my intention of summarizing the whole culture of classical Greece in approximately the number of pages that were given, respectively, to the cultures of Mesopotamia, Egypt, India in its first age, and China through the Han Empire. In Part Five, however, I shall be dealing more fully with Greek literature and art.

XXII

Sic transit . . .

WHAT IS NOTABLE about the first 5,000 years of civilization, from the Sumerians to our present, is its instability, the failure to establish on a basis of permanence any one kind of social and political organization, any form of literary or artistic expression, any normative belief or attitude. The laws that govern the physical universe are changeless; and the evolution of life over three to four thousand million years has shown a consistent progress from less developed to more developed; but the five or six thousand years of civilization have represented the ultimate failure of every attempt to resolve chaos by the establishment of an order conceived in the mind. Every civilization that has succeeded in realizing itself has succeeded only temporarily, teetering for a moment on the summit of its achievement, then falling.

A thesis of this work is that, in the evolution of life on earth, order arises out of chaos, and this is borne out by a record that, as far as our knowledge goes, extends over thousands of millions of years. Even allowing, however, for the ever increasing acceleration of evolution, we must still suppose that 5,000 years is too short a time to serve as a basis for conclusions with respect to the long-term trend of evolution. The curve of a graph, when seen at a distance and as a whole, may appear to show a steady and invariable upward progress; but if a small section of it is looked at through a magnifying glass it may appear wavy, sometimes rising, sometimes declining; and an extremely close-up view of an ascending curve may show it descending only.

No one can doubt that there has been distinct progress, from the Sumerians to our present, in the undertaking of mind to bring order out of chaos by the development and realization of normative conceptions — perhaps because each civilization, basing itself on the ruins of its predecessors, starts from a higher standpoint. But the progress has been uneven, wavering, greater in some fields (e.g., natural science) than in others; and, above all, we cannot say that it has, as yet, established itself securely in any respect.

So the Graeco-Roman civilization, one of the most successful known so far, was a failure like every other. It reached a pinnacle of achievement on which it balanced momentarily before it declined to its fall.

It is tempting but meretricious to attribute the decline of this civilization simply to the wastage of incessant warfare. The pinnacle of achievement is to be identified with Athens in the immediate aftermath of the Persian wars, during which the city had been captured by the Persians and largely destroyed; and, in any case, there was as much warfare in the rise as in the fall of Greece.

Neither can the decline be attributed simply to the internecine strife among the Greek states, for such strife accompanied the rise as well.

The rise of any civilization is marked by developments that, continuing past an optimum, go too far. We have seen how the evolution of democracy in Athens exemplifies this. But so does the evolution of literature and art.

Every art may be regarded as a product of tension between what the artist seeks to express and the means available to him for its expression. This is implicitly acknowledged where the means of expression are, by deliberate intention, arbitrarily limited, as in the case of such a poetic form as the sonnet, limited as it is to fourteen lines of iambic pentameter; for there would be no sense to this if the removal of the restriction would enable the poet to do better.

For example, the ancient Greeks had a normative idea of the male body that their sculptors tried to represent in stone, beginning about the middle of the seventh century B.C. The first so-called *kouroi* (statues of youths) that they produced were awkward in form, stiff in posture, and crude in detail because the sculptors had not yet sufficiently mastered the skills by which the resistance of the stone was overcome. This is to say that their attempts to express the normative idea were limited by an excessive resistance in the means of expression. Over a period of two centuries, however, the skills of the sculptors developed until they were able to carve the stone with a delicacy so great as to create the illusion that it was not stone at all but yielding flesh. The optimum in this changing balance between what the artist is trying to represent and the resistance of the material or the means comes about the middle of the fifth to the middle of the fourth century B.C. After that, however, he finds himself increasingly freed, by the development of his technical skill, from the restraint that is an element in all art. He is therefore impelled, rather than to repeat what has already been accomplished, to go to the limit allowed by his technical mastery, depicting nudes with bulging muscles and swollen veins in contorted attitudes of struggle, the best known example being the Laocoon in the Vatican Museum, which was carved in the second century B.C. It would be hard to dissent from the accepted view that, excellent as it is, what it typifies represents a decline from the *kouroi* and Apollos of the fifth century B.C. The optimum balance between expression and the resistance to it has been passed.

Moreover, there is a sense in which direction is lost with accomplishment, and inspiration with the loss of direction. By the latter part of the seventh century B.C., the basic form of the Greek temple, a normative idea in stone, had become established. However, the relative crudeness of execution in the early examples, which made them inadequate representations of the idea, meant that the idea remained as an inspiration to those who, in successive representations, improved the execution until, in the fifth century, they built the Parthenon, which was perfect of its kind. In such a final realization of the idea, it loses its power to inspire continuing effort, since such effort can no longer improve on the results of earlier efforts. Therefore, when men are again moved by a like inspiration, it will be on the basis of an entirely different normative idea, such as that which inspired, at last, the construction of the great Gothic cathedrals.*

One surmises, albeit with rather more hesitation, that the untroubled belief in a body of religious mythology, which characterizes the youth of a civilization, provides an inspiration that lessens as an increasing sophistication produces an increasing scepticism. In Book II of Plato's *Republic,* Socrates speaks with scorn of the false belief in the traditional gods and goddesses that is imparted to school-children by requiring them to read Homer; and in a wave of conservative reaction, following the Athenian defeat in the Peloponnesian War, Socrates was condemned by the Athenian Assembly for not believing in the gods in whom the state believed, and for corrupting the young by his scepticism. One who is himself a sceptic and who sides with Socrates may, nevertheless, observe that the traditional religion represented, albeit in childish terms, a complex of normative ideas that provided an inspiration and a basis for the de-

---

* I simplify here as, necessarily, throughout. The point might be made that the Parthenon is perfect in expressing the normative idea of the Doric temple, which is not quite the same as the normative idea of the Ionic temple, as represented by the temple of Athena Nike on the Athenian Acropolis. Perhaps one could say that normative ideas may be classified as genera, species, and subspecies. This type of analysis could, however, degenerate into quibbling.

velopment of the Greek civilization. The beauty of Apollo or Aphrodite, the wisdom of Zeus or Athena, constituted models for imitation, not only in stone but in statecraft and in personal conduct.*

Whatever the causes may be, every civilization so far has, in its limited life-history, risen only to decline, its trajectory resembling a parabolic curve. It is as if mankind were repeatedly attempting to attain some heights unattainable as yet, leaping again and again, only to fall again and again.

In the past few chapters we have seen the rise of the Graeco-Roman civilization to its apogee. What remains is to trace, however briefly, its subsequent decline and fall.

*

In the early stages of any civilization the formal organization of society is chiefly local — as when it is organized around individual feudal lords in their strongholds, or around city-states. In the course of time, however, as the civilization develops, a wider organization tends to become predominant, the local organizations gradually losing their autonomy until they have been reduced to mere subdivisions.

Concurrent with this tendency is that of the local societies to lose their purpose as a consequence of already having realized their potential. From the pinnacle of their achievement they decline. Moreover, the norms of behavior that provided the basis of social order when society was still relatively simple and primitive tend to lose their power over the minds of the people, with increasing disorder the consequence. But life without order is intolerable, because without order there is no security, and without security no one engages in such sowing as is justified only by the expectation of reaping.

When self-discipline, based on universally accepted norms of behavior, breaks down because the norms do, and in the degree to which it breaks down, force, centralized and imposed from above, must necessarily take its place, since the alternative of anarchy is intolerable. That force can assume, as it has, a variety of shapes into which we need not go here.

* Socrates objected to the examples of immorality also provided by the gods — e.g., the adultery between Ares and Aphrodite (see *The Odyssey*, Book VIII, 266–365). The immorality with which Yahweh is associated in some passages of the Old Testament is surely no less shocking (e.g., Judges 11:30–40 and Ezekiel 9:6). However, unless our gods are shown to have human weaknesses like our own, we cannot identify ourselves with them. This is the significance of Jesus's cry on the cross, which appears to represent a lapse from faith: "My God, my God, why hast thou forsaken me?" (Matthew 27:46.)

Anarchy in the relations among local societies, such as the Greek
city-states, also tends to be resolved, at last, by the imposition of a
centralized force.* So it is that every civilization ends in military empire under some variety of Caesarism. Such an empire is quite generally anticipated, before the time is fully ripe for it, by some military conqueror who creates a personal empire that commonly fails to
survive him. There was the ephemeral Akkadian empire of Sargon
I in Mesopotamia, which anticipated the Assyrian Empire; there was
the Ch'in Empire of Shih Huang Ti in China, which anticipated the
Han Empire; and there was the empire of Alexander the Great,
which anticipated the Roman Empire.†

These ephemeral personal empires are generally founded by
someone who comes from the margins of the civilization he con-
quers, neither quite belonging to it nor altogether barbarian.
Sargon I came from barbarian territory just north of the area covered by the Sumerian civilization; the Ch'in state, from which Shih
Huang Ti came, had been a half barbarian realm on the western
frontier of China; and the Macedonia of Alexander the Great, on
the northern marches of the Greek area, was a land that the Greeks
proper tended to regard as barbarian.

King Philip of Macedonia, the father of Alexander, began the
conquest of Greece after his accession to the throne in 359 B.C.
Upon his assassination in 338, Alexander continued his father's
course of military expansion until he had, by the time of his death in
323, extended the Macedonian empire beyond the banks of the
Indus, well into central Asia, and over Egypt, Libya, and Cyrenaica.
So, for a moment, Egypt, Mesopotamia, and the Indus Valley were
under one sovereignty, from which only China, of the original four
areas of civilization, was excluded.

The legacy of Alexander's military achievement, however, was not
order but confusion, for his overextended empire fell into fragments upon his death.

The next great imperial power to rise and embark upon a course
of unlimited military expansion was Rome, which incorporated
Greece into its Empire in 146 B.C.

The period of 177 years from 323 to 146 B.C., known as the Hellenistic period, was not one of cultural sterility. Even in the graphic
arts, which had reached a pinnacle in fifth-century Athens never

* The variety and the degrees in which the tendencies I am describing manifest themselves are such that one must resist the temptation of either dogmatism or excessively
narrow definition. These tendencies do not correspond to the precise laws of mechanics that apply over a wide range of inanimate nature.
† It is too early to say whether the Napoleonic empire was anticipatory in the same
sense.

since surpassed, the Hellenistic period produced such masterpieces as the Hermes of Praxiteles (second half of the fourth century), the Aphrodite of Melos, and the Winged Victory of Samothrace in the Louvre (both c. 200 B.C.).

Philosophy, which is stimulated by circumstances of disenchantment and despair, reached its highest point in Athens immediately after her defeat and downfall in the Peloponnesian War, which ended in 404 B.C. It was then that Plato wrote his dialogues, and it was not until after 390 B.C. that he founded his Academy, the first school of philosophy. His pupil, Aristotle, who was to become the tutor of Alexander the Great, was not even born until c. 384 B.C. We may also credit the sordidness of an increasingly disordered and militaristic civilization with the rise of those philosophies, Stoicism and Epicureanism, that sought the good life for the individual in a detachment from his surroundings that allowed him to cultivate the resources of his own soul. The one was founded by Zeno of Citium, the other by Epicurus, about the beginning of the third century B.C.

Moreover, the natural sciences flourished as never before in Alexandria, the city Alexander had founded in Egypt. Here Euclid developed geometry, Eratosthenes measured the circumference of the earth, and Aristarchus is believed to have formulated the theory (which was to be discredited until Copernicus revived it some seventeen centuries later) that the earth circled around the sun. Alexandria, in fact, became a center of scholarship, based on documentation in its great library, such as the world had never before known.

XXIII

Rome

IF THE HISTORY OF CIVILIZATION seems capricious, a history of accidents, we may plausibly believe that this is because we can as yet see so little of it, because we can view it only as a nearsighted flea in an elephant's ear can view the elephant.

We saw in Part One how, if we regard matter close up, focusing on subatomic particles as separate entities, the role of accident, defined by the Uncertainty Principle, is prominent; but that it disappears as an ever widening view shows the subatomic particles combined to form atoms, the atoms combined to form molecules, and the molecules combined to form still larger entities.* Again, in a distant view that embraces millions of years, a view in which individual millennia are not even discernible, we see how the evolution whereby life was enabled to emerge from the water onto dry land, the evolution that entailed the development of the amniotic egg, was consistent in its direction, not representing accident but an inevitability that was implicit in it.† However, if we could view that evolution close up, from generation to generation, the accidental circumstances that disappear from the larger view would surely be prominent.

It may be that some future observer, viewing the history of civilization in a perspective that embraced the next million years, would see a consistent line of development from which the accidental circumstances of the close-up view had disappeared.‡ Limited as we still are, however, to a close-up view that includes only five or six thousand years, we can hardly see more than the chaos of accidental circumstances that dominate the close-up view of anything, whether it is the constitution of matter or the evolution of life on earth.

* See Part One, Chapter XII above.
† See Part Three, Chapter II above.
‡ This might be a line of development whereby life emerged into outer space from its previous confinement to this planet as it had once emerged from water onto dry land.

Inevitably, therefore, we find ourselves dealing with accidental particulars that seem all-important — e.g., the fact that the Greeks, who might have lost the Battle of Salamis, won it, thereby being enabled to realize the achievements that they could hardly have realized if, in consequence of losing it, they had become part of the Persian Empire. As, then, we chronicle the accidents that appear in an excessively detailed view of history, and gain thereby the impression that it is little more than the chaos of particulars which was all H. A. L. Fisher saw in it,* we should recall that the elephant as a whole represents an order, manifested by its total form and symmetry, that does not appear in the view to which the flea is confined.

*

The picture we have of the Mediterranean basin, in the years from 700 B.C. to 300 B.C., is of an area in which a diversity of primitive nations or tribes, speaking a diversity of languages and representing a diversity of customs, attach themselves to the soil here or there for the practice of agriculture, only to be displaced, perhaps, by others that are on the march. All is flux and uncertainty, except where some nations have succeeded in planting civilizations that are more or less enduring — such as the Egyptians, some of the Middle Eastern peoples, and increasingly the people who are called Greeks because of the language they have in common. It is in these circumstances of flux that the Greeks realize the momentary glory represented by the culture of Athens in the fifth and fourth centuries B.C. It is in these circumstances, too, that those marginal Greeks, the Macedonians, establish their sway, for what is but a fleeting instant of history, over a region that extends across the entire eastern Mediterranean and into central Asia.

By 700 B.C. Greeks had established themselves at the southern end of the Italian peninsula. North of them were a variety of nations or tribes whose names still have their echoes: Umbrians, Sabines, Veneti, Ligurians, Latins, and the Etruscans who may have come by sea from the eastern Mediterranean. These people of central and northern Italy built fortified villages on defensible hilltops here and there, engaged in the practices of agriculture and warfare, traded by sea and land under circumstances more or less precarious, and came into contact not only with one another but also with Phoenicians, with Greeks, and with Gauls. To the extent that they acquired the elements of advanced culture, those elements were predominantly Greek. Indeed, until the fall of the Roman Empire, the culture of the peninsula would be what had sprung from the Greek rootstock

* See p. 331 above.

(which is what justifies us in identifying as a single civilization what we call the Graeco-Roman or Classical civilization).

Some kilometers up the Tiber River on the west coast of Italy are a few hills, seven of which would come to constitute an historical group, that had villages of shepherds and farmers on their summits as early as 1000 B.C. The inhabitants of the Palatine Hill and others adjacent to it were probably Latins, while those of the Quirinal were probably Sabines. One can imagine how, as their populations increased, the villages tended to grow together, becoming districts in a single urban complex. Sometime in the seventh century B.C., a marsh between the Capitoline and Palatine hills was drained to make a market-place and place of assembly called the Forum, and a defensive wall was built about the surrounding complex. So Rome was founded. Presumably there was nothing to make it stand out among the other towns in Italy and the Mediterranean basin generally. However, whether by accident or not, it, rather than some other settlement, was to become the center of an empire, comparable to the Han Empire of China, which extended from Scotland to the Persian Gulf, from the Straits of Gibraltar to the Caspian Sea.

*

In circumstances of military insecurity, sovereign societies, whether cities or empires, are moved to push their frontiers outward against one another, thereby driving danger back. They are also moved to expand by the temptation of wealth beyond their frontiers. So Rome was to expand against all who opposed or rivaled her until her frontiers — on the Firth of Forth, the Rhine, the Danube, the western shore of the Caspian Sea (on the eastern shore of which a Chinese army would encamp in A.D. 97) — would also include the entire Mediterranean as a Roman lake.

Presumably, in the mutual conflict that the dynamics of expansion entails, any of countless settlements, towns, or city-states around the Mediterranean might have emerged victorious instead of the little settlement on the seven hills. What was predictable was merely that one comprehensive military empire would be formed, by whatever community, since the formation of such an empire has represented the last stage of every civilization to have run its course so far.

The constant growth of Rome, first as a city and then as an empire, engendered continually new problems that called for the exercise of exceptional political, administrative, and military skills, skills that the Romans consequently developed to a high degree. Internally, there was an almost continuous state of latent civil war between various classes of the growing and changing population, between patricians and plebeians mainly, that expressed itself in unbridled competition among opposing political leaders, who became skilled in the political arts of demagogy and conspiracy. The government of what came to be urban masses, and the management of large military forces, entailed a growth of bureaucracy and an ever increasing role for administrative ability. More than most centers of government in most times, Rome was in a state of continual turmoil and crisis that brought out a capacity for improvisation, giving occasion to those who had the opportunistic disposition and the skills needed in crisis management. So Rome became a forcing ground for the production of the kind of leadership that empire requires. The great Romans were not thinkers or artists but men of action.

What is striking — and it is significant for all civilization so far — is that Rome never became truly stabilized. It lived, so to speak, from year to year, in a condition of chaos latent or overt, surviving by making shift with every new emergency. By surviving thus from year to year, however, it survived for over a thousand, from the middle of the seventh century B.C. to the middle of the fifth after Christ — but always like one who teeters on a tightrope.*

The preoccupation of the Greeks with normative ideas, which was the source of their inspiration, was relatively lacking in the Romans, who were more preoccupied with practical solutions for the practical problems of everyday life. Where the greatest achievement of the Greeks might be represented by a temple, that of the Romans would be represented by an aqueduct. Where the Greeks dreamed of the good life, which meant a life of harmony and beauty, the Romans were content to apply themselves to the competition for power and wealth, regarded as sufficient ends in themselves. They tended to regard culture as merely an embellishment of life, valued by the wealthy and great for its outward show, and they looked to the Greeks for its supply, ordering copies of Greek statues for their homes, using cultivated Greek slaves to provide their children with it.

All this illustrates the fact that inspiration is lost with its realization. The Romans did not need to create harmony and beauty for themselves because they could buy it ready-made from their Greek clients — nor could they, in any case, have improved on what the Greeks had already accomplished.

---

* I here disregard as nominal only, or essentially so, its continuation for another thousand years in Byzantium, or to our times in the institution of the papacy, or as the capital of Italy — or, for that matter, in the Russian Empire of the czars (i.e., the Caesars) that considered itself the continuation of the Byzantine Empire by virtue of Ivan the Great's marriage to the niece of the last Byzantine emperor.

Every age has poets, philosophers, artists, and so did the old age of the Classical civilization; but not every age has a Euripides, a Plato, or a Phidias. The great men of Rome, her political and military leaders, would cultivate the arts for their own greater glory, as had Nebuchadnezzar, as had Rameses II, which meant that they would not content themselves with what was not pretentious.

Having originally been under a king, like Mycenae under Agamemnon, the growing city on its seven hills transformed itself into a republic in the sixth century B.C. At first the republic was under the domination of the patricians, who kept the other principal class, that of the plebeians, in misery. Gradually, in the state of latent civil war that was chronic, the plebeians gained increasing political power. But this development of democracy, as in the history of Athens, went past an optimum to degenerate, at last, into something like the rule of mobs under the control of rival demagogues. The resulting anarchy was resolved, as always, by the dictatorship of one man, a dictatorship finally established by Julius Caesar in 45 B.C. His successor, Caesar Augustus, gave Rome the constitution of an empire — that is to say, a state under the absolute rule of an emperor. The emperors who succeeded him came in time to depend entirely, for their power, on such military forces as were loyal to them, so that in its last centuries Rome became a militarized state organized under military leadership for the practice of military government.

Almost from the beginning of the imperial rule, however, the Empire had already become overextended. The effective patrolling of its frontiers from Scotland to the Euphrates was too great a task to be carried out from one center. Therefore it tended to break up internally as rival Caesars, leading rival armies, contended for the supreme power. In A.D. 395 it was permanently divided into a western empire, with its capital at Rome, and an eastern with its capital at Byzantium on the Bosporus. Meanwhile, the outer barbarians (including the Huns who were playing the same role in China) were infiltrating or invading the empire across the thousands of kilometers of its porous frontiers. Acquiring the military and other skills of the Romans, they came to outnumber and overwhelm the old Romans of the old Rome on its seven hills. A Germanic nation, the Visigoths, sacked the Rome of the seven hills in A.D. 410. Another, the Vandals, sacked it again in 455. In 476, a barbarian chieftain called Odoacer deposed the last emperor in Rome, making himself king of Rome in his place. So the Graeco-Roman civilization at last came to an end, like the Mesopotamian in 539 B.C., like the Egyptian in 332 B.C.

XXIV

Philosophy and Religion in China

WHEN THE EVOLUTION OF MIND, embodied in man, had reached a certain point, five or six thousand years ago, civilizations began to form on the earth's surface as if they were natural growths (which, in the longest view, they surely were). One formed at the head of the Persian Gulf, another in the Nile Valley, others in the Indus Valley, the valley of the Yellow River, Central America, and South America. Each appears to have been subject, like biological organisms, to a life history. Each had an initial period of vigorous and hopeful growth; each, if it ran its full course, succumbed at last to an exhaustion like that of old age, as if some vital principle that had accounted for the drive and purpose of its youth had gone out of it. After these first civilizations, others continued to form and run their course — in the Mediterranean, in western Europe, in the Far East.

All civilizations represent a victory over the natural environment achieved by the common endeavor of men organized for the purpose. The man-apes of 30 million years ago had depended on and lived off of the unaltered natural environment, just as the primates of the Amazon forest do still. They had no protection against rain or cold, and their only food was what they found occurring of itself in the natural environment. Animal husbandry, agriculture, and architecture represented, then, a course whereby man, at a more developed stage, made himself increasingly independent of the natural environment, partly by artificially shielding himself against it (e.g., architecture), partly by subjugating and exploiting it (e.g., agriculture).

Civilization in this aspect (which takes no direct account of cultural features, such as poetry and painting) produced a rapid proliferation of the human population by protecting it against the hazards of the natural environment that had, until then, limited its increase. It may be that the entire human population when the first civilizations began was 10 million, but that it had grown to 300 million by the time of the Han and Roman empires.* Therefore, although the first civilizations grew at scattered points on the earth's surface, separated from one another by wilderness, as their populations increased they expanded, overspreading the intervening areas of wilderness so as to come increasingly into contact with one another — until, by our own time, civilization had at last become continuous around the earth. Assuming that no global catastrophe occurs between now and then, an historian of the year 8000 will surely regard the years from 4000 B.C. to A.D. 2000 as the period of multiple civilizations, a period that was merely preliminary to the formation, by the latter date, of the one worldwide civilization. (Perhaps, for an historian of the year 800,000, the period from 4000 B.C. to A.D. 2000 will simply have disappeared from view.)

If this is so, what is most significant about the history of civilization over the past 1,500 years is the merging of the several different and distinct civilizations into one worldwide civilization. And in that case, what should chiefly engage our attention, as we survey the past 1,500 years, is the way in which the spreading civilizations have borne upon one another, by conflict or accommodation, to produce what is at last one civilization with local variations or subcultures.

In the previous paragraph I referred to the "merging" of the several civilizations. What has actually happened, however, is that the Western, which had been only one among several, has in its expanding imperial phase overspread the entire globe, so that it has at last been adopted by all peoples everywhere.

Until this development in our present, the two principal civilizations of the past thousand or fifteen hundred years have been the Far Eastern or Chinese and the Western. Since the Western was to inherit the earth, in my account of these years I take the Chinese first, so as to conclude with the Western.†

*

* According to one estimate, the human population of the earth when agriculture began, about 8,000 years ago, was 8 million; by A.D. 1 it was 300 million; by 1750, 800 million, by 1800, 1,000 million, by 1850, 1,300 million, by 1900, 1,700 million, by 1950, 2,500 million, and by 1974, 3,900 million (A. J. Coale, *Scientific American*, September 1974, p. 43).

† To say that the Western civilization has inherited the earth is not to say that the West has achieved the political government of the earth. The China of our day, although it is adopting Western science and technology, although it is industrializing itself on the Western model, although it has made a Western ideology its official ideology, and although it is participating in a Western design for international organization, is not less but more independent of Western political domination as a consequence.

In categorizing, as one necessarily must, an ultimately uncategorical reality, I have thought to be most faithful to that reality by referring to two Chinese or Far Eastern civilizations, one from about 1100 B.C. to the fall of the Han Empire in A.D. 221, the other from A.D. 589 to the beginning of the twentieth century. Just as the Western civilization that arose about A.D. 1000 inherited from the Graeco-Roman civilization, so the second Chinese civilization inherited from the first; but this Chinese inheritance was so massive that one might, if one wished, regard the second as a revival and continuation of the first after almost 400 years of eclipse.*

We refer to the period in western Europe from the fall of Rome in 476 to the eleventh century as the Dark Ages because the old order had broken down, a new order had not arisen to take its place, and life had in large measure returned to the barbarian level. So it was with the period in China from the fall of the Han Empire in 221 to the sixth century.†

The Dark Ages in Europe had stimulated the rise of monasticism, for the only escape that the sensitive individual could find from barbarism was to take refuge, with other like-minded individuals, in a monastery where he might still cultivate letters and a rudimentary learning, joining himself to a monastic brotherhood for the purpose of keeping alive, within the monastic shelter, the flicker of culture, until the day when the phoenix of civilization arose again from the ashes in which it had been consumed. In China, too, the fall of a civilization and the return to barbarism stimulated the rise of monasticism, for the same reasons and in the same way.

As the European monasticism was associated with Christianity, which gave men courage to endure the evils of this life by upholding the hope of a better life after death, so the Chinese monasticism was associated with a religion that performed a like service. I told in a couple of paragraphs at the end of Chapter XIII how Buddhism, originally a philosophy rather than a religion, was born in India in

---

* If one separates the two civilizations only by the period of virtually total anarchy that followed the fall of Loyang in the north (A.D. 315), one can reduce the interval to the seventy years before the rise of those northern nomads, the Wei. We must not, however, be more precise than the reality itself in our account of it.

I refer to the second civilization as Chinese, although Far Eastern might be the better term, since it includes a Japanese branch that represents achievement in some respects equal to what we properly regard as the main stem, and since it may also be thought of as including, if only as a marginal fringe, Korea, Manchuria, Mongolia, Tibet, Burma, and Annam. Within the limitations of the present account, however, I shall describe only developments within China proper.

† The thorough reader will here wish to reread the quotation on pages 399–400 above in which Professor FitzGerald compares and also contrasts this period in China to the Dark Ages in Europe.

the sixth century B.C., apparently as a response to circumstances in which this life seemed hopeless. What it offered its followers was the hope that they might eventually, after however many reincarnations, escape the evils of this life by attaining the condition called Nirvana.

According to the historical tradition, the Buddhism that was to become dominant in China was first imported from India in A.D. 65 by the Han Emperor Hang Ming Ti, who sent an embassy to India to bring back its scriptures and sacred images. However that may be, it presumably came to China by the only route in use up to that time, from northwest India through Hellenized Persia and across central Asia north of Tibet. We may doubt that, as it had already evolved by this time, it would have been recognized by its nominal founder, Gautama Buddha; and once in China (after it had died out in its native India), it would evolve still further to suit the Chinese needs, becoming divided into sects as Christianity became divided into sects (as every religion and ideology, including Marxism in our time, comes to be divided into sects).* In its basic Chinese form, Gautama was merely the reincarnation of one of a multitude of Buddhas who had succeeded each other from infinite time past and would continue to do so through an infinite future, not only in this one speck of a world that is all we know, but in innumerable other worlds as well. As this Chinese Buddhism evolved, the Buddhas would acquire in the minds of the devout the attributes of gods; and at last one Buddha, Amida, would tend to supplant all the others, thereby exemplifying the tendency of monotheism to replace polytheism in that period of world history which began 6,000 years ago and may, conceivably, have come to an end in our present. (The worship of Amida, however, which in effect represented the foundation of a new religion, did not arise until the tenth century.)

The Buddhism imported by a Han emperor in the first century was consequently available for the consolation of the thoughtful after the Han Empire fell, offering the hope of escape in another life from the suffering not to be escaped in this one. The monasteries into which the thoughtful could retreat were, for the most part, Buddhist monasteries.

The other religion that was to become dominant in the second Chinese civilization, except that it was native to the soil, had an origin similar to that of Buddhism. As we saw in Chapter XV, Taoism was a philosophy rather than a religion, founded in China — by the legendary Lao Tzu, according to tradition — at the same time that

---

* In our time, China would import Marxism and then sinify it as, twenty centuries earlier, it had imported Buddhism and sinified it.

the philosophy called Buddhism was being founded in India by the legendary Gautama — again, according to tradition. It had been individualistic and hermitic, seeing no possibility of the good life in society, from which it followed that the wise individual would withdraw from it, perhaps to a monastery where he could engage in solitary contemplation, perhaps to a mountaintop where he could live the solitary life of a hermit — in either case conforming his individual self not to the sordidness of an artificial society but to the basic harmony of nature identified as the Tao.

Just as Buddhism, originally a philosophy, came to be a religion that focused men's aspirations on an afterlife, so did the philosophy of Taoism. It came to promise immortality in an afterlife, unknown to its founders, by the magical operation of certain alchemistic practices. As a religion, like Buddhism, it achieved a popularity that no philosophy as sophisticated as the original Taoism could possibly have achieved.

In previous chapters we have identified the foundation of civilization with a single normative complex in the form of a religion that provides an explanation of being, which explanation endows human life with a corresponding significance, which significance has implications for the organization of society and the conduct of the individual. We have also noted that, although philosophy and religion may properly be regarded as distinct from each other, there is not always a sharp dividing line between them.

The second Chinese civilization, rather than being identified with one religion only — as the Arab civilization was identified with Mohammedanism, as Western civilization has been identified with Christianity — was identified with an ethical philosophy, Confucianism, and two religions, Buddhism and Taoism. The Confucianism, associated with ancestor worship and the imitation of an idealized past, would be the official ideology of the scholars who, until the twentieth century, would constitute the Chinese government — for admission to the civil service would depend on passing examinations in the Confucian classics and Confucian doctrine. It would be the ideology of the cultivated. Buddhism would be a widely accepted and well established religion, but not the only one, for it would be in competition with Taoism, which would appeal to the least sophisticated elements in the population by its alchemy, its astrology, its magical practices and promises.

Perhaps we should consider that, from the beginning of the first Chinese civilization to what I shall call the end of the second, the basic religion of China was ancestor worship, together with all that was involved in the concept of the Mandate of Heaven. But this could not satisfy all the elements in the population, and therefore there had from the start been the local divinities, gods of the streams or the vegetation, and in time there had been the varying forms of Buddhism and Taoism.

In any case, the cohabitation of three normative schemes tended to obviate the extremes of religious or ideological intolerance that have been notable in the history of Islam and Christendom alike. Many Chinese, as a matter of practical accommodation, referred to the three, with a casuistical logic, as three ways to one goal.

XXV

The Resurrection of the Phoenix

> Out of the spent and unconsidered Earth
> The Cities rise again.
>
> — *Rudyard Kipling*

ALTHOUGH THE ROMAN EMPIRE had at last fallen in the fifth century, the normative idea of the single worldwide empire, with Rome its capital, had persisted throughout the Dark Ages and, indeed, for many centuries after, becoming only gradually dimmer in men's minds as one generation succeeded another. So it was that, at the end of the eighth century, when Charlemagne had momentarily succeeded in bringing western Europe under his single rule, he went to Rome to be invested with the imperial crown, thereby associating himself with the restoration of normality and, *ipso facto*, legitimacy based on the normative model of tradition.

During the Chinese Dark Ages, from A.D. 221 to the end of the sixth century, every military adventurer or bandit chieftain who succeeded in establishing a temporary rule over an important part of what had been one China proceeded to call himself Emperor and the founder of a dynasty in succession to the Han rulers, thereby testifying to the persistence of an idea long after its embodiment had fallen into ruin.

In the West — despite Charlemagne, and despite the pretension represented by the largely nominal institution that Voltaire said was neither holy, nor Roman, nor an empire, and which was not brought to the end of what had become a wholly nominal career until 1806 — in the West, then, a new Roman Empire would never truly rise up again out of the ashes of the old. The case was different in China, where the normative idea would again, after the lapse of centuries, receive its embodiment.*

---

* The term "embodiment," in this context, is to be taken in a special sense. A state is the "embodiment" of a normative idea as a particular performance of *Hamlet* is an embodiment of the play by Shakespeare. See Part Five, Chapter XIV below.

In 589 a general would unify China momentarily, as Charlemagne would momentarily unify Europe a couple of centuries later, but the Sui Dynasty that he thereby founded would crumble after his death like the Carolingian dynasty after the death of Charlemagne. Thereupon, the man who is plausibly accounted the greatest statesman of Chinese history made himself emperor under the name of T'ang T'ai Tsung, and so founded the T'ang Dynasty (618–907), which is plausibly accounted the most notable dynasty of Chinese history.

The Chinese state of the T'ang Dynasty — like the Chinese state of the Han Dynasty, like Greece, like Rome, like Mesopotamia and Egypt — could never be stabilized, but survived only through a series of crises as one ruler succeeded another in the struggle for power. For ten years in the middle of the eighth century civil war raged, to be won at last by the representative of the T'ang Dynasty with the aid of foreign military forces that included even an Arab contingent sent by the caliph — so small had the world grown! But the T'ang court never recaptured its full authority over the whole realm. For a century it made shift to deal with excessively independent provincial governors and invading barbarians from Tibet. Chaos became increasingly the rule until, at the end of the ninth century, the realm became entirely subject to the marches and countermarches of rival armies. When the last T'ang emperor abdicated in 907, China had finally sunk back into the state of fragmentation and confusion in which it had languished before the establishment of its unity by the first T'ang emperor in 618.

Again the normative idea was without embodiment.

*

From 907 to 960, when there was no central government, a fragmented China was under the simultaneous rule of rival military adventurers, each of whom would make himself momentarily dominant over as much of its territory as his army could grasp. The chaos this represented tends to be disguised by the disposition of the Chinese historians to make the actual conform, if only nominally, with the normative idea. So the ruler of the largest piece of China at any particular moment was to be identified by the historian as Emperor of China and the founder or inheritor of a dynasty. This imposition of a nominal order on an actual chaos accounts for the fact that the half century of chaos following the fall of the T'ang is known as the Period of the Five Dynasties, and is subdivided into a succession of dynasties, the longest of which is said to have lasted seventeen years, the shortest four.

The chaos of the so-called Five Dynasties prevailed in northern China (roughly north of the Yangtze basin), the traditional center of Chinese civilization, rather than in the south. During the long decline of the T'ang Dynasty from 763, when the capital city of Ch'ang An was captured and sacked, to its final dissolution in 907, the south enjoyed a relative degree of peace and order, with the consequence that the traditional dominance of the north was permanently lost. (The growing relative importance of the south would be further promoted in later centuries when maritime communications with the West, through the southern ports, would tend to replace those across the land routes of central Asia.) So it was that, while the north was torn by civil war and experiencing the growing barbarity that goes with such a condition, the south, for the most part, continued under its provincial governors to enjoy a relative peace and to sustain the cultural activities that had flourished under the T'ang Dynasty as never before.

It has happened on more than one occasion in history that the experience of a well-nigh intolerable insecurity during a period of intensive disorder has provoked in a population a universal inclination to support any rule by which order may be restored — and this especially where the idea of a normative order has become firmly established in tradition. So it was that a certain Chao Kuang-yin, notable for his trustworthy and conciliatory disposition, founded the Sung Dynasty (960–1127) on the basis of general assent rather than by force.

In keeping with the manner of its foundation, the Sung empire tended to be pacifistic in its policy, the civil element predominating over the military. It was also identified with the period of the greatest refinement in Chinese culture and the greatest elegance in Chinese manners; so that, in connection with it, one thinks of fourth-century Greece or eighteenth-century Europe. Perhaps one could say that there was even a whiff of decadence in the atmosphere of the Sung court.

The Achilles heel of Sung China was on its northeastern frontier, where the territory from Peking to the Great Wall, and the mountain passes from Mongolia—the territory that contained the defenses of China against attack from the north — had been left in the hands of barbarian nomads, whom the Sung proceeded to appease with an annual subsidy not easily to be distinguished from tribute money; so that present peace was bought at the price of future safety.

In 1126, nomadic tribes called the Kin poured over the virtually defenceless northern frontier of China and, overcoming the decayed military power of the Sung, captured the capital, the Em-

peror, and the court; after which they continued on across the
Yangtze. In 1141 a peace treaty partitioned China again, dividing it
into a Kin Empire of the north and a Sung Empire of the south.
Expressing this in the dynastic terminology of the Chinese historians, we say that the Sung Dynasty came to an end in 1127, and that
the ensuing period of partition (1127–1280) was that of the Kin Dynasty and the Southern Sung Dynasty, each with its half of China.

The Southern Sung may properly be regarded as a continuation
in the south for some three more generations of the Sung Dynasty,
characterized as it was by the same high level of cultural activity, the
same refinement, and the same pacifism.

*

The reader will appreciate the constant disposition manifested in
these pages to discover a pattern or life-history, from birth to death,
implicit in every civilization that has run its course so far. There is
an inspired first stage in which a civilization arises out of barbarism,
as in the case of the Greeks from 800 to 400 B.C. This is followed by
a stage of over-ripeness, exemplified by the Hellenistic period. Finally there is the stage of military empire, represented by Rome in
the example of the Graeco-Roman civilization. If there are differences in important particulars between the way this pattern appears to have manifested itself in various civilizations, the pattern in
its broadest terms may still be representative of reality.

The reader will also have been aware of an uncertainty, sometimes
amounting to scepticism, that has kept the author from being dogmatic in applying this pattern. It is, therefore, in a quasi-speculative
spirit that we may consider the following application of the pattern
to the second Chinese civilization. The T'ang period represents the
inspired first stage; the Sung represents the stage of over-ripeness;
and what follows the Sung, as we are about to see, is a military empire never yet equaled, either before or after, in the extent of its
conquests or in the brutality that characterizes all such empires.

The Mongol Empire of Genghis Khan — which included eastern
Europe, central Asia, all of China, Siberia, Manchuria, and Korea —
conquered and incorporated China in 1280; and, although it broke
into fragments after the death of Genghis Khan, China continued
under Mongol rule (nominally the Yüan Dynasty) until 1368. The
Mongols adopted Chinese culture as the Romans had adopted Greek
culture, so that one may say that — as throughout Chinese history,
no less in the case of the Kin than in that of the Mongols — the
conquered conquered their conquerors by their cultural superiority;
which is to say that the civilization went on living after a fashion.

The period of Mongol rule (denominated the Yüan Dynasty, 1280–1368) was followed by a native dynasty, the Ming (1368–1644), which was followed by another dynasty of barbarian (but ultimately sinified) conquerors, the Manchu (1644–1911), which lasted into the lifetime of many who are still living as these lines are written, including their author.* It may not be altogether fanciful to compare the period after the fall of the Mongol Empire in China to the thousand years during which Byzantium persisted, as a nominal Rome, after the fall of the western Roman Empire, Byzantium having itself been likened to the dead tree that remains standing in the forest. There was in China a persistence of civilization, as in the case of Byzantium, and cultural production continued, but the great inspiration that had been the life-giving principle of the civilization was gone. By the end of the nineteenth century the dead tree had at last become too rotten to remain standing. Its official fall took place in 1911.

* At this point — in a history of life on earth which had its beginning three to four thousand million years ago, and which has been examined at ever closer range and, consequently, in terms of ever smaller periods of time — we at last come down to the present of still-living individual organisms.

XXVI

The Second Chinese Civilization:
Poetry and Painting

UNDER THE MANCHUS (1644–1911), China was to become a hermetic society, pursuing a policy of excluding foreigners and foreign influences, until at last in the nineteenth century, having gradually become too weak to resist, it was overwhelmed by the expanding West. During these three centuries it also came to believe that there was no need for it to look beyond its frontiers, for the world outside of China was regarded as having nothing to offer either of cultural or of economic value. Throughout the previous 3,000 years, however, the openness of China to foreign influences was notable. Perhaps all civilizations are more subject to foreign influences than one would gather from what their own historians write. Surely, however, if one thinks in terms of two traditions, one represented by the succession of civilizations on the western side of Eurasia, the other by the succession on the far eastern side, there is an important drift of influence over three millennia from west to east, as well as a counter-drift that may, up to the thirteenth century, have been no less important. In Chapter XVII we saw that a large part of what remains of the artistic production of the first Chinese civilization shows influences from western and central Asia. In Chapter XXIV we saw how one of the two principal religions of China originally came to it from India by way of western and central Asia. In the eighth century the T'ang, having been temporarily overthrown by rebellion, were restored by a mixed army that included Arabs. (One does not, however, hear of European potentates being supported by military contingents from China; although in the first century B.C. a Chinese commander installed a Greek king in what is now Pakistan.*) In this perspective, the hermetic character of China over the past three centuries appears out of character.

Never were foreigners more welcome or appreciated than at the height of the second Chinese civilization in the T'ang Dynasty

* See pp. 3ı 7–398 above.

(618–907). The streets of the T'ang capital, according to Professor FitzGerald, "were frequented by men of the most diverse races, from Siberian tribesmen to the jungle peoples of southern India, Greeks, Arabs, Persians and Japanese." * (Again, one does not hear of the streets of Paris being frequented by Chinese.) In the eighth century, the Arabs founded a sizeable Moslem community in China that was to persist into the twentieth century. As early as the seventh century, Christian missionaries had established Nestorian Christianity in China. In the tenth century, however, as the T'ang Dynasty was in its final decline, a reaction against the toleration of foreign religions set in and they were subjected to official persecution. After that, China was conquered by the Mongols and its long decline was under way.

The distinction of Chinese civilization was never in the fields of mathematics, science, or technology. Perhaps this is because the conservative disposition represented or engendered by Confucianism was not conducive to innovation and the search for new knowledge. It may also be because, in the minds of the educated Chinese, the very concept of science was associated with the pseudo-sciences practiced by Taoism, the religion of the uneducated, thereby becoming an object of scorn. The Taoist priests deceived the ignorant by the hocus-pocus of their astrology, of an alchemy that guaranteed immortality in an afterlife, and of medical practices that were closer to magic than to science. If they had been accepted by the Confucian scholars, the astrology, alchemy, and medicine of the Taoists might have led to genuine scientific progress, as in the West, where astronomy, chemistry, and modern medicine arose out of similar pursuits. Indeed, such scientific progress as was made in China was made by the Taoist priests; but their intellectual context was so disreputable in the eyes of the learned as to cause them to be undervalued. Consequently, when the magnetic compass was invented it was enlisted in the service of superstition rather than being put to any useful service; and for a long time after gunpowder was invented it was used only to make firecrackers that would drive away evil spirits.

Beginning in the seventeenth century, however, when China was entering its final hermetic phase, Western science began a spectacular progress that, applied to technology, would generate the power, at last, to overwhelm a civilization that had sunk into somnolence.

The explanations by which we account for anything in this world serve, at best, for no more than to push the unexplained down to a deeper level. We can say that the Chinese produced no Archime-

* C. P. FitzGerald, *China: A Short Cultural History,* New York, 1950, p. 325.

des, no Darwin, and no Fulton because Confucianism opposed the progress of thought or because Taoism discredited science. While acknowledging the presumed validity of such answers, the philosophical reader will not be satisfied with them. Just as two individuals may from birth show quite different aptitudes, one being gifted in poetry, the other in engineering, so it appears to be with civilizations. The question this begs may, perhaps, be answered by reference to the normative ideas on which civilizations are respectively based.* Anyone who compares the Parthenon frieze and a Chinese landscape painting, in terms of the normative ideas they respectively represent, may well conclude that the Greeks were more likely than the Chinese to concern themselves with numerical relations and music, while the Chinese were more likely than the Greeks to concern themselves with disembodied ideas (e.g., the Yin and the Yang, or a Heaven that, unlike Olympus, cannot be pictured) and with the distinction between reality and illusion (as in the quotation from Chuang Tzu on page 394 above). Viewing the Parthenon frieze, one is aware of nothing beyond what is depicted, but the Chinese landscape shows a world that must extend indefinitely beyond the horizon that delimits visibility. One cannot imagine the Greeks depicting empty sky, for that, in their logic, would be to depict nothing.†

*

By general consent, the T'ang period was the great age of poetry, distinguished by numerous poets, among whom the two greatest were Li Po (701–762) and Tu Fu (712–770).

> Li Po after one measure [of wine] produces one hundred
> poems;
> He sleeps in a wine shop at Ch'ang An market-place;
> The Son of Heaven summons him to the Presence; he does not
> board the boat;
> He styles himself "Official who is an Immortal of Wine." ‡

Presumably this quotation from Tu Fu represents about the nearest

---

* The question this in turn begs may, perhaps, be answered by reference to the respective environments in which normative ideas arise: e.g., the spectacle of the stars in the night sky is more likely to play a part in the thinking of those who inhabit Arabia than in that of those who inhabit Alaska, which in turn may lead the Arabians to a greater cultivation of astronomy and mathematics.

† For a further discussion of the Greek logic, contrasting it with that of our own civilization, see pp. 468–471 below.

‡ Translation from Tu Fu by Florence Ayschough in *Tu Fu, the Autobiography of a Chinese Poet*, 1929, pp. 83–85; quoted by C. P. FitzGerald, op. cit., p. 348.

approach that may be made in the English language to the sense and character of Chinese poetry. We should, however, take account of the fact that Chinese poetry must be radically different in character from Western poetry.

There are persons who can read a foreign language that they don't know how to pronounce, which means that they must be able to dissociate it from sound, specifically from its sounds as spoken. When they read poetry in such a language, they don't hear its music but enjoy it, rather, for what there is in it that is not music — its thoughts and the images it evokes. (So a person who had been stone-deaf from birth might still take pleasure in reading poetry.) Within the limits of such an appreciation, poetry has nothing to do with song. Presumably Chinese poetry (at least after about 800 B.C.) has relatively little to do with song; for there is no one way of pronouncing the characters in which it is written, just as there is no one way of pronouncing the character "3," which is pronounced as "three" in English, as "trois" in French, and in as many other ways as there are other written languages to which it belongs. (Note that, because sound is not what counts, my addition of two syllables to the first line of the poem quoted above has not damaged it as the addition of two syllables would damage any line in the poetry of Tennyson or Keats.)

On the other hand, the differences in the pronunciation of written Chinese are limited to the range of differences represented by the various dialects of what is all one language. Similarly, the various pronunciations of the character "3" are all monosyllabic, and all begin with a consonantal sound at least akin to the English "th" (e.g., "t" or "d"), followed by the English consonant "r" or its equivalent in other languages. Moreover, the same poem in English will not sound the same when read by an American from Alabama as when read by a Yorkshireman.

The fact that the language of poetry was primarily a written language meant that the ranks of the poets were recruited only from the small class of scholars who had mastered an ideographic script which required years of study. The "mute inglorious Miltons" must have been more numerous in China than in the West, where it has been possible for a Robert Burns to flourish.

Much of the T'ang poetry, and notably that of Li Po, was inspired by and reflects the philosophical attitudes of the Taoism that enjoyed a certain dominance at the time. The poet, looking into himself, found higher values that were incompatible with the sordidness of a crowded and excessively organized society. Therefore he turned away from such society to nature, idealizing the life of withdrawal, dreaming of remote hermitages by mountain streams.

This attitude and this inspiration are most notable, however, in the Chinese landscape painting that is, surely, one of the greatest achievements of civilization so far, on a level with the highest artistic attainments of Greek or of Western civilization. Although we say that the inspiration for this painting was Taoist, we must suppose that it represents in graphic form an ideal, proper to Chinese civilization, that Taoism represents in philosophical terms. Such painting could lead to the Taoist philosophy as readily as the Taoist philosophy could lead to such painting.

In all these paintings, a relationship is established between the natural landscape and human life. Typically, they were painted on silk scrolls that were unrolled to reveal a continuing and changing scene of mountains, forests, and watercourses of one sort or another. What impresses at first view is the immensity of the natural scene, the height of the mountains, the depth of the gorges. The human element may be overlooked in the first view, so that only on closer examination does one see a man driving two mules along a forest path, an arched bridge over a stream, or a temple perched on an outcrop of rock. Although this human element may be almost lost in the natural, when discovered it never appears intrusive, as if it did not belong, any more than, in nature itself, processions of ants on the forest floor seem intrusive. The viewer is aware that, despite the disparity of scale, there is a proportion and even a sort of established balance between man and nature. The muleteer and his charges, the bridge, or the temple, so far from taking away from the naturalness of the setting, constitute an intrinsic aspect of it. Something would be missing from nature itself if they were not there.

What this represents, in a word, is a harmony — not a harmony between nature, on the one hand, and man on the other, but a harmony within nature. "The great unifying aim has been to express *Tao*, the Way — the basic Chinese belief in an order and harmony in nature. This grand concept originated in remote times, from observation of the heavens and of nature — the rising and setting of sun, moon, and stars, the cycle of day and night, and the rotation of the seasons — suggesting the existence of laws of nature, a sort of divine legislation that regulated the pattern in the heavens and its counterpart on earth." * The Tao is the equivalent of the Western Logos.

I have here mentioned what seems to me at once most typical and most striking in the one art that best enables outsiders to appreciate how great was the second Chinese civilization, surpassing any of the first civilizations (the four of the Old World and the two of the New)

* Mai-Mai Sze, *The Tao of Painting*, New York, 1963, p. 3.

insofar as we can judge from what remains of them. But human life is not viewed only from a distance in Chinese painting. The artist might, let us say, have taken a relatively close-up view of the man leading the two mules, in which case we would have had a genre painting — like the Egyptian painting in Thebes of a hunting scene (see page 372 above), or like a seventeenth-century Dutch painting of skaters on a pond. It would still, however, have been representative of the harmonious integration of man and nature in the paintings I have described.

There is, in the Boston Museum of Fine Arts, a short scroll by Shen Chou (1427–1509) on the right side of which several persons are sitting at table in an open pavilion among trees at the edge of a body of water that extends leftward to the end of the scroll. Almost all the left half of the scroll is blank, representing water or sky indistinguishably; but in the upper left-hand corner, so small that it might escape notice entirely, is a disc, somewhat paler than its pale background, that represents the moon. The title of the painting (really a colored drawing, as is true of all the scrolls) is "Contemplating the Moon." It is accompanied by a poem, which makes the point that in youth one contemplates the moon of mid-autumn negligently, but in old age with the question in one's mind of how many more such autumn moons one may hope to see. What this typifies is the literary and philosophical character of Chinese painting. Walter Pater wrote a prose poem about Leonardo da Vinci's "Mona Lisa" more than three centuries after it was painted, thereby supplying his own literary and philosophical accompaniment. But the Chinese painter is two in one, at once a Leonardo and a Walter Pater.*

It is only in the close-ups of scenes from court life that the association of man and nature is missing, because nature is missing. They are, however, Confucian rather than Taoist. They depict an artificial life disciplined by the formalities that the Confucians call rites. They represent the beauty of courtly grace, which has its own reality.

*

We have seen how unstable Chinese civilization has always been in its political organization — no different in this from other civilizations. In its culture, however, the high standards it has achieved have persisted for many centuries after their achievement. Poetry declined after the T'ang Dynasty, and painting after the Sung, but with a slowness that made the decline perceptible chiefly in the increasingly imitative, repetitious, and therefore unoriginal and uninspired char-

* See p. 506.

acter of the work as the centuries passed. The painting of the Italian Renaissance held its high level for hardly more than a century, and this is true as well of seventeenth-century Dutch painting; but the ups and downs of Chinese painting were more gradual. This stability is one aspect of a civilization that has always been distinguished alike by the advantages and the drawbacks of its distinctive conservatism.

XXVII

The Dark Ages in the West

EVERY CIVILIZATION, as we have noted, is the product of an inspiration associated with some normative order of the mind that takes the form of a religion or an ideology. Such an order inspires men to strive for its realization in the world external to the mind. It inspires them to create a culture that represents it in the formalities governing social relations, and in a variety of other forms, political, literary, artistic. There comes a point in this process of creation, however, when the potential of the original conception has been realized — e.g., in the T'ang state, or in the Parthenon. Such realization is followed by the loss of inspiration, for the achievement of a goal means the loss of a goal. Successive generations tend to repeat, to imitate the past because they cannot improve on it, or they become preoccupied with the continuing development and display of merely technical skills. (The sculptor of the Laocoon has surpassed the sculptor of the Parthenon frieze in technical skill, but has lost much of the normative vision by which the former was inspired.) Ultimately, as the order inspired by the normative vision breaks down, sheer military force becomes the basis of the order that takes its place. By a curious paradox, tyranny and military empire are the expression of an inwardly developing anarchy at the same time that they are the answer to it. The empire that is based on military force, however, is never able to limit itself. So it becomes overextended, and a certain rottenness at its core spreads. At last, what remains of the civilization is the dead tree that, even if it continues to stand for a thousand years, is doomed to ultimate decomposition.*

* In the normative pattern I have here sketched, of the rise and fall of a civilization, I can be neither dogmatic nor precise. I can only say that, seen from a distance through squinted eyes, civilizations appear to have a tendency to go through some such life-history as this, although individual cases vary in particulars and, perhaps, in more than particulars. I shall be reluctant, therefore, to quarrel with those of my readers who, knowing the truth as I do not, read such a paragraph as the above and announce that in this I am wrong. ("Bless us," said Browning's Fra Lippo Lippi, "they must know!")

At the end of Chapter XXIII we saw how, in the fifth century, the Graeco-Roman civilization fell — although, to change an earlier metaphor, shoots from the original stock kept on cropping up from runners it had previously put out.

We refer to the following 500 years in Europe as the Dark Ages.* The central government that had maintained the Pax Romana had broken down. The invading barbarians, everywhere in the ascendant, set up their barbaric and evanescent kingdoms, the Ostrogoths in the Italian and the Visigoths in the Iberian peninsula, the Franks and Burgundians in what is now France, the Angles, the Saxons, and the Jutes in what is now England. All was flux, nor was there any part of Europe, west of Constantinople, in which a secure enough order was established to make possible the development of civilization. For men do not even begin to build on ground from which they may expect to be driven before there is time to finish.

In the seventh century, with the foundation of the Mohammedan religion, the Arabs began that explosive expansion that was to carry them eastward into China, westward across North Africa, into the Iberian peninsula, and on into northern France, where they were stopped, at last, by the Franks under Charles Martel in 732. In the ninth and tenth centuries the wild Magyar horsemen repeatedly raided Europe from the east. Beginning at the end of the eighth century, the ship-borne Vikings from Scandinavia began raiding Europe every year, invading it along its coasts and up its rivers, pillaging and burning the huddled settlements that lay exposed to their depredations. In the ninth century they besieged Paris and ravaged all of what is now northern France. In 844 they attacked Spain, and in 860 destroyed Pisa on the west coast of Italy. In the tenth century they established themselves in what is now Normandy. In the eleventh century they conquered England and southern Italy. So western Europe was constantly invaded and ravaged from all sides during the years of what we call the Dark Ages — by Saracens, by Magyars, and by Vikings.

This was not a case of civilized people beset by barbarians, for it

* All historians are hampered by an established but misleading terminology based on the old tripartite division of history into ancient, mediaeval, and modern — ancient covering the history of the Graeco-Roman civilization, mediaeval the period called the Middle Ages, from the fall of Rome to the Italian Renaissance (c. 1400), and modern from the Renaissance to the present. For my own part, I have thought it best to divide the centuries from the fall of Rome to the Renaissance into the Dark Ages (400–1000) and the Middle Ages (1000–1400). The term "Dark Ages" has been criticized even in its application to the period from 400 to 1000. There can be no question, however, about the generally prevailing darkness, at least in western Europe, from the fifth to the eleventh century — in spite of the fact that an occasional monk lighted a candle, and that Charlemagne lighted a bonfire (which, however, went out again right away). Nighttime is not to be identified as daytime simply because one can point to stars, or even a moon, in the sky.

was the barbarians who had overwhelmed the Latin empire who were now harried by other barbarians, Magyars and Vikings, and by the relatively civilized Saracens from Arabia. So it was a time of barbarism and anarchy, suggesting the condition described by Thomas Hobbes as the war of every man against every man.

> In such condition [Hobbes wrote], there is no place for industry; because the fruit thereof is uncertain: and consequently no culture of the earth; no navigation, nor use of the commodities that may be imported by sea; no commodious building; no instruments of moving, and removing, such things as require much force; no knowledge of the face of the earth; no account of time; no arts; no letters, no society; and which is worst of all, continual fear, and danger of violent death; and the life of man, solitary, poor, nasty, brutish, and short.*

*

During all these centuries the principal basis of the new civilized order that would come into being was a new religion, which had been founded in the first century of our era by Paul of Tarsus and others who subscribed to the teachings of the prophet Jesus. It was monotheistic, like the Judaism out of which it grew, but it interposed between human beings and a deity who had become too remote an avatar in the person of Jesus himself. In Jesus God had assumed human form so as to share the human experience; or, from another point of view, in Jesus he had sent his son to mediate between him and a mankind that had been doomed by Adam's disobedience. What Jesus offered mankind, on condition that it follow his teachings, was salvation from the consequences of Original Sin, of that evil which we all know in ourselves, and which is in us from birth.

Partly, one surmises, because Jesus had spoken for poverty against wealth, promising a blessed immortality to the poor that would be denied to the rich, the new religion spread among the masses of the Roman Empire. It appealed to those who could expect only suffering in this life by the prospect, after death, of a Heaven in which they would be compensated for their sufferings. It was a religion suited to a world that had become hopeless.

The establishment of the religion entailed the organization of a church, and the organization of a church would, as it transpired, perpetuate the normative idea of the centralized Roman Empire, which would continue to dominate men's minds for centuries after the Empire itself, as a secular and political structure, had fallen. Thus the organization of the Roman Empire was the model for the

* *Leviathan*, Part I, Chapter 13.

organization of the Church. As the Empire had, in principle, been universal, so the Church was "catholic" (from the Latin for universal). As the Roman Emperor had been supreme, so the Bishop of Rome, eventually under the title of Pope, was accorded supreme power as the vicar of Christ on earth. As the supposed successor to St. Peter (see Matthew 16:18–19) he held the keys to the Kingdom of Heaven. So it was that, when the Roman Empire was dead, it lived still in the Christian Church. Men to whom the normative idea of order was the Roman order could find it only in the Church, to which they would therefore turn the more naturally.*

Ethics, the rules of propriety that should govern the conduct of people, are central to any normative order that constitutes the basis of a civilization. Confucianism, for example, emphasized loyalty — of the son to the father, of the subject to the emperor, of the living descendants to the ancestral dead. Christian ethics were based on a dichotomy, a contradiction, and a consequent tension between the animal and the divine in humanity. Man had been created in God's image, but had fallen from his paradisal estate by acquiring knowledge of a divided realm of being in which good and evil oppose each other. So he became a split personality — a beast, but with a soul that made him susceptible of redemption.

To the men and women who lived in the centuries after the fall of Rome, then, the world was not only the world of the Hobbesian insecurity, but also a licentious world in which man's animal nature had the ascendancy over his spiritual nature. The apparently irremediable wickedness as well as the insecurity of the present world was the reason why there could be no hope except in a heavenly kingdom to which, by God's mercy, one might be admitted after one's departure from the present world.

One response that sensitive and conscientious persons make to such political and moral anarchy is withdrawal. They may, as individuals, withdraw to a chapel in the woods, there to lead the hermit's life, or they may band together to create a monastic island of order in a sea of chaos, in either case renouncing this wicked world. It is not surprising, therefore, that the fall of Rome was followed by the rise of monasticism. The founder of the principal monastic order was St. Benedict (c. 480–547). He began as a hermit, but others were attracted to him by his holiness so that he found himself, at last, organizing monastic societies and formulating the rules of the order

* The theoretical status of the papacy, as I have here described it, has in practice been modified by the casuistry involved in centuries of politically motivated theological disputation that goes on still today. Such casuistry, however, or the exegesis through which it operates, is generally the art of interpreting statements to mean the opposite of what they say. Here I am concerned only with what they say.

that was to spread, in monastic islands, all over western Europe. Communities of nuns were similarly founded, one by Benedict's sister Scholastica. Benedict and Scholastica were, in their way, performing the mission of mankind to bring order out of chaos.

Culture, as we have seen, is traditional and cumulative from generation to generation. Much of the cultural heritage of mankind has been lost, however, by such natural processes as decay, by war, by vandalism, and by catastrophes like the Chinese Burning of the Books or the fire that consumed the library of Alexandria. The great service performed by those who retreated into monasteries during the Dark Ages was to preserve the cultural heritage by copying classical texts on parchment or vellum and thereby making libraries. One reason why the darkness was not unrelieved during those centuries is that the monks, in their relative isolation from the prevailing barbarism, kept the lights of literacy and learning alive.

*

When we were viewing the history of life on earth in the perspective of hundreds of millions of years we saw in it an evolution that represented what appeared to be an inevitable order. Viewing the history of civilization in the perspective of a few millennia, it has been only in the speculative, tentative, and uncertain fashion represented by the first paragraph of this chapter that we have been able to discern any like order in it. When, finally, we have narrowed down our perspective to the lifetime of an individual, a Pericles or a T'ang T'ai Tsung, the role of accident, representing chaos rather than order, appears to predominate.

The reader will have in mind the equation between this aspect of temporal extension and the like aspect of spatial extension represented by the Uncertainty Principle discussed in Chapters XI and XII of Part One. At the level of elementary particles, the role of accident predominates; but, as the particles combine to form ever larger combinations, an ever increasing order manifests itself, which justifies us in concluding that order is progressively imposed upon an underlying chaos.

Although I strain my mind to see something other than accident in the historical phenomenon called the Carolingian Renaissance, lasting but one generation, I cannot do so.* Presumably it would not have occurred except for the accident that an extraordinarily en-

_____

* The best I can do is to find a suggestive parallel, at the beginning of the second Chinese civilization, in the foundation by Yang Chien, just before the T'ang Dynasty, of the Sui Dynasty that collapsed after his death, as in the case of Charlemagne's empire. See p. 449 above.

ergetic and able individual, best known as Charlemagne, became king of the Franks by hereditary succession in 771. He proceeded to unify virtually the whole of Europe (excepting the Iberian Peninsula, Britain, Scandinavia, and the eastern fringe) under his rule. Then, in 800, he had himself crowned Emperor of Rome by the Pope, thereby restoring, as he thought, the lapsed normality represented by the Roman Empire.

The term "Carolingian Renaissance" properly applies to the cultural revival that Charlemagne sponsored and directed. He brought the scholar Alcuin from York in Britain to his court, where he assembled other such luminaries from all over Europe to create a court academy for the revival of arts and letters.

However, all that he built collapsed after his death in 814, and the two centuries that followed may, in fact, be considered the darkest of the Dark Ages.

Then, beginning about the year 1000, the Dark Ages came to their final end with what we may regard as the birth of a new civilization.

XXVIII

The Normative World of the West

IT WAS CHIEFLY in the ninth and tenth centuries that Europe was subjected to the depredations of the invaders from all sides. In such circumstances, where there is no law or no effective means for its enforcement, and no adequate large-scale organization for defence, so that every settlement on river-bank or plain is naked to its enemies, who may descend upon it at any time without warning; where the crops men have planted or the food they have stocked may be burned by pillaging bands; where the men may at any time be slaughtered and the women carried off — in such circumstances human communities have always reacted in the same way. People cluster about some strong man among them, who undertakes to defend them in return for their service. This is the basis of any feudal system, whether in China, in Japan, in the Middle East, or in Europe.

Typically, at least in Europe, the strong man provides a fortress castle into which those who keep the flocks and work the land can retreat at the approach of the invader. Supporting him and his establishment in return for his protection, they become his serfs, attached to the land that he claims and defends. As the area so defended becomes larger a hierarchical order develops. A principal feudal lord — king or duke or count — exercising jurisdiction over a wide territory, requires the service of lesser feudal lords, who perhaps require in turn the service of still lesser lords, until one gets down to the serf at the bottom of this social pyramid, this hierarchical organization for the maintenance of order and security. When that happens, the Vikings, for example, who raid up the rivers of the Frankish land are confronted with fortress-castles not to be reduced except by siege-warfare; or they encounter bands of knights on horseback, full-time professional warriors, who are up to dealing with them.*

* What I have described here in schematic terms is a basic initial order that is bound to develop spontaneously in response to an intolerable situation of anarchy and corre-

The development of feudalism may be regarded as a first step in the resolution of such anarchy and insecurity as Hobbes described. On the bare bones of the feudal system grows a body of customary law governing land-tenure and mutual obligations, as well as a complex of formalities applicable to birth, to marriage, to death, to the conduct of social relations in almost every aspect.

The relative security provided by a feudal system makes the further building of a civilization possible. With a reasonable expectation that the circumstances in which they find themselves will continue, men can project and embark on works that may, like the Gothic cathedrals, take generations for their completion.

In these situations, when all is yet to build, order engenders order. As a network of increasingly established feudal relationships makes peaceful travel more secure, commercial and other exchanges develop over ever wider areas. Towns grow up as market centers and centers of manufacture, where commerce is regulated, where craftsmanship is organized and cultivated. All this entails the rise of a new class of persons outside the feudal system, a class of town-dwellers or bourgeoisie.

The growing towns, constantly accumulating wealth, require architectural structures for religious worship on a scale greater than can be accommodated by a village church or a wayside chapel, and this in itself contributes to an increasing demand for craftsmanship of various sorts, and an increasing challenge to it.

The concentration of people in towns is intellectually stimulating. Further removed as they are from the animal existence that their forebears lived, concerned with the competitive cultivation of artificial skills, facing increased demands for the education of the young to meet the relatively complex needs of town life, and being crowded together so that they are constantly subjected to the stimulation of discussion, their minds are continually exercised, trained, and enlarged. The new cities become centers of thought and learning. Universities grow up as naturally as mushrooms in the woods, unplanned. So the conscious striving of the mind to bring order out of chaos is added as an increasingly concentrated factor in the development that began automatically with the establishment of primitive feudal relationships.

What I have here outlined is the basic dynamics involved in the initial development of a civilization. There must also be, as we have seen, a normative conception that serves as an ideal model to be realized in the conduct of men's lives, in the organization of their

sponding insecurity. Its particular development in the particular circumstances of a certain time and place will take particular forms that vary from the basic scheme I have here outlined.

societies, and in all the forms of cultural creation. When we are dealing with a civilization that, unlike the Sumerian, is built upon the accumulated remains of former civilizations, and in contact with other still-living civilizations, a certain eclecticism is inevitable in the formation of such a conception. We have already noted a Roman contribution to the normative conception on which Western civilization was based in the organization of the Christian Church. A variety of other contributions was to be made by the neighboring Arabic civilization in philosophy, in mathematics, in astronomy, in medicine. By the middle of the eighth century the Arabs had already undertaken the study and absorption of virtually the whole of Hellenistic science and philosophy, much of which was consequently transmitted through them to western Europe. Paraphrases of Aristotle by Ibn Sina (980–1037), better known as Avicenna, and commentaries on him by Abu'l-Walid Muhammad ibn-Rushd (1126–1198), better known as Averroës, being translated into Latin, were largely responsible for giving the philosophy of Aristotle, in however corrupt a form, a unique intellectual authority in mediaeval Europe.

Having cited examples of the Greek and Roman heritages, among many others, on which the new civilization drew, I must add that these heritages were so transformed, either in the process of transmission or in that of adoption, as to have only a nominal or superficial identity with their originals. Just as a bank building in twentieth-century New York, although its entrance is flanked by Doric columns, is not Greek architecture, so the Aristotle of the twelfth century is not Aristotle. All we can say is that Aristotle made a superficial contribution to mediaeval philosophy as Greek architecture made a superficial contribution to twentieth-century architecture. The same may be said, surely, of the Christianity of St. Paul, which was reshaped by a succession of Church fathers (e.g., St. Jerome, St. Ambrose, St. Augustine) and Church councils.

*

Perhaps we may say of every civilization, as of every individual, that it has a unique mind of its own in the sense of having its own view of the great external realm in which we mortals find ourselves, and of our place in that realm. The Graeco-Roman civilization, for example, tended not to give the value of reality to what was intangible or unbounded, such as empty space. Unlike Western mathematicians, Greek mathematicians could not deal with a putative entity called "minus five" as they dealt with "plus five" — for how can less than nothing be? They could not, in their computations, have used the square root of minus one, as Western mathematicians do, because minus one has no square root. Reality, for the Greeks, consisted of tangible bodies with clear boundaries. Divinity, for example, was not something to be associated with a formless concept like that of the Chinese Heaven or Spinoza's omnipresent deity, but rather with such clearly bounded and localized forms as those of Zeus and Athena. The figures of Greek sculpture were self-contained, complete in themselves, enclosed by definitive outlines, independent of any such indefinite background as that from which the figures in a painting by Rembrandt emerge only partially. Such concepts as that of dividing three by zero to obtain infinity belonged to a nightmare world rather than to the world of bounded and measurable realities.

Western civilization, by contrast, has been constantly attracted to the idea of the limitless. A Greek temple has a Euclidean roof-line, representing a boundary as firm as that of a triangle, but a Gothic cathedral is capped by steeples and spires that diminish gradually toward the infinitesimal (which is never reached) as they point upward toward infinity (which is never attained).* A Gothic cathedral has no ceiling. Its piers do not, like Greek columns, end at lintels, but open out gradually into branches that lose themselves in the obscurity of the vaulting above. The whole evolution of Gothic architecture was in the direction of replacing the bounding walls of the church with the glass through which the radiance of infinite space could enter. By contrast with such a musical instrument as the lyre, the purpose of that exclusively Western instrument, the cathedral organ, seems to be to fill endless space with sound that never ceases, or that fades away in reverberations. The purpose of the great bells that are hung in the steeples is to fill the empyrean with their humming — a humming that dies out in ever more distant realms of space, approaching but never attaining the limit of silence.

In Aristotle's cosmos continuous movement in a straight line was excluded because it implied infinity, the unmeasurable, so that movement had to be circular like that of the planets. In the cosmos governed by Newton's First Law of Motion, however, all movement that was not subjected to extrinsic influences continued in a straight line to infinity. It was not until the late stage in Western civilization represented by Einstein's Relativity that the rectilinear and infinite Newtonian cosmos was replaced, but replaced by another that would surely have been no less unacceptable to the Greeks, if only because it was not subject to absolute measurement.

A strong tendency, at least, throughout the history of Western civ-

* See Viollet-le-Duc's drawing of "The Complete French Cathedral" on the next page.

ilization has been to do away with boundaries, to achieve the bound-less. Even the present work, with its scepticism of categorical boundaries, represents a holism that is typically Western, and that the Greeks would, one surmises, have found uncongenial if not re-pugnant. Plato's "ideas" — e.g., of justice or of beauty — were each as complete in itself and as well defined as a brick.

No doubt one can find all sorts of tendencies in every civiliza-tion — pantheism in the philosophy of Zeno the Stoic, discreteness and measure in Michelangelo's David — but what must concern us is the dominating and defining features of a civilization, its peculiar features, those that are typical in the sense that they are most distinc-tive of its world outlook, its normative order. The normative order on which a civilization is based tends, however, to lose its integrity after it has been realized. So the Parthenon in Athens is more representative of the Classical civilization than the Pantheon in Rome, the Cathedral of Chartres is more representative of Western civilization than the Church of the Madeleine in Paris.

Beside the Western disposition to obliterate or transcend limits is another defining tendency no less marked. The normative world of Western civilization is a dynamic world of thrusts and tensions, a world of forces that actively oppose each other, so that whatever equilibrium is attained is not the static equilibrium of an Egyptian pyramid or a Greek temple but the dynamic equilibrium of opposed and mutually balanced forces. In the normative society described by Dante in *De monarchia,* there is one universal and therefore unlimited state (an ideal version of the state founded by Caesar Augustus), but the society is presided over by two equal potentates who alike derive their authority from God: the Pope, who is responsible for the spiritual governance of mankind, and the Emperor, who is responsible for its secular governance. The implication here is of a dynamic equilibrium between two realms, the spiritual and the temporal, each with its own separate government. (One can hardly imagine Solon, or the Plato who wrote *The Republic,* designing a society in these terms, since neither had ever conceived of such a separation between spiritual and temporal.) *

The basic polarity in Western civilization is the ethical polarity on which Christian theology was formed. Man had been created by God in his own image. Succumbing, however, to the Satanic seduction of the serpent in the Garden of Eden, he had fallen from this paradisal estate by acquiring the knowledge of a polar world divided between good and evil. In terms of this polarity, men are born evil but strive for the salvation that will entitle them, after the Last Judgement, to enjoy the rewards of the virtuous in Heaven rather than suffer the punishments of the unredeemed in Hell.

To a remarkable degree, evil, in this conception, is associated with sexuality — which presumably does not exist in Heaven and did not exist in the Garden of Eden before the fall of man. (Note that the acquisition by Adam and Eve of the knowledge of good and evil immediately made them aware, for the first time, of their nakedness, prompting them, as reported in Genesis 3:7, to hide the evidence of their sexuality behind aprons that they made of fig leaves.)

For two thousand years, then, from St. Paul to Tolstoy, the ideal of virginity (or, failing that, of a more qualified and therefore more

* Note, however, that the spiritual and temporal in Dante's world are parts of one whole, like the two legs on which a man walks.

attainable chastity) has been upheld throughout the West.* The
suppression of the sexual impulse that this entailed caused the natural attraction between persons of opposite sex to take the sublimated
form of an ideal love, which is a principal theme of Western poetry,
as friendship, based on loyalty, is a principal theme of Chinese poetry.†

*

The normative world of Western civilization is represented by
Gothic architecture as the normative worlds of the Graeco-Roman
and Chinese civilizations are represented, respectively, by the Greek
temple and the Chinese landscape.

Both the Parthenon and the Cathedral of Chartres were built as
sanctuaries to which the human society might resort for communion
with divinity; yet they represent conceptions so different that they
cannot be compared with each other in terms of better or worse.
The Greeks would surely have considered Chartres a monstrosity,
violating the rule of measure in all things; while its own builders,
one supposes, would have found the Parthenon too tightly bounded
for the accommodation of divinity — as if one should try to fit the
God of the infinite into a closet.

The Greek temple was built, so to speak, from the outside in, its
designers being concerned with its external appearance rather than
its interior. The Gothic cathedral, by contrast, was built from the inside out, its builders being concerned with its interior first of all, and
only finally with its exterior. What the interior of the Gothic cathedral was designed to produce was a sense of limitless space, of space
that is not walled in but that, illuminated by "a dim religious light," is
gradually lost, with distance from the observer, in an increasing obscurity.

Just as the structural basis of the Greek temple is the column-and-
lintel, so the structural basis of the Gothic cathedral is the arch. The
so-called "true" arch, composed of separate wedge-shaped stones,
remains standing because each side leans with equal weight against
the other. The equal pressure from either side holds the keystone
in place — and, in fact, holds all the stones in place, even without
cement. What this amounts to is an inward "thrust" from either side

* See 1 Corinthians 7, and the Introduction to Tolstoy's *Kreutzer Sonata*.
† The concept of man as a fallen angel, or as a beast with a soul, was one of the main
determinative elements in Western civilization only until the end of the nineteenth
century, when it began to break down. The breakdown is associated with the replacement of the Creation story in Genesis by Darwinism, the materialism preached by
Marx, and the acceptance of human sexuality identified with Freud (in whom it was,
however, a pessimistic or a despairing acceptance).

that balances the thrust from the other. One can also think in terms of an outward thrust; for the weight of the keystone is equally distributed or communicated in both directions, being continuously transmitted from stone to stone down to the base on either side. Here is a dynamic equilibrium of thrust and counter-thrust, by contrast with the dead-weight equilibrium of column-and-lintel construction.*

If one places a series of identical round arches against one another in a row one gets a so-called barrel vault. The simplest vaulted chamber one could construct would consist of two parallel walls spanned by such a vault. The walls would have to have a certain thickness and solidity to receive the outward thrust from the vault without being pushed over; and the higher they were the thicker and more solid they would have to be, so that a practicable limit to their height would quickly be reached.

Little light could enter such a chamber except from its two ends, for the removal of enough stones from the vault would cause its collapse, since they are needed to receive and transmit the thrust and counterthrust, while the removal of stones from the walls to make windows of any size might weaken them dangerously in their role of supporting the heavy vault, with its outward thrusts.

Imagine, now, two identical barrel-vaulted chambers that cross each other at right angles, as the transept of a cathedral crosses the nave. If one stands inside the square area that represents the crossing and looks up, one sees that the two interpenetrating vaults meet each other along two arched lines (called groins) that run diagonally from each corner to the one opposite, the two crossing each other at their respective apexes in the middle. A weight, such as that of a spire, placed over the center of the crossing, where the diagonal groins cross, would be distributed equally four ways, along the groins to the four respective corners of the crossing, as if the groins were themselves arches (and, indeed, in most Romanesque and Gothic churches such groins are covered, on the inside, by ribs of stone that do constitute arches). A weight placed elsewhere over the crossing, but still along the center line and apex of either vault, will

* What I have just described is simply an architectural expression of Newton's Third Law of Motion: *When two bodies interact, the forces exerted by each on the other are equal and opposite.* Each side of the arch presses against the other with equal force; two adjacent stones press reciprocally upon each other with equal force. The Gothic cathedral and Newtonian physics represent the same normative order in different terms. It is also represented by the atom of Western physics, which has become a tense complex of opposing and balanced forces, lacking any sharp outline, by contrast with the hard, massy, indivisible atom of the Greeks, as inert and as sharply bounded as a block of marble. Presumably the normative order of the Greeks would have prevented them from discovering the atom as we know it, or as we suppose it to be.

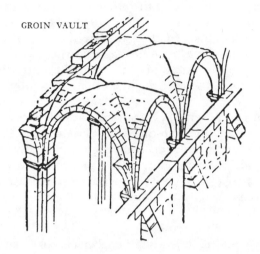

GROIN VAULT

be distributed equally two ways, down the vault on either side to the two diagonal groins, one on each side, and along them to the two respective corners. A weight placed at a point below the apex of either vault will be carried down to the groin below it, and then down the groin to the corner from which it springs. In sum, wherever a weight is placed on the crossing of the two vaults, it will be carried down to one or more of the four corners, so that four corner-posts, without walls between them, are all that are needed. The com-

pound vault over the crossing, divided into four parts by the diagonal groins, is supported like a canopy exclusively at its four corners.

Next let us cut one of the cross chambers off at the line of the wall on either side of the other, leaving it no longer than the other is wide. In that case, the other chamber would be lighted by a vaulted opening on either side where the truncated chamber had been cut off. (One might, if one chose, fill such an opening with stained glass — which is to be viewed from within rather than from without.)

Suppose next that the one long chamber is traversely penetrated by other like chambers of exactly its width — cut off, that is, at its walls — one after another, side by side. What one would then have would be one long vaulted chamber divided into square bays, each separated from its neighbor by a transverse arch (what remained of the original barrel vault), each with a vault divided into four parts by the two diagonal groins that crossed it from each corner to the opposite corner, each with a longitudinal arch on either side to span the opening. Now the entire thrust of the vault over each bay would be carried to the four piers, one at each corner, on which it rested like a canopy. The entire weight of the complex vault, made up of a succession of bays down the length of the chamber, instead of being carried by a continuous wall on each side, would be carried by two rows of piers, with openings between the piers in each row to let in light from outside.

Each pier in one of the rows, except those at the end, would receive, from the two longitudinal arches connecting it with the piers on either side, two thrusts that, being directly opposed, neutralized each other. It would also receive two thrusts along the two diagonal groins or ribs that sprang from it, and these thrusts would only partially neutralize each other, pressing outward against the pier for the rest. Finally, each pier would receive the outward thrust from the transverse arch that connected it with the corresponding pier in the other row. Since the net effect of the five thrusts it received would be to push it outward, this outward push would have to be countered by a buttress of sufficient thickness and weight on the outside.

Suppose, however, that this long vaulted chamber or nave is flanked by an aisle on either side, as in any Gothic cathedral. In that case, the buttress for each pier might have to be separated from it by the width of the aisle, to support it only by means of a stone arch or bridge (a "flying buttress") crossing from it over the aisle to the top of the pier, thereby supplying the inward thrust to balance the net outward thrust from the complex of interior vaulting.

So far I have described this schematic structure in terms of round arches and barrel vaulting only. But the height of round arches or

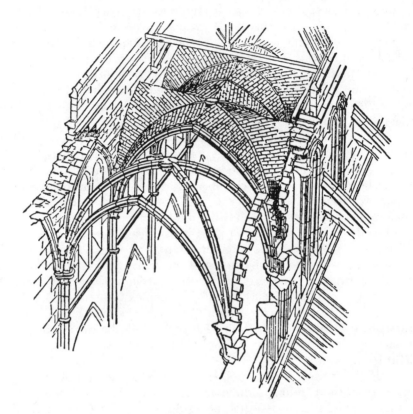

barrel vaults is limited by their width, of which it is always half. If, then, one wishes to gain more height for the vaulting and the arched openings alike, one might substitute pointed for round arches. This device would also make it possible, by its flexibility, to make the height of the transverse arches (as well as the longitudinal arches) the same as that of the longer diagonal groins or ribs, so that the vaulting of the nave may be all at one level (like the inside of a boat's hull upside down).

The account I have just given of the structural problems that confronted the architects of the mediaeval cathedrals, and their solution, is also a schematic account of the evolution of church architecture from the earliest round-arched and barrel-vaulted Romanesque churches (c. A.D. 1000) to its fullest realization in the great Gothic cathedrals of the thirteenth century — stone canopies walled by glass — with their pointed arches and vaults, such as those of Paris, Chartres, Amiens, and Rheims.

The finished product, represented by any of these four, is a dynamic complex of thrusts and counter-thrusts carried longitudinally, transversely, and diagonally, from the crossing of the transept or the apex of each bay outward through the stone arcs of the flying buttresses and eventually into the ground on both sides — all the thrusts (longitudinal, lateral, and diagonal) mutually countering and neutralizing one another in a grand equation representing the dynamic stability that has enabled these structures to stand for centuries.

The inside of any of these cathedrals, symbolically comprehending infinite space, is what counts, the outside consisting essentially of stone scaffolding (buttressing).

They are also dynamic structures, entailing the constant tension of polar opposites, like the religion of sin and salvation, like Dante's ideal society of spiritual and secular powers in dynamic balance, like all of Western physics from Newton through Heisenberg. One may plausibly believe that Western civilization, more than any other (unless it be the Mohammedan), has glorified dynamism.

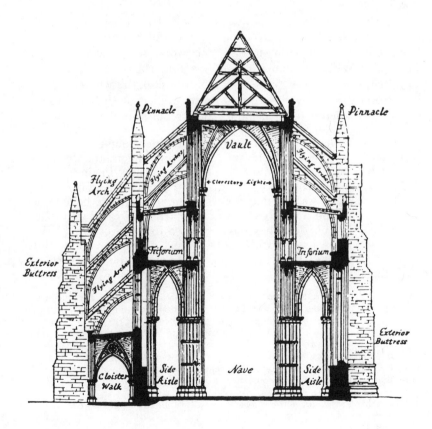

A civilization is far more than a merely utilitarian artifact to provide physical security and economic benefits. It is a common undertaking to translate a normative vision into reality. It is born of an irresistible inspiration in the common mind that overrides doubt and confusion to unite a whole society in such an undertaking. So the Athenian society was moved when it built the temples of the Acropolis, and so the French society was moved when it built the Cathedral of Chartres. The ecumenical completeness and integrity of such an inspiration, rising above petty or utilitarian motives, give such an endeavor a purity distinctive of a stage in the history of a civilization that may be regarded as its finest moment — a moment that is truly momentary, for it will never be repeated, however much the civilization may thereafter grow in wealth, in power, or in technical mastery. This is what distinguishes the building of the great thirteenth-century cathedrals from the building of, let us say, the Louvre, or the Empire State Building in New York, or even such a fine piece of ecclesiastical but eclectic architecture as St. Paul's Cathedral in London.*

The sheer expense of building the Cathedral of Chartres was met by contributions from all over the Kingdom of France, thereby justifying the statement that it was "the work of France and of all France."† When its construction was undertaken (after a fire in 1145 had destroyed its predecessor on the site), the whole society of the region was involved and, in a sense, unified by the common endeavor. In a letter to a colleague, the Archbishop of Rouen wrote:

> The inhabitants of Chartres have combined to aid in the construction of their church by transporting the materials. . . . Who has ever seen! — Who has ever heard tell, in times past, that powerful princes of the world, that men brought up in honour and in wealth, that nobles, men and women, have bent their proud and haughty necks to the harness of carts, and that, like beasts of burden, they have dragged to the abode of Christ these waggons, loaded with wines, grains, oil, stone, wood, and all that is necessary for the wants of life, or for the construction of the church? ‡

* I say that the inspiration rises above petty or utilitarian motives, not that it does away with them. In this flawed world of our habitation everything has an underside. In 1194, when a fire destroyed in large part the Cathedral of Chartres as it then was, among the arguments advanced for its reconstruction was that the political importance and economic prosperity of the city of Chartres depended on its status as a religious center. (See Otto von Simson, *The Gothic Cathedral*, New York, 1962, pp. 164–167.) The political and economic benefits, however, were by-products of the impulse that brought people from outside to worship at Chartres.
† Simson, op. cit., p. 180.
‡ Henry Adams, *Mont-Saint-Michel and Chartres*, Boston, 1933, pp. 101–102.

I have chosen the Gothic cathedral — that "cosmos in stone," as Dr. Simson calls Chartres — to epitomize the normative vision on which Western civilization is based. Indeed it is a microcosm of Western civilization, with its aspiration to infinity, its complex balance of forces, and its associated tensions.

A civilization realizes itself in architecture at a relatively early stage in its evolution. When it realizes itself in science, it is likely to do so at a later stage, after the hold of dogmatic religion has been loosened by scepticism — e.g., the great age of Greek science was the Hellenistic, the great age of Western science has been from the seventeenth to the twentieth century. Eventually, however, vision and inspiration are lost. Then, at last, the civilization becomes no more than an artifact for the production of power and wealth.

XXIX

The Expansion of the West

EVERY CIVILIZATION tends to spread geographically, especially in its final imperial phase. This tendency varies in the degree of its dynamism. It was stronger in the Mesopotamian, the Graeco-Roman, and the Arab civilizations than in the conservative Chinese civilization — which never, be it noted, took to ships and spread overseas. (Were not the Chinese, when they built their Wall to wall others out, walling themselves in as well?) It is not surprising that Western civilization, with its aspiration to infinity and its dynamism, should have been the most expansive of all, finally spreading to encompass the whole globe, even reaching into outer space to establish a first contact with other planets.

We may think of this expansion as beginning with the birth of the civilization, because the first of the series of Crusades, penetrating the Middle East, was launched in 1095. In the thirteenth century embassies were sent to Genghis Khan, head of the Mongol Empire; and Marco Polo, having sojourned at the court of Kublai Khan, returned to report on the Chinese civilization. Before the end of the fifteenth century Columbus had discovered the Americas and Vasco da Gama had sailed around the Cape of Good Hope to India. In the first quarter of the sixteenth century the expedition originally commanded by Magellan circumnavigated the globe — from Spain around the southern end of South America to the Philippines, then past the Cape of Good Hope to return to Spain. At the same time, the two New World civilizations, the Mayan-Aztec and the Incaic, were destroyed and replaced by the expanding civilization that proceeded to establish itself over the length and breadth of the American continents.

The increasing domination of the earth by what had begun as a civilization confined to Europe led, in the eighteenth and nineteenth centuries, to the creation of the great European empires in Africa and Asia as well as America. By 1911 Europeans had reached both the North Pole and the South Pole.

The first civilization, which began some 6,000 years ago, spread from the head of the Persian Gulf over Mesopotamia and into Asia Minor. The present civilization has spread from Europe over the entire globe.

*

If the history of life on earth represents the progressive emergence of order from chaos, if the advent of mind in the course of that history represents a new stage in which life consciously undertakes to produce such order, and if civilization represents this undertaking, then it should not be surprising if the latest civilization showed some advances on the earlier.

No one living today is in a position to make such comparative judgements except tentatively and with the utmost diffidence. I do not myself think that, in the graphic arts, Western civilization can be said to have exceeded the achievements of Greece, or the achievement represented by Chinese landscape painting. Nor can I say that it has exceeded the Graeco-Roman or the Chinese civilization in literary achievement. I would guess, however, that in a detached judgement it would be regarded as having equaled them in these fields — although, as we see right away if we try to judge between the Parthenon and the Cathedral of Chartres, the possibilities of such comparison are limited.*

On the other hand, I have no doubt that the achievements of Western civilization in the associated fields of mathematics, the natural sciences, and technology so far exceed those of any other civilization as to represent virtually a new order of accomplishment. And these achievements (some of which were the subjects of the first three parts of this work) are associated with the expansion of Western civilization until it has become the first worldwide civilization — until, indeed, it has taken what may be the first steps in an expansion beyond the planet to which the life we know has hitherto been confined.

Until the fifteenth century, the expansion of Western civilization had taken place like that of other civilizations, overland and along oceanic coasts. However, the dry lands of the earth are but islands on a planet that is over two thirds ocean, so that any sudden worldwide expansion was hardly possible until men were ready to navigate

---

* This does not mean that they do not exist. I find no difficulty in judging between the Parthenon and the Egyptian Temple of Amon.

the open oceans.* This required navigational aids, of which the magnetic compass was of prime importance. Although it had existed for centuries, the first use of it for navigation over the open seas appears to have been by Vikings in the twelfth century. Without it, Columbus could hardly have set out deliberately, as he did in 1492, over an ocean of which no end was known. In the eighteenth century, two Englishmen invented respectively the sextant, an instrument that enabled a navigator to determine his latitude, and the chronometer, which allowed him to determine his longitude even after he had been many weeks away from land.† About the same time, medical science discovered a way of overcoming the dietary deficiency that caused ships' crews to die of scurvy on long voyages — so that Captain Cook, the first to cross the Antarctic Circle, was able to make voyages that kept men at sea for years. In the following centuries, accelerating scientific and technological developments enabled men to navigate the atmospheric envelope of the earth, and at last to go beyond it into outer space. Who would have believed, when men first crossed the Antarctic Circle, that in less than two centuries they would be visiting the moon?

In the perspective that shows particular civilizations, which last one or two thousand years, it is Western civilization, specifically, that expands to encompass the entire globe. However, in the perspective of some 5,000 million years, which comprehends the entire history of life on earth — the development of eukaryotic cells, their combination to make multicellular organisms, the emergence of mind, and mind's creation of civilization — in such a perspective it is civilization itself that, beginning in a river-valley here or there, has now expanded to encompass the globe and, perhaps, to go beyond it.

The expansion we are viewing here, however, is not merely this geographical expansion. It is, more fundamentally, the expansion of the knowledge life has acquired of itself and its setting. Presumably, after some 6,000 years of the development of civiliza-

---

* Antarctica is the only isolated continent. Africa is connected with Eurasia, the Americas are almost connected with it at the Bering straits, and Australia is almost connected with it by chains of islands. Probably well before Columbus, the Polynesians had begun to spread across the Pacific from island to island in their outrigger canoes. Vikings, probably carried off course, reached North America about the year 1000, but made no settlement. This does not alter the fact that the worldwide expansion of Western civilization was the result of a departure from the coastlines and adventure over the open oceans.

† If one knows when it is noon at any charted location on the earth's surface (e.g., Greenwich), then one can calculate one's longitude by the position of the sun or of the stars at that moment. Hence the requirement for such a time-keeper as the chronometer, which can be relied on still to give Greenwich time, for example, with reasonable accuracy many weeks after leaving the last known location on the earth's surface.

tion — viewed in the large perspective as an undifferentiated whole — it was ready for this general expansion, which we associate in the first instance with the progress of science.

*

The burgeoning of scientific knowledge begins quite abruptly in the sixteenth century. (Here we again reduce our momentarily expanded perspective to the close-up view.) From the beginning of Western civilization, which it is convenient to date from the year 1000, all thinkers had accepted the body of Christian dogma, upheld by the authority of what was still the only Christian Church in the West, as representing fundamental truth, and had sought to explain the world exclusively by deduction from it. While this total commitment to the dogmatic aspects of a normative vision could produce the purity of Gothic art and of such intellectual structures as those of Thomas Aquinas and Dante, it forbade the free use of the mind in the quest of scientific knowledge. With the opening up of the age of physical exploration, however, an age of intellectual exploration opened up as well.

We may suppose that the order and security produced by Western civilization in its first five hundred years caused men to become less preoccupied than they had been with otherworldly matters — specifically with the afterlife described in the Christian teachings — and so to turn their attention increasingly to the world of their present life, which now appeared to have more hopeful possibilities than it had had at the end of the Dark Ages. A new breed of humanistic philosophers, exemplified by Erasmus, began to concern themselves with the actual life of man on earth, Sir Thomas More going so far as to imagine, in his *Utopia,* an ideal society that was not in the Kingdom of Heaven but on this earth itself. So the authority of the Church, which continued to regard the present life as no more than a stage of testing for the next one, lost intellectual conviction and tended to be left behind by the intellectual progress made outside its rule.

The Greeks, who lived in a commonsense mathematical world of positive integers only (so that for them a fraction was only a proportion between two integers, as in a rectangle that is 2 meters wide by 3 long), took to geometry in part because of the frustrations posed by arithmetical computation. (In geometry it suffices to say that the area of a second square constructed on the diagonal of a first square is twice that of the first square — this being a special case of the Pythagorean theorem, that the square on the hypotenuse of a right-angle triangle equals the sum of the squares on the other two sides.

But, if one wanted to proceed from this to determine arithmetically, by square roots, the proportion of the diagonal to the side, one would end up with a figure that could never be precisely determined, like ⅓ of 100, which is 33.333 . . . , with an infinite number of threes following the decimal point, and this would have been a nightmare to the Greek mind.) The Greek contributions to mathematics were limited, therefore, to what did not require elaborate and indefinite arithmetical calculations, so that there was no imperative need for the place-value system of notation that had been invented by the Mesopotamian civilization almost 2,000 years before Euclid.* Surely, however, the physics, the astronomy, and the cosmology of the West, together with all the associated technology, depended entirely on the facility of computation provided by the place-value system; nor would the Western mind be put off it by the confrontations with infinity and infinitesimals that it entailed (as when one calculates the figure for 100 divided by 3 or the square root of 8). Western scientific thought would not long remain limited to the common sense of the Greeks. The civilization that could appreciate the Gothic spire, which diminishes toward infinity, would not consider that the square root of 8 was outside the limits of sanity, or that the atom had to be indivisible.

It is a curious example of how civilizations are cumulative, each benefiting from the accomplishments of its predecessors, that the Mesopotamian place-value system, unknown or unaccepted by Greeks and Romans, was transmitted to the Hindu civilization of India, from the Hindu civilization to the Arab, and from the Arab to the Western, which it reached by the twelfth century. Here it was slow in establishing itself, but it had at last done so by the sixteenth century, when the real need for it arose.†

Natural science was born in the West when Western thought liberated itself from such exclusive dependence on Christian dogma as characterizes theology. It was born when thinkers could base themselves on the observation of nature instead. Copernicus (1473–1543), a contemporary of Columbus, explored outer space, recording the observed movements of the sun and the other astral bodies that traversed the sky in their regular courses. On the basis of such observation, then, and contrary to the teachings of the Church, he concluded that the earth circled around the sun rather than the sun

* See page 351 above.
† The English biographer John Aubrey, born in 1626, wrote: "All old accounts are in numerall letters. Even to my remembrance when I was a youth, Gentlemen's Bayliffs in the Country used no other, e.g. i. ii. iii. iiii. v. vi. vii. viii. ix. x. xi. etc: and to this day in the accounts of the Exchecquer" (*Aubrey's Brief Lives*, O. L. Dick ed., London, 1950, p. xxxiii).

around the earth, and that the apparent daily movement of the sun and the stars was produced by a spinning of the earth.

It is noteworthy that this discovery, the circumnavigation of the earth, and the general replacement of Roman by Arabic numerals all occurred at the same time. It was, in fact, a time of general liberation from the restrictive orthodoxy of the Middle Ages, marking their close. The invention of printing by moveable type allowed the members of a wide public to interpet the Bible for themselves, and made widely available the writings of such humanist philosophers as Erasmus and More. Italian sculptors and painters began to study anatomy in order to represent human bodies as they are, rather than such idealized forms, some with wings attached to their shoulders, as decorate the façades of the Gothic cathedrals. All this was like a discovery of nature, of the natural, by a civilization that had, until then, been preoccupied with the supernatural. There is an association between Copernicus's presentation of the true relationship between sun and earth, and the carefully observed musculature in Antonio del Pollaiuolo's bronze of Hercules holding Antaeus off the ground.*

Aristotle had represented the universe as a hollow sphere, with the earth at its center and the stars fixed to its inner surface. Newton, in the seventeenth century, represented it as infinite, and introduced the concept of gravitation to account for departures from uniform motion in a straight line.

For the development of Western science since Newton I have only to refer the reader to the first three parts of this work. That development represents an enlargement, not only in the physical sense, but in the sense of liberation. Perhaps its greatest achievement — in modern mathematics, in relativity theory, and in quantum theory — is its liberation of the mind from a common sense that is merely subjective, representing only the limitations of the observer's natural endowments for the direct apprehension of external reality.

*

The prime motive behind the study of nature since the fifteenth century has been the mind's need to know, to understand — as when a child, told that the world was made by God, asks who made God. The need to know is one of the defining characteristics of mind. A negative and metaphoric way of putting this is to say that the mind abhors the vacuum of ignorance. Consequently, in the absence of true knowledge it fills that vacuum in ways that do not bear examination. The commonest is to fill it, so to speak, at one remove — as

* Professor George Edgell of Harvard used to point out that if we had only the legs of the Hercules we could still tell that they were carrying the weight of two bodies.

when we believe that what we do not ourselves know or understand is known or understood by those whom we regard as our betters: our parents (if we are children), or priests, or professors. Those who are credited with the knowledge we lack may, in their turn, themselves credit surrogates — as when the priest, who supplies the answers to the questions of his flock, has obtained them through a course of training from those whom he, in his turn, regards as his betters.*

Another way that the vacuum is filled entails the kind of social competition, associated with boasting, in which we are tempted to make a show of what will pass for knowledge. So, in discussion, we habitually advance as unquestioned knowledge whatever will give the impression of being so, even though it should, in fact, be no more than a guess.† In doing this, all but the most sophisticated among us impose on ourselves as on our auditors. Nevertheless, these devices are but means of avoiding the recognition of an ignorance that, if recognized, would increase the burden of anxiety which is inseparable from mind.

The mind's need to know is associated with what I have conceived to be its mission, that of bringing order out of chaos. Of necessity, however, it is also preoccupied with the practical problems of living in the present; and for those of us who represent this particular preoccupation to the exclusion of others, the natural sciences are justified, not in themselves, but by the practical applications that are by-products of their cultivation.

The development of science since Newton, although it has been motivated by the mind's need to know, has in fact resulted in technological advances that must have a notable place even in the perspective of over 3,000 million years. It is, then, to these advances, and their implications for the history of life, that we turn in the following chapter.

* In this respect professors do not differ from priests, or the specialized academic communities from churches. (This is why so many of the fundamental advances in understanding are made by persons who, like Darwin and Einstein, do not form part of the academic communities in their fields.)

† One knows the foibles of others by experiencing them in oneself. Because I am credited with a special knowledge of birds, it will happen that, on a walk in the country with a friend who does not have such knowledge, he will ask me the identity of a bird we had merely glimpsed. Partly because of what he expects of me, I find myself prompt to respond with the name of a species — only to have to admit to myself, when I have had time for thought, that the answer I gave with such assurance was no more than a questionable guess. Like priest or professor, I automatically live up to the role attributed to me by others, even if I do so only in pretence.

XXX

The Domestication of the Earth

WE HUMANS HAVE ALWAYS MADE a sharp distinction between our own and all other species on the basis that it alone possesses an attribute of transcendental significance, which has been variously defined. That attribute is what some have called "soul," what we have here called "mind." It constitutes one basis for the distinction we all make between man and nature.

This latter distinction also represents the view that man does not live in a state of nature, although he once did (and although some primitive humans, like the Australian aborigines, still come close to doing so). Here the traditional distinction, since the age of world-wide exploration began, has been between the naked and the clothed, which is a valid distinction if we regard it as symbolic only. For nature did indeed make man naked, so that he should be exposed to the elements; but man frustrated nature's design by improvising clothes to cover his nakedness. Implicit in this view is a fundamental opposition between man and nature, between what is artificial and what is natural. Civilization is artificial. It is opposed to the state of nature, and in its progressive development it seeks to overcome and subjugate nature.

This opposition between man and nature dates back only to man's first indulgence in the practices that would lead to civilization, such as that of clothing himself in the skins of other animals. It is, however, but part of a larger opposition, the opposition between organism and environment that dates back to the beginning of life itself. Presumably the first prokaryotic cells were vulnerable to exceedingly small changes in their local environments, changes in the chemical composition or temperature of the water they inhabited, or in the amount of ultraviolet radiation that reached them. In the process of evolution by natural selection, however, they and their successors became ever more independent of particular environmental conditions. The history of life on earth may be regarded as the history of such increasing independence.

As we saw in Part Three, Chapter II, until some 300 million years ago all life was confined to water, dying if the water in which it lived dried up. Then the development of lungs and feet overcame this particular vulnerability, producing the amphibians that were able to live part of their lives, at least, out of the water. A hundred and fifty million years later, an offshoot of the amphibians, the reptiles, became altogether independent of the water by developing the amniotic egg, which packaged the watery environment that the embryo still needed for its initial development, protecting it against the dry external environment by a shell. Less than a hundred million years later, with the advent of the birds and the mammals, life gained a relative independence of changes in the temperature of the environment by the development of means to control internal temperature.

May we not say, then, that the whole evolution of life has been in the direction of making organisms increasingly independent of their environment — or, rather, of particular environments to which they are, in the beginning, bound? Until a few million years ago this increasing independence was achieved by the blind process of natural selection alone. However, with the advent of mind, natural selection began to be supplemented, in the case of our own species, by the deliberate improvisations that constitute the artifices of civilization as distinct from the processes of nature.

Where men live today in a state of advanced civilization, a baby born prematurely (prematurely separated, that is, from the specialized environment of the womb on which it naturally depends) is placed in a contrivance called an incubator, especially fabricated for the purpose, in which the environment it needs has been artificially packaged, and within which it is protected from an inimical external environment, of which it is thereby made independent. There is no difference of function between the incubator and the amniotic egg; but the latter was produced by natural selection over millions of years, whereas the former was produced virtually instantaneously by the artifice of mind.

Until some 300 million years ago, life was confined to the water. Then, by natural selection, it was made independent of the water so that it could survive in the air over dry land. Until our present, life was confined to the atmospheric envelope of our planet. Now, however, by an artifice of the mind similar to the incubator, it has been made independent of the atmospheric envelope so that it can survive in outer space — as in the case of the organisms of our own species who, encased in special clothing that contains a special environment, have visited the moon and walked on its surface.

When we make the distinction between the state of nature and the state of civilization, we are, in more specific terms, referring to the distinction between the provision made by the process of natural selection and the provision made by mind in the exercise of its capacity for conscious improvisation, the conscious improvisations of the mind being artificial, in our terminology, as opposed to natural.

When honeybees build a hive, within the specialized and contrived environment of which they may spend their lives (the queens, in many cases, never leaving it at all), they appear to be doing what men do when, for example, they build an apartment house. But we do not say that, within the hive, the bees are not living in a state of nature, although we do say this of the men who live in an apartment house. What is the difference? The difference is that the hive is the direct product of natural selection in that its design is contained in the genes of the honeybees, who realize it mindlessly; whereas the design of the apartment house is not contained in the human genes but is, rather, a consciously contrived improvisation of the mind, which seeks by such creation to overcome and subjugate nature.

*

The image of the egg, the incubator, or the apartment house implies the persistence unchanged of a natural environment from which the organism withdraws as a snail into its shell. The fabricated environment does not alter or diminish the natural environment any more than the specialized and enclosed environment of a submarine alters or diminishes the great ocean within which it is, by its insignificance, lost. In fact, however, civilization is now altering, displacing, and replacing the natural environment of the entire earth.

For the first thousand million years of its existence this earth was of mineral composition only; nor could a disembodied observer of the time have foreseen that the first cells, which were spreading in a few shallow pools of water, microscopic and apparently insignificant in terms of the vastness of the earth, were the beginning of a development that would remake the entire planetary surface and its atmospheric envelope as well.

This development reached one culmination a million years ago. (In the whole scope of time involved it makes no difference whether we say a hundred thousand or a million years.) Meanwhile, however, life had given rise to mind. The disembodied observer of the earliest men, who embodied it, could hardly have foreseen, however, that through the agency of civilization it would remake the surface of the planet, and perhaps its atmospheric envelope, as they had already been remade once before.

One reason why the disembodied observer of 3,500 million years ago could not have foreseen that life would remake the surface of the planet was that the cells which represented it were so few, so small, and so limited in their distribution. Similarly, the disembodied observer of a million years ago could not have foreseen that mind would remake the surface of the planet, because the hominids which represented it were so few and so limited in their distribution. The original life, however, took thousands of millions of years to produce any considerable change in the earth's surface, whereas mind (in accordance with the rule of acceleration set forth in Chapter I above) is now producing such a change with the abruptness of a cataclysm.

If we go back a million years, the human population of the entire earth was probably a few thousand or a few hundred thousand.* Ten thousand years ago, when agriculture and animal husbandry were beginning, it may have been 8 million. In A.D. 1 it may have been 300 million, in 1750, 800 million. This last date represents the point at which the great scientific and technical efflorescence of civilization was getting under way (as agriculture and animal husbandry had been getting under way in 8000 B.C.). From 800 million in 1750 we go to 1,000 million in 1800, 1,300 million in 1850, 1,700 million in 1900, 2,500 million in 1950, and 4,000 million in 1976. At the rate of increase in the early 1970s, the population would double in 35 years. (At the average rate from 8000 B.C. to A.D. 1, it would have taken some 2,000 years to double.)

Representing these figures by a graph showing growth from a million years ago to the present, what one gets is a curve that is almost horizontal for a million years until, almost at the present, it turns abruptly upward in an approach to the vertical. If one takes only the last 10,000 years of these million, the curve begins to angle up more steeply at A.D. 1, but at about 1800 turns abruptly upward to approach the vertical. Finally, if one takes just the period since 1750, it rises in a smooth upward curve that is ever steeper to the present, and that would rapidly approach the vertical if extrapolated beyond the present.†

What may properly be referred to in the long perspective as the

---

* It makes no difference in the overall picture whether it was 50 thousand or 500 thousand in the year 1,000,000 B.C. The population figures in this paragraph, all but the latest of which are no more than calculated estimates of orders of magnitude, are taken from "The History of the Human Population" by A. J. Coale in *Scientific American*, September 1974.

† The present referred to is 1975, when these words are being written. The sophisticated reader will appreciate the fact that the rate of increase has almost reached an unsurpassable limit. (A vertical curve would represent an infinite increase in zero time.)

population explosion beginning in the eighteenth century is the consequence of a fall in the death-rate rather than a rise in the birth-rate. It is not that more infants are born but that more survive long enough to grow up and breed. They survive because of the scientific researches that Western civilization began to pursue at the end of the Middle Ages, when observation and experiment took the place of deduction from a mythic authority.

The development of biological science, in particular, has had this effect on the death-rate. The study of anatomy (represented by Pollaiuolo's bronze of Hercules and Anteus) led to knowledge of the hidden organs and processes of the body's interior; which led, in turn, to the ability to diagnose and correct malfunctioning in the body that would otherwise cause death. When Leeuwenhoek, in 1674, made a microscope through which he discovered the world of micro-organisms, he took the first step toward a knowledge of the microbial agents of deadly diseases.* That knowledge led, in turn, to an increasing ability to control these agents and thereby save life.

Biological science also discovered means of increasing food production, so that lack of food was not the check on the growth of population which it would otherwise have been. Add to this that the spread of Western civilization around the globe opened new lands for settlement and for the cultivation of food by the increasingly productive means that biological science was discovering.

Finally, developments in transportation and communication made possible exchanges over wide areas, so that food consumed in Europe might be produced in South America, while medical supplies produced in Europe might be used for the cure of disease in South America — and this kind of thing too, by increasing the effective use of the production that supported human life, allowed the human population of the world to increase.

One way to envisage the transformation of the earth by mind is to imagine oneself surveying all the continents over the millennia from an airplane that circumnavigates it constantly. Beginning 10,000 years ago, one sees an occasional small clearing in the wilderness where men have planted crops and built shelters for themselves and their animals. These clearings widen in parts of the earth until they are grain-fields continuing for hundreds of kilometers, spotted with settlements. Marshes are drained, lakes are created, and roads begin to wind across the changing landscape.

By the twentieth century, the most conspicuous development over important parts of the earth would be the spread of urban communities. Just as the first manifestations of agriculture may have been

* See p. 188 above.

small clearings surrounded by endless forests, so the first towns, sharply defined by their enclosing walls, had been no more than occasional dots in the endless expanses of countryside. And just as the little clearings had grown to become fields of grain that extended beyond the most distant horizons, so the towns now grew into urbanized regions that spread beyond the horizons to cover ever larger areas of what had been countryside.

Much would be missed in the view from the airplane: the changes in the fauna, many species of mammals and birds disappearing from wide areas or altogether, others that had been rare and local in their distribution becoming abundant and widespread. Some species were being changed (in their genotypes and therefore in their phenotypes) by adaptation to the artificial environments of civilization — e.g., the house sparrow and the Norway rat. The viewer might also fail to perceive that some of the remaining forests, coming under the management of men, were no longer the natural growths they had been but were acquiring the character of cultivated plantations; or that some of the large mammals had been reduced to living in reserves, as in zoological gardens, under the care and protection of mankind, the new collective master of the earth. More and more, however, the planet would assume the aspect of a man-made artifact.*

In the second half of the twentieth century, this domestication of the earth would, by its constant acceleration, have become cataclysmic in its pace. Even the composition of the oceanic fauna — fish and whales and seabirds — would be undergoing revolutionary alteration, while the chemistry of the ocean waters was being changed and films of oil, however fine, were spreading over them. The atmospheric envelope of the earth, too, was beginning to undergo changes in composition, until one could no longer be sure of the survival, intact, of the high layer of ozone on which most life depended for the reduction by filtration of the ultraviolet radiation that reached the earth's surface.

Except for the changes attributable to biological science, those in the earth's surface and atmosphere since 1750 had been brought about by accelerating technological developments associated with what we call "the industrial revolution" (but which, in a larger per-

---

* As I was writing this in a Swiss Alpine village, an osprey or fish hawk passed over on fall migration, traveling southwest. It had undoubtedly come from the region of the Baltic, and it was about to pass to the west of Mont Blanc on a course that would take it to the Mediterranean coast of France and probably on to North Africa. Its whole passage had been, and would continue to be, over a conspicuously man-made world of crowded cities, towns, highways, and cultivated lands. Almost everywhere that it landed, to feed or spend the night, it would have been among civilized men.

spective, may prove to be more than that). Waterpower and windpower had already been submitted to man's use in watermills and windmills, while the energy latent in wood had been used by burning to provide heat; but after the seventeenth century, with such inventions as the steam engine and the internal-combustion engine, the energy contained in coal and oil began to be used, not only for heat and light, but also as a substitute for muscle power that went far beyond the capacity of muscle. Electricity was generated and put to all sorts of use. And, by the middle of the twentieth century, the virtually unlimited energy contained in the nucleus of the atom had been brought into use.

The same revolution manifested itself in the domain of transport and communications. At the beginning of the eighteenth century it would have taken many months to send a message around the world, but by the twentieth it could be done in one second. In the sixteenth century it took Magellan's expedition three years to circumnavigate the earth; in the twentieth it was done in three hours.

What we have been tracing here is two parallel and associated developments. One is the transformation of the earth by mind in connection with what may be regarded as the domestication of nature by man. The other is the increasing withdrawal of men into an artificial environment produced by mind. Having suggested the course of the former development as seen through the eyes of the observer in the earth-circling airplane, let me now suggest the parallel course of the latter development.

A million or more years ago the first men lived like the baboons in a completely natural environment, exposed to the wind and the weather. Over the millennia they contrived clothing and shelters for protection from the rigors of this environment, and learned to use fire for heat and cooking. As villages and then towns developed, more people spent more of their lives indoors — that is to say, withdrawn from the natural environment into an artificial and amniotic environment. The "industrial revolution" that got under way about 1750 required, increasingly, that industrial workers and managers be brought together in large concentrations that had to be provided with commercial services, and this was facilitated by the development of communications and transport, allowing an ever wider geographical division of labor. As urban areas spread over the landscape an ever larger proportion of the human population was withdrawn into them from the surrounding countryside.

In 1825, London was the only city in the world with a population of one million. By 1975, fast as the human population was growing, the number of cities with a population over a million was growing three or four times faster, and growing in size as well as number. And the time was rapidly approaching when more people would be city-dwellers than country-dwellers.

Although no human beings, except for an insignificant remnant of savages, were living in a state of nature by the beginning of the twentieth century, the predominant rural population still lived under the governance of natural phenomena. The lives of those engaged in agriculture were dominated, the year around, by the seasons, by the vagaries of the weather, and by the fruitfulness of the soil. The huts or houses into which they withdrew at night and on other occasions were small compared to the surrounding earth and sky — as the submarine is small compared to the surrounding ocean. But the people who live inside the great urban conglomerations are increasingly in the position of the embryo in the egg, the infant in the incubator, the mariner in a submarine, the space-traveler in his space-craft. They have withdrawn almost completely into an artificial world, and what they still see of the natural world they see, so to speak, through the windows that protect them from it. Even the atmosphere they breathe has been artificially treated. This represents the furthest point reached so far in the long evolution of life toward an ever greater independence of immediate environmental conditions.

*

In Part One we surveyed the physical universe to the spatial-temporal limit of our vision, which is 10,000 million light-years outward in space and backward in time. In Parts Two, Three, and Four we have now surveyed the evolution of life on earth from its apparent beginning to the limit represented by our own particular present. There was no sense of a chaotically abrupt stop in our survey of the physical universe when we got to the limit of 10,000 million light-years; and, although we would have liked to know what lay beyond this limit, it was so far away as not to arouse any intimate concern or any suspense hard to bear. The unfinished history of earthly life, however, cut off so arbitrarily at a date that, in the long view, is altogether accidental, that does not represent the close of a chapter or even the end of a sentence, leaves this an unfinished work. And this is the more painful because the acceleration of the evolution we have been following has reached the point where even a decade might make a difference. It is as if Shakespeare's *Hamlet* should stop with Act IV, Scene 7, line 127. For lack of a better alternative, imagination would have to take over, weighing alternative possibilities in terms of their plausibility by the test of such an order as had seemed to be developing in the work up to that point. This, then, is the burden of the next and final chapter of Part Four.

XXXI

The Unknown Future

> O! that a man might know
> The end of this day's business ere it come;
> But it sufficeth that the day will end,
> And then the end is known.
>
> — *Shakespeare*

OUR THEME HAS BEEN the progressive emergence of order from chaos. In a view that embraces the three or four thousand million years from the first prokaryotic cells to the first men this progress is manifest. When we reduce our perspective to the million years since the appearance of the first men, however, we cannot, without some reservation and uncertainty, say that the progress as a whole has been manifest, although there have been many manifestations of it. Mind has turned away from the natural order in quest of a civilized order that, at the moment where we have to break off, has not yet been achieved. The departure from the natural order has even entailed, and continues to threaten, a certain proliferation of chaos. It is as if life, having abandoned one order for the purpose of achieving another, found itself between the two at the moment when our history breaks off.

What cannot be in doubt is the continued striving toward order. Until the advent of mind, the evolution of life represented an unconscious drive toward an ever greater and more complete order. With the advent of mind that drive became conscious. It is the basic fact of evolution, perhaps the basic fact of being, and we must expect it to continue. One is tempted to believe that it progresses toward some final realization — but, if that is so, we cannot say whether the final realization lies a few thousand years ahead, a few million, or untold thousands of millions. We may suppose that, in any short periods of time (relative to the entire span of this evolution), there will be temporary breakdowns of the evolving order, entailing retrogression. Within these terms we may now speculate about the future.

*

What we call history begins with the more-or-less independent birth of local civilizations here and there around the globe, the first appearing some 6,000 years ago. These civilizations have spread until, at last in our own time, we see what is basically one civilization covering the entire earth and transforming it. This worldwide civilization provides an artificial environment into which human life is withdrawing, and if we assume its continuance we must expect that whatever other life survives will also be drawn into it, since there will be no alternative environment for its habitation.

One possibility is that this civilization will break down, as civilizations have always broken down in the past. Indeed, we have reason to speculate that civilizations have life-histories, like organisms, from infancy through youth to old age and death. In that case we would have to regard our civilization as entering old age. The implication is that we might, in the next two or three centuries, see a considerable proliferation of disorder throughout the world.

In the worst view, which is not altogether implausible, this disorder would be far greater and more damaging than anything that had preceded it. This is because our civilization has developed a power of destruction, represented by nuclear weapons, that could in a few days, if responsible control were lost, destroy a large part of life on earth and, perhaps, make much of the earth uninhabitable to all except a few primitive forms. It might destroy the environment, including the composition of the atmosphere on which most life, as now constituted, depends.

In this worst view, one can with some straining imagine a return to something like the condition of the earth 3,000 million years ago, in which life is represented only by such primitive forms as bacilli, perhaps including a few that live by photosynthesis.

In a view that embraced all time and the universe, even the catastrophic extinction of life on one among many millions of planets that support it might be inconsequential, like the death of one fish in an ocean that contains millions. Or the setback of evolution by 1,000 million years might seem of limited consequence in a view that embraced 10,000 million years. There would still be time for life on earth to try again, so to speak. Perhaps mind would evolve again, and more successfully, in some species different from our own.

It is also possible that, without the particular catastrophe I have described, the proliferation of our kind will exhaust the fertility of the earth, transforming much of it into desert. We would be like the plagues of locusts that, in their passage, consume everything edible, so that they have to move on or starve — but we, perhaps consuming even the seed-stock, and having no other planet to which we could move, would starve, so that our numbers would be drastically reduced and we might, like the dinosaurs before us, become extinct. Then, over hundreds of thousands of years, the earth might be expected to recover its fertility, enabling life to resume its progress.

‚Another possibility — to be realized in another hundred years, or in a thousand, or a million — is that the life we know will no longer be confined to the planet of its origin. The increasing independence of the immediate environment that civilization represents opens up vast possibilities for extraterrestrial habitation. In an amniotic container, which is not beyond what we could construct by our developing technology, we might be able to put a whole city into space. There are prospects, not implausible, of a transparent shell (an amnion) in the form of a wheel perhaps hundreds of kilometers in circumference and many kilometers thick, within which a community of men, with attendant plants and animals, might thrive. Revolving on its axis, it would, by what we call centrifugal force, provide the equivalent of the gravitational attraction that now binds us to the earth. It would contain an atmosphere suited to our needs, presumably the same as the natural or unpolluted atmosphere of the earth. Those who lived in it would depend on solar radiation as the source of the energy they needed. They would cultivate food under artificial conditions that were free of the capriciousness associated with earthly weather. Eventually there might be any number of such amniotic wheels in space, maintaining communication with one another — and no limit to the possibility of their proliferation.*

There are other like prospects that are not inconceivable, prospects entailing the proliferation of life in the space that surrounds the earth — such as that of altering the existing atmosphere of other planets, or providing them with an atmosphere where they lack it, in order to make them livable for earthly life.†

So much for imagined possibilities, which one could multiply indefinitely. I myself see reason to believe that, whatever the future may hold, it will not be what any of us have anticipated. The reason is that this seems to have been our experience ever since mind devel-

---

* In the footnote on p. 163 I speculated that colonies of human individuals might, by symbiosis, become superorganisms. Is it not conceivable that the colonies of human beings and other organisms contained, respectively, in such amniotic wheels as I am here imagining might each, by symbiosis, develop into a single organism — as the eukaryotic cell, by symbiosis, developed out of the association of prokaryotic cells?
† See p. 101 above.

oped to the point where it began to engage in prediction. What people in the past foresaw, if only in their speculations, that the whole earth, including its atmosphere, might be transformed by man? What thinker before Malthus (1766–1834), who lived only yesterday, foresaw that the population of mankind might increase to the limit of the earth's capacity for its support — and he stood discredited until the middle of the present century. Who before Jules Verne foresaw the possibility that men would land on the moon — and for him it was no more than a fantasy in which he indulged his imagination a century before it actually happened.* Experience shows that the unanticipated is what happens. I incline to believe that this will be true in what I may paradoxically call the foreseeable future as it has been in the past.†

While the course of events cannot be predicted, even in general terms, there is one prediction, not of the course of events, that may, I think, be made with some assurance. Mankind everywhere is coming loose from its cultural moorings, from the foundations of its psychological security. Hitherto there has generally been a normative order to which people were brought up — as in the case of those who built Notre-Dame de Chartres to give expression to what they believed to be God's own order. They have been able to conduct their lives, regulate their behavior, and make their decisions on the basis of such an order; for it has presented them with an established hierarchy of values and a basis for distinguishing good from bad, right from wrong. Such a normative order has been founded on tradition and has derived its authority from custom.

Tradition and custom, however, require time to become established, generally such time as is reckoned in centuries. If the conditions of life to which particular traditions or customs respond change gradually enough, they can evolve with it. But they cannot be replaced overnight or in one generation. Consequently, if they are abruptly rendered obsolete and unworkable by abrupt changes in the conditions of life, people will have lost their old moorings without having gained new ones. Then, in the common metaphor, they will be at sea. They will have no established hierarchy of values for distinguishing good from bad, right from wrong. They will have no established basis on which to conduct their lives, regulate their behavior, and make their decisions. Then they will lose their mental stability, they will be prey to a succession of outlandish fashions in

---

* *De la terre à la lune* was published in 1865. Men first landed on the moon in 1969.
† One may imagine, as an extreme example of the unanticipated, that life from elsewhere in the universe might come within our purview and, in one way or another, determine our future.

thought, they will be swept one way and then another by convulsive mass movements representing the capriciousness of mob psychology under the influence of insecurity or even panic.

One of the consequences of such a situation is social anarchy; and social anarchy always and necessarily evokes the organization of such government as keeps order by force and fear — Caesarian government or, under modern conditions, the police-state with all the means of compulsion and intimidation at its disposal. The police-state, with its imposed order, is not the opposite of anarchy but its complement.

In the first chapter of the series on civilization, which this one concludes, I called attention to the rule of acceleration in the evolution of all life on earth over the three or four thousand million years of its existence — and in the evolution of civilization (which is part of the evolution of life) over the past 6,000 years. Then, in the chapter preceding this one, I called attention to the curves, representing this acceleration, that were rising sharply toward the vertical in our own time. The acceleration has at last brought the pace of change to a point at which tradition and custom, which constitute the basis of civilized order, can no longer keep up. Under the circumstances, I foresee a proliferating chaos of the mind and of human society the world over in the period immediately ahead. Perhaps some manifestation of the unexpected, which is always what actually happens to falsify prophecy, will falsify this expectation. Perhaps some factor that I have not foreseen, or to which I have attached no importance, will become all-important and prove itself determinative for the future of life on earth. But it is hard to see how an increasing chaos can otherwise be averted.

*

Let the reader note the confirmation of the holistic thesis in the aspects of being we have reviewed so far. When, in Part One, we examined the very small, item by item, we saw how it represented the chaos of the Uncertainty Principle; but how the ever greater combination of the items that in themselves represented chaos represented an ever greater order in terms of statistical probability, until the equivalent of a perfect order was attained. This perfect order was what we saw when we examined physical being in the large, as provisionally represented by the Theory of Relativity.

Again, when we traced the evolution of life from the first organic molecules, submicroscopic in their dimensions, to the immense and organized assemblages of such molecules in the most advanced organisms of our time, we saw the same progressive construction of an increasingly wide and elaborate order out of an elemental chaos.

This was the theme of Parts Two and Three. If it has not been nearly so evident in Part Four, that is because in Part Four we have been dealing with such small portions of space and time — this one planet over the past 6,000 years, viewed in terms of centuries and even decades — out of who knows how many thousands or millions of millions of years? Even so, there has been evidence of an increasing order in the history of civilization (however wavering the progress), from the Babylonian ziggurat to the Cathedral of Chartres, from the paintings of the early Egyptians to those of the T'ang Dynasty in China, from the physics of Thales in the sixth century B.C. to that of Einstein in our own time.

If the holistic thesis is valid, however, it is absolutely valid only in terms of the whole of being in time and space. The smaller the proportion of the whole that the observer comprehends in his view, the more partial and uncertain are its manifestations. A single tree represents a very partial order, one leaf of the tree represents an order even more partial, one cell of the leaf an order still more partial — until, by such reduction, one comes down to that notional particle, the single quantum, which represents no order at all, which represents chaos.

Over the span of universal time and distance, beyond our vision, there may well be one perfect order, which we, within the limits of our vision as it is, and in terms of what time means to us, see in process of realization. In that process, it may be, life arises untold millions of times on untold millions of planets, only to fail, at last, in the great majority of cases. If it should fail in our case, the failure would not invalidate the thesis and, in a view of the whole, might appear altogether negligible — like the 999 salmon eggs that do not contribute to a new generation for every one that does. Or, if, in our case, the process should suffer a setback of a thousand million years, that too might be a negligible incident in the perspective that comprehends the whole. On the other hand, the very fact that life in general, and our kind in particular, having spread until it has covered the earth, is now moving out into space — this very fact opens up a new vista for hope and for the suspense that attends on hope.

*

I have now completed my survey of being — as best I could and from the parochial point of view to which the reader and I, alike, are bound. That survey, with the anxieties that it arouses for our immediate future, may seem to offer no basis for comfort. The search for truth, however, must come first, and then we may derive such comfort from it as we can.

There are grounds, I think, for deriving substantial comfort from the picture of being as I have presented it — even if it were only such comfort as we may properly derive from the meaning of tragedy.* What is clear in the picture is direction. A fundamental tenet of Christian theology is that we should find out what the will of God is and, having done so, accord our own will to it. If, within our parochial limitations, we can discern a direction in being, then there is no reason why our own lives should be without direction.

The direction we discern is from chaos to order. In Part Five I shall attempt to show how progress in this direction is served by the cultivation of literature, music, and the arts, no less than by that of science — or, to put it conversely, how literature, music, and the arts may be understood in terms of it.

> I think it not improbable that man, like the grub that prepares a chamber for the winged thing it never has seen but is to be — that man may have cosmic destinies that he does not understand.
>
> — *Oliver Wendell Holmes, Jr.*

* I shall elucidate this in Part Five, Chapter V.

PART FIVE

What Mind Creates

The Middle Ages never forgot that all things would be absurd if their meaning were exhausted in their function and their place in the phenomenal world, if by their essence they did not reach into a world beyond this. This idea of a deeper significance in ordinary things is familiar to us as well, independently of religious convictions: as an indefinite feeling which may be called up at any moment, by the sound of raindrops on the leaves or by the lamplight on the table.

— *Johan Huizinga*

I

Mona Lisa and
the Grapes of Zeuxis

> . . . to say what might be said of every
> work of art and of every natural object, that
> it could be made the starting-point for a
> chain of inferences that should reveal the
> whole universe, like the flower in the cran-
> nied wall.
>
> — *George Santayana*

MIND, which has only begun to emerge from the process of evolution, is a faculty for bringing order out of chaos. The totality of the
order it has produced so far, represented by the civilizations that
were the subject of Part Four, embraces a diversity of categories,
including, in addition to religion and social organization, the natural
sciences and the arts.

We assume that the proper object of the natural sciences is to discover an existing order, not to invent one, so that the Copernican
order, for example, is valid only to the extent that it represents what
is literally so.* We assume that the arts, by contrast, are free to represent imaginative invention, so that where they also represent some
independently existing truth they do so incidentally or indirectly,
perhaps in symbolic terms, as in the tale of the blind men and the elephant.

At this point let it suffice that, whether or not this represents a
substantial distinction, it does represent a formal one. The artist,
unlike the scientist, is not formally bound to describe only what is literally so. Since we have to classify the products of mind for heuristic purposes, this formal distinction will serve as a convenient basis
for separating the arts, which we are about to examine, from the
sciences.

In referring to the arts we are here using the term in a broad

* See, however, Part One, Chapter III above, particularly pp. 11–12.

sense to include painting, sculpture, architecture, music, and the whole range of fictional literature at least, whether in prose or verse. We are concerned to determine what kind of order they bring out of chaos, and to what end. The best way of going about this may be to examine the effect that specific works of art have on the mind, beginning with those that represent what is particular and going on to others that are progressively more abstract.

*

Leonardo da Vinci's "Mona Lisa" is, ostensibly, nothing more than the portrait of a Florentine merchant's wife. We may suppose that the artist was commissioned to paint it so that there would be an enduring record of her appearance as an individual, simply what she looked like. Now, if it is true that order is found in the combination of particulars, rather than in the particulars themselves, then the depiction of a particular individual in terms of her individuality is likely to be less representative of order than the depiction of what, by its very lack of such specificity, stands for a type or species. We might therefore suppose that such truth as the "Mona Lisa" contains is in the fidelity with which it represents, not some larger order of being, but one insignificant individual. In a famous comment on this portrait, however, Walter Pater wrote:

> Hers is the head upon which all "the ends of the world are come," and the eyelids are a little weary. . . . All the thoughts and experience of the world have etched and moulded there . . . the animalism of Greece, the lust of Rome, the reverie of the middle age with its spiritual ambition and imaginative loves, the return of the Pagan world, the sins of the Borgias. She is older than the rocks among which she sits; like the vampire, she has been dead many times, and learned the secrets of the grave; and has been a diver in deep seas, and keeps their fallen day about her; and trafficked for strange webs with Eastern merchants; and, as Leda, was the mother of Helen of Troy, and, as Saint Anne, the mother of Mary; and all this has been to her but as the sound of lyres and flutes, and lives only in the delicacy with which it has moulded the changing lineaments and tinged the eyelids and the hands.

This comment reports the effect of the "Mona Lisa" on Pater's mind, which would not be precisely the same as its effect on someone else's mind. In the Florentine merchant's wife he saw Leda and St. Anne, who in this context are symbolic figures that represent aspects of femininity or aspects of worldly experience. This is to say that,

seeing something more than the individual in the individual portrayed, seeing in her both Leda and St. Anne, he saw in them something more as well. What they in their turn represented to him, we
may suppose, was profane and sacred love respectively. (Leda had
served the lust of a god and given birth to a pagan suckling, while
the conception with which St. Anne was identified is known as the
Immaculate Conception.) Here are symbols beyond symbols, receding into infinite distance. The "Mona Lisa," it appears, has a reso-
nance in the mind, like the note of a bell that repeats itself in harmonics which spread out into the empyrean, sounding still when the
sounding of the note has ceased.

No two persons, asked to say what they saw in the "Mona Lisa"
beyond the individual portrayed, would report the same thing. One
might be reminded of the Fall of Man recounted in Genesis, seeing
in the merchant's wife the eternal Eve, forever sure of being able to
win her man away from the service of God himself. Another might
see in her the traditional strength of woman's will on which the apparently stronger men of all ages have leaned; or a Helen who could
take pride in a power that had brought about the destruction of
Troy and the ruin of the House of Atreus. Still another might see
in her simply the smug vulgarity of the *nouveaux riches* in all times
and places. And indeed she might well evoke all these in addition to
Leda and St. Anne. The point is that in the minds of all sensitive
observers an expanding series of resonances is set off, perhaps only
unconsciously, so that the particular subject, inconsequential in itself,
is enlarged by ever widening circles of association. The genius of
Leonardo, seeing beyond the surface, painted the surface so that the
rest of us might see beyond it too.

*

I have chosen for my first example of the effect the arts have on the
mind what, contrary to its factitious fame, is surely below the level of
the greatest works of art. It has no grand theme, it lacks scale. The
very fact that it enlarges from such a small beginning, however, has
been a reason for choosing it to illustrate the enlarging effect of
works of art.

For still further examples of enlargement from the particular I
now allow myself to quote the following statement, which begins
with the citation of an incident trivial in itself.

"Not long ago," Clifton Fadiman wrote, "I happened to observe a mother lifting her eight-year-old boy in her arms. As
she did so she laughed, and said, 'You're getting so big you'll be

lifting me soon.' It was the simplest of statements. Yet I felt something transiently touching about the scene merely because millions upon millions of mothers reaching back into the dawn of history must have said the same thing to their children at some time and because other millions will say it in the remote future long after this mother and child are dead."

It is this recognition of oneself in others, this discovery of experience common to all men, that contributes the moving element in humanistic art. This, we say, is universal experience. What the American mother said in the twentieth century a Jewish mother said in the days of Joshua, and if the language was different the difference was superficial only. And the Egyptian mother who was to lose her firstborn before the prediction of his growth could come true; the Chinese mother in the mud compound on the banks of the Yellow River, in the time of Confucius or two thousand years later — it is all the same; the Japanese mother in the corner of her garden under the cherry blossoms, in the evening of too warm a day as at last the sun sinks upon the horizon; the Viking mother on the banks of the fjord, whose man has gone south in the long-boat for the raiding season, and who says to the little boy that he will have to be her man now until his father comes back (wondering, as countless women have, whether he ever will); the African mother, naked at the river's edge, placing her son astride her hip; the Roman matron or the English lady or the Macedonian peasant woman; the American Indian mother outside the tepee on the Great Plains, or my wife — all know the thought, the attitude, the emotion, the essential experience.

It is the same with Pieter Bruegel's painting of a frolic at the village tavern, the children playing games, slipping between their elders' feet, getting into mischief, and half their elders merely bigger children than they — as it might be today, in the low countries as it might be here. Or Vermeer's painting of the maidservant, the brawn of her arm pouring the milk from the pitcher as the afternoon sun comes through the kitchen window to make the scene golden — just like the peasant girl in our kitchen now, stopping to shoo away the children who want to know, eternally, when it will be ready. The scene repeats itself for thousands of years (the golden light of the sun on evenings then as now), while the individuals who enact it are replaced generation after generation, different and forever the same. Vermeer's peasant girl is taking her turn in an eternal pageant.*

---

* From my *Men and Nations*, Princeton, 1962, pp. 110–111. The quotation of Fadiman is from his Introduction to Tolstoy's *War and Peace*, New York, 1942, p. xxix. The Bruegel painting referred to may be either "The Wedding Dance" in the Detroit Institute of Arts or "Peasant Dance" in the Kunsthistorisches Museum of Vienna. The Vermeer is "Maidservant Pouring Milk" in the Rijksmuseum, Amsterdam.

Here again is testimony to the enlargement from the particular that makes the particular meaningful. This enlargement, like all enlargement, has implications of the order arising from the accumulation of particulars that, in themselves, represent chaos — as witness the reference to "an eternal pageant" at the end of the quotation. In literal terms, Vermeer's "Maidservant Pouring Milk" represents nothing more than a particular girl engaged in a particular act at a particular moment. But the viewer is aware of her as "taking her turn in an eternal pageant." A "pageant" is the acting out of a formal order, and the word "eternal" tells us that the formal order she is acting out goes on through the ages, with new actors in every generation. Thus there is an ever widening circle of associations beyond the particular.

The truism that art imitates nature does not tell us what it is in nature that art imitates. It was said in praise of a Greek painter, Zeuxis, that he painted bunches of grapes with a verisimilitude so perfect that the birds flew down to peck at his painting. We may well ask, however, what is the worth of such literal imitation in itself, where there is nothing more. Bunches of grapes have been imitated so perfectly in wax, for the ornamentation of dining-room tables, that the observer mistakes them for the reality, and artificial flowers have been made to look just like real ones, but we do not call such imitation art in the sense in which we have been using the term here. We do not call it art because it does not teach us to see its subject in larger terms than we otherwise would, because it does not associate it with a larger order.

*

One aspect of the larger order that art evokes is temporal. A work of art fixes what is fleeting.

Even as I write these words my eye falls on the reproduction in today's newspaper of a drawing by the French nineteenth-century painter J.-F. Millet that shows a man pushing a loaded wheelbarrow.* It may be regarded as a study in mechanics. The man has lifted the barrow by its two handles, which are gripped in his hands so that its weight pulls down on his arms. He is leaning forward, opposing his own weight to the barrow's inertial mass, so that, if it were not for the resistance of that mass, he would fall forward; and he is also pushing with his feet against the ground in order to overcome the resistance and force the barrow forward. Newton's three Laws of Motion are each exemplified here, as is the relationship, explained by Einstein, between inertial and gravitational mass. The

* *Journal de Genève*, 6 December 1975.

contending weights of barrow and man are, so to speak, visible. There is an equilibrium of dynamic and inertial forces. The impression is of a monumental quality in what is, after all, the most banal of spectacles, one that each of us has seen in real life a thousand times over.

Why is this so impressive in the artist's representation, although we have overlooked it on the innumerable occasions when we have seen the actuality of a man pushing a wheelbarrow?

The artist's representation has this effect because it transcends the here-and-now by catching and fixing the passing moment. It represents "the instant made eternity." Not only does it overcome the transience of the moment, it overcomes the transience of life itself. The actual laborer who was the model for the drawing has been dead, one supposes, for a century; but others, unborn at the time, may still be seen enacting what he did. This sketch that I have taken so casually for an example suggests a permanent order in being, the vision of which lifts me above the chaos of the here-and-now. The passing moment, transfigured, has become an eternally commemorative monument.

*

Let me take one more example of particularistic art, a painting that represents nature literally, and consider its effect on the mind in what are, to begin with, personal terms.

Occasionally, when my wife and I have an opportunity to visit Holland, we spend two or three days driving about it. Few countries can match the monotony of the Dutch scenery; for all one sees is flat fields of green with canals crossing them in straight lines, an occasional windmill or group of farm buildings, an occasional village with church-steeple, some individual trees here or there — and over all a sky in which, on a pleasant day, clouds sail like galleons, their shadows following on the landscape below. Viewing such scenes, however, we repeatedly find ourselves moved, even to the point of exaltation, for they seem to us beautiful in a special way.

What is the source of the special beauty we see in such ordinary scenes?

To answer the question I must begin by saying that we first saw it, not in the scenes themselves, but in paintings by Dutch landscape painters of the seventeenth century. The emotion we feel when we see the actual scenes is the effect of recognition — what someone has called the shock of recognition.

One of my favorite paintings is the "View of Haarlem" by Jacob van Ruysdael in the Mauritshuis in The Hague. It shows, as from above, the flat distances of the Dutch landscapes with the fields and the features they contain dwindling in perspective. In the background is the town of Haarlem, itself made small by the extent of the surrounding countryside and the immensity of the sky. In the middle distance, behind a farmhouse, human figures that seem no bigger than ants are stretching out strips of linen to dry. Over all is an infinite sky containing clouds that mottle the landscape over which they pass with shadows and bursts of sunlight. As we ourselves travel, now, across the real Dutch landscape, we repeatedly see what is essentially the same scene — the same sky, the same cloud-shadows and bursts of sunlight, the same fields and farmhouses. If anyone asks why what we see is so beautiful and moving to us, I must answer that it is so because it imitates the painting.

Now this is a strange answer, for obviously the landscape came first and it is the painting that imitates it. What concerns us here, however, is the effect on the mind, and from that point of view it is the landscape that imitates the painting. We would not have appreciated the immensity of the sky over the flat fields of Holland if we had not had our attention called to it in the first instance by such a painter as Ruysdael. He made it possible for our minds to be illuminated by the celestial illumination of the actual landscapes.

A few kilometers from the museum in which the "View of Haarlem" hangs the observer can see the reality itself. Ruysdael, one would say, pointed out in his painting what was so obvious that there was no need to point it out. But it had not been obvious until he had pointed it out. The fact is that, unless the artist calls our attention to certain aspects of reality, we do not see them.

The painting somehow epitomizes reality, heightens it, purifies it, brings it into focus. It isolates the scene by putting a frame around it, and concentrates it by the composition of elements within the frame. In the absence of the boundary provided by the frame, and of a point of focus provided by the composition, the wandering eye would have had no place to rest. If one had stood beside the artist at his easel, seeing what lay under his eyes, the actual scene would have appeared as part of an indefinite continuity in all directions rather than a self-contained whole.

Moreover, the importance of allowing the eye to rest in time as well as space becomes evident when one imagines the "View of Haarlem" as a moving picture, the clouds and people set in motion. The value of the painting as a work of art would vanish with its stability. As it is, the passing scene has been given the permanence of a monument.

"I think that I shall never see / A poem lovely as a tree," wrote

Joyce Kilmer. If a tree is lovely, however, it is only because a poem
or some other work of art has taught us to see it as such.

*

We saw in the "Mona Lisa" how a work of art expands in the mind,
even from the most insignificant beginning. Pater's poetic comment
on the painting was itself a work of art that served its expansion, and
that itself became expanded in our own minds to include the Fall of
Man. In the Chinese tradition, the painter might supply his own poetic commentary. I close this chapter by calling attention to the
scroll by Shen Chou, referred to on page 458, which shows on
the right side several persons sitting at table in an open pavilion
among trees at the edge of a body of water that extends leftward to
the end of the scroll. Almost all the left half of the scroll is blank,
representing water or sky indistinguishably; but in the upper left-
hand corner, so small that it might escape notice entirely, is a disc,
somewhat paler than its pale background, that represents the moon.
The scroll has written upon it a poem, which makes the point that in
youth one contemplates the moon of mid-autumn negligently, but in
old age with the question in one's mind of how many more such autumn moons one may hope to see. Some 500 years and 6,000
moons later, the painting still speaks the same truth.

II

Normative Ideas

LEONARDO DA VINCI was commissioned to paint the portrait of a particular woman so that there would be an enduring record of her as she had been in her transient actuality at a particular moment. Unlike the "Mona Lisa," the Aphrodite of Melos is not the portrait of a particular woman.

What is it then?

We suppose it to be the image of a goddess, a woman of the imagination rather than a woman of flesh-and-blood.

The Greeks, as represented by Plato, believed that primary reality consisted of ideas, each perfect in itself, each manifested in the visible world by any number of imperfect imitations.* We may think of the Greek gods and goddesses as Platonic ideas endowed with personality by the myth-making proclivities of a simple people. There was, for instance, an idea of man, to which the name Apollo had been given, of which actual men were imitations more or less imperfect; and there was an idea of woman, Aphrodite, of which actual women were imperfect imitations. Although an artist might undertake to portray a particular woman who was but an imperfect copy of Aphrodite, he might logically prefer to portray the perfect original, as it existed in his imagination, instead. By so doing he would be imitating reality directly rather than at one remove.

Artists in all times have done this, even though they did it on the basis of other conceptions than those of the Platonic philosophy. An "idea" in that philosophy is what we call a universal as opposed to a particular. Even though an artist believed that universals were derived from particulars, rather than the other way around, so that the idea of woman was secondary to the multitude of visible women that gave rise to it, he might still wish to portray the perfect idea itself rather than the imperfection of what he saw in any actual

* See pp. 425–427 above.

woman. In that case he would think of himself as abstracting the one from the many.

We need not concern ourselves at this point with whether the many are derived from the one or the one from the many. Suffice it that, in terms of human psychology, we all live by normative ideas, by ideas of what is normal, which we find imperfectly represented in the multitudinous and transient manifestations of the visible world. I have in my mind, for example, the idea of a straight line as extension in one dimension and one direction only; but any representation of it produced by a pen on paper is bound to be imperfect, since it will have two dimensions, however narrow it may be, and since it will waver, even though its wavering should be so slight as to be perceptible only through a microscope.

Again, I have in my mind the idea of a circle, which is a line everywhere equidistant from a point. When I see a line on paper like the following, which would fit this definition except that it bends inward at one place, I regard that line as an imperfect representation of the normative idea of a circle.

Why should I not regard it, rather, as the essentially perfect representation of the normative idea of just such a shape as it has?

The answer is that there is no normative idea that corresponds to such a shape, as there is a normative idea that corresponds to the shape of a circle. Normative ideas are ideas of regularity, which can therefore be defined in terms of the rules they represent (as the circle represents the rule of equidistance from a point). It follows that what is irregular, what obeys no rule, cannot correspond to a normative idea. Normative ideas obey rules, whether we call them rules of logic, rules of symmetry, or laws of nature. So it is that the first of the two following figures represents a normative idea because

it can be defined by a rule, while the second does not because it cannot be so defined. This is as much as to say that the first represents order, the second chaos.* Mind, as we have observed, is the faculty for bringing order out of chaos. The normative ideas that it entertains are associated with order, as is the consequent distinction between perfect and imperfect.

The Aphrodite of Melos embodies and, in a sense, eternalizes a normative idea of woman in the minds of the ancient Greeks. It has bilateral symmetry, its proportions are harmonious, and it is expressive of a certain anatomical logic, the legs being just right to support the rest of the body, the displacement of one part from the center of gravity being compensated by the displacement of other parts to maintain the equilibrium of the whole. All this represents essentially the order epitomized by the circle, or by the equilateral triangle illustrated above, but with an elaborate combination of balanced parts into one whole that makes the Aphrodite the expression of a more developed order — just as a falcon is the expression of a more developed order than a bacterium. What the sculpture represents, then, is a normative idea, rather than a particular woman in her imperfect actuality.

"It is widely supposed," writes Kenneth Clark, "that the naked human body is in itself an object upon which the eye dwells with pleasure and which we are glad to see depicted. But anyone who has frequented art schools and seen the shapeless, pitiful model that the students are industriously drawing will know that is an illusion. . . . A mass of naked figures does not move us to empathy, but to disillusion and dismay. We do not wish to imitate; we wish to perfect." † One can perfect, however, only by a standard associated with a normative idea.

The human body represents an order that has emerged progressively from chaos in the course of biological evolution. Such beauty as we see in it is the effect produced in the mind by the contemplation of this order. Any particular example in flesh-and-blood, however, is imperfect by whatever normative standards we may apply. If we apply a standard of symmetry we may find that in a particular woman one shoulder is higher than the other; if we apply a standard of proportion we may find that in a particular woman the torso is too heavy for the legs. Our critical minds make a distinction, then, between better and worse, based on the imagined perfection of a normative order. The Aphrodite is a rendering of that imagined perfection in stone.

*

* Note how the mind seeks for order in the second figure by impositions of the imagination — e.g., seeing in it the head of a beast, with open mouth, facing to the left.
† *The Nude: A Study in Ideal Form,* New York, 1956, pp. 5–6.

By the standard of the Aphrodite, we do not wish to imitate the "mass of naked figures" but "to perfect." This is to say that what we wish to imitate is the normative idea represented, in our example, by the Aphrodite.

Now, such imitation is not only possible, it actually occurs. It occurs in the most immediate if superficial sense when young women, imitating consciously or unconsciously, hold themselves with the poise and grace of the Aphrodite.* It occurs when they cultivate a figure as much like the Aphrodite as possible, whether by exercise or dieting.† Finally, it occurs where men, their taste formed on the ideal model represented by the Aphrodite, prefer as their mates those young women who approach it, thereby producing, by sexual selection, a genetic strain that shows its influence. So it is that the sculptor not only creates a statue in stone, by creating such a statue he also creates women in flesh-and-blood.

The Aphrodite is not the most obvious example of this because, while its poise can be imitated directly and immediately by flesh and blood, its physical shape can be imitated only partially and over a period of time, first by exercise, diet, and dress, ultimately by such sexual selection as would be effective only over a span of generations. If, however, we could return to sixteenth-century Tuscany we would undoubtedly find the Mona Lisa's smile (which also occurs on the face of St. Anne in Leonardo's "The Virgin, the Child, and St. Anne," as well as in paintings by his imitators) on the faces of actual women. Somerset Maugham once wrote that the Englishmen in Kipling's stories of India were less representative of Englishmen in India at the time they were written than of those who came after — from which he concluded that Kipling not only created fictional characters, he created actual men.

Each of us, in the process of growing up, develops a normative idea of himself that he imitates. The idea may be based in part on the models provided by actual persons whom we admire — such as the mature man whom, in a typical situation, a growing boy regards with hero-worship. It is certainly based as well, however, on human-

---

* The power of such direct imitation has notable possibilities. Children adopted in infancy and genetically unrelated to their foster parents nevertheless grow up to look like them, if only because they have unconsciously imitated such of their attributes as facial expression.

† Imitation of this sort is so effective that, in any particular population, the prevailing physical form of women may change from generation to generation in response to changes of fashion that are simply changes in the models accepted as normative. So the deep-bosomed, wasp-waisted, and large-hipped women of Victorian times were replaced in the 1920s by linear women with flat figures like those of boys. Over such a short run, it is true, such imitation depends largely on artificial devices, such as dress.

istic works of art, especially in the field of fiction. So it is that the artist creates real persons.

Copernicus, in the model he made of the solar system, imitated what we may call existential reality. While the sculptor, the painter, or the teller of tales may himself abstract from existential reality, it is existential reality that imitates the model he makes.

I know of no grounds for believing, with Plato, that in the realm of being as a whole particulars are derived by imitation from universals. In what the mind creates, however, there can be no doubt of it.

III

Aphrodite and the Upland Sandpiper

BECAUSE PEOPLE MODEL THEMSELVES on norms represented to them by the works of artists, it can be said that, through the agency of artists (among others), mind creates people. Mind is able to do this because of the extraordinary plasticity of our species. Unlike such other species as the army ant, *Eciton burchelli*, its form and behavior are not fixed. So it is that a whole human society can show one kind of behavior at one moment, under the influence of a particular normative idea, and altogether different behavior the next moment, when it has fallen under the influence of another. Responding to the normative idea upheld by Adolf Hitler, the German society behaved in one way, but when that idea was discredited by defeat in warfare it adopted overnight the normative idea upheld by the victors and, in accordance with it, behaved in an altogether different way. One cannot describe a standard behavior of *Homo sapiens* as one can of *Eciton burchelli*, because it has no standard behavior. Its behavior depends, rather, on whatever normative ideas happen to prevail at a particular moment. The behavior of the army ant is natural, having been determined by natural selection, while that of our species is artificial, responding with seeming capriciousness to the widely varying inventions of mind.

The distinction I am making here is best understood as a distinction between animals of the wild and domestic animals. Until recently, the process of evolution has depended entirely on natural selection, which has produced the wild animals. In the most recent times, however, mind has begun to take over. It has done so with deliberation in the case of such domestic species as dogs and barnyard animals, which today are largely what our species, as the custodian of mind, has made them. The species produced by mind may be distinguished from the wild species by their variety of form and character. Thus the domestic dog, although regarded as all one species, varies from the little chihuahua to the St. Bernard, while the common barnyard fowl (whose wild ancestor still thrives in the forests of southern Asia) varies from the Jersey White Giant to the Cochin bantam, with new varieties being constantly produced in accordance with such new ideas as occur to those who breed them. The Chinese bred the Pekingese dog over the centuries to represent a highly stylized conception of a lion, also represented in their sculpture, that they had in their minds. There is a Platonic implication in this priority of the ideas.

By the test of variety, our own kind must be classed with the domestic as opposed to the wild species, even though its variety is not the result of such artificial selection, deliberately practiced, as entered into the production of most domestic breeds. The variety represented, for example, by the difference between Hottentots and typical Scandinavians is the product of geographical separation and adaptation, respectively, to different natural environments. Even within one breeding population, however, the variety is incomparably greater among human individuals than among those of any wild species. Even children of the same two parents vary widely, some having blue eyes and others brown, some having straight hair and others curly, some square-built and others lean.* This variety represents in large part the mixing of varieties that had originally developed in geographical isolation from one another. But it also represents the civilization that has increasingly insulated our kind against the natural environment that imposes natural selection; for, where such selection was completely operative, the variety would quickly be reduced, in each geographical habitat, to a standard that represented the best adaptation to that habitat. Blue eyes, for example, would quickly be eliminated in lands of bright sunlight, where brown eyes, having the advantage, would become standard. Today, however, a blue-eyed man who worked in an office in a North African city would control the amount of light in his artificial environment and, when he went outdoors, would wear dark glasses, thereby circumventing by artifice the severities of natural selection.

Aristotle maintained that the city-state was nature's norm for man as the hive was for the bee. Perhaps a follower of Plato would have said that the Aphrodite of Melos represented the eternal norm for

---

* "When we look to the individuals of the same variety or sub-variety of our older cultivated plants and animals, one of the first points which strikes us, is, that they generally differ much more from each other, than do the individuals of any one species or variety in a state of nature. . . . I think we are driven to conclude that this greater variability is simply due to our domestic productions having been raised under conditions of life not so uniform as, and somewhat different from, those to which the parent-species have been exposed under nature." (Charles Darwin, *The Origin of Species,* London, 1859, p. 7).

the female of our species, an idea of which all particular women were imperfect copies. None of us would make such a claim today, however, if only because we know that the form of the human body is not like something established forever by God at the Creation, but that it is, rather, one among innumerable, constantly changing manifestations of an evolution that has gone on for 3,500 million years and that continues.

In fact, as is to be expected in a species so varied, the Aphrodite is only one among many normative ideas that have been invented by the human mind for the female form. The female nudes depicted in Indian sculpture of the second century, with their globular breasts, their narrow waists, and their big hips angled sharply to one side, represent another such idea. The Eve in the van Eycks' Ghent altarpiece (painted in 1432), with her little breasts and her belly like a deep bag, represents still another. What these examples represent is so many normative ideas designed to set a standard where no standard will hold.

How different is the case of the upland sandpiper, *Bartramia longicauda!* Leaving aside variations so slight as to be virtually unnoticeable, every upland sandpiper is identical in its appearance with every other, so that one could not, as Leonardo did in the case of the "Mona Lisa," paint the portrait of one individual as such — for the portrait one painted would be of all other individuals as well. Any illustrated field guide to North American birds shows, not *an* upland sandpiper but *the* upland sandpiper. The illustrator of a field guide that included our own species, however, could not represent it by just one image intended to portray all its individuals, including Hottentots and Scandinavians; nor could he even, by one image, portray all Scandinavians or all Hottentots only.

Again, one can describe the upland sandpiper in precise terms that fit every individual, noting that it is 28 centimeters long from the tip of its bill to the tip of its tail, with black eyes and bill, with yellow feet, etc. Who, however, could give the exact dimensions and coloring of man — even if he confined himself to the description of one family, consisting of parents and grown children?

Moreover, because every upland sandpiper is like every other one, there cannot be different normative ideas of it, nor such a separation between the perfect idea and the imperfect imitation as there is in the case of man. (This gives point to the statement made by D. H. Lawrence that, if a man were as much a man as a lizard is a lizard, he would be more worth looking at.)

*

I have now made two points about works of art. The first is that they have an enlarging effect on the mind of the observer, teaching him to see the world in larger terms than he otherwise would. The other is that they shape him by setting up normative models for his imitation. With these two points in mind, I now cite the following description by W. H. Hudson of the upland sandpiper on the Argentine pampas:

> All its motions are exceedingly graceful: it runs rapidly as a corncrake before the rider's horse, then springs up with its wild musical cry to fly but twenty or thirty yards away and drop down again, to stand in a startled attitude flirting its long tail up and down. At times it flies up voluntarily, uttering a prolonged bubbling and inflected cry, and alights on a post or some such elevated place to open and hold its wings vertically and continue for some time in that attitude — the artist's conventional figure of an angel.
>
> These birds never flocked with us, even before departing; they were solitary, sprinkled evenly over the entire country, so that when out for a day on horseback I would flush one from the grass every few minutes; and when travelling or driving cattle on the pampas I have spent whole weeks on horseback from dawn to dark without being for a day out of sight or sound of the bird. When migrating its cry was heard at all hours from morning to night, from February till April; and again at night, especially when there was a moon.
>
> Lying awake in bed, I would listen by the hour to that sound coming to me from the sky, mellowed and made beautiful by distance and the profound silence of the moonlit world, until it acquired a fascination for me above all sounds on earth, so that it lived ever after in me; and the image of it is as vivid in my mind at this moment as that of any bird call or cry, or any other striking sound heard yesterday or but an hour ago. It was the sense of mystery it conveyed which so attracted and impressed me — the mystery of that delicate, frail, beautiful being, travelling in the sky, alone, day and night, crying aloud at intervals as if moved by some powerful emotion, beating the air with its wings, its beak pointing like the needle of the compass to the north, flying, speeding on its seven-thousand-mile flight to its nesting home in another hemisphere.*

This passage represents an upland sandpiper (individual and species without distinction in this case) as the Mona Lisa or the Aphrodite represents a woman. In doing so, it teaches the reader to see

* *A Hind in Richmond Park*, New York, 1923, pp. 158–161.

what extends beyond the visible, which he would not otherwise have seen.

In the strictest sense, what anyone actually sees with his eyes is only variations of light. A baby, when it first opens its eyes, sees areas of lighter and darker, moving or still. At first, however, it does not know how to interpret this confusion of lights and shades, so that the world of its vision is meaningless and, consequently, chaotic. With the passage of the days the initial chaos is overcome by learning. The infant learns that a whitish patch of a certain shape represents its foot. In like manner it learns in time to identify people around it, eventually distinguishing particular individuals, one from another. It becomes aware of a real world which it comes to think that it actually sees, overlooking the fact that all it sees in fact is light, which it automatically translates into people and things. (It does not think of the patch of light as *representing* its foot but as *being* its foot.) This is equally true for the sounds, smells, tastes, and sensations of touch that it experiences.

What the baby first opened its eyes on was chaos; but the process of learning is, from the start, that of bringing order out of chaos.

Primitive people, shown the first photograph they have ever seen, are said to see it only as areas of light and dark on a flat surface. They have not learned to interpret these lights and darks as representing familiar three-dimensional objects. Whether this is true or not, what is true is that all people who know how to read have had to be taught to interpret the bizarre assortment of black marks on white paper (such as the reader has under his eyes), to translate them from nonsense into sense, from chaos into a meaning that represents order. There are mathematical equations which represent only chaos to me, who have not learned to interpret them, that may seem sublime to a mathematician because of some logical order they communicate to his own specially trained mind.

May we not say that there is, in our entire experience, no element of order that we apprehend as such except in consequence of having learned to do so?

Works of art have a role in this process of learning. Fairy-tales not only teach the young child to see the world in terms of a distinction between what is beautiful and what is ugly, they set the standards for it. (Thus the nineteenth-century children's stories in the West were likely to associate blue eyes and blond hair in a girl with the beauty of innocence, while evil people were apt to be described as dark.) For centuries the Chinese, exposed to the work of their landscape painters, thereby learned to regard nature as something incomparably larger than the little people they themselves were, like ants crawling about the roots of trees — but as something with which they could and must, nevertheless, establish an harmonious relation. The whole ordering of their traditional society, under the Son of Heaven, reflected this view, so that we may plausibly say that the landscape painters communicated a normative vision that constituted the basis of the social order.

Because Hudson's representation of the sandpiper was in words rather than paint, he could be explicit about what, in his view, extended so far beyond the visible (as Pater was explicit in the case of the "Mona Lisa"). A painting would have represented a particular scene at a particular moment, whereas Hudson's prose embraces the years — and, within each, what was heard "at all hours from morning to night, from February till April; and again at night, especially when there was a moon." Here is temporal enlargement. There is also spatial enlargement, for the account refers to the bird's "seven-thousand-mile flight to its nesting home in another hemisphere."

Anyone who has been taught to see the upland sandpiper by Hudson is bound to see it quite differently, then, from one who has had no such teaching. To an Indian on the pampas before the arrival of European man, the sandpiper may have had little significance except as food to be enjoyed for the catching. Its habit of holding its wings vertically after alighting would not have appealed to him as it would to one who was familiar with the representation of angels in the sacred art of the Europeans. Nor would he have known that the birds he saw flying north in the austral autumn were on their way to another continent 7,000 miles away, there to nest and raise their young. (Hudson himself would not have known this a hundred years earlier.)

The Indian of the pampas was confined to a smaller world than Hudson, so that the sandpiper would have had a lesser meaning for him. The same may be said of the average gaucho in Hudson's day, who would perhaps hardly have noticed the sandpiper at all — or would have remained unmoved by it. Perhaps the reader and I, too, would remain relatively unmoved by a sight of the sandpiper if Hudson's cultivation, sensitivity, and breadth of vision had not been communicated to us, teaching us how to see.

Hudson's vision, for its part, was not entirely self-generated. In the formation of his own mind he had been taught to see by the accumulated works of a long tradition. It is likely that he was not unacquainted with the words of Jeremiah the Prophet: "Yea, the stork in the heaven knoweth her appointed times; and the turtle and the crane and the swallow observe the time of their coming; . . ." *
And, when Hudson read or heard this passage, did he not also think

* Jeremiah 8:7. The reader knows that "the turtle" is the turtle dove, but I mention it here because so many others do not.

of the words of the Preacher: "To every thing there is a season, and a time to every purpose under the heaven . . ."? *

My point is that what the cultivated man has learned to see is as much more than the reflected light from the sandpiper as the infant's foot is than the light patch it appears to be before its interpretation has been learned. There is enlargement from the particular, and the enlargement, in its degree, represents the emergence of order from chaos.

*

In addition to saying that works of art have an enlarging effect on the mind of the observer, I have said that they shape him by setting up normative models for his imitation. This is true of some works of art, such as Kipling's tales of India or the Aphrodite of Melos. Surely, however, it is not true of others, such as Hudson's description of the upland sandpiper!

If only for the sake of the argument, I grant that it is not true of Hudson's description. Immediately I have done so, however, I find that I must qualify. Hudson's sandpiper is not itself a model for the reader's imitation, but Hudson's way of looking at it is. His vision is the model he sets up for imitation. That vision is of a large normative order extending over the annual cycles of the seasons and across two hemispheres. By reading Hudson, and other literary artists who have described birds in like terms, my mind is formed to see as they see, react as they react. When I, myself, have written about birds, it has been in terms of a larger vision for which they provided models. I, coming in a later generation, was created by them as the Englishmen in India, a generation after Kipling, were created by him.

* Ecclesiastes 3:1 and 2, but continuing through 8.

IV

The Epic Vision

WORKS OF ART vary from the particularistic, exemplified by the "Mona Lisa," to the abstract, which may be exemplified by Bach's "Musical Offering" or the Parthenon. Traditionally, the most particularistic form of art has been painting, for it has traditionally been confined to particular subjects — e.g., a Florentine woman or a scene in Holland. Sculpture is better adapted to what is more abstract, for even where it is completed with paint (as in the Egyptian head of Nefretete), it cannot, like painting, represent such settings as land and sky. Literature has a wide range between the extremes of particularism and abstraction, but it can hardly represent every leaf on a tree as painting can. The setting for Hudson's sandpiper was simply "the pampas," whereas a painting of it against its natural background would have had to depict a particular scene on the pampas.

Another criterion by which works of art may be classified, however roughly, is that of scale. I do not use the term with reference primarily to physical size, although such size may count — as when one compares the small-scale loveliness of the Maison Carrée at Nîmes with the grandeur of the Parthenon. Nor is scale necessarily to be equated with quality, for in that case we would have to prefer the Baths of Caracalla to the Parthenon. Theme or subject counts. Thus Leonardo's "Last Supper" is greater in scale than his "Mona Lisa," quite apart from its size, because it represents, not one undistinguished individual but, rather, a conjunction between the human and the divine at an epochal moment in the historic tradition on which a whole civilization is based.

There is a sense in which every great civilization has its roots in the large-scale literature we call epic. The two associated Homeric epics, *The Iliad* and *The Odyssey,* were basic to the Classical civilization as the Bible has been to our Western civilization. Both are on a scale that removes them from the category of such works of art as we have been considering so far. This is to say that we are moving on, now, from the small-scale examples with which this examination of artistic creation began. What I am concerned with here is the effect of works of art on the mind, and it is in these terms that I now take *The Odyssey* as an example of the epic vision.

*

What accounts for the sense of fulfillment with which one finishes *The Odyssey*?

The happy ending might explain it. After ten years of agonizing frustration, through which the reader suffers with him, Odysseus wins his way back, at last, to his wife, his son, and his kingdom, to which he restores the order that had broken down in his absence.

We have all experienced a thousand times the satisfaction that happy endings provide — in the fairy-tales of our childhood, in light fiction, in the movies, even in the cartoon-strips of newspapers. This is the satisfaction we feel when we come to the end of *The Odyssey*. By a delicious anticipation, moreover, we taste it throughout the long tale of the hero's sufferings and frustrations — for, as in the case of *Hamlet*, no one reads *The Odyssey* without knowing in advance how it is going to end. Our pleasurable anticipation becomes more intense as chapter-by-chapter Odysseus approaches the day when he will land on the shores of Ithaca, overthrow the usurping suitors, and be reunited with his wife and son. At last, when all that we knew would happen does happen, we feel ourselves more than ful-filled, exalted.

As far as it goes, this seems to me a valid explanation of the satis-faction one feels at the end of *The Odyssey*. But there must be more to it than that; for if our satisfaction is deeper and more abiding than what we derive from just any tale with a happy ending, then the explanation, however valid in itself, is not enough.

The happy ending of *The Odyssey* is associated with a normative vision, and this, surely, is what lifts it to a higher plane of literature. All of us, living as we must in a world of disorder, strive for the real-ization of a normative order that we cherish in our minds, a concep-tion of what God or nature intended us to be, a conception of how God or nature intended us to live. All of us, consequently, inhabit two worlds at once: the existential world of accident, conflict, sordid-ness, and breakdown, the world of greed and hatred, of cowardice and treachery — this on the one hand, and on the other a world of the imagination in which a Pythagorean harmony prevails, in which all men fulfill the roles reserved for them in the sublime pageant of life as it was intended to be, as we have sometimes thought it must have been before men fell into evil, as we hope it will be at the end of all our striving.

Each of us has in his mind a conception of propriety that contrasts with the world of his actual experience, even though we disagree in our respective conceptions (as our ideological conflicts show). For some, such propriety is represented by the vision of St. Paul; for others, by that of Karl Marx. Some have found it in Hitler's *Mein Kampf*, others in *The Little Flowers of St. Francis of Assisi*. Some have found it in the ideal Confucian order, in which men are organized about the family unit, others (e.g., the Plato who wrote *The Republic*) in the ideal order represented by Sparta, where they were organized in barracks.

The normative order of the Homeric vision is one that has, so far, prevailed in a wide variety of disparate societies separated from one another in time or space. It is a hierarchical order within which men and women have each their obligations of leadership or obedience according to their place in the whole. As has generally been true of agricultural societies, the fundamental unit is the family, based on the lifelong mutual attachment of husband and wife. The organized societies of the Homeric world were small and local, exemplified by Pylos and Sparta, by Ithaca, by Troy and Mycenae. In each the husband and father who was the head of the leading family was also king. He was responsible for the leadership and protection of the community, while the others had the duty of obedience according to their respective stations, whether as sons, as soldiers, as artisans, as thralls, as wives, or as handmaidens. The kings themselves might be loosely leagued together, with bonds of mutual obligation not unlike those among the lords of our own feudal age, 2,000 years after Homer's day. The expedition to Troy under Agamemnon's leadership represented the discharge by him and the other kings of a collective obligation to uphold the union between Menelaus and his wife Helen. Each had once been Helen's suitor; in their mutual rivalry Menelaus had won her; all had accepted the legitimacy of the victory so won; and all had agreed to uphold the normative order as represented by the relationship between husband and wife so established.

What *The Iliad* recounts is a catastrophic disruption of this normative order in consequence of pettiness on the part of gods and men alike. Aphrodite had engendered the catastrophe by promising Paris the enjoyment of an illegitimate union with Helen if he would award her, rather than Hera or Athena, the golden apple of victory as the most beautiful of the goddesses. In payment of that bribe she had enabled him to steal Helen from Menelaus and carry her off to Troy. This was the act that, by disrupting the normative order, would have such terrible and far-reaching consequences.

Odysseus, still in full enjoyment of that order as the king in far-away Ithaca — with his young wife, Penelope, and his new-born son, Telemachus — foreboded these consequences, and tried to evade his obligation of involvement like many draft-evaders since (by feigning insanity), but without success. He, too, had to abandon his normal life and go to Troy.

The Iliad is a partial account of the existential chaos represented by the ten years' siege of Troy, ending in sordid death and destruction for Greeks and Trojans alike. What Priam, the Trojan king, and his family have to suffer is too horrible to contemplate. But to the leader of the Greeks, Agamemnon, comes a doom on the same scale. Returning to his home after ten years, he is taken in ambush and murdered by his wife and her lover, who thereby set off a new succession of sordid disasters that will afflict his line for generations to come. All this in consequence of the disruption of the normative order by the dirty little deal between Aphrodite and Paris.

A like disorder threatens finally to engulf the house and line of Odysseus in Ithaca. With the throne empty, and the place of Penelope's husband vacant in her bed, a lawless crew of upstarts from Ithaca and the surrounding islands make themselves at home in Odysseus's palace, spurn his son, and lay siege to the unhappy Penelope. This is the situation that is revealed to the reader at the beginning of *The Odyssey,* and we then follow Odysseus as, against heartbreaking obstacles and setbacks, he strives for ten years to win his way back to his home, where in the end he will redeem a wife who has been faithful as the wives of Menelaus and Agamemnon were not, where he will kill the usurpers and restore the normative order that had been disrupted when Paris carried off Helen. This, and not some merely personal triumph, is the happy ending.

As in virtually all societies that in the past have upheld the institution of monogamous marriage, the husband is allowed more latitude than the wife. *The Odyssey,* while it is clear as to Penelope's successful resistance to the suitors, does not suggest that Odysseus had any compunctions about accepting Circe's invitation to share her bed during the year that he lived with her. Yet this in no way diminishes the reader's impression of his unwavering devotion to Penelope, his loyalty to their lifelong marriage. One feels that, in what is essential, he remains as faithful to her as she to him. He also lived with Calypso, as her prisoner for seven years on the island of Ogygia, and she offered him immortality if he would consent to remain forever as her husband, but he was not tempted. His single-minded purpose to return to the normative order, of which his marriage was an essential part, never weakened. And the marriage itself is no less solid for these evanescent affairs when at last the partners have been reunited.

If this double standard is to be justified at all, it is by the common observation that men can, more easily than women, enter into passing affairs that leave them emotionally unmarked.

*

If *The Odyssey* is not merely a tale of adventure, neither is it one of those modern novels that has for its purpose the description of our daily life. What it describes, rather, is life lifted to the level of a heroic ideal. There is one crucial incident, however, that would be worthy of the most sophisticated psychological novelists of our time.

All through the twenty years of their separation Odysseus and Penelope had hoped against hope, and had constantly longed for the day of his homecoming; but to neither had it occurred that, if the day came at last, it might entail embarrassment or disappointment. One has only to consider the situation, however, to see that it was bound to entail an awkward pause, at least, when the two met. After twenty years neither could be, still, the same person the other had known, which means that they would meet as strangers. This would put in doubt whether the mutual knowledge and understanding that constituted the real marriage-bond still existed. The resumption of intimacy could not be taken for granted.

Penelope is in her upper chamber, quite unaware of the fact that the old beggar who has entered the halls is Odysseus in disguise, unaware of the fact that behind locked doors he has just encompassed the death of the suitors. Now the old nurse, laughing hysterically, comes to break the news to her. Penelope at first refuses to believe it, then is seized with shyness. Uncertain, hesitating, half alarmed, she agrees to follow the old woman down to the hall, but says disingenuously, "I will go to see my son," adding, "so that I can see my suitors lying dead — and the man who killed them." *

> She spoke, and came down from the chamber, her heart pondering much, whether to keep away and question her dear husband, or to go up to him and kiss his head, taking his hands. But then, when she came in and stepped over the stone threshold, she sat across from him in the firelight, facing Odysseus, by the opposite wall. . . .

Odysseus, too, is reserved now. Twenty years have passed, and he, too, cannot know whether this woman is still his wife. He sits at the other side of the hall looking down on the ground. It is an

---

* The quotations are from the translation by Richmond Lattimore, New York, 1966. I have, however, given them the format of prose rather than set them in the broken lines of the original.

awful moment, wholly unexpected, and upsetting to the unseasoned Telemachus. He upbraids his mother, saying that "no other woman . . . would keep back as you are doing from her husband who, after much suffering, came at last in the twentieth year back to his own country."

> My child [says Penelope], the spirit that is in me is full of wonderment, and I cannot find anything to say to him, nor question him, nor look him straight in the face. But if he is truly Odysseus, and he has come home, then we shall find other ways, and better, to recognize each other, for we have signs that we know of between the two of us only, but they are secret from others.

Because Telemachus is in the way, his father asks him to leave.

When he is at last alone with Penelope, except for the presence of the old nurse, Odysseus begins: "You are so strange. . . ." He blames her, as Telemachus had, for keeping back from her husband "who, after much suffering, came at last in the twentieth year back to his own country."

Penelope, answering, also begins with "You are so strange. . . ." Both are looking for the key that will unlock their old identities and thereby restore their union. Odysseus finds it, at last, by describing peculiarities of their marriage bed that only he among men can know. Immediately a common memory restores the past to the living, the living to the past. Penelope's "knees and her heart went slack." Then "she burst into tears and ran straight at him," throwing her arms about his neck and kissing his head.

> He wept as he held his lovely wife. . . . And as when the land appears welcome to men who are swimming, after Poseidon has smashed their strong-built ship on the open water . . . so welcome was her husband to her as she looked upon him, and she could not let him go from the embrace of her white arms.

"The gods gave us misery," she tells him, "in jealousy over the thought that we two, always together, should enjoy our youth, and then come to the threshold of old age."

And so they "gladly went together to bed, and their old ritual." And when they "had enjoyed their lovemaking, they took their pleasure in talking, each one telling his story."

This is part of the happy ending.

*

Here am I in the twentieth century reading something called *The Odyssey* by someone called Homer. The world I live in is a man-made world that extends all around this aquaterrestrial globe, its surface spotted with cities bound together by networks of roads, of air-lanes, and of sea-lanes. Over a large part of this world most of the population have never seen such vanishing remnants as may still be found of the natural world. In the man-made world people now live like bees in their own architecture, in extensive complexes of cement, macadam, and asphalt. They are supplied with food brought in to them from unknown sources, often halfway around the globe; they are clothed through like procedures; they are protected, educated, trained, and given medical care by the anonymous powers and procedures of the states to which they respectively belong.

The size of the human population is 4,000 million, which means that it is now crowding the planet. Its societies are unstable, so that they are always falling into some kind of disorder, news of which is instantly communicated all around the world, together with pictures. Airplanes fly from city to city, shunting people around the planet. If there is a breakdown in a city called Paris the effects are immediately felt at what once were remote cities like Tokyo and Buenos Aires. (Odysseus never got so far.)

Here am I, one man in 4,000 million, finding a corner by myself where I can read Homer's *Odyssey*. This literary relict is a product of life around the shores of the Aegean Sea some 3,000 years ago. The world was just about unpopulated then, almost all wilderness, and the Aegean people didn't even know that they lived on a globe. Their explorations did not go beyond the vicinity of the Mediterranean, embracing an area that we traverse today in half an hour.

They were not civilized like us, but barbarous, like the pre-Columbian Indians of North America, like the Vikings, like the Picts and Scots. Their settlements were strongholds on the coast, but set back from the seashores so that assailants in their hollow oared boats would have to beach and go inland in order to attack them. A large part of their activity was making war, which they appear to have done by single combat (perhaps quite a few going on simultaneously in one field) with bronze swords, spears, battle-axes, and rocks. Those who won seemingly had no compunctions about despoiling their victims in various ways. They carried off one another's women, and when the lord of the place wasn't around (perhaps because he had gone off to help fetch back someone else's wife) interlopers might move into his domain, devour his substance, and besiege his own wife.

Reading *The Odyssey* today, we are uncomfortably aware of all that strikes us quite otherwise than it must have struck the people of the time. Today we cannot regard it as proper for Odysseus, introducing himself to the Phaeacians, to say: "I am Odysseus, son of Laertes, known before all men for the study of crafty designs, and my fame goes up to the heavens" — although we know that this kind of boasting is routine in primitive and warlike societies. We are bound to feel uneasy, as well, at the way he makes the most of his sufferings to invite the pity and the gifts of others. Finally, the deaths inflicted on Melanthios and on the delinquent women servants at the end of Book XXII seem repulsively brutal to us, as apparently they did not to those who told the tale.

And yet, these are superficial matters merely. In the end we have to acknowledge something fundamental and imperishable, something that remains for us what it must have been for the men of 3,000 years ago, a common essence under the accidentals of manner and attitude. I think of the scene of Odysseus's and Penelope's reunion. And I return to the vision of a normative order toward which men struggle across the wide realms of chaos in which they are plunged, today as 3,000 years ago. This is what remains common in the midst of diversity: the vision of a harmonious and orderly society, the fulfillment of lifelong marriage, the regular succession of the generations, the consummation of life in the rhythm of creation, courage and endurance rewarded, the fruits of fidelity realized, the parable of man's striving toward a goal forever the same.

We are all of us born into an existential chaos out of which we struggle to emerge into some order that we may identify with a natural propriety. The lifetime monogamous association between the sexes may, in time, prove to be less well adapted to life in the dense urban conglomerations than some other pattern of relationship, perhaps such a pattern as Plato outlined in Book V of *The Republic*. It does, however, constitute one possible order that, as such, opposes the existential chaos. Because I have come, like so many others, to cherish it, I derive a comforting reassurance from testimony in its favor that goes back as far as 3,000 years. Although Homer lived in a society so different from mine that I cannot put myself in his place, here is intimate personal experience that he and I have had in common. The history of the homecoming of Odysseus, and the normative conception that gives it meaning, arouses in me the poignant experience of recognition. The very fact that the recognition takes place across such a wide gulf of time gives me a greater assurance of the stability of the normative vision that Homer and I have in common.

The Odyssey is a parable of man's striving to emerge from the existential chaos into an ideal order, represented by the Kingdom of Ithaca when it is under the governance of legitimacy. The poem represents the emergence of man, in consequence of his courage and persistence, from a world of discord into a world of harmony. It is creative, foreshadowing the possibility of a happy end for all mankind.

This is what accounts for the sense of fulfillment with which one finishes *The Odyssey*.

V

The Tragic Vision

IF WE WERE TO LIST the formal categories of literature in an order of greatness, what *The Odyssey* represents would have to come second, first place being reserved for tragedy. While *The Odyssey* has a happy ending, tragedy is formally characterized by an unhappy ending. Moral nobility, which triumphs in *The Odyssey*, is doomed to defeat in tragedy. The weakness of the happy ending is that it does not represent reality. "They married and lived happily ever after" is necessarily untrue, if only because it disregards human mortality. *The Odyssey* ends with the reunion of Odysseus, Penelope, and Telemachus; but in real life it could have ended only with their deaths and the ultimate passing of all they had striven so heroically to attain.

An unhappy ending is not enough in itself to make a tragedy, as pieces of fiction that are merely sordid show. What tragedy in the strict and traditional sense of the term displays is the inevitable defeat of moral nobility in a corrupt world; and the greatness of the tragedy is proportionate to the nobility that is defeated. (The downfall of Othello is tragic, but that of Iago is merely sordid.) Moreover, while it is true in formal terms, in terms of plot, that tragedy ends in the defeat of what is noble, every true tragedy leaves in the mind, when it is over, a suggestion that in some larger sense the defeat was really a victory. Indeed, it is because of this suggestion, however dimly apprehended, that when all is over we find ourselves uplifted rather than depressed.

This last point, making a distinction between what is merely formal and something that transcends it, may be exemplified by reference to one of the classic Greek tragedies. Thucydides recounts how, during the Peloponnesian War, an Athenian expedition conquered the Aegean island of Melos. The Athenians, brutalized by years of fighting, then proceeded to put the Melian men to death, after which they sold the women and children into slavery. This action was condemned as a crime, not only by the enemies of Athens but also by many Athenians. Thucydides, himself an Athenian, identified it with the moral downfall of Athens that preceded its political and military downfall.

The most profound condemnation of the Athenian action, however, was expressed by another Athenian, Euripides, in his play, *The Trojan Women*, produced in Athens a few months after the obliteration of Melos. *The Trojan Women* presents the fall of Troy, but those who attended its performance would have had in mind, as the author did, the fall of Melos. It displays the barbarous behavior of its author's fellow Greeks in killing the Trojan men and carrying the women off into slavery. The paradoxical message of the play is that the real victory, which is the moral victory, belonged to the Trojans who were killed or enslaved, while the Greeks had suffered a self-inflicted defeat. ("How are ye blind, ye treaders down of Cities . . . yourselves so soon to die!") *The Trojan Women* is remarkable because it equates true victory with fidelity to a normative conception, rather than with the merely formal victory that will quickly turn to ashes in the mouths of those who taste it. The fall of the House of Atreus proceeds from the ostensible victory of the Atreides and their associates over the Trojans, just as the fall of Athens is about to proceed from its ostensible victory over the Melians.

Again, in Melville's *Moby Dick*, Captain Ahab sets himself to destroy that embodiment of evil, the white whale, knowing that in the final confrontation it will destroy him. Even as he sinks beneath the waves in physical defeat, however, it is clear that he has won a moral victory, which his shipmates, putting their own safety first, preferred to forego.

One way or another, the theme of all tragedy is the struggle, forever defeated and forever renewed, to realize a normative order in a world of anarchy. Although each attempt ends in defeat, when all is over and life has returned to its usual course what transpires is that the attempt, in itself, has constituted a victory in defeat — just as the death of Socrates constituted a victory in defeat.

In any case, there is a purification. As the Greeks are corrupted by victory, the Trojans, in themselves no better than the Greeks, are purified by defeat. King Lear, whose *hubris* had led him into corruption, is purified and enlarged by his consequent sufferings. It is in these terms that we should understand, as well, the association between crucifixion and redemption.

*

Hamlet exemplifies the tragic vision as *The Odyssey* does the epic vision. Its theme, like that of *The Odyssey*, is the conflict between two worlds, an orderly world under the rule of legitimacy, and a chaotic world at the mercy of personal opportunism. Before the events with which the play opens, the Kingdom of Denmark had enjoyed the legitimate rule of its King Hamlet, with his faithful consort (Queen Gertrude) at his side, and with their son (Prince Hamlet) as the heir who, at the next turn in the regular revolution of the generations, might be expected to succeed his father on the throne. These three stand as the counterparts of Odysseus, Penelope, and Telemachus in the Kingdom of Ithaca before the Trojan War.

It was the adultery of Menelaus's queen, Helen, that brought about the breakdown of the normative order represented by the rule of Odysseus in Ithaca. The breakdown of the normative order represented by the rule of King Hamlet in Denmark results from the usurpation by his brother Claudius, who, after killing him clandestinely, has taken both his throne and his queen for himself.

When the play opens, Claudius's usurpation appears to have been completely successful. It has been accepted by everyone, unless an exception be made for Prince Hamlet, whose behavior has implications to the contrary that leave Claudius still uneasy. This general acceptance represents no more than the disposition of people everywhere, based on self-interest, to associate themselves with power, whether legitimate or illegitimate. In fact, everyone knows in his heart that the replacement of the old king by the new was not altogether according to rule. Quite aside from the atmosphere of conspiracy in which the new king moves, his marriage to his brother's widow constitutes at least a qualified violation of the rule against incest, an impropriety compounded by the fact that it was not delayed to allow for the customary period of mourning. However, although everyone knows in his heart that the succession was not achieved without some violation of legitimacy, only Hamlet knows the details.*

According to the normative order of the times in which he lived, the chief responsibility for restoring legitimacy lies with Hamlet as his father's heir. When Macbeth killed King Duncan and usurped his throne, Duncan's sons escaped and organized, from outside the

* My statement of what everyone knows in his heart is based on evidence implicit in the play. For example, in the very first scene it transpires that all who know about the visits of the old king's ghost are instinctively in favor of reporting them, not to the new king as their formal duty requires, but to Prince Hamlet. (They recognize that, as one of the sentries puts it, "something is rotten in the state of Denmark.") My statement that Hamlet knows the details is based not only on what he is told by his father's ghost (which may be regarded as merely a playright's device for revealing the inner mind), but also on his immediate response: "O my prophetic soul!" Before that, when he had first been told of the ghost's visits, his response had been: "Foul deeds will rise, though all the earth o'erwhelm them, to men's eyes."

realm, a military expedition to overthrow him. Hamlet, prevented by his usurping uncle from leaving his court, knows that according to the normative tradition, at least, his proper role is to avenge his father's murder by killing the murderer.

At this point, however, the basic conflict of the plot, between Claudius and Hamlet, is complicated by the inner conflict that divides Hamlet against himself. If either Laertes or Fortinbras, each a man of action rather than of thought, had been in Hamlet's place, he would have proceeded without compunction to carry out the role assigned him by tradition. But Hamlet is an introspective thinker, and thinking arouses in him speculative doubts that postpone, inhibit, and finally prevent action.*

The elimination of Claudius, if it was to be followed by the restoration of the normative order, would have had to be planned and executed as a conspiracy more or less elaborate. The paradox of Hamlet's position was that, to realize the normative world in action, he would have had to embrace all the sordid devices of the corrupt existential world. He would have had to adopt the pragmatic means of secrecy, double dealing, hypocrisy, and violence. He would have had to give himself entirely to the struggle for personal power, thereby corrupting himself — so that he might, as he feared, have ended as Nero did.†

Torn as he is by inner conflict, an increasingly wild Hamlet behaves in an increasingly capricious fashion, which so alarms the king, at last, that he conspires to send him to England, where he has arranged to have him killed. But the ship in which he sails is captured by pirates and Hamlet is returned to Denmark. This is the turning point of the play — not so much in terms of its plot as in terms of a transformation in Hamlet's character or state of mind.

---

* The psychological and philosophical subtleties involved here are set forth in a short book on *Hamlet* that I wrote some years ago and that will someday be published, I hope, if not before my death then after. Here, within the limitations of one chapter, I have no choice but to describe Hamlet's situation in excessively crude terms for which I ask the reader's indulgence.

† On his way to the confrontation with his mother in Act III, Scene 4, Hamlet warns himself: "let not ever the soul of Nero enter this firm bosom: let me be cruel, not unnatural; I will speak daggers to her, but use none." Has no one ever noticed the parallel to which this points in all its fulness? The young Nero had been distinguished, like Hamlet, by his qualities of soul and intellect, although in his final years he gave rein to those inordinate passions on account of which it might have been better if his mother, in the words Hamlet speaks of himself, "had never borne" him. The husband his mother took in second marriage had the name Claudius, and since he was her uncle the marriage was incestuous, as Hamlet considered his own mother's second marriage to be. Nero, the child of her first marriage, became the stepson and heir of the Emperor Claudius just as Hamlet, also the child of a first marriage, became the stepson and heir of King Claudius. In the end, Nero killed his mother, and we see in Hamlet the fear that he might do likewise.

Except for the momentary flare-up in Act V, Scene 1, when he leaps into Ophelia's grave to grapple with Laertes, Hamlet's inner conflict is no longer in evidence. It has at last been resolved, and in its resolution he has risen to a high plane of philosophical detachment in which he is at peace with himself. His serenity in this final act represents the purification that all tragedy achieves in the end.

In the grave-digger's scene, when he contemplates the disinterred skull of the court jester whom he remembers affectionately from his childhood, something approaching a godlike view of human existence forms in him. Later, reviewing the circumstances of the tragedy in conversation with Horatio, he surmises the existence of "a divinity that shapes our ends, rough-hew them how we will." Although he anticipates that his death is at hand, in the supposedly sporting duel he is about to engage in with Laertes, he rejects Horatio's plea that he forestall it, remarking that "there's a special providence in the fall of a sparrow. If it be now, 'tis not to come; if it be not to come, it will be now; if it be not now, yet it will come: the readiness is all."

Throughout the first four acts, Hamlet, still a prisoner of the here-and-now, had been prey to the chaos of immediate circumstances. In the fifth he has risen above them to a higher standpoint, and in the expanded vision that it affords he is able to see an order in the fall of a sparrow.

*

The effect of tragedy, which is reserved for the final act, is to lift us out of the sordid existential world of our daily lives to a higher world of the mind. It concludes with a sort of apotheosis; for, in what is ostensibly an unhappy ending, the ultimate triumph of the normative world is enacted.

In lifting us up to a higher level of being, tragedy opens up an enlarged vision in which we can begin to see the order that arises from what, in the close-up view, had been only a chaos of particulars. That order is summed up in Hamlet's statement that there is a special providence in the fall of a sparrow.

But is there, in fact, a special providence in the fall of a sparrow?

We should not take Hamlet's statement literally, for it is no more than a poetic expression of his sense that there is an order in being. Indeed, we must not take it literally, for it refers to a particular — i.e., any particular sparrow — whereas order, as we have seen, is to be associated in its degree only with the ever-larger combination of particulars. Because the immortality of species depends on the mortality of the individual, we may say that the succession of the generations, entailing the passing of each, makes death itself a part of the natural order. The way that the death of a particular sparrow comes about may be an accident, as the moment when a particular atom of thorium-234 decays is an accident (see Part One, Chapter X), but its death is still representative of an order that decrees the death of all sparrows, as the atom's decay is representative of an order that decrees the decay of all such atoms.

In any case, what is being affirmed is simply the existence of an order, the precise nature of which may remain beyond our understanding. Hamlet, whose disposition is agnostic, is expressing his belief that the sparrow plays out its part in an unknown order in which he, too, must play out his part. This order transcends the chaos that we know in the here-and-now.

*

The subject of this chapter is the tragic vision, and in it I have already referred to the purification that all tragedy achieves in the end.

Nowhere is the tragic vision more completely realized than in Michelangelo's marble "Pietà" at St. Peter's in Rome. The mother holds in her lap the limp and lifeless body of her son, which has been taken down from the cross, her head bowed and her hand raised in a gesture of acceptance. Peace has come at last, for this is the end of Act V. The whole composition is permeated with the feeling of a divine love associated with a loss that is also divine. (There is a special providence in the loss of this son, if not in the fall of a sparrow.) It has that tranquility of an inevitable ending which is the mark of tragedy — for here is tragedy in stone on a level with the literary tragedies of Euripides and Shakespeare.

VI

The Counterpoint of Two Worlds

WHAT TRAGEDY OSTENSIBLY PRESENTS to our view is the eventual failure of every attempt to realize a normative order amid the chaos of
the existential world. We might conclude from this that it was basically nihilistic, so that we should expect to come away from it feeling
depressed rather than uplifted. In fact, however, it constitutes affirmation rather than negation, for what it represents is an exaltation of human nobility in defeat.

On a lower level than tragedy, there is a body of literature that we
may categorize as the literature of disillusionment. One reason why
it is on a lower level is that, rather than being primary, it arises by reaction against the unrealism of inspirational writing, with its false
optimism. The literature of disillusionment is cynical, nihilistic, and
embittered; yet, just as one may prefer a bitter taste to a sweet, so
many of us derive a comfort and a courage from it that are not to be
had from the inspirational writing that has no other purpose.

I shall begin with an example so brief that I can quote it in its entirety, the poem by Coventry Patmore called "Magna est Veritas."

> Here, in this little Bay,
> Full of tumultuous life and great repose,
> Where, twice a day,
> The purposeless, glad ocean comes and goes,
> Under high cliffs, and far from the huge town,
> I sit me down.
> For want of me the world's course will not fail;
> When all its work is done, the lie shall rot;
> The truth is great, and shall prevail,
> When none cares whether it prevail or not.

This falls into two parts. The first six lines have withdrawal for their
theme. The poet, like one who withdraws from a battle that continues without him, has detached himself from "the huge town" to

find peace, at last, by the edge of a little bay where time is marked by the ebb and flow of an ocean that extends beyond the limits of human vision. The reader does not need me to point out the parallel with the Hamlet of the fifth act who, by his detachment, has at last found peace in a higher standpoint and a wider view. Nor will the reader be unaffected by the rhythm and the balance of antitheses — tumultuous life and great repose, purposeless and glad, coming and going — which give an impression of perpetuity. The rhythm and balance pertain to nature; they are not merely of the poet's invention. What the poet has found beneath the high cliffs is a world under the rule of some large order.*

The last four lines prick the bubble of the cant phrase on which we are all brought up: "Magna est veritas, et praevalebit." In setting the truth of experience against the pretended truth of mere rhetoric, they are purgative. A piece of humbug has been eliminated from our system, and we feel the better for it. This purgation is relevant to our concern with whether the order we find in literature is true or invented. In achieving it, the last four lines validate the first six.

*

The literature of disillusionment had a particular vogue after the First World War, when its most notable exemplifications were parodies of the heroic literature that generations of schoolchildren had been brought up to regard as sacred.† They mocked this literature by showing how sordid the real world was by contrast to the ideal world with which it had beguiled us.

T. S. Eliot exemplified this postwar literature of disillusionment by parodying traditional English poetry in "The Waste Land." He had already begun to give expression to the contrast between the ideal and the real by means of simple but startling juxtapositions, as in his poem, "Sweeney among the Nightingales." The scene is a tavern

---

* In "Dover Beach," another poem of disillusionment, which the reader should read at this point if he can, Patmore's contemporary, Matthew Arnold, represents a like withdrawal to the shore of a sea that, in its ebb and flow, provides the same sense of an eternal order beyond the strife of mankind.

† This was the age of what was called "debunking," in which T. E. Lawrence, introducing his translation of *The Odyssey*, denigrated the work he had nevertheless translated. ("The author misses his every chance of greatness, as must all his faithful translators. . . . Perhaps the tedious delay of the climax through ten books may be a poor bard's means of prolonging his host's hospitality." As to the three principal characters, they are: "the sly cattish wife, that cold-blooded egotist Odysseus, and the priggish son. . . .") In his *Greek Myths*, Robert Graves, of the same generation as Lawrence, expressed his doubt that Penelope had, in fact, remained faithful to Odysseus during the twenty years of their separation — leaving us to conclude that, on the basis of evidence known only to Mr. Graves, Homer had been mistaken about her.

where Sweeney and another man are engaged in drink and de-
bauchery with a couple of women who make their living that way.
The poem is contrapuntal, one voice (to use the term only in its
musical sense) representing what was represented by the first six
lines of Conventry Patmore's poem, the other representing the sordidness identified with Sweeney. Here are the first four verses:

> Apeneck Sweeney spreads his knees
> Letting his arms hang down to laugh
> The zebra stripes along his jaw
> Swelling to maculate giraffe.
>
> The circles of the stormy moon
> Slide westward toward the River Plate,
> Death and the Raven drift above
> And Sweeney guards the horned gate.
>
> Gloomy Orion and the Dog
> Are veiled; and hushed the shrunken seas;
> The person in the Spanish cape
> Tries to sit on Sweeney's knees
>
> Slips and pulls the table cloth
> Overturns a coffee-cup,
> Reorganised upon the floor
> She yawns and draws a stocking up;

So it goes until the next to last verse, the second half of which provides a shock of beauty that depends on the contrast with what had
gone before:

> The host with someone indistinct
> Converses at the door apart,
> The nightingales are singing near
> The Convent of the Sacred Heart, . . .*

Here is the contrast between the chaos of Coventry Patmore's "huge
town" and the order he finds in the world of nature outside it.

For most of us, English lyric poetry begins with Spenser in the sixteenth century, when it still represents such an innocent delight in
dreams of the poetic imagination as children take in fairy-tales.

---

* I have stopped with these lines because the last two quoted have for me an inexplicable magic that I hesitate to go beyond. Having hesitated, I now give the four final
lines of the poem, which follow them.

> And sang within the bloody wood
> When Agamemnon cried aloud,
> And let their liquid siftings fall
> To stain the stiff dishonoured shroud.

This is perfectly represented by Spenser's musical "Prothalamion," with its constant refrain: "Sweet Thames run softly, till I end my song." The poet describes how, walking out one day

> Along the shore of silver streaming Thames,
> Whose rutty bank, the which his river hems,
> Was painted all with variable flowers,
> And all the meads adorned with dainty gems,
> Fit to deck maiden bowers,
> And crown their paramours,
> Against the bridal day, which is not long:
> Sweet Thames run softly, till I end my song.

The poet of "The Waste Land" describes how:

> The river's tent is broken; the last fingers of leaf
> Clutch and sink into the wet bank. The wind
> Crosses the brown land, unheard. The nymphs are departed.
> Sweet Thames, run softly, till I end my song.
> The river bears no empty bottles, sandwich papers,
> Silk handkerchiefs, cardboard boxes, cigarette ends
> Or other testimony of summer nights. The nymphs are
>   departed.
> And their friends, the loitering heirs of City directors;
> Departed, have left no addresses.
> By the waters of Leman I sat down and wept . . .
> Sweet Thames, run softly till I end my song, . . .

Again, Andrew Marvell, in his appeal "To His Coy Mistress" not to delay the fulfillment of their love, wrote:

> But at my back I always hear
> Time's wingéd chariot hurrying near; . . .

And in John Day's "The Parliament of Bees" there is a description of a painting which represents a forest-scene so vividly that

> . . . of the sudden, listening, you shall hear
> A noise of horns and hunting, which shall bring
> Actaeon to Diana in the spring, . . .

The poet of "The Waste Land" writes:

> But at my back from time to time I hear
> The sound of horns and motors, which shall bring
> Sweeney to Mrs. Porter in the spring.

What is surely the masterpiece of all such contrapuntal writing, W. H. Auden's "The Shield of Achilles," is too long to be quoted here in its entirety. It is based on a description, in Book 18 of *The Iliad,* of the shield that Hephaestus, the smith of the gods, made for Achilles at the request of the latter's mother, Thetis. The shield depicts landscapes and seascapes and all varieties of human activity.

> On it he wrought in all their beauty two cities of mortal men. And there were marriages in one, and festivals. They were leading the brides along the city from their maiden chambers under the flaring torches, and the loud bride song was arising. The young men followed the circles of the dance, and among them the flutes and lyres kept up their clamour as in the meantime the women standing each at the door of her court admired them. . . .
> And the renowned smith of the strong arms made elaborate on it a dancing floor, like that which once in the wide spaces of Knosos Daidalos built for Ariadne of the lovely tresses. And there were young men on it and young girls, sought for their beauty with gifts of oxen, dancing, and holding hands at the wrist.*

Auden's poem, written at a time when the Nazi tyranny had turned Europe into a prison and a torture chamber, represents Thetis looking over the shoulder of Hephaestus at the shield he is making, expecting to see the idyllic scenes described by Homer but seeing something quite different. There are as if two voices, the one responding to the other.

> She looked over his shoulder
>   For ritual pieties,
> White flower-garlanded heifers,
>   Libation and sacrifice,
> But there on the shining metal
>   Where the altar should have been,
> She saw by his flickering forge-light
>   Quite another scene.
>
> Barbed wire enclosed an arbitrary spot
>   Where bored officials lounged (one cracked a joke)
> And sentries sweated for the day was hot:
>   A crowd of ordinary decent folk
>   Watched from without and neither moved nor spoke

---

* Translation by Richmond Lattimore, Chicago, 1951. I have here taken the liberty of presenting this translation in the format of prose rather than in the broken lines of the original.

As three pale figures were led forth and bound
To three posts driven upright in the ground.

The mass and majesty of this world, all
 That carries weight and always weighs the same
Lay in the hands of others; they were small
 And could not hope for help and no help came:
 What their foes liked to do was done, their shame
Was all the worst could wish; they lost their pride
And died as men before their bodies died.

So the poem goes back and forth between the ideal and the actual.

We may be grateful that English literature has, in addition to its Spensers and Marvells, its Eliots and Audens; nor should we try to choose between them, since there is no need to do so. We may plausibly maintain, however, that the latter have added something to the former; for, as the sordid is the more vivid in its reality because it is contrasted with what is idyllic, so the idyllic is the more vivid in its reality because it is contrasted with what is sordid. More truly in Eliot than in Spenser, the nightingales are singing near the Convent of the Sacred Heart.

*

> Why rushed the discords in but that har-
> mony should be prized?
>
> *— Robert Browning*

If James Joyce had not given his most celebrated novel the title *Ulysses,* its reader would have no way of knowing that it had been written as the parody of a classic. There is no explicit counterpoint in the text itself, no going back and forth between the sordid and the idyllic. Indeed, the idyllic is lacking except as it is implied by the title's suggestion of what the author had in mind.

In *Ulysses,* Homer's hero is replaced by Mr. Leopold Bloom, a lumpish Jewish salesman in Dublin, whose mind contains little more than a jumble of trivialities, including his concerns with his own animal needs. Penelope is represented by Molly Bloom, a piece of ripe female flesh with a mind that wallows in such thoughts as never rise above the mean and the lecherous.

Ulysses belongs to the kind of fiction that has as its sufficient object to show life as it really is experienced by actual people in the privacy of their own minds — the privacy being stripped from their minds for the purpose of revealing a stream of consciousness, like an alimentary canal, through which half-digested sensations and recollections follow one another in a more-or-less incoherent succession.

I could dismiss *Ulysses* as one of those pretended works of art that are nothing of the sort. It is nihilistic in its conception, directed against the normative visions of traditional literature because, presumably, they do not correspond to the sordid reality. I could dismiss it the more readily in that, on the face of it, it does not fulfill what I have regarded as the creative mission of mind. There are many works of nihilism that I would dismiss on this basis, such as pretended poems that indulge in ugliness of sound and imagery for its own sake, and do nothing more. But *Ulysses* does do something more. It depicts one kind of reality with a persuasiveness not to be denied, opposing that reality to the normative vision represented by *The Odyssey*. It tells us that Homer was false to the reality for which Joyce stands by banishing from the vision of life he presented a multitude of facts that did not fit it — such as the need of all people, even heroes, to relieve themselves periodically by the evacuation of what accumulates at the bottom of the alimentary canal.

I do not doubt that here Joyce does for us in some measure, albeit with unrelieved insistence and at excessive length, what Coventry Patmore does when, to the cant saying that "the truth is great, and shall prevail," he adds: "when none cares whether it prevail or not." Such realism is purgative.

Perhaps there is a further justification in the paradoxically interdependent and sometimes intimate relationship of opposites that we have already noted. In a world without evil there would be no good, nor any evil in a world without good; for each is what it is by contrast with the other, and so each depends on the other. ·Again, of two persons brought up to the practice of Christian devotions, who rebel against their upbringing, one may show his rebellion by simply abandoning devotional practices, while the other shows his by opposite devotional practices, practices that represent the worship of Satan rather than God. A shrewd judgement will conclude that the second has not really broken with his religion as the first has.

The life Joyce depicted in *Ulysses* was sordid in his own evaluation, and if it was sordid for him then it must have been so by contrast to the normative world that his mind continued to inhabit, even though he was ostensibly revolting against it. Only an idealist could have written *Ulysses*. Having read it, one turns from it, as Hamlet turned from the life of the Danish court, to the larger world that it ostensibly belies.

> So gladly from the songs of modern speech
> Men turn, and see the stars, and feel the free

Shrill wind beyond the close of heavy flowers;
And, through the music of the languid hours,
They hear like ocean on a western beach
The surge and thunder of the Odyssey.*

*

I confess that, in justifying *Ulysses* as a valid work of art, I have gone beyond the point where I feel sure of my judgement. Written within my lifetime, it made its appeal chiefly to a generation of intellectuals who assumed that a work of fiction had fulfilled its function if it showed life at a particular time and place (e.g., Dublin, June 16, 1904) as it really was — if, so to speak, it simply photographed existential reality. This assumption, however, seems to me inadequate. As the premise for judgement it would invalidate virtually the whole fictional literature of mankind from the beginning.

The members of the generation to which *Ulysses* made its appeal had been brought up to the expectation that they would meet impossible standards of thought and behavior, standards that could be met only in outward seeming, hypocritically. Ladies and gentlemen in the Victorian Age had been supposed not to have animal needs or any thoughts except such as might occur to angels in Heaven. The sexual appetite was represented as bestial and therefore as unworthy of proper people. Consequently, all who felt themselves expected to live up to such standards, and who pretended that they did, suffered from a secret sense of guilt when they were consumed by desires and teased by thoughts that they regarded as signs of wickedness peculiar to themselves. After the First World War, however, there was a general revolt of intellectuals against the unrealizable norms that had been upheld by society, and the associated hypocrisy. So they embraced the teachings of Freud, who told them that all people, not just themselves as individuals, were dominated by concupiscence, and they were immensely relieved to have a writer represent the realities, which they had known in themselves as guilty secrets, as being in fact normal and common to all. Those who read *Ulysses* were thereby relieved of guilt. It was welcomed because it contributed to destroying an unrealizable normative order that, having become established, had been the cause of moral suffering. We are justified, therefore, in regarding it as nihilism.

We shall find it enlightening, here, to examine *Ulysses* as a work of negative art, metaphorically representing the worship of Satan rather than God — as negation rather than affirmation. I observed above that it stripped the privacy from people's minds to reveal a stream of

* "The Odyssey" by Andrew Lang.

consciousness through which half-digested sensations and recollections follow one another in a more-or-less incoherent succession. This is to say that what is found in the stream of consciousness is an incoherence that betokens a large measure of chaos. (The quasi-incoherence of the language in which Joyce wrote, appropriate to its subject, is also suggestive of chaos, as opposed to the order found in the language of traditional literature.*)

Under the circumstances, we may well understand why, where Homer's *Odyssey* covers ten years, Joyce's *Ulysses,* which is more than twice its length, covers only one day. The significance of this may be appreciated by my repetition here, from Part One, Chapter XII, of the last three paragraphs but one.

If, descending the scale of magnitude, we progressively analyze being down to its smallest components of time or of space we find that, as we approach the extreme of ultimate granularity, we discover a condition representative of chaos. Going back up the scale, we find order emerging progressively from the underlying chaos as the ultimate grains combine in larger and larger combinations, until at last chaos has become imperceptible and only the overlying order remains in evidence.

The phenomenon this represents has always been so familiar in our daily life that one wonders why its centrality in human experience has not become a matter of common knowledge and acceptance. One example will suffice.

Suppose I draw a circle with pencil on paper, using compasses. Viewing that circle from a sufficient distance, so that I see it in the large, it appears to me to be a perfect circle. The closer and more detailed my view, however, the more likely I am to notice little imperfections, irregularities caused by the roughness of the paper or by lack of perfect steadiness in the hand that guided the instrument. If I take a magnifying glass to it I shall find it even more imperfect; and if, at last, I use a miscroscope, I shall no longer be able to see a circle at all, only a

---

* The following are typical samples. Bloom, riding in one of the carriages of a funeral cortege, is reminded, by a remark of one of his fellow travelers, of a son who had died in infancy. He muses to himself about how he had been conceived. "Must have been that morning in Raymond terrace she was at the window, watching the two dogs at it by the wall of the cease to do evil. And the sergeant grinning up. She had that cream gown on with the rip she never stitched. Give us a touch, Poldy. God, I'm dying for it. How life begins." Again, looking out the carriage window: "Gasworks. Whooping cough they say it cures. Good job Milly never got it. Poor children! Doubles them up black and blue in convulsions. Shame really. Got off lightly with illness compared. Only measles. Flaxseed tea. Scarlatina, influenza epidemics. Canvassing for death. Don't miss this chance. Dogs' home over there. Poor old Athos! Be good to Athos, Leopold, is my last wish. Thy will be done. We obey them in the grave. A dying scrawl. He took it to heart, pined away. Quiet brute. Old men's dogs usually are."

chaos of smudges on the paper. It is, however, out of the chaos of these smudges, representing the very small, that the order represented by the circle as a whole is built. The circle stands for the order that overlies chaos; the smudges stand for the chaos that underlies order.

The life of Odysseus, viewed in the long perspective of the years, represents an heroic order. Viewed close-up, in terms of its successive instants, it is but a sequence of smudges.

> On the earth the broken arcs; in the heaven, a perfect round.
>
> — *Robert Browning*

VII

The Fall of a Sparrow

NIHILISM, in the example of Joyce's *Ulysses,* discredits the heroic order, which we would fondly discover in human life, by examining that life close up, in terms of the very small. Tennyson's "In Memoriam" stands in contrast to *Ulysses,* for it attempts to exorcise by enlargement the implications of chaos in a particular experience.

According to the normative order we all have in mind, one generation after another goes through the successive stages of infancy, childhood, adolescence, maturity, and final old age. In a close-up view, however, which shows those particles of being, individual persons, accident is common — as when a promising child is struck and killed by an automobile. So it had been with Tennyson's friend, Arthur Hallam, whose sudden death at the age of twenty-three had cut off, at its beginning, what had promised to be an exceptionally distinguished career.

The implications of chaos in this experience provoked in Tennyson's mind a train of agonized philosophical thought that he set down over the years in the stanzas of "In Memoriam." That train begins with the question whether the life of the individual is meaningless, of no value in nature.

> Are God and Nature then at strife,
>   That Nature lends such evil dreams?
>   So careful of the type she seems,
> So careless of the single life;
>
> That I, considering everywhere
>   Her secret meaning in her deeds,
>   And finding that of fifty seeds,
> She often brings but one to bear,
>
> I falter where I firmly trod,
>   And falling with my weight of cares
>   Upon the great world's altar-stairs
> That slope thro' darkness up to God,

> I stretch lame hands of faith, and grope,
> And gather dust and chaff, and call
> To what I feel is Lord of all,
> And faintly trust the larger hope.

From faint trust he goes on to near despair.

> 'So careful of the type'? but no.
> From scarped cliff and quarried stone
> She cries, 'A thousand types are gone:
> I care for nothing, all shall go.
>
> 'Thou makest thine appeal to me:
> I bring to life, I bring to death:
> The spirit does but mean the breath:
> I know no more.' And he, shall he,
>
> Man, her last work, who seem'd so fair,
> Such splendid purpose in his eyes,
> Who roll'd the psalm to wintry skies,
> Who built him fanes of fruitless prayer,
>
> Who trusted God was love indeed
> And love Creation's final law —
> Tho' Nature, red in tooth and claw
> With ravine, shriek'd against his creed —
>
> Who loved, who suffer'd countless ills,
> Who battled for the True, the Just,
> Be blown about the desert dust,
> Or seal'd within the iron hills?

The poet alternates between despair and trust, between faith and scepticism.

> Oh yet we trust that somehow good
> Will be the final goal of ill,
> To pangs of nature, sins of will,
> Defects of doubt, and taints of blood;
>
> That nothing walks with aimless feet;
> That not one life shall be destroy'd,
> Or cast as rubbish to the void,
> When God hath made the pile complete;
>
> That not a worm is cloven in vain;
> That not a moth with vain desire
> Is shrivell'd in a fruitless fire,
> Or but subserves another's gain.

> Behold, we know not anything;
> I can but trust that good shall fall
> At last — far off — at last, to all,
> And every winter change to spring.

I said in Chapter I that Vermeer's "Maidservant Pouring Milk" appeals to us because it suggests a rhythmic order of being, represented by the succession of the generations, in which each of us, when his turn comes, plays his part and then moves on — as in a pageant. Because the death of Tennyson's friend before he could play his part, rather than being suggestive of such an order, was suggestive of chaos, the underlying theme of "In Memoriam" is the underlying theme of all human culture, of mind itself. It is the theme of order *versus* chaos. The poet is driven to bring the one out of the other, seeking to discover an order in nature if he can, creating it where he cannot — as the painter composes a landscape to achieve balance and harmony, as the sculptor eliminates the imperfections of the human body.

> There rolls the deep where grew the tree.
> O earth, what changes hast thou seen!
> There where the long street roars, hath been
> The stillness of the central sea.
>
> The hills are shadows, and they flow
> From form to form, and nothing stands;
> They melt like mist, the solid lands,
> Like clouds they shape themselves and go.
>
> But in my spirit will I dwell,
> And dream my dream, and hold it true;
> For tho' my lips may breathe adieu,
> I cannot think the thing farewell.

This is to say that, although he cannot know, he will balance doubt with faith. On this basis he concludes:

> . . . I see in part
> That all, as in some piece of art,
> Is toil coöperant to an end.

So he comes to his final stanza.

> That God, which ever lives and loves,
> One God, one law, one element,
> And one far-off divine event,
> To which the whole creation moves.

The teleology of his conclusion is out of fashion in our day, for reasons as good as those that determine the fashion of any day. In our ignorance we have no basis for either accepting or rejecting it. Tennyson himself presents it as no more than speculation supported by faith. All that counts in our present context, however, is that the poet is driven to create an order of the mind, whether it does or does not correspond to external reality. Here he is concerned, in particular, with the temporal aspect of order, which is to say that he is concerned with movement. Like his contemporaries, Herbert Spencer, Charles Darwin, and T. H. Huxley (whose lecture "On a Piece of Chalk" should be read in connection with the two stanzas that begin: "There rolls the deep . . ."), he was concerned with the progressive movement called evolution.

What is significant here, where we are drawing a contrast with Joyce's *Ulysses,* is that Tennyson, in his striving to bring order out of an ostensible chaos, represented by the accidental death of his friend, enlarges from this particular to the scale of the evolution of all life on earth. There may be a special providence in the fall of a sparrow — but, if so, it is not to be found in the fall of a particular sparrow. Order is built out of chaos by the combination of such particulars.

*

In the previous chapter I remarked that the incoherence of Joyce's language, appropriate to its subject, was suggestive of chaos as opposed to the order displayed by the language of traditional literature. Joyce was denying a normative order by showing the incoherence of life as it is experienced up close, and he improvised a language that represented this theme. Because Tennyson was doing the opposite, finding an order in the incoherence of life as seen only in its immediacy, he resorted to such regular rhymed stanzas as suited the conception of "one God, one law, one element,/ And one far-off divine event."

Form, as we shall see in the chapters that follow, is ultimately inseparable from content.

VIII

Content and Form

SINCE THOUGHT COMES INTO BEING only as it is composed in the mind, there can be no thought without composition; and, since composition is a matter of form, it follows that there can be no thought without form. Form and content, to speak in more general terms, are inseparable.

Because words are the medium in which we compose our thoughts, language is only secondarily a means of communication. Primarily, it is the means by which we think; and the forms of language, themselves shaped by the requirements of thought, in turn limit if they do not determine the thought that depends on them.

By examining competent writing of all sorts, we find that the composition of thought tends, as if of itself, to assume forms suitable to the thought composed. I open a textbook on physics, written by a scientist with no literary pretensions, and this is the first sentence on which my eye falls: "Two waves arriving at the same point may strengthen each other if they are crest to crest and trough to trough, or they may cancel each other out if the crest of one coincides with the trough of the other." * The sentence rises to a crest, only to fall off again. Because Darwin considered himself a poor writer, and was indeed deficient by the standards of his time and place, I choose my second example from his *Origin of Species*.

> It is interesting to contemplate a tangled bank, clothed with many plants of many kinds, with birds singing on the bushes, with various insects flitting about and with worms crawling through the damp earth, and to reflect that these elaborately constructed forms, so different from each other, and dependent upon each other in so complex a manner, have all been produced by laws acting around us.†

* Kenneth W. Ford, *Basic Physics*, Waltham (Mass.), 1968, p. 583.
† 6th ed., New York, 1915, p. 305.

This sentence rises as if to a plateau, sustains itself at that level, and declines at last to a rounded conclusion, like a piece of music returning to the keynote on which it began.

Neither the physicist nor the biologist, we may be sure, was consciously shaping the language to conform to the thought. It was the thought that, as of itself, gave shape to the language, thereby making of thought and language an indivisible whole. When Darwin's subject was the anatomical parts of *Ophrys muscifera,* for example, his language was pedestrian. The sentence I have quoted necessarily rises above the pedestrian because its subject is the variety of living forms that would imply chaos if they were not, in fact, parts of a single order under the laws of nature. When Joyce is describing the semi-coherent succession of Leopold Bloom's thoughts, his language does not remain coherent for the length of a normal sentence. Contrast this with the sentences of Gibbon, recounting the long decline and fall of Rome, which march one after another as if to the beat of music.

Finally, I quote another historian, as he introduces his account of a war that has, for him, the shape of tragedy.

> These pages recount dazzling victories and defeats stoutly made good. They record the toils, perils, sufferings and passions of millions of men. Their sweat, their tears, their blood bedewed the endless plain. Ten million homes awaited the return of the warriors. A hundred cities prepared to acclaim their triumphs. But all were defeated; all were stricken; everything that they had given was given in vain. The hideous injuries they inflicted and bore, the privations they endured, the grand loyalties they exemplified, all were in vain. Nothing was gained by any. They floundered in the mud, they perished in the snowdrifts, they starved in the frost. Those that survived, the veterans of countless battle-days, returned, whether with the laurels of victory or tidings of disaster, to homes engulfed already in catastrophe.*

If the historian, here, had thought of himself as chronicling a conflict involving only wooden figures on a chessboard, such language would not have occurred to his mind. His vision, however, was of a vast field of action on which human aspirations, defeated, ended in human suffering on a scale unimaginable in its immensity. It was this conception that shaped his language.

*

* Winston S. Churchill, *The Unknown War,* New York, 1931, p. 1.

Setting aside what serves for laundry lists, all language, whether prose or verse, entails rhythm, and rhythm implies movement. Movement exists to begin with in nature. On the astronomical scale, it appears to be determined by mechanical laws. The rhythmic movement of the earth around the sun, for instance, is invariable as a matter of the mechanics that govern it, not subject to accelerandos, ritardandos, pauses, or any irregularities at all. It may be significant that, on the astronomical scale, this is the only kind of movement there is.

Another kind of movement, which occurs on the mundane scale, is represented by the waves that break, one after another, on an oceanic shore. This rhythm, rather than being invariable like clockwork, manifests irregularity within regularity, for no two waves are ever quite the same. And what is true of the rhythm of the waves is true as well, and without exception, of all the rhythms associated with living matter. It is true of my heartbeat, of a fox running, of a bird flying. Like the waves, the wingbeats of gull or crow manifest irregularity within regularity. This kind of living rhythm is what Alfred North Whitehead was referring to in the following statement.

> A rhythm involves a pattern, and to that extent is always self-identical. But no rhythm can be a mere pattern; for the rhythmic quality depends equally upon the differences involved in each exhibition of the same pattern. The essence of rhythm is the fusion of sameness and novelty; so that the whole never loses the essential unity of the pattern, while the parts exhibit the contrast arising from the novelty of their detail. A mere recurrence kills rhythm as surely as does a mere confusion of detail.*

Auguste Renoir, the painter, was referring to the same kind of irregularity in nature when he said:

> The Earth is not round. An orange is not round. None of its segments has either the same form or the same weight. Open them and they will not have the same number of seeds, and the seeds will not be alike. . . . I do not want a column to be any rounder than a tree.†

May we not say categorically that all forms of art imitate, not the mechanical perfection of the astronomical universe but the ir-

* *The Principles of Natural Knowledge,* Cambridge, 1925, p. 198. Quoted by C. H. Waddington in *Aspects of Form,* L. L. Whyte, ed., London, 1968, p. 46.
† Translated from the French of *Renoir* by Jean Renoir, Paris, 1962, pages 232, 233, and 236.

regularity within regularity that characterizes living nature? No distinction can be made in this respect between prose and poetry — and, indeed, there is no line to be drawn between the two, as there is between prose and verse.* Let the reader at this point read Ecclesiastes 1 and 12, The Song of Solomon, I Corinthians 13 (all in the King James translation), and Lincoln's Gettysburg Address. Half the poetry of Walt Whitman has the rhythm of successive waves on a sandy shore — each running up the sloping shingle, to be followed by another that does the same.

> When lilacs last in the dooryard bloom'd,
> And the great star early droop'd in the western sky in the night,
> I mourn'd, and yet shall mourn with ever-returning spring.

This rhythm associates the pulse of the waves, regular in its irregularity, with ever-returning spring and the memory of him we mourn.

What is explicit in words — whether in the sentence from the textbook of physics or in Whitman's poem — is implicit in the rhythm, and in the other non-verbal elements of composition (which we have not yet examined). This suggests that one might dispense with the words altogether, leaving the remaining elements of composition to express the same meaning, albeit in less explicit terms. The dirge Whitman wrote to mark the death of Abraham Lincoln, from which I have quoted above, might have been given what was merely a more abstract expression by being composed, without the accompaniment of words, for the organ. (Let the reader think, here, of the lamentation expressed by the second movement of Beethoven's Seventh Symphony, or of "Åse's Death" from Grieg's incidental music to a work in which that death is explicit, Ibsen's *Peer Gynt*.)

Having begun these chapters on what mind creates by citing examples of particularistic art, we have now moved to the point where we are ready to consider examples representative of the opposite extreme, that of abstraction.

---

* The formal difference between prose and poetry is often a matter of whether it is presented to the eye in continuous or broken lines. The second half of the passage from Pater that I quoted in Chapter I, although presented by him as prose, was recast into successive lines of irregular length by W. B. Yeats for inclusion in his anthology, *The Oxford Book of Modern Verse* (Oxford, 1936). Quoting from Lattimore's translation of Homer in Chapter IV above, I did the opposite, rearranging his broken lines to form the continuous lines of prose. Although presented visually as poetry, Lattimore's translation is no more poetic than that of *The Odyssey* by Butcher and Lang, which is presented visually as prose.

IX

The Elements of Music *

> All art constantly aspires toward the condition of music.
>
> — *Walter Pater*

I TAKE WALTER PATER'S STATEMENT at the head of this chapter to represent the common view that music is the purest of the arts. What, however, do we mean by purity?

Perhaps there is an analogy in the relationship of mathematics, which is unadulterated in its abstraction, to natural science. In mathematics two plus two make four, whereas in science it must be two of something, whether apples or galaxies. This is to say that in mathematics numbers stand by themselves as nouns, while in science they are adjectives that, as such, have to lean on nouns that are extraneous to mathematics.

Describing the music of an imaginary culture, a writer has said that its rhythms imitate "movement apart from what moves: the quick running step of the fox, but without the fox; the repeated dip, tug, and release of the willow tips in the running stream, without willows or stream; the drift of a cockle boat on the rippled surface of a pond, without boat or pond." † The musical intervals stand by themselves as nouns rather than adjectives.

*

Music is experienced as a coherent succession of sounds — not just any sounds but sounds called musical because each represents a particular pitch on the scale from low to high. If I drop a rock on a cement floor, the resulting sound, lacking an identifiable pitch, is not musical; but the sound produced when I pluck the stretched

* What I have to say about the art of music in this chapter refers only to Western music, which I believe, although on an insufficient basis of knowledge, to represent the most advanced development of music in the cultural evolution of mankind so far.
† L. J. Halle, *Sedge*, New York, 1963, p. 51.

string of a violin is musical because it does have an identifiable pitch — e.g., the A above middle C. Pitch, then, is one of the elements of music.

We don't think of pitch as existing in time, but we do associate it with spatial extension, however irrationally, since we refer to a particular pitch as being higher or lower according to the position that its symbol, in our notation of music, would occupy on the written page — the A "above" middle C, for example, being higher up. So we think of intervals between pitches as if they were spatial, although they are not.*

The other basic element in music is what we experience as a temporal interval: short or long rather than high or low.

In written music, according to our notation, the one element is placed on what we may call a "north-south" line (an axis in mathematical terminology), the other on a "west-east" line. Since music is extension in time, the movement from west to east is more fundamental than the differences between farther north and farther south, which is to say that the intervals of time are more fundamental than those of pitch. One can produce a rhythmic piece of music on the west-east axis alone, all on one pitch of a kettle-drum — indeed, one can produce such a piece of music with no pitch at all, beating on a piece of wood with a couple of drumsticks (thereby producing an exception to the first sentence of this section) — but one can produce no music on the north-south axis alone, since it has no extension in time. Rhythm, it follows, is more fundamental than pitch. It is the basis of all music.

The temporal relationships on which rhythm is based are measurable and can be expressed in arithmetic. Thus (in the convenient American nomenclature) there are whole notes, half notes, quarter notes, eighth notes, sixteenth notes, etc., these names representing the fractions of the duration of a whole note for which each stands.

The length of time allowed for each note, according to these fractions, is only one of the elements in rhythm. Another is the special emphasis that we think of as a beat. A piece of music composed in what is called four-four ($\frac{4}{4}$) time will be divided into measures that have room for four quarter notes or the equivalent. There will be four beats to the measure, with at least an implied special emphasis

---

* This explanation, although the best I can devise, seems to me inadequate. A passage in music that rises to a summit, tips over, and comes running down again gives the impression in its initial rising of the tension that actual climbing (e.g., mountain climbing) entails, and in its subsequent descent of the relative relaxation that actual coming down entails. Perhaps this has to do with the fact that higher frequencies require more energy than lower for their production, but this seems implausible to me.

on the first to mark the beginning of each measure. In such classical music as tends to adhere rigidly to these mechanics, the listener can distinguish the successive measures and the number of beats within each.

With two or more instruments playing in conjunction, different rhythmic intervals may be combined so that they fit into one another. One instrument may play a succession of eighth notes, four to each of a succession of half notes being played by another instrument, or it may play triplets — i.e., three notes to each half note of the other instrument.

Although I describe all this in terms of a mechanical perfection, like that of the astronomical universe, the reader will have in mind the element of irregularity within regularity, involving accelerandos, ritardandos, and special emphases to achieve particular kinds of expression. A perfect example of such irregularity, albeit from poetry rather than music, is in the three stanzas of Auden's "Shield of Achilles" that I quoted on pages 544–545. The second and third are in iambic pentameters, each line containing five beats on alternate syllables, beginning with the second. ("Barb'd wíre enclós'd an árbitráry spót . . .") In the first line of the third stanza, however, an irregularity occurs that has an extraordinarily powerful and dramatic effect — as if the voice of the poet, which had been speaking in a calm monotone, was suddenly lifted by a swelling emotion within him. And the stanza does not quite settle back to normal again until the fourth line. Such expressive irregularity occurs in music as well, which would otherwise be as lifeless as clockwork.

One form of expressive irregularity in music is rubato, which may entail emphasizing a particular note by holding it a trifle longer than the others. (For example, holding the top note in a long passage that rises to a peak, only to descend again, is like pausing at the top of a mountain, when one has just climbed it, before continuing down the other side. Rubato marks the achievement of the summit.) Or rubato may entail the slower and consequently more expressive playing of a whole passage.

Another form of expressive irregularity is syncopation, in which suddenly one note or all the notes in a sequence fall between the beats rather than on them.

Without such variations from regularity a piece of music would hardly hold one's interest more than the ticking of a clock. The avoidance of monotony, however, is not their most important function. They are the devices by which the meaning of a piece of music is expressed. It follows that the irregularity within the regularity is essential.

Although we do not hear it as such, pitch, which we have arbitrarily identified with spatial rather than temporal intervals, is in reality a rhythmic phenomenon, extending in time, no less than the element of music we have been referring to as rhythm. What we hear as the A above middle C is a vibration (of the air against the eardrum) with a frequency of 440 cycles per second. This is about 370 times the frequency of a normal heartbeat. If, now, we imagine someone whose life processes, including those entailed in perception, are 370 times as fast as normal, he would hear the vibrations of a tuning fork that sounded A = 440 as having the frequency of a normal heartbeat. The duration of each cycle might be equivalent to the duration of a whole note in a piece of music. If, then, this tuning fork were accompanied by another, sounding the octave above A = 440, he would hear it as a series of vibrations twice as frequent as those produced by the first, thereby fitting into the intervals of the first as half notes fit into whole notes. Such a person might give a description of pitch, and the relationships among different pitches of different instruments playing together, that was virtually identical with the description I have just given of rhythm and the relationships among the rhythms of different instruments playing together.

The fact that the elements of music are all composed of temporal intervals, which are numerically measurable and so have a numerical relationship to one another, is what associates music with mathematics.

The irregularity within regularity that characterizes the rhythmic combinations of music is not lacking from the combinations of pitch. Two pitches may be more or less consonant or dissonant in relation to each other, which is to say that two frequencies, as a matter of arithmetic, may fit together perfectly (as sixteenth notes fit into half notes, eight to one) or imperfectly (as seventeenth notes, if there were such things, would fit into half notes). Consider, then, the arithmetical relationships of the various pitches in music.

If each musical sound were confined to one pitch, as in the case of the tuning fork that gives A = 440, it would impress the auditor as excessively dull or lifeless. But a violin string that sounds A = 440 simultaneously sounds, although less conspicuously, a series of higher tones (the harmonic series) that we call harmonics or overtones.* In addition to the fundamental tone (A = 440), it sounds the octave (A = 2 × 440 = 880), the twelfth (E = 3 × 440 = 1,320), the fifteenth (A = 4 × 440 = 1,760), the seventeenth (C♯ = 5 × 440 = 2,200), the nineteenth (E = 6 × 440 = 2,640), etc. Because the respective

* See pp. 61–63 above.

frequencies of the harmonic series are multiples of the domineering fundamental frequency, so that they fit into it (although not necessarily into one another) without fractional remainders, as sixteenth notes fit into half notes, they are consonant with it, making a predominant harmony when sounded with it. If, however, one sounds together C = 2,077 and C♯ = 2,200 the dissonance is extreme; the two seem to the ear to clash rather than harmonize because the one does not fit into the other. They do not match, as the hypothetical seventeenth notes don't match with the half notes.

The construction of the various scales on which music is based is such that the intervals are not mathematically as perfect as my account would lead one to believe. For reasons we need not go into here, the tones of the harmonic series are not all, in fact, exact multiples of the fundamental tone, and in any case they are not, for the most part, consonant with one another. The only perfectly consonant interval is the octave, the others, with their harmonics, ranging from a high degree of consonance to extreme dissonance. Moreover, the theorists all appear to agree that the relative consonance or dissonance, as experienced by the listener, depends not only on the mathematical factor I have here set forth but also on the training of the ear, which may be habituated to hear as pleasant, if not harmonious, intervals that in mathematical terms are exceedingly dissonant. The perfect consonance of the octave, while not unpleasant, gives the same impression of lifelessness as the sound devoid of overtones produced by a tuning fork. It lacks the irregularity within regularity that we associate with a living as opposed to a dead order.

The fact that a violin string tuned to A = 440 also gives the octave, the twelfth, the fifteenth, etc. is not an accident but the manifestation of a logical order based on the same correspondence between wavelength and frequency that characterizes electromagnetic radiation.* Since all electromagnetic radiation travels at a fixed velocity in a vacuum, the shorter the distance between waves (i.e., the wavelength) the greater the frequency with which they pass a given point in a given time (or strike the eye or a radio-antenna). Since sonic waves (synonymous with vibrations) travel at a fixed velocity in any uniform medium, the shorter the waves the higher the frequency. A violin's A-string, vibrating in its total free length, does so at a frequency of 440 per second. Stop the string at its midpoint, however, by pressing it down against the fingerboard, and, just as the length of string that vibrates will be halved, so the wavelength will be halved and the frequency doubled, thereby sounding the octave. Allow only a third of its length to vibrate and the frequency will be multiplied by three, giving the twelfth. Allow only a quarter to

* See p. 60 above.

vibrate and the frequency will be multiplied by four, giving the fifteenth. And so on.

It happens that, when a violin string is set in vibration, it does not vibrate only in its entire length — itself assuming, at the extremes of its vibration, the shape of a wave with its crest at the midpoint and the troughs at either end. There is a subordinate vibration (a vibration within a vibration) of its two halves, the midpoint of the total length being a trough with respect to this vibration; there is a still more subordinate vibration of the three thirds; etc. That is why the notes of the harmonic series are sounded, along with the fundamental note, as overtones.

What applies to a violin string applies as well to the column of air that vibrates within a wind instrument, like the flute. (It also applies to bells, with the exception that in a big church bell the most prominent tone is not that of the fundamental but that of its octave, the first harmonic, the fundamental note sounding as an undertone to the first harmonic, called the clang tone, with which we identify the bell's nominal pitch.)

It will be seen that musical tone is not only a matter of mathematics but also of physics. The way the string or the enclosed column of air vibrates, and the way its vibrations are propagated through the atmosphere, is determined by such laws of physics as we dealt with in Part One. This was first appreciated by the Greek school of Pythagoras in the sixth century B.C., which discovered the relationship between the various lengths of a vibrating string and the various pitches thereby produced, noting that the simpler the mathematical relationship (the 1 to 2 relationship being simpler than, say, the 4 to 5) the greater the concordance between tones. The Pythagoreans were so carried away by the correspondence between music and the operations of natural law that they were disposed to identify music not only with the vibration of strings but also with the movement of planets in their orbits. (And indeed the identification does have a certain validity inasmuch as music represents basically the same natural order, based on rhythm, as that which causes the planets to move as they do in their orbits.) The result was the conception of a music of the spheres, which could not be apprehended by us men, with our gross sensibilities, but was, presumably, audible to such beings as had a greater measure of divinity.

In a play that is infused with music throughout, Shakespeare's *Merchant of Venice,* Lorenzo says to his bride, Jessica:

> How sweet the moonlight sleeps upon this bank!
> Here will we sit, and let the sounds of music
> Creep in our ears: soft stillness and the night

Become the touches of sweet harmony.
Sit, Jessica: look, how the floor of heaven
Is thick inlaid with patines of bright gold:
There's not the smallest orb which thou beholds't
But in his motion like an angel sings,
Still quiring to the young-eyed cherubins;
Such harmony is in immortal souls;
But, whilst this muddy vesture of decay
Doth grossly close it in, we cannot hear it.*

*

In Part One, Chapter IX, describing the "harmonic series" manifested by the vibrations of an atom's electron, I compared it with the like phenomenon manifested by the vibrating string of a violin. If the Pythagoreans had known what we do about atoms and their attendant electrons they would surely have postulated an unheard music of the atoms. The two phenomena represent one basic order in the universe, which justifies me in concluding this chapter with the two concluding paragraphs of the chapter in Part One.

The Pythagoreans believed that the planets in their rhythmic rounds produced an inaudible music, what they called "the music of the spheres." If there is not, in fact, an inaudible music of the planetary spheres, there is, in a real sense, an inaudible music of the atoms. The harmonic series is a mathematically definable phenomenon that is one of the fundamental elements in all music. Precisely the same element pervades the world of the very small, even though it does not, in this case, manifest itself as sound. It is the same phenomenon; and it is, as we shall see, one of the bases of order in the universe.

The universe is everywhere filled with rhythm and harmony. Because, in a large view, rhythm and harmony are one, being the constituents of music, the universe is everywhere filled with music.

* I have quoted this passage more fully than the occasion required because it exemplifies the concluding point of the last chapter. The rhythms of the poetry represent the music that is its subject as textbook prose would not.

X

The Shape of Music

> We all lead lives which are discontinuous, frag-
> mented. We are the prey of one emotion after
> another. Gradually, in the course of experi-
> ence, we begin to make a whole, a single per-
> sonality, out of the disparate elements of which
> we are constructed. The great composers are
> demonstrating that such reconciliation is pos-
> sible; and words are a very poor way in which
> to paraphrase their achievements. Ultimately,
> this may be why great music has such unri-
> valled power to exalt, to console, and to make
> sense out of the disorder of our day-to-day ex-
> perience.
>
> — *Anthony Storr* *

ANY MUSICAL COMPOSITION that is complete in itself has a beginning,
a middle, and an end — like any other coherent work of temporal
art, such as *The Odyssey, Hamlet,* or Coventry Patmore's "Magna est
Veritas." In music, however, the beginning and end are generally
marked by what is as definite as the period at the end of a sentence.
Typically, the composition begins and ends on the keynote of the
key in which it is composed. If it is composed in B major or B
minor it begins on B and ends on B, however widely it may roam in
between. This sequence of beginning, middle, and end may be
likened to an airplane that takes off from the firm ground, goes
through a variety of evolutions in the air, until at last it descends and
comes to rest on the ground from which it took off. It cannot come
to rest in the air but only when it has returned to its starting point.
Similarly, a composition starts from a keynote, goes through a variety of evolutions that may entail several changes of key, but can

* *Times Literary Supplement,* London, 20 November 1970, p. 1364. Compare this statement with my remarks (see p. 548 above) on the deliberate display of incoherence in
Joyce's *Ulysses.*

come to rest again only by returning to the note from which it started.* The effect on the auditor is one of tension followed by relief from tension. While the music is in space the auditor follows its course with a suspense that is at last resolved when it returns to where it began. When that happens, he is left with a gratifying sense of completion.

This sense of completion is one element in the appeal of all temporal art (as a sense of completeness is an element in the appeal of all spatial art). I have already given *The Odyssey* and *Hamlet* as examples. In the case of the first, the protagonist, after a series of adventures that keep us in suspense, returns at last to where he began, united once more with his wife and son as king in Ithaca. In the case of *Hamlet*, although the protagonist dies young he has, before his death, achieved a final state of peace with himself after an inner conflict that has kept us in suspense. The tension has been resolved. What aroused the philosophical anguish of the Tennyson who wrote "In Memoriam" was that his friend had been cut off in mid-career, leaving a life broken off like a piece of music arrested in the middle of a passage, unresolved.

Just as there are rhythms within rhythms, so in music there are paragraphs within chapters, sentences within paragraphs, and phrases within sentences — all characterized in varying degree by the sequence of tension and relief, by this sort of rise and fall. The generally unwritten marks of punctuation that delimit these entities within entities are the occasional notes or chords on which it is possible, both rhythmically and harmonically, to come to rest. Because a dissonant chord entails the tension of conflict, one cannot come to rest on it. But one can come to rest on a consonant chord, since its components are at peace. One can come to rest on the tonic chord (i.e., the chord of the keynote), somewhat less satisfactorily on that of the dominant (a fifth above the tonic), but not at all on that of the next note above or below the tonic, for then the auditor would be left up in the air.

All this and more can be illustrated by one of Johann Sebastian Bach's simple exercises in composition, the Two-Part Invention for keyboard in A minor. It is composed as a constant exchange between two voices, one performed by the left hand and the other by the right. The two pass themes back and forth between each other as if they were balls. Or the two may be likened to partners in a dance who dance alternately, the non-dancing partner stamping out the time with his feet until his turn to dance comes, when they reverse roles.

* What I am describing is subject to such exception as the occasional substitution of the dominant for the tonic or keynote. But this does not change the general rule.

The piece is in four-four time. Left hand starts it by sounding the keynote, A, which is the signal for right hand to go. Thereupon right hand plays the initial theme in sixteenth notes.

What is this theme?

It consists of eight successive notes, two groups of four which would correspond to the first two beats of the four-beat measure except that the whole thing begins a sixteenth of a measure late, with the initial E, and is completed equally late with the C that is already in the second half of the measure.

At mid-measure, then, or rather a sixteenth after, left hand repeats the theme an octave lower, after which, in the second measure, essentially the same performance by the two is repeated, with first right hand and then left playing the theme.

Note that the part played by the right hand can come to rest at two points only: at the return to the tonic A which falls on the first beat of the second measure, and at the second return which falls halfway between the third and fourth beats of the second measure. (The same observation applies to what the left hand plays, but displaced forward by half a measure.) This is to say that, if one had to interrupt right hand (or left hand), these would be the points at which one could do it with the least disastrous consequences. If one did it immediately after, say, the fourth sixteenth note in the first measure, the B, the effect would be chaotic, leaving the music up in the air, the passage unresolved. (This is what the death of Arthur Hallam meant to Tennyson.)

After the repetitions of the initial theme in the first two measures, right hand introduces (with the dominant E) another theme of eight successive notes (beginning one sixteenth of a measure after the first beat), which left hand then plays, but differing from right hand this time by beginning with the A. In the fourth measure they repeat the third, as in the second they repeated the first, but this time the repetition is one tone lower. And in the next two measures (five and six) they continue the repetition, dropping down one tone at half-measure intervals, but in a simplified version, concluding with the simultaneous C by both hands in the middle of the sixth measure. The effect has been of coasting down to a point of momentary pause.

From here to the middle of the eighth measure, the first two measures are repeated, but two tones higher, after which the second theme is brought in again by the left hand. Beginning with measure nine, however, there is a succession of modulations from the key of A minor, briefly evoking other keys, and a dissonance is sounded halfway between the second and third beats in measure nine (the combination of G and the adjacent A) and at the same point in measure ten (F♯ and G). (These dissonances are spice. Note how lacking in piquancy, by contrast, is the octave of A halfway between the third and fourth beats of the eighteenth measure.)

So the piece goes on, briefly modulating from E minor to D minor in the fourteenth measure, but returning gradually to the tonic by the eighteenth, when the measure with which the piece opened is repeated. In nineteen the two hands together begin a series of descending phrases in sixteenth notes, which the right hand carries on through twenty-one to its end in the middle of twenty-two. At this point the piece takes off again, as in the first measure, but now for its final evolution. Higher and higher it rises, until at the midpoint of twenty-four it begins its final descent, sinking more and more slowly (in the performance) to come to rest at last on the keynote from which it had taken its initial departure in measure one. We have experienced fulfillment.

*

I have now described, as best I can, a piece of pure music in terms of its formal structure, its "shape." However, we have such an inadequate vocabulary for the description of auditory experience, by comparison with the one we have for describing visual experience, that we are constantly having to borrow from the latter, unsuitable as it may be, to give an account of music. I am compelled to suggest that the music evokes the picture of an airplane taking off and landing, or of two dancers who pass a ball back and forth to the rhythmic stamping of feet. This, however, is to adulterate by implication what is pure music. Someone, I have noted, has said that a piece of music describes the quick running step of a fox, but without the fox. Bach's exercise in composition is an experience of the ear, not the eye. Consequently, when we have evoked airplane or dancers to describe it, we should proceed to forget them in order to restore, in appreciation, the purity of the music.

Yet all the arts are one, and music is ultimately inseparable from those that present themselves to the eye rather than the ear. This is what gives validity to the "unheard music" evoked in Keats's mind by the Grecian Urn. We shall see further on how the elements of music are in the Parthenon frieze, and in the Parthenon itself. We have already found them in poetry and in prose.

It is generally safer to evoke music for the description of what is visual than to evoke what is visual for the description of music. There may be some derogation from a piece of music in saying that it describes the quick running step of a fox, but there is no derogation from the gait of the fox in saying that it is like music. This is because music is the most abstract of the arts, and what is abstract may represent an ideal as what is concrete cannot, since what is concrete is always imperfect by the standard of the ideal. The abstract is compromised by association with the concrete, but the concrete is enhanced to the extent that it is associated with an abstract and ideal order.*

Nevertheless, all music is not as pure in its abstraction as Bach's exercises in counterpoint. Vivaldi's "Four Seasons," in certain passages, seems almost a painting in music, so vivid is its evocation of an autumn hunting scene or falling snow. With this in mind, I shall here describe, in the only terms that the vocabulary makes available, one more piece of music, altogether different from Bach's compositions, the "Kol Nidrei" of the more recent composer, Max Bruch.

*

* Because "ideal" in many usages comes close to being synonymous with "normative," which is a key term in this work, I here note that the two may differ in meaning if "normative" is limited to what is considered fully attainable in practice. The ideal does not have to be fully attainable in practice.

I am unable to describe a piece of music except by comparison with what is extraneous to it, like the quick running step of the fox. But when the fox has served the purpose for which it was evoked, that of describing the music, it must be forgotten. For the music represents the ideal as the fox does not.

In my description of the Two-Part Invention, which is abstract and formal music, I did not attempt to convey, what I hardly understand myself, the moving quality of its phrases and passages, the emotions they arouse when properly performed either on the keyboard or in the mind.* Bruch's "Kol Nidrei" is far from being either as formal or as absolute in its abstraction as the Two-Part Invention. Its minuscule greatness for me is in the expression of certain emotions associated with attitudes that may be termed philosophical — as is the case in some passages of "In Memoriam," where, however, the use of words allows the philosophical attitudes to be made explicit. In describing it, therefore, I am bound to be more explicit than the music. I am bound to identify the music with what it evokes in my own mind, which goes beyond what is actually in it. This is the fox that, when it has served its descriptive purpose, must be dismissed and forgotten.†

"Kol Nidrei" is an adagio in D minor for solo 'cello with orchestral accompaniment; but at a key point it is marked by a brief and terrible dialogue — like the dialogue between Job and the Almighty, in which our sympathy is entirely with Job. In my own mind I go so far as to think of it as having the same philosophical theme as The Book of Job, that theme being the unanswerable question why a just and omnipotent God treats his own creations with such cruel and capricious injustice.

The solo 'cello is announced by the orchestra in a hushed preliminary passage of eight measures that begins on the dominant (the second A above middle C) and, coming down in a series of steps, would end on the keynote except that, after holding it a moment, it slips down another half step. This leaves the auditor in suspense, as an introduction should.

After a moment of silence, the 'cello begins by a passage of four measures that presents itself as a gently plaintive question, beginning and ending on the tonic.‡

---

* I say when properly performed. Performers are tempted to play Bach's allegros at high speed, but they sacrifice expression in doing so. If, merely as an experiment, one plays a Bach allegro as if it were an adagio, one is likely to discover an emotional content that one had not known was there.

† A warm and moving performance is given by Pierre Fournier with the Orchestre Lamoureux of Paris under Jean Martinon on phonograph record 138669 of the Deutsche Grammophon Gesellschaft.

‡ In case the reader is not familiar with the tenor clef in some of the passages shown on the next page, he should note that middle C is on the second line from the top.

After this has been repeated an octave lower, the emotional intensity of the questioning voice is raised somewhat in a second passage that is also repeated (with a slight variation) an octave lower.

A third passage represents another slight rise in the intensity with which the question is asked.

Then the question is repeated with the diffidence of its original form.

It is at this point that the answer comes, performed in an implacable unison that is off-key, at least by implication. It takes the form of two thunderous measures in the tone of the Almighty's crushing reply when he "answered Job out of the whirlwind, and said, Who is this that darkeneth counsel by words without knowledge?"

The 'cello responds with a short phrase of pure pathos — whereupon the thunderous answer is repeated:

The 'cello replies with a long and plaintive passage, accelerando and crescendo, in which one has the impression of an underlying passion that is steadily rising. Apparently unable to accept the verdict which has been delivered with such finality, it repeats verbatim, so to speak, its opening question. Now, however, it has won an ally by the eloquence and justice of its appeal. The first violin of the orchestra echoes the end of the question, but with a special emphasis (expressed simply by lowering one of the notes a half tone). Thus encouraged, the 'cello becomes more confident in stating its position. All this culminates, quite suddenly, in what is the turning point of the drama. The key shifts from the minor to the major, and there is a confident increase in animation, the orchestra now having actively taken the part of the 'cello. For some eight measures, while the 'cello is silent (listening), the violins, together with the harp, perform a series of rising arpeggios and melodic runs in the new key of D major — at which point the 'cello comes in, no longer timid and plaintive but confident and serene. It appears to express at least a resigned acceptance of the paradox of fulfillment through suffering — but the tranquil final note of the piece, on A (the fifth of the tonic chord), is one of fulfillment only.

In this ending there is the same sense of serenity and completion that one feels in *Hamlet.* Injustice continues, but the protagonist has risen above it. He has come to the "little bay . . . under high cliffs." His question remains unanswered, as Tennyson's question remains unanswered, but he has achieved an inner peace by which he transcends it. "The nightingales are singing near the Convent of the Sacred Heart."

Because the limitations of language have appeared to leave me no choice, I have now described the "Kol Nidrei" in terms of a human drama that I have invented for the purpose and which the composer certainly did not have in mind. I have equated it very roughly with The Book of Job, of which it reminds me, but I daresay I could have equated it with *Hamlet* instead. There is the same pattern of questioning and conflict ending in peace and fulfillment at a higher level of being. However that may be, as the fox should be forgotten when he has served his descriptive purpose, so should my drama now be forgotten, the music alone remaining.

*

What I have described here are two short and simple pieces of music, one that in formal terms is no more than an exercise, the other an adagio for solo 'cello. It would have been beyond my capacity to describe any of the great monuments of our musical heritage — such as Mozart's Coronation Mass in C major or Rachmaninoff's Second Piano Concerto in C minor — for these lift us up to the ineffable level of religious inspiration.

XI

The Abstract Order

WE BEGAN OUR INQUIRY into the significance of the mind's artistic creation by considering examples that were concrete and particularistic in what they ostensibly represented: a Florentine housewife, a maidservant pouring milk, a scene near Haarlem. What we found was that in each case the particular subject seemed to represent something larger than itself, something that comprehended, perhaps, worldwide and millennial aspects of human experience; and we found that this enlargement tended to make manifest aspects of the order that one apprehends only in the comprehensive view.

From this extreme of the ostensibly concrete and particular we proceeded to the extreme of abstraction illustrated by Bach's Two-Part Invention. As mathematics is the expression of a logical order in itself, it was the expression of a rhythmic order manifested in time and by variations of pitch. It was marked by variety within a framework of uniformity, by irregularity within regularity.

We had already seen that these abstract and formal elements of a temporal order were not confined to music, for we had found them in poetry and prose as well, where they were associated with explicit statement. If, now, we enlarge our view, we shall also find them in what has spatial rather than temporal extension — for the temporal and spatial, being but aspects of a single order, may be translated into each other.

To illustrate this last point, I here present (see next page) the printed score of a fragmentary passage from the harpsichord cadenza in the first movement of Bach's Fifth Brandenburg Concerto. This score translates the oral into the visual, and the reader will see at a glance that the translation has essentially the same beauty as the original, that the music is beautiful to look at. One sees the rhythm, one sees the high and low, one sees the irregularity within regularity. One sees in what is spatial what one hears in what is temporal.

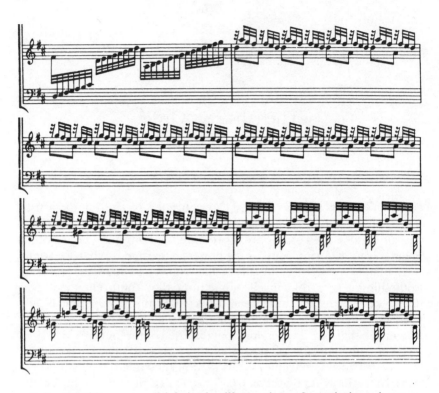

From Bach's score, which is the illustration of music in print, we turn to that illustration of music in stone, the Parthenon. On a platform rising in three equal and receding steps stands a rectangular arrangement of equally spaced columns, each divided equally in its circumference by vertical flutings. These columns support a plain architrave above which is a frieze composed of fluted triglyphs alternating with sculptured metopes. Above the frieze comes the cornice that, seen from either end of the rectangular structure, constitutes the base of the isosceles triangle formed by the roof.

The element of rhythm is patent here, as in the score of the harpsichord cadenza, as in the performance of the Two-Part Invention. There is the same repetitive regularity. But where is the irregularity within regularity? For the columns, like their flutings, all appear to repeat one another exactly at equal intervals.

The irregularity, in this case, is provided by a changing perspective. The flutings on each column appear to narrow as they recede around it on either side. If one looks at the front of the building (its west end) from a point directly opposite the center, its eight columns will appear to be more widely spaced at the center than at the ends.

If, then, one moves to the left, the change in perspective as one moves will appear to bring the columns at the right closer together, until they overlap, and the columns of the long north side will appear in a receding perspective that progressively diminishes their size and the spaces between them. Moreover, there is an inner row of columns at both ends, seen through the outer row, the two rows shifting in relation to each other as the observer moves. So it is that, as one walks around the building, it changes constantly in all its relationships. From the point of view of the observer it exists in time as well as space, for to see it as a whole he has to walk around it; and when he does so it moves like music.

The fluted triglyphs above the fluted columns are spaced like quarter notes against half notes, one above each column and one above each space between columns, providing variety in regularity.

The rhythm, the variety, the diminuendos of perspective, the irregularities within regularity — all these are even more conspicuously manifested in a great Gothic cathedral to anyone who walks about inside it or circumambulates its exterior. On the inside, the columns that bound the nave are like two rows of forest trees receding in the distance, their branches interlacing overhead. At Chartres, each column appears as a cluster of trunks in its lower part, above which it is made up of multiple stems, bound together at regular intervals, that separate higher up to make the branches. Between each cluster of trunks on the lower story is a pointed arch repeated by other arches in the upper story and by the vaults over all. Above each arch, in the next story up, the triforium, is an arcade of four arches supported by pillars (four quarter notes to each whole note), and above each quarter-note arch, in the next story up, the clerestory, is a compound window divided by two pointed arches (separated by a mullion) and framed by one pointed arch that rises over and embraces them. All this is changed into different proportions and relationships in the rounded apse, which one sees at the far end like a clearing in a forest as one looks east.

*

The distinction between spatial and temporal art is not as distinct as I have made it seem. One can look at the score of the Bach cadenza as one looks at the west end of the Parthenon, taking it all in at a glance, or one can read it, measure after measure, as one does a book. The Parthenon frieze is like a musical score, to be read as such from one end to the other.

It is a continuous strip of bas-relief, about a meter high, that runs continuously around the four sides of the structure inside the outer

colonnade, at the level of the ceiling.* What it probably depicts is
the quadrennial Panathenaic procession in which Athens celebrated
the birthday of the patron goddess by presenting a new robe to
clothe her image in the Parthenon. As represented on the frieze,
the procession begins at the center of the west end (the front end to
those who come onto the Acropolis through the gate of the Propy-
laia, as the procession itself would have come onto it). It moves in
two branches, around the north and south sides of the building respectively, to meet in the center of the east end, where the presentation of the robe takes place.

On either side of the point where the presentation takes place, facing toward the corners and the approaching procession, the Olympian gods and goddesses are seated to receive it. The procession is
headed by a line of girls, all but the foremost bearing libation bowls
or jugs. After them come the animals being led to the sacrifice,
cattle and sheep, followed by a line of elders, who are followed by
horse-drawn chariots with charioteers. The end of the procession is
composed of youths on horseback, some wearing tunics, some
naked.

One does not have the impression of a formal parade but of a
procession as it is being formed, with marshals getting the members
into line, with some of the horsemen or charioteers mounted and
others still dismounted. There are flute players and lyre players
making music for all to move by, but the movement is not that of a
march. Some of the horses and some of the cattle for the sacrifice
are hard to control. There is disorder within a basic order, infor-
mality within formality.

Music itself is not more musical than this sculptural frieze. The
procession of girls makes one theme, with variety and repetition, the
procession of horsemen another. Certain motifs are repeated with
variations, like that of a youth, mounted or dismounted, whose head
is turned back and his left hand raised in what may be a signal to
those who follow. The very movement of the horses straining
against their bridles, stepping and prancing and rearing up, is
music, their bent forelegs repeating one another and the bent legs
of their riders, with variations. The attitudes of the riders, relaxed
and balanced, give the impression of their gentle movement up and
down, like the waves of the sea, as the horses advance under them.
Here, then, is sculpture, one of the graphic arts, that extends in time
and moves like music.

*

* I describe it as it was before the ruin and dismantlement of the Parthenon.

Music entails movement and movement takes place in time. Since all movement is relative, it makes no fundamental difference whether the primary movement is in the work of art (as in the case of the Two-Part Invention) or in the observer (as in the case of the Parthenon or the Parthenon frieze). But movement in time can be implicit rather than actual, as in the case of a painting that the observer comprehends in one glance. I know of no painting by Raphael that does not exemplify this. Let me, however, particularize.

A repeated subject of Greek and Roman art was that of the so-called Three Graces: two female nudes facing the observer, connected by a third between them with her back to him, the three with their arms raised, in some cases to rest on one another's shoulders. Although they are certainly not in violent movement, but in sinuous and relaxed poses, one thinks of them as dancers, accompanied by the unheard music which Keats admired. This subject or motif or theme of the Three Graces was taken up by the painters of the Renaissance. A rather freely rendered example is that of the three girls in Botticelli's "Primavera" who are holding hands and dancing in a ring. A more classical example is that of Raphael's "Three Graces" at Chantilly. The two outermost, facing the observer, rest their weight, respectively, on the outermost leg, which causes the hip to swing out to the same side, and tilt their heads outward to look at the apple which each carries in a partly outstretched hand. The middle Grace, her back to the observer, conforms in her pose to the one on the observer's right rather than the one on the left; for she rests her weight on her right leg, her hip being swung to that side, and carries the apple in her right hand, toward which she tilts her head. If one were to indulge in the artifice of "reading" this painting from left to right, its rhythm would approximate that of a dotted half note followed by two eighth notes. For so the three heads are spaced, and below them the three apples, and below the apples the three hips. There is a sort of counterpoint between the Grace at the left and the two at the right, or a movement back and forth, and another such opposition between the one in the middle and the two facing the other way, so that all three move at the same time together and apart. Unlike the Botticelli figures, the three appear to be at rest for the moment, as in a *tableau vivant* — but the movement is implicit in their rest, and the music implicit in the movement. All this one sees at a glance, as one may see one measure of a musical score at a glance.

*

We have now surveyed artistic creation, in its various media, from the concrete and particular to the formal and abstract. The main conclusions we have drawn are (1) that works of art enlarge our vision by an implied generalization from the particular, thereby making apparent the order that is wanting in the very small, and (2) that in their formal elements they epitomize the order discovered by enlargement.

One aspect of the enlargement achieved by a work of art is temporal. It rescues an otherwise fleeting reality from time. It presents the observer with "the instant made eternity" — as in the painting of a bird that is always on the wing but never passes. This is what impressed Keats about the procession on the Grecian Urn. It is what impresses the observer of the cavalcade, forever forming and never to be formed, on the Parthenon frieze. This fixing in perpetuity of what is in itself fleeting was Shakespeare's justification for his sonnets.

The importance of this stability in time was impressed on us when we imagined Ruysdael's "View of Haarlem" as a moving picture, the clouds and people set in motion. Michelangelo's "Pietà" also enshrines in time a climactic moment that would be lost if the mother should begin to caress the son.

This stability in time is no less necessary to any piece of poetry or music, for what it shows us is an attitude that is forever there. "For ever wilt thou love, and she be fair!" So long as the poem survives we can be sure that "the nightingales are singing near the Convent of the Sacret Heart." "Here, in this little Bay," the poet has found his permanent rest. King Lear's transcendence of his initial *hubris,* culminating in a love for his dead daughter like the mother's love of her crucified son, has by Shakespeare's art been made eternal. The peaceful acceptance in which the "Kol Nidrei" ends is final.

We have also had occasion to see, as throughout this work, how arbitrary are the categories into which we are constrained — by the nature of language and by the corresponding heuristic requirements — to arrange experience. The Parthenon frieze, which is sculpture, is as much like music as it is like the "Pietà," which corresponds to *Hamlet* as a representation of tragedy. The Gothic cathedral has much in common with the organ music of Buxtehude (both of them extending to infinity, as we saw on page 469).

Even in the larger categorial distinctions, such as we make between art and science, we have already had occasion (on pages 88–89) to note a certain artificiality. This particular distinction, in terms of its limitations, is the theme of the next chapter.

XII

Art and Science

> I do not share the common fallacy of an an-
> tagonism between science, literature and art
> . . . Creative imagination is the vital factor
> in all of them. . . .
>
> — *George Ellery Hale*

ALTHOUGH WE ASSUME a categorical distinction between art and
science, I here raise the question of what basis there may be for making it as sharp as we do.

To answer the question we must know what we mean by "science."
What is the practice of science? What do scientists do?

The majority of practicing scientists are research scientists. This is
to say that they make observations or conduct experiments designed
to elicit precise factual information. (At this point I open the first
scientific journal that comes to hand and find, on the page at which I
open it, a table giving the weights and other measurements of 122
eggs of the least tern examined at seven specified sites in California
in 1969, 1970, and 1971.) Such information does not, in and by itself, contribute to the reduction of chaos. It may provide material
on which to base understanding, but it provides no understanding in
itself.

Besides research scientists there are theoretical scientists. An example of the latter is Einstein, who never in his life, as far as I can
determine, made observations or conducted physical experiments.
All the work he did, which entailed largely the testing of hypotheses
by the logic of mathematics, could be done with pencil and paper
alone. And the mathematics was itself secondary to the creative
imagination by which he produced the hypotheses to be tested. Just
as we imagine the poet taking solitary walks during which his ideas
come to him, so we can imagine Newton or Einstein, Darwin or
Mendel, Copernicus or Galileo. "The real key to the theory of rela-

tivity," writes one of Einstein's biographers, "came to him unexpectedly, after years of bafflement, as he awoke one morning and sat up in bed. Suddenly the pieces of a majestic jigsaw puzzle fell into place . . ." * All creative minds, whether of poets or scientists, know what it is to have a vision on the road to Damascus.

We have the example of Darwin to show that a theoretical scientist and a research scientist can inhabit the same body. He was by disposition both a formulator of hypotheses and a collector of facts. "From my early youth," he wrote, "I have had the strongest desire to understand or explain whatever I observed, — that is, to group all facts under some general laws. . . . I have steadily endeavoured to keep my mind free, so as to give up any hypothesis, however much beloved (and I cannot resist forming one on every subject), as soon as facts are shown to be opposed to it." Referring to his discovery of the way coral reefs are formed, he wrote: ". . . the whole theory was thought out on the west coast of S. America before I had seen a true coral reef. I had therefore only to verify and extend my views by a careful examination of living reefs." As to his theory of the origin of species by natural selection: "In October 1838 . . . I happened to read for amusement Malthus on *Population,* and being well prepared to appreciate the struggle for existence which everywhere goes on from long-continued observation of the habits of animals and plants, it at once struck me that under these circumstances favourable variations would tend to be preserved, and unfavourable ones to be destroyed. The result of this would be the formation of new species. Here, then, I had at last got a theory by which to work. . . ." At the time, however, he omitted to ask himself why species, once formed, diverged progressively, let alone to think of the answer that they diverged because they became adapted to different environmental circumstances. "It is astonishing to me," he wrote, "except on the principle of Columbus and his egg, how I could have overlooked [this problem] and its solution. . . . I can remember the very spot in the road, whilst in my carriage, when to my joy the solution occurred to me. . . ." †

Darwin, himself, undertook the observations of natural phenomena required to verify his hypotheses, while in Einstein's case such verification was done by others, to the extent that it could be done at all, in connection with the theory of gravitation — e.g., by Eddington when, taking advantage of an eclipse of the sun in 1919, he measured the deflection of starlight predicted by that theory.

* Banesh Hoffmann, *Albert Einstein,* New York, 1972, p. 69.
† *The Autobiography of Charles Darwin,* London, 1958, pp. 141, 98, and 120–121 respectively.

Physics, however, differs from biology in that the material for verification extends to largely inaccessible worlds outside our mundane experience — either the world of intergalactic distances or that of the infinitesimal. Consequently, the possibilities of verification by observation and experiment are more limited. In fact, the General Theory of Relativity and the Uncertainty Principle alike are hardly susceptible of such verification. This justified Einstein's colleague, Max Born, in writing of the General Theory that "its connections with experience were slender. It appealed to me like a great work of art, to be enjoyed and admired from a distance." *

Surely the great creative minds in the history of natural science — Copernicus, Kepler, Galileo, Newton, Maxwell, Darwin, Mendel, Einstein, Heisenberg — are as much akin to artists like Phidias, Dante, Michelangelo, and Bach as to those who accumulate data on the dimensions of terns' eggs. Must we not consider it a defect of our excessively categorical language that it lumps them with the latter as "scientists" in opposition to the former as "artists"?

The difference between theory and research in science is the difference between synthesis and analysis: the one puts together and the other takes apart. A research scientist disassembles a watch to measure and catalogue its parts; whereas a theoretical scientist, seeing a chaotic variety of scattered parts, puts them together in his imagination to make a single whole, which represents such an order as provides, like any work of art, the aesthetic satisfaction to which theoretical scientists themselves have repeatedly testified.†

An artist, too, puts together the elements of what then presents itself as an harmonious whole.

The minds of all the great scientists have been governed by the artist's synthesizing vision. So it is that the following statement by Einstein, in its conception of an order that, lying behind phenomena, can be directly apprehended by the mind, evokes Plato rather than Francis Bacon, the father of empiricism. "It is my conviction that pure mathematical construction enables us to discover the concepts and the laws connecting them, which give us the key to the understanding of the phenomena of nature. Experience can, of course, guide us in our choice of serviceable mathematical concepts; it cannot possibly be the source from which they are derived. In a certain sense, therefore, I hold it to be true that pure thought is competent to comprehend the real as the ancients dreamed." ‡

---

* Quoted by R. W. Clark in *The Life of Albert Einstein*, London, 1973, p. 198.
† See the quotation from P. A. M. Dirac on p. 89 above.
‡ Lecture at Oxford in June 1933, quoted by Philipp Frank in *Einstein: His Life and Times*, New York, 1965, p. 282.

Research and theory are both necessary. Few of us would willingly return to the period from St. Augustine to Calvin when theory was the product of deduction, not from observed reality but from the dicta of ancient writings considered sacred. However, the positivism of our times, together with the specialized training of research scientists for research alone — a training that, in itself, is understandably opposed to the exercise of imagination — has gone to another extreme, engendering the belief that the only business of science is to describe and classify phenomena. This has led to a general favoring of what we call the Aristotelian approach, as opposed to the Platonic represented by the above quotation from Einstein. Theoretical physicists have been almost the only ones to uphold, in our day, the thesis that the business of science is to discover a pre-existing order in being, an order characterized by its essential simplicity, its harmony, its aesthetic appeal. They have been concerned with natural law, which must be tested by observation and experiment to the extent possible, but also by its logical consistency in terms of whole systems — the logic entailed being, for the most part, a mathematical logic. (It is surely no accident that almost all theoretical physicists are amateurs of music.)

Here, for example, is a statement by Heisenberg about scientific method:

In the scientific work of this century we still follow essentially the method that had been discovered and developed by Copernicus, Galileo and their successors in the 16th and 17th centuries. This method is sometimes misunderstood and called empirical science and contrasted with the speculative science of former centuries.

In fact Galileo turned away from the traditional science of his time which was based on Aristotle and took up the philosophical ideas of Plato. When he argued for experience he meant experience illuminated by mathematics. Galileo, as well as Copernicus, had understood that by moving away from immediate experience, or by idealizing experience, we may discover mathematical structures in the phenomena and thereby gain a new simplicity as a basis for a new understanding. Aristotle, for example, had stated correctly that light bodies fall more slowly than heavy bodies. Galileo claimed that all bodies fall with the same speed in empty space and that their fall can be described by simple mathematical laws. Fall in empty space could not be observed accurately in his time but Galileo's claim suggested new experiments.*

* *Physics Bulletin*, June 1974.

What empirical experience showed was that light bodies fall more slowly than heavy bodies, and there was no experience to show that it was otherwise in a vacuum. Therefore Galileo, formulating his theory on the basis of an ideal order in his mind, was, if anything, going counter to such experience as was available. It was not until much later that it became possible to subject the theory, not only to the testing of a certain logic, but also, by an experiment that required relatively advanced technology, to the test of actual observation.

Max Planck, the original begettor of quantum mechanics, wrote:

> On the one hand, every hypothesis — as a factor in the picture of the external universe presented by the physicist — is a product of the freely speculating human mind; and, on the other hand, there are no physical formulae whatsoever which are the immediate results of research measurements. The opposite is the case. Every measurement first acquires its meaning for physical science through the significance which a theory gives it. Anybody who is familiar with a precision laboratory will agree that even the finest and most direct measurements — such as those of weight and current — have to be corrected again and again before they can be employed for any practical purpose. It is obvious that these corrections cannot be suggested by the measurement process itself. They must first be discovered through the light which some theory or other throws upon the situation; that is to say, they must arise from an hypothesis.*

At the time Planck was defining the quantum in mathematical terms (not foreseeing its physical significance), the Michelson-Morley experiment to measure the speed of light through Newton's absolute space was being performed over and over again, with constantly refined techniques, because its failure to conform to the predictions of Newtonian mechanics implied some fault in the method of measurement. It was Einstein's Theory of Relativity, coming several years later, that finally showed the fault to be in the Newtonian theory rather than in the experiment. But the unexpected results produced by the experiment were not what led to the Theory of Relativity, for Einstein, if he had heard of it at all, did not have it in mind.

History records that the measurements of the deflection of light made by Eddington and his associates during the solar eclipse in 1919 confirmed Einstein's General Theory; but they were not really the basis on which it was accepted by the scientific world. Eddington

* *Where is Science Going?*, London, 1933, pp. 92–93.

himself later said that "we do not need to observe an eclipse of the sun to ascertain whether a man is talking coherently or incoherently." * The 1919 measurements would not have been considered significant if there had been no theory to support them (i.e., no theory to support them in supporting the theory); and, in fact, the margin of possible experimental error was so great that they were far from proving the theory.†

A scientific theory must conform to such observations as can be trusted, and should be put to trial by such observations as can be devised. Especially in the realm of physics, however, where so much observation must be mediated by an instrumentation that makes it exceedingly indirect, the consistency and completeness of the logic behind the theory is the first requirement. Even in biology, where observation and experiment pose less of a problem, logic comes first. Darwin's theory of natural selection and Mendel's theory of genetic inheritance had to be logically presentable to begin with.

Before returning to the question with which this chapter began, and in preparation for doing so, I offer one more quotation from Heisenberg.

> When we represent a group of connections by a closed and coherent set of concepts, axioms, definitions and laws which in turn is represented by a mathematical scheme we have in fact isolated and idealized this group of connections with the purpose of clarification. But even if complete clarity has been achieved in this way, it is not known how accurately the set of concepts describes reality.
>
> These idealizations may be called a part of the human language that has been formed from the interplay between the world and ourselves, a human response to the challenge of nature. In this respect they may be compared to the different styles of art, say of architecture or music. A style of art can also be defined by a set of formal rules which are applied to the material of this special art. These rules can perhaps not be represented in a strict sense by a set of mathematical concepts and equations, but their fundamental elements are very closely related to the essential elements of mathematics. . . . Here again, the question of how far the formal rules of the style represent that reality of life which is meant by the art cannot be decided

---

* Haldane Lecture of May 26, 1937, quoted by R. W. Clark in *Einstein*, London, 1973, p. 228.

† In 1962, at a meeting of the Royal Society of London, a group of scientists concluded that the difficulties of making such measurements as had been undertaken in 1919, when those difficulties were not fully understood, were so great that eclipse observers should no longer attempt it. See Martin Gardner, *Relativity for the Million* (an account of Relativity that should not be judged by its title), New York, 1962, p. 103.

from the formal rules. Art is always an idealization; the ideal is different from reality — at least from the reality of the shadows, as Plato would have put it — but idealization is necessary for understanding. . . .

Therefore, the two processes, that of science and that of art, are not very different. Both science and art form in the course of the centuries a human language by which we can speak about the more remote parts of reality, and the coherent sets of concepts as well as the different styles of art are different words or groups of words in this language.*

*

This chapter began with the question of what basis there was for making as sharp a distinction as we commonly do between the visions represented, respectively, by works of art and works of science.

In either case, the vision is of a comprehensive order, self-consistent or mutually harmonious in its elements, offering an aesthetically satisfying completeness within its own terms. In either case, it transcends the here-and-now to which mindless animals are confined. In either case, therefore, it has the effect of lifting us above the chaos of our daily preoccupations. In either case, the vision is logical in a fundamental sense.

How, then, does the artistic vision differ from the scientific?

The answer, I think, is that the scientific vision is expected to represent a literal truth while the artistic vision may be true only in a symbolic sense, as if truth should be made manifest through counterparts that are not true. The tale of the five blind men and the elephant is not a true story but a story that nevertheless tells a truth. Michelangelo's representation in paint of God infusing life into the body of the first man does not show an event that actually took place, but it does represent the concept of a divinity in man (which I take to be true in a sense that I shall later set forth), a concept associated with the myth that he was made in the image of a divine creator. *Hamlet,* although not literally true, shows us how the human spirit may be refined and elevated through suffering and frustration. Even the little Two-Part Invention by Bach represents, in abstract terms, the logical order on which all scientific theory is predicated.

Because literal truth is hardly relevant to the artistic vision (the question whether the "Mona Lisa" represents its subject literally, warts and all, is beside the point), the artistic vision is not susceptible to such testing by observation and experiment as we apply to the scientific vision when we can.

* *Physics and Philosophy,* London, 1959, pp. 96–98.

Our conclusion at this point must be that the distinction between the scientific and the artistic vision is not as great as we have come to assume. In the next chapter we shall find reason to doubt whether there is any categorical dividing line at all between them.

XIII

History as Art or Science

> It is, of course, impossible for an historian to give
> too much, or even enough, time to research, but
> it seems to me not impossible that he may some-
> times give proportionately too much of his time
> and mental energy to research itself, at the ex-
> pense of the thought and art that should be de-
> voted to making use of the results of research.
>
> — *G. M. Trevelyan*

IN THE LAST CHAPTER I drew a distinction between analysis and synthesis, between taking things apart and putting things together.
The analyst makes detailed observations, of which he accumulates
records; and this is so far from being an imaginative activity that it
properly requires, as a matter of disciplinary training, the exclusion
of imagination. By contrast, it is in the imagination of the synthesist
that all comes together to make one whole. So it was that Darwin,
contemplating the endless variety of the lives led by different plants
and animals, suddenly had a grand imaginative vision of how all
species alike originated. So it was that Newton, associating in his
imagination the confinement of the moon to an earthly orbit with
such phenomena as the fall of an apple to the ground, brought these
apparently disparate facts together in his theory of a mutual attraction that operates indifferently among all masses everywhere.

The experience is the same as that of what artists have called inspiration, whereby a grand conception suddenly enters the mind as
if it were a revelation communicated by a god. We may suppose
that, in fact, it is always the product of long gestation, largely in the
subconscious mind, and that the prime element in at last bringing it
to birth is the synthesizing imagination. However that may be, it is
an experience that associates all those who have the imaginative capacity for it, whether we denominate them artists or scientists, distinguishing them from all others, not excluding those scientists who
confine themselves to research.

The reader will have noted that much of what I wrote in the last chapter and in the opening of the present one has had the objective of freeing our minds from the trammels of a vocabulary that is too crude in its categories. What Copernicus and Darwin practiced used to be called natural philosophy rather than natural science, and if this terminology had survived it would have provided a basis for distinguishing what I have called the theoretical scientists from the researchers. An Einstein, then, would have been a philosopher, by distinction from a researcher in a laboratory, to whom the name scientist would have been confined.

The distinction I have been making is, in a word, between those whose contribution to human understanding takes the form of a vision and those whose contribution takes the form of data.*

*

The much debated question whether history is an art or a science arises out of the semantic difficulty I have been discussing. Thucydides was a man of vision whose nearest counterpart, to my mind, was Shakespeare. All the great historians since have been distinguished by a large vision, so that we are justified in classifying their works as literature, like our traditional epic and dramatic literature. Other historians, in the tradition of Herodotus, have been primarily anecdotalists (although I do not draw a sharp line between the two kinds here); and this also puts their works in the category of literature, associating it with the literature of those who tell tales for the entertainment or edification of the public.

History, however, is distinguished from fictional literature, as the vision of a Newton is distinguished from that of a Michelangelo, by its objective of representing literal truth. Goethe's *Faust* does not pretend to be an account of what actually happened, but Gibbon's *Decline and Fall* does. To find out what actually happened requires research, and it is at this point that we confront history as a science.

The parallel with the equivocation we have found in natural science is, I think, exact. The academic training of an historian today is in research, which entails concentration on analysis and a proper mistrust of the imagination. The researcher examines such evidence as there may be scientifically in order to accumulate data

* If this distinction implicitly honors the man of vision above the researcher, it does not thereby denigrate the latter; just as the competent craftsman suffers no denigration when we accord first honors to the occasional genius. Moreover, the distinction is basically between two kinds of pursuit rather than two kinds of men. Galileo, Newton, Darwin, and Mendel were "natural philosophers" who also practiced research. What cannot be doubted is that both pursuits are necessary — and necessary, specifically, to each other.

on what actually happened in history. These data provide a basis for the synthesizing imagination of the historian as a literary artist; and also a basis for testing particular items, at least, in the synthesis he produces.

Historical research, however, is not like the measurement of terns' eggs. For one thing, like research into the atom, it may have to make do with evidence that is distant by several removes from its object. The physicist, unable to see electrons, may have to depend on deducing their presence from the oscillation of a needle on a dial. He deduces the existence and character of a nuclear particle, perhaps, from the path left in a bubble chamber as that path is recorded on a film produced by a photographic apparatus. The historian, similarly, may know of an historical happening only because a trace left in the memory of an observer has descended to him in the form of hearsay.

There is another sense in which historical research differs from the measurement of terns' eggs and also from research into the atom. It deals with what, unlike egg or atom, no longer exists to be observed. Today's hydrogen atom is identical with yesterday's, so that the observation of yesterday may be repeated today. But every historical circumstance is unique. Such traces as it may have left behind in its passing constitute all the evidence of it that the researcher will ever have. The object of his research is gone, never to return.

Furthermore, most of this unrepeatable historical evidence is unreliable, as the testimony of any human reporter is unreliable by comparison with that of the physicist's pivoting needle. We know that ten persons who observe a fight in the street will give ten different accounts of it.* And much is bound to remain hidden even from the most expert observer on the spot. Although movie cameras had recorded the fight in the street from all angles, so that it could be reconstructed blow by blow, we still could not see directly into the minds of the combatants. Even their facial expressions might be deceptive; since either might, for example, be disguising a real fear and manifesting a confidence or a fury he did not feel in order to intimidate his opponent. Nor could the testimony later formulated by either, as to his state of mind at the time, be given much credence. Scientific exactness in historical research is, then, virtually confined to the authentication of documentary materials; but the authentication of a text, for example, provides no evidence

* The reader who doubts this should read Chapter VIII, on fallacies of testimony, in F. L. Wellman's classic, *The Art of Cross-Examination*, New York, 1941. See also Chapter I of my *Society of Man*, New York/London, 1965.

that what it says is true. Under such circumstances, the pure re-searcher himself can hardly avoid the exercise of a personal judge-ment based on his intuitive knowledge of human nature, of how people tend to behave in such circumstances as he is trying to recreate.

These obstacles in the way of the researcher who tries to recover the past matter less, however, insofar as they apply to details that, in-teresting as they may be in themselves, have no importance in terms of the long view. The reader will have gathered from Part Four, Chapter VII, that I do not share the view light-heartedly expressed by Pascal when he remarked that if Cleopatra's nose had been shorter the whole face of the earth would have been changed. It may be that history in the large has an inevitability that is the prod-uct of natural selection among the innumerable accidental circum-stances that might or might not have been as they were — just as the eagle on the heights represents an inevitable order that has emerged over thousands of millions of years from the chaos of quantum uncertainty.

At this point I quote two passages from a work that was written before the larger theory they illustrate had formed as such in my mind. Introducing a history of the Cold War, I wrote:

In the close-up view of human society the role of accident seems to predominate. An airplane carrying the future ruler of Algeria falls into the hands of the French, who are trying to sub-due the revolt of which he is a leader; or the Prime Minister of Great Britain has to undergo a prostatectomy at a moment criti-cal for the British Government; or the Secretary General of the United Nations is killed in an airplane crash. When we read about such accidents in the newspapers, hours after they have occurred, they seem decisive. As we are able to detach our-selves and broaden our perspective, however, they come to seem inconsequential. Finally, when we achieve the large historical view we see Algeria, for example, emerging with a logical inevi-tability from its colonial history, and the capture of Ben Bella by the French, if not forgotten, is seen to be an accident of no ul-timate significance for the secular movement that is its context.

In the larger view a pattern, an order of some sort, becomes apparent. Roman history from day to day must have seemed a succession of accidents to the men on the spot. We ourselves, however, can see how Rome was rising, over a period of cen-turies, to dominate the Mediterranean world and half Europe: we can see how, by this very process, it was becoming overex-tended and in various ways corrupt; and we can see how at last it crumbled away. There is something more here than a meaningless succession of events. There is a movement, a progression, a development. The events fall into patterns that are logical.

Later in the same work I wrote: "We must assume a range of choice in the actual play of events. But the range may be small at any one time (although cumulatively large over the generations), . . ." *

*

I suggest that the emergence of order out of chaos is recapitulated in human history, which in this respect represents the tendency of nature as a whole. More specifically, I suggest that the Uncertainty Principle applies on the scale of minutiae in history as on the scale of the quantum in physics (see Part One, Chapter X).

The historical researcher is preoccupied with such particular details as, being subject to the Uncertainty Principle, might have been otherwise than they were. The writer of history on a large scale may be concerned with a secular evolution over the centuries that, by contrast, appears to have a certain inevitability. By way of exemplification, let me apply this distinction to what could be an actual case-history.

Suppose that a researcher, marshaling the available evidence, seeks to reconstruct the way in which Napoleon Bonaparte, on a particular day at a particular hour, made his decision to have the Duke of Enghien arrested and shot. Did he consult his advisors, either separately or in council? — and, if so, what was the position taken by each? The evidence, consisting of later testimony by those who had been there, might be conflicting, in which case the researcher either has to accept frustration or exercise a personal discrimination based on his own subjective judgement. Even if stenographic transcripts had been kept, the wise researcher would be left to wonder what balance each advisor might have been striking between being honest and being politic in the advice he gave. Nor could he know whether the decision was made as it was because Bonaparte had, perhaps, slept badly the night before, and would otherwise not have been made as it was.

The execution of the Duke of Enghien has no historical importance in itself, deriving its significance entirely from its historical context. It contributed to the mounting hostility against Bonaparte outside France that would eventually cause his overthrow. See, now, how the Uncertainty Principle applies.

The thought passing through Bonaparte's mind, which was the

* *The Cold War as History*, London/New York, 1967, p. xi and pp. 75–76 respectively.

immediate cause of the order he gave, might have been otherwise than it was. The particular decision that came of it, which increased the growing hostility against him, might not have been taken. In a larger view, however, we see that the hostility would have developed as it did anyway, and we may well believe that, whether sooner or later, it would have reached the point at which it had elicited the strength to overcome him. In a still larger view we see the action and reaction, over a period of years, of a society experiencing too sudden an upheaval, an upheaval that circumstances of still longer range had made virtually inevitable. The French Revolution, the rise of Bonaparte to re-establish order in France by means of a dictatorship, the overextension of his power that led to his fall, and the attempted restoration of the *ancien régime* — all this seems, in terms of its dynamics, to be a well-nigh inevitable train of events arising out of antecedent circumstances. (If it had not been Bonaparte it would have been someone else who exercised the dictatorial receivership after France had fallen into chaos.) So we may conclude that the secular movement of French history over a period of a generation had a certainty that any particular incident in its course lacked. This resembles the situation in which the life-span of a particular atom of thorium-234 is uncertain, but the life-span (more precisely, the half-life) of a lump of thorium-234, containing untold millions of such atoms, is not.

If we examine what happened in history detail by detail, regarding each separately, we find it utterly uncertain in the sense that it might not have happened as it did. If, however, we gradually back away to take an ever wider view, the details gradually dwindle into insignificance and the uncertainty disappears. So an order in the large arises out of chaos in the very small. I have already cited the metaphor of the curve described by a series of plotted points on graph paper, which cannot be seen if the points are examined one by one, close up, but which becomes apparent when we stand back from it. In the comprehensive view we achieve by standing back it makes no difference that any particular point might have been elsewhere than it is.

*

I return now to the distinction between historical research, which is analytical, and the writing of history in the large, which is based on syntheses achieved by the creative imagination. Just as the Theory of Relativity did not arise gradually in Einstein's mind out of innumerable minute observations put together, like the stones of a cathedral, until it was complete, so the particular vision of an historian is not produced by putting together, one upon another, the innumerable details revealed by research. For such details, in the absence of a large context, represent a chaos that is not resolved into order by their multiplication alone. As in the cases of Darwin, Einstein, and every other creative thinker, the vision, however long prepared in the unconscious mind, suddenly emerges into consciousness like Athena from the head of Zeus; and it is only after this has happened that the historian, on the basis of the design it provides, assembles and marshals the details by which he represents it. "It was at Rome, on the 15th of October 1764," wrote Edward Gibbon, "as I sat musing amidst the ruins of the Capitol, while the barefooted friars were singing vespers in the temple of Jupiter, that the idea of writing the decline and fall of the city first started to my mind." *

Indeed, the vision has to come first, in history as in natural science, since otherwise there would be no basis for the necessary selection among an infinitude of separate facts, or for their ordering.

Suppose that, as a rigorously impartial historian, one attempted to list all the occurrences in the city of Geneva on April 15, 1798, gathering one's material from personal diaries, letters, account books, parish records, etc. One would set down indiscriminately whatever items came to light, such as: that a housewife on the Rue des Granges, cooking the midday meal, accidentally upset a saucepan of boiling water, thereby scalding her right hand; that a shoemaker on the Place de la Taconnerie completed a pair of boots for the bishop; that a notary on the Rue des Chaudronniers received a visit from his cousin who lived in Coppet — and so *ad infinitum*. The impartial historian, eschewing value judgements, would also set down, on a basis of equality with all the other items, the arrival of a column of troops representing the French Revolution, their entrance into the city through the Porte Neuve, and the consequent annexation of Geneva to the French Republic.

Is it not evident that the historian, no less than any artist, has to compose his picture in advance as a basis for selecting and arranging the items that are to enter into it? The only basis on which he can do so is a prior vision that provides the design.

*

There can be no one vision of what happened in history that is the right one, so that all others must be wrong. For the historian can do no more than reproduce certain aspects of what happened, and although the aspects chosen by one are not those chosen by another, their different choices may be equally valid.

Two painters undertaking to paint the same landscape will paint it

* *Autobiography*, London, 1911, p. 124.

from different points of view if they set up their easels at different sites; but both points of view are equally true. Again, although they set up their easels at the same site, the objective of one may be to include all the details as he knows them to be from previous close-up examination, so that he paints, as a matter of fidelity to truth, the individual leaves of trees, even though they are too distant to be seen individually. The other may think of himself as painting the light reflected from the scene, rather than its material reality in itself, so that what he shows is the general radiance, as it comes to his eye, omitting the details that are lost in that radiance. Although their finished paintings represent two different visions of one reality, they may be equally true to it.

Leopold von Ranke said that his objective was to write history "as it actually happened," and surely this should be the overriding objective of all historians; but each must still decide what aspect of history he will attempt to present "as it actually happened," and from what point of view. One historian of the fifteenth century in Europe may focus on the multitudinous individual human beings — their aspirations, their frustrations, their joys and their sorrows, their triumphs and defeats — while another focuses on a few figures regarded as heroic. Still another may give prime importance, over heroes and ordinary people alike, to the changing technology of warfare (e.g., the advent of the pike, the long-bow, and artillery) that did so much to bring the mediaeval way of life to an end; while still another concentrates on the growth of commerce as communications improved and became more secure, as towns developed, and as a money economy became dominant. For one historian history is made by human beings, for another it is made by institutions, for a third it is made by abstract social forces. Nations or individuals may be the chief actors, depending on the historian's point of view. (J. C. L. Sismondi, acknowledging a complimentary copy that Michelet sent him of his *Histoire de France,* wrote: "I cannot accept a personality in the peoples that makes the personality of individuals disappear." *)

I have said that different points of view or different ways of treating the same subject may be equally valid. This does not mean that they necessarily are so; and indeed it is clear that, aside from the question of validity, some points of view are superior to others in the detachment, the breadth, or the worldly understanding they represent. Thus a history of England for children, listing the kings according to whether they were good or bad, represents a more naïve point of view than the *History of England* that G. M. Trevelyan wrote for adults. Herbert Butterfield has observed that

* Cited in G. P. Gooch, *History and Historians in the Nineteenth Century,* London, 1952, p. 173.

a partial, selective story of the seventeenth-century constitutional struggles in England might prompt the reader to strong parliamentary predilections in the case of one author and to royalist conclusions perhaps in the case of another. But if one could see the whole story in its fulness and complexity one would cease to hanker after this kind of judgment or decision. Everything else would be submerged in one's sense of what Froude calls "the tragedy of humanity itself". No attempts to summarise an age by means of formulas and general theses can be anything but harmful unless we keep in mind that jungle of life for which they provide the merest abstraction and diagram. No selective account, such as we find in ecclesiastical history, or when we study the development of the idea of sovereignty — no schematisation, no patterns of process or evolution — can avoid giving rise to misconceptions, unless we perpetually refer these things back to the general narrative and sink them into that broader stream of human life which the literary historians were so concerned to reproduce.*

The reader will see for himself that these questions of point of view bear on the imaginative vision of each particular historian and have nothing to do with a science that excludes imagination and value judgements.

*

One reason why we cannot properly separate history as science from literature as art is that no line can be drawn between the writing of history and the writing of fiction. We regard *The Iliad* as fiction, yet the basic story it recounts is confirmed by archaeological evidence. Thus the ruins of Agamemnon's Mycenae still stand, and excavations have shown that there was a Troy which, as Homer said, was destroyed by fire. On the other hand, Plutarch is classified as an historian, for biography is a form of history, yet we must doubt whether the Lycurgus whose biography he wrote ever lived at all.

The historian who writes about individuals has only a limited number of clues to what they were really like, outwardly or inwardly. On the basis of those clues he creates a character in the same way that a novelist does. He fills in what is missing by surmise based on an imagination disciplined by his understanding of the way human beings tend to behave in such circumstances as he has undertaken to describe. The result is that the same historical figure is given a different character by every historian. Richard III of England is represented by one as a villain, by another as a conscientious ruler. Peter Geyl, in a book entitled *Napoleon: For and Against*, has cited the

* *History and Human Relations*, London, 1951, pp. 237–238.

widely diverse characters respectively attributed to Napoleon by some thirty historians.* Nor can any of those characters be more than fictional approximations. We may be sure that the real Napoleon, whom we shall never know, was different in many ways from all of them.

All public figures become legends in their lifetime, at least in some degree, and the legend survives rather than the man.

If we can never know the character of the real Napoleon it is not simply because the time has passed when that was still possible. Even if we had lived in his time and known him personally, there would have been much in his character about which we could only have speculated. He would have been to us like the iceberg that is four-fifths hidden. Even his two successive wives, if consulted, would surely have given different reports of his character. If those of us who have been happily and inseparably married for decades may often be at a loss to know what is going on in the minds of our respective wives or husbands, how can we know what really went on in the mind of Julius Caesar as he stood on the banks of the Rubicon, or of Cleopatra when she decided to participate in the Battle of Actium? To give an account of either Caesar or Cleopatra we have to exercise the imagination and intuitive understanding of the novelist. There is a sense, then, in which all history that deals with human characters is historical fiction.

Surely this is equally true of those pages of historical writing that do not deal with human characters. To make sense they must entail a logic of cause and effect that is also the product of their authors' imaginations, however disciplined by knowledge of the world and a determination to come as close as possible to the vanished reality.

*

The point I have been making in these chapters is that the arts liberate us from imprisonment in the here-and-now. They enlarge us. We have seen how even such a particularistic work as the "Mona Lisa," the portrait of one unmemorable person, may do this. We have seen how the Parthenon, Michelangelo's "Pietà," Bruch's "Kol Nidrei," and Vermeer's "Maidservant" do it. The great works of history, whether small or large in their coverage, also do it. Johan Huizinga's *The Waning of the Middle Ages* is full of genre scenes or accounts of daily life and thought in the fifteenth century that together constitute a sort of bridge between us and people who lived so long before our time. Reading it as we might look at the painting of a seventeenth-century Dutch genre scene, we feel our lives extended

* London, 1949.

beyond their span, we become part of something larger than ourselves.

Quite a different kind of historian, Thucydides, represented the
Peloponnesian War as Shakespeare represented the tragedy of King
Lear or of Othello, thereby enlarging, for example, those readers
who, living through the strikingly similar tragedy of the First World
War, were able to rise above it in their minds so as to see it in the
same elevating and ultimately consoling terms — terms that are consoling because they seem to represent an order in being.

Oswald Spengler, in his *Decline of the West,* surveyed all history,
worldwide and from the beginning, in such a distant perspective that
human beings disappeared from it altogether, but showed it as a succession of tragedies whereby the West of the twentieth century was
associated with the Greece of which Thucydides had written. We
who are buffeted by the chaotic circumstances of our daily lives,
reading Spengler as we read Thucydides or Shakespeare, feel ourselves lifted above these circumstances to the view of a large order
that gives meaning to our lives because, as these works show us, we
are part of it.

The question whether history is a science or an art can arise only
in the English language, which imposes an opposition between the
two that hardly exists, if at all, in other languages (The German
Wissenschaft and the French *science* are closer to what we call "scholarship" than to the narrower meaning of "science" in English.) This
is significant because it shows how the artifice of language may impose categorical distinctions on a reality that knows them not. Since,
then, the question is unnecessary, rather than answering it we
should dismiss it. The writing of history is the literary representation of the past, what happened in it and what it was like, to the
extent that the historian can recreate it. The closest approximation
to the truth is what the writer of history should try to achieve, under whatever label.

Having begun this chapter with a quotation from G. M. Trevelyan, I shall close it with another. "Truth is the criterion of historical study; but its impelling motive is poetic. Its poetry consists in its
being true. Work that out and you will get a synthesis of the
scientific and literary views of history." *

* Both quotations are from *Clio, a Muse,* London, 1930, pp. 194 and 103 respectively.

XIV

Social Construction

ONE OF THE THEMES of this work has been that our categories are more-or-less superficial impositions on a reality that is, at bottom, uncategorical. So, as we saw in the last two chapters, no sharp dividing line can be drawn between fiction and history, and Einstein's Relativity is a work of art no less than Shakespeare's *Hamlet*. Similarly, no sharp line can be drawn between creation in the domain of social construction and fictional creation. This last point may be proved by three examples that together close the supposed gap between what is and what is not fiction.

In Plato's *Republic,* Socrates sets forth the constitution of what, taking account of human limitations, he regards as an ideal society or state. It is composed of three distinct classes: the guardians, a ruling class that sees to its security and the maintenance of order; the soldiers, who defend it against external enemies; and the common people, who provide the economic goods and services. Provision is made for the education appropriate to each of these classes, and the way of life for each is prescribed. The equality of men and women is institutionalized, the women receiving the same education as the men. Regulations are established for marriage and the care of progeny. The myths in which the members of the society shall be taught to believe are prescribed.

All this, however, is presented as no more than a piece of fiction. Socrates, although based on an historical model, is a fictional character, like the characters in Shakespeare's historical plays. There is no suggestion that the constitution of the ideal state he has imagined could be promulgated, that it could serve as the constitution of an actual state.

The author of my second example, Sir Thomas More, was a courtier and statesman at the court of King Henry VIII. Just as Shakespeare's Hamlet grew disgusted with the sordid reality of the Danish court, so More (an idealist like Hamlet) grew disgusted with the sordid reality of the English court. He took refuge from this reality by imagining another and a better land, a land for which he invented the name "Utopia" (Greek for "nowhere"), and in the book of that name he described the constitution of the Utopian society. As in the case of Plato's *Republic,* More's book was merely fictional, even though some of its characters were drawn from actual persons. Published in 1516, it became immensely popular, presumably because it offered its readers an escape in imagination from the sordid environment of the real society in which they lived.

More's imaginary state had several radical features. One was religious freedom. Another was public education provided by the state for both sexes alike. These features were almost unthinkable (in modern parlance they were utopian) in the England of Henry VIII. But in the England of four centuries later religious freedom and public education for both sexes had become established. We may plausibly believe that More's *Utopia* contributed to shaping the evolution of the English society in which these features were finally realized. It set forth a conceptual order that made its impress increasingly on men's minds, until they began, at last, to translate it into reality. The reader will see the correspondence here with the point made by Somerset Maugham, cited in Chapter II, that the Englishmen in Kipling's tales of India were less representative of the Englishmen in India at the time than of those who came after.

I take as my third example a document that belongs to essentially the same genre as Plato's *Republic* and More's *Utopia.* This one opens with the words:

> We, the People of the United States, in Order to form a more perfect Union, establish Justice, insure domestic Tranquility, provide for the common defence, promote the General Welfare, and secure the Blessings of Liberty to ourselves and our Posterity, do ordain and establish this Constitution for the United States of America.

It then goes on to provide, among other things, that no law shall be made "respecting an establishment of religion, or prohibiting the free exercise thereof" — and I mention this because it shows a connection with that other work of art, More's *Utopia.*

The authors of the Constitution of the United States were remarkably similar to More in background and attitude. Jefferson, for example, was like More a lawyer, a diplomat, and an idealist who was reacting against the arbitrary and sordid tyranny practiced in the name of a capricious king. One supposes that if More had been in the position of Jefferson and his associates, he would have proceeded much as they did. Given the opportunity that was theirs but not his, instead of drawing up the constitution of a society that must remain a dream, they drew up the constitution of a society to be realized forthwith.

Like *The Republic* and *Utopia*, the Constitution of the United States is a work of literary art. It differs from them in that it was meant to be enacted, as indeed it was enacted forthwith. In this respect we may compare it with *Hamlet*. *Hamlet* presents an imagined society in which there are several offices that are filled by a variety of fictitious individuals: a King (Claudius), a Queen (Gertrude), a Prince (Hamlet), a Lord Chamberlain (Polonius), Citizens, etc. This example of fictional art was, however, designed to be enacted. Accordingly, along come some real persons in the guise of professional actors. They walk out onto the stage reserved for the enactment and severally proceed to act out the parts in accordance with the script. One assumes the role of the King and does what the King is supposed to do; another of the Queen — and so forth.

The Constitution says: There shall be "a President of the United States of America. He shall hold his Office during the Term of four Years, and . . . be elected as follows. . . ." The procedure of his election is then prescribed. Along comes an actor called, let us say, Thomas Jefferson. He goes through the prescribed procedure, whereupon he assumes the role of the President of the United States of America. In that role he follows the script of the Constitution, essentially as the actor who takes the role of the King in *Hamlet* follows Shakespeare's script. For example, the Constitution says that the President of the United States of America "shall nominate, and by and with the Advice and Consent of the Senate, shall appoint Ambassadors, other public Ministers and Consuls, Judges of the supreme Court . . . ," etc. So the actor who takes the part, in this case Thomas Jefferson, proceeds to nominate and appoint ambassadors, other public ministers and consuls, judges of the Supreme Court . . . , etc.

This Thomas Jefferson is only one actor in the performance of the script called "The Constitution of the United States of America." Another, whom we may call Workaday Jones, plays a lesser role, that of a citizen. The constitution sets forth certain rights and certain duties of citizens. In his role as a citizen, then, Workaday Jones exercises those rights and discharges those duties.

More's *Utopia* was for reading only. *Hamlet* realizes itself alike whether it is read or performed on a stage. The Constitution of the United States was for such performance as was not make-believe.

Any organized society is a work of art that takes the initial form of a concept in the mind. The United States of America and Utopia are alike in this. But the United States, unlike Utopia, was given a live performance. So, when we see by the latter example the whole process of creation in the domain of social construction — from the concept in the minds of authors like Jefferson, to the communication of that concept in a script called "The Constitution of the United States of America," to its enactment by real people in the real world — we see that it does not differ fundamentally from fictional creation. *The Republic, Utopia, Hamlet,* and the Constitution may be associated as examples, all belonging to one broad category, of the mind's creativity.*

Social construction, no less than music or landscape painting, represents the replacement by mind of a blind process for bringing order out of chaos.

* This chapter has been adapted from my book *The Society of Man,* New York/London, 1965, pp. 40–44, where its theme is more fully developed. I have developed it and associated themes in two other books of political philosophy as well: *Men and Nations,* Princton, 1962, and *The Ideological Imagination,* Chicago/London, 1972.

XV

The Question of Truth

SUCH ORDER as the mind brings out of chaos takes the form of imaginative visions that lift us above the here-and-now to a wider view. This is true alike of the visions we customarily term scientific (e.g., Einstein's vision of a four-dimensional universe or Darwin's of evolution) and of those we term artistic (e.g., Michelangelo's "Pietà," *Hamlet*, or Beethoven's Ninth Symphony).

In Chapter XII we asked what basis there was for our customary distinction between the scientific and the artistic. This led us to define the scientific vision as representing what we assume to be the literal truth about an external world that exists independently of our observation, that would exist whether we knew of it or not. In that world the earth literally does circle around the sun, and the life upon it literally has evolved over some 3,500 million years by the process of natural selection. Therefore we think of Copernicus and Darwin not as inventors but as discoverers of the order of nature.*

Having thus defined the scientific vision, we went on in Chapter XII to say that "the artistic vision may be true only in a symbolic sense, as if truth should be made manifest through counterparts that are not true." At this point we turned aside, for a whole chapter, to examine the question whether the historian's profession was a science, or an art, or neither, or both. Having done so, we must now return to the question of what the artistic vision represents, a question we had hardly more than broached at the end of Chapter XII.

We suppose that science represents literal truth only, not going beyond it. Art, however, if it represents literal truth at all, does go beyond it, and all its value is in going beyond it. Thus the painting of a bunch of grapes by Zeuxis or the image of Napoleon in Mme. Tussaud's waxworks is not an expression of artistic vision precisely

---

* We should bear in mind that this view of science, as representing an independently existing order in nature, is based on the unprovable assumptions set forth in Part One, Chapter III, "The Problem of Knowing."

because, although representing a literal truth, it does not go beyond it. On the other hand, the literal truth represented by the "Mona Lisa" is secondary to something larger and more universal that we find implicit in it.

We cannot be precise about what a work of art tells us beyond the literal truth of its ostensible subject, if it has one, and each of us would define what it tells us differently. All of us alike, however, are aware of meanings hard to define that widen in our minds like ripples on a pool. To change the metaphor, we are all aware of overtones that grow fainter in their succession until we can no longer hear them.

In the present context it does not matter that we can no longer accept Genesis as literal truth, any more than it would matter if we learned that the "Mona Lisa" was not a faithful representation of the woman who sat for it, its value residing, not in literal truth but, rather, in a complex of implications by which each of us may understand himself and the nature of mankind as a whole. It tells us of an Original Sin in consequence of which mankind has ever since been flawed and condemned to suffering and the ultimate defeat of death. It gives symbolic expression to the plausible and widely held conception of a humankind that is possessed of a potential dignity, which we may call divinity, but denied its full or lasting realization by the unconquerable element of corruption that also possesses it. (This is the basis of tragedy, for it is what ultimately brings downfall and death even to the greatest and noblest of human enterprises. All Shakespeare's tragedies have this for their theme.) In symbolic terms, we may account for the need of government and the nature of politics by Original Sin. Original Sin dominates "The Waste Land" and *Ulysses*.

In the legend of the Tower of Babel, Genesis speaks of the inescapable misunderstanding and consequent disorder entailed in the diversity of mankind, enlarging our vision to encompass a detached awareness of the human condition that lends a certain nobility to our participation in it. The Book of Job likewise lifts us up to a universal view of injustice that, by giving this context to the particular injustices from which we suffer, makes them easier to bear.

Again, the Passion of Christ, as recounted in the New Testament, in addition to speaking of divinity, speaks of suffering and death as the consequence of Original Sin, the figure of Christ being the epitome as well as the paradigm of mankind. All this is in Michelangelo's "Pietà" — and how much more as well! There is the sense of resignation and peace when the agony has at last reached its end, as in the conclusion of *Hamlet*. (It is like the return to the keynote that marks the close of a movement in music.) I could go on to speak of the "Pietà" as Pater spoke of the "Mona Lisa," showing how its meaning expands in successive resonances towards infinity.

There is a more abstract quality in the "Pietà" as well. It has what we think of as grace, associated with rhythm and symmetry. In this it resembles music — as does the Parthenon frieze, as does the Parthenon itself. This, however, is not a separate quality but integral with everything else that the work represents.

I have already shown how, in abstract terms, what is in the Parthenon is in a Two-Part Invention by Bach, how what is in the Book of Job is in Bruch's "Kol Nidrei" — and, indeed, in a large sense one has the impression that all these works represent some single order (the "central order" represented by the Bach D minor Chaconne and referred to by Heisenberg in the quotation that concludes Part One). When we come to the Parthenon and the Two-Part Invention, however, we are no longer in the realm of representational art at all. Here order is presented pure, as if abstracted from the existential world that a landscape or portrait painting represents.

In what sense might the order that we find in such works be true?

Heisenberg, in his reference to the "central order" revealed by the Chaconne, asserts that there is such an order, even that it constitutes the basic design of the universe. But this conception is too generalized to be susceptible of such proof as, by the application of logic to observation, we are able to give to the thesis that the earth orbits the sun. To be sure, rhythm and symmetry are basic to the universe, for we find them all about us — in the orbiting of the planets and their spherical shape, in the waves of the sea and the wavelike manifestations of electromagnetic radiation, in the succession of the generations of life, in the hexagons of the honeycombs made by bees, in the shapes of honeysuckle flowers, galaxies, and snowflakes. To reduce the whole matter to its simplest terms: by symmetry and rhythm we mean regularity, and without regularity no universe is conceivable.

We also see all around us the irregularity within regularity. For the earth is not perfectly spherical, the succession of the generations or of the waves of the sea is not precisely fixed in its timing, the compartments of the honeycomb are not uniformly perfect, the shape of galaxies and snowflakes are never absolute in their symmetry.

There can be no doubt, then, of a parallel between the order we see in the universe and the order we see in works of art. But the parallel is general, so that it would be absurd to say that the Parthenon, for example, represents specifically the symmetry of the solar system, or that the Chaconne represents the rhythmic succession of the seasons. Speaking in broad terms, however, rather than in terms of particulars, we can say that the order in the universe has its counterpart in the mind, which is moved to express that counterpart in works of art. The Parthenon, as an epitome of such rhythm and symmetry as are in the mind and in the universe alike, represents the apparent fact of an order throughout the realm of being, and is true in that sense.

*

We have seen that any work of art tends to have widening implications, like overtones in music. Therefore, if the question of truth arises, it arises at different levels. At the lowest level one asks about a portrait whether it is a true likeness in the physical sense. At another, one asks whether it gives a true impression of its subject's personality — e.g., the intellectual seriousness of Thomas More or the narrow-minded coarseness of Henry VIII as depicted in the respective portraits by Holbein. (Even though we have no direct knowledge of either man, their respective careers offer a basis for judgement; so that most of us could not imagine Holbein's Henry VIII writing *Utopia,* while we can easily imagine his Thomas More doing so.) At another level likeness is irrelevant and one asks whether the paintings represent types of humanity that we know as such in our own experience — as Falstaff represents one type and Hotspur another in *King Henry IV.* I, myself, looking at the portraits of More and Henry VIII, might conjure up in my mind philosophical implications that were valid even though Holbein had not seen them in the terms in which they presented themselves to me. Looking at them, I might be moved to think in each case of the descendant of the man-apes who in a tentative fashion had begun to clothe himself in the accouterments of civilization, whereby he separated himself from the beasts of the field to rise above them. In such a context, the respective costumes in which each had clothed his nakedness would seem to represent what we call human dignity, but more pretentious and therefore equivocal in the one case, more authentic in the other.

The reader will see that these excessively remote implications which I have drawn from the two portraits have a strong subjective element, representing the mind of the man who has observed them at least as much as they do that of the portrait painter who, nevertheless, provided a sound foundation for them. So Pater's description of the "Mona Lisa" is as much Pater as it is Leonardo, but not necessarily false on that account. What he saw was there to see, as was much else, perhaps, that someone else would have seen. Some of us see what he called attention to, and others do not. Those of my readers whose minds are enough like mine will accept the implications I have drawn from the two Holbein portraits, while others whose minds are sufficiently unlike mine will regard them as an indulgence in fantasy. And who can say whether they are true as, supposedly, the vision of Copernicus is true?

It is a paradox that all the great works of art have a profound meaning for the cultivated observer, but that it tends to be a different meaning for each, and one that may, moreover, change radically from one age to the next. If I may use such general terms, what the eighteenth century (e.g., Samuel Johnson) saw in Shakespeare was different from what the nineteenth century (e.g., Swinburne) saw in him, which was different, in turn, from what most of us who live in the second half of the twentieth century see in him. (I find myself appalled at the common belief of the Victorians that Imogen, in *Cymbeline,* is perhaps the greatest female character in the history of literature; but they would doubtless be appalled at my own view that Shakespeare's Cleopatra is the greatest.) All agree in seeing a profound meaning in these works, but that meaning is different for every age and to some extent for every observer.

A work of art may be likened to a note struck on some resonant instrument that propagates an endless series of harmonics. The respective tones of the series produce sympathetic resonances in the mind of the listener to the extent that it is attuned to each of them, which means that it produces different resonances in different minds. My mind sings with the chords that *Hamlet* sets off in it, but I know only too well that such chords as it may set off in other minds are quite different. So it is that none agree on *Hamlet's* meaning while all agree on its greatness.

*

We have been trying to come to grips with the question of truth in works of art. Abstract works, we have said, make manifest the presumed fact of an order in the universe (the "central order"), so that we may regard them as being true in this sense even though they are not true in any other sense. When it comes to representational works of art what counts is their implications; but we find it hard to define those implications or even to agree on what they are. There are some implications, however, that we can define, and that we ought to be able to agree on. I can illustrate this by two contrasting examples of how human nature is represented in literature.

The first example is a story for children, Perrault's fairy-tale of Cinderella and her wicked step-sisters. Like all fairy-tales, it assumes that mankind is divided into two separate and opposed species, the good and the wicked. Every child brought up on these tales, deriving his conceptions of the world from them before he has any worldly experience of his own from which to derive them, makes the same assumption and tends to apply it to the interpretation of real life. When I became old enough for fairy-tales the First World War was being fought, and I knew with the absolute knowledge of my worldly ignorance that we Americans were the good people and the Germans the bad.

At a later stage in my life I became familiar with the plays of Shakespeare. What they represented as the truth about mankind was more subtle and more equivocal than what Cinderella represented. Their characters seemed each to contain both good and evil, perhaps in varying proportions. Iago in *Othello* is a rare example of a villain apparently as pure in his wickedness as any figure of fairy-tale. Edmund in *King Lear* would be another, except that in the end, as he lies dying, he shows a virtue that had all along been hidden under his wickedness. Imogen, Perdita, Hermione, Portia, and others of Shakespeare's heroines appear to represent an unadulterated virtue, but they are not characters into whom we see as deeply as we see into Queen Gertrude, for example, or Cleopatra. (This is true of all the characters in fairy-tales, none of whom is deeply realized, or could be within the limits of the form, and it is also true of Iago.) The more profoundly realized characters in Shakespeare are all in a state of inner conflict between impulses of good and impulses of evil. No one can doubt that Macbeth is a man of outstanding virtue who, succumbing to a momentary temptation, re-enacts irrevocably the Fall of Man, with Lady Macbeth in the role of Eve. (Even she is not purely wicked, for she draws back from murdering Duncan on account of his resemblance to her father, and in the end she earns our compassion by a troubled conscience that no villainess of fairy-tale would possess.)

Here, then, are two opposed conceptions of human nature represented, respectively, by quite different works of literary art. Both take for granted a conflict between good and evil, but in the first the conflict is between persons who are all good and others who are all evil, while in the second it is an inner conflict, one that goes on between impulses of good and impulses of evil within each person. What choice should we make between these two opposed conceptions by the criterion of what human nature truly is?

In deciding on which choice to make, we lack any such objective process of testing as is available in choosing between the Ptolemaic and Copernican views of the relation between the sun and the earth.

Lacking it, each of us must depend on the impression of human nature that has, over the years, on the basis of experience and exposure to the arts, formed in his own mind; or on a consensus of the cultivated, which is to say external authority; or on some combination of both.

In the examples I have given, a consensus of the cultivated would surely favor the conception represented by *Macbeth* over that represented by the story of Cinderella. Such a consensus would be possible, however, only because the alternatives are so extreme; and even so it would be short of unanimity, for I have known cultivated Germans to maintain that the Jews were all evil and cultivated Jews to maintain that the Germans were all evil. If we took opposed examples that were less extreme, the choices between them would be more uncertain. Is the pessimistic view of human nature presented in Voltaire's *Candide* or Flecker's *Hassan* true or untrue? Is the hopeful view of human nature presented in Shakespeare's *The Tempest* true or untrue? Is the view of human nature we find in Thornton Wilder's *Bridge of San Luis Rey,* or in Melville's *Moby Dick,* or in Dostoyevsky's *Brother Karamazov,* or in Chaucer's *Canterbury Tales,* or in Joyce's *Ulysses,* or in Kipling's *Kim* true or untrue? No clear answer can be given, and that for the most fundamental of reasons, a reason which we must now introduce.

*

There is no one human nature except in the broadest terms. Just as our kind in its physical structure, although possessing the same organs in the same arrangements, varies from the African Pygmy to the Scandinavian, so human nature, as manifested by human behavior, varies. In this case, however, I do not refer to genetic variations, as between races, which I take to be relatively minor. Even within one genetic stock the variety of human nature is notable. The children of the same parents (as many of us can testify from personal experience) have each a unique individuality that becomes evident in the first weeks if not days after birth. No two human beings in the whole world, identical twins excepted, are even close to being the same.* Moreover, given the inborn individuality to begin with, human nature is malleable to a degree. By the time anyone has grown to adulthood, his individuality has undergone a shaping by experience that may be the predominant factor in determining it.

* Degrees of sameness or difference depend on the scale against which they are viewed, and where the question is one of human individuality they are not truly subject to measurement. What I mean here by saying that no two individuals are even close to being the same is simply that, even on the most casual acquaintance, the difference between any two would be readily apparent.

If one could experiment as freely with human beings as with guinea pigs, it might prove possible by the separate and controlled upbringing of identical twins to make an Iago of one and an Othello of the other. This influence of upbringing, moreover, might be demonstrated not only on the scale of individuals but on that of whole societies. Indeed, it has been demonstrated, although not under experimental conditions, time and again.

The protean character of human nature in such that a whole society can be transformed in its behavior, almost from one day to the next, by the appeal of a normative idea. From 1918 to 1933 the German people were under the government of one normative idea represented by their political leaders. From 1933 to 1945 they were under the government of quite a different normative idea represented by a different leadership. The replacement of this second idea in 1945 resulted in another like change in the behavior by which human nature is manifested.

The American people, feeling a high degree of self-confidence, showed one pattern of behavior from 1945 to 1950, after which certain developments on the international scene caused them to lose the self-confidence that had determined that pattern, and consequently to adopt a different pattern through most of the 1950s. (I think of individual colleagues of mine who, before 1950, were without exception honorable in their behavior, but who, under the influence of a sudden sense of insecurity, feeling their careers threatened by the so-called McCarthyism of the time, or tempted to take advantage of it, adopted quite another mode of behavior during the few years when it was dominant.)

The Japanese have been one thing under one set of circumstances, quite another under another — and that more than once in their history.

During the 1950s and the first half of the 1960s, the students in American universities were notable for their docile conformity to established standards of value and conduct; but then, suddenly, under the sway of new ideas, they began to engage in widepread violence against those standards.

In fairy-tales, as in all literature for the childlike mind, character never changes. By contrast, in Shakespeare it changes definitively under the stress of circumstances. Macbeth, having always behaved himself honorably, becomes inescapably committed to criminal behavior. Lear, having been a capricious tyrant, acquires humanity and rises to a certain philosophical elevation. Cleopatra, from being a frivolous wanton, achieves an unparalleled sublimity of spirit in the end. It is because Shakespeare knew so well the potentialities and the variability of human nature that his works must be considered closer than the tale of Cinderella to the truth. But all the greatest writers whose primary concern has been to give a rounded and realistic account of human nature have represented it in essentially the same terms.

The protean character of human nature accounts for a curious reversal, resembling a time-reversal, between fiction and reality. Human nature is, in some measure, what the writer of fiction makes it to be. The works of novelist and playwright, and of all who see visions that bear on humanity, provide normative models on which actual human beings shape themselves. The New Testament provided in Jesus a normative model on which some persons have shaped themselves, while the legend of Siegfried the warrior provided a different model on which others have shaped themselves. I have already cited Somerset Maugham's statement that the Englishmen in Kipling's tales of India were less representative of the actual Englishmen at the time he was writing than of those who, living a generation later, had been formed on the models he created — so that he could be said to have created human nature rather than merely reporting what it was. His fiction became true *ex post facto*.

In the next and final chapter of Part Five we shall see what conclusions we can come to on the questions raised in this chapter, questions which had been forming in the fourteen that preceded it.

XVI

The Creation of Order

SCATTERED ACROSS A REALM OF SPACE that extends at least 10^{10} light-years in every direction are some 10^{20} stars, many doubtless attended by planets of which an estimated 10^{10} must be so similar to our own that we may well suppose them to support the same kind of life. Life on our own planet, beginning with rudimentary cells, has developed over the past 3,500 million years at an accelerating pace, until in recent times it has acquired the attribute of mind.* Mind seeks to bring order out of the chaos of raw experience, whether by the discovery of an order existing independently or by its own invention. Implicit in this use of the mind is a liberation from the here-and-now to which mindless life is confined. For there can be no order that does not have extension beyond the here-and-now, nor any liberation from the here-and-now except in terms of an order that extends beyond it. Therefore we must equate the liberation from the here-and-now with that evocation of order, real or imaginary, which is the faculty of mind.

Until the emergence of mind, the evolution of life represented the response of species to the natural environment as it was. With the emergence of mind, however, the one species that had acquired it began to transform the entire surface of the earth, suiting the environment to itself. This is to say that it began to displace and replace the natural environment by an artificial one of its own devising.

When, in Part One, we were considering being on a time-scale of 10^{10} years and on a distance-scale of twice that many light-years we were able to detect in it aspects of a perfect order defined by natural law. When we were considering life on our own planet over a period of 3,500 million years, we were still able to see in it the order represented by the theory of evolution, in which accident, however, appears to play some part as the unforeseeable plays some part in the world of the very small. When our scale had been reduced to

* See Part Three, Chapters VI and IX.

some 10,000 years we had an increasing impression of uncertainty or capriciousness in what happened. And now, when we consider how life in our present, as measured on a time-scale in which decades count, is replacing the natural environment with an artificial one, we feel that all is subject to the accidents that make life unpredictable. Approaching the day-to-day (which is the equivalent of the very small in the world of physics), we are increasingly confronted by the play of something like the Uncertainty Principle — of what we may, indeed, call the Extended Uncertainty Principle, the Uncertainty Principle extended to a different world of phenomena. We are in the position of the research historian who, trying to reconstruct the particular circumstances surrounding the death of the Duke of Enghien, comes to the conclusion that they could as well have happened otherwise than they did. This day-to-day world appears to be largely capricious, a world in which indeterminism reigns.

The mind seeks to bring order out of chaos, and we equate chaos with indeterminism. If the world of cosmic time and distance represents a determined order, the mind's apprehension of that order may be regarded as discovery rather than invention. If, by contrast, the world measured in decades represents the chaos of indeterminism, any order that the mind brings out of that chaos may well be regarded as its own creation — which is to say that it may be regarded as invention.

In Chapter IV I said that *The Odyssey* is a parable of man's striving to emerge from the existential chaos into the normative order represented by the Kingdom of Ithaca when it was under the governance of legitimacy. The normative order is that of the family which is basically composed of a man and woman who are mated for life, of their children, and of the household that includes servants or retainers of one sort or another. In the agricultural and feudal setting with which we may identify this social unit, the commanding role is played by the husband and father, who is responsible for the welfare of all, for their living and for their defence against military attack. The mutual attachment called love, and the traditionally defined obligation of obedience — of children and servants to the presiding couple, of the wife to the husband — provide cohesion and effectiveness in cooperation. By extension and adaptation, this pattern of family relationships applies to the minuscule kingdoms of the Homeric scene, such as Ithaca under the rule of Odysseus, Pylos under Nestor, Sparta under Menelaus, and Mycenae under Agamemnon.

In Homer, this order is regarded as nature's norm rather than as the invention of men, so that any departure from it, such as Helen's adultery, leads to terrible consequences. It is regarded as representing the only proper and natural way for men to live, just as the order of the hive represents the only proper and natural way for bees to live. We, however, who have a perspective that Homer lacked, must doubt that it did, in fact, represent nature's norm, just as we must doubt Aristotle's dictum that man was intended by nature to live in city-states. I suggest that it was, rather, the invention of mind, devised to meet the circumstances of time and place, rather than the discovery of natural law. In the artificial urban environment that is today spreading around the earth, this social order is breaking down because the environmental circumstances to which it corresponded are changing.

In the last chapter I said that Genesis gave symbolic expression to "the plausible and widely held conception of a humankind that is possessed of a potential dignity, which we may call divinity, but denied its full or lasting realization by the unconquerable element of corruption that also possesses it." This conception, however, is plausible to me personally because it belongs to the Judeo-Christian cultural tradition in which I was brought up. Presumably it would not have been as plausible to a Greek of Homer's day, to a Sumerian whose mind had been formed on the Epic of Gilgamesh, or to a Chinese bought up in the Confucian tradition. I conclude that, being valid primarily in terms of one passing culture among many, it does not, any more than Aristotle's city-state, represent the discovery of an independently existing order in nature — that it represents, rather, the mind's invention.

We have noted that mind has now begun to replace the natural environment with an artificial one of its own devising. The construction of such an environment is necessarily based on prior concepts in the mind, just as the construction of a building is based on the architect's prior design. Each such concept represents a normative order arising in the mind and serving as a basis for reconstructing the environment.

For the purpose of exposition I have just referred to individual concepts as if each came in a separate package containing a discrete whole. In fact, however, what the creative mind produces is a conceptual complex that constitutes a generalized world outlook, a more or less vaguely defined view of the nature of being, of man's place in it, of the values to be cultivated or cherished, of how human society should consequently be organized — all expressed, as often as not, in delphic terms. Mahavira, Gautama Buddha, Confucius, and Jesus are each associated with such a world view; as are Homer, Plato, Thomas Aquinas, Dante, and Calvin; as are Hobbes, Locke, Jefferson, Rousseau, Hegel, Karl Marx, and Sigmund Freud (who represented the concept of Original Sin in a new form).

When it comes to the values associated with any such view, the values for the realization of which we live and for the pursuit of which we formulate norms of human behavior and social organization, we look to the arts in the most inclusive sense of the term. The Parthenon or Mozart's Coronation Mass represents the harmonious order that we would wish to govern our lives, as does Vermeer's "Maidservant" in its suggestion of an everlastingly repeated way of life, as does the painting by Shen Chou, "Contemplating the Moon," in its evocation of the autumnal experience that every generation has in its turn. Ruysdael's "View of Haarlem" teaches us to value the element of spaciousness in our environment. The 13th chapter of St. Paul's First Epistle to the Corinthians, the Funeral Oration of Pericles as rendered by Thucydides, Lincoln's Second Inaugural Address, and Melville's *Moby Dick* represent, respectively, certain ethical values. Shakespeare's *As You Like It* or Thoreau's *Walden* speaks for certain values associated with a simpler life than that of courts or cities.

*

The mind is not an organ, like the brain, but a faculty associated with the brain. We can define it as the faculty for producing order, whether an independently existing order that it discovers or an invented order.

If only in formal terms, those who are called theologians, philosophers, or scientists pretend to be discoverers. Thomas Aquinas and Calvin, Socrates and Hegel, Vico and Spengler, Ptolemy and Copernicus, Pliny the Elder and Darwin — all thought of themselves as engaged in the enterprise of discovery. Most readers of this book, like its author, do not accept this claim on the part of the theologians because, in their case, it is based on the premise of a divine revelation that we regard as belonging to the realm of legend. Many of us regard the enterprise of the philosophers in the ontological domain as representing speculation about an externally existing reality, some of which we find plausible and of fundamental value for understanding, but none of which is to be regarded as discovery in anything approaching an absolute sense. On the other hand, we may well accept the offerings of the natural scientists as representing the discovery of an independently existing reality because we have already accepted, if only as a practical necessity, the unprovable assumptions (set forth in Chapter III of Part One) on which they are based.*

* I leave out the social sciences because, dealing as they do with such a narrow range of experience — i.e., human society in the present — they are confronted by the Extended Uncertainty Principle mentioned earlier in this chapter, and are, consequently, largely immersed in chaos.

Natural science, which on these grounds has the best claim to represent discovery, is by its nature cumulative and progressive. The vision of Copernicus is closer than Ptolemy's, Darwin's is closer than Pliny's, and Einstein's is closer than Newton's to the truth. We must, however, take account of the fact that, in the long view, mind has only just now arrived on the scene of earthly life. Since it is only beginning to discharge its function, we may plausibly believe that, if the progress of science has occasion to continue, the respective visions of Darwin and Einstein will be superseded — not, perhaps, in the sense that they will have been disproved but in the sense that they will have been modified for absorption into a more developed vision, as Newton's has been modified for absorption into Einstein's.

This is to say that, in considering discovery and invention, we cannot regard what claims to be discovery as being so in an absolute or final sense. It is so in a formal sense, and in some cases we may regard it as being so in a relative sense as well.

We are dealing here with categories that are not as categorical as we make them seem for purposes of exposition. We have said that there are, on the one hand, works of science, and on the other hand, works of art, and that the works of science, although they represent discovery in a formal sense, do not represent it absolutely or with such certainty as forbids scepticism. We would say that works of history, which we refrained from classifying as either science or art, represent discovery in a formal sense, but necessarily entail a major element of surmise, much of which is indistinguishable from invention.

The discovery represented by works of science and history, ostensibly or in a formal sense, is the discovery of what we take to be literal truth. Works of art, on the other hand, even if they happen to represent such truth incidentally, derive their value, rather, from the representation of some truth beyond it. Since discovery is associated with literal truth, and since literal truth is not of primary importance in works of art, invention enters into their production as a major element. Although Shakespeare, in his *King Richard II*, was ostensibly representing a literal truth, he was representing it only in the broadest outline, and felt free to fill that outline with the purest invention. A landscape painter also feels free to depart from literal truth, as when, for example, he omits a tree in the actual scene that would upset the balance of his composition. (If a portrait painter feels less freedom to depart from literal truth, that may be merely because of the terms on which his painting has been commissioned.) When it comes to an abstract piece of music or architecture, the question of literal fidelity to a particular truth does not arise at all.

Up to this point we have been largely groping for the significance of human creativity in the arts and sciences, varied as they are. In doing so, we have been coming to a number of partial or tentative conclusions. Now at last, however, we must see what we can produce as a final reckoning.

*

If the realm of being we inhabit represents an order that exists independently of our observation, that order, as we have seen, manifests itself only in the very large. It manifests itself in terms of such time and space as we measure in light-years. In the realm of the very small, the underlying chaos, represented by the Uncertainty Principle, prevails. Because we have minds, however, we are impelled to use them toward the end of bringing what order we can out of this chaos. If we accept certain unprovable assumptions, we can conclude that, in part, we discover order. For the rest, however, we create it ourselves.

The order we create generates and develops in our minds as imaginative visions that extend beyond the here-and-now, within the confines of which order is not possible.

All of us live in two worlds at once, the chaotic world by which we are buffeted in our daily lives and an orderly world of the imagination that transcends it. Because our minds function only in terms of order — indeed, exist only as expressions of it — our failure to achieve such transcendence would produce mental breakdown. It follows that our dependence on a visionary order of some sort is complete.

The two worlds, however, interact. On the one hand, the existential world provides the raw materials for the world of the imagination — as actual countryside provides the raw material for the landscape painting, as actual human behavior provides the raw material for the playwright — and, on the other, the world of the imagination tends to impose such order as it produces on the existential world — as when the natural environment is replaced by the artificial one of the mind's designing, as when actual persons imitate the behavior of fictional characters.

Works of art, including works of science, teach us to see. They are the wings that lift us above the chaos of the here-and-now to a higher standpoint. Whatever is worthwhile in life depends on what they enable us to see, which we would not see otherwise. So all art invests our experience of actuality with meaning that it would not otherwise have. It creates the meaning.

This meaning, over the whole range of art and actuality, shapes our individual and collective lives, determines our behavior, provides the designs for the ever developing civilization by which mind has lifted life above the level of the beasts to such levels of awareness as we associate with divinity.

If we take the term art in the largest sense, overriding the categories into which we arbitrarily break it down, so that Einstein's Relativity is a work of art no less than Shakespeare's *Hamlet,* then we must recognize that mind and art are inseparable. Mind exists in terms of the visions that are embodied in works of art, and human life, at least, is organized accordingly. These visions are of the mind's own creation, although we assume a correspondence, however remote and imperfect, between them and an order external to the mind. We assume it but do not know that it is so.

It is on the basis of these visions, which life has created through the newly developed agency of mind, that it has now embarked on the enterprise of transforming the surface of the earth. Within the limits that are inescapable, the order that we, as the possessors of mind, have just begun to establish on earth, and that we may find ourselves extending beyond it, is of our own design and our own making. In this perspective the works of art we produce are not just finished creations in themselves but sources of creative radiance by which life, through the agency of our species, is remaking the world.

It is too early to give the account of an enterprise just begun. Assuming that it continues, that it is not cut off by some catastrophe, we would wish to view it from the standpoint of a million years hence. However, since this standpoint is not accessible to us we must do the best we can from the standpoint of our own present — which is what we shall do in the three chapters of what is necessarily a truncated Part Six.

PART SIX

Implications

I know nothing but this, that things
fleeting and transitory should be spurned,
that things certain and eternal should be
sought.

— Saint Augustine of Hippo

I

The Extended Uncertainty
Principle

WE HAVE SEEN that, in the physical universe as a whole, order is built out of an underlying chaos represented by the elementary particles in themselves. It arises out of the combinations of those particles on an ever larger scale. By the time we have reached the scale of the atom we have already risen far above the underlying chaos, for the atom is symmetrical in the balance of its positive and negative charges, as well as in other respects, and is obedient to the logic associated with certain laws of nature. But this is just a beginning in the progress from chaos to order, because, for one example, atoms combine to form molecules, which enter into the ever larger and more elaborate combinations out of which life arises. Life in turn evolves from prokaryotic cells to the ever larger and more elaborate order represented by its highest forms so far. That order is what we perceive as the beautiful. It is represented for me at the moment by just one feather of a peacock's tail, 85 centimeters long, its multicolored "eye" framed by a setting of sinuous plumes, that lies before me on my desk. One would say it was a work of art rather than the product of a nature acting haphazardly. Put it together with its companion feathers to constitute the peacock's tail, then give the tail its setting in the entire organism, which opens it in a fan as it bows in a ritual reserved for special occasions, and we have a symbol of the order that has, over thousands of millions of years, been arising out of the underlying chaos.

The above paragraph speaks of a progression from a primitive chaos to an ever more elaborate order. On the scale of the universe itself, there is no basis for regarding this as a temporal progression, for we do not know that the universe began in chaos or whether it had any beginning at all. We have no reason to believe that there was an initial moment when all elementary particles existed uncombined, after which their ever increasing combination began. In fact, we cannot imagine a beginning to being, or to order, and we may properly doubt that, independent of our own perceptions, there is a temporal extension that moves ever in one direction out of an eternal past into an eternal future. Perhaps, like the fish that are confined to the middle depths of the sea, we are prisoners in a limited ocean of space-time, unable to know what lies beyond it. However that may be, in terms of the wide universe the progression from an underlying chaos to an ever increasing order is a notional rather than a temporal progression, the word "progression" implying that order is superior to chaos, an assumption we necessarily make.

However, when we limit our view to the 3,500 million years of life on this one planet, the progression is temporal as well as notional. On this planet, an ever increasing order emerges out of chaos with the passage of time.

Up to a certain point, that increasing order appears to be produced blindly, for it is based on mutations that occur by accident, and the natural selection that operates among the variety of forms so engendered is automatic and unconscious, not animated by a purpose. At the point we have now reached, however, natural selection has thus produced mind, which is a conscious faculty for deliberately creating order. This is to say that what is blind has, in its blindness, produced what is not blind.

We may think of mind as a faculty for discovering an already existing order in nature, on the one hand, and, on the other, for creating an order of its own devising. The consequent distinction between discovery and invention is at least convenient. Thus it is convenient to refer to the "discovery" that gravitation is a force of attraction between bodies, although the very concept represented by the word "force," reflecting our experience of pulling and pushing within the confines of our immediate commonsense world, may be regarded as no more than a convenient invention that serves the heuristic purpose of metaphor. An all-knowing intelligence would, perhaps, regard this as merely our way of explaining to ourselves, in terms that represent our present limitations, what appears to happen in the realm of being.

In any case, within the minuscule scope of our own planet, the evolution of life has at last produced, in mind, a conscious agency for creating, out of chaos, an ever more perfect order. It is as if the order progressively produced by the automatic process of natural selection were itself, at last, taking over from that process by consciously assuming the function it had been carrying on unconsciously. Apparently the order already developed so far has reached the stage where it can undertake its own further development.

*

The Uncertainty Principle, as understood and accepted today, applies directly only to the realm of particle physics. A counterpart of this principle, however, appears to apply as well in the realm of the evolution of life by means of natural selection. For natural selection operates among the products of what appear to be accidental circumstances. Molecules arise from the accidental collisions and consequent combinations of atoms, the accidental initial combinations grow into increasing agglomerations by successions of like accidents, and, as the agglomerations increase, those that have accidentally come to assume a certain size and form become self-perpetuating. Competing for survival, some through accidental mutation acquire advantages that favor them in the screening by natural selection that now comes into play. By this process, which begins with accident, life emerges and evolves from a lesser to a greater organization. Sexual combination provides a new basis for natural selection, accelerating the evolutionary progression in the direction of an order ever greater in its scale and formal elaboration. Eventually, in succession to the early and haphazard agglomerations of molecules, we have elephants and peacocks. Still, however, natural selection takes place among the products of genetic mutations caused by accidental circumstances at the level of the very small. It screens accidents.

We may plausibly suppose that the classes of fishes, birds, and mammals emerged from the screening process with a certain inevitability to fit those particular aspects of the earthly environment to which they are adapted. When a large part of the earth's surface was dry land it was inevitable that life, evolving by natural selection, should emerge from the water in forms suited to its occupation. As, however, we go from the general to the particular in our examination of living forms, evolution appears progressively less than inevitable. We may say with some confidence that the emergence of the class Aves was inevitable, but we cannot say with equal confidence that the emergence of the peafowl was inevitable; for the peafowl evolved to occupy a particular and casually existing niche in the earth's environment, while birds evolved to take advantage of the atmospheric mantle in which the entire planet is wrapped. So, as we go progressively from class to species, from species to subspecies, and from subspecies to individuals, the role of accident appears to increase. Thus an individual human being is the product of an accidental combination of two particular germ cells among hundreds of millions made available for such combination in a single act of copulation alone. It was no more certain that the particular individual would be brought into being than it was certain that a particular atom of thorium-234 would decay at a particular moment.

Note that the justification for saying that the combination of the two particular germ cells was accidental is based on the Uncertainty Principle in physics. Long before that principle was discovered, the French scientist Laplace had written: "An intelligence that, at a given instant, was acquainted with all the forces by which nature is animated and with the state of the bodies of which it is composed, would — if it were vast enough to submit these data to analysis — embrace in the same formula the movements of the largest bodies in the Universe and those of the lightest atoms: nothing would be uncertain for such an intelligence, and the future like the past would be present to its eyes." According to this, the conjunction of the two particular cells that produce a particular individual would be predetermined rather than accidental. It is the invalidation of Laplace's dictum by the Uncertainty Principle that requires us to regard the conjunction as accidental.

The uncertainty of the Uncertainty Principle is manifested as well by the particular mutations resulting, even in the highest organisms, from such accidental collisions as those of particles coming from outside with particles composing the nucleic acids in the germ cells.

It is, then, a plausible hypothesis that the Uncertainty Principle in physics has its counterpart in biology (which is, after all, continuous with physics). We have already seen that it has its counterpart in the realm of human history.* I use the term "counterpart," refraining from applying the term "Uncertainty Principle" itself outside the realm of physics because that would implicitly compromise the present precision of its meaning. Hereafter, however, I shall refer to the "Extended Uncertainty Principle." The Extended Uncertainty Principle must be considered, in the present state of our knowledge, as a philosophic rather than a scientific principle, to the extent that such a distinction has meaning. But then, the Uncertainty Principle in physics is on the borderline between physics and metaphysics. Both principles or, rather, both aspects of the same principle, belong to the realm of what used to be called natural philosophy.

In all aspects of being, then, it appears (a) that order is built on an underlying chaos, and (b) that the Uncertainty Principle, associated with the phenomena studied by physics, is representative of that chaos in relation to other phenomena as well — here, however, in the nominal form of the Extended Uncertainty Principle.

*

Although I have not dwelt on it so far, another principle appears to emerge from the holistic vision as it develops — viz., that diversity is

* See pp. 592–594.

built progressively on an underlying uniformity. As we have seen, one photon is absolutely identical with another, so that it might, indeed, be regarded as the same photon where circumstances of time and place did not forbid.* This lack of individuality prevails still at the atomic level, one helium atom being indistinguishable from another. When we reach the visible orders of magnitude, however, individual distinction has already appeared. We may be sure that no two snow crystals are absolutely identical. Individual distinction must be minimal among bacteria of the same immediate descent; but as one examines ever more developed forms of life, from bacteria to birds and mammals, the increasing elaborateness of their organization, ultimately entailing millions of differentiated cells, is associated with an increasing diversity.

I daresay the requirements of the close adaptation to common environmental circumstances produced by natural selection limit individual differences among the members of species that live entirely in a state of nature. Anyone who has watched tight schools of small fish, or a flock of sanderlings flying over the surf — all members of the group moving together, changing direction simultaneously in evident response to a common impulse — can see that they represent, still, something short of the individuality that characterizes our own kind. This pressure of the environment for conformity, operating through natural selection, must vary in its intensity from species to species. Animals that have escaped from the pressures associated with a state of nature — which is to say man and his domestic animals — develop the most extreme forms of individuality known among living creatures. Casual observation will reveal virtually no individual differences among the members of a colony of rock pigeons in the wild; but the pigeons of our city streets, which are descended from them, vary conspicuously as individuals. So do we descendants of the man-apes, having largely escaped from the pressures of the natural environment, vary alike in our physical forms and our psychological constitutions.†

*

As we noted in Part Four, Chapter I, certain processes of the universe as a whole appear to obey a rule of acceleration. However that may be, it is certain that the evolution of life has been accelerating from the beginning. The increasing diversity associated with evolution, by offering a constantly wider range of choice for natural selection, has constantly hastened the process. And as life, in its develop-

* See pp. 52–53.
† See pp. 518–520.

ment, has changed the mundane environment, it has thereby opened up new possibilities for an ever wider diversity and a consequently accelerating evolution. The very process of evolution, creating new and ever larger possibilities for itself, is self-accelerating, like that whereby the stars and planets are formed. One factor here has been the development of means whereby life has come increasingly to insulate or free itself from the pressures of the natural environment. The advent of the amniotic egg, with its protective shell, was one step in that direction. The advent of means whereby organisms could control their internal temperatures was another. The creation of civilization, best represented in this respect by its cities, was a continuation and extension of this process at an ever more rapid rate, supplementing internal temperature control with control of the immediate external temperature, entailing such insulation against the wide realm of nature as resembles that provided by the amniotic egg.

*

Having now surveyed the knowledge of being that mind has achieved in the first 50,000 years of its existence, we find ourselves in the position of a man who, following a forest path to find out where it emerges, is overtaken by the darkness of night. We can go no farther, nor can we see ahead. It remains, then, for us to take stock of our position and, on that basis, to draw what conclusions we can.

II

What Might Be

THE OUTSTANDING FACT in our present situation is that mind, confined to our own species, is now assuming command of our planet, taking over from the blind process of natural selection the direction of the evolution of life.

I have just referred to "mind" as if it were an entity in itself, like some brooding prescience in the sky that had the ability to oversee and direct the course of life on the earth below. In fact, however, it is but an imperfectly developed faculty for bringing order out of chaos with which the individual members of our species, in their thousands of millions, are unequally endowed. It is, moreover, a faculty that depends on intensive cultivation by a long process of education if it is to realize its potential and to be exercised as responsibly as possible. The chance of disaster for life on earth, foreseen in the last chapter of Part Four, gains plausibility from the inadequacy of mind, even in its highest manifestations, to the responsibility that, in the course of evolution, seems now to have fallen upon it. However that may be, we have no choice but to do the best we can with what we have.

I am not here concerned to prescribe what human society should do for the realization of its prime mission as the custodian, for life in general, of the faculty that has emerged only so recently in its evolution. At this point I do no more than to suggest what in ideal terms, disregarding the practical difficulties of our immediate present, would be the best organization and disposition of society for the realization of that mission.

We have seen that, virtually within our own lifetime, mankind has been brought under a single civilization and has coalesced into what is becoming a single worldwide society, however loose, largely in consequence of the technological developments produced by that civilization in the field of communications and transport. Such a society would ideally have a confederal organization — perhaps like the evolving organization of the Swiss cantons from the eighteenth century to our own time, a period in which centralization has developed gradually at the expense of local autonomy.

Ideally, the worldwide society would depend for its cohesion on an overriding common purpose. Such a purpose is essential to the cohesion of any group, whether a football team, a national society, or an organization of allied states like the league of Greek city-states that combined to resist the Persian attempt at their conquest. Let me exemplify this in the simplest terms. We may imagine a group of half-a-dozen disorderly and quarreling schoolboys who, walking along a country road, come upon an automobile stuck in a ditch, the driver struggling to get it out again. Immediately the boys join together, their bickering forgotten, to lift and push the car out of the ditch and back onto the roadway, working together with exhilaration and moral satisfaction in combining their strength so effectively to a constructive common purpose. We have seen how, when a nation is at war, its people tend to forget the differences among themselves in order to combine for the overriding purpose of avoiding defeat or achieving victory; or how the inhabitants of a city struck by an earthquake, as was the case of San Francisco in 1906, are inspired to combine their efforts in the common task of rescue and restoration.

In the society that I am here imagining, the overriding common purpose would not be that of meeting a desperate emergency. A better model than the common resistance of the Greeks to the Persian invasion is the common enterprise of the Athenians in rebuilding their city after the Persians had been repulsed. Or we might take that of the common undertaking by a wide national community to build the Cathedral of Chartres, a model which resembles my imagined example of the boys joining in a common undertaking to get the car out of the ditch.*

Another condition I would make for the overriding common purpose is that it not be self-serving in a materialistic sense. Here, again, the example of Chartres applies. Surely all human experience supports the ancient wisdom according to which economic abundance, in itself, does not make for the good life in the sense of a life that, in realizing the highest human potential, provides a corresponding satisfaction. Therefore I exclude as inadequate the purpose of achieving an ever higher standard of living for us all. The achievement of the good life, which might conceivably be lived on bread and cheese, should have priority over the achievement of the more abundant life as an overriding purpose to inspire a worldwide society that holds the future of life in its custody.

* See p. 478 above.

What, then, might the purpose be, under the ideal conditions I am imagining?

If the mission of mind is to bring order out of chaos by the progressive enlargement of its world, then the purpose should be defined accordingly. It must, however, have a certain specificity if it is to provide a clearly defined target at which the whole society of man can aim.

We have seen how life, beginning as a microscopic speck somewhere on earth 3,500 million years ago, has expanded at an ever accelerating rate until, in our own time, it has at last come to wrap the entire planet earth as in a mantle, transforming its surface and creating its atmosphere. We have also seen how, at a late stage, our own species, as the custodian of mind, has come to dominate all life, itself proliferating and becoming ever more crowded within its terrestrial limits until, in our own present, it is just beginning to spill over those limits, embarking on the first exploratory excursions into interplanetary space.

In the perspective of thousands of millions of years, and taking account of the constant acceleration in the expansion and development of life, what could be more logical than that, at the moment when it has at last filled up its home planet, it should continue its expansion into the empty space that surrounds it — just as the life of 3,500 million years ago, having at last filled up the seas, rose out of them to spread over the empty land? And, in fact, it is just taking the first steps in this direction.

In Part Four, Chapter XXXI, I pointed out that, by making itself increasingly independent of the immediate environment, life has opened up vast possibilities for extraterrestrial habitation. "In an amniotic container, which is not beyond what we could construct by our developing technology, we might be able to put a whole city into space. There are prospects, not implausible, of a transparent shell (an amnion) in the form of a wheel perhaps hundreds of kilometers in circumference and many kilometers thick, within which a community of men, with attendant plants and animals, might thrive. Revolving on its axis, it would, by what we call centrifugal force, provide the equivalent of the gravitational attraction that now binds us to the earth. It would contain an atmosphere suited to our needs, presumably the same as the natural or unpolluted atmosphere of the earth. Those who lived in it would depend on solar radiation as the source of the energy they needed. They would cultivate food under artificial conditions that were free of the capriciousness associated with earthly weather. Eventually there might be any number of such amniotic wheels in space, maintaining communication with one another — and no limit to the possibility of their proliferation." In

Part Two, pages 101–102, I pointed to other possibilities as well for the unlimited expansion of life beyond the confines of the earth and, ultimately, beyond the solar system.

Under the ideal circumstances I am imagining, such an expansion into outer space would be the common purpose in the realization of which mankind would be united as the people of France were united in the realization of grandiose plans for the building of a cathedral.

For the first time in history, mankind commands the resources for such an undertaking. To the extent that the common purpose, by uniting mankind, made military expenditures unnecessary, human and material resources would be released for its realization. Such an enterprise, in itself, might be expected to generate the rapid development of ever more advanced technological means for its achievement — just as the competition for improved means of waging war has, especially since 1939, produced the technological revolution represented by ballistic missiles, by present-day computers, and by the associated miniaturization of electronic devices for the performance of a variety of services.

When I consider the alternative possibilities that present themselves for the future of mankind and of life in general, this seems to me the most promising. It promises to solve all the dilemmas that are posed for us today by lack of adequate space and adequate resources for an ever expanding population. And it appears to be illimitable in its possibilities; for there are no bounds to how far life might spread over the millions of years to come, making itself independent of a solar system that will not last forever; and there is the prospect of ultimately entering into contact with the life that must exist here, there, and elsewhere in the universe.

Finally, there is no other prospect as promising for what I have conceived to be the mind's mission, that of bringing order out of chaos by the progressive enlargement of the world it comprehends. Once in outer space, we will have enlarged our horizons as would the dwarf flea if it were to expand its vision from the limits of the single cell to encompass first the leaf, then the tree, then the forest, and then whatever lay beyond.

*

The picture I have just sketched, of one worldwide society moved by the common purpose of enlargement beyond its earthly confines, might be realized in another five hundred or another million years. It is as plausible a prospect, over the long run, as that life on earth will be set back a thousand million years. However, it will not occur in the immediately foreseeable future unless there should be some radical change of mind amounting to a transfiguration — and, although such a change could take place, we have no basis for expecting it.

All the signs indicate that our civilization is just entering that final stage in which inspiration and its accompaniment of creativity are lost, in which men become exclusively concerned with the administration of wealth and power for their own sake. On the face of it, this represents the dynamics of history, associated with a certain ineluctable logic.

All civilizations, while still creative, have been based on a hierarchical ordering of society. In such an ordering, a small educated class has presided over an intellectually and politically inert majority that has carried on the menial tasks of providing material goods and services. This is to say that the achievements of mind, and the attendant satisfactions, have generally been identified with a cultivated minority supported by an uncultivated majority. This hierarchical organization in a society that is thriving has generally seemed legitimate in the eyes of those who composed it, high and low alike. It has been regarded as representing propriety, what God or nature intended, like the society of the beehive with its several distinct castes. In times of trouble and destabilization, however, or when the poverty of the poor has approached the limits of tolerance, the normative idea of a basic egalitarianism, associated with a concept of social justice, has arisen in men's minds. In fourteenth-century England, during the peasants' revolt, they asked:

> When Adam delved and Eve span,
> Who was then the gentleman?

And during the Black Death that preceded the peasants' revolt, the people of Europe were impressed by the fact that death was indiscriminate in carrying off nobles and commoners alike.

In the life-history of every large-scale society or civilization, I think, traditional hierarchies have tended to give way before the mounting demand, in the common mind, for an ever more perfect equality. We saw this exemplified in the history of Graeco-Roman civilization and, more particularly, in that of Athens.* It was given its classic expression for our own civilization by Alexis de Tocqueville, who in the 1830s made it the theme of the Introduction to his *De la démocratie en Amérique,* where he pointed out that Western civilization, since the eleventh century (which is to say from the beginning), had been steadily evolving in the direction of an ever greater

* See pp. 418–421.

equality, concluding: "The gradual development of equality in men's condition therefore is equivalent to a decree of Providence . . . ; it is universal, it is enduring, it is beyond human control. . . ."

I have already noted that Caesarism marks the last stage of every civilization that runs its full course. So far from being unrelated to egalitarianism, it is complementary to it in its ultimate development. For the entire population of a society cannot, in the name of equality, occupy the seat of government and exercise rule all alike, nor can it control and operate a delicate system of limited government entailing built-in restraints on its own power. Therefore, what tends to happen is that one man, speaking in the name of the people and exerting a demagogic appeal, establishes his dictatorship on that basis — as was the case in Russia after 1917. "As for me," Tocqueville wrote, "when I consider the point at which several European nations have already arrived and toward which others are tending, I am led to believe that soon there will be no place among them for anything except liberal democracy or the tyranny of the Caesars." *

The same egalitarian tendency manifests itself in the relations between a civilization and the surrounding nations, outside its frontiers, regarded as barbarians. In its late imperial phase the civilization typically extends its sway over them, becoming overextended in the process. It absorbs them in increasing numbers. They, for their part, acquire the skills of the civilization that had given it an initial ascendancy over them, thereby ceasing to be altogether barbarian and tending to do away with the distinction on which their initial social inferiority had been based. At last they may rise to such actual rulership as was symbolized by the coronation in Rome of the Gothic chieftain, Odoacer, after he had deposed the last of the Caesars.

We have noted that our own civilization, originating north of the Mediterranean, has at last extended itself over the entire globe. Those varied peoples in Africa, Asia, and elsewhere who originally came under its sway as colonial subjects have in some measure acquired its skills, have achieved their independence, and have proliferated increasingly within its traditional frontiers. At the same time, the concept of equality, originally limited to individuals, has been extended to nation-states, being enshrined in the preamble of the Charter of United Nations, which refers to "the equal rights of men and women and of nations large and small. . . ." †

The words "equality" and "democracy" are virtually synonymous

---

* Both quotations of Tocqueville are my translations from the edition published in Paris in 1951, revised in 1960, Vol. I, pp. 4 and 329 respectively.

† See *Sovereign Equality among States: the History of an Idea*, by Robert A. Klein, Toronto, 1974.

in this context, so that the increasing achievement of equality within a society, whether that of a city-state or of a civilization, is the achievement of an ever more complete democracy.

When democracy first begins to develop it is, typically, a limited democracy, one in which political power is limited to an educated minority — as was the case in Periclean Athens, in Republican Rome, in the United States of the Founding Fathers, and in nineteenth-century Britain. Whatever the shortcomings of such a democracy in terms of social justice, it has a certain relative workability in that it is under the direction of those who represent the cultivation on which the uses of the mind depend. It makes for the progress of civilization, as we have defined it in these pages, even though it may do so at the cost of suffering for the majority (exemplified by the hunger of the Roman plebeians in the second century B.C., or by the misery of the British slum-dwellers in the nineteenth century).

By the process I have been outlining, however, limited democracy evolves, at last, into mass democracy. When that happens, political power comes to depend on a mass opinion that is incapable of the delicate, informed, and balanced judgements generally required in reaching the decisions on which the progress or even the survival of the society may depend. Competition for political leadership generates an ever more irresponsible demagogy, entailing an ever more irresponsible conduct of government. Indeed, leadership becomes followership as those who are competing for the suffrage of the masses succumb to the temptation of identifying themselves publicly with whatever the masses, in their ignorance and excitement, may be clamoring for, rather than seeking by persuasion to enlist their support for such measures as may be necessary for the security and well-being of the society.* The consequence is such disorder and disaster as leads, at last, to what is the equivalent of a receivership in bankruptcy — i.e., such rule as we have here called Caesarism, which maintains an ascendancy over the masses by force, by fraud, or by such devices as bread and circuses. Even before matters have gone so far, however, the cultural creativity of the civilization has been lost, partly because of the passing of the innocence that allowed religious myths to be taken literally, partly because the higher hopes of a young civilization have evaporated, partly because that creativity was identified with the inclinations and tastes of an élite, partly because the preoccupation of the masses is with material benefits and vulgar show. Society, under a purely pragmatic leadership, comes to be exclusively concerned with the immediate achievement of such

---

* This is the theme of Thucydides' history, in which he attributes the downfall of Athens to the decline in the quality of leadership associated with mass democracy.

benefits and of such show. Great works of engineering may be accomplished, like the Roman roads and aqueducts, or great works of display, like the Hanging Gardens of Babylon, but they have a different character from the works of art and science that marked an earlier stage of civilization, for they are not to be identified with the achievement of the larger vision.

*

In the days when the bulk of mankind was directly engaged in agriculture, the preoccupation with present problems, to the exclusion of the larger vision, took the form of a primary concentration on the struggle to cope with those manifestations of nature that threatened or prevented success in the annual production of crops. For an increasingly urbanized mankind, in its amniotic seclusion from nature on earth and from the universe beyond, the preoccupation with the present takes the form of a concentration on social struggle in which various groups seek the rectification of their particular grievances or the triumph of causes that, whether good or bad, afford the individual the assurance or the sense of power that goes with finding oneself part of an immense group, the members of which march shoulder-to-shoulder toward a common goal.

So far in history, however, the notable achievements of mind — whether in the arts, the sciences, or statecraft — have generally been associated less with mass movements than with individuals who, by their individual distinction, have stood apart from the groups in which individualities are merged and lost. The outstanding manifestations of mind have been not in a popular or fashionable consensus but in individuals like Solon, Thucydides, Shen Chou, Dante, Michelangelo, Shakespeare, Bach, Galileo, Descartes, Darwin.

In thus recognizing the role of the distinguished individual, however, we must also recognize how entirely it depends on the cultural context of time and place. John Milton, brought up in a cultural desert, would have been no more than the "mute inglorious Milton" of Gray's "Elegy." Although the Parthenon and the Parthenon frieze undoubtedly owed much to the genius of Phidias, that genius could be exercised as it was because it found itself in the momentary setting of Periclean Athens, which afforded it both a cultural context and scope for its expression. The building of the Cathedral of Chartres, although it owed much to the earlier vision of Abbot Suger, almost represents an exception to the rule that the most distinguished achievements of mind are to be associated with individuals rather than with mass movements. (There was a chief builder and architect, but his name has been lost.) Again, the development of cosmology was at something of a standstill from the 1880s until Einstein came along with his Theory of Relativity, but both J.-H. Poincaré and H. A. Lorentz had already almost hit upon it, and we must suppose that someone else would at last have done so if the accident of Einstein's birth had never occurred. Alfred Russell Wallace hit upon the theory of evolution by natural selection at the same time as Darwin, and in any case it had already been in gestation for a couple of generations.

Note, however, that the indispensable social and cultural context of the achievements identified with individuals was associated, in each case, not with the popular masses that constituted the society as a whole but with a cultivated élite. In the two generations before Darwin, during which Darwinism was in gestation, the rank and file of the British people did not even know that there was a problem to be solved. It may be that in 1905, when Einstein published his Special Theory, the number of those who were aware of the problems with which it dealt could have been brought together in one hall — although the entire population of the earth at the time was over 1,500 million. The rank and file of the inhabitants of Athens in the days of Aristotle made no contribution to the cultural infrastructure on which his achievement was based. The cultural context of Michelangelo's work was a small oligarchy, supplemented by a few fellow artists, that was capable of appreciating it.

*

At this point I ask the reader to cast his mind back to the last chapter of Part Four, entitled "The Unknown Future." There we noted that until the most recent times — say the last million years out of 3,500 million — the progress of life toward an ever increasing order was based on a natural selection that operated blindly on accidentally produced variations. This process, however, has now produced mind, which is a faculty of producing order by what has come increasingly to represent conscious and purposeful action. Mind, at the present stage, has turned away from the natural order in quest of a civilized order that has not yet been achieved.

Up to what we may regard as our immediate present the history of civilization has been that of multiple civilizations, more or less separated from one another, which began to spring up here and there around the earth, everywhere replacing the natural with an artificial environment of the mind's devising. The whole process of transformation entailed is now proceeding at such a rate, in accordance with the rule of acceleration, that it threatens to end in breakdown and chaos — like a machine that spins faster and faster until it flies apart.

The mind cannot adjust itself quickly enough to circumstances that change so rapidly, being unable to cope in the decreasing time available with all the increasingly urgent problems that the change engenders — such as the uncontrolled proliferation of the human population and the overwhelming of the earth by the waste products of industrial activity. I shall not, however, repeat here all the plausible possibilities of disaster that I mentioned in the last chapter of Part Four.

Civilization has always depended on one normative order or another that has governed the minds of those who have lived by it. Such an order is enshrined in tradition, and the formation of tradition requires such time as is measured in generations. In the past the secular change of circumstances by which traditions are rendered obsolete has, except in times of total breakdown, been gradual enough to allow for the continuous adaptation, from generation to generation, of the traditions that correspond to them. This is no longer the case, so that today we see the normative order in men's minds, on which civilization rests, crumbling into confusion, with all the consequences of psychological insecurity and disorientation that are bound to ensue.

Moreover, the one remaining civilization of our day, having run the cycle of other civilizations up to this point, appears to be entering its last phase. With the general breakdown of belief in the Christian mythology on which it had been formed — like the breakdown of belief in the Olympian gods of the Greeks — we can expect an increasing breakdown in the self-discipline of populations. In that case, there will be, on the one side, unprecedented concentrations of populations tending to degenerate into mobs, and on the other unprecedented means provided by our technological progress for the enforcement of tyranny. Increasing anarchy will engender the less intolerable alternative of Caesarism, and under the contentions of rival Caesars and would-be Caesars our societies will sink back into barbarism.

If this should be our immediate future, who can say how it will be resolved? In the last chapter of Part Four I foresaw that there might be a cataclysmic setback to the thousands of millions of years of evolutionary progress. I do in fact foresee only too clearly a breakdown of civilization and a time of troubles ahead, but not at all what may lie beyond that time. In Revelation 20, St. John the Divine predicted a time when "Satan shall be loosed out of his prison, and shall go out to deceive the nations which are in the four quarters of the earth, . . . to gather them together to battle: the number of whom is as the sand of the sea." After Satan had thus had his fling, however: "I saw a new heaven and a new earth: for the first heaven and the first earth were passed away. . . ."

In the like revelation of the future that came to Karl Marx, the revolution he foresaw would be followed by a transitional period when all that was vile in mankind would be released from the imprisonment of traditional self-discipline to expend itself in unbridled excesses. But this would be merely preliminary to the final advent of a new heaven and a new earth.*

I daresay this parallel between Christian and Marxist mythology represents a common logic, according to which the evil in mankind has to be purged by dissipation before mankind can finally enter the Kingdom of Heaven. I repeat the prediction here because it is not implausible, nor is it at odds with the protean character of human nature referred to on pages 610–612.

*

In the first part of this work we were viewing existence on a scale of thousands of millions of light-years. In the second we viewed it on our single planet only, and over a span of 4,000 million years. In the third our perspective was reduced to tens of millions of years, in the fourth and fifth to some 6,000 years. Now, at last, we have come down to our infinitesimal present, say a few decades; and, even though we try to view that present in the perspective of the 6,000 years past, uncertainty reigns in the form of the Extended Uncertainty Principle.

At the moment when these words are being set down, the possibility that our kind will unite in the pursuit of any single purpose that serves the mission of mind, such as the one set forth earlier in this chapter, is wholly implausible; for we are too divided, and too preoccupied with the practical problems that confront us with an immediate urgency. In considering the possibilities of the immediate future, however, we should properly take account of present circumstances for which history offers no precedents, and of man's protean nature. This, then, is what we shall do in the next chapter.

* As his thinking developed, Marx replaced this "crude Communism" with "the dictatorship of the proletariat." See *Karl Marx: Early Writings*, T. B. Bottomore, ed., London, 1963, pp. 152–155.

III

The Individual

THIS ENTIRE WORK, now at its end, has been directed only at the achievement of such understanding as is possible to us at this stage in the development of life on earth. Prescription has been no part of its purpose. While I am not without views on what should be the preferred direction for the worldwide society of man to take, I leave them implicit, for the most part, in what understanding has been achieved. In such understanding, however, there are also implications for the life of the individual, and these I do undertake to make explicit in this final chapter, which should be regarded as an epilogue rather than as part of the main text.

*

From the birth of the human individual to his death, a state of tension exists between him and the society of which he forms a part. On the one hand, he feels himself to be a self-contained entity, with daylight all around him. On the other, he not only depends on the society within which he finds himself, he owes his character as an individual largely to the formation it has given him. If he engages in thought, he does so in the terms it has provided, without which he would be mindless.

If human societies were as established and mindless as those of the honeybee, this tension would not exist. There would be no question of how the individual should conduct himself. Each bee conforms to a normative model that is, for all practical purposes, unalterable, providing no range of choice. All human societies, by contrast, being artificial, are makeshift, provisional, subject to trial-and-error — from which it follows that they are endlessly changeable and constantly changing. The proprieties they represent are subject to dispute among the individuals and groups of which they are constituted. The result is that there is no established model with unalterable norms to govern the individual's life. On the contrary, at any given moment there is a range of opinion on what is proper or improper, and this confronts each with the continual necessity of choice.

To the degree that a society at any moment is an integrated whole, it is under the governance of a consensus with respect to what constitutes propriety in the conduct of the individual. The traditional acceptance of the tenets of Confucianism in China provides one example, the traditional acceptance of Christian ethics in Europe another. In the latter case there was, until the end of the fifteenth century, a single church with a priesthood that prescribed the individual's conduct. The prescription, however, tended to be based on ideals that were imperfectly attainable, so that the conduct of the individual could never quite conform to what was expected of him, and this in itself entailed tension between him and society.

Because of the acceleration of evolution, which has now reached a point of crisis in the ever more rapid development of civilization, we have at last entered upon a time when behavior is no longer tightly controlled by custom, or consensus stabilized by tradition. We must therefore expect a growing intellectual disorientation in every society, manifesting itself in a social chaos that will be intensified by the mob-psychology that arises among urban concentrations of people. Disoriented mobs will be swept this way and that by capricious movements of opinion or belief. Fanaticism will flourish and bigotry prevail. Under such circumstances, the freedom that depends on tolerance of diversity will tend to give way, thereby posing a problem for any thinking individual.

In any society, the unexceptional individual conforms automatically to the attitudes and opinions of the group with which he finds himself immediately associated. However, since the standards of the many, especially in matters of basic belief and basic values, are apt to be more primitive than those of the distinguished few, the distinguished few may find conformity especially difficult. The classic example of refusal to conform, when the issue was joined, is that of Socrates, who paid for his refusal with his life. Although he necessarily thought in the traditional terms of the Athenian society by which he had been shaped, that society had become disoriented. Even if this had not been the case, there would have been a sufficient latitude and changeableness of normative prescription in it, as within any human society, to call for constant adaptation, and to allow the individual a range of freedom in the exercise of which he might find himself opposed to the majority. Here, then, is a particularly dramatic example of the strain that always exists, although generally in lesser degree, between the individual and the society to which he belongs.

The individual is responsible in the first place, not for the conduct of society but for his own conduct only. He is responsible for what he does with the freedom that he, unlike the mindless insect, has no choice but to exercise. He may exercise it by giving it up in the measure of the possible — perhaps by joining a monastery, a military organization, or some other social institution in which his conduct is prescribed. Or he may inwardly give up his freedom of choice by committing himself to some body of dogma, no matter what it happens to be. The individual who has given himself to a doctrinal cause, by which he is associated with others in an extended group, might as readily, according to the accidents of circumstance, have given himself to the opposite cause. What counts for him is the sense of solidarity with others — more precisely, the satisfaction he gets from losing his individuality in the mass, thereby relieving himself of the burden of freedom that the mind otherwise imposes.

Virtually all of us study conformity in order to identify ourselves with those immediately around us and to feel ourselves accepted by them. The loneliness of Socrates at his trial, consequent on his determination to follow the logic of his own mind, is not for us.*

I am here addressing myself to the individual who feels compelled to use his individual mind in such a way as forbids unthinking conformity with whatever may, at a particular moment, be the prevailing opinion of the group with which he happens to find himself associated.

The standards of the many, as I observed above, are apt to be more primitive than those of the few, who are therefore bound to find conformity difficult. The individual, then, in the measure of his distinction, will wish to achieve a certain detachment from what we may call the mass mind. Since the mass mind tends to be governed by the problems, the views, and the intellectual fashions of the passing moment, this means that the individual will wish to achieve a degree of detachment from the here-and-now.

At this point, the argument that has been based on the strain between the individual and society joins the argument that has been virtually the theme of this work, beginning with the reference to the dwarf flea in the first chapter. It also explains why the outstanding manifestations of mind (as we noted on pages 636–637) have been, not in a popular or fashionable consensus, but in individuals like

---

* I know how many readers of this book will judge the points it makes by whether they are in conformity with what is taught in the schools, with "what we all say," and mark them right or wrong accordingly.

Solon, Thucydides, Michelangelo, Shakespeare, Newton, and Darwin. The mass of men are preoccupied with the problems of the here-and-now, whether those of getting a living or those represented by the social issues of the passing day. If their objective were to achieve a large understanding of those problems (which normally is not the case), they would do better to stand back from them so as to gain perspective. Where the objective is the highest of all, that of bringing order out of chaos, such perspective is basic. The grand order that is implicit in *Moby Dick* or the "Pietà," in the Funeral Oration of Pericles or Lincoln's Second Inaugural Address, in Bach's "Trauer-Ode" or Mozart's Coronation Mass, that is implicit even in the little exercises composed for keyboard by Bach or Domenico Scarlatti — this order emerges with the enlargement from the here-and-now in which most of us are imprisoned. (Such enlargement is, therefore, the proper purpose of a general education.)

Socrates, Michelangelo, Newton, and others lived in circumstances of social turbulence but rose above them — like the seabird rising out of the turbulence of the sea into the clear sky overall — so as to achieve the detached and comprehensive view. I here cite two examples as epitomizing this capacity for detachment.

1. Beginning on the 10th of October, 1806, 200,000 French troops under Napoleon, 127,000 Prussian and Saxon troops under Hohenlohe — all massing for the Battle of Jena that would take place on the 14th — were swarming around Weimar, where Johann Wolfgang von Goethe, as the diary he kept mentions, was engaged in osteological study and the collection of minerals. In his entry for the 14th he does mention the fact that at 5 p.m. "cannon balls flew through the roofs," but there is no other mention of what is happening in the here-and-now, and one gets the impression that the issue over which the cannon balls flew, whatever it was, had nothing to do with him.

2. In June 1940, as Hitler's *Wehrmacht* swooped down on Paris, Wanda Landowska was recording a series of harpsichord sonatas by Domenico Scarlatti at her home in St-Leu-la Forêt outside Paris, in the path of the *Blitzkrieg*. Although she was Jewish, and therefore game for the Nazis, she turned a deaf ear to those who, fleeing all around her, implored her to go with them. She finished recording the twenty sonatas she had left to do, and then, her work done, took her departure with the Nazi hordes almost upon her. In the recordings subsequently published, the sound of the harpsichord is drowned out for a moment, in the middle of the D-major sonata, by the rumble of anti-aircraft artillery. Mme. Landowska, herself, appears not to have been

aware of the interruption. The serenity of the sonata, as she performs it, and the evenness of her tempo, are unaffected.*

*

When we considered Joyce's *Ulysses,* contrasting it with Homer's *Odyssey,* we saw, if only in symbolic terms, how the life of the hero loses its heroic quality when viewed close up, in the chaos of its minutiae, in the incoherent succession of its fleeting instants. (Marshal Catinet, when he remarked that no man is a hero to his valet, was making the same point.) If we regard Thomas More as a saint and a hero, it is because our perspective allows us to see his life as a whole. In the long view that is ours, all that was inconsequential has disappeared, leaving clear to our vision the great occasions to which he rose and the nobility of his spirit and his intellect. Presumably, however, like all of us he occasionally suffered from malfunctioning of the digestive system, sexual imaginings sometimes possessed his mind to the exclusion of everything else, or he became excessively preoccupied by some such triviality as the fact that he was served stale bread for breakfast. Even the greatest life, viewed at point-blank range, viewed as it is lived from minute to minute, must appear predominantly sordid and trivial. But the details of anyone's life are evanescent, so that in the example of Thomas More they have long since disappeared.

I offer these remarks to introduce the paradox that, although one's life seems unrewarding in detail, it may turn out to be profoundly rewarding as a whole. Most of the days of my own life I have begun in a state of anxiety and aversion at the thought of the day's duties, and in coping with them I have suffered from a continual sense of inadequacy. If some ghostly monitor, stop-watch in hand, had kept a continuous record of my life, minute by minute, it would show that the minutes of happiness were far outnumbered. So, by the statistics of the very small, he could show that this particular life had been unrewarding. And yet, now that I look back from the threshold of old age at this life as a whole, seeing how it has evolved through a consistent development as if by some kind of preordination, I conclude that it has been distinctly rewarding. In the long perspective that shows the whole, the day-to-day trivialities tend to disappear, and what remains is the growth of a quasi-religious vision produced by cumulative experience and knowledge over so many years, including exposure to the enlargement offered by the arts and sciences.

* Adapted from my paper, "The Question of Commitment," published by the California Arms Control and Foreign Policy Seminar in 1973, which also appeared in *The Virginia Quarterly Review,* Spring 1973.

There is no question here of choosing between the close-up and the distant view in terms of which represents reality. Both represent it. The only question is that of the value to be attached, respectively, to the one and the other.

If we accept the thesis that the mission of mind is to bring order out of chaos, and if we also accept the principle that order arises in its degree from the combination of the minute elements that represent chaos, we will conclude that what counts is the life of the individual as a whole, that its fleeting instants are of no consequence. This conclusion entails the rejection of a doctrine that has its classic statement in Horace's advice that we should live for the day, not looking to the morrow: *Carpe diem, quam minimum credula postero.* Anyone who, following Horace's advice, undertakes to live only in the here-and-now, without looking beyond it, will live what, in the end, must prove to have been a miserable and fragmented life.

The individual who seeks refuge from the increasing disorder of a declining civilization can attempt to achieve it, in accordance with Horace's advice, by the pursuit of such momentary pleasures as provide a fleeting forgetfulness; but the end of such a course is a wasted life. His other alternative is that of withdrawal, like Coventry Patmore escaping "from the huge town" to the shores of "this little Bay"; like the Stoics and Epicureans, who undertook to make themselves independent by the mastery of desire; like the Taoist philosophers who retired to remote solitudes where they led lives of detached contemplation; like those who, during the passing Dark Ages in Europe, retreated into monasteries. While the policy of withdrawal finds no acceptance in our immediate day, it is likely to find increasing acceptance with the passage of the years ahead. And if our civilization is indeed to be overwhelmed by the transitional reign of evil predicted alike by St. John the Divine and Karl Marx, the trustees of the hope of the future will be those who have withdrawn, in this fashion, to cherish the true mission of mind.

*

> For we know in part, and we prophesy in part.
> But when that which is perfect is come, then that which is in part shall be done away.

The objective of this work has been to achieve such understanding as the mind is capable of at the present stage of its evolution. It has been written in the spirit of scepticism entailed by the belief that, with one exception, we can have absolute knowledge of nothing.

The exception was stated by Descartes in three words: *Cogito, ergo sum* — I think, therefore I am.

However, even though this is all any of us can be sure of, it may at least be extended — as when I say, "I think certain thoughts, therefore those thoughts are." Indeed, it may be extended in more specific terms, as: "My thoughts encompass divinity, therefore divinity is." The divinity that my thoughts encompass is associated with the order that arises out of chaos.

Although each of us can have unquestionable knowledge only of his own existence and his own thinking, none has any basis for a positive belief that, in fact, there is nothing outside himself. On the contrary, each of us necessarily assumes the existence of a wide realm of being to which he belongs. As we expand our knowledge of this realm, we have ever increasing reason to see it in terms of one sublime order that awaits full realization.

INDEX

Index

I HAVE here indexed the main concepts presented in the text, distinguishing by boldface those few that together constitute the philosophy set forth in it. I have also included a selection of proper names (without giving every reference to them in the text) and random particulars to which the reader might wish to return. Certain broad topics (e.g., China, Religion) have not been included because the reader can find where they are treated by perusing the table of contents.

Having read the book through, some readers may find it rewarding to browse in this index and, on that basis, to trace the development of particular points through repeated but scattered references.

L.J.H.